Finding The Right Pitch III

A Guide To The Study Of Advanced Harmony

David Nivans

California State University Dominguez Hills

World Bet Books

Copyright © 2016 David Nivans

All rights reserved. No part of this publication may be reproduced, transmitted, stored in a retrieval system or a database in any form or by any means, be it graphic, electronic, or mechanical, including but not limited to photocopying, recording, scanning, digitizing, or otherwise, without prior written permission of the publisher.

World Bet Books
www.worldbetbooks.com
worldbetbooks@gmail.com

ISBN 978-1-937214-02-9

Library of Congress Control Number: 2013935287

This book is printed on acid-free paper.

To the Memory of

Wally Bower

1929–2008

About the Author

David Nivans took his Ph.D. in historical musicology from University of California Los Angeles. He taught courses in music fundamentals, harmony, counterpoint, musicianship, world music, music appreciation, music and art appreciation, music history, and surveys of popular music, jazz, rock, and film music.

In addition to *Finding The Right Pitch III: A Guide To The Study Of Advanced Harmony* (ISBN 978-1-937214-02-9)

David Nivans is the author of

Introduction To Music Fundamentals And Lead-Sheet Terminology
(ISBN 978-1-937214-03-6)

Finding The Right Pitch: A Guide To The Study Of Music Fundamentals (Workbook Included)
(ISBN 978-1-937214-00-5)

Music Fundamentals Workbook For Finding The Right Pitch: A Guide To The Study Of Music Fundamentals
(ISBN 978-1-937214-04-3)

Finding The Right Pitch II: A Guide To The Study Of Basic Harmony (Workbook Included)
(ISBN 978-1-937214-01-2)

Basic Harmony Workbook For Finding The Right Pitch II: A Guide To The Study Of Basic Harmony
(ISBN 978-1-937214-05-0)

World Bet Books
www.worldbetbooks.com
worldbetbooks@gmail.com

TABLE OF CONTENTS

Abbreviations xiii

Chapter 1   Primary Borrowing 1

    The Three forms of Minor 1

    The Harmonic Minor Mode 1

    The Melodic Minor Mode and Its Ascending and Descending Forms 2

    Finding the Variable Scale Degrees of the Melodic Minor 4

    The Formation of Triads in the Melodic Minor 4

    Extended Major 5

    The Formation of Triads in the Extended Major Mode 6

    Triad Formats for the Extended-Diatonic Major-Minor System 6

    The Application of the Triad Formats for the Extended-Diatonic Major-Minor System 7

    The Formation of Seventh Chords in the Melodic Minor 8

    Notation for Inversions of Tonic and Subtonic Sevenths 10

    Important Functions and Uses of Seventh Chords in the Extended Major 12

    Important Functions and Uses of Seventh Chords in the Melodic Minor 12

    Seventh-Chord Formats for the Extended-Diatonic Major-Minor System 13

    The Application of the Seventh-Chord Formats for the Extended-Diatonic Major-Minor System . . 14

    Primary Borrowing within the Cadential $^6_4$ Chord and the Generic Use of Accidentals 15

    The Picardy Third 16

    Melodic Chromaticism 17

Chapter 2   Apparent Chords 19
Generic Figured Bass 19
Using Generic Figured Bass for the Melodic Succession from ♭7 to ♯7 in Minor 23
Non-Dominant Apparent Chords 24
Placing the Real Chord Before the Apparent Chord 27
Exact Figured Bass 32

Chapter 3   Applied Chords 35
The Subtonic and Mediant in Minor 36
Tonicization, Modulation, and Lower-Level Keys 36
The Applied Tonal Harmonic Dominant [THD] 37
Cross Relations 38
The Applied Tonal Melodic Dominant [TMD] 39
The Leading Tone of the Dominant 41
The Applied Dominants of the Mediant in Minor and in Major 42
Applied Dominant Sevenths in Sequential Succession 42
The Transferred Resolution 48
The Modal Dominant Seventh Chord 50
The Modal Dominant Triad 52
Chord Progressions 54
Harmonic and Contrapuntal Progressions 55
Lower-Level Keys within Lower-Level Keys 56
Cadences 58
Harmonic and Contrapuntal Cadences in the Main-Level Key 58
Contrapuntal Half Cadences in Lower-Level Keys 60
Authentic Cadences in the Main-Level Key 62
Authentic Cadences in Lower-Level Keys 63

Chapter 4 Small Form 65

    The Period 65

    The Antecedent and Consequent Phrases 66

    Interruption of the Melodic and Harmonic Structure 66

    The Motive 66

    Small One-Part Form: the Parallel Period 68

    Small One-Part Form: the Contrasting Period 70

    Continuous Periods 71

    Small Two-Part Form: the Rounded Binary 72

    The Descending 5—6 Sequence and the Retroactive Dominant 77

    Motives 79

    The Repeated Period 80

    A List of Small Forms 82

Chapter 5 Degree-Inflected Chords (Altered Triads and Sevenths) 89

    Type I: The Altered Tonal Harmonic Dominant (THD) 89

        The Augmented 6th of the THD 90

        The Degree-Inflected THD and the Whole-Tone Scale 90

        The Degree-Inflected THD in Minor 91

        Inversions of the Degree-Inflected THD 92

        The Applied Degree-Inflected THD 93

    Type II: The Neapolitan 6th Chord 94

        Chord Symbols 94

        The X-Chord Function of the Neapolitan 6th 95

        Filling in the Diminished 3rd 95

        The Phrygian Supertonic Itself 97

        Using the Submediant before the Neapolitan 6th 99

        The Neapolitan 6th and the Phrygian Supertonic in Major 102

Type III: Common-Tone Fully Diminished Seventh Chords 103

    The Common Tone 103

    The Common-Tone Fully Diminished Seventh in Minor 104

    Using Exact Accidentals in Front of the Roman Numeral Instead of Generic Accidentals .. 105

    The Common-Tone Fully Diminished Seventh as a Pedal Embellishing Chord 106

    Voicing the Fully Diminished Seventh Chord 107

    Fully Diminished Seventh Chords in Succession 108

Type IV: Augmented 6th Chords of the Tonal Melodic Dominant (TMD) Family (Triads) 110

    Augmented 6th Chords of the Tonal Melodic Dominant (TMD) Family (Seventh Chords) . 112

Type V: The "Ethnic" Augmented 6th Chord 115

    The Contrapuntal Origin of the Ethnic Augmented 6th 116

    The Italian Augmented 6th (IA6) 117

    The German Augmented 6th and the German Doubly Augmented 6th (GA6 and GDA6) .. 120

    The French Augmented 6th (FA6) 121

    The Exceptional Augmented 6th (EA6) 122

    Inversions 123

    The Augmented 6th as an Applied CLT Chord 124

    The Augmented 6th as a Pedal Embellishing Chord 125

    The Augmented 6th as a Mediant Embellishing Chord 126

    Disjunct Resolutions 127

    Alternative Descriptions for the Ethnic Augmented 6th Chord 128

Type VI: Raising and Lowering the Third of Diminished Chords Other Than the TMD 129

    Raising and Lowering the Third of the Common-Tone Fully Diminished Seventh 131

A Review of the Six Types of Degree-Inflected Chords 134

Chapter 6 Secondary Borrowing 137

Type I: Complete Interchangeability of the Extended Major with the
Parallel Extended Minor 137

Type II: Complete Interchangeability of the Extended Major with
Parallel Non-Major-Minor Modes 138

Type III: Sonoric Substitution (Chord Substitution) 139

Interpreting Major Triads of Secondary Borrowing As Applied Dominants 140

General Uses for Chords of Secondary Borrowing 140

Mediant Embellishing Chords of Secondary Borrowing 141

Melodic Embellishing Chords of Secondary Borrowing 142

The Mediant as an X-Chord of Secondary Borrowing 144

The Chopin Prelude in E Major, Op. 28, No. 9 145

Harmonic Transformation and Reinterpretation 149

The Secondary Melodic Progression (SMP): Ascending Melodic Structure 150

The Late Middleground of Chopin's Prelude in E Major, Op. 28, No. 9 152

The Contrapuntal-Structural Chord 153

The Acclimation of Secondary Borrowing 154

An Early Middleground of Chopin's Prelude in E Major, Op. 28, No. 9 155

The Linear Melodic Progression (LMP) 156

Double-Function Chords 158

Chapter 7 The Sequence 161

The Descending 5th: Root-Position Seventh Chords (Harmonic Bass) 161

The Tritone and the Descending 5th 162

The Descending 5th: First and Third Inversions (Contrapuntal Bass) 163

The Descending 5th: First and Third Inversions (Contrapuntal Bass, Out of Key) 165

Transferring the Resolution in the Descending 5th: (Rising 2nd-Falling 3rd) 167

Root-Position and First-Inversion Chords (Descending 5th):
    Falling 3rd-Rising 2nd 168

Root-Position and First-Inversion Chords (Descending 5th):
    Falling 3rd-Rising 2nd (Out of Key) 170

First-Inversion and Root-Position Chords (Descending 5th):
    Rising 2nd-Falling 3rd 171

First-Inversion and Root-Position Chords (Descending 5th):
    Rising 2nd-Falling 3rd (Out of Key) 173

The Ascending 5—6 173

The Ascending 5—6 (Chromatic Bass) 178

Root-Position Variants of the Ascending 5—6 (becoming 12—7):
    the Applied TMD/CLT 182

Root-Position Variants of the Ascending 5—6 (becoming 5—8):
Falling 3rd-Rising 4th 184

Root-Position Variants of the Ascending 5—6 (becoming 5—8):
Falling 3rd-Rising 4th (Out of Key) 185

Root-Position Variants of the Ascending 5—6 (becoming 5—10):
Rising 4th-Falling 3rd 187

Root-Position Variants of the Ascending 5—6 (becoming 5—10):
Rising 4th-Falling 3rd (Out of Key) 189

The Ascending 5th 191

The Ascending 5th (Out of Key) 193

Avoiding the Problems of the Ascending 5th 195

Root-Position and First-Inversion Chords (Ascending 5th):
Falling 2nd-Rising 3rd 196

Root-Position and First-Inversion Chords (Ascending 5th):
Falling 2nd-Rising 3rd (Out of Key) 198

The Descending 5—6 200

The Descending 5—6 (Out of Key) 202

Avoiding the Problems of the Descending 5—6 204

Root-Position Variants of the Descending 5—6:
Falling 4th-Rising 2nd 206

Root-Position Variants of the Descending 5—6:
Falling 4th-Rising 2nd (Out of Key) 207

The Three-Chord Pattern (Out of Key) 208

Invention Number 13 in A Minor 210

    Essential and Nonessential Melodic Tones 210

    Modulation to III 211

    Exchanging the Parts: Invertible Counterpoint 212

    The Prolongation of the Mediant 214

    The Return of A Minor 216

    The Middleground 218

Leaving Home 220

Chapter 8 Modulation 221

Techniques of Modulation: Pivot, Sequential, and Abrupt Modulation 221

The Distance of Modulation 223

The Root Relationship Between Tonics: Melodic, Mediant, Tonal,
and Tritone Modulations 223

The Distance Between the Key Signatures: Degrees of Relationship
Between the Two Tonics 223

Determining the Distance Between Key Signatures: Modulation to a Related,
Remote, or Distant Key 224

Sequential Modulation Revisited 226

Pivot-Chord Modulation 227

The Status of the Pivot within the Tonal Contexts of the Old and New Keys 228

Finding and Using the Right Pivot 228

Comparing the Diatonic Pitch Content of the Two Keys 233

The Brahms Intermezzo in A Major, Op. 118, No. 2 234

Using the Picardy Third to Produce Chords of Secondary Borrowing 241

Enharmonic Reinterpretation, Chromatic Voice Exchange, and the "Omnibus" Principle 243

Opening Up the Omnibus 244

Consecutive Parallel Dominant Sevenths 246

Modulating with the Fully Diminished Seventh 249

Abrupt Modulation 251

The Chopin Prelude in E Minor, Op. 28, No. 4 252

Structure and Prolongation in Chopin's Prelude in E Minor 257

Local Harmony and Structure in Prokofiev's "Classical Symphony," Op. 25, III 261

The Chord Scale and the Mode Scale 262

The Harmonic Minor Chord Scale 261

Local Harmony and Structure in Prokofiev's "Classical Symphony," Op. 25, III (Return) 264

Modulation Is Prolongation 268

Chapter 9 Chords of "Higher Power" 269

    General Considerations 269

    The Governing Ninth Resolving within the Succeeding Chord 270

    Resolution of the Ninth Resolving within the Same Chord 272

    Frozen Nonharmonic Tones 275

    The Basic Anatomy of the Ninth, Eleventh, and Thirteenth 278

    Distinguishing Real and Apparent Chords of Higher Power 278

    Sequential Sevenths and Ninths: Descending 5ths 280

    Sequential Sevenths and Ninths: Root-Position Variants of
        the Ascending 5—6 (becoming 5—8) 283

    The Chord of the Ninth: Structure, Inflections, and Description 285

    Inflecting the Higher Extensions 287

    Chords of Addition 288

    Descriptions of Ninths, Elevenths, and Thirteenths in Commercial Music and Jazz 289

    Chords of the Ninth 290

    The Altered Fifth and Altered Ninth 291

    The Altered Fifth and Altered Ninth Together 293

    Chords of the Eleventh and Thirteenth 294

    Altered Eleventh and Thirteenth Chords 295

    The Added 6th and Added 9th 299

    The Polychordal Potential of the Higher Powers 300

Epilog: Wallace H. Bower, Jr. 303

Index 307

Abbreviations

BCP Basic Contrapuntal Progression
A progression containing a contrapuntal leading-tone chord (CLT) formed above the leading tone, scale degree 2, or scale degree 4 in the bass addressing the final tonic by means of stepwise motion, upwards or downwards (see p. 55).

BHP Basic Harmonic Progression
A progression that contains a tonal harmonic dominant (THD) addressing a stable tonic (see p. 55).

BMP Basic Melodic Progression
A stepwise melodic descent to scale degree 1 from either scale degree 5 or 3. The melodic progression is incomplete if scale degree 1 is not achieved (see p. 107).

CLT Contrapuntal Leading-Tone Chord
A chord of the tonal melodic dominant (TMD) or the tonal harmonic dominant (THD) formed above the leading tone, scale degree 2, or scale degree 4 in the bass. The complete abbreviation for each chord is TMD/CLT or THD/CLT. The CLT chord is part of a contrapuntal progression, functioning either as a neighbor chord (complete or incomplete) or as a passing chord (see. p. 39).

CS Contrapuntal-Structural Chord
A chord which in any other circumstance would fulfill the function of contrapuntal prolongation at the middleground rank; however, in its new role of supporting a structural melodic tone, this contrapuntal chord is elevated to the rank of middleground or background structural progression, becoming thereby a contrapuntal-prolonging chord with added structural significance (see p. 153).

DF Double-Function Chord
A chord which, in any other circumstances, would fulfill the function of harmonic prolongation at the middleground rank; however, in a new role of supporting a structural melodic tone, this harmonic chord is elevated to the rank of middleground or background structural progression, becoming thereby a harmonic-prolonging chord with added structural significance (see p. 158).

Ext P Extended Passing Chord
A chord occurring as part of a bass motion that fills in the interval of the 4th or 5th between unlike-rooted chords (see p. 74).

HEMB Harmonic Embellishing Chord
A chord between two statements of the same root-position chord. The prolonged root-position chord in turn displays a rising 4th-falling 5th or rising 5th-falling 4th root-and-bass or bass-only relationship to the prolonged chord. Any harmonic bass motion must not produce a basic harmonic progression in the main- or lower-level key, however. Note: some theorists classify this chord—since it supports a neighbor, passing, or inverted pedal-embellishing tone in the melody—as a chord of contrapuntal rather than harmonic prolongation (see p. 132).

LMP Linear Melodic Progression
An upward or downward stepwise expression of a melodic interval or chord, fully harmonized (see p. 156).

MEMB	Mediant Embellishing Chord
	A chord of contrapuntal prolongation standing between two statements of the same root-position chord. The prolonged root-position chord in turn displays a rising 3rd or falling 3rd root-and-bass or bass-only relationship to the prolonged chord (see p. 132).
SCP	Secondary Contrapuntal Progression
	A progression that elaborates any basic contrapuntal progression with the inclusion of an intermediary X-chord between the initial tonic and the final *contrapuntal* dominant (see p. 55).
SD	Subdividing chord
	A chord occurring as part of a bass motion that fills in the interval of the 6th, 7th, or octave between like-or unlike-rooted chords (see p. 68).
SHP	Secondary Harmonic Progression
	A progression that elaborates any basic harmonic progression with the inclusion of an intermediary X-chord between the initial tonic and the final *harmonic* dominant (see p. 55).
SMP	Secondary Melodic Progression
	A chord-supported structural melody that has a stepwise ascent from scale degree 5 to scale degree 1 (see p. 150).
TEMB	Tone-Embellishing Melodic Succession
	Chord-supported melodic activity involving either neighbor motion above or below a tone, or repetitions of a tone (inverted pedal embellishment), or combinations of neighbor tones and repeated tones (see p. 116).
THD	Tonal Harmonic Dominant
	Minimally, a major triad built on scale degree 5 of any extended major or minor mode in any main-level or lower-level key. The THD, if in root position, is a potential member of a harmonic progression or, if inverted, of a contrapuntal progression (see p. 12).
TMD	Tonal Melodic Dominant
	Minimally, a diminished triad built on the leading tone of any extended major or minor mode in any main-level or lower-level key. The TMD is a member of a contrapuntal progression only (see p. 12).
X	X-chord
	A chord which occupies the antepenultimate (or intermediate) position between the initial tonic and the final dominant as a member of either a secondary harmonic progression or secondary contrapuntal progression. This intermediate chord of harmony is found above scale degrees 2, 3, 4, or 6 and is never a tonic or dominant-family chord (see p. 55).
X-DF	X-Double-Function Chord
	A chord which normally fulfills the function of a regular X-chord member of a middleground or background harmonic or contrapuntal progression; however, in a new role of supporting a prolonging-embellishing tone (i.e., a complete or incomplete upper or lower neighbor, which has replaced an expected structural melodic tone), this otherwise intermediate chord of harmony assumes a hybrid status—it becomes a chord of weakened harmonic influence supporting a decorating tone (see p. 158).

Chapter 1   Primary Borrowing

The previous volume in this series, *Finding The Right Pitch II: A Guide To The Study Of Basic Harmony,* explored the essential principles and practices of pure diatonicism by studying the major mode, the minor mode, and the so-called church modes. The present text provides an introduction to the principles of chromatic harmony, or advanced harmony.

One of the simplest forms of chromaticism involves the formation of chords in major that incorporate elements of the parallel minor mode, a process referred to variously as "modal borrowing," "modal exchange," "modal mixture," or for us, "primary borrowing."

Although the technique of primary borrowing is generally taught as a basic type of chromaticism, this book places it within the category of diatonicism, albeit an *extended* form of diatonicism. The exchange of certain elements between the major and minor modes yields what is termed here "the extended-diatonic major-minor system."

Primary borrowing produces some of the pitch content for two of the three forms of the minor mode, namely, the harmonic minor and the melodic minor. Similarly, placing certain elements of the minor mode into a composition in major extends the pitch content of the major mode. In order to understand how this process works from both directions (major to minor and minor to major), our study of primary borrowing begins with a review of the minor mode.

The Three Forms of Minor

The minor mode has three forms, the harmonic minor, the melodic minor, and the natural minor, which is also known as the pure minor and the Aeolian mode. The natural minor can be located on the piano keyboard by finding the A octave in any register. As shown in example 1–1, the natural minor in the A octave consists of white keys only; no black keys are involved and no pitches inflected. Since the pitches E to F and B to C constitute the only two places within the octave where there are half steps between two adjacent white keys, the combined distribution of whole steps and half steps across the A octave produces a profile of half steps between scale degrees 2 and 3 and scale degrees 5 and 6.

Example 1–1: the natural minor

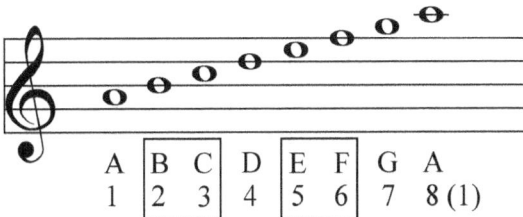

The Harmonic Minor Mode

The harmonic minor and the natural minor are almost identical—except for one *very* important difference. The natural minor employs the subtonic, which is one whole step below the tonic. The harmonic minor, on the other hand, borrows the leading tone from the parallel major; which in effect raises the subtonic by one half step and produces a half step between scale degrees 7 and 8 (examples 1–2a and 2b).

The harmonic minor's use of the leading tone (instead of the natural minor's subtonic scale degree) intensifies the melodic motion upwards to the tonic note. Moreover, the drive upwards by half step from scale degree 7 to scale degree 8 helps to firmly establish the key center. Conversely, the subtonic scale degree lacks the leading tone's compelling drive to move upwards by half step to the tonic; thus, the key center is more clearly defined in those modes that employ the leading tone and more difficult to hear in modes that have subtonics, such as the natural minor.

Example 1–2: the harmonic minor and its parallel major

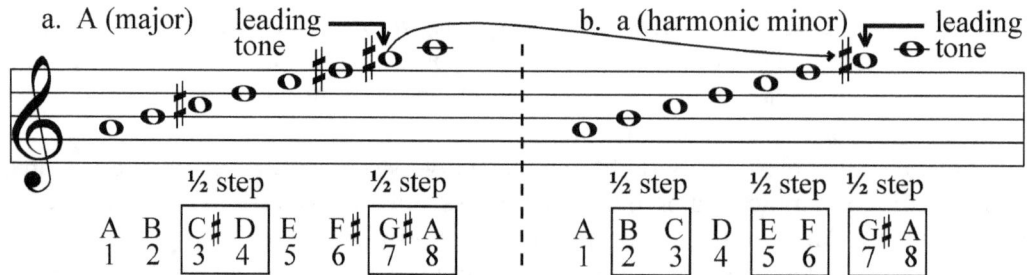

The harmonic minor retains all of the pitch content of the natural minor *except* for the incorporation of the major mode's leading tone. This one difference, however, produces a very unusual mode and scale. First, the harmonic minor has half steps between scale degrees 2 and 3, scale degrees 5 and 6, and scale degrees 7 and 8—a mode and scale with three pairs of half steps. Secondly, by raising the subtonic one half step to produce a half step approach to scale degree 8, an augmented 2nd (1½ steps) is created between scale degrees 6 and 7 (see example 1–3a below). The augmented 2nd is far more difficult to sing than either the major or minor 2nd.

The Melodic Minor Mode and Its Ascending and Descending Forms

When a melody in the harmonic minor moves upwards towards scale degree 8, composers usually raise scale degree 6 by one half step in order to eliminate the augmented 2nd that would otherwise occur between scale degrees 6 and 7 (example 1–3).

Example 1–3: eliminating the augmented 2nd in the harmonic minor

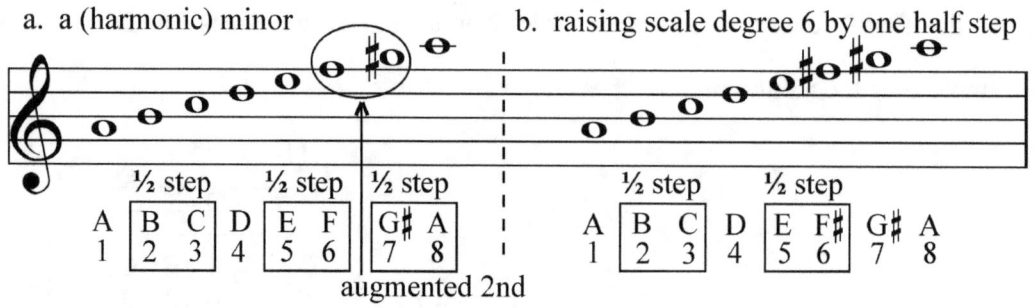

Raising scale degree 6 by one half step to avoid the augmented 2nd of the harmonic minor results in an upper tetrachord with a profile of half steps and whole steps that is identical to the upper tetrachord of the major mode, that is: whole step, whole step, half step (example 1–4). Borrowing the upper tetrachord of the major mode produces what is referred to as the "ascending" form of the melodic minor. Whenever the melodic activity of a composition written in the minor mode moves upwards in the direction of scale degree 8, the ascending form of the melodic minor is usually preferred.

Notice that the key signature for c minor in the second measure of example 1–4 has three flats but that an A♮ (rather than an A♭) is used to avoid the augmented 2nd that would occur in the harmonic minor between scale degrees 6 and 7 (A♭ to B♮). Henceforth, we refer to scale degrees 6 and 7 as "raised 6" and "raised 7" when the ascending melodic minor is used. The symbols for raised 6 and raised 7 are ♯6 and ♯7.

Example 1–4: borrowing the upper tetrachord of major to produce the ascending melodic minor

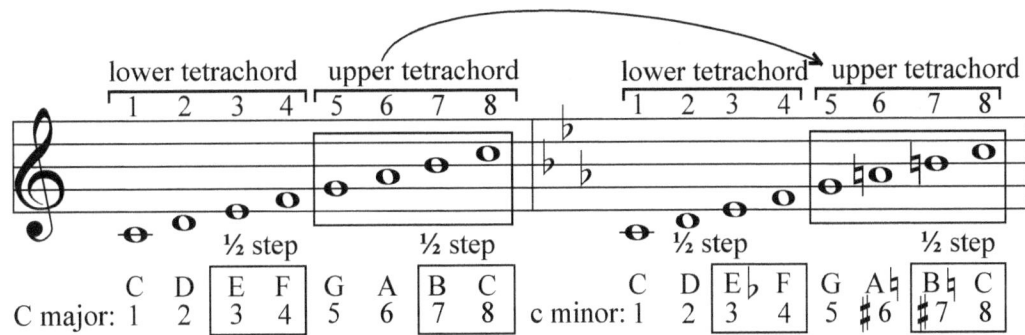

The sharp (♯) in front of the number is a "generic" symbol; its use does not necessarily mean that the pitch itself carries a sharp. Indeed, in 1–4 above, the pitches for ♯6 and ♯7 are A♮ and B♮. Scale degrees ♯6 and ♯7 are not reflected in the minor key signature. If, therefore, a composition is written in a key such as c minor, which has three flats in its key signature (B♭, E♭, and A♭), the music will probably also include an A♮ and/or a B♮, particularly when the melody moves upwards towards scale degree 8. Strictly speaking, then, if the pitches borrowed from the parallel major are taken into account (♯6 and ♯7), the melodic minor is not a pure seven-tone diatonic scale, but rather an extended scale consisting of nine tones. (In this text, we arrange the two forms of the melodic minor into a single ascending nine-tone scale and call the resulting configuration the "extended minor.")

When the minor mode descends towards scale degree 5, scale degrees 6 and 7 are each lowered by one half step from their raised counterparts, scale degrees ♯6 and ♯7. Lowering scale degrees 6 and 7 produces what is called the "descending" melodic minor (example 1–5). We call the lowered forms of scale degrees 6 and 7 "lowered 6" and "lowered 7" to distinguish them from their raised counterparts, scale degrees ♯6 and ♯7. The symbols for lowered 6 and lowered 7 are ♭6 and ♭7. Notably, the pitch content of the descending form of the melodic minor is identical to that of the natural minor.

Let us consider the key of c minor in example 1–5 to see how the process of lowering scale degrees 6 and 7 works. The ascending form of the melodic minor in the key of c minor shows A♮ and B♮ as scale degrees ♯6 and ♯7. But when the c-minor scale moves down in the direction of scale degree 5 (G) in the descending form of the melodic minor, both the A♮ and B♮ are lowered by one half step to A♭ and B♭.

Example 1–5: the ascending and descending forms of the melodic minor

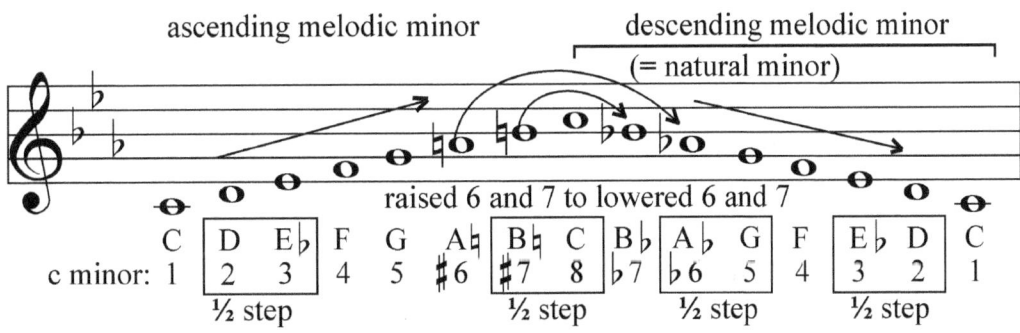

The use of scale degrees ♭6 and ♭7 intensifies the melodic motion downwards to scale degree 5 by creating a half-step approach from scale degree ♭6 to scale degree 5. We term scale degrees 6 and 7 raised or lowered and apply symbols to them (either ♯ or ♭) because on each of these scale degrees, the melodic minor has two different versions of the same letter name. For example, in c minor, scale degrees 6 and 7 may be either A♮ or A♭ and B♮ or B♭, according to whether the tones are either raised or lowered. The sharp or flat in front of the number merely indicates that there are two pitches with the same letter name and that one pitch is either raised or lowered *in relation to the other pitch.*

Having two versions of the same letter name, scale degrees 6 and 7 are *variable* tones in the melodic minor; we therefore refer to scale degrees 6 and 7 as "variable scale degree 6" and "variable scale degree 7." A more complete and specific verbal description of the variable scale degrees in the melodic minor would be as follows: "variable scale degree raised 6," "variable scale degree raised 7," "variable scale degree lowered 6," and "variable scale degree lowered 7."

It is important to understand that the flat (♭) in front of the numbers 6 and 7 does not necessarily mean that the pitch itself carries a flat; again, the flat is a generic symbol. For example, compare the keys of c minor and a minor. In c minor (1–5 above), the lowered variables happen to take flats (A♭ and B♭), whereas in the key of a minor (example 1–6), the lowered variables do not carry flats (F♮ and G♮).

Example 1–6: in minor, raised variables are not reflected in the key signature

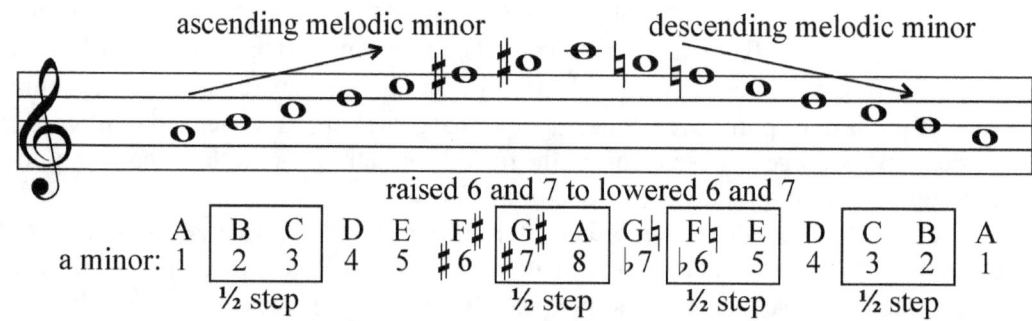

Finding the Variable Scale Degrees of the Melodic Minor

Variables ♯6, ♯7, ♭6, and ♭7 may be located in any key according to the following guidelines:
(1)   ♭6 is one half step above scale degree 5 (and a minor 6th above scale degree 1).
(2)   ♭7 is one whole step below scale degree 1 (and a minor 7th above scale degree 1).
(3)   ♯6 is one whole step above scale degree 5 (and a major 6th above scale degree 1).
(4)   ♯7 is one half step below scale degree 1 (and a major 7th above scale degree 1).
(5)   ♭6 and ♭7 are one half step lower than ♯6 and ♯7.
(6)   ♯6 and ♯7 are one half step higher than ♭6 and ♭7.
(7)   ♯6 and ♯7 are *never* included in the key signature of the minor mode.
(8)   ♭6 and ♭7 are *always* included in the key signature of the minor mode.
(9)   ♯6 and ♯7 correspond to scale degrees 6 and 7 of the parallel major mode.
(10) The pitch content of the descending melodic minor is exactly the same as the natural minor.

The Formation of Triads in the Melodic Minor

The pitch content of melodic minor, which has nine tones, produces thirteen triads, a richer vocabulary of chords than any pure seven-tone diatonic scale. The increased number of triads in the melodic minor is attributed to the presence of variable scale degrees 6 and 7 as either the root, third, or fifth elements of each chord.

Except for the tonic triad, the basic quality for triads in the melodic minor is determined by the presence of a variable scale degree and identified with uppercase and lowercase Roman numerals and the addition of either the plus sign for the augmented triad or the superscript circle for the diminished triad. If the root of the triad is a variable scale degree, then the Roman numeral is preceded by either a flat or a sharp, just as the individual pitches for the variable scale degrees of the melodic minor are indicated as either ♯6 and ♯7 or ♭6 and ♭7. (In example 1–7, filled-in note heads designate the variable scale degrees as the root, third, or fifth of the triad. The natural sign applies only to the chord to which it is attached.)

As we have said, the use of a sharp or a flat in front of the variable scale degree does not necessarily mean that the pitch carries either a sharp or a flat; rather, the sharp or flat indicates that the pitch is either raised or lowered. We apply the same principle to the flat or sharp in front of the Roman numeral. Thus, the major triads of the melodic minor are represented as III, IV, V, ♭VI, and ♭VII, the minor triads as i, ii, iv, and v, the diminished triads as ii°, ♯vi°, and ♯vii°, and the augmented triad as III+.

Example 1–7: thirteen triads formed in the melodic minor (ascending and descending forms merged)

Extended Major

The extended major makes use of tones borrowed from the parallel minor mode, namely, scale degrees 3 and lowered 6. These tones are common to all three forms of minor. Primary borrowing from minor to major produces an extended scale consisting of nine tones. (In example 1–8 below, filled-in note heads identify the borrowed scale degrees).

We refer to the borrowed tones as "borrowed lowered 3" and "borrowed lowered 6"—and not as "flat 3" or "flat 6." The symbols for borrowed lowered 3 and borrowed lowered 6 are (♭3) and (♭6). The parentheses enclosing the borrowed tones are central to the terminology used in this book. And as with the raised and lowered signs in minor, the flat in front of the number does not necessarily mean that the pitch itself carries a flat (1–8b).

Example 1–8: the nine tones of the extended major mode

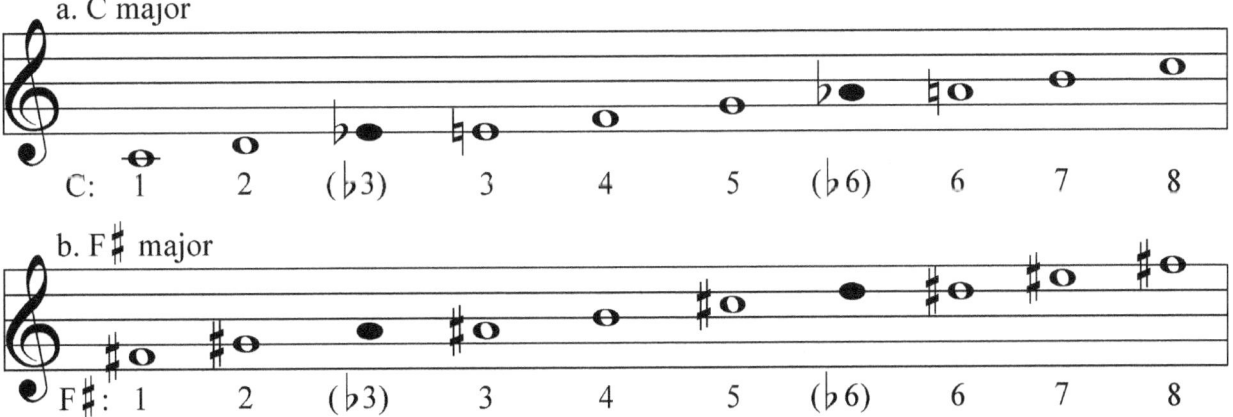

The Formation of Triads in the Extended Major Mode

The nine tones of the extended major mode produce fourteen triads, twice the number of triads found in the seven-tone diatonic major scale. Except for the triad of the leading tone, the basic quality for triads in each scale degree area of major is determined by the presence or absence of borrowed tones, (♭3) and (♭6).

The notation for triads is similar to that employed in the melodic minor but with the addition of parentheses to designate borrowed elements for chord symbols (Roman numerals) and scale degrees (Arabic numerals). Thus, (i), (ii°), (iv) and (vi°) indicate triads containing a borrowed tone other than the root. (In example 1–9, filled-in note heads identify the borrowed scale degrees as the root, third, or fifth of the triad.)

However, if the root of the chord is the borrowed tone, then not only is the chord symbol enclosed in parentheses but it is also preceded by a generic flat. When (♭3) is the root of the triad, the chord is expressed as (♭III+) and when (♭6) is the root the triad, the chord is written as either (♭VI) or (♭VI+).

Example 1–9: fourteen triads formed in extended major

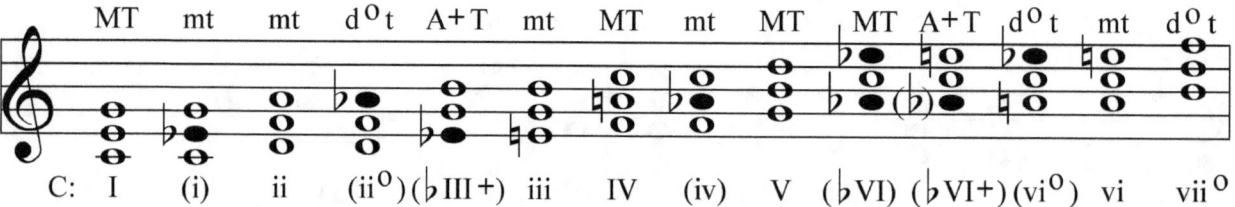

Triad Formats for the Extended-Diatonic Major-Minor System

Examples 1–10 and 11 illustrate triad formats for specific triad qualities that occur in extended minor and major. In minor (1–10), there are five major triads, four minor triads, three diminished triads, and one augmented triad. In the next section, we shall find a useful application for these formats.

Example 1–10: the triad format for extended minor

Major Triad	Minor Triad	Diminished Triad	Augmented Triad
III	i	ii°	III+
IV	ii	♯vi°	
V	iv	♯vii°	
♭VI	v		
♭VII			

It should be noted that the III+ may address the ♭VI in a falling perfect 5th or rising perfect 4th root and bass relationship. In this instance, we describe the III+ as a "modal dominant" to the ♭VI, despite the fact that the augmented triad is rarely autonomous and its viability as a chord questionable. (The modal dominant is any chord within a diatonic scale having either a perfect or tritone falling 5th or rising 4th root relationship to the following chord other than the tonal dominant to the tonic.) If not used as a modal dominant triad of ♭VI, the III+ is usually found in conjunction with either i^6 or V. (For discussions of the limitations of the augmented mediant and the properties of the modal dominant, see Chapter 8 of *Finding The Right Pitch II: A Guide To The Study Of Basic Harmony*. For the latter, see also Chapter 3 of this text, pp. 50–53.)

The major mode (1–11) yields four major triads, five minor triads, three diminished triads, and two augmented triads. Seven of these triads are the result of primary borrowing.

Example 1–11: the triad format for extended major

Major Triad	Minor Triad	Diminished Triad	Augmented Triad
I	(i)	(ii°)	(♭III+)
IV	ii	(vi°)	(♭VI+)
V	(iv)	vii°	
(♭VI)	v		
	vi		

Both augmented triads are rare in major. The (♭III+), if not used as a modal-dominant triad of (♭VI), is usually found in conjunction with either the (i^6) or V. The (♭VI+), if not used as a modal-dominant triad of (ii°), is usually found in conjunction with the (iv^6). (In most circumstances, the diminished triad in root position should be avoided because of the tritone 5th between the root and the chord fifth. However, adding a chord seventh to the diminished triad renders its expression in root position acceptable.)

The Application of the Triad Formats for the Extended-Diatonic Major-Minor System

Using the formats presented in examples 1–10 and 11 enables us to see how any given triad can assume a different context according to key. Examples 1–12 and 13 place major, minor, diminished, and augmented triads rooted on C into various key contexts for extended major-minor. For instance, in 1–12, a C-major triad can be I in C major, IV in G major, V in F major, or (♭VI) in E major.

Example 1–12: triad contextualization for extended major

Major Triad (C E G)	Minor Triad (C E♭ G)	Diminished Triad (C E♭ G♭)	Augmented Triad (C E G♯)
C : I	C : (i)	B♭ : (ii°)	A : (♭III+)
G : IV	B♭ : ii	E♭ : (vi°)	E : (♭VI+)
F : V	A♭ : iii	D♭ : vii°	
E : (♭VI)	G : (iv)		
	E♭ : vi		

In 1–13, a C-major triad can be III in a minor, IV in g minor, V in f minor, ♭VI in e minor, and ♭VII in d minor.

Example 1–13: triad contextualization for extended minor

Major Triad (C E G)	Minor Triad (C E♭ G)	Diminished Triad (C E♭ G♭)	Augmented Triad (C E G♯)
a : III	c : i	b♭ : ii°	a : III+
g : IV	b♭ : ii	e♭ : ♯vi°	
f : V	g : iv	d♭ : ♯vii°	
e : ♭VI	f : v		
d : ♭VII			

Example 1–14 combines the contextualization for extended major and minor into a single format. Without looking at examples 1–12 and 13 above and using the combined format in 1–14, can you assign the correct keys to the major, minor, diminished, and augmented triads in both major and minor modes?

Examaple 1–14: combined triad contextualization for extended major and minor

Major Triad (C E G)		Minor Triad (C E♭ G)		Diminished Triad (C E♭ G♭)		Augmented Triad (C E G♯)	
Major	Minor	Major	Minor	Major	Minor	Major	Minor
: I	: III	: (i)	: i	: (ii°)	: ii°	: (♭III+)	: III+
: IV	: IV	: ii	: ii	: (vi°)	: ♯vi°	: (♭VI+)	
: V	: V	: iii	: iv	: vii°	: ♯vii°		
: (♭VI)	: ♭VI	: (iv)	: v				
	: ♭VII	: vi					

The Formation of Seventh Chords in the Melodic Minor

The addition of the chord seventh to the triads of the melodic minor increases the number of chords to sixteen. In actual practice, however, the melodic minor's capacity for seventh chords falls somewhat short of its potential, as two of these sixteen seventh chords cannot be used and another two rarely occur in music literature. (For a discussion of the limitations of certain seventh chords in the melodic minor, see *Finding The Right Pitch II: A Guide To The Study Of Basic Harmony*, Chapter 8.)

Example 1–15 demonstrates how the addition of the chord seventh increases the number of chords on three scale degrees: the tonic, subtonic, and leading tone. Variables ♭6 and ♯6 form sevenths for two subtonic chords (♭VII ♭7 and ♭VII ♯7) and for two on the leading tone (♯vii o 7 and ♯vii ø 7). Variables ♭7 and ♯7 become seventh components of two tonic chords (i ♭7 and i ♯7)—six chords.

In four of the six chords cited above, when a variable comprises the seventh, we need to account for the additional element in the chord symbol. On the tonic and subtonic, the chord symbols carry either a flat or a sharp in front of the figured-bass 7: i ♭7, i ♯7, ♭VII ♭7, and ♭VII ♯7. We will consider the symbolic representation of these chords in more detail in the next section; for the present, know that the flat or sharp in front of the 7 indicates that the seventh element of the chord is either a lowered or raised variable and is occurring at the interval of a 7th above the bass (and root).

Despite the presence of a variable as the seventh element of the leading-tone chords, no additional descriptive terminology is needed beyond the inclusion of a superscript circle. The superscript circle with a diagonal slash (ø 7) represents the half-diminished seventh; the circle without the slash represents the fully diminished seventh (o 7).

When using a raised variable, the principle difficulty occurs if it is also the chord seventh because the linear demands of the variable to move upwards conflicts with the harmonic tendency of the dissonant 7th to resolve downwards. Accordingly, in minor, some seventh chords are either rare or unusable.

Upon close inspection of example 1–15, we find that the addition of variable ♯6 above the respective fifths of the leading-tone triad and the subtonic triad renders impractical the use of both resulting seventh chords, the ♯vii ø 7 and the ♭VII ♯7 (marked "not used"). Further, the viability of two other seventh chords is also questionable (marked "very rare"): the tonic seventh chord with variable ♯7 as its seventh component (m-M7) and the augmented-major seventh of the mediant with ♯7 as its fifth component (A-M7) are rarely used (see below, p. 12). (In 1–15, the filled-in note heads identify the variable scale degrees that constitute the root, third, fifth, or seventh of each chord.)

Example 1–15: the seventh-chord content of the melodic minor

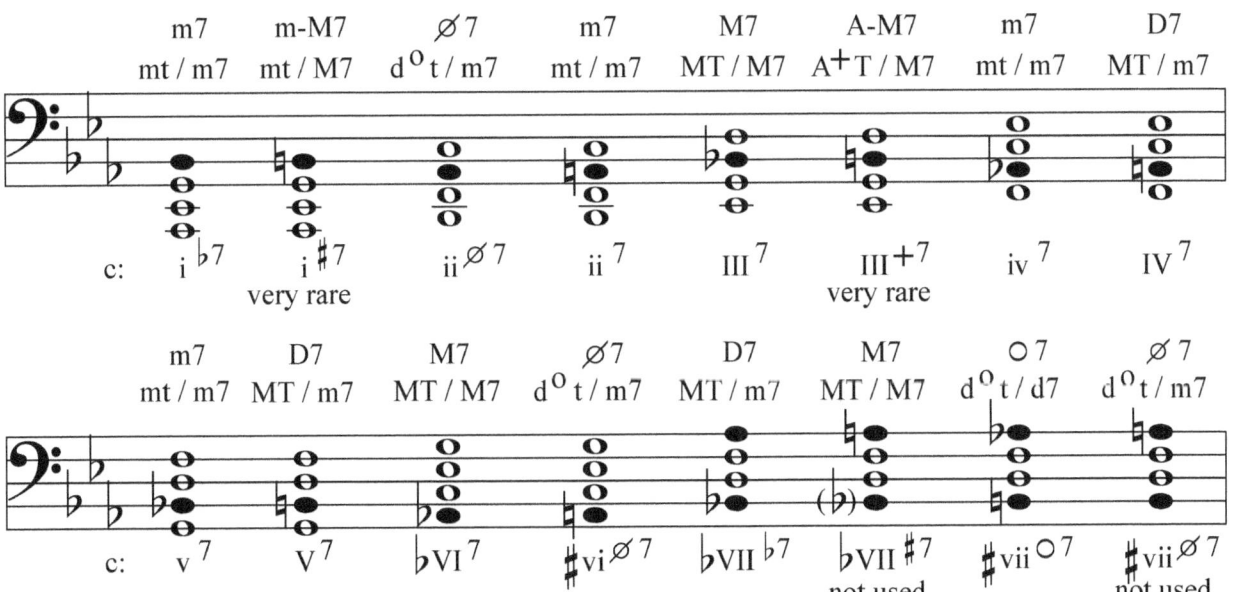

Notation for Inversions of Tonic and Subtonic Sevenths

The chord symbol for the tonic minor seventh is i ♭7. The flat in front of the figured-bass 7 for the chord indicates that variable ♭7 is occurring at the interval of a 7th above the bass (and root). When the i ♭7 inverts, the description becomes somewhat more complicated because we want to account for the variable scale degree that forms the seventh component of the chord. The same problem confronts the inversions of the i ♯7, ♭VII ♭7, and ♭VII ♯7.

Example 1–16 demonstrates how we shall indicate the presence of the variable when either the tonic or subtonic seventh chords invert. These are the only two areas of the melodic minor in which the chord symbol requires a sharp or flat in front of the figured-bass 7. Since the ♭VII ♯7 is not used and the status of the i ♯7 as a viable seventh chord questionable, we shall focus on the descriptions for the inversions of the i ♭7 and the ♭VII ♭7. (Filled-in note heads designate variable scale degrees.)

When either the i ♭7 or the ♭VII ♭7 inverts (examples 1–16a through 16f), we indicate the quality of the seventh by placing the symbol for lowered 7 in parentheses (♭7) above the traditional figured bass, identifying the position of the chord and designating it to be of the "lowered variety." Similarly, we indicate the inversions of the i ♯7 or the ♭VII ♯7 with the symbol for raised 7 in parentheses (♯7) above the standard figured bass, identifying both chords as being of the "raised variety" (examples 1–16g through 16l). However, since neither chord is likely to appear in music literature, our concern is with the tonic and subtonic sevenths that are found in common practice, the i ♭7 and the ♭VII ♭7.

Example 1–16: inversions of the i ♭7, ♭VII ♭7, i ♯7, and ♭VII ♯7

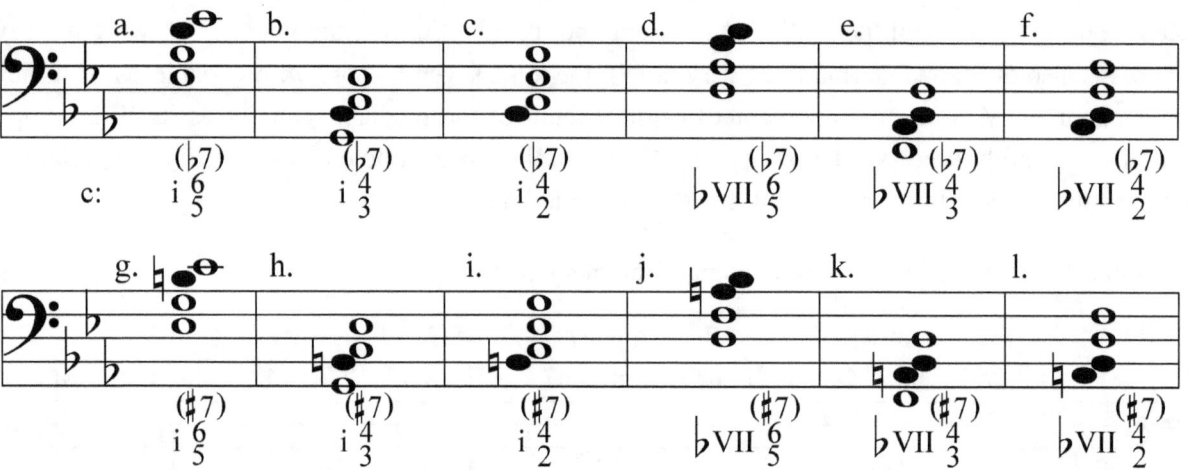

The Formation of Seventh Chords in the Extended Major

The addition of the chord seventh to the fourteen triads of the extended major mode increases the number to seventeen. As shown in example 1–17, every scale degree area except for the dominant borrows tones from the parallel minor mode, which in major become (♭3) and (♭6). Ten of the chords contain at least one borrowed tone; the (iv ♭7) and the (♭VI 7) each have two. (In 1–17, filled-in note heads indicate borrowed tones as the root, third, fifth, or seventh of each chord).

Example 1–17: the seventh-chord content of the extended major mode

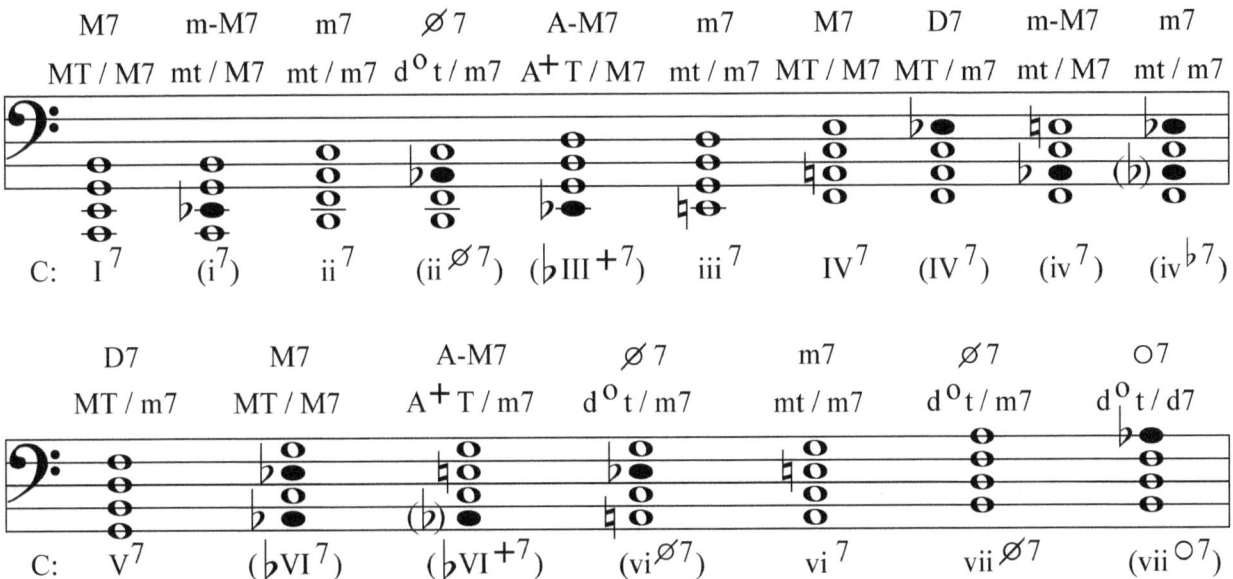

The similarities between two of the chords in the subdominant area require an adjustment to the figured bass. The minor seventh of the subdominant, (iv ♭7), takes a flat in front of its figured-bass 7 so that it can be distinguished from the (iv 7), the minor-major seventh chord. The flat in front of the 7 indicates that (♭3) is occurring at the interval of a 7th above the bass (and root). We call this chord the subdominant "lowered seventh variety." The inversions of the (iv ♭7) use the same method of notation as that of the i ♭7 or the ♭VII ♭7 (example 1–18).

Example 1–18: inversions of the (iv ♭7)

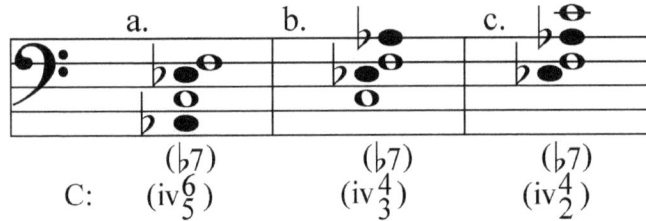

The (IV 7) requires no additional symbols. The upper case Roman numeral tells us that the underlying triad is major while the parentheses refer to (♭3) occurring at the interval of the 7th above the bass (and root).

All of the remaining borrowed chords are enclosed in parentheses. However, some of these chords take an additional descriptive symbol: a plus sign for the augmented-major seventh, a superscript circle with a diagonal slash for the half-diminished seventh, and a circle without the slash for the fully diminished seventh.

Important Functions and Uses of Seventh Chords in the Extended Major

The dominant chord in major stands in a falling perfect 5th or rising perfect 4th root and bass relationship to the tonic chord and contains as its chord third the leading tone. So constituted, the V produces two optimal conditions for affirming the tonality of a music composition: the compelling melodic drive upwards from the leading tone and the strong harmonic motion of the falling perfect 5th or rising perfect 4th in the bass. Because of its function as the chief definer of the tonality, the V chord, with or without its chord seventh, is termed here the "tonal harmonic dominant" (THD).

The leading-tone seventh, which is found in all positions, may also define the tonality. Sharing three pitches in common with the dominant seventh, it stands in a rising minor 2nd root relationship to the tonic. For example, in C major, the root, third, and fifth of the leading-tone triad (B D F) are the same pitches as the third, fifth, and seventh of the corresponding dominant seventh (G B D F).

Because of its key-defining function and common pitch content with the dominant, the leading-tone seventh functions in most cases as a dominant chord. As such, all of the chords built on the leading tone belong to the "dominant family" of chords. To be sure, there are circumstances in which the chord of the leading tone may not be functioning as a dominant but rather serving some other purpose within a particular musical context. Still, in most cases, the leading-tone seventh is appropriately recognized as a chord of the dominant family; accordingly, we further describe it as the "tonal melodic dominant" (TMD).

In addition, the vii $\varnothing^7$ (B D F A) in C major may stand in a falling perfect 5th or rising perfect 4th root and bass relationship to the iii chord (E G B) and function thereby as a modal dominant. The (vii$\circ^7$), however, can function only as a TMD and never as a modal dominant. (As we have said, the modal dominant is any chord within a diatonic scale having either a perfect or tritone falling 5th or rising 4th root relationship to the following chord other than the THD to the tonic. If we extract the vii $\varnothing^7$ and the iii from the context of C major and assume that E G B is the tonic of E Phrygian, then a half-diminished seventh consisting of the tones B D F A would serve as the modal dominant of the E-minor triad.)

The augmented triad with the major 7th, formable in both the mediant and submediant areas, rarely occurs. The ($\flat$III + ^{7}) is used as a modal dominant of ($\flat$VI), the ($\flat$VI + ^{7}) as a modal dominant of (ii$^{\circ}$). Sometimes the ($\flat$III + ^{7}) is found in conjunction with either the (i ^{6}) or V ^{7}. The ($\flat$VI + ^{7}) may be linked to the (iv ^{6}). The seventh chord of the leading tone never functions as a modal dominant of ($\flat$III + ^{7}) because the root relationship between the two chords is a diminished 4th (an acoustical major 3rd). Both the (ii $\varnothing^7$) and the (vi $\varnothing^7$) can be expressed in all chord positions.

Important Functions and Uses of Seventh Chords in the Melodic Minor

The dominant chord in minor, with or without its chord seventh, can use either variable $\flat$7 and $\sharp$7 as its chord third, resulting in either a major or minor triad. The major triad of the dominant, the V, contains as its chord third the leading tone and functions as the THD. The minor triad of the dominant, the v, is used primarily as a passing chord with variable $\flat$7 in the bass; it never defines the tonality.

As we have said, the leading-tone seventh also defines the tonality and is recognized as a chord of the dominant family, the TMD. The leading-tone seventh (or triad) can never serve as a modal dominant of the mediant because the root relationship between the two chords is a diminished 4th (an acoustical major 3rd). On the other hand, the mediant chord in minor, the III ^{7}, may be addressed by a modal dominant chord of the subtonic, the $\flat$VII $^{\flat 7}$; for both chords stand in the falling perfect 5th or rising perfect 4th root and bass relationship to each other. The subtonic may also be used in first inversion as a passing chord. The III + ^{7} is sometimes connected to the i ^{6}. Finally, as in major, both the ii $\varnothing^7$ and the $\sharp$vi $\varnothing^7$ are expressed in all chord positions.

Seventh-Chord Formats for the Extended-Diatonic Major-Minor System

Examples 1–19 and 20 illustrate seventh-chord formats for specific chord qualities that occur in extended minor and major. In minor (1–19), there are three major sevenths, three dominant sevenths, four minor sevenths, three half-diminished sevenths, one minor-major seventh, one augmented-major seventh, and one fully diminished seventh. In major (1–20), there are three major sevenths, two dominant sevenths, four minor sevenths, three half-diminished sevenths, two minor-major sevenths, two augmented-major sevenths, one fully diminished seventh. As we have said, some of the seventh chords in minor are either not used or rarely encountered in the music literature. However, all of the potential seventh chords are included in the formats to maintain pedagogical consistency

Example 1–19: the seventh-chord format for extended minor

Major Seventh	Dominant Seventh	Minor Seventh	Half-Diminished Seventh
III^7	IV^7	i$^{\flat 7}$	ii$^{\varnothing 7}$
$\flat$VI^7	V^7 (THD)	ii^7	$\sharp$vi$^{\varnothing 7}$
$\flat$VII$^{\sharp 7}$ (not used)	$\flat$VII$^{\flat 7}$	iv^7	$\sharp$vii$^{\varnothing 7}$ (not used)
		v^7	

Minor-Major Seventh	Augmented-Major Seventh	Fully Diminished Seventh
i$^{\sharp 7}$ (very rare)	III+^{7} (very rare)	$\sharp$vii$^{\circ 7}$ (TMD)

Example 1–20: the seventh-chord format for extended major

Major Seventh	Dominant Seventh	Minor Seventh	Half-Diminished Seventh
I^7	(IV^7)	ii^7	(ii$^{\varnothing 7}$)
IV^7	V^7 (THD)	iii^7	(vi$^{\varnothing 7}$)
($\flat$VI^7)		(iv$^{\flat 7}$)	vii$^{\varnothing 7}$ (TMD)
		vi^7	

Minor-Major Seventh	Augmented-Major Seventh	Fully Diminished Seventh
(i^7)	($\flat$III+^{7})	(vii$^{\circ 7}$) (TMD)
(iv^7)	($\flat$VI+^{7})	

The Application of the Seventh-Chord Formats for the Extended-Diatonic Major-Minor System

Using the formats presented in examples 1–19 and 20 enables us to see how any given seventh chord can assume a different context according to key. Examples 1–21 and 22 place the seven seventh-chord qualities rooted on C into various key contexts for extended major-minor. Thus, in 1–21, a C-major seventh can be I^7 in C major, IV^7 in G major, or (♭VI^7) in E major. In 1–22, a C-major seventh can be III^7 in a minor, ♭VI^7 in e minor, or (theoretically) ♭VII$^{\sharp 7}$ in d minor.

Example 1–21: seventh-chord contextualization for extended major

Major Seventh (C E G B)		Dominant Seventh (C E G B♭)		Minor Seventh (C E♭ G B♭)		Half-Diminished Seventh (C E♭ G♭ B♭)	
C	: I^7	G	: (IV^7)	B♭	: ii^7	B♭	: (ii ⌀7)
G	: IV^7	F	: V^7	A♭	: iii^7	E♭	: (vi ⌀7)
E	: (♭VI^7)			G	: (iv♭^{7})	D♭	: vii ⌀7
				E♭	: vi^7		

Minor-Major Seventh (C E♭ G B)		Augmented-Major Seventh (C E G♯ B)		Fully Diminished Seventh (C E♭ G♭ B♭♭)	
C	: (i^7)	A	: (♭III+^{7})	D♭	: (vii°7)
G	: (iv^7)	E	: (♭VI+^{7})		

Example 1–22: seventh-chord contextualization for extended minor

Major Seventh (C E G B)		Dominant Seventh (C E G B♭)		Minor Seventh (C E♭ G B♭)		Half-Diminished Seventh (C E♭ G♭ B♭)	
a	: III^7	g	: IV^7	c	: i♭^{7}	b♭	: ii ⌀7
e	: ♭VI^7	f	: V^7	b♭	: ii^7	e♭	: ♯vi ⌀7
d	: ♭VII$^{\sharp 7}$	d	: ♭VII♭^{7}	g	: iv^7	d♭	: ♯vii ⌀7
				f	: v^7		

Minor-Major Seventh (C E♭ G B)		Augmented-Major Seventh (C E G♯ B)		Fully Diminished Seventh (C E♭ G♭ B♭♭)	
c	: i$^{\sharp 7}$	a	: III+^{7}	d♭	: ♯vii°7

Example 1–23 combines the seventh-chord contextualization for extended major and minor into a single format. Without looking at examples 1–21 and 22 above and using the combined format in 1–23, can you assign the correct keys to the seven seventh-chord types in both major and minor modes?

Example 1–23: combined seventh-chord contextualization for extended major-minor

Major Seventh (C E G B)		Dominant Seventh (C E G B♭)		Minor Seventh (C E♭ G B♭)	
Major	Minor	Major	Minor	Major	Minor
: I ^{7}	: III ^{7}	: (IV ^{7})	: IV ^{7}	: ii ^{7}	: i ♭^{7}
: IV ^{7}	: ♭VI ^{7}	: V ^{7}	: V ^{7}	: iii ^{7}	: ii ^{7}
: (♭VI ^{7})	: ♭VII ♯^{7}		: ♭VII ♭^{7}	: (iv ♭^{7})	: iv ^{7}
				: vi ^{7}	: v ^{7}

Half-Diminished Seventh (C E♭ G♭ B♭)		Minor-Major Seventh (C E♭ G B)		Augmented-Major Seventh (C E G♯ B)		Fully Diminished Seventh (C E♭ G♭ B♭♭)	
Major	Minor	Major	Minor	Major	Minor	Major	Minor
: (ii ⌀^{7})	: ii ⌀^{7}	: (i ^{7})	: i ♯^{7}	: (♭III +^{7})	: III +^{7}	: (vii °^{7})	: ♯vii °^{7}
: (vi ⌀^{7})	: ♯vi ⌀^{7}	: (iv ^{7})		: (♭VI +^{7})			
: vii ⌀^{7}	: ♯vii ⌀^{7}						

Primary Borrowing within the Cadential $^6_4$ Chord and the Generic Use of Accidentals

Finding The Right Pitch II: A Guide To The Study Of Basic Harmony presented two different ways to describe the linear activity of certain types of $^6_4$ chords. The conventional approach provides a literal account of what tertian structures are formed above a stationary bass. The other method offers a more functional description of harmonic events in which the intervals of the 6th and the 4th are interpreted as nonharmonic tones forming chords more apparent than real.

The conventional interpretation, shown in example 1–24a, maintains that the first part of the cadential $^6_4$ is a tonic triad in second inversion followed by a root-position dominant triad or seventh. The functional perspective, however, sees the 6th and the 4th above the bass as nonharmonic tones of elaboration. Accordingly, what we have in 1–24a is not a C-major triad in $^6_4$ position, but rather, the arrival of the dominant pitch in the bass, over which two nonharmonic tones on the strongest beat of the measure occur. The nonharmonic tones delay the appearance of the dominant's chord third and fifth. The use of the Roman numeral V indicates the dominant bass while the circle around the figured-bass $^5_3$ marks the completion of the dominant with all chord tones present. The second-inversion tonic is an apparent chord.

Example 1–24b demonstrates the notation for the cadential $^6_4$ when borrowed ($\flat$3) is employed. Since the borrowed tone, E$\flat$, assumes the interval of a 6th above the bass within the apparent chord, we put a flat in front of the figured-bass 6. Remember that the use of the flat in front of the number does not necessarily mean that the pitch itself carries a flat. Instead, the functional description in 1–24b implements the *generic use of an accidental*, which tells us that the tone in question is lowered within the context of the key and mode. If the key had been C$\sharp$ major instead of C major, then ($\flat$3) would have been E$\natural$ and the figured-bass 6 would still have taken a flat.

Example 1–24: conventional and functional descriptions for the cadential $^6_4$

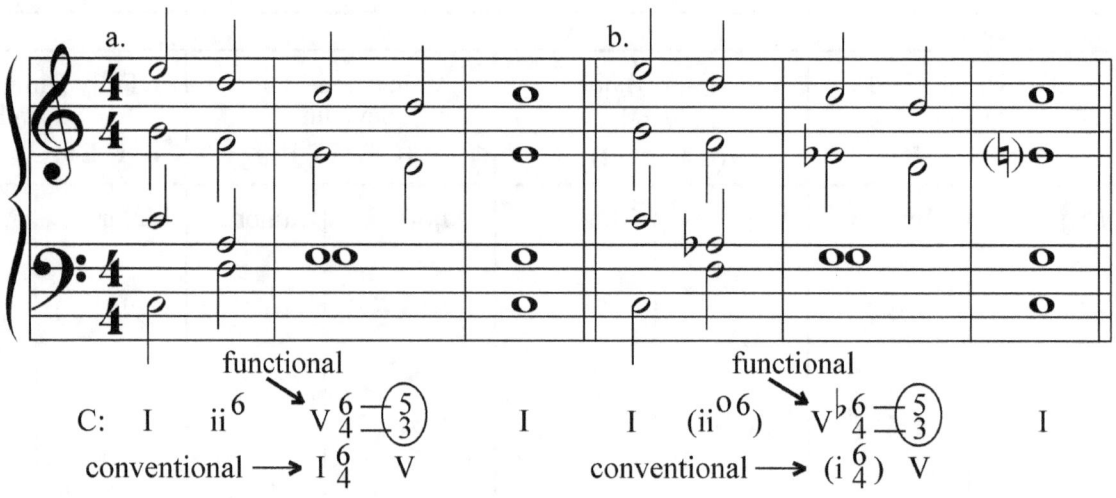

The Picardy Third

Around the beginning of the sixteenth century, composers began to show a preference for ending minor compositions with a major triad on the tonic. This practice continued for about two hundred years of music composition. The assignment of the major tonic triad in a composition written in the minor mode was later referred to in French as the *tierce de Picardie*, in English, the Picardy third. Within the context of the minor mode, the tonic triad is viewed as having a raised 3rd, raised one half step from the characteristic minor 3rd between the root and third of the chord.

The Picardy third is a common form of primary borrowing that incorporates scale degree 3 of the major mode into minor. Example 1–25 illustrates a chord progression that uses the Picardy third in the final tonic chord. Play the progression on the piano and you will hear how powerful the Picardy third sounds within the prevailing minor mode. Moreover, the cadential $^6_4$ in minor enhances the effect of the major triad of the final tonic. (The P under the I indicates the Picardy third.)

Example 1–25: ending a progression in minor with a major tonic

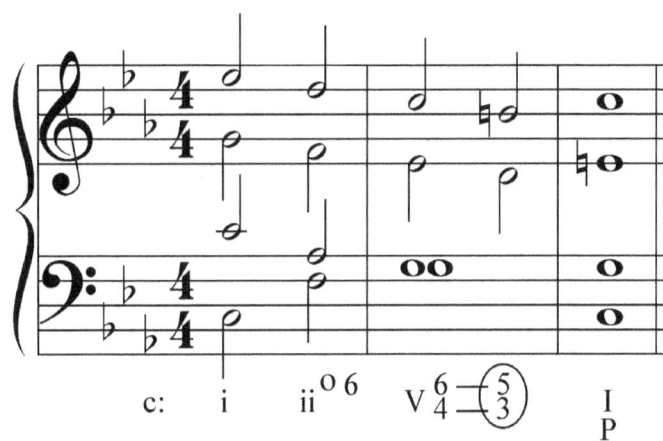

In the next chapter, we shall encounter a class of linear-harmonic operations similar to that of the cadential $^6_4$. Indeed, certain linear activities, often involving borrowed tones, produce tertian structures that appear to be chords but whose status as such is questionable. Upon closer examination, these chords turn out to be collections of pitches containing one or more nonharmonic tones that together comprise all of the literal components of a chord.

Our task is to explore the differences between real and apparent chords and to put forward a notation for their functional description. But first, we conclude this chapter with a type of simple chromaticism that often informs the harmonic dispositions of both real and apparent chords.

Melodic Chromaticism

The chromatic scale in example 1–26 is a model of melodic chromaticism. It contains pairs of pitches with two different versions of the same letter name: in the ascending form, C–C♯, D–D♯, F–F♯, G–G♯, and A–A♯ (1–26a); and in the descending form, B–B♭, A–A♭, G–G♭, E–E♭, and D–D♭ (1–26b). Most of the scale exhibits alterations of notes with accidentals, a process known as pitch inflection.

Example 1–26: pitch inflection in the chromatic scale

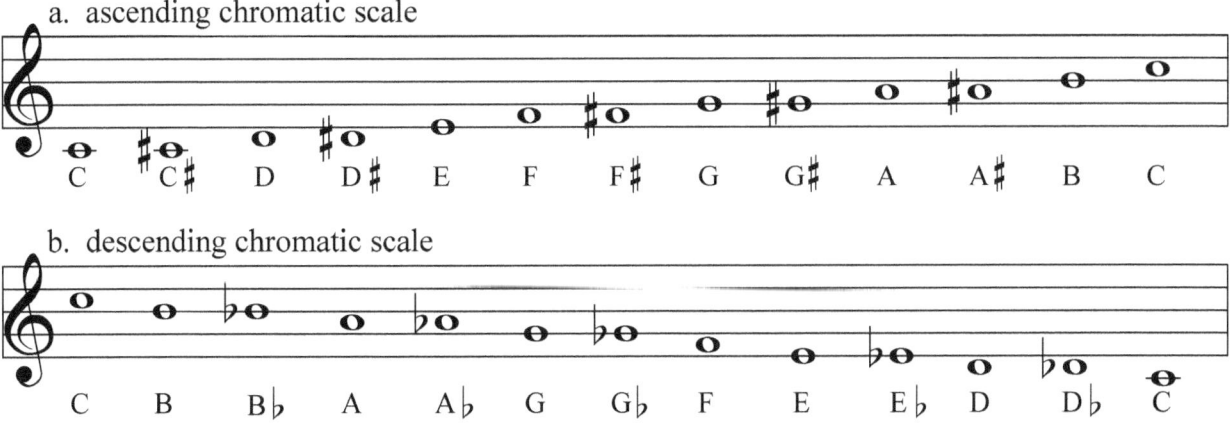

Chromatic pitch inflection involves raising or lowering diatonic pitches in half-step increments. Such chromatic additions may or may not effect a change of key. Often, these additions have an ornamental function and pose no threat to the stability of the governing tonic; rather, they serve to embellish a tone or to intensify the linear motion between tones. As given in example 1–27, the most common types of melodic chromaticism consist of complete or incomplete neighbors and passing tones.

Example 1–27: chromatic pitch inflection

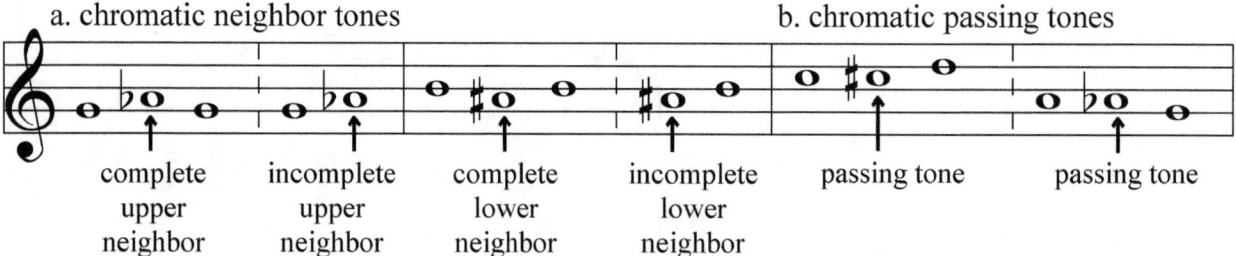

Chapter 2   Apparent Chords

Chords are by-products of linear motion. Sometimes, melodic chromaticism and other linear activities may produce a collection of pitches that together comprise all the literal components of a chord but whose existence as such presents certain challenges to both listeners and music analysts. Acquiring the knowledge and ability to distinguish between real and apparent chords and then implementing a functional notation that accounts for the linear events from which they arise count among the most significant challenges.

As we saw in Chapter 1, the cadential $^6_4$ both delays and elaborates the tonal harmonic dominant (THD) with an apparent tonic chord in second inversion. In Example 2–1, an apparent seventh of the leading tone delays the formation of the dominant. Ultimately, a harmonic conversion takes place between two chords of the dominant family: the tonal melodic dominant (TMD) and the tonal harmonic dominant. The TMD connects to the THD when the former's chord seventh moves down to scale degree 5, producing what shall be referred to here as a "conversion dominant" (A or A♭ down to G).

In 2–1, the functional description is given in row A, the conventional interpretation in row B. Row A shows how the apparent leading-tone seventh elaborates the dominant through conversion. The circle around the figured bass marks the completion of the dominant with all chord tones present. (Although not featured in 2–1, the conversion dominant could also proceed in the reverse order, from the THD to the TMD.)

Example 2–1: conversion from apparent half-diminished/fully diminished TMD to THD (in major)

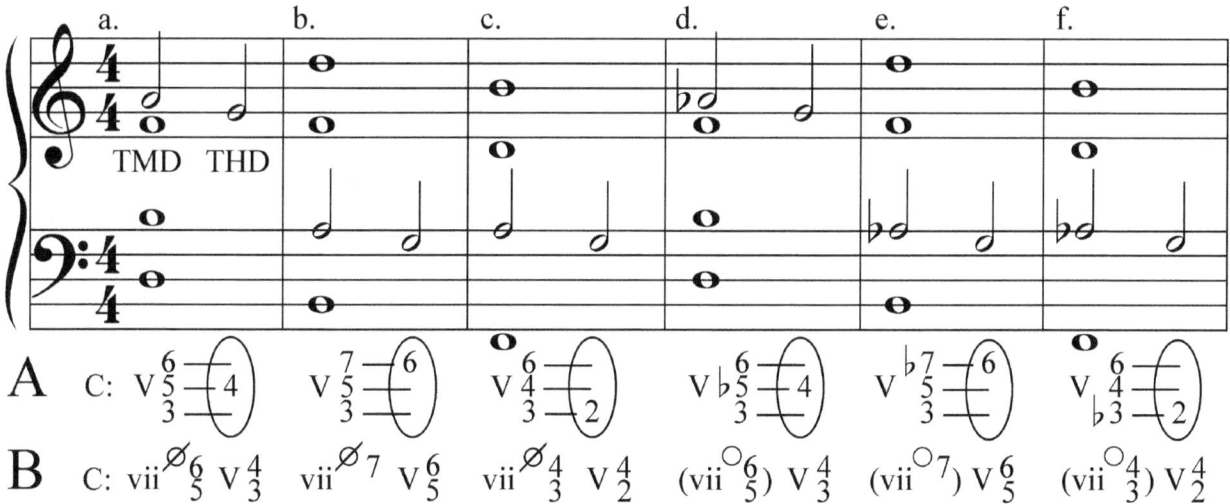

Generic Figured Bass

Examples 2–1d, 1e, and 1f demonstrate the generic use of the flat in conjunction with figured bass and Roman numerals. Example 2–1d places a flat in front of the figured-bass 5 to indicate that (♭6) is written at the interval of a 5th above the bass. Borrowed (♭6) assumes the interval of a 7th above the bass in 2–1e and a 3rd above the bass in 2–1f. (Note: If stationary and uninflected, both the 3rd and 5th above the bass are sometimes omitted in the generic figured bass.)

The half-diminished seventh chord of the leading tone is not used in minor and is therefore excluded from example 2–2. The fully diminished seventh, however, functions as an apparent seventh when it forms a connection with the dominant chord. The seventh of the leading-tone chord in 2–2 moves down by half step to scale degree 5, the root of the THD (A♭ down to G).

Since variable ♭6 (A♭) forms the seventh of an apparent chord, we must account for its presence with a generic flat in front of the figured bass. Thus, in 2–2a, ♭6 occurs at the interval of a 5th above the bass, in 2b at the interval of a 7th, and in 2c at the interval of a 3rd. The question is: why not also inflect the figured bass to account for B♮, variable ♯7? When using accidentals generically with Roman numerals, inflect the figured bass *only* when it clarifies the linear operation. Since B♮ is the chord third of the dominant, the uppercase Roman numeral V accounts for ♯7.

Example 2–2: conversion from apparent fully diminished TMD to THD (in minor)

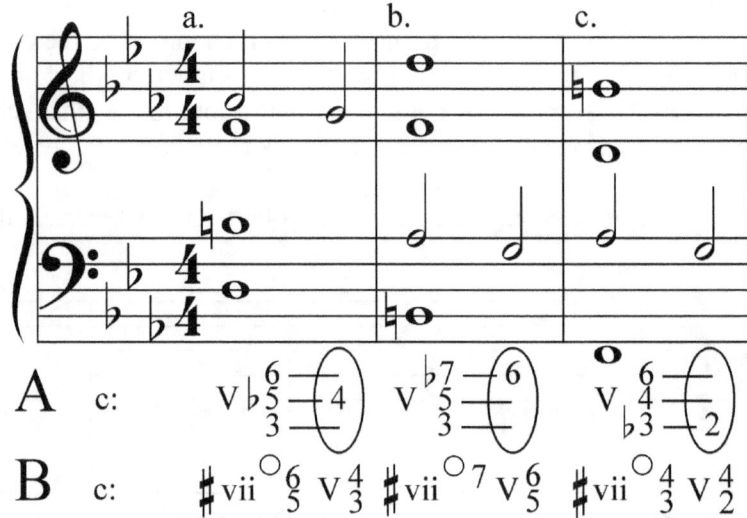

Example 2–3: apparent chord to half-diminished TMD (in major)

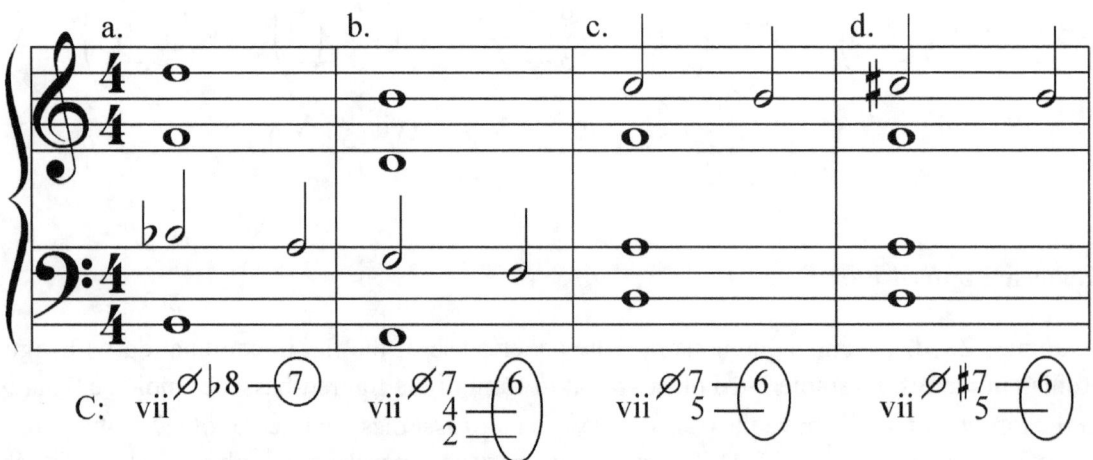

Example 2–3 above displays some unusual vertical formations preceding the completion of the leading-tone half-diminished seventh. (Note: There are no alternative chord symbols for some of the chords in this chapter.) In 2–3a, the B♭ in the tenor voice takes a flat in front of the number 8 because it is a lowered chromatic tone occurring at the interval of an octave above the bass. However, the B♭ is enharmonically

Chapter 2 Apparent Chords 21

equivalent to A♯, which gives us a diminished triad with an acoustical major 7th above the B♮. In 2–3d, the C♯ stands a 7th above the bass as a raised chromatic tone within a complex of pitches that sounds like a minor triad with a major 7th. The chord's figured bass needs a sharp in front of the number 7.

Example 2–4, also in C major, illustrates the borrowed fully diminished seventh of the leading tone. Both the parentheses and superscript circle attached to the Roman numeral account for the A♭, borrowed (♭6). No inflection of the figured bass is needed. However, in 2–4a, the B♭ is a lowered chromatic tone, which is indicated in the figured bass with a flat in front of the number 8. At the interval of a 7th above the bass, the C♯ in the soprano of 2–4d is a raised chromatic tone within what appears to be a diminished triad with a major 7th. As in 2–3d, the figured bass has a sharp in front of the number 7.

Example 2–4: apparent chord to borrowed fully diminished TMD (in major)

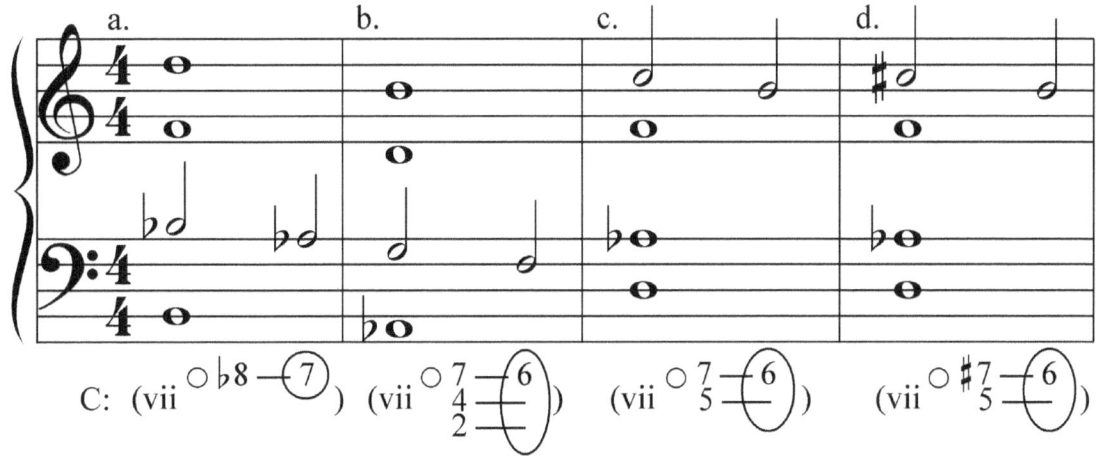

Example 2–5 places the fully diminished seventh of the leading tone within the context of c minor. The B♮ is represented by the sharp in front of the Roman numeral, designating variable ♯7 as the root of the chord. The superscript circle attached to the Roman numeral determines the tone of the chord seventh (A♭). Since the B♭ in 2–5a is variable ♭7 and stands an octave above the bass, the figured bass requires a flat in front of the 8. The figured bass in examples 2–5b and 5c remains uninflected. Example 2–5d, however, has a raised chromatic tone (C♯), which must be indicated in the figured bass with a sharp in front of the number 7.

Example 2–5: apparent chord to fully diminished TMD (in minor)

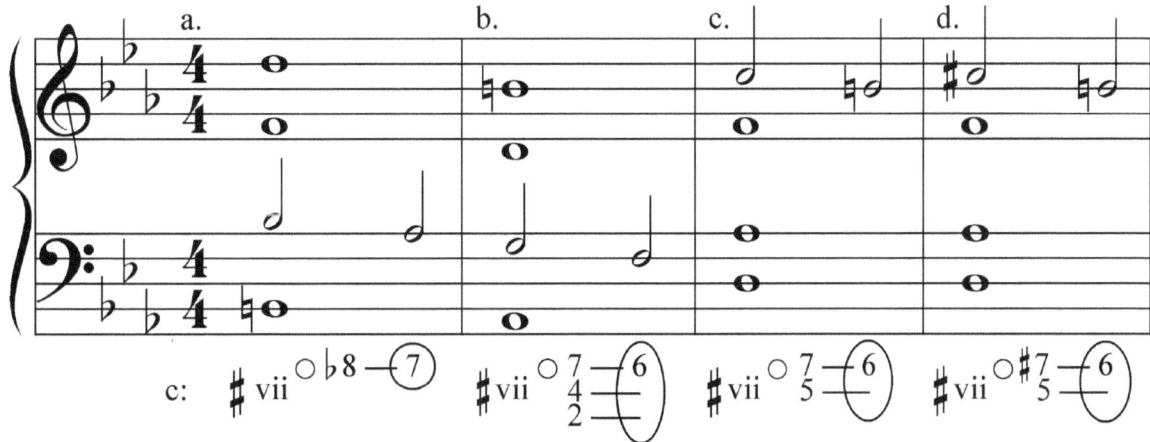

22   Chapter 2   Apparent Chords

In example 2–6, we resist the temptation of assigning a chord-symbol identity to the apparent chord. Instead, let us recognize that the linear activity involving the 6th above the bass (E or E♭) delays the completion of the THD triad (2–6a) or seventh (2–6b, 6c, and 6d). Examples 2–6c and 6d contain (♭3), E♭, which requires an inflection of the figured bass. The tone E♭ stands above the bass as a consonance and may therefore move either upwards (2–6c) or downwards (2–6d). The number 6 takes a flat because the borrowed E♭ is lowered within the context of C major.

Example 2–6: apparent chord to THD (in major)

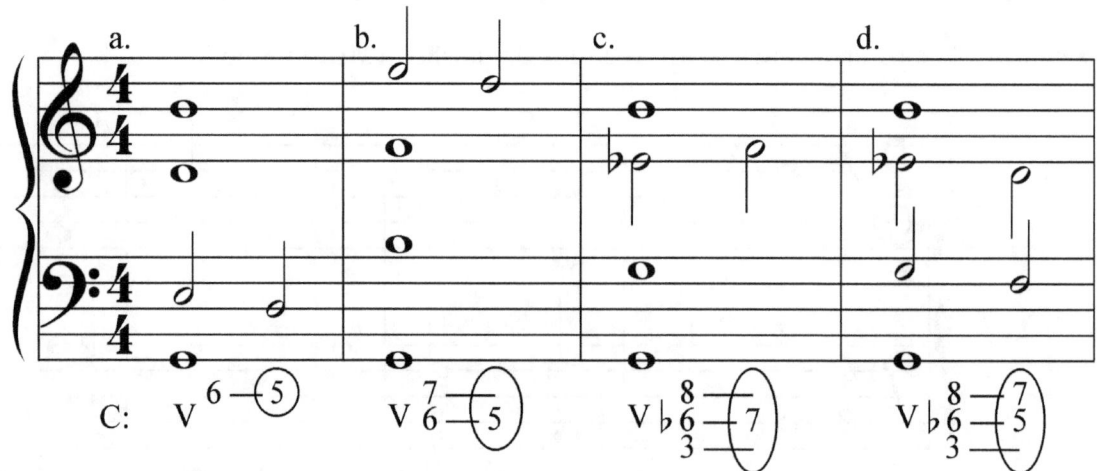

Although B♮ contradicts the key signature of c minor as variable ♯7 in example 2–7, the uppercase V confirms its place in the chord's disposition. The chord symbol and generic figured bass in 2–7 is identical to that of 2–6 above; except that in 2–7, there is no need to inflect the number 6 with a flat because E♭ is scale degree 3 of c minor.

Example 2–7: apparent chord to THD (in minor)

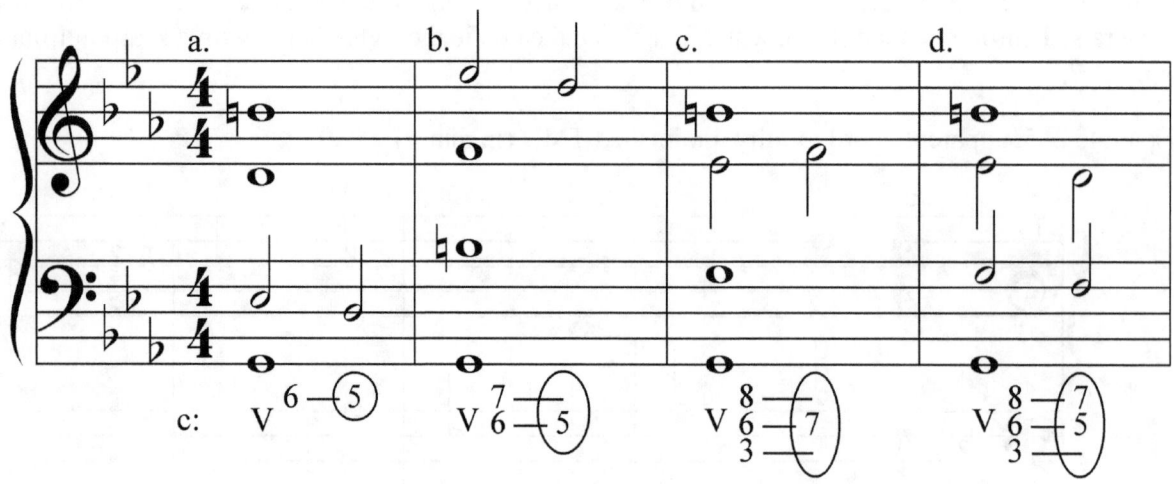

Using Generic Figured Bass for the Melodic Succession from ♭7 to ♯7 in Minor

Adding generic figured bass to Roman numeral chord symbols provides an accurate functional description of the connections between real and apparent chords. However, the generic approach is best employed by avoiding unnecessary inflections of the figured bass and relying (whenever practicable) upon the chord symbols introduced in the foregoing pages. Most of the examples in this chapter show the apparent chord leading to the real chord. But as we shall later discover, it is also possible to proceed from the real chord to the apparent chord.

Although Roman numerals and generic figured bass account for virtually all of the chord structures in the extended major-minor system, at least one rendering of generic figured bass is less than ideal. As with the previous examples, it involves a chord of the dominant family.

In example 2–8a, an apparent III^6 chord precedes the completion of the dominant seventh on beat 3. The soprano voice exhibits a succession of pitches from variables ♭7 to ♯7 (B♭ to B♮). There is no problem representing ♭7 with a generic flat in front of the number 3. Moreover, as we have said, the uppercase V accounts for ♯7 (B♮) as the chord third.

However, since there is a succession from ♭7 to ♯7 in the same voice, a generic sign is required to indicate the change from one tone to the other. Designating ♯7 with a sharp in front of the number 3 would be awkward following the inflection of 3 with a flat and also confusing because the uppercase V confirms the chord third as B♮.

The only sign that remains available is the natural, used here to indicate that the chord third reverts to what the chord symbol (the uppercase V) already tells us. In 2–8, the inclusion of the natural is essential because it clarifies the motion from ♭7 to ♯7. An alternative would be to repeat the number 3 and precede it with the natural sign in parentheses (see the bottom line of the example).

Examples 2–8b, 8c, and 8d transpose the chord formation in 8a to the keys of f♯, f, and g♯ minor. For all three transpositions, we use a generic natural to represent E♯, E♮, and F𝄪—variable ♯7 in each respective key. At the end of this chapter, we shall see how providing exact figured bass instead of generic figured bass adds an unnecessary layer of complexity to the description of the operation.

Example 2–8: using generic figured bass with the melodic succession from ♭7 to ♯7

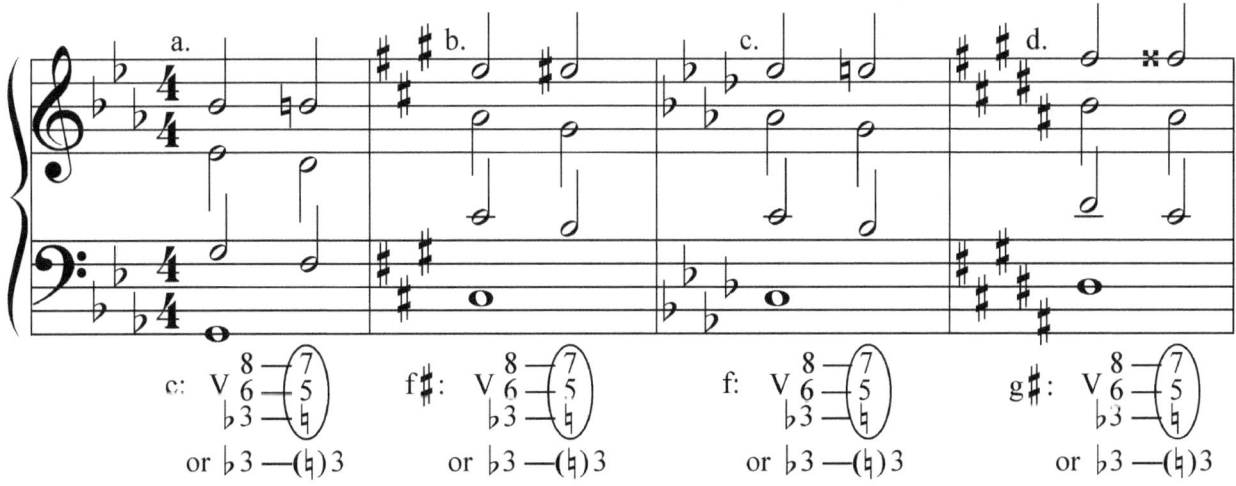

There are other ways to represent the linear activities that produce the harmonic disposition shown in 2–8; however, the method put forward in this text inflects the figured bass in a consistent and uniform way and only when all other options for chord symbols have been exhausted. The case of the Roman numeral,

24   Chapter 2   Apparent Chords

the presence or absence of parentheses (indicating whether or not the chord is borrowed), superscript circles (with or without the diagonal slash), and/or a sharp or flat in front of the Roman numeral (generic signs) account for all of the components of the real chord. Further, a circle enclosing the figured bass confirms the linear operations that constitute the real harmonic structures.

Non-Dominant Apparent Chords

This section explores some of the apparent chord formations other than those of the dominant family. Example 2–9 presents various expressions of the tonic, preceded by apparent subdominant and mediant chords. In 2–9b, a flat in front of the figured-bass 6 indicates that borrowed (♭6) is written at the interval of a 6th above the bass. Example 2–10b uses the same generic designation for variable ♭6. In both examples 2–10c and 10d, a sharp in front of the 5 accounts for the presence of variable ♯7 in the apparent chord. We also represent ♯7 with a generic sharp in example 2–12a below. (Notice that the 5 in 2–9d does not need a generic sharp because B is a diatonic scale degree in C major.)

Example 2–9: apparent chord to tonic (in major)

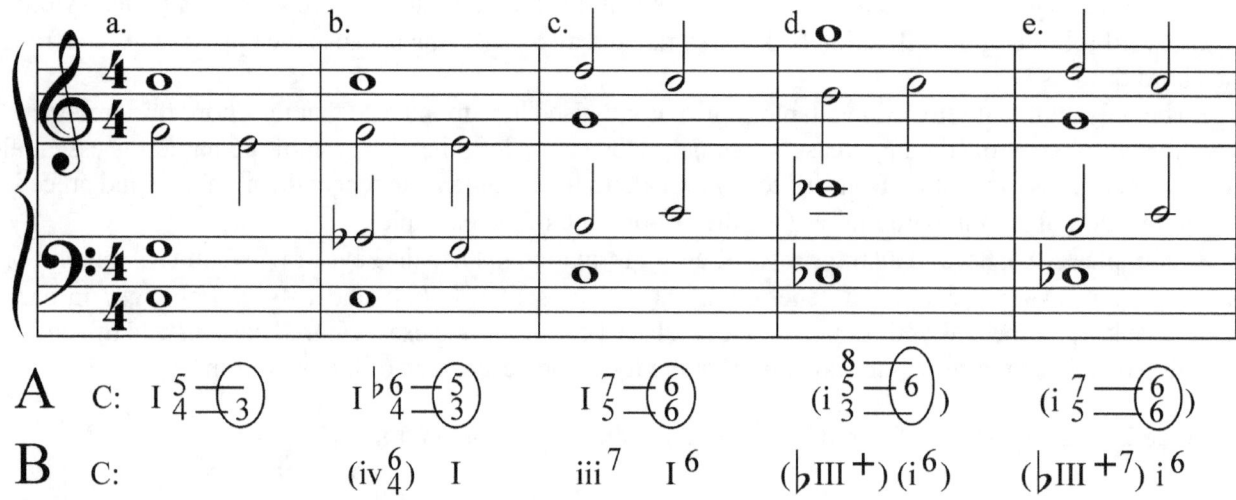

Example 2–10: apparent chord to tonic (in minor)

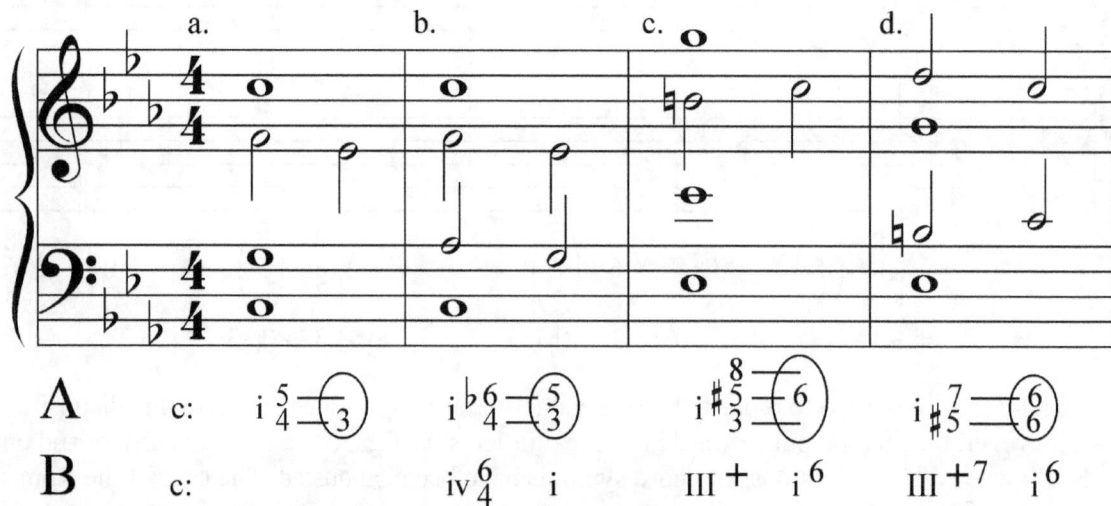

Chapter 2 Apparent Chords   25

Examples 2–11 and 2–12 focus primarily on chords of the tonic and supertonic. As in examples 2–9 and 2–10, the real chords are preceded by apparent mediant and submediant chords. The chords in 2–11 require no inflections of their figured bass. In all instances, the chord symbol accounts for the pitches.

The E♭ in example 2–11a and the A♭ in 11d are borrowed elements, indicated as such by the parentheses, case of the Roman numeral, and the superscript circle (in 2–11d and 11e). Notice the apparent ninth chord in 2–11c, which involves 9—8 and 7—6 motions into a first-inversion supertonic (see also 2–12c).

Example 2–11: apparent chord to tonic or supertonic (in major)

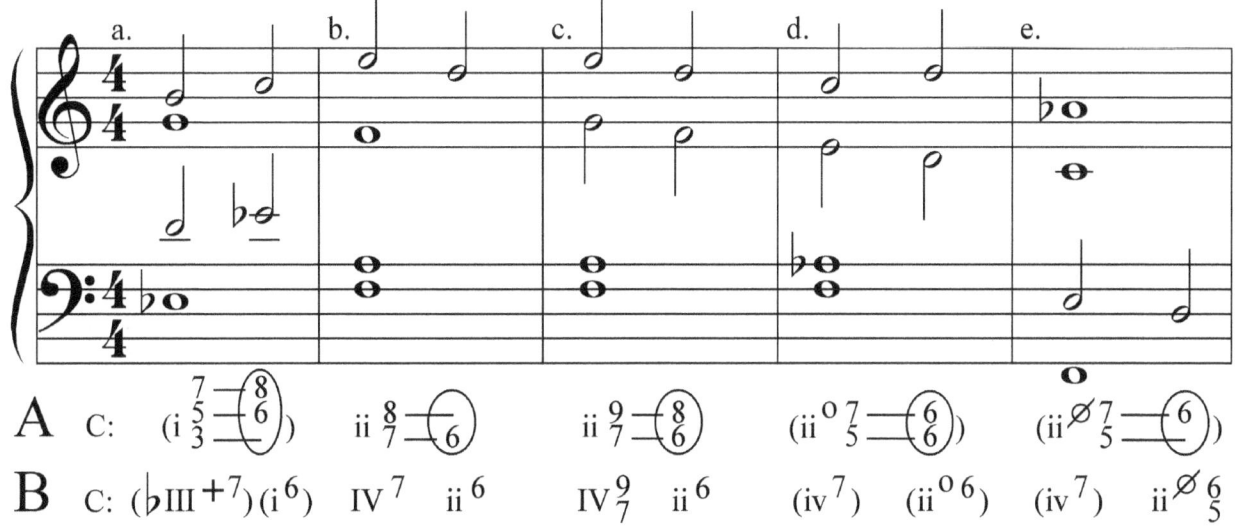

Example 2–12: apparent chord to tonic or supertonic (in minor)

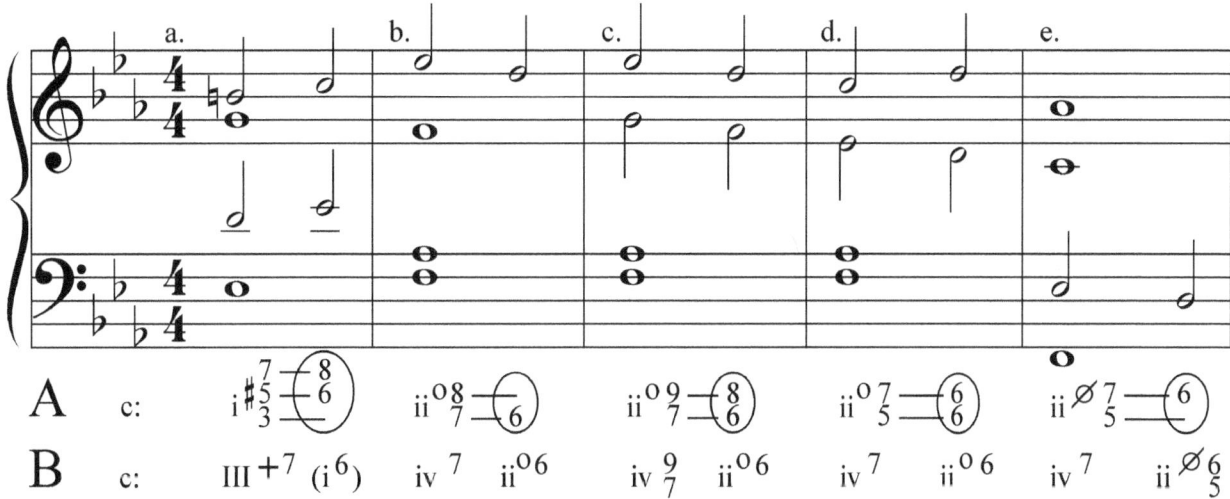

Examples 2–13 and 2–14 feature subdominant and submediant chords. The real chords are delayed by apparent supertonic, subdominant, and submediant chords. Example 2–13c displays the only apparent chord necessitating an inflection of the figured bass; a flat in front of the number 5 represents borrowed ($\flat 3$).

Shown in 2–13b, the apparent augmented-major seventh of the submediant, ($\flat VI+^7$), is not formable in minor without borrowing scale degree 3 of the parallel major. For the present, we shall defer incorporating the major mode's mediant scale degree into minor (except for the Picardy third) and accordingly omit the augmented-major seventh from example 2–14. (The use of major's scale degree 3 in the parallel minor will be discussed later.)

Example 2–13: apparent chord to subdominant or submediant (in major)

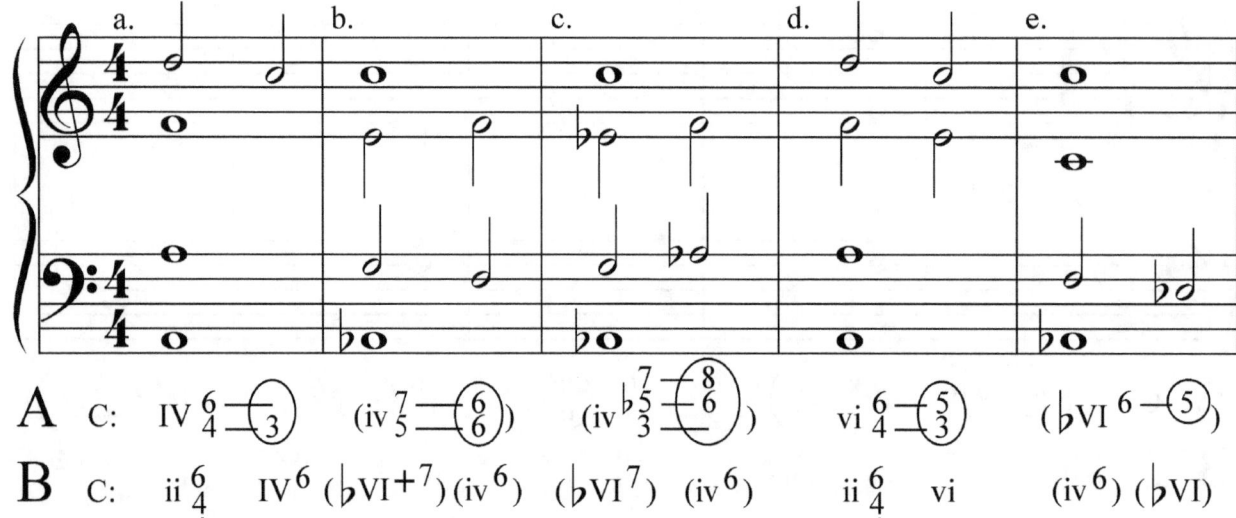

Example 2–14: apparent chord to subdominant or submediant (in minor)

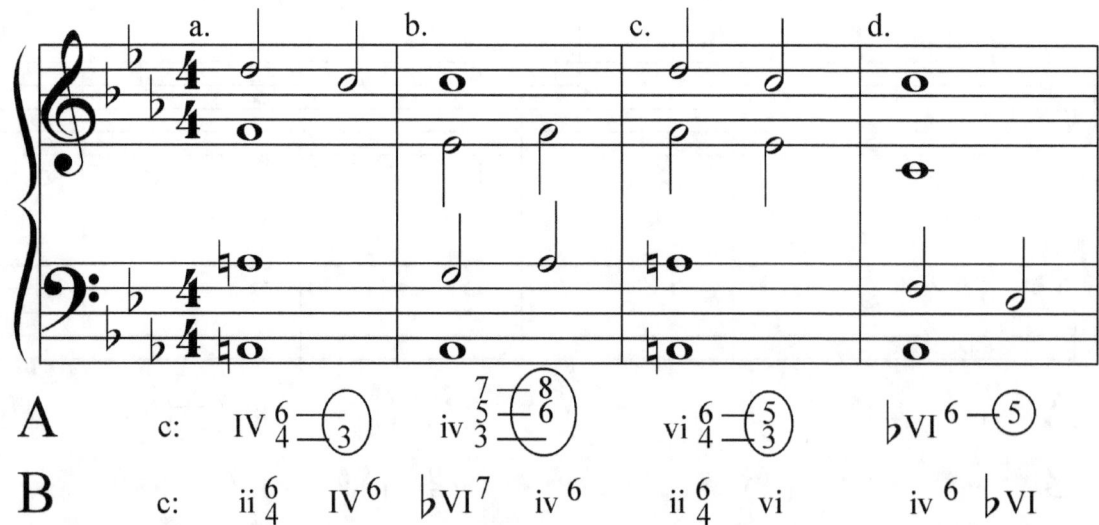

Example 2–15 demonstrates seventh chords of the subdominant and supertonic in both major and minor. The subdominant (examples 2–15a and 15c, row A) requires a flat in front of the 3 to account for the chromatic 3rd above the bass (E$\flat$/G$\flat$). In 2–15a, the borrowed E$\flat$ is indicated by the parentheses enclosing Roman numeral IV. In 2–15c, the uppercase IV identifies the chord third as A$\natural$ ($\sharp 6$).

In the soprano and alto voices of example 2–15a and 15c, an augmented 5th proceeds to a perfect 5th. Unequal parallel 5ths are usually acceptable except when they occur between outer voices. In examples 2–15b and 15d, an apparent minor seventh of the subdominant (row B) delays the completion of the supertonic half-diminished seventh. The superscript circle with the diagonal slash and the parentheses (in major) stipulate the pitch content of the real chord. The circled figured-bass tells us that we have an inverted seventh.

Example 2–15: apparent chord to subdominant or supertonic (in major and minor)

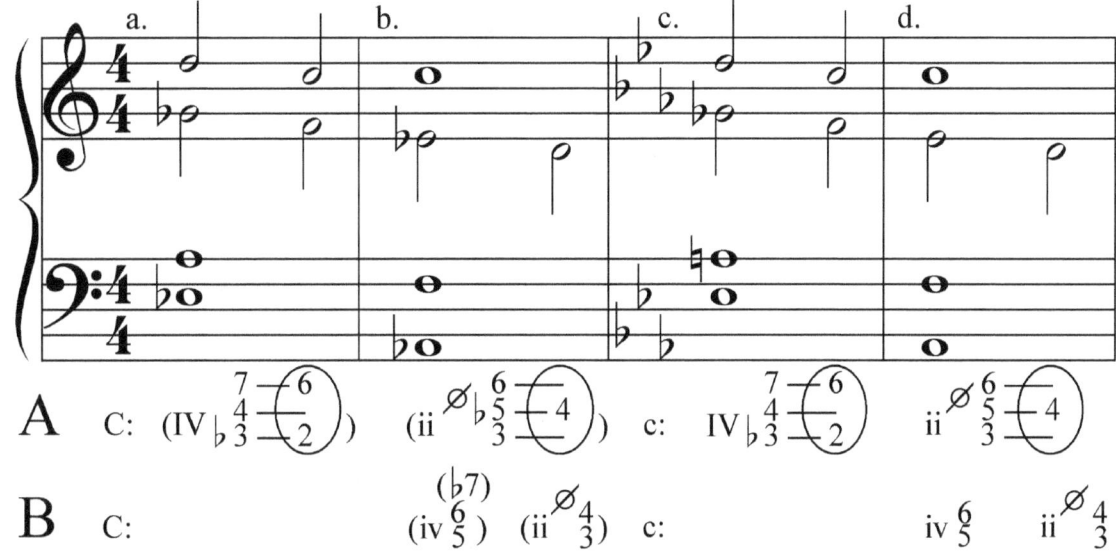

Placing the Real Chord Before the Apparent Chord

In this section, we examine some dispositions in which the real chord precedes the apparent chord. Example 2–16 has five expressions of the tonic triad followed by an apparent submediant. The flat in front of the 6 in examples 2–16c and 16d represents borrowed (♭6), A♭.

Example 2–16: tonic to apparent submediant (in major)

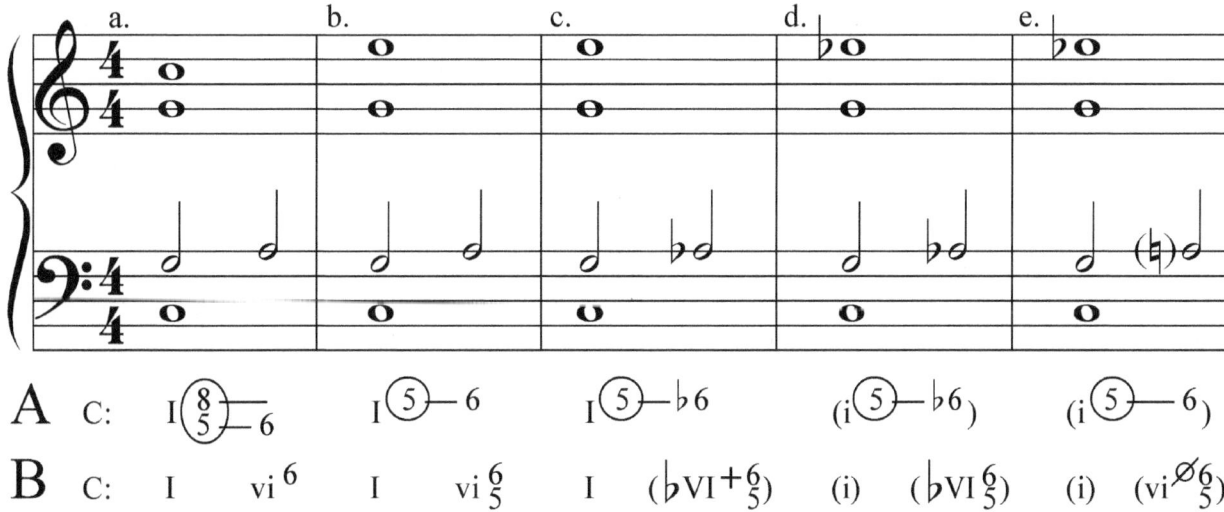

28   Chapter 2   Apparent Chords

In example 2–17, both the number 6 and numerals VI and vi take generic accidentals to designate lowered and raised variables. The superscript circle with the diagonal slash (2–17b) confirms the quality of the apparent seventh as half-diminished.

Example 2–17: tonic to apparent submediant (in minor)

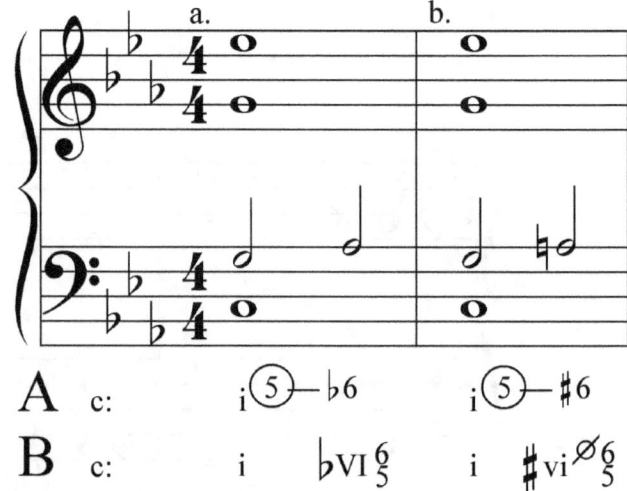

Example 2–18 exhibits apparent seventh chords of the supertonic (18a, 18b, 18c, and 18d) and subdominant (18e). Notice the use of borrowed E♭ as the chord seventh of the subdominant in 2–18b. This subdominant is the lowered seventh variety of the chord, consisting of a minor triad and a minor 7th from root to seventh (see above, p. 11). As shown in 2–18d, when this chord inverts, we indicate the quality of the seventh by placing the generic symbol for lowered 7 in parentheses above the figured bass. Thus, the real chord is the subdominant lowered seventh variety in first inversion.

Example 2–18: submediant or subdominant to apparent supertonic or subdominant (in major)

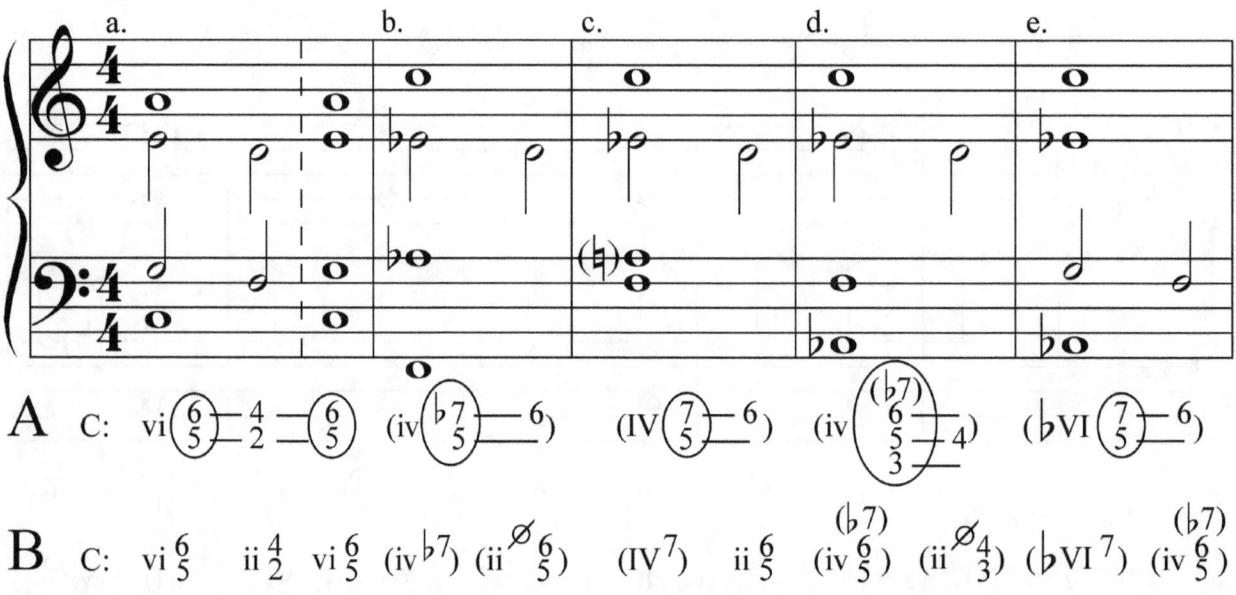

Example 2–19 places the seventh chords of 2–18b, 18c, 18d, and 18e into the parallel key and mode of c minor. The chords in 2–19a, however, differ slightly from those of 2–18a and are selected on the basis of their potential formation within the descending melodic minor. The half-diminished seventh of the supertonic elaborates, or embellishes, the major seventh of the lowered submediant.

Example 2–19: submediant or subdominant to apparent supertonic or subdominant (in minor)

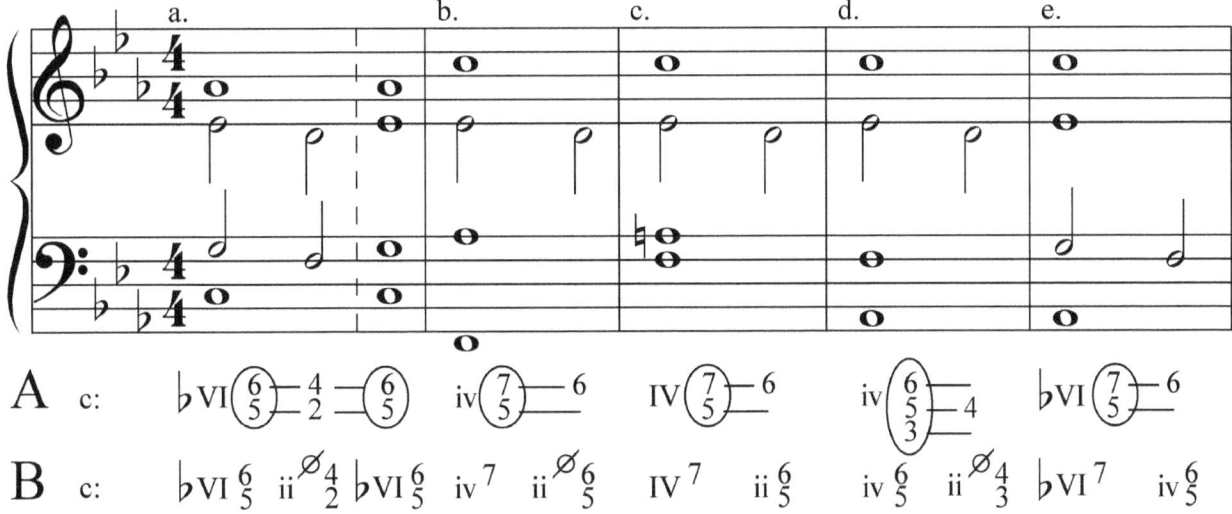

Example 2–20 illustrates seventh chords of the leading tone, dominant, and tonic in C major. As in some of the previous chord formations, borrowed ($\flat 6$) appears as the seventh of the real chord in 2–20b, as the seventh of the apparent chord in 20c and 20d, and as the third of the apparent chord in 20e. In 2–20b, the chord seventh of the fully diminished seventh is confirmed as A$\flat$ by the parentheses denoting borrowed ($\flat 6$) and the superscript circle identifying the overall quality of the chord.

Example 2–20: TMD, THD/CLT, or tonic to apparent TMD or subdominant (in major)

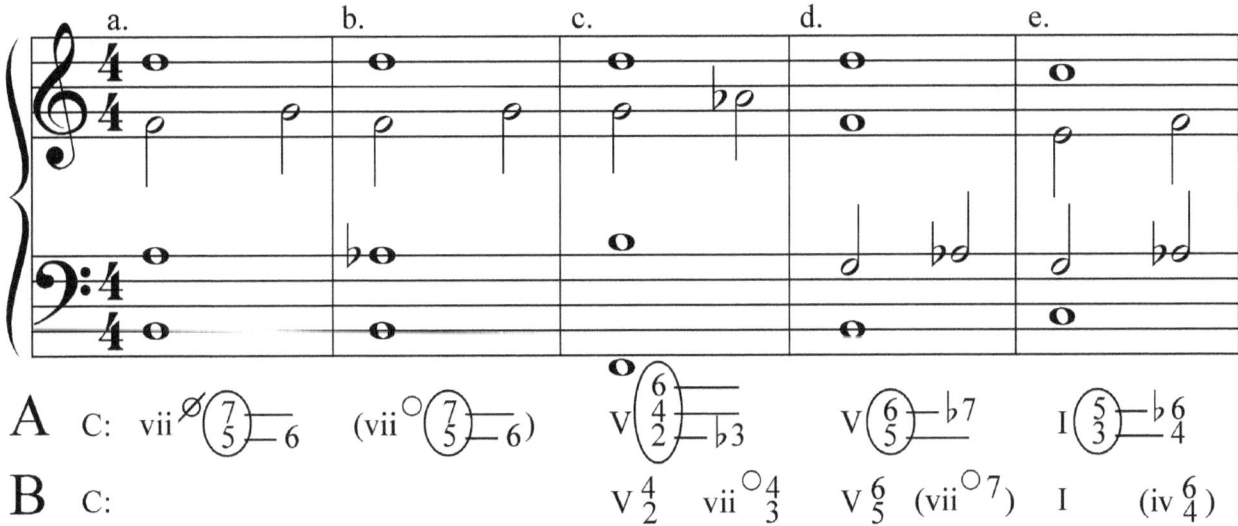

30   Chapter 2   Apparent Chords

Examples 2–21b, 21c, 21d, and 21e in c minor correspond to examples 2–20b, 20c, 20d, and 20e in C major. In 2–21a, we replace the half-diminished seventh of 2–20a (which is not used in minor) with two chords: an apparent subtonic and a real subdominant; the former embellishes the latter. The uppercase V in examples 2–21c and 21d accounts for the B♮, variable ♯7 and the chord third of the dominant. In 2–21b, the generic sharp in front of the vii represents the B♮. Variable ♭6 takes a generic flat in the figured basses of 2–21c, 21d, and 21e (row A).

Example 2–21: subdominant, TMD, THD, or tonic to apparent subtonic, TMD, or subdominant (in minor)

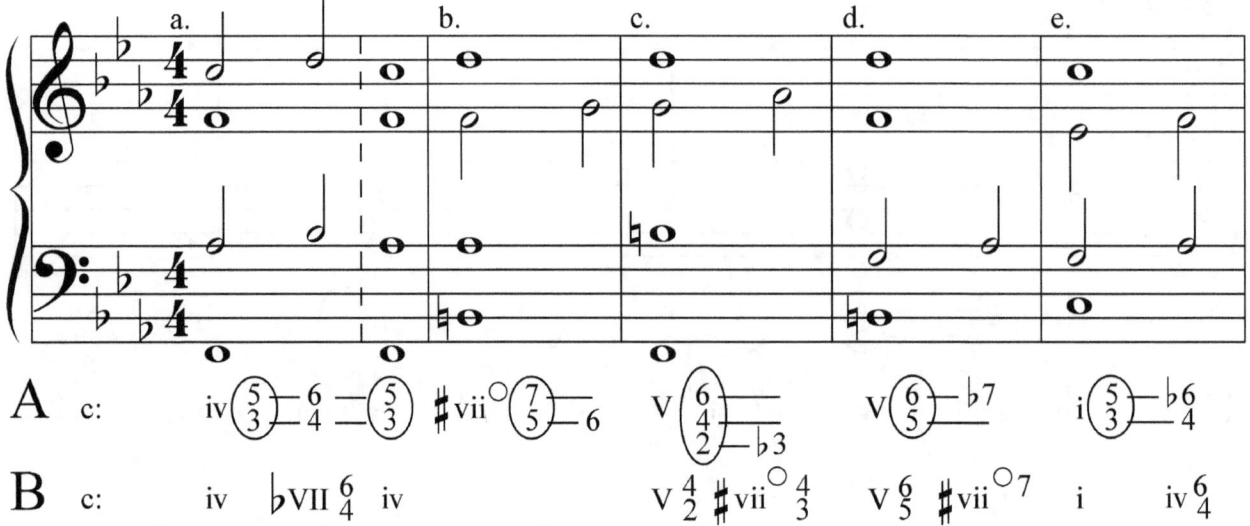

Using the same type of pedal embellishing motion (that is, motion above a stationary bass) shown in 2–21a above, examples 2–22 and 23 exhibit tonic triads in conjunction with apparent triads of the subdominant and submediant.

Example 2–22: tonic to apparent subdominant or submediant (in major)

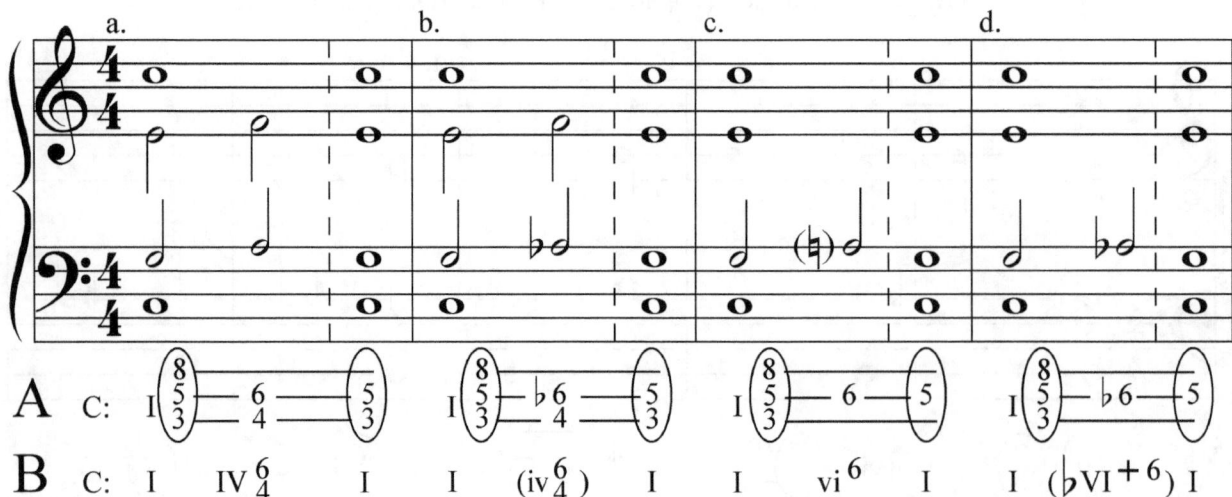

Example 2–23: tonic to apparent subdominant or submediant (in minor)

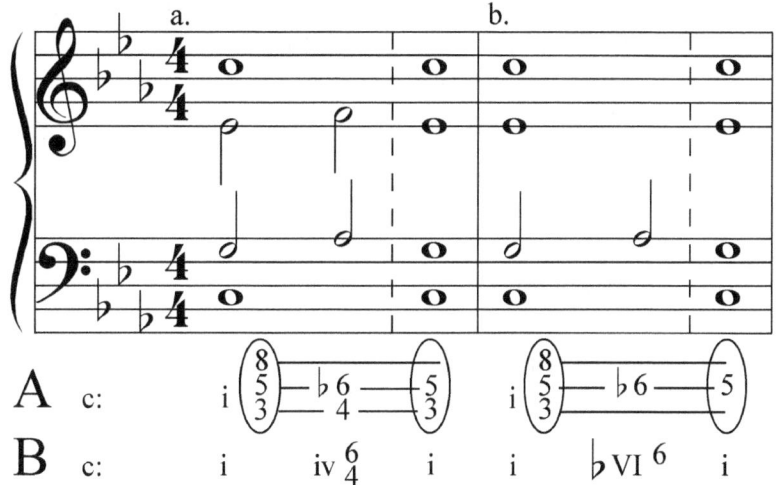

The apparent chords of the supertonic in example 2–24 contain 8—9—8 motions above a stationary bass. It should be noted that the position of this apparent supertonic is actually that of a third-inversion seventh chord. The figured bass in row A expresses the interval of the 2nd as a 9th, but the actual position of the chord is understood as either $\begin{smallmatrix}6\\4\\2\end{smallmatrix}$ or $\begin{smallmatrix}4\\2\end{smallmatrix}$.

Example 2–24: tonic to apparent supertonic (in major)

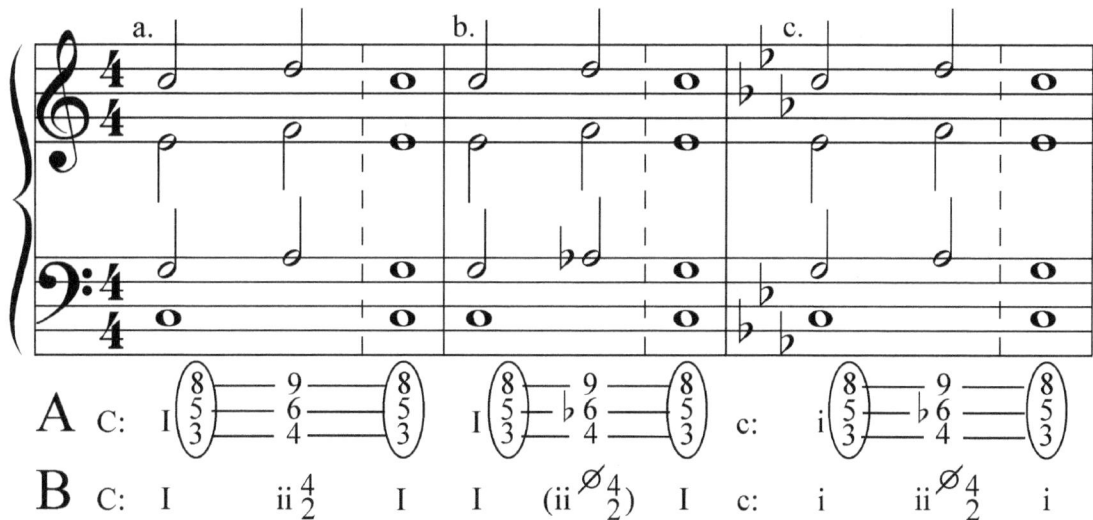

Exact Figured Bass

The practice of using exact figured bass originated in the Baroque period (1600–1750). The Baroque system of figures is also known as thoroughbass or basso continuo. Baroque composers usually did not provide complete accompaniments for their music. Rather, they placed Arabic numbers and other symbols below the bass line to indicate what pitches should be used to perform the accompaniment.

Although the details of the accompaniment were left to the skill and judgement of the figured-bass player, the numbers stipulated the intervals to be executed above the bass while the symbols indicated chromatic pitches. Thus, exact figured bass reflects the specific pitches in the music, without regard to their function or meaning. If the pitch is in the key signature, then no accidental is attached to the Arabic number. However, if the pitch contradicts the key signature, then either a sharp, double sharp, flat, double flat, or natural precedes (or sometimes follows) the number. Any accidental attached to the figured bass determines the accidental used in the music.

Reading exact figured bass is not unlike interpreting the chord symbols that appear in commercial lead sheets; for both practices, the player makes no attempt to analyze the music. Rather, the only objective is to "realize" (that is, interpret and play) the specific pitches in the score without understanding the context or meaning of those pitches. The following guidelines summarize the principles of exact figured bass (some symbols mentioned below are not used in this text):

(1) Arabic numbers indicate numerical intervals above the bass.
(2) The Arabic number does not identify the register for the top note of the indicated interval.
(3) Any accidental in the music that contradicts the key signature takes the same accidental in the figured bass. The accidental is placed either before or after the Arabic number. Accidentals include ♯, ×, ♭, ♭♭, ♮. In this text, accidentals are not placed after the number.
(4) An accidental that is not attached to an Arabic number refers to the interval of a 3rd above the bass.
(5) A plus sign following a number indicates that the tone is raised. The plus sign, as applied here, is not used in this text.
(6) A slash through a number or a small vertical line attached to the number designates a raised tone. Neither symbol is used in this text.
(7) The absence of any figured bass usually means that a root-position triad occurs above the bass pitch.
(8) When the number 6 appears alone in the figured bass, it is usually an abbreviation for $^6_3$; therefore, the interval of the 3rd above the bass is also assumed.

Example 2–25 presents some possible renderings for chords using exact figured bass without Roman numeral chord symbols.

Example 2–25: exact figured bass

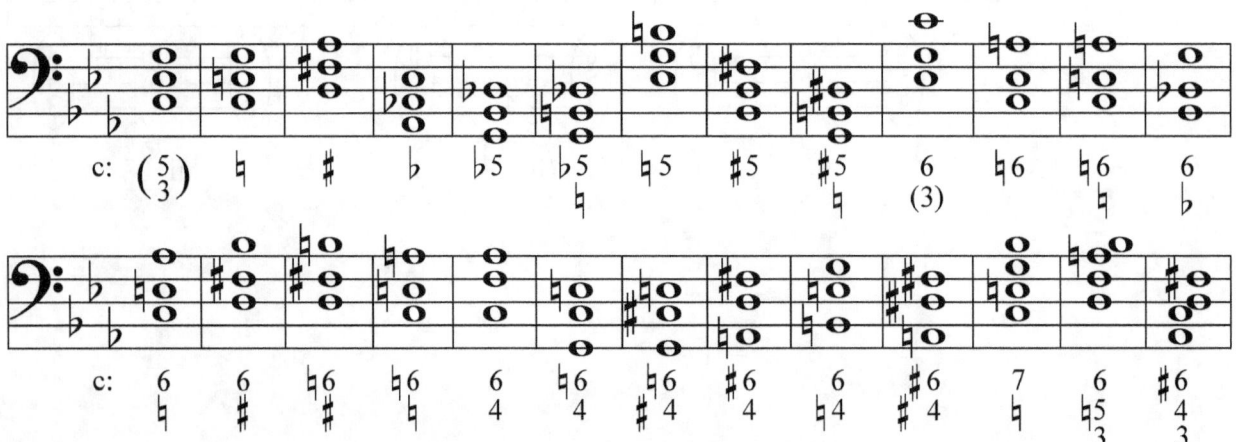

Example 2–26 illustrates the use of exact figured bass with the previous chord formations and chord symbols of example 2–8 above. If the music has a natural, then the figured bass has a natural. The same principle also applies to any other accidentals. In 2–26a and 26b, the number 3 is not preceded by a flat (unlike example 2–8) because the pitch standing a 3rd above the bass is in the key signature. With exact figured bass, there is no attempt to recognize the tone as variable ♭7 occurring at the interval of a 3rd above the bass, as the number 3 and the key signature provide all of the necessary information for an accurate reading.

As with generic figured bass, the number 3 may be omitted from the exact figured bass if the tone is uninflected. Additionally, as stated in guideline 4 above, an accidental that is not attached to a figured-bass number always refers to the interval of a 3rd above the bass. In 2–26, however, we include the figured-bass 3 for the 3rd above the bass because the soprano voice *moves* to an inflected tone (if a tone contradicts the key signature, then it needs an inflection in the figured bass).

Thus, in 2–26a, when the real chord forms on beat 3, the natural in the figured bass refers to a pitch that takes a natural occurring at the interval of a 3rd above the bass (B♮). The fact that variable ♭7 (B♭) moves to variable ♯7 (B♮) is of no consequence to the reader/performer. Example 2–26c also uses a natural sign to designate the interval of a 3rd above the bass (E♮). In 2–26b, a sharp in the figured bass indicates the E♯ in the soprano; in 2–26d, a double sharp in the figured bass represents F𝄪.

Example 2–26: exact figured bass for the chord formations and chord symbols presented in example 2–8

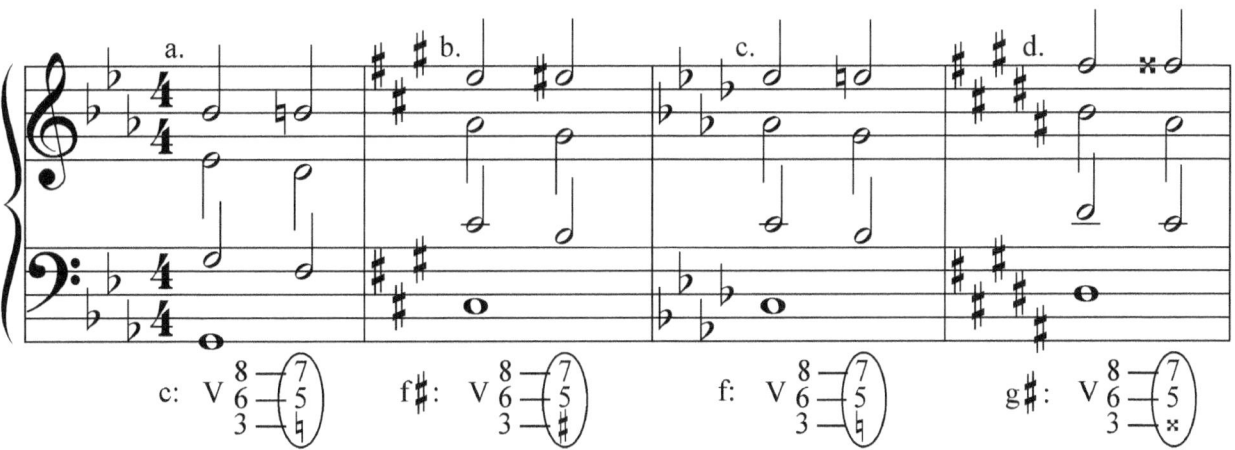

Chapter 3 Applied Chords

At the conclusion of Chapter 1, we observed that chromatic pitch inflection may or may not effect a change of key. Indeed, these additions often have an ornamental function and pose no threat to the stability of the governing tonic; rather, they serve to embellish a tone or to intensify linear motion between tones.

Example 1–27 illustrated a type of chromaticism between pitches that fills in a whole step with an intervening half step. In the example, the motion from C to D is intensified by C♯ (C C♯ D), a chromatic passing tone; our attention is drawn to the C♯ and to the D. The effect of the C♯ is momentary, however, because it exists as an isolated melodic event, rather than as a chord tone.

In Example 3–1a below, the C♯ passes from the root of a C-major triad to the root of a D-minor triad. Although the C♯ intensifies the motion between chords, notice that it fails to avert the parallel 5ths between the tenor and bass, as an unaccented passing tone is too insignificant an event to overcome the perfect 5ths occurring on primary accents. In 3–1b, C♯ no longer stands alone; for adding an A to the tenor line produces an A-dominant seventh in first inversion (C♯ E G A). Once the C♯ assumes the status of a chord tone, the harmony to which it belongs acquires the capability to correct faulty motion.

The A-dominant seventh in 3–1b treats the D-minor supertonic as if it were a tonic chord and constitutes thereby what is referred to as an "applied chord," specifically, an applied dominant. The notation for applied chords is a pair of brackets, [ ].

In this chapter, we learn that the diatonic relationship between the tonic and dominant, found in every major and minor mode, can be applied chromatically to any nontonic major or minor triad. ("Secondary dominant," an alternative expression, is not used in this text, as there are chords in this category of chromaticism that are not part of the dominant family.)

There are three factors to consider when using applied dominants:
(1) the chord third of any major triad is the potential leading tone of a major or minor key;
(2) any nontonic major or minor triad may become a temporary tonic of a "lower" order, *if* the chord is addressed by its own tonal harmonic dominant (THD) or tonal melodic dominant (TMD);
(3) the third of the THD should never be doubled. However, the root of the TMD *triad* may be doubled when it occurs as part of a chordal sequence. Moreover, the prohibition against doubling such sensitive scale degrees as the leading tone, variables in minor, and borrowed lowered 6 in major may be rescinded when those tones are roots of triads functioning as modal dominants (see below, pp. 50–53).

Example 3–1: averting parallel 5ths with a voice-leading chord above a chromatic passing tone (C♯)

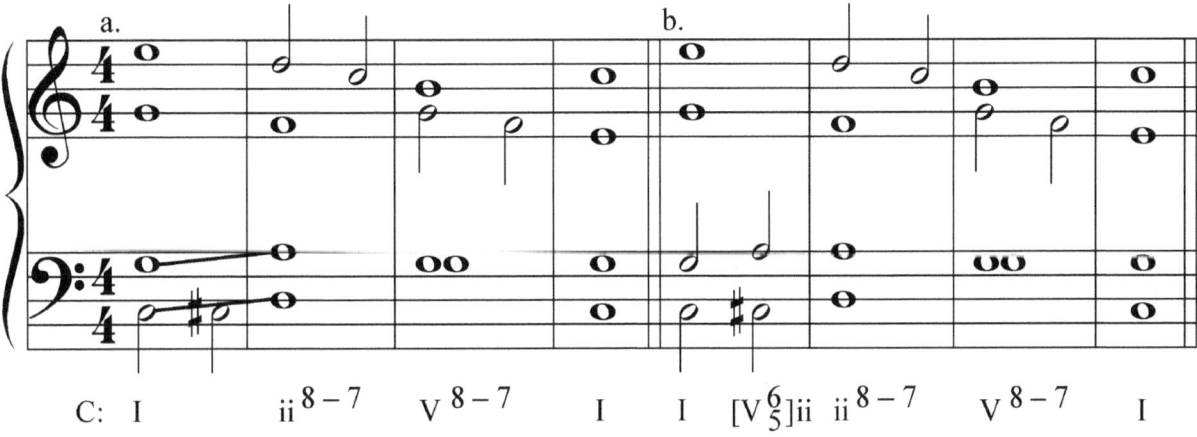

In 3–1b above, the C♯ in the bass is the chord third of the A-dominant seventh and the leading tone of both D major and d minor. The dominant seventh therefore functions as the V_5^6 of C major's supertonic, d minor. The applied dominant is indicated with brackets as $[V_5^6]$, followed by the Roman numeral ii to represent the supertonic. There are two traditional alternatives to using brackets for the representation of applied elements: "V_5^6 / ii" and "V_5^6 of ii."

The Subtonic and Mediant in Minor

As stated earlier, the diatonic relationship between the tonic and dominant can be applied chromatically to any nontonic major or minor triad. Notably, this relationship occurs diatonically in minor between the subtonic triad and the major triad of the mediant. In example 3–2, the ♭VII♭7 articulates and strengthens the III without disturbing the integrity of the "main-level key." In fact, no chromatic tones are needed to address the mediant with its own applied THD, as ♭VII♭7 is also [V 7]III. Similarly, [vii°6]III is ii°6 of the main-level key.

Example 3–2: the subtonic as an applied dominant of III

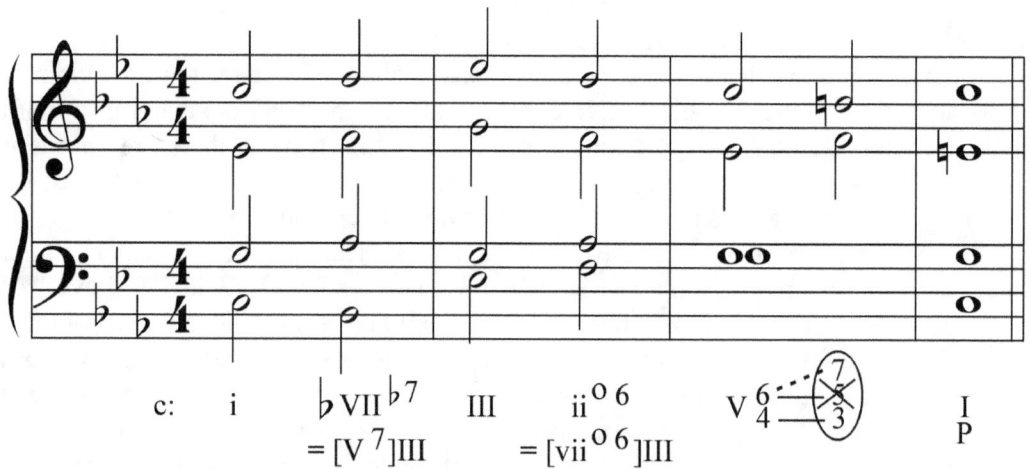

In 3–2, the subtonic chord contains D, the leading tone of the mediant, E♭. The leading-tone moves up to E♭ to give momentary emphasis to the E♭-major triad of the mediant. However, the focus returns to the main-level key of c minor with the onset of the cadential $^6_4$. Unlike the applied dominant of the supertonic in 3–1b, which approaches the D-minor chord contrapuntally with C♯ (that is, by stepwise movement), the B♭ root of the applied dominant in 3–2 initiates a harmonic approach. (Movement in the bass of either a perfect or tritone 5th and 4th is called harmonic motion.)

Tonicization, Modulation, and Lower-Level Keys

Both examples 3–1b and 3–2 display the principle of tonicization, which involves treating any nontonic major or minor triad of the main-level key as a temporary tonic. *Diminished and augmented triads cannot serve as temporary tonics.* We should exercise caution, however, when using the word temporary in this context because its denotation fails to provide us with a measurable span of time. For now, the process of temporary tonicization consists of the applied dominant and the chord it addresses.

Ultimately, if the tonicization of the nontonic chord continues beyond a certain threshold of time, it will produce a key change, a *modulation* to a new key. Some theoreticians maintain that if the tonicization is limited to one phrase of music or less, then the modulation is "transient," or "transitory." However, if the tonicization extends beyond a single phrase, then it may well constitute an actual change of key, a real modulation. Modulations to nontonic areas involve harmonic and contrapuntal progressions that should be understood as representing keys of a lower order. The various excursions into "lower-level keys" that may occur in a composition are intended to enhance, expand, and enrich the expression of the main-level key.

The Applied Tonal Harmonic Dominant [THD]

In 3–3a, the applied dominant (A C♯ E G) takes a harmonic approach to the supertonic, d minor. In the first measure, we have a dissonant clash between the C bass (beat 1) and the C♯ tenor (beat 3). When a chromatic half step occurs as the result of an applied dominant, it is usually best to maintain chromatically altered versions of the same tone in the same voice.

The diatonic pitch (C) from which the chromatic tone (C♯) emerges may be duplicated in another voice (C), creating a conflict between two different versions of the same pitch in different voices, an *apparent* cross relation (see the dotted lines in 3–3). When another voice duplicates one of the two pitches, the clash of tones in different voices is acceptable provided the succession between diatonic and chromatic versions of the same pitch remain in the same voice (C in the bass against C to C♯ in the tenor).

Still, moving the non-chromatic duplication (C) to another tone mitigates the harmonic conflict. In the voice opposing the succession of diatonic and chromatic activity, stepwise motion away from the duplicated pitch is best; however, as shown in 3–3, a departure by leap also works (C down to A in the bass).

Example 3–3b presents an alternative voicing that allows the employment of the cadential $^6_4$. We exercise this option by dropping the applied leading tone of d minor (C♯) to scale degree 5 of d minor (A), producing a 5th-to-unison motion between the bass and tenor. Denying the resolution of the leading tone scarcely weakens the momentary emphasis of the d minor, while the cadential $^6_4$ brings a strong articulation of C major, the main-level key.

Example 3–3: diatonic pitch duplication (C) opposes the succession of diatonic and chromatic activity

C: I   [V^7]ii   ii$^{8-7}$ V^7 I   I   [V^7]ii   ii$^{8-7}$ V$^{6\,\text{-}\,7}_{4\,\text{-}\,3}$ I

When using applied dominants, it will likely produce a succession of pitches involving one diatonic tone and one chromatic tone of the same letter name (C to C♯ in examples 3–1 and 3–3). As we have said, chromatically altered versions of the same tone should be maintained in the same voice. However, this disposition may not always be possible or even desirable. In such cases, the diatonic pitch will occur in one voice while the chromatic tone is placed in another voice, producing a cross relation.

Cross Relations

Example 3–3 above demonstrates how conflicts between two different versions of the same pitch may arise when an applied dominant occurs in root position. Example 3–4a contains three root-position chords and two in first inversion. The chord third (G♯) of the [V$^6_5$] stands in a cross relation with the preceding chord fifth (G♮) of the I^6 (3–4a); notice that *neither tone of the cross relation is duplicated in an opposing voice*.

The applied dominant approaches the submediant contrapuntally after leaping upwards a major 3rd. The bass of the applied dominant (G♯) contains the leading tone of the chord it addresses (the submediant). The strong tendency of the leading tone to move to a tonic pitch (in this instance, a temporary tonic) helps to lessen the harsh effect of the cross relation. It is better to avoid this effect in the outer voices unless the departure from the cross relation is by step *in the soprano voice* (G to F in 3–4b). Leaping away from the cross relation yields a poor result (G to E in 3–4c).

Some theoreticians may object to the unequal 5ths between the tenor and alto voices of 3–4a (A/E to B/F) and between the alto and soprano voices of 3–4b (C/G to B/F); however, we allow them as long as they do not occur between the outer voices. Moreover, in this instance, the succession of parallels is perfect 5th to diminished 5th. Subsequently, the diminished 5th contracts to a 3rd, as expected.

Example 3–4: acceptable and unacceptable cross relations

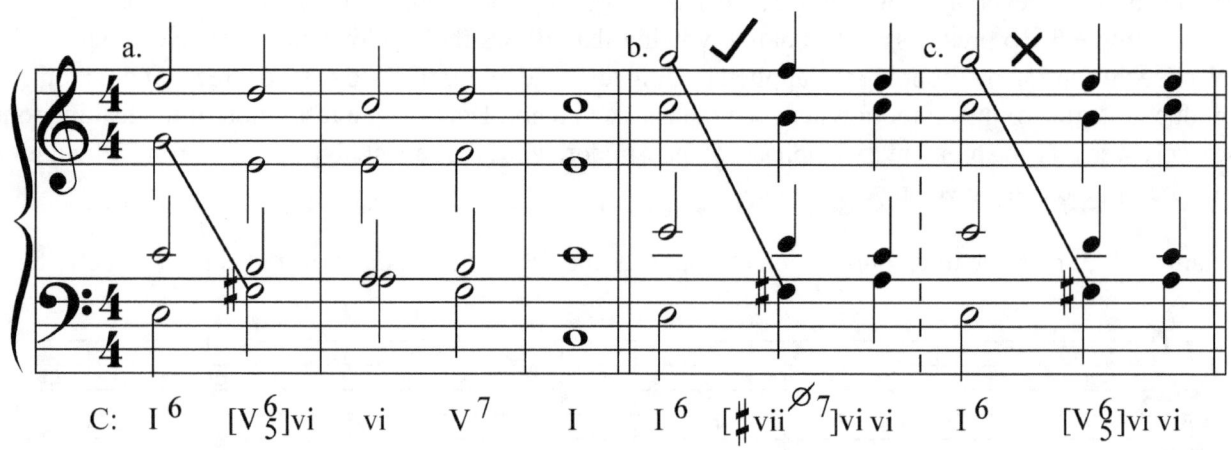

Example 3–5: passing elements between conflicting pitches weakens the effect of the cross relation

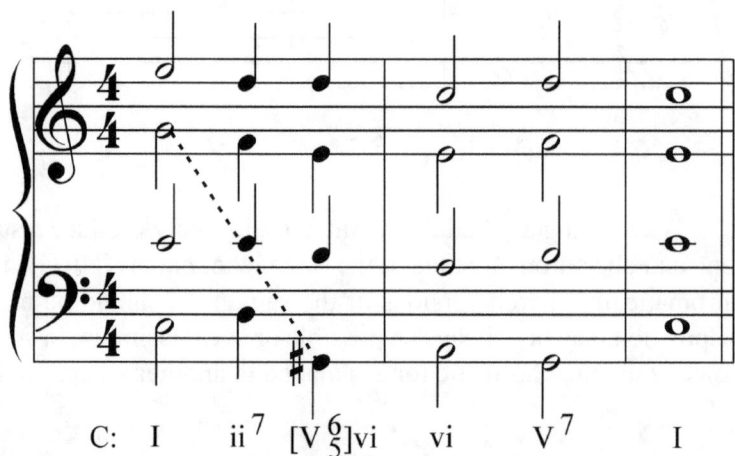

Another way to weaken the effect of the cross relation involves inserting either a passing tone or chord between the conflicting pitches in order to separate them, as an intervening passing tone or chord prevents the harmonic clash from continuing. In example 3–5 above, a passing chord of the supertonic breaks up the cross relation between the G and the G♯. The addition of the supertonic also improves the voice leading in the soprano and alto (compare examples 3–4a and 3–5, measure 1). The downward leap of the diminished 5th (D to G♯) is acceptable if limited to the bass.

The Applied Tonal Melodic Dominant [TMD]

Earlier in this chapter, we observed that any nontonic major or minor triad may be tonicized by its own tonal harmonic dominant (THD) or tonal melodic dominant (TMD). As we have seen, applied dominant sevenths in root position stand in a harmonic bass relationship to the nontonic chords they address. Examples 3–1, 3–4a, and 3–5 show how an inverted dominant seventh can effect a contrapuntal approach to a lower-level tonic.

In *Counterpoint In Composition* (New York: McGraw-Hill, 1969), Felix Salzer and Carl Schachter describe *chromatic* leading-tone chords as "contrapuntal equivalents of the applied dominant" (pp. 210–211). Salzer and Schachter call this chord the "contrapuntal leading-tone chord." We shall abbreviate the contrapuntal leading-tone chord as "CLT."

Finding The Right Pitch II: A Guide To The Study Of Basic Harmony broadened the definition of the chord's operation to include any *diatonic* framework in which a chord of the dominant family approaches the main-level tonic by step. This section focuses on TMD/CLT chords functioning as applied dominants of lower-level tonics, a procedure closer to Salzer and Schachter's original concept.

CLT chords may serve as either upward or downward passing chords or as complete or incomplete upper or lower neighbor chords. Example 3–6 illustrates the TMD triad in $^6_3$ position as an applied CLT chord of C major's supertonic. (An applied dominant of the supertonic in minor is impractical because the probable lower-level tonic would be a diminished triad.)

Since the applied TMD in 3–6 is a diminished triad, remember that the $^5_3$ and $^6_4$ positions of the chord are usually avoided because of the tritone interval between the bass and one of the upper voices. (Notice the permissible succession of unequal 5ths in the alto and tenor voices, C♯/G and D/A.)

Example 3–6: TMD/CLT chords applied to the supertonic

C: [vii^{o6}]ii   ii   [vii^{o6}]ii   ii^6

Once the TMD triad becomes a seventh chord, any position of the chord is acceptable, including the root position. In 3–7b, the potential hazard of parallel 5ths prevents us from connecting the applied half-diminished TMD in first inversion to the root-position subdominant (as a lower-level tonic). Thus, in order to avoid faulty motion, the chord of resolution has to be the IV^6.

Example 3–7: all positions of the half-diminished TMD applied to the subdominant

C: [vii$^{\varnothing 7}$]IV   IV   [vii$^{\varnothing \frac{6}{5}}$]IV   IV^6 [vii$^{\varnothing \frac{4}{3}}$]IV   IV   [vii$^{\varnothing \frac{4}{2}}$ I$^{\frac{6}{4}}$ or V^7]IV

In major, the chord of the leading tone is a half-diminished seventh; however, as we observed in Chapter 1, the leading tone cannot have the half-diminished seventh in minor, as the chord carries variable ♯6 as its seventh (see above, p. 9). The linear demands of ♯6 to move upwards to ♯7 and the harmonic tendency of the dissonant 7th to resolve downwards renders the chord useless. Therefore, in minor, the fully diminished seventh serves as the TMD; for its seventh component is variable ♭6, which seeks to move down to scale degree 5. As we have seen, it is possible to bring the fully diminished seventh chord of the leading tone into the extended parallel major as (vii$^{\circ 7}$).

In example 3–8b below, having the fully diminished seventh as the applied TMD enables us to connect to the subdominant in *root position* because the 5th that occurs between its chord third and seventh is diminished, resulting in a permissible succession of unequal 5ths, G/D♭ to F/C. If a half-diminished seventh were used instead of the fully diminished seventh, then the 5th between the chord third and seventh would be perfect, resulting in parallel 5ths from the TMD to the subdominant (G/D to F/C).

Example 3–8: all positions of the fully diminished TMD applied to the subdominant

C: [(vii$^{\circ 7}$)]IV   IV   [(vii$^{\circ \frac{6}{5}}$)]IV   IV   [(vii$^{\circ \frac{4}{3}}$)]IV   IV^6 [(vii$^{\circ \frac{4}{2}}$)   I$^{\frac{6}{4}}$ or V^7]IV

In Example 3–9, an applied fully diminished seventh of the leading tone addresses C major's submediant (a minor). Once again, in 3–9b, we have unequal 5ths between the chord third and seventh of the applied TMD and the chord root and fifth of the submediant (B/F to A/E). If a half-diminished seventh were used instead of the fully diminished seventh, then the 5th between the chord third and seventh would be perfect, resulting in parallel 5ths from the TMD to the submediant (B/F♯ to A/E).

Example 3–9: all positions of the fully diminished TMD applied to the submediant

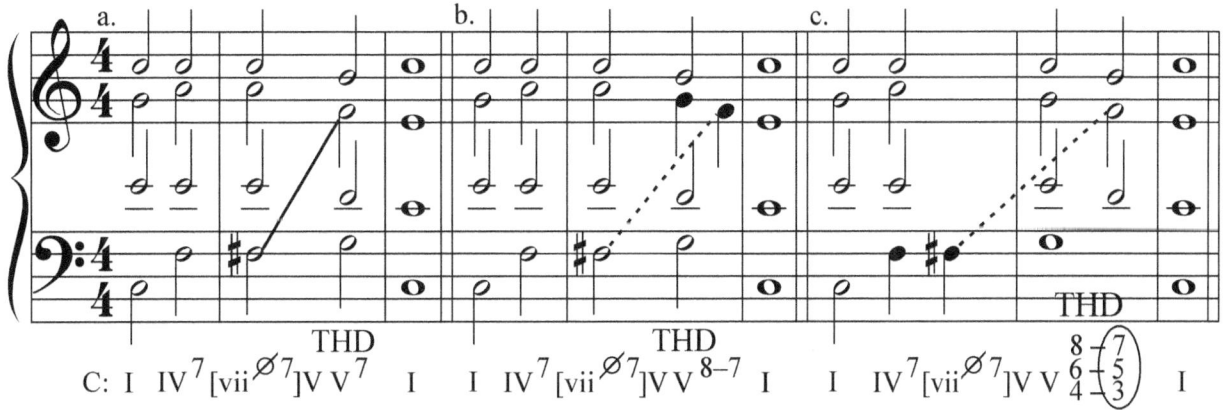

The Leading Tone of the Dominant

The contrapuntal approach to the tonal harmonic dominant of the main-level key is usually accomplished by having what would be called scale degree ♯4 ("raised 4") in the bass. In example 3–10, ♯4 is F♯. The harmony containing ♯4 can be either an applied THD (expressed as a CLT chord) or TMD/CLT chord. As we have said, never double the third of the THD or the root of the TMD (except when the TMD occurs as part of a chordal sequence).

Example 3–10 illustrates the formation of an applied vii∅⁷ of the main-level THD. In 3–10a, measure 2 presents a cross relation between F♯ and F♮ in the bass and alto. The strong tendency of the leading tone (F♯) to move to the lower-level tonic (G) helps to lessen the harsh effect of the cross relation. In 3–10b, an 8—7 motion above the bass produces the dominant seventh and softens the cross relation as a result of the intervening G. The cadential $^6_4$ in 3–10c places an apparent chord between the F♯ and F♮.

Example 3–10: the cross relation between scale degrees 4 and ♯4

The Applied Dominants of the Mediant in Minor and in Major

The foregoing examples illustrate how applied dominants address the lower-level tonic triads of the supertonic, mediant, subdominant, and submediant. All harmonic and contrapuntal approaches to these temporary tonics require the introduction of chromatic leading tones, *except* when the applied dominant addresses the major mediant of the minor mode.

As mentioned earlier (see above, p. 36, example 3–2), the ♭VII♭7 and the ii°6 of the main-level key in minor can be employed as applied dominants of the mediant: the [V 7]III and the [vii °6]III. The applied dominant of the mediant is more common in minor than in major because it occurs naturally (that is, diatonically) without using chromaticism and because of the way the tritone seeks to resolve in minor.

In minor, the tritone involves scale degrees 2 and ♭6. The diminished 5th contracts to the root and third of the mediant chord while the augmented 4th expands to the third and root (example 3–11a: D/A♭ to E♭/G and A♭/D to G/E♭). In major, the tritone involves scale degrees 7 and 4. The diminished 5th contracts to the root and third of the tonic chord while the augmented 4th expands to the third and root (3–11b: B/F to C/E and F/B to E/C). Therefore, with respect to the tendency of the tritone to move to certain intervals within the mode, the mediant chord is tonicized more readily in minor than in major.

Example 3–11: the mediant chord is tonicized more readily in minor than in major

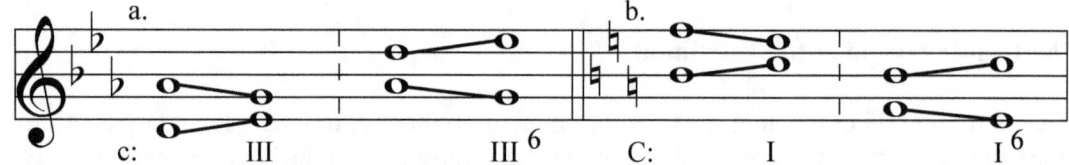

Applied Dominant Sevenths in Sequential Succession

This section examines the formation of successive applied dominants. Although this succession can occur with triads instead of seventh chords, we are concerned here with harmonies that have the dissonant 7th, which seeks to move down by step in the same voice to the chord that immediately follows, according to the procedure outlined below.

When two seventh chords stand in a falling 5th or rising 4th root relationship to each other, it is possible to form a two-chord pattern of overlapping resolutions in which the seventh of the first chord moves to the third of the second chord while the third of the first chord becomes the seventh of the second chord. This operation is called interlocking seventh chords. When the chords are in root position, the pattern forms a descending harmonic bass line that is subsequently repeated at different pitch levels. (As displayed in 3–14 below, the harmonic bass line of interlocking seventh chords contains a stepwise descent in the bass on the primary accent of each measure, from the I 6 to the THD, from E to G: E–D–C–B–A–G.)

Interlocking seventh chords demonstrate one application of a procedure known as the sequence, which includes a variety of techniques. Some sequences are melodic, harmonic, or both. A sequence consists of a pattern that is repeated at different pitch levels in order to shift all of the voices upwards or downwards. The original pattern and its duplications exhibit consistent intervallic relationships in all or most of the voices above the bass. Since interlocking seventh chords produce harmonic textures, they form one type of *harmonic* sequence, or chordal sequence.

Example 3–12 is a *melodic* sequence involving three ascending pitches that cross over the normal fourfold division of the quarter note into sixteenths, producing a rhythm of four beats against three beats (beats 1–3 of measure 1). The dotted lines and brackets mark off the three-note pattern, which occurs five times before reaching the goal of middle C. (For a more conventional instance of melodic sequencing, see example 4–15 below, measures 5–6, treble clef.)

Example 3–12: melodic sequence

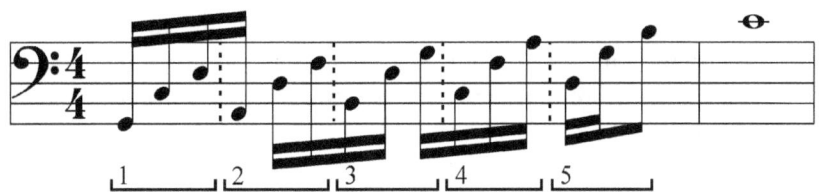

The harmonic pattern in example 3–13 below consists of interlocking seventh chords and is sometimes referred to as a descending 5th sequence because all of the voices proceed downwards through a falling 5th and rising 4th (or rising 4th and falling 5th) root movement between chords. Example 3–13a shows the formation of successive applied dominants evolving from an 8—7 motion above the bass. The third of each applied dominant resolves upwards to the following temporary tonic (C♯ to D and F♯ to G).

Ultimately, the harmonic framework maintains a consistent succession of intervallic relationships, including a 5th-to-octave motion between the outer voices, the bass and soprano. The root of each temporary tonic moves down one whole step (8—7) to become a passing 7th (D to C♮ in the tenor and G to F♮ in the alto). This operation converts the applied triad into an applied dominant seventh of the next chord. (The 5th-to-octave pattern of intervals in the outer voices sounds somewhat empty; however, the context of interlocking sevenths renders the pattern acceptable.)

With respect to the chord symbols, the [V] is used twice, first for the supertonic and then for the dominant. We do not recognize the supertonic in the bass of measure 3 (3–13a) as a lower-level tonic because the ii readily becomes a dominant seventh chord directing its motion towards the next chord, the THD in measure 4.

The underlying triad of the initial [V $^{8-7}$]ii in 3–13a is formed by melodic chromaticism in the tenor (C♯). In the alto of measure 2, the seventh (G) passes from the octave to the chord third of the [V $^{8-7}$]V. The seventh of the second applied dominant (C♮, measure 3, tenor) passes to the chord third of the THD in measure 4. In the alto of measure 4, the seventh of the THD (F) passes to the chord third of the tonic in measure 5. The interlocking pattern of seventh-chord resolutions generates a sense of forward motion pushing the harmonies to their final destination.

Example 3–13b illustrates a skip in the compositional process whereby that which has been established through common practice is shortened, or contracted. An abbreviation of the 8—7 motion eliminates the octave resolution (measures 3–4), leaving the resultant seventh as a standalone member of the chord (D/C in the bass and tenor of measure 3 and G/F in the bass and alto of measure 4). A re-articulated suspension from the initial tonic produces the chord seventh of the first applied dominant (G, measures 1–2, alto).

Example 3–13: the 8—7 motion contracted to a 7th

44   Chapter 3 Applied Chords

Example 3–14 is based upon the pattern of interlocking sevenths presented in 3–13b. The pattern produces overlapping resolutions in which the seventh of the first chord moves to the third of the second chord while the third of the first chord becomes the seventh of the second chord.

Thus, one chord *finishes* a 7 3 motion in one voice (C down to B, measure 2, soprano) while simultaneously *initiating* a 7 3 motion with the next chord in a different voice (F down to E, measures 2–3, alto). In four voices, this two-chord pattern is maintained with root-position sevenths by alternating a complete seventh chord with an incomplete seventh chord (or an incomplete seventh chord alternating with a complete seventh chord). A complete seventh chord has all chord tones present; an incomplete seventh omits the fifth and doubles the root. (The complete-to-incomplete succession of seventh chords also occurs in example 3–13 above. In 3–14, complete and incomplete are abbreviated as comp. and incomp.)

The tritone between scale degrees 4 and 7 in major presents certain difficulties, as 3–14 confirms. When using applied dominants on these scale degrees, the seventh of the first chord does not take a downward resolution because the tone is enharmonically equivalent to the third of the next chord. Moreover, scale degree 7 supports a half-diminished seventh, a chord that cannot be tonicized. (In measures 3–4 below, the E♭ is re-interpreted as D♯. The exclamation mark attached to the bracket underscores the problematic nature of the tritone area.)

Example 3–14: descending 5th sequence of applied dominant sevenths, harmonic bass (in major)

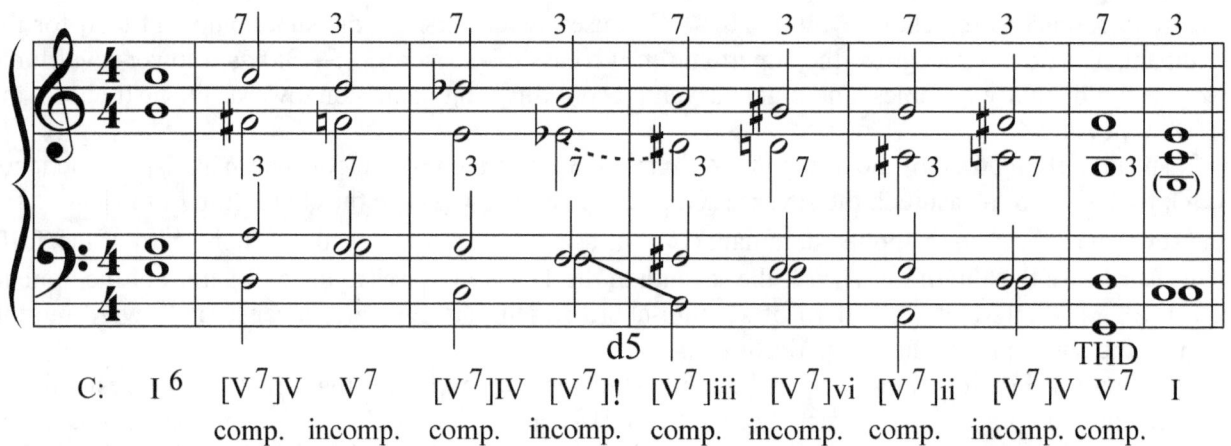

Example 3–15: alternative options for the stationary chord seventh, harmonic bass (in major)

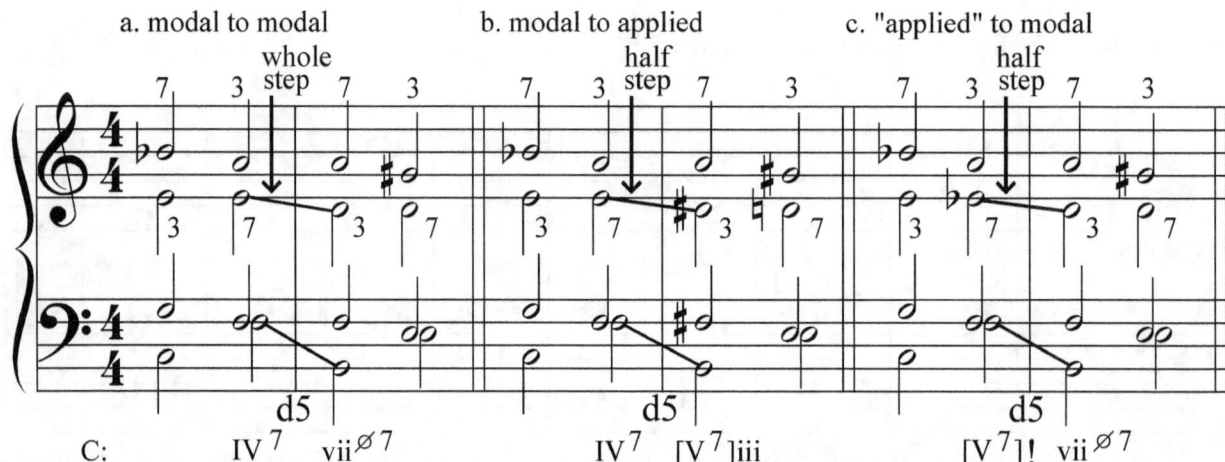

Chapter 3 Applied Chords   45

Example 3–15 above displays options for the tritone area that allow the stationary seventh of the chord to resolve downwards. Example 3–15a replaces both chords of the tritone with two modal dominants ("in the key" seventh chords), whereas 3–15b has one modal dominant and one applied dominant. Example 3–15c exhibits one applied dominant and one modal dominant.

Executing the sequence in its original form, without exercising any of the solutions in 3–15, leaves us with the stationary chord seventh, the least desirable option. In any case, we cannot establish a lower-level dominant-to-tonic relationship in the tritone area because the interval of the falling perfect 5th or rising perfect 4th is not present.

It would be well to avoid placing the stationary seventh that occurs in major (or even in minor) near the beginning of the descending 5th sequence. A location closer to the middle or end of the sequence allows the momentum of the previous interlocking sevenths to more effectively drive the succession of harmonies forward.

In example 3–16, we find the stationary seventh in minor near the end of the descending 5th sequence. Here, the tritone area involves scale degrees 2 and ♭6. As in 3–15, example 3–17 has the three options for resolving the seventh element of the chord downwards by step or by half step.

Example 3–16: descending 5th sequence of applied dominant sevenths, harmonic bass (in minor)

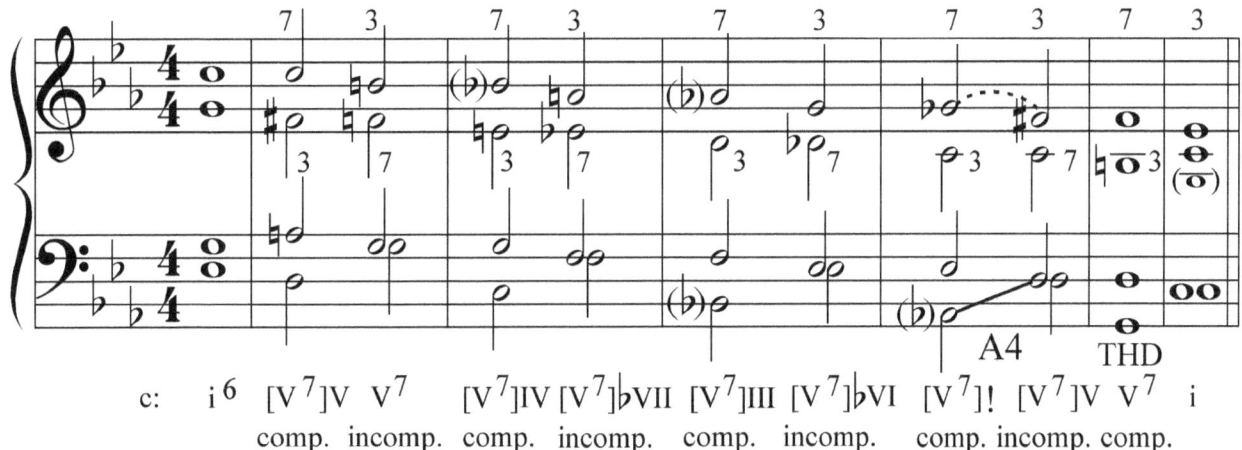

Example 3–17: alternative options for the stationary chord seventh, harmonic bass (in minor)

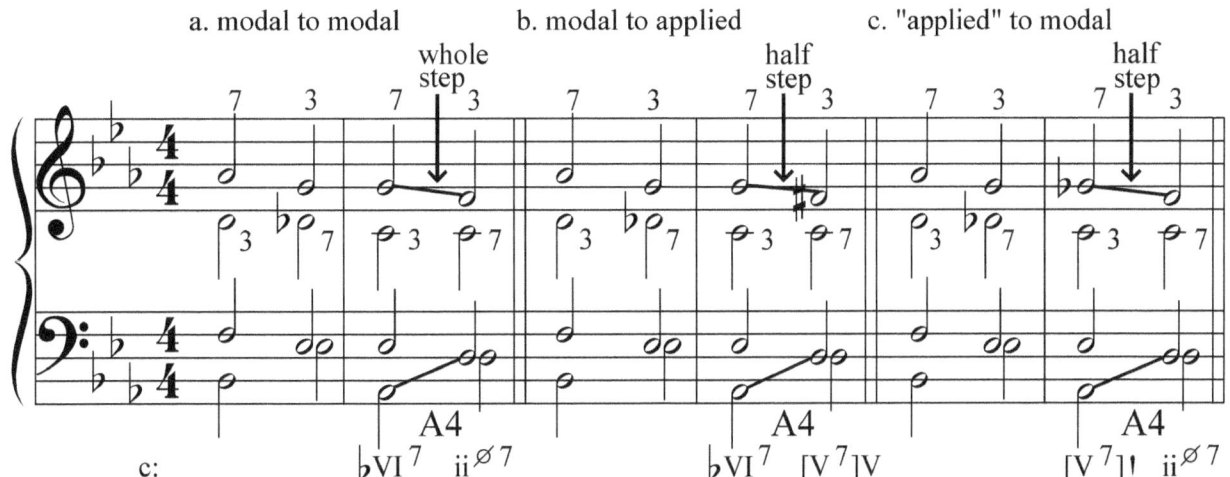

46   Chapter 3 Applied Chords

As shown in example 3–18, if one of the two chords of the two-chord pattern of interlocking sevenths is inverted, then the chord succession must consist of two *complete* seventh chords instead of an alternation of complete and incomplete sevenths. The descending 5th sequence of applied dominants in 3–18 obtains a contrapuntal bass by adding a chord fifth on beat 3 of measures 2–5, converting each incomplete applied dominant to an inverted seventh with all chord tones present. The problem of the stationary chord seventh in the tritone area can be averted with the options in example 3–19.

Example 3–18: descending 5th sequence of applied dominant sevenths, contrapuntal bass (in major)

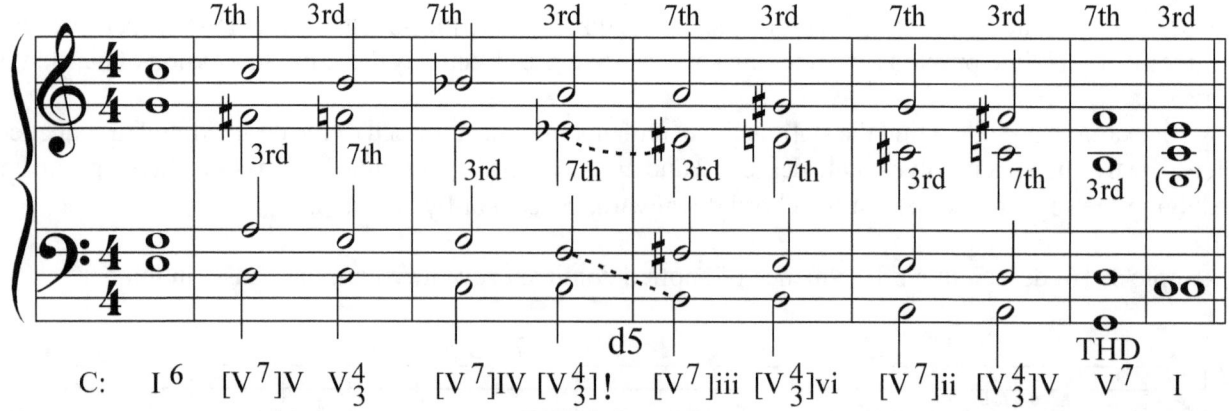

Example 3–19: alternative options for the stationary chord seventh, contrapuntal bass (in major)

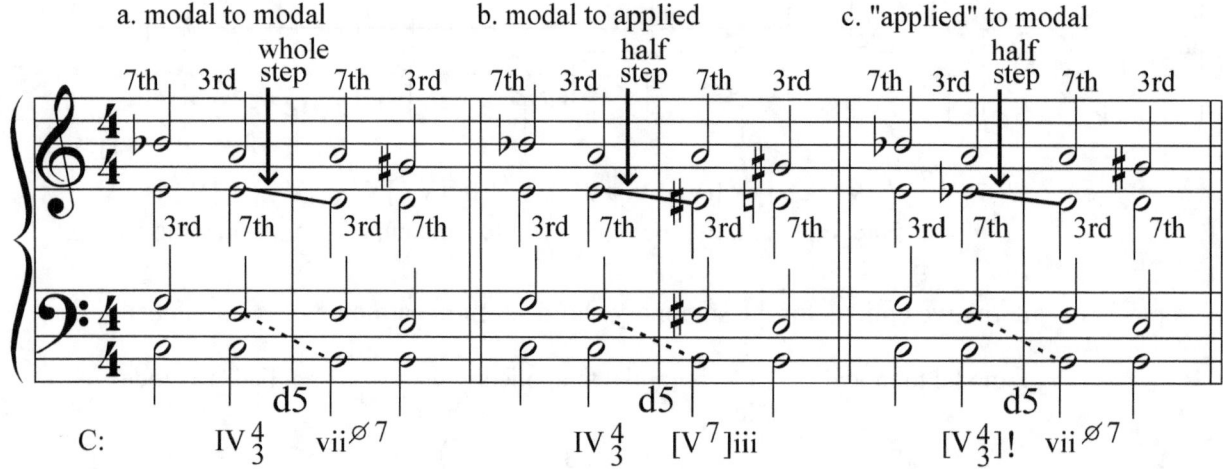

In example 3–20, another complication becomes evident in the tritone area of minor when the applied dominant of the dominant is complete, with all chord tones present. Notice that on beat 3 of measure 5, the bass moves from scale degree ♭6 to ♯6 (A♭ to A♮), producing a dominant seventh in second inversion: A C D F♯. Although this motion within the descending 5th sequence of applied dominants is acceptable, an alternative solution would be to hold on to ♭6 when the [V$^4_3$]V arrives.

However, including ♭6 in the chord would result in the following pitches: A♭ C D F♯, a chord that falls within the category of chromaticism known as the augmented 6th. For now, we shall avoid using the chords of the augmented 6th. With this restriction in place, example 3–21 provides options for moving the seventh of the tritone area down.

Example 3–20: descending 5th sequence of applied dominant sevenths, contrapuntal bass (in minor)

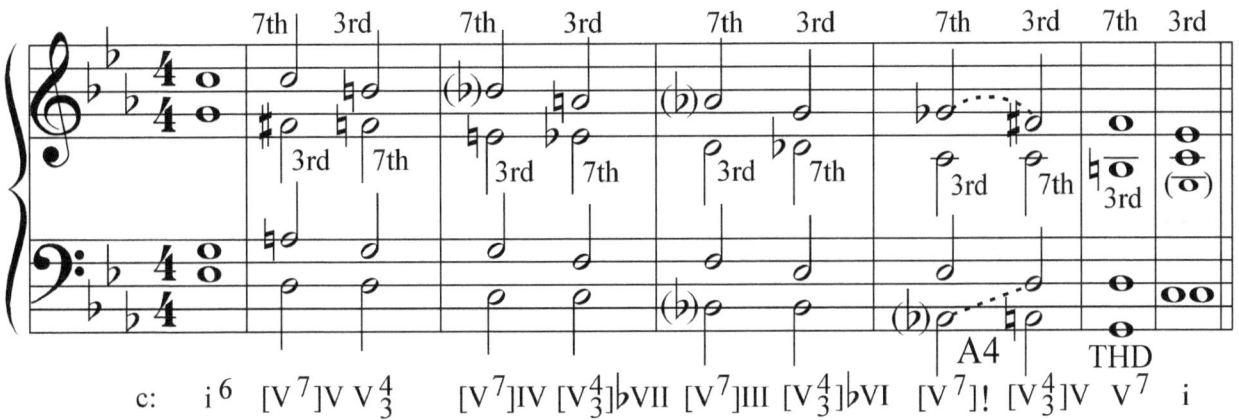

Example 3–21: alternative options for the stationary chord seventh, contrapuntal bass (in minor)

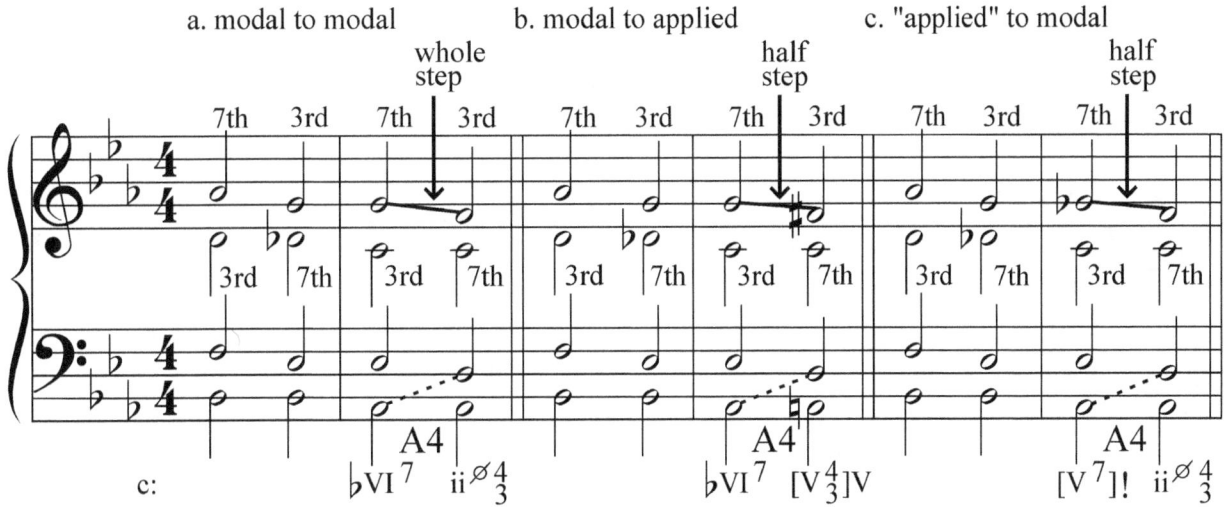

48   Chapter 3   Applied Chords

The Transferred Resolution

Example 3–22 shows a descending 5th sequence of applied dominants with a contrapuntal bass (as in examples 3–18 and 3–20 above). Earlier, we said that if one of the two chords of the two-chord pattern of interlocking sevenths is inverted, then the chord succession must consist of two *complete* seventh chords instead of an alternation of complete and incomplete sevenths. In 3–22, the seventh of the first chord moves to the third of the second chord *in the same voice* (the tenor) while the third of the first chord becomes the seventh of the second chord *in the same voice* (the soprano).

Example 3–22: descending 5th sequence of applied dominant sevenths, contrapuntal bass (in major)

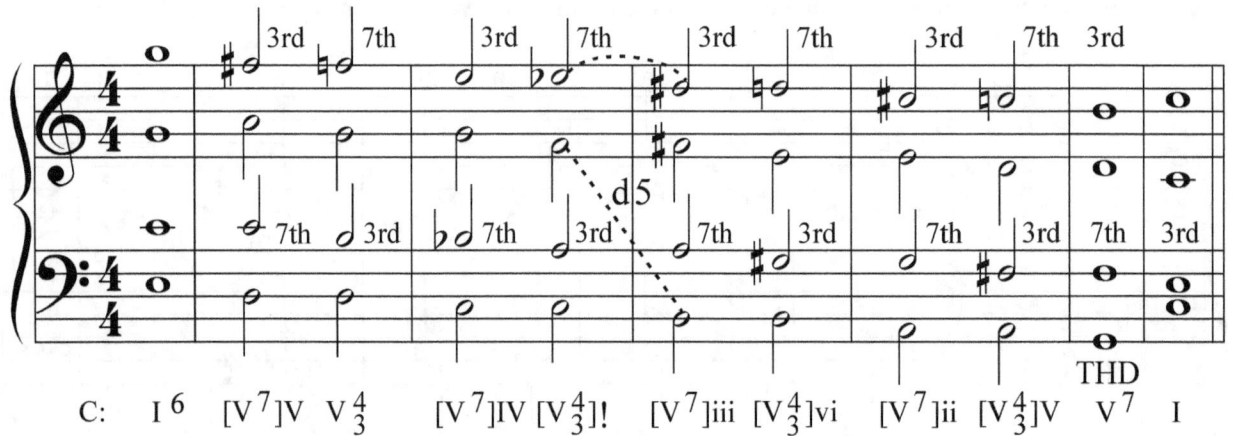

A less common practice, demonstrated in example 3–23, transfers the resolution of the first chord's seventh in the tenor to the bass of the second chord. The transferred resolution takes place within an outer-voice framework of alternating 10ths and 12ths. In the tenor, notice the downward leap of a 3rd into the first chord seventh of measures 2–6 (D to B♭, C to A, B to G♯, A to F♯).

Example 3–23: descending 5th sequence, contrapuntal bass, transferred seventh resolution (in major)

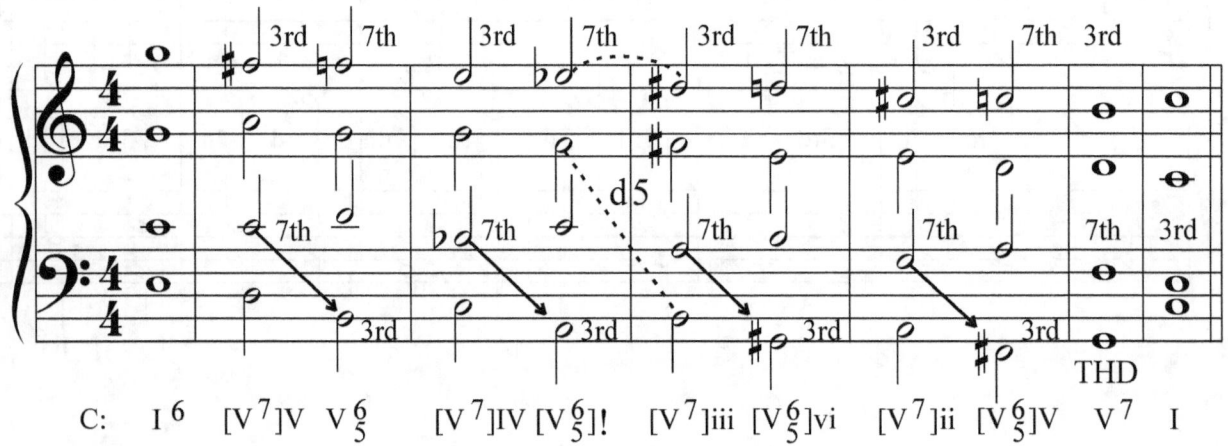

In example 3–24, both the transferred resolution and the downward leap into the first chord seventh (as in measures 2–6 of example 3–23, tenor voice) are avoided by omitting the seventh of the first chord of the two-chord pattern. The options for managing the stationary chord seventh in example 3–25 should be applied to the sequence in 3–23.

Example 3–24: descending 5th sequence, contrapuntal bass, alternating triads and sevenths (in major)

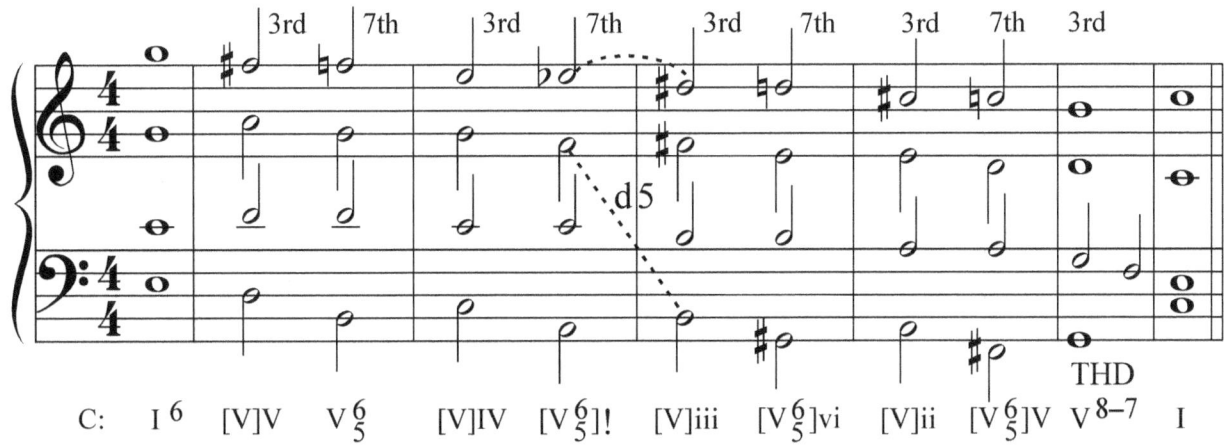

Example 3–25: alternative options for the stationary chord seventh, contrapuntal bass (in major)

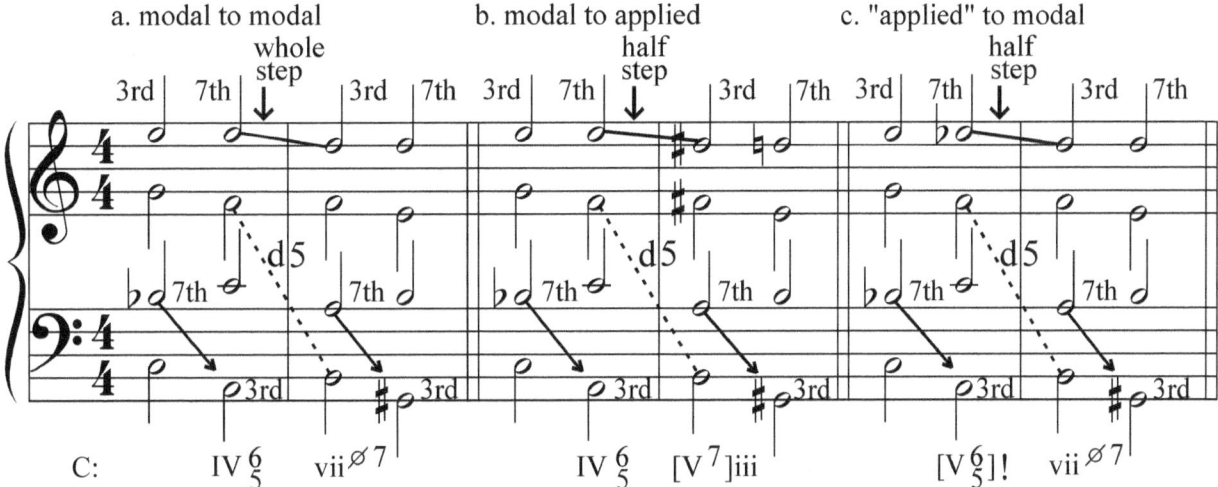

Example 3–26 presents the transferred resolution of 3–23 in the parallel minor. In example 3–27, we have the three options for the stationary chord seventh.

Example 3–26: descending 5th sequence, contrapuntal bass, transferred seventh resolution (in minor)

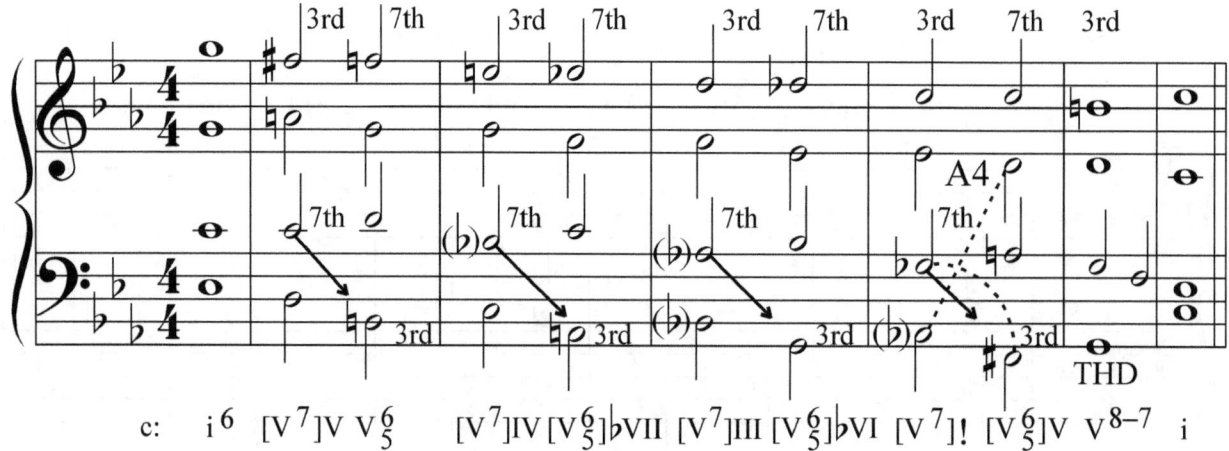

Example 3–27: alternative options for the stationary chord seventh, contrapuntal bass (in minor)

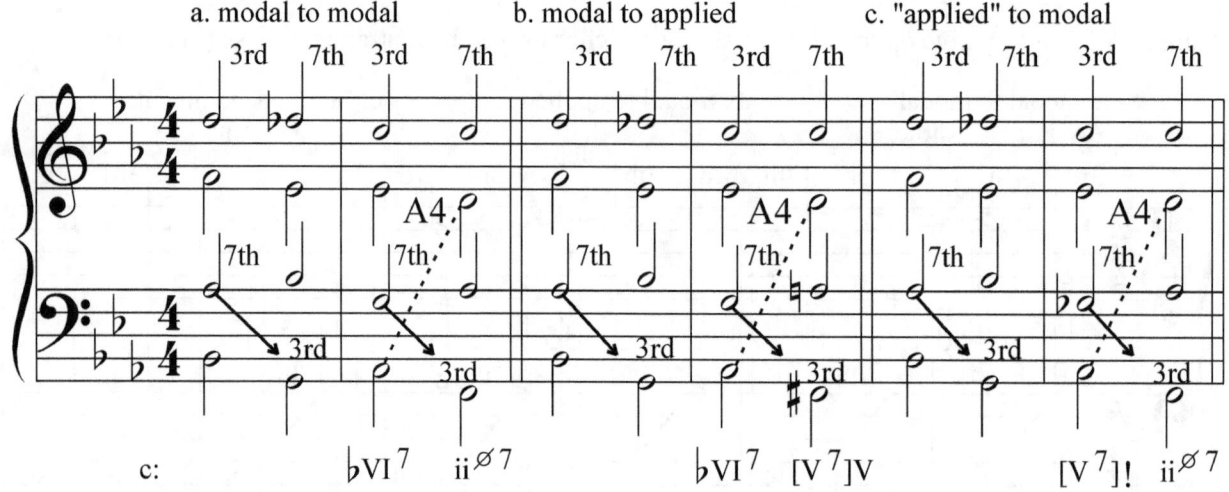

The Modal Dominant Seventh Chord

In this section, we remove all of the chromaticism of the previous sequences of applied dominants and examine the chords of the descending 5th sequence within the diatonic context of the major-minor tonal system. With the chromaticism removed, a diatonic succession of interlocking seventh chords remains. Each chord stands in either a perfect or tritone falling 5th or rising 4th root relationship to the next chord. Drawing upon the tonic-dominant relationship within the church mode system, we describe this succession of chords as a chain of "modal dominants."

The modal dominant is any triad, seventh, or chord containing extensions above the seventh within a diatonic scale that has either a perfect or tritone falling 5th (or rising 4th) root relationship to another chord. The relationship between the tonal harmonic dominant and the tonic, however, is excluded from the category of the modal dominant.

In measure 2 of 3–28, the pattern of interlocking sevenths begins in C major with a D-minor seventh addressing a G-dominant seventh: the ii ^{7} proceeds to the V ^{7}. In G Mixolydian, scale degree 5 projects a D-minor seventh. The seventh chord of the Mixolydian tonic is a G-dominant seventh. From a modal perspective, the ii ^{7} (D-minor seventh) can be understood as the modal dominant of the V ^{7} (G-dominant seventh). Thus, in C major, the V ^{7} is addressed with its own modal dominant, the ii ^{7}.

In measure 3, the tonic major seventh serves as the modal dominant of the subdominant (C major's Lydian area). The subdominant major seventh constitutes the modal dominant of the leading-tone (C major's Locrian area). The leading-tone half-diminished seventh in measure 4 becomes the modal dominant of the mediant (C major's Phrygian area).

The mediant minor seventh in measure 4 is the modal dominant of the submediant in measure 5 (C major's Aeolian area). The submediant minor seventh is the modal dominant of the supertonic (C major's Dorian area). And so, the pattern of interlocking sevenths in 3–28 (and in 3–29) demonstrates a succession of "in the key" modal dominants, each seventh chord constituting a modal dominant to the next in the series (by virtue of the falling 5th or rising 4th root relationship between them).

Every diatonic mode contains a tritone between two of its scale degrees. The tritone prevents the succession of modal dominants from leading away from the main-level key, as the root movement would otherwise proceed through a consistent series of falling perfect 5ths and rising perfect 4ths (or rising perfect 4ths and falling perfect 5ths).

Example 3–28: descending 5th sequence of modal dominant sevenths, harmonic bass (in major)

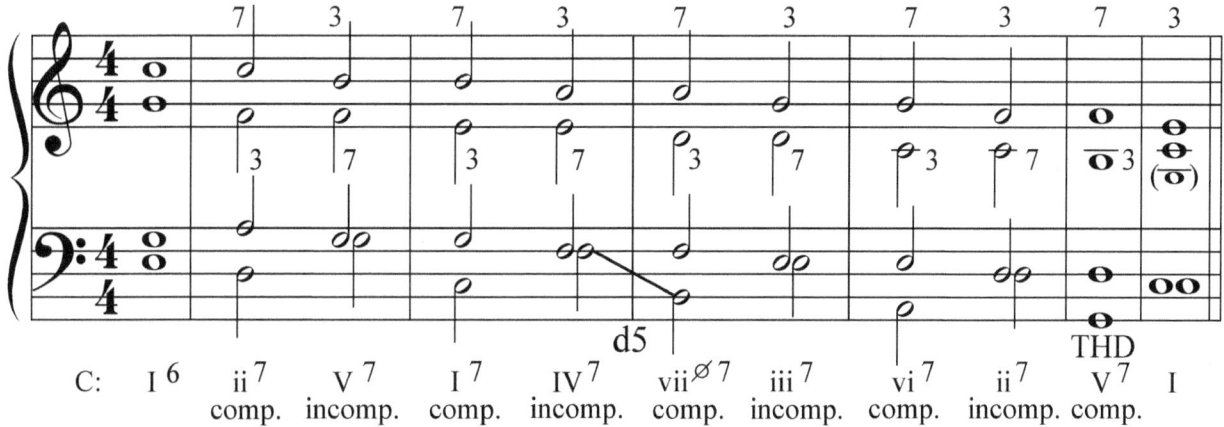

Example 3–29: descending 5th sequence of modal dominant sevenths, harmonic bass (in minor)

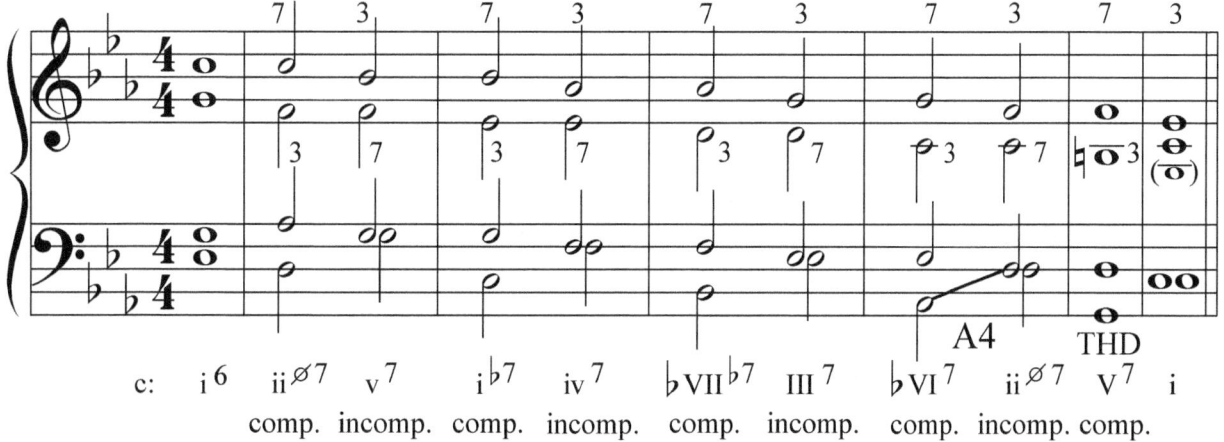

Examples 3–30 in major and 3–31 in minor exhibit a descending 5th sequence of modal dominants with a contrapuntal bass. In both examples, the seventh of the first chord moves to the third of the second chord while the third of the first chord becomes the seventh of the second chord.

A review of examples 3–14 through 3–21 underscores the ease with which the modal dominants of examples 3–28 through 3–31 may be converted into applied dominants. The harmonic framework maintains a consistent succession of intervallic relationships. Moreover, the structure of the sequence does not depend on either the presence or absence of chromatic tones.

Example 3–30: descending 5th sequence of modal dominant sevenths, contrapuntal bass (in major)

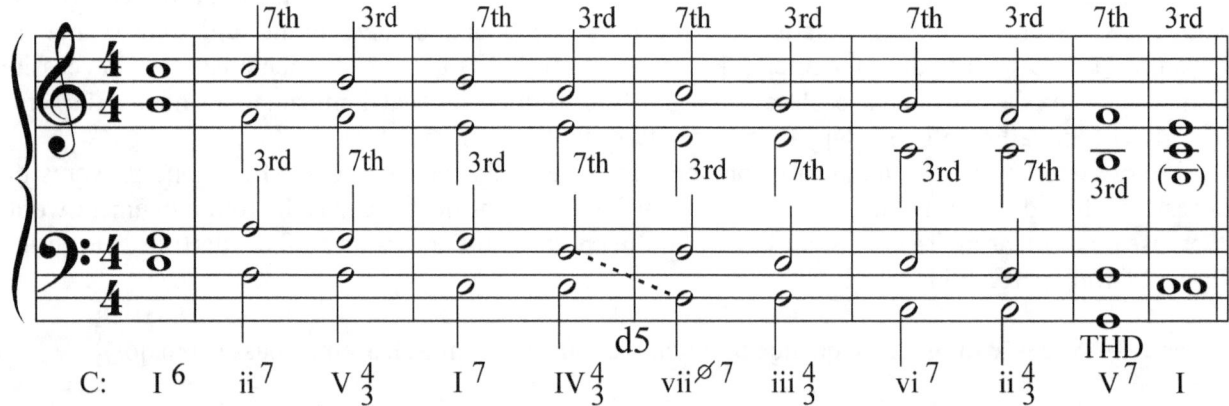

Example 3–31: descending 5th sequence of modal dominant sevenths, contrapuntal bass (in minor)

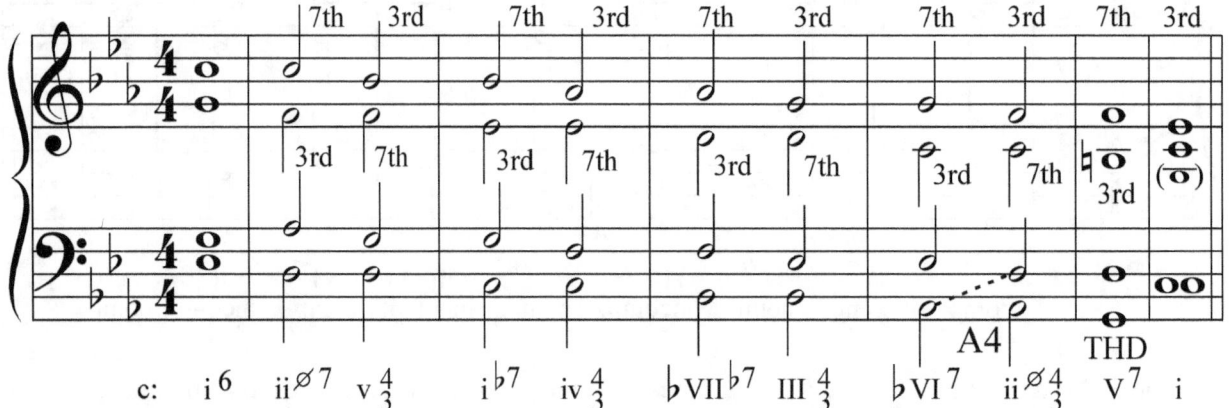

The Modal Dominant Triad

At the beginning of this chapter, we mentioned the possibility of having a descending 5th succession of modal-dominant triads. In examples 3–32 and 3–33, we have triad frameworks in both major and minor respectively. When sevenths are not used, the disposition of the four voices yields more disjunct motions.

Although the 5th-to-octave (or octave-to-5th) pattern of intervals in the outer voices sounds somewhat stark, the harmonic framework of the descending 5th sequence and the forward motion produced by its falling 5th-rising 4th succession of chords helps to mitigate the weaker aspects of the texture.

And while caution should be exercised when using diminished triads in root position, the momentum of the two-chord pattern informing the descending 5th sequence shifts the focus away from the dissonant tritone above the root of the diminished triad (3–32, measure 2; 3–33, measure 4). An instructive exercise would be to convert the triads into seventh chords and then assess the differences between the two textures.

Example 3–32: descending 5th sequence of modal dominant triads, harmonic bass (in major)

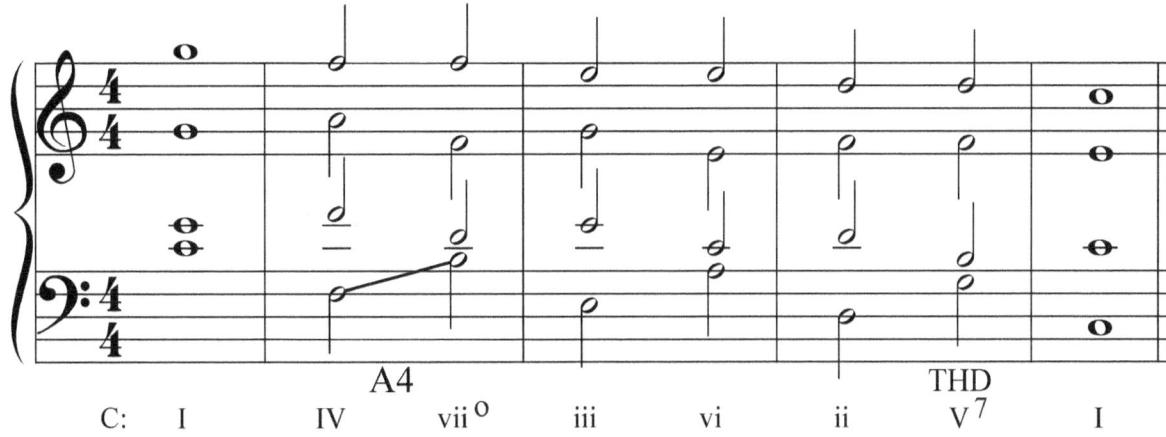

Example 3–33: descending 5th sequence of modal dominant triads, harmonic bass (in minor)

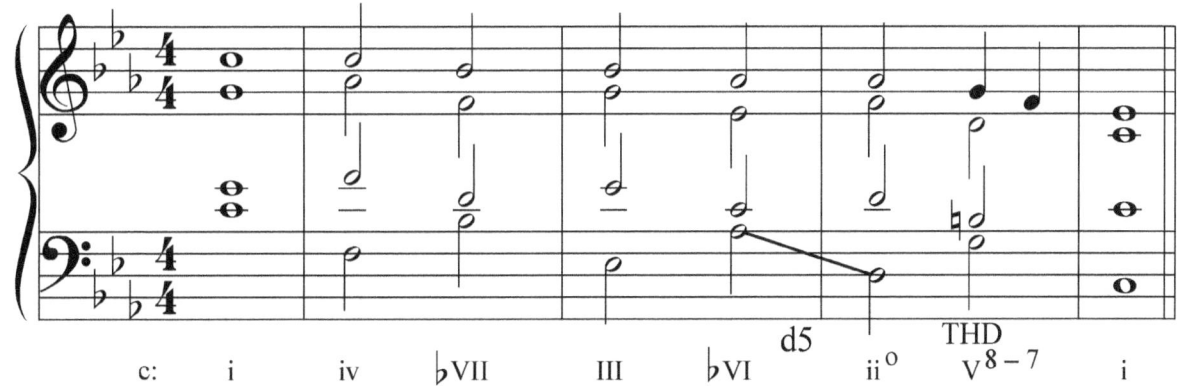

The direct (or hidden) 5ths in example 3–34 underscore the hazards of starting with an unfavorable voicing and pattern of intervals when implementing a chain of modal dominant triads; however, adding sevenths to the texture can improve the connections between chords. Another problem, particularly in minor, is the potential augmented 2nd that may arise when a chord containing variable ♭6 is followed by a chord that contains variable ♯7. Variable ♭6 should descend to scale degree 5 rather than move upwards to ♯7.

Example 3–34: the hazards of using a chain of modal dominant triads

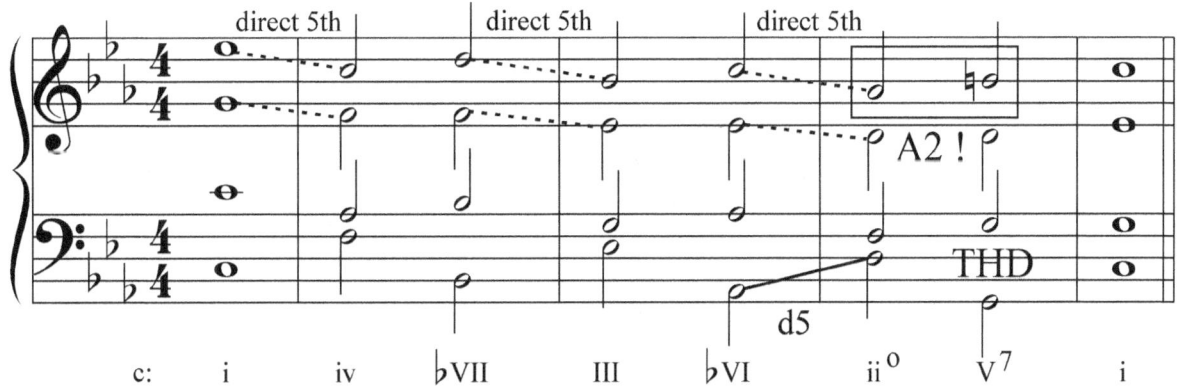

Chord Progressions

We began this chapter with a preference for the term applied dominant over secondary dominant because there are chords in this category of chromaticism other than those of the dominant family. Virtually any chord may be applied to any major or minor triad (possibly with upper extensions such as the seventh and ninth). This section examines lower-level progressions containing non-dominant chords as well as those of the tonic and dominant.

Example 3–35 presents a very common harmonic operation in which the dominant is preceded by an inverted supertonic. The lower-level progressions in 3–35 do not have an initial tonic chord and are therefore described as incomplete progressions. When the supertonic connects the initial tonic to the dominant within a *complete* progression, the chord is often called an intermediate harmony. One of the most important functions of the intermediate harmony is to support the melodic activities of the top voice.

In this text, we avoid the term intermediate harmony because many progressions, both main level and lower level, lack the initial tonic. Allowing for incomplete progressions, an alternative expression describes the chord of the supertonic as a "pre-dominant" chord. In Chapter 7 of *Finding The Right Pitch II: A Guide To The Study Of Basic Harmony*, we call these pre-dominant harmonies "X-chords."

Example 3–35: incomplete secondary contrapuntal progressions with the supertonic as X-chord

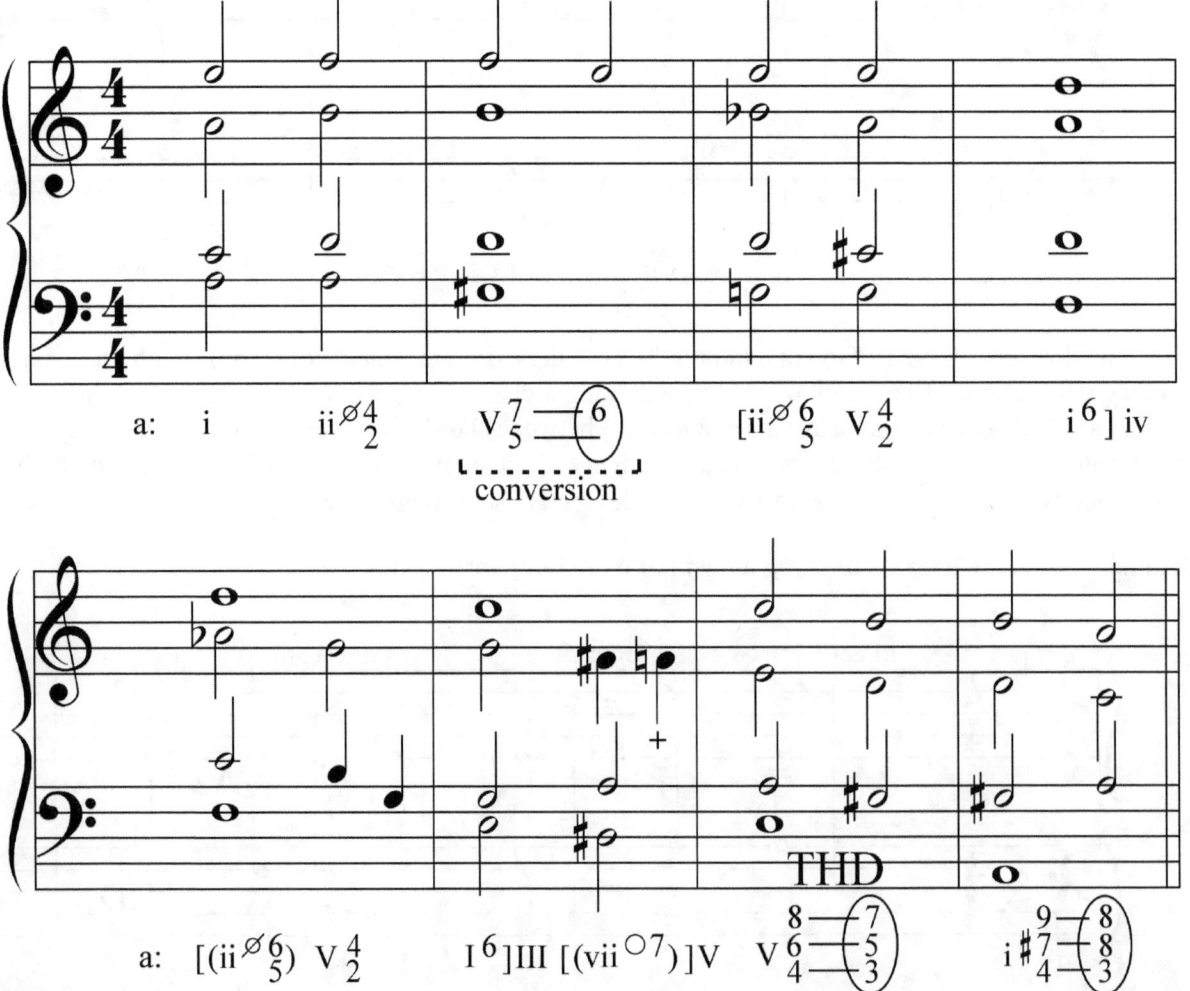

Composers draw upon the areas of the supertonic, mediant, subdominant, and submediant for these intermediary or pre-dominant chords, each of which constitutes an interchangeable value within either a complete or incomplete harmonic or contrapuntal framework. Since the value of the intermediary chord varies from one progression to the next, it assumes the status of what in mathematics would be called X, "the unknown quantity."

When the progression is complete, the X-chord occupies an intermediary position between the initial tonic and the penultimate chord of the dominant family. As a component of either a complete or incomplete progression, the supertonic, mediant, subdominant, and submediant chords may each become X-chord values within the following types of harmonic or contrapuntal frameworks (as before, the contrapuntal leading-tone chord is abbreviated as CLT):

(1) major: I – X – V – I   or   X – V – I
(2) minor: i – X – V – i   or   X – V – i
(3) major: I – X – CLT – I   or   X – CLT – I
(4) minor: i – X – CLT – i   or   X – CLT – i

Before we leave the foregoing example, let us examine its a-minor progression more closely. Notice the use of unequal 5ths between the soprano and alto voices (measure 1). The succession of parallels is perfect 5th to diminished 5th. Subsequently, the soprano (F) suspends into the next chord (measure 2), a conversion dominant proceeding from an apparent fully diminished seventh of the leading tone to a dominant seventh in first inversion (G♯ B D F becomes G♯ B D E).

In measure 3, an incomplete progression begins in the lower-level key of d minor, the subdominant of a minor. The progression is introduced with a half-diminished supertonic in first inversion. The progression is then repeated in C major, the mediant of a minor. Both progressions are part of a descending contrapuntal bass and both end with the V$^4_2$ (CLT) proceeding to the tonic in first inversion.

In the tenor of measure 5, the chord third of the applied dominant skips down to the root (B to G), which also anticipates the chord fifth of the lower-level tonic. An applied leading-tone seventh of the THD brings us back to a minor. In measure 6 (beat 4, alto), a passing tone on F♮ forms an diminished 10th with the bass (D♯ to F♮). The diminished 10th contracts to an E octave and leads thereby to the cadential $^6_4$ of a minor. The progression ends with the third, fifth, and seventh components of the dominant seventh suspended into the tonic triad, producing multiple 9—8, 7—8, and 4—3 motions over the bass. (The progressions cited here are demonstrated in Chapters 7 and 8 of *Finding The Right Pitch II*.)

Harmonic and Contrapuntal Progressions

Our study of harmony is concerned with four types of chord progressions, all of which have a chord of the dominant family in the penultimate position (either the V or a CLT):

(1) the basic harmonic progression (BHP)
   (a) major: I – V – I   or   V – I
   (b) minor: i – V – i   or   V – i
(2) the basic contrapuntal progression (BCP)
   (a) major: I – CLT – I   or   CLT – I
   (b) minor: i – CLT – i   or   CLT – i
(3) the secondary harmonic progression (SHP)
   (a) major: I – X – V – I   or   X – V – I
   (b) minor: i – X – V – i   or   X – V – i
(4) the secondary contrapuntal progression (SCP)
   (a) major   I – X – CLT – I   or   X – CLT – I
   (b) minor   i – X – CLT – i   or   X – CLT – i

These progressions often exhibit stepwise melodic descents in the soprano voice, conjunct motions that are, to a considerable extent, the skeletal frameworks of far more elaborate melodies. Indeed, melodies consisting primarily of scale-like formations may fail to hold the attention of the listener. On the other hand, an engaging melody usually contains both conjunct and disjunct motions with leaps that are likely (though not always) followed by a reversal of direction. Actual melodies rise and fall at the will of the composer, typically presenting more rhythmic variety than those illustrated in this text. Such devices as nonharmonic tones and chordal skips are also common (see *Finding The Right Pitch II*, Chapters 3 and 9).

The use of conjunct and disjunct motion, varied rhythmic patterns, and nonharmonic tones all count among the elements that make up the outer skin or flesh surrounding the bare bones of a musical work. The details that comprise the musical surface of a composition help to establish its individuality; moreover, the details of a musical composition make it accessible to the listener.

The harmonic and contrapuntal progressions that accompany melodies are seldom limited to three or four chords. Still, the study of harmony should begin with the simplest of melodic and harmonic constructions. While a much wider variety of chord progressions may occur in music than those put forward here, the four general types of progressions cited above form the underlying harmonic and contrapuntal frameworks for the music literature of the common practice period.

Lower-Level Keys within Lower-Level Keys

Example 3–36, in c minor, approximates the harmony of the first phrase of Frédéric Chopin's Prelude in E Minor, Op. 28, No. 4 (measures 1–12). (Chopin ends the first phrase of the Prelude on the dominant. Example 3–36 ends with a tonic chord. In Chapter 8, we shall study the entire work in the original key.)

The lower-level progression in c minor's subdominant (f minor) is enriched by an excursion into the subdominant's subtonic (E♭ major). Example 3–37 clarifies the relationship between the keys: f minor is iv of c minor and E♭ major is ♭VII of f minor, represented by brackets within brackets.

Example 3–36 has a descending contrapuntal bass spanning the distance between two positions of the tonic chord (first-inversion and root-position). As in 3–35 above, the passage ends with multiple suspensions into the tonic chord. (Chopin's actual ending to the Prelude does not use *multiple* suspensions.) All four voices move conjunctly except for measure 7, which re-voices an apparent augmented-major seventh *en route* to the iv ^{6} on beat 3 (expressed as a lower-level tonic). The iv ^{6} is the X-chord of the main-level key.

Generic figured bass accounts for the nonharmonic tones that produce the apparent chords. Exact figured bass is provided above the chord descriptions. Throughout most of 3–36, three out of four voices of each chord are sustained into each successive chord. The remaining voice moves by half step, except for measure 7 which contains the re-voiced chord. Measure 8 establishes the main-level THD (the V chord in measure 1 is a passing chord).

In broad terms, the chromatic harmony in 3–36 occurs between the initial i ^{6} and the iv ^{6} (measure 7). The contrapuntal bass, chromatic movement between voices, and expression of lower-level keys (whose tonic resolutions are denied) expand the motion to the iv ^{6}. This expansion *prolongs* the motion from the tonic to the subdominant.

In the example, an apparent chord on beat 1 of measure 2 sounds like a dominant seventh in second inversion with a lowered fifth (G B D♭ F); on beat 2, the chord proceeds to the half-diminished supertonic of f minor (G B♭ D♭ F). As in example 2–8 (Chapter 2), the expression of generic figured bass in 3–36 presents certain difficulties (measure 2). The B♮ is scale degree ♯4 in f minor, a chromatic tone (occurring at the interval of a 6th above the bass). The B♭ that follows on beat 2 is scale degree 4 of f minor.

The sharp in front of the 6 on beat 1 correctly represents ♯4. Since we are trying to avoid the awkward succession of ♯6 to ♭6 (B♮ to B♭) in the generic figured bass, the natural in parentheses attached to the following 6 is the best option for indicating that the chord third of the supertonic reverts to f minor's "natural" scale degree 4, B♭.

The third beat of measure 2 initiates a conversion dominant in f minor that ends in measure 3. The conversion dominant is repeated in E♭ major in measures 4–5. Neither conversion resolves to its respective tonic. A contrapuntal approach of a lower-level effects the arrival of the X-chord, the iv ^{6} (measure 7). The resolution to the main-level tonic takes place only after its THD is established (measures 8–9).

Ultimately, the excursions into lower-level keys in 3–36 constitute prolongations of chords of differing rank within the tonal hierarchy of c minor, the main-level key. The underlying harmonic framework of the highest order, or rank, belongs to the category of the secondary harmonic progression, with the subdominant serving as the X-chord: i ^{6} – iv ^{6} – V ^{7} – i.

Example 3–36: the chromaticism of Chopin's Op. 28, No. 4 (based on the harmony of measures 1–12)

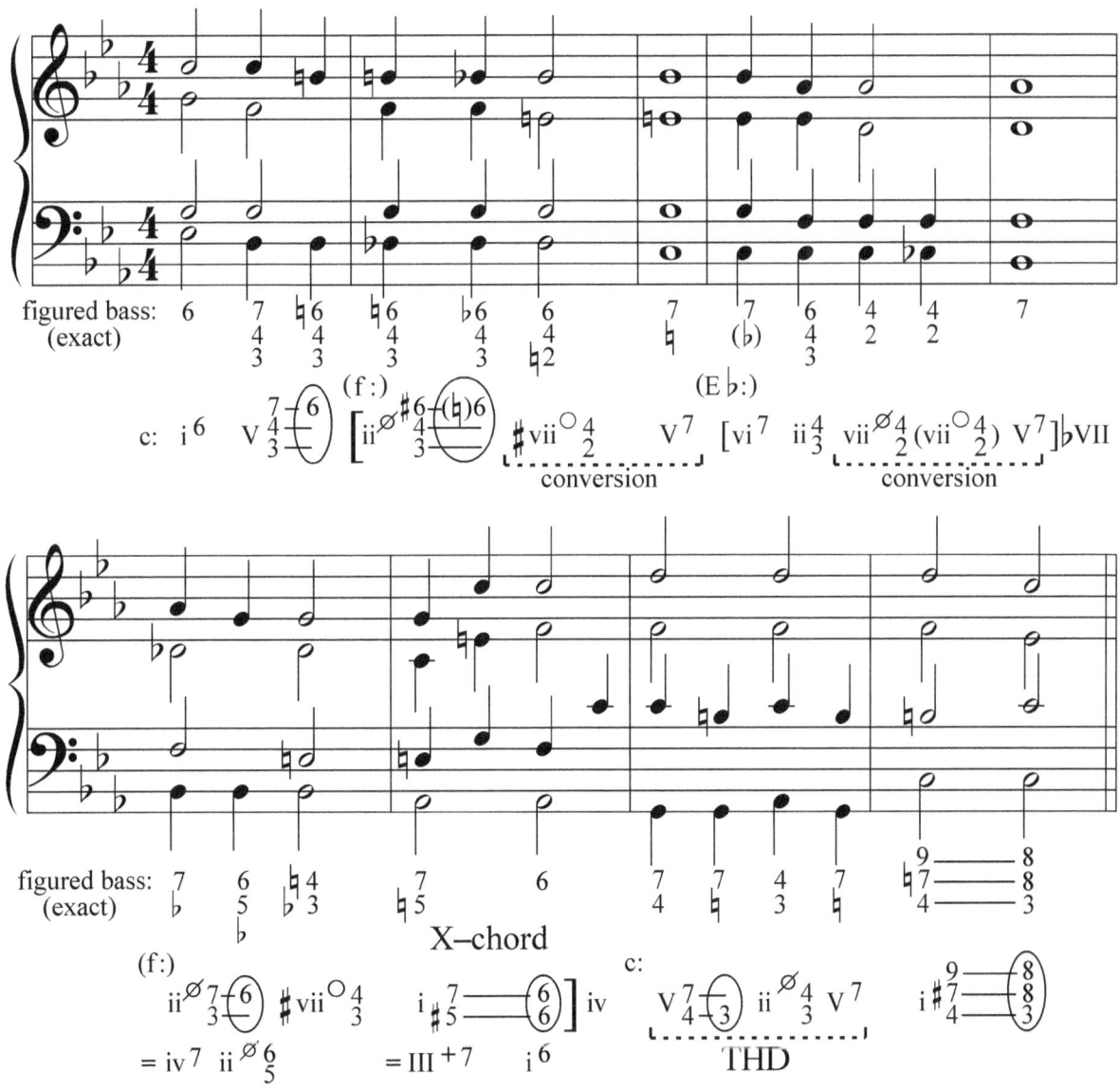

Example 3–37: summary of key relationships for example 3–36

c: [[   ] ♭VII] iv
         (E♭)   (f)

Cadences

In Chapter 6 of *Finding The Right Pitch II: A Guide To The Study Of Basic Harmony*, we observed that the cadence is a two-chord pattern that forms the end of a musical phrase. The phrase is the smallest element of musical form in which a combination of melodic, rhythmic, and chordal components together comprise the beginning, middle, and end of a musical thought. The ending may be permanent or temporary, whether or not the activity within the phrase is continuous or segmented into smaller units known as sub-phrases. These sub-phrases, if present, may also contain endings marked off by cadences.

The first part of the two-chord pattern is called the *approach chord* because it addresses the second chord, known as the *cadential chord*. The approach chord may include dissonant upper extensions beyond the root, third, and fifth of the basic triad, such as the seventh and the ninth. Since the cadential chord constitutes either a permanent or temporary ending, dissonant chords are usually avoided here because consonant chords more effectively convey a state of rest. There are two basic types of cadences, each defined according to how the approach chord addresses the cadential chord:

(1) If the approach to the cadential chord in the bass involves either a falling 5th or rising 4th motion (or a falling 4th or rising 5th motion), then we describe the cadence as a harmonic cadence.

(2) If the approach to the cadential chord in the bass involves the melodic interval of a major or minor 2nd, then we describe the cadence as a contrapuntal cadence.

None of the cadences in *Finding The Right Pitch II* involve applied chords; they are all diatonic. This chapter concludes with an exploration of the possibilities for using applied chords to tonicize the cadential chord. But first, it would be well to review some of the most common dispositions for both authentic cadences and half cadences in the main-level key, starting with the latter.

Harmonic and Contrapuntal Half Cadences in the Main-Level Key

The half cadence, also known as the semicadence, consists of a cadential chord other than the tonic; it is often analogized to a comma in speech, a stopping point that nonetheless seeks continuation to complete the musical thought. The half cadence exhibits either a harmonic or contrapuntal bass relationship between its two chords.

For the harmonic half cadence in major, illustrated in examples 3–38a through 38f, the tonic or the supertonic constitute the most common approaches to the cadential chord. The dominant triad or the cadential $^6_4$ are the most frequently used cadential chords. When either the dominant or the cadential $^6_4$ appears as the cadential chord, a triad rather than a seventh chord is preferred because a consonant chord establishes a feeling of repose more successfully than a dissonant one.

In minor, the tonic often serves as the approach chord of choice (examples 3–38g, 38h, and 38i). The diminished supertonic can be used as an approach chord but not in root position, as the diminished 5th formed above its root is too dissonant. When, however, a 3rd is added above the fifth, transforming the diminished triad into a half-diminished seventh chord, the harshness of the diminished 5th above the root is mitigated (3–38j).

The contrapuntal half cadence, shown in examples 3–39 and 3–40, presents more varied possibilities for the approach chord, while the cadential chord is expressed in either root position, first inversion, or as a cadential $^6_4$. The approach to the cadential chord is usually made from above or below by step. Although the limitations of space preclude a complete listing of all the available approach chords for the contrapuntal half cadence, examples 3–39 and 3–40 demonstrate a few of the simplest ways to address the cadential chord.

Example 3–38: the harmonic half cadence in the main-level key

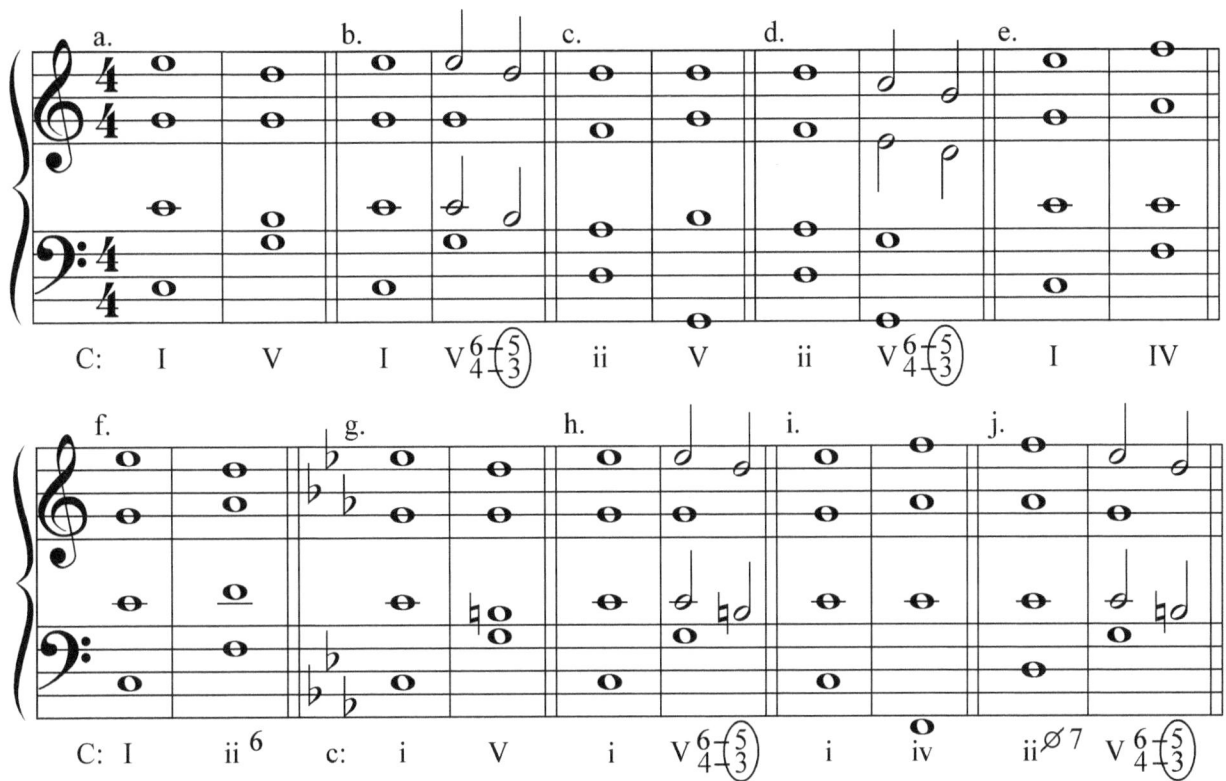

Example 3–39: the contrapuntal half cadence in the main-level key

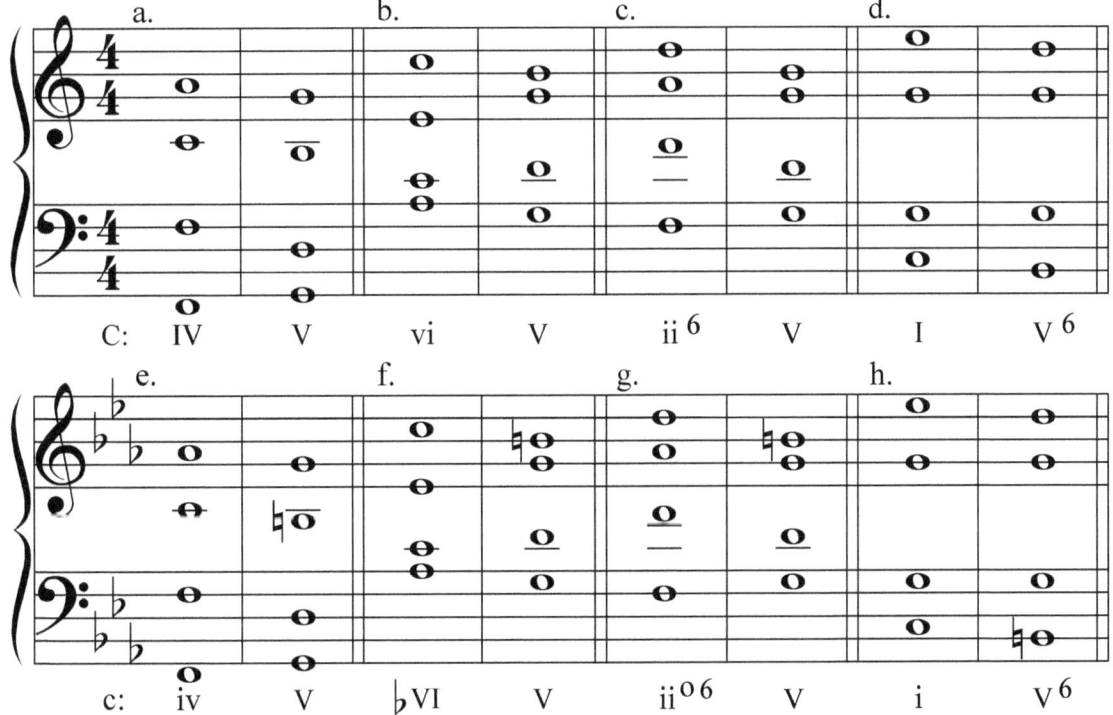

Example 3–40: the contrapuntal half cadence in the main-level key (using the cadential $^6_4$)

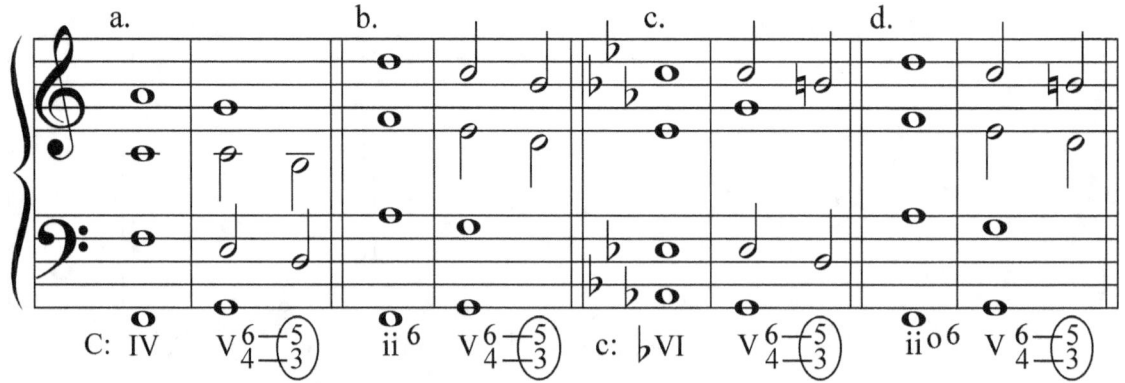

The approach chord in the examples of half cadences displayed above are all triads; but it is also possible for the approach chord to carry a seventh, as in example 3–41.

Example 3–41: approaching the cadential chord with a seventh chord

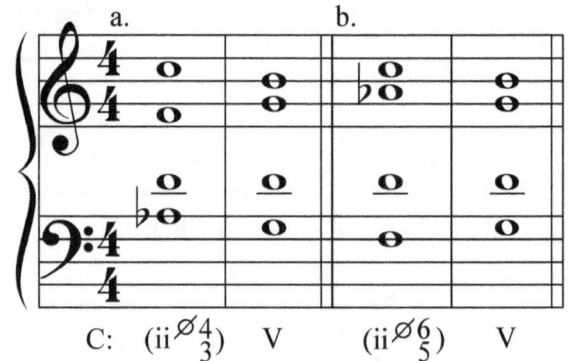

Contrapuntal Half Cadences in Lower-Level Keys

In the foregoing sections, we considered various half cadences in the main-level key. The same basic principles of voice leading and chord disposition can be used to tonicize the cadential chord, which is usually the dominant. When a musical phrase ends with a half cadence in the main-level key, we describe the operation as being "on" the chord (example 3–42a). If the dominant is the cadential chord, then the half cadence is *on* the dominant.

The opposite condition would be a half cadence "in" the chord, that is, in the dominant (as in 3–42b). Once the dominant has been tonicized, the musical context determines whether the key change is extensive enough to qualify as a true modulation or something more transient.

Example 3–42b displays a contrapuntal approach to the cadential chord (G B D), effected by a chromatic passing motion in the bass (F–F♯–G). In the main-level key of C major, the F♯ is scale degree ♯4; in the dominant key of G major, F♯ is the leading tone. The chord on which the F♯ stands is an applied dominant seventh in first inversion. The half cadence is therefore *in* the chord of the dominant.

Example 3–42: the half cadence on the chord versus the half cadence in the chord

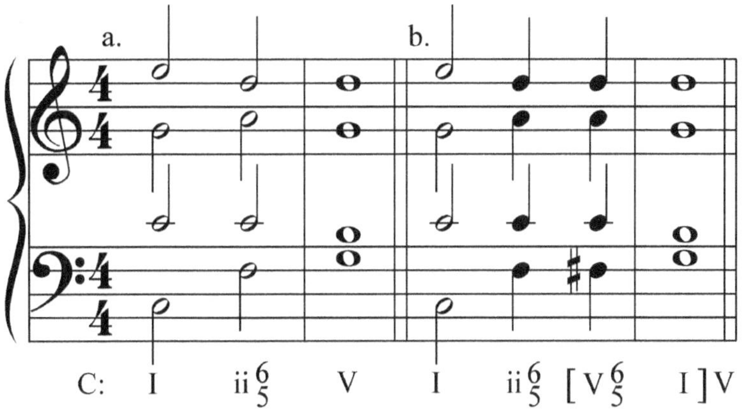

[musical example: C: I ii$^6_5$ V | I ii$^6_5$ [V$^6_5$ I]V]

The half cadence *in* the chord is always a contrapuntal cadence. Examples 3–43, 44, and 45 present various dispositions of half cadences in the chord of the dominant. Although the applied half cadences in the following three examples count among the most common usages, there are many other alternatives to what is put forward here. For instance, when an applied leading-tone seventh chord addresses the cadential chord (as in examples 3–43c and d, 44c and d, 45c and d), you may encounter either a half-diminished seventh or a fully diminished seventh in the literature (a half-diminished leading-tone seventh in minor, however, is not used).

The half cadence in the chord can also be described as a contrapuntal perfect authentic cadence or contrapuntal imperfect authentic cadence *of a lower level*. This alternative description is possible because the cadential chord assumes the status of a lower-level tonic. If the passage containing the tonicized chord remains in the new key long enough and a sense of modulation achieved thereby, then the half cadence in the chord is re-interpreted as a contrapuntal perfect or imperfect authentic cadence of a lower level. In 3–43, the G-major triad is the lower-level tonic and therefore becomes available as the cadential chord for a variety of "tonic-oriented" cadences. (The most prevalent types are discussed in *Finding The Right Pitch II*.)

The contrapuntal perfect authentic cadence has scale degree 1 in both outer voices (as in 3–43a), whereas the contrapuntal imperfect authentic cadence has a scale degree other than the tonic in at least one of its outer voices (as in 3–43b, 43c, and 43d). Of all the applied half cadences in examples 3–43, 44, and 45, only examples 3–43a and 3–45a also constitute contrapuntal perfect authentic cadences; the remaining contrapuntal cadences belong to the imperfect authentic category.

Example 3–43: contrapuntal half cadences in the dominant chord

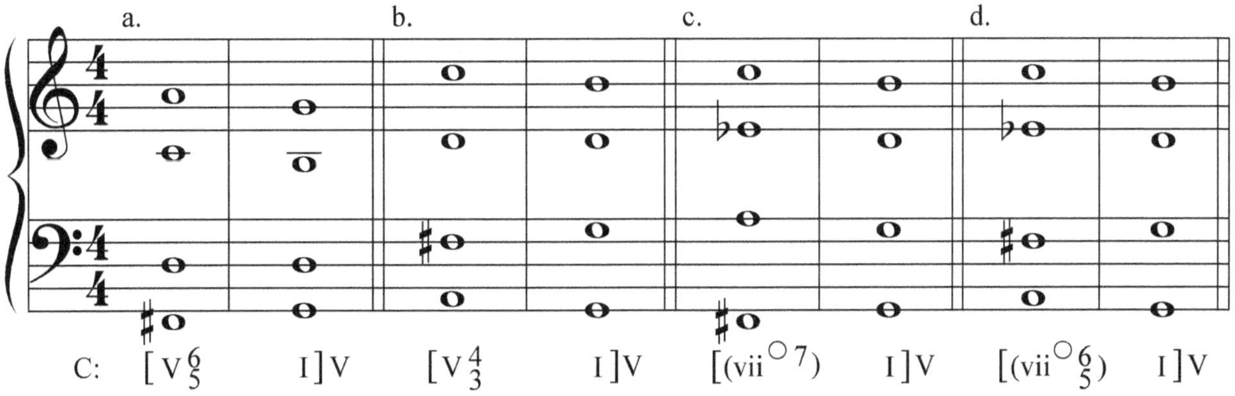

[musical example: C: [V$^6_5$ I]V [V$^4_3$ I]V [(vii^{o7}) I]V [(vii$^{o6}_5$) I]V]

In example 3–44b, notice the unresolved 7th in the soprano (C). The V$^4_3$ chord is part of a contrapuntal progression that supports a motion in parallel 10ths between the bass and the soprano voices. The dissonant 7th continues upwards into a 10th. The melodic activity between the bass and an upper voice overrides the traditional downward resolution.

Example 3–44: contrapuntal half cadences in the dominant chord

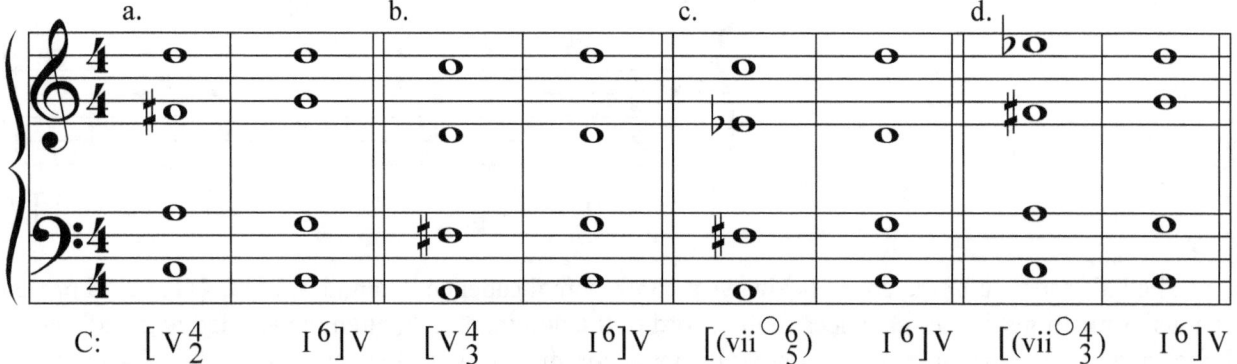

Examples 3–45c and 45d contain a correctly misspelled tone in the alto voice, namely, D♯. The chord seventh of the borrowed leading-tone seventh chord is E♭ (F♯ A C E♭); however, since the alto moves to E♮ in the cadential $^6_4$ chord, it is better to have a D♯ leading upwards to E♮ than to backtrack E♭ to E♮. A word of caution: the composer may or may not correctly misspell the chord.

Example 3–45: contrapuntal half cadences in the dominant chord (using the cadential $^6_4$)

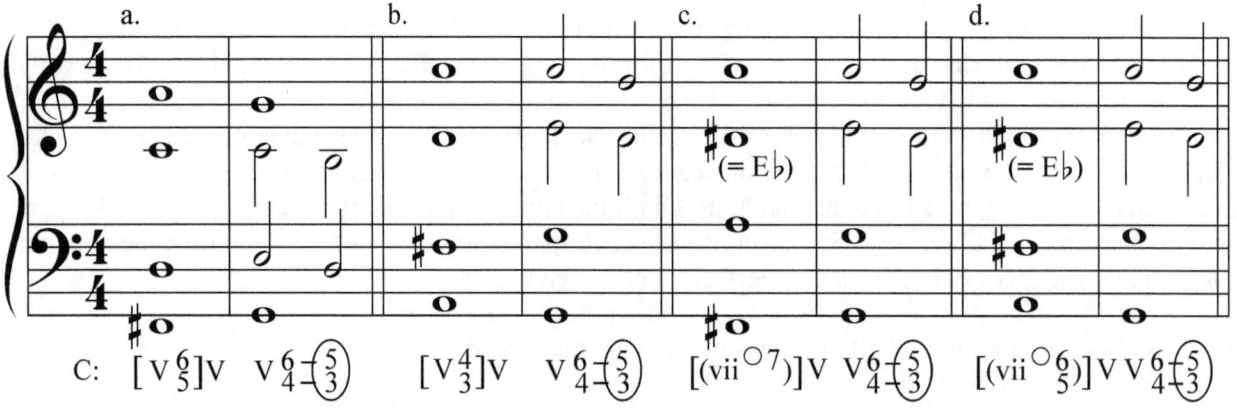

Authentic Cadences in the Main-Level Key

The approach chord of the authentic cadence is a dominant-family chord. The cadential chord is the tonic chord. There are two general classes of authentic cadences, each defined according to how the approach chord addresses the cadential chord: harmonic authentic cadences and contrapuntal authentic cadences. Additionally, within the general category of the authentic cadence, there are two subclasses, each grouped according to what scale degrees appear in the bass and soprano voices: the perfect authentic cadence and the imperfect authentic cadence. The most permanent-sounding close to a musical phrase is produced by the authentic cadence, particularly, the perfect authentic cadence.

The harmonic perfect authentic cadence is described generally as a "closed cadence," or "full cadence" (example 3–46). Having either a falling 5th or rising 4th root and bass relationship between its approach chord and cadential chord, the harmonic perfect authentic cadence produces a sense of finality not present in other cadences because it has scale degree 1 in both outer voices of the tonic chord. The finality of the harmonic perfect authentic cadence makes it the most effective device for establishing an actual modulation. (The chief characteristic of the harmonic imperfect authentic cadence is the appearance of either scale degree 3 or 5 in the soprano voice of the tonic chord.)

Example 3–46: the harmonic perfect authentic cadence in the main-level key

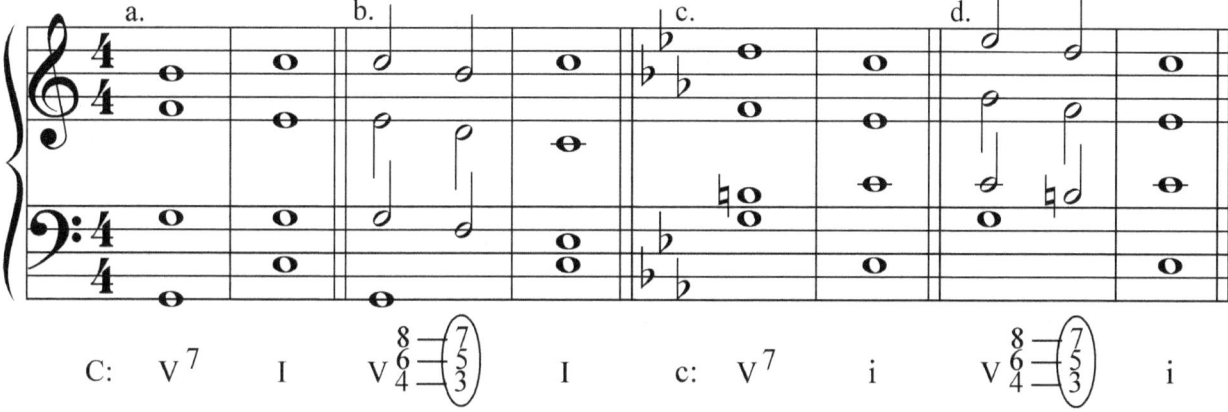

Authentic Cadences in Lower-Level Keys

As stated earlier, an applied half cadence may also be interpreted as either a contrapuntal perfect authentic cadence or contrapuntal imperfect authentic cadence of a lower level. Examples 3–43a and 3–45a above have applied contrapuntal perfect authentic cadences, while all of the remaining cadences in examples 3–43, 44, and 45 exhibit contrapuntal imperfect authentic cadences.

Although a change of key may be produced by using an applied contrapuntal cadence, the most convincing modulations occur when the new key is confirmed by a harmonic perfect authentic cadence of a lower level, such as those featured in example 3–47.

Example 3–47: the harmonic perfect authentic cadence in the dominant and in the mediant

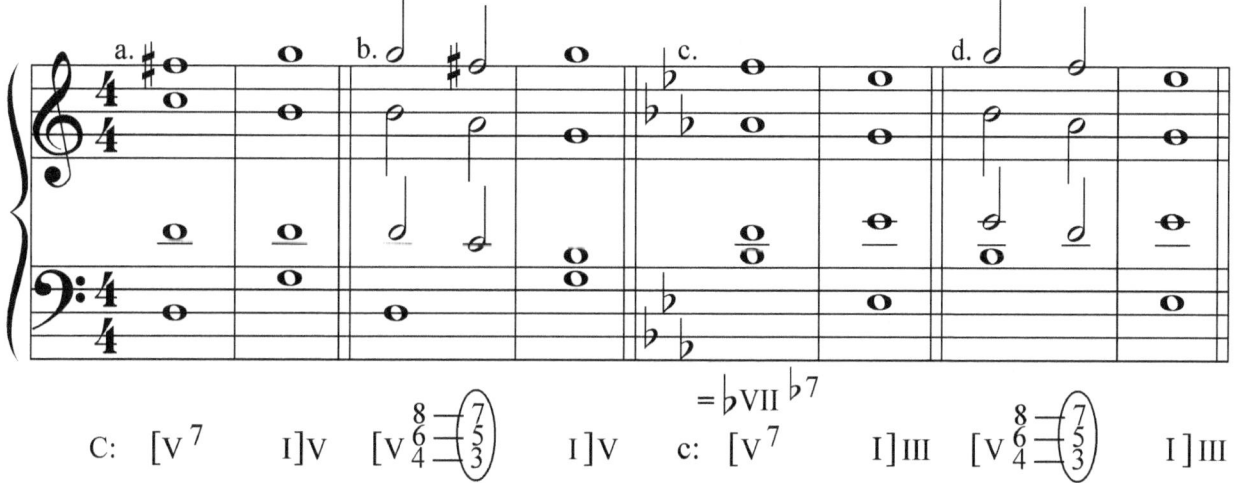

In major, as depicted in 3–47a and 47b, the most common key area for tonicization or modulation is the dominant. The choice of the dominant is due to its close relationship to the tonic. Standing at the interval of the perfect 5th above the tonic and serving as the primary definer of a composition's tonality, the dominant scale degree forms the strongest relationship with the tonic. The prominence of the perfect 5th within the harmonic series produces the field of attraction between the dominant and the tonic. Accordingly, the most natural change of key in major involves a prolongation of the dominant chord and/or its key.

In minor, as illustrated in 3–47c and 47d, there is a decided preference for the mediant. All potential lower-level tonics are established with the introduction of chromatic tones, *except* when the subtonic triad or seventh addresses the mediant chord in minor. As a diatonic member of the key and mode, the subtonic chord sounds like an applied dominant of the mediant *without the addition of chromaticism.*

Revisiting example 3–2 above as example 3–48a below, we know that the ♭VII♭7 and the ii°6 of the main-level key in minor can be employed as applied harmonic and contrapuntal dominants of the mediant: [V 7]III and [vii°6]III. Thus, both the ♭VII♭7 and ii°6 of the main-level key have a diatonic function within the key of the mediant, the relative major. Chords that provide a smooth and convincing connection from one key to another are known as "pivot chords" (see below, p. 74).

The progression between the subtonic and mediant chord in 3–48a forms a harmonic perfect authentic cadence in E♭ in measure 2. Once the motion *into* the III chord is accomplished, the progression may continue in the new key; however, additional chords in E♭ major would be needed to delay the return of c minor. In 3–48a, the appearance of the cadential $^6_4$ in the main-level key prevents the tonicization of the mediant from lasting more than one measure.

In 3–48b, the ♭VII♭7 once again articulates and strengthens the III; but instead of proceeding to the cadential $^6_4$ of the main-level key (as in 3–48a), two applied CLT chords forming upper and lower neighbors effect contrapuntal prolongations of the III chord from above and below E♭: [vii°6]III and [V$^6_5$]III.

And so, at what point do we use brackets to show the motion into the lower-level key of E♭? Identifying the exact place of the key change is not as important as understanding the process that makes the move to the relative major so effortless. In 3–48b, the motion into III begins with the ♭VII♭7 serving as [V 7]III.

Using ♭VII♭7 and ii°6 as dominant-family chords in the new key provides a very direct though transparent way to proceed from the minor mode to its relative major. As we shall see later in this study, establishing an X-chord as the pivot to the new key is preferable to establishing a dominant-family chord as the pivot, though the latter method certainly works (as in 3–48b).

Example 3–48: using ♭VII♭7 and ii°6 as pivots to the relative major

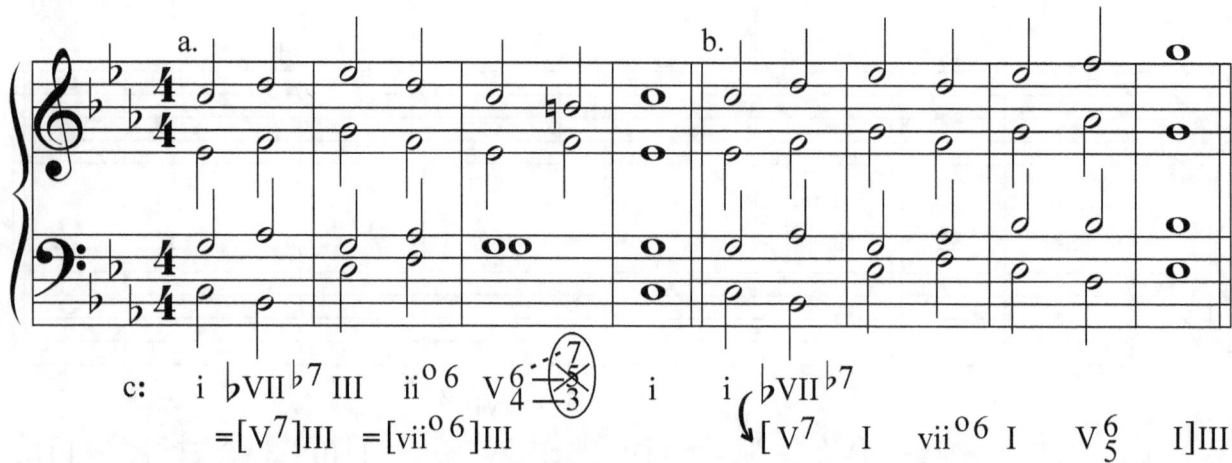

Chapter 4 Small Form

Tonal music, like literary prose, is organized into phrases, sentences, and paragraphs. These constituent parts are brought together in various combinations to produce musical form. The elements of music (such as pitch, melody, rhythm, meter, harmony, and texture) create musical form by means of three basic techniques: repetition, contrast, and variation.

Repetition unifies a musical composition by providing the listener with points of orientation, frames of reference that convey a sense of familiarity. Contrast helps to maintain and focus the attention of the listener by providing variety. Variation is the most flexible of the three techniques in that it endows a composition with both unity and variety.

A new section of music may be either a complete contrast from a previous section or it may simply constitute a variation of a previous section. But regardless of the degree of contrast or similarity between sections, each formal component is supported by some kind of harmonic and/or contrapuntal structure in which excursions into lower-level keys may occur.

Using keys of a lower order adds tonal contrast to a musical segment of a composition. At the musical surface, the repetition of a melody in a different key can produce just enough contrast to engage the listener. At a deeper level, the tonality of a larger section of music may herald a change in the form of the composition. Additionally, tonality can indicate the return of material heard previously. In these circumstances, tonality articulates both large and small events in the form.

Small forms emerge from combinations of phrases which in turn may coalesce into sections yielding large formal designs. Tonicization is often associated with the smaller events, whereas modulation tends to support the larger events. In between these two extremes, the tonal plan of the composition provides the underlying framework for the elements of music to interact throughout the various layers and dimensions of the form.

In this chapter, we encounter the components of form comprising the musical surface, such as motives, phrases, and periods. Formal analysis of these essential elements can yield valuable information about the musical content of a composition. However, regardless of how we account for these surface events, deeper harmonic and/or contrapuntal structures determine the true nature of a composition's overall shape. Our discussion of form starts from this premise.

The Period

Musical phrases are marked by cadences just as commas, semicolons, and periods punctuate linguistic structures. Cadences in which the cadential chord is a chord other than the tonic are often compared to the comma or semicolon, as they indicate that the musical phrase seeks continuation in a subsequent phrase to complete the musical thought. The half cadence, also known as the semicadence, is the most notable musical equivalent of the comma or semicolon.

In language, the period conveys the strongest sense of completion or closure. In music, the most permanent-sounding close is the harmonic perfect authentic cadence (HPAC), which is usually described as a "closed cadence," or "full cadence." The perfect authentic cadence assumes the function of the linguistic period, marking the end of the musical idea. All other cadences are "open cadences." Open cadences are incomplete and seek continuation and resolution to a closed cadence, an HPAC.

In some of the music of the common practice period, cadences are important destinations; they are *goals* of arrival with form-building properties. The practice of articulating phrases with open and closed cadences leads to the creation of small forms consisting of two or more interdependent phrases. When two phrases are connected by a combination of open and closed cadences, the resulting segment of music is commonly referred to as a "period."

The Antecedent and Consequent Phrases

Example 4–1 illustrates the period structure of the first sixteen measures of Mozart's Sonata No. 16 in C Major (K. 545), second movement. The segment consists of two eight-measure phrases (phrase 1 and phrase 2 in the example), each phrase dividing into two four-measure sub-phrases. The first phrase of the period structure is known as the antecedent phrase (in 4–1, measures 1–8). The second phrase is called the consequent phrase (measures 9–16).

In 4–1, the second phrase grows out of the need for completion produced by the contrapuntal half cadence of the first phrase. The closed cadence of the second phrase resolves the tonal tension arising from the antecedent's dominant. Together, the two phrases are usually described as having a "question-answer" dynamic. The relationship between the cadences of the antecedent and consequent phrases thus produces the interdependent structure of the period.

Interruption of the Melodic and Harmonic Structure

As we have said, the creation of small form is associated with the practice of articulating phrases with open and closed cadences. The contrapuntal half cadence in measure 8 is open (4–1); it demands continuation. On beat 2 of measure 8, the melody ends on scale degree 2 as the dominant chord is reached (see the circled A in 4–1). For the progression to complete itself with the tonic chord in the next measure, scale degree 2 should proceed down to scale degree 1 (G). However, when the tonic returns in measure 9, the melody begins on scale degree 3 (B), *not scale degree 1*.

Therefore, the tonic chord in measure 9 is not the completion of the first progression, but rather, the beginning of a *second* progression. The first progression is *interrupted* by the onset of the second, which repeats most of the tonal framework of the first. (Later in this text, the technique of interruption is represented by attaching carets to scale degrees, with two vertical bars marking the point of the division. A chord of harmony supports the division.)

The first progression is incomplete. And yet, the tonal tension produced by the interruption on the dominant *binds* the two phrases together by making the weaker contrapuntal cadence of the first phrase (measure 8) dependent upon the HPAC of the second phrase (measure 16).

The Motive

The texture of the excerpt in 4–1 consists of a combination of triad arpeggiations and conjunct motions. The triads and sevenths in the left hand (bass clef) constitute the accompaniment while the right hand (treble clef) takes the melody. The triads in the right hand have a motivic quality that contributes to the unity of the composition (see the brackets in 4–1).

The "motive" is a self-contained intervallic and/or rhythmic unit, subject to transposition and transformation, and clearly recognizable at the musical surface. The motive serves to unify and give coherence to components within a single phrase or especially between two or more phrases. (The motive is similar to a related figure known as the "motto," a self-contained intervallic and/or rhythmic unit, less subject to transformation and used primarily to differentiate larger sections of a music composition.)

As shown in example 4–1, the triad motive in the right hand undergoes transposition (in both phrases), reduction of note values to sixteenths (in phrase 2), and transformation. In measures 6 and 14, the descending arpeggiation of the tonic triad is transformed into an ascending figure by changing the register of one chord tone (G). Though the alteration of the motive is modest, the change greatly intensifies the expression of the melody leading up to the cadences at the end of each eight-measure phrase. Additionally, we find the triad embedded in two stepwise passages: the first descending through the subdominant triad (example 4–1, measure 7), the second ascending through the tonic scale (measure 10).

Chapter 4 Small Form

Example 4–1: Mozart, Sonata No. 16 in C Major (K. 545), II, measures 1–16

Small One-Part Form: the Parallel Period

Let us take a closer look at the first sixteen measures of Mozart's Sonata No. 16 in C Major (K. 545), second movement. For convenience, the music of example 4–1 is reproduced on the following page as example 4–3. The period shown in the example constitutes a small one-part form. All one-part forms have one perfect authentic cadence.

The specific variety of period in 4–3 is known as a parallel period. The word parallel refers to the similarity of the two phrases. Since the two phrases are related more than they are dissimilar, we assign a lowercase letter a to both phrases. If the second phrase is a modification of the first, then we also assign a prime character (') to the lowercase a and call it "a prime."

Example 4–2a displays the general form of the parallel period (each curved line and lowercase letter represents a musical phrase), which ends with an HPAC. (Had the phrases exhibited less similarity, we would have assigned a lowercase letter b to the second phrase instead of retaining the same letter. This second type of small one-part form, the contrasting period, is discussed in the next section.)

Although the parallel period consists of two musically related phrases, there are likely to be some differences between the phrases because the cadences of their underlying harmonic frameworks are usually different: the first phrase ends generally (though not always) on the dominant and the second phrase ends on the tonic. Therefore, adjustments may be required to accommodate the different goals of motion at the end of each phrase. However, despite any adjustments or variations between phrases, each phrase of the parallel period typically begins with the same basic idea, hence the description a a'.

The formal diagram for the period that opens the second movement of the C-Major Sonata is shown in 4–2b. Phrase a extends from measures 1–8 and ends with a contrapuntal half cadence on V (½). Phrase a' comprises measures 9–16, is an elaboration (or variation) of the first phrase, and concludes with an HPAC.

Since the progression of the antecedent phrase has an interruption of the melodic and harmonic structure, we can describe the two phrases as a parallel period "with interruption." The interruption produces a *noncontinuous* period structure, one in which the initial progression and its melody is suddenly stopped in the first phrase and then repeated as the beginning of the second phrase. An incomplete secondary harmonic progression (SHP) supports the first phrase. (The X-chord, IV, appears in measure 7.)

Within the incomplete SHP, the initial root-position tonic is prolonged from measures 1–6 by means of a CLT chord functioning as an upper neighbor (UN chord) in measures 1 and 5 and a pedal embellishing subdominant $^6_4$ in measure 3. Two basic contrapuntal progressions (BCP) sustain the prolongation of the tonic (measures 1–4 and 4–6). The interrupting dominant occurs in measure 8.

In measure 6, the tonic chord moves into its first inversion through a subdividing chord (a bass motion that fills in the interval of the 6th, 7th, or octave between like- or unlike-rooted chords). The subdominant X- chord in measure 7 extends across three beats. In measure 8, the cadential $^6_4$ completes itself in two beats.

The complete SHP supporting phrase a' is virtually the same as the incomplete SHP of phrase a, except that the supertonic X-chord in measure 15 is compressed into one beat so that the cadential $^6_4$ can occur on the second and third beats. This placement sets up the arrival of the HPAC in measure 16 (completing the SHP). Reducing the five-beat duration of the subdominant X-chord and the dominant in the first phrase to three beats in the second phrase (with its own supertonic X-chord and dominant) preserves the eight-measure symmetry of both phrases.

Example 4–2: the parallel period in Mozart's Sonata No. 16 in C Major (K. 545), II, measures 1–16

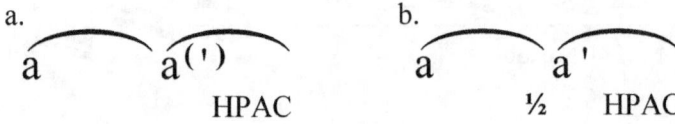

Example 4–3: Mozart, Sonata No. 16 in C Major (K. 545), II, measures 1–16, parallel period

70   Chapter 4   Small Form

Small One-Part Form: the Contrasting Period

As demonstrated in example 4–4, it is possible to have a noncontinuous period *without* interruption in which the *tonic closes off the first phrase*. The example contains measures 1–10 of the first movement of Mozart's Sonata No. 5 in G Major (K. 283). Here, each phrase is supported by its own basic contrapuntal progression (BCP) in the tonic (the dominant is expressed as a CLT chord). The tonic chord in measure 4 constitutes both the end of the first progression and the beginning of the second. Closing off the first phrase with the tonic creates a noncontinuous *sectional* period.

The contrapuntal imperfect authentic cadence at the end of the first phrase (CIAC, measure 4) is just weak enough to carry the music forward and to allow the second phrase to close convincingly with a strong HPAC in measure 10.

Example 4–4: Mozart, Sonata No. 5 in G Major (K. 283), I, measures 1–10, contrasting period

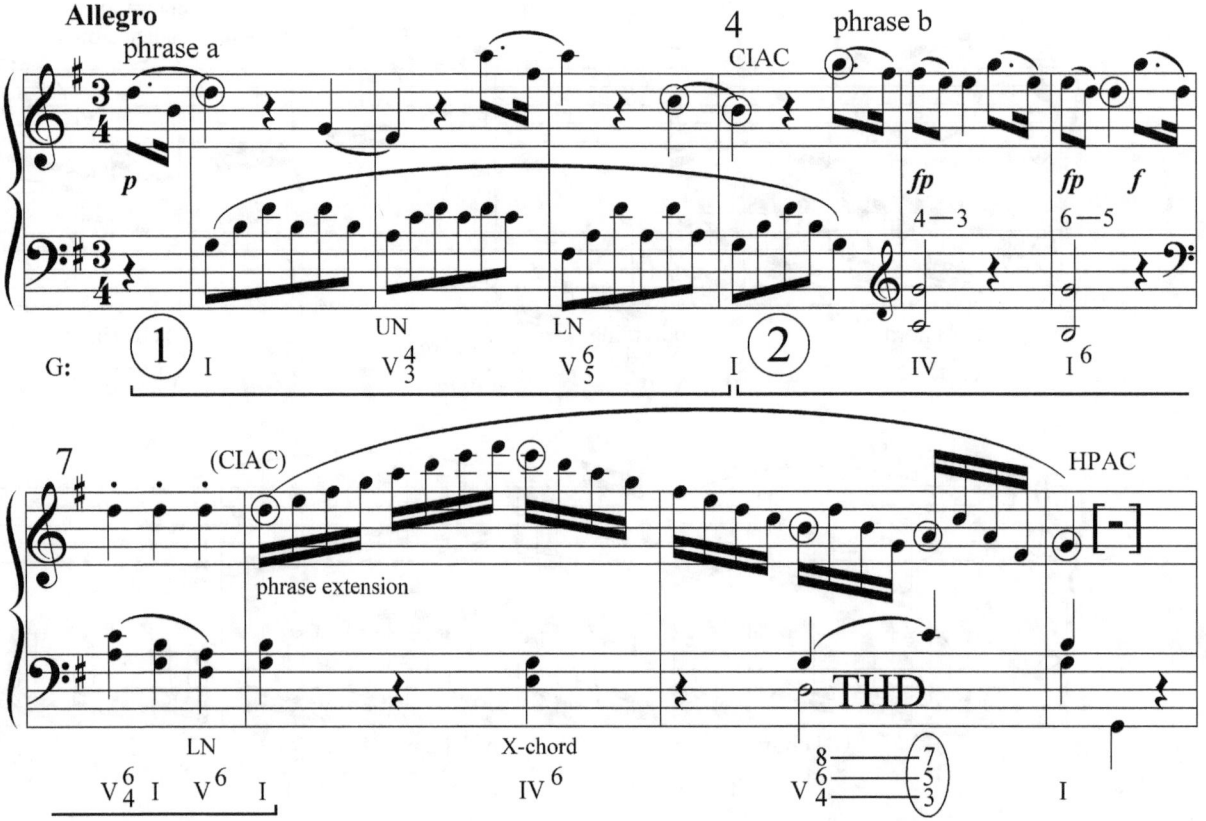

Since the melodic structures and accompaniments of the two phrases are more dissimilar than they are related, we can describe their combined form as that of a contrasting period (represented by the letters a b in example 4–5).

Example 4–5a illustrates the essential characteristics of the contrasting period (two dissimilar phrases and one HPAC). Example 4–5b shows the formal diagram for the first ten measures of Mozart's Sonata in G Major (K. 283, I). Unlike the symmetrical phrasing of measures 1–16 of the C-Major Sonata (example 4–3, K. 545, II), measures 1–10 of the G-Major Sonata (example 4–4) are configured asymmetrically: phrase a is 4 measures long; phrase b is 6 measures long (including a phrase extension of three measures).

Example 4–5: the contrasting period and Mozart's Sonata No. 5 in G Major (K. 283), I, measures 1–10

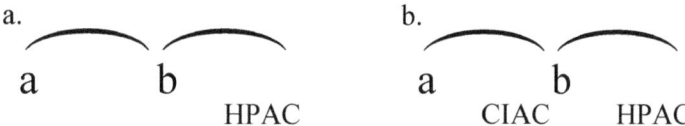

As we have observed, the contrapuntal imperfect authentic cadence in measure 4 (CIAC) demands continuation. After beginning on scale degree 5 (D) with the right hand jumping from one register to another (measures 1–4), the first phrase closes on the tonic with scale degree 3 (B) in the melody (measure 4). The tonic chord is prolonged by upper and lower neighbor chords of the dominant in measures 2–3 (UN and LN), producing a BCP with a stepwise melodic descent from scale degrees 5 to 3 (D–C–B, see the circled pitches in 4–4).

The leap upwards to the tonic note (G) on beat 3 of measure 4 is not a goal, but rather an anticipation of the subdominant's chord fifth in measure 5 and the beginning of the second phrase. A stepwise descent consisting of the tones G–F♯–E–D brings the melody back to scale degree 5 in measure 6. The descent is animated by 4—3 and 6—5 suspensions (measures 4–6) over subdominant and tonic chords.

Ultimately, two contrapuntal progressions (numbered 1 and 2) support melodic activity above and below scale degree 5 and prolong the tonic chord from measures 1–8. Throughout the first eight measures and despite its conspicuous absence from measures 2–5, scale degree 5 is retained as the most important melodic tone until the arrival of the phrase extension in measure 8. (A phrase extension is an alteration of the expected length of any phrase by an addition before the cadence, or at the cadence itself, or after the cadence.)

The contrapuntal imperfect authentic cadence in measure 8 is not strong enough to bring the phrase to a convincing conclusion. Accordingly, the phrase extension executes a secondary harmonic progression (SHP) supporting a stepwise descent in the melody from scale degrees 5 down to 1 (D–C–B–A–G, circled pitches in 4–4). The IV^6 occurring on beat 3 of measure 8 supports scale degree 4 (C) in the melody and is therefore elevated to the status of an X-chord.

Continuous Periods

In the foregoing examples, we have seen how noncontinuous periods (both parallel and contrasting) may exist with or without interruption. In these circumstances, a combination of harmonic and/or contrapuntal progressions underlie the noncontinuous period. But it is also possible for a single *uninterrupted* progression to sustain both phrases of the period, resulting in a *continuous* period. Uninterrupted progressions usually support continuous periods with applied chords tonicizing such elements as the X-chord and/or the V.

A single progression supporting a two-phrase design produces a period whose form is described as continuous because *the tonic does not close off the first phrase*; and, there is *no interruption of the melodic and harmonic framework*. In a continuous period, the second phrase typically proceeds with a lower-level excursion into a nontonic area instead of returning immediately to the tonic.

There are three basic ways to effect a continuous period using a *single uninterrupted progression*, all of which consist of nontonic prolongations of a lower order:
(1) prolongation of the X-chord at the end of the first phrase (a nontonic close to phrase one);
(2) prolongation of the X-chord at the outset of the second phrase (preceded by a nontonic close to phrase one in which a "retroactive" dominant relates back to the initial tonic, commonly known as a "back-relating dominant" and discussed later in this chapter);
(3) prolongation of the dominant area from the end of the first phrase into the second phrase (a continuation of a nontonic key between phrases, as shown in examples 4–6 and 4–7 below in a type of small two-part form called the "rounded binary").

72 Chapter 4 Small Form

Small Two-Part Form: the Rounded Binary

Binary form is music divided into two sections. The simplest way to differentiate the two sections is to repeat each section with the use of repeat signs. When a composition is divided into two parts with repeat signs, its form is described as having a "two-reprise" design. In binary form, a harmonic perfect authentic cadence marks the end of each section. (Formal diagrams for the basic binary design are shown in example 4–20 below.)

The third movement of the Mozart Sonata No. 6 in D Major (K. 284) begins with two repeated sections (examples 4–6 and 4–7). Each section consists of two four-measure phrases. The first section ends with an HPAC in V (measure 8), the second section ends with an HPAC in the main-level key (measure 17). (The D: symbol in example 4–7 is intended to indicate the main-level key. What is actually heard at the beginning of section two is not D major as a main-level tonic.)

The first phrase of section one concludes with a contrapuntal half cadence *on* V (measure 4), whereas a contrapuntal half cadence *in* V concludes the first phrase of section two (measure 12). (The statement and balancing references in examples 4–6 and 4–7 are explained on the following page.)

Before we study the formal design displayed in examples 4–6 and 4–7, it would be well to understand that the terminology associated with the sectional and continuous tonal plans discussed in conjunction with the period can also be applied to binary forms. Thus, if the first part of the binary composition ends in the tonic, then the binary form is *sectional*. If, however, the first part ends in a key other than the tonic, then the binary form is *continuous*. Usually, the first section of a continuous binary ends in V if the mode is major and in III if the mode is minor.

Example 4–6: Mozart, Sonata No. 6 in D Major (K. 284), III, measures 1–8, section one

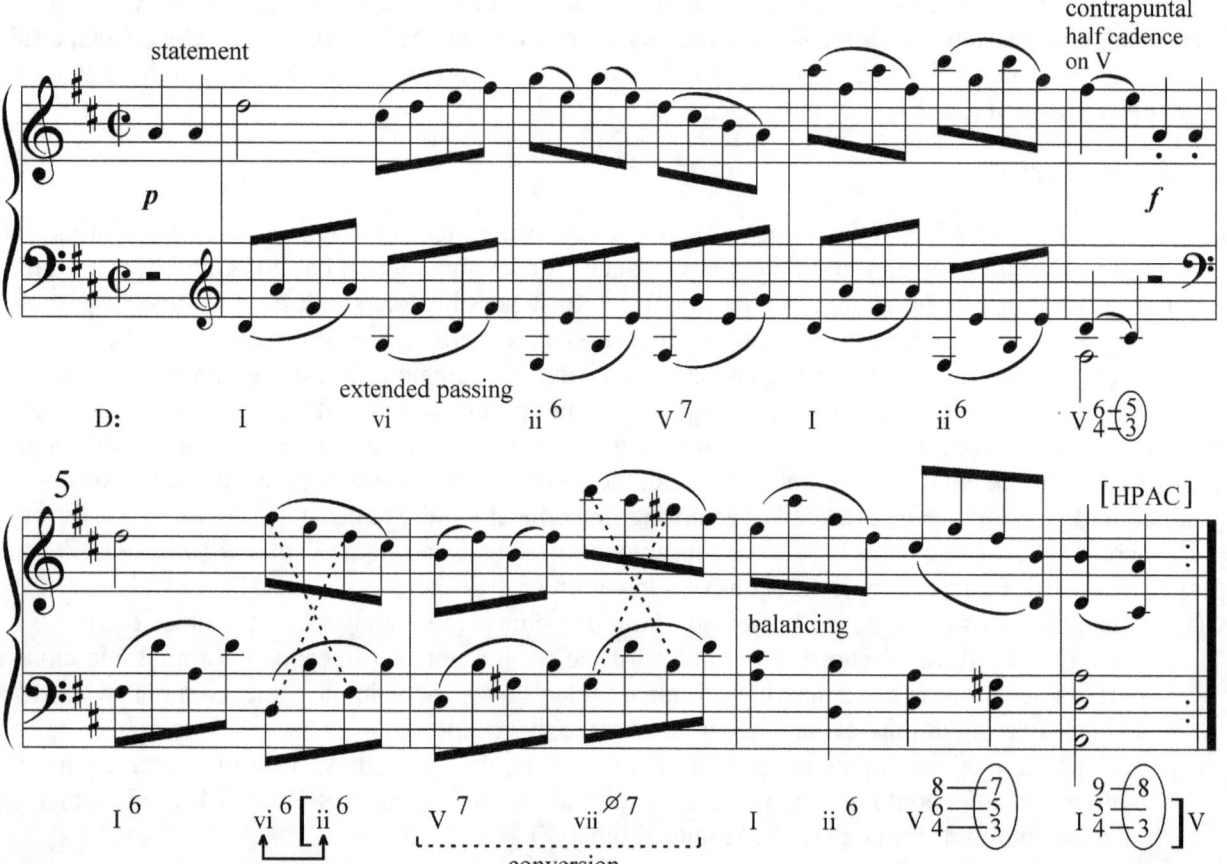

Chapter 4 Small Form

The first seventeen measures of Mozart's Sonata in D Major (K. 284, III) constitutes a continuous binary because section one ends in the dominant rather than in the tonic. Notably, this excerpt is more than just a continuous binary because some of the material from section one returns to form the last phrase of section two (measures 13–15).

Therefore, two significant factors are in play. First, the return of the opening idea (measures 1–2) after the contrasting material of measures 9–12 produces what is referred to as a "rounded" binary. As shown in example 4–8a (p. 74), the rounded binary is expressed with the three-part letter scheme a b a (or a b a'); an HPAC concludes each repeated section. (Since the phrase structure of the rounded binary exhibits a three-part design, it is sometimes called an "incipient" ternary.) The basic operation of the rounded binary involves a statement of music, departure, and restatement of the beginning. The departure usually consists of new material supported by excursions into lower-level keys.

The second factor to consider is the restatement of material from the end of section one (4–6 above, measures 7–8) at the end of section two (4–7 below, measures 16–17), transposed from the dominant to the tonic. Using the closing measures of section one to conclude section two creates what some theoreticians call a "balanced" binary.

The binary form in the D-Major Sonata is continuous, rounded, and balanced. However, it should be remembered that binary form may be neither continuous, nor rounded, nor balanced. Indeed, as we have said, the first section may close in the tonic and yield a sectional binary, which may or may not also be rounded and/or balanced.

Example 4–7: Mozart, Sonata No. 6 in D Major (K. 284), III, measures 9–17, section two

Example 4–8: the rounded binary

a.
⌢⌢⌢   b. ⌢⌢⌢⌢
a   b   a⁽′⁾   a   a'   b   a"
HPAC   HPAC   ½ on V [HPAC] ½ in V HPAC
or [HPAC]

The formal diagram for Mozart's D-Major Sonata is shown in example 4–8b above; measures 1–17 are reproduced in example 4–9 below. Two progressions support the opening phrase (measures 1–4):

(1) an SHP in measures 1–3 that proceeds from the tonic to the ii^6 (X-chord) by way of an extended passing chord on beat 2 of measure 1 (a bass motion that fills in the interval of the 4th or 5th between unlike-rooted chords); and,

(2) an incomplete SHP in measures 3–4 with a contrapuntal half cadence *on* V (using the same supertonic X-chord as the first progression).

The end of the second phrase in section one (measures 7–8) contains both the progression and the thematic material used for balancing the end of section two (measures 16–17), transposed from the dominant to the tonic. Each ending contains an HPAC.

At the beginning of the second phrase (measures 5–6, a'), two interesting events merit comment.

(1) Although the first two beats of the second phrase could be interpreted in D major, the harmonic motion to A major, the dominant, becomes immediately apparent. The vi^6 of D major also serves as the ii^6 of A major. Within the context of both D major and A major, the B-minor triad in measure 5 is a pivot chord, a chord that provides a smooth and convincing connection from one key to another. Additionally, the D-major tonic may be viewed as the subdominant of A major, another pivot relationship.

(2) Notice the voice exchange between the hands on the second beat of measures 5 and 6 (see the dotted lines in 4–9); it prolongs the B-minor pivot chord in measure 5 and the half-diminished leading-tone seventh of A major in measure 6.

Let us consider the incomplete SHP in D major (the second half of phrase a) leading up to the contrapuntal half cadence on V (measures 3–4). The I and ii^6 unfold over a duration of two half notes. When this progression returns in A major in measures 7–8, the harmonic rhythm between the I and ii^6 is compressed into one half note to optimize the placement of the HPAC ending section one. Since the progression that closes section one forms the balanced portion of section two, this rhythmic compression (measures 7–8) is retained in measures 16–17.

The second section (measures 9–12) begins with the contrasting b phrase. Because of the active nature of its harmony, the b phrase marks what we call a departure from the first two phrases. (Some theoreticians describe this passage as a "digression" because it marks a harmonic and/or thematic *departure* from the initial idea.)

The departure unfolds within a sequence of applied dominants and retroactive dominants, which together produce a passage that transitions back to the tonic in phrase a ". Ultimately, phrase b constitutes a prolongation of the dominant by sequential activity, pivot relationships between the tonic and the dominant (D major is A major's subdominant), and CLT chords.

The harmonic activity of the departure (measures 9–12) ends with a contrapuntal half cadence *in* V; the cadential $^6_4$ of D major is approached by [vii^{o6}]V in measure 11 (G♯ B D, with B in the bass). (We shall revisit this portion of section two below.)

In measures 13–17, the material of phrase a is restated (a ") with the last two measures transposed to the tonic D major and modified in order to balance the end of section two with the end of section one. Thus, the contrapuntal half cadence of measures 3–4 is replaced with an HPAC in measures 16–17 (using the balancing material of measures 7–8).

Example 4–9: Mozart, Sonata No. 6 in D Major (K. 284), III, measures 1–17, rounded binary

76   Chapter 4   Small Form

As shown in example 4–10, the opening phrase of section two (measure 9) is heard initially in A major because that is the key in which the first section ends. But despite the HPAC in A major (measure 8), the b phrase begins with an uncertain path, as it proceeds through a descending 5th sequence of applied dominants (B–E–A–D in the bass). Quarter notes 1 and 3 (measure 9) take dominant sevenths, each of which resolves to a major triad (on E and D). What is the identity of the D-major triad in measure 9? Although tonicized by its own dominant seventh, D major is also the subdominant of A major.

In measure 10, a sequence consisting of retroactive dominants prolongs the vi and IV of D major. (In measure 11, the sequence continues in the right hand with longer note values, a process known as "augmentation.") In the left hand (measure 10), the F♯ on the fourth eighth note of beat 1 relates back to B; the D on the fourth eighth note of beat 2 relates back to G. Since the G has no meaning in the key of A major, Mozart provides an element of stability in measure 11 by tonicizing D major with its own dominant, just before the cadence in V at the end of phrase b.

Notice the vi chord on beat 1 of measure 10, which occurs within a series of parallel 10ths between both hands. In phrases a and a ", the vi serves as an extended passing chord involving a descending motion consisting of D–B–G in the left hand. The last quarter note of measure 9 initiates the same motion (D–B–G) through measure 10 before reaching the V $^6_5$ of D major. Another significant motion is the octave transfer of B in the left hand from the first quarter of measure 10 down to the last quarter of measure 11, passing through the tones B–G–D–B. (This transfer supports an attendant transfer of D in the right hand, passing through D–B–F♯–D.) At the end of measure 11, the B supports a CLT chord of A major, the [vii °6]V (that is, B G♯ D). A major becomes both a goal and a preparation for the return of the tonic key.

Example 4–10: section two of Mozart's Sonata No. 6 in D Major (K. 284), III, measures 9–17

The last phrase (a ") rounds off the form with a return to the opening material. The harmonically active departure that both precedes and compels this return is often described as a "retransition" (to D major in this instance). The retransition connects phrase b to phrase a ". (In general, the restatement of the initial idea may be either literal or modified. The beginning of the third movement of the D-Major Sonata presents a rounded binary in which the restatement is modified.)

The Descending 5—6 Sequence and the Retroactive Dominant

In Chapter 3, we said that the sequence consists of a pattern that is repeated at different pitch levels in order to shift all of the voices upwards or downwards. The original pattern and its duplications exhibit consistent intervallic relationships in all or most of the voices above the bass. Ultimately, the function of the sequence is to prolong either a single chord or the way from one chord to another. Let us consider the sequence in example 4–11, as it forms the basis of the retroactive dominants in measure 10 of the D-Major Sonata.

Example 4–11a shows the voice leading from which the retroactive dominants emerge. The final disposition (without chords) appears in example 4–12a. Example 4–11 displays the descending 5—6 sequence. The numbers representing the motion of the 5th proceeding to the 6th takes a dash because one voice is stationary. In this instance, the stationary tone is above the moving voice; so configured, the top voice constitutes an "inverted pedal embellishing tone" (the stationary tone is located in an upper voice).

One of the problems with the descending 5—6 is that somewhere in the course of the series, a diminished 5th occurs. Usually, composers skip the diminished 5th (C♯/G in 4–11a). The omission produces a descending 3rd in the lower voice (D–B). Removing the fourth 5—6 from the series (A/E to G/E) results in a second descending 3rd (B–G) and yields thereby two melodic 3rds in the lowest voice (D–B and B–G). The descending 3rd is an integral component of the descending 5—6.

As example 4–11b demonstrates, the descending 5—6 supports a two-chord pattern. Notice that the second chord of each pair is a first-inversion triad. The triads of the leading tone and the dominant are omitted from the series. The first-inversion triads paired with the omitted chords are removed as well. Taking out the two dominant-family chords helps to de-emphasize the main-level key. The downward leaps of the 3rd (D–B–G) underscore the operation of the 5—6 and support the presence of the I, vi, and IV chords (see the boxes in 4–11b).

Omitting the second and fourth statements of the descending 5—6 creates potential direct 5ths between the I, the vi, and the IV (see the arrows pointing to F♯ and D in 4–11b). Since all three chords are in root position, direct (or hidden) 5ths result: C♯/A to B/F♯ and A/F♯ to G/D.

Example 4–11: the descending 5—6 sequence

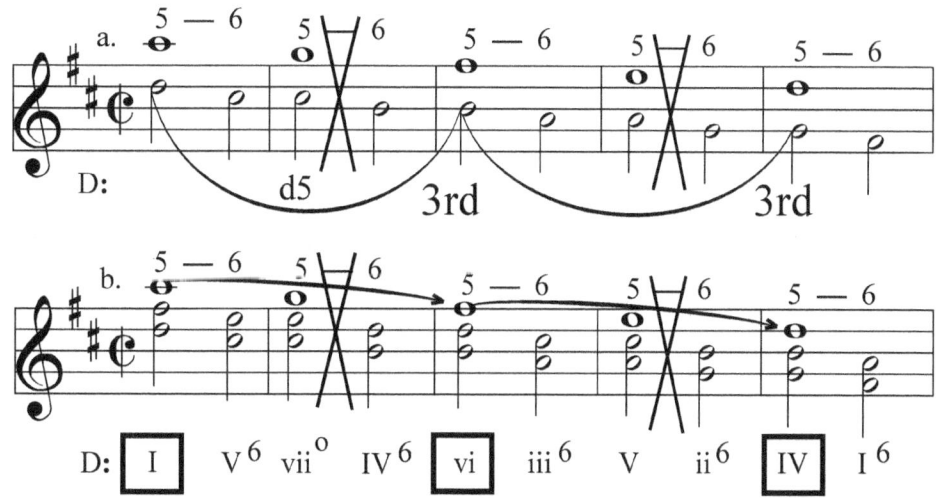

78 Chapter 4 Small Form

In example 4–12a, a variant of the descending 5—6 affords a solution to the problem of direct 5ths. The motion down to the 6th is replaced by the octave; in other words, the first-inversion chords of the 5—6 become root-position chords of the 5—8. Once the moving voice produces an octave with the stationary voice, the approach to the vi and to the IV can be effected by contrary motion.

Adding the major triad to the 5—8 operation, as in 4–12b, produces an applied dominant that relates back to the preceding chord (modal dominants can also be used retroactively). In this circumstance, the retroactive chord effects a harmonic prolongation of the chord it follows. The backward arrows in 4–12b point to the chords prolonged retroactively, namely the I, vi, and IV.

Although the 5—8 variant solves one difficulty associated with the 5—6, it creates another: possible parallel 5ths between the retroactive dominant and the succeeding chord (in 4–12b: A/E to B/ F♯ and F♯/C♯ to G/D). When a rising 2nd root and bass relationship occurs between two chords, the 5th intervals of each chord may lead to wrong parallel motion. Observing careful voice leading overcomes this potential hazard. In measure 10 of the D-Major Sonata, Mozart simply passes through the sequence in parallel 3rds (or 10ths), avoiding 5ths altogether (see measure 2 of example 4–13a below).

Ultimately, the descending harmonic 3rds in measure 10 are based upon the operation in 4–12c. The whole notes in 4–12c on F♯ and D do not correspond to the actual score; however, both pitches form the roots of the retroactive dominants. In any case, a very simple contrapuntal framework (in which F♯ and D *are* integral components) underlies the melodic motion in descending 3rds (D–B–G) and the harmonic prolongations of the vi and the IV.

Example 4–12: the descending 5—6 sequence and the retroactive dominant

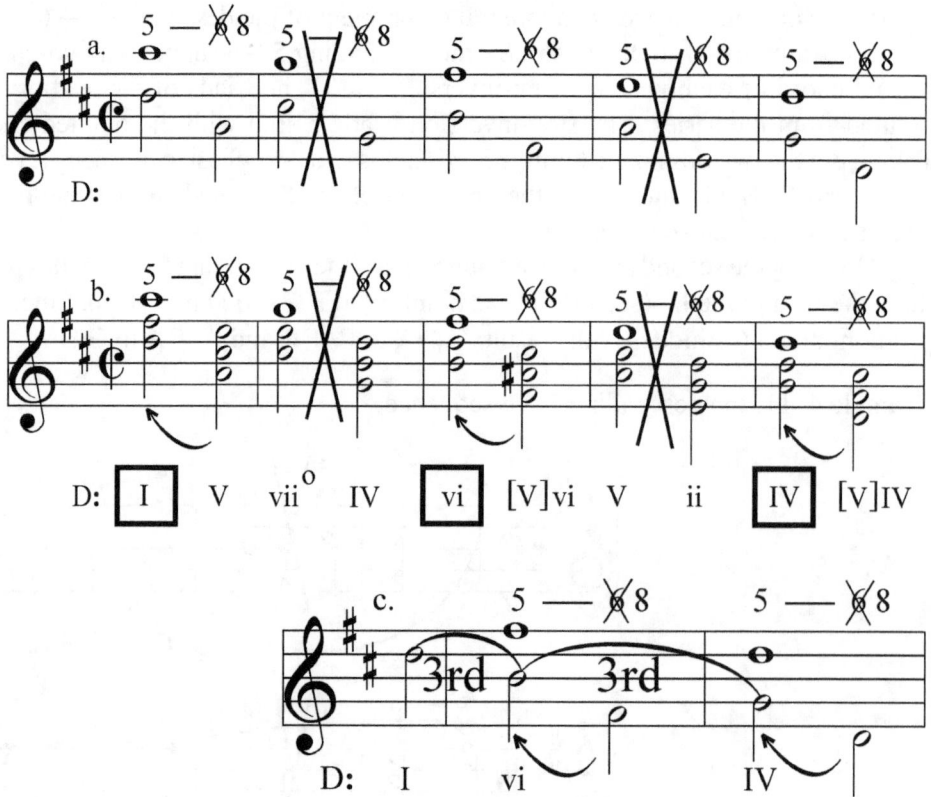

Example 4–13b shows the underlying intervallic patterns for the two sequences in measures 9–10 that support the beginning of phrase b (K. 284, III). In measure 9, we have the 7 3 motion of the descending 5th sequence in the outer voices. Although this sequence uses applied dominants, a succession of modal dominants would maintain the same intervallic patterns. The retroactive dominants in measure 10 require more interpretation (4–13b, second measure). As stated above, the F♯ and D are important factors in the 5—8 variant of the descending 5—6, despite the absence of these pitches from the top line.

Example 4–13: Mozart, Sonata No. 6 in D Major (K. 284), III, measures 9–10 (beginning of phrase b)

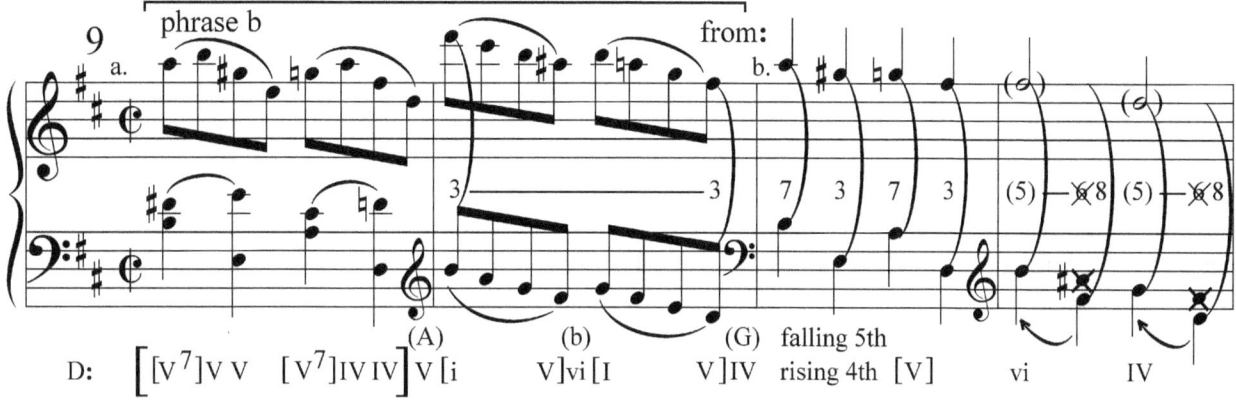

Motives

Example 4–14 illustrates the principal motives that help to unify the formal design of Mozart's D-Major Sonata. One approach to labeling these motives is to start with letters from the end of the alphabet in order to avoid the letters used for phrases, which typically begin with a, b, c, and so on.

Indicated as Z in 4–14a, the interval of the rising 4th may be called a "head motive," as it begins the composition. Motive Z undergoes immediate modification by having its span filled in with conjunct tones (note the use of the prime character to reflect an alteration of the original). In measure 2, Z inverts (Z'); that is to say, the motive is turned upside down (again, as a filled-in 4th). Motive Y is introduced in measure 2 as a descending melodic 3rd. In measure 6 (example 4–6 above), Y inverts to become an ascending 3rd. In measure 9 of 4–14b, Y is used in combination to produce motive X, which also serves to balance the end of each form section.

Example 4–14: motives Z, X, and Y

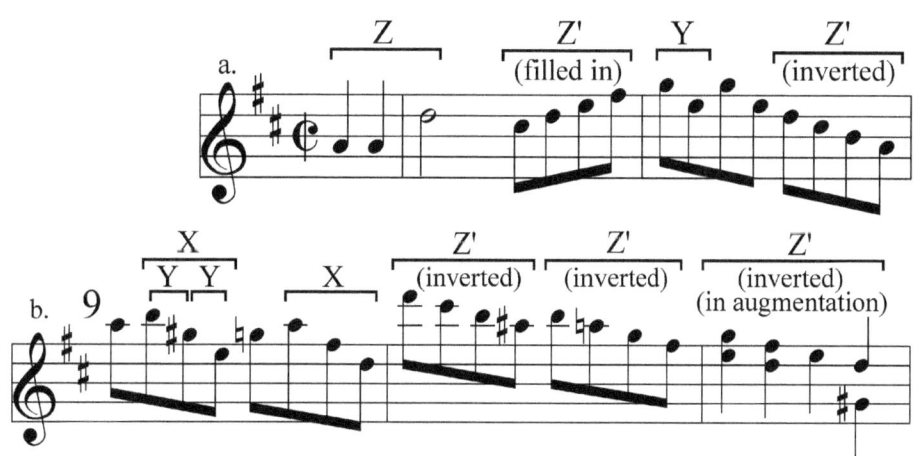

The Repeated Period

In example 4–15, we have a contrasting period in the first eight measures of the Sonata No. 35 in C Major by Haydn, first movement. The eight measures contain two four-measure phrases with a half cadence on V in measure 4 and an HPAC in measure 8.

A motion from the tonic to the dominant comprises the harmony of the first phrase (a). The principle melodic tone is the G, which unfolds into the D at the half cadence on V in measure 4. (G moves through the chord tones of the I and V before reaching D.) Beginning on the upbeat of measure 4, the second phrase (b) continues with the dominant chord. (As shown in examples 4–4 and 4–9 above, all of the phrases from the first ten measures of Mozart's Sonata No. 5 in G Major and the first seventeen measures of his Sonata No. 6 in D Major, III, begin with upbeats.)

Haydn's prolongation of the V in measures 4–5 (example 4–15) creates a harmonic link between phrases a and b, binding them together as a continuous contrasting period, supported by two progressions:

(1) a BHP (basic harmonic progression, I–V–I, measures 1–5); and,
(2) an SHP (secondary harmonic progression, I– ii^6–V–I, measures 5–8).

The dominant prolongation from measures 3–5 belongs to the BHP. The final tonic of the BHP in measure 5 constitutes the initial tonic of the SHP. The SHP moves through a voice exchange, with a V$^4_2$ standing between two positions of the tonic chord (see the dotted lines in 4–15).

In measures 5–6, the motion in the left hand takes an upward leap from C to F. The tone F (the chord seventh of the dominant) is a substitution for the passing D, which appears instead in the melody. Placing the D in the left hand would have yielded a passing motion consisting of C–D–E (see the D in parentheses in measure 6).

Example 4–15: Haydn, Sonata No. 35 in C Major (Hob. XVI), I, measures 1–8

In measures 1–8, the right hand takes a descent from G to C (see the circled pitches) supported by tonic, dominant and supertonic chords. The ii^6 in measure 7 is the X-chord of the SHP. The ii^6 supports D, scale degree 2. Notice the approach to the HPAC in measure 7. On the third quarter, the right hand moves to B, the leading tone, instead of maintaining the common tone D from the preceding supertonic. The leading tone serves as a substitute for scale degree 2. (In measure 7, the line from D down to B indicates the voice leading; the missing D is in parentheses.) The descent from G becomes G–F–E–D–B–C instead of G–F–E–D–D–C.

Example 4–16 presents the next eight measures of Haydn's C-Major Sonata. The melody is almost exactly the same as the first eight measures. However, the accompaniment is more active and the harmony is somewhat different. A neighboring dominant in measure 11 prolongs the initial tonic. The half cadence in measure 12 exhibits a contrapuntal approach to the V^6. As in measures 3–5, a dominant prolongation connects phrases a' and b' (measures 11–14).

A root-position dominant supports phrase b' in measure 13. On the third quarter of that measure, Haydn replaces the earlier voice exchange (example 4–15, measures 5–6) with a pedal embellishing $^6_4$. A BHP extending from measures 9–14 ends with a vi chord, a chord that becomes a substitute for the tonic. The vi keeps the harmony from achieving full closure while serving as both the end of the BHP (measures 9–14) and the beginning of the SHP that concludes this excerpt. Two progressions of a lower order stand within the BHP spanning measures 9–14: a BCP (I–V$^4_3$–I, measures 9–11) and a BHP ending on vi as a substitute for I (I–V^7–vi for I, measures 11–14).

It is only with the appearance of the vi in measure 14 that the E in the melody of phrase b' assumes part of the descending line (G–F–E–D–B–C). (In measure 5, the E of the descending line was heard with the tonic chord in root position. In measure 14, the E anticipates its vi chord by one sixteenth note.) The vi also stands in a modal dominant relationship to the ii^6 X-chord, itself a modal dominant of V.

Example 4–16: Haydn, Sonata No. 35 in C Major (Hob. XVI), I, measures 9–16

Although we might be tempted to classify the opening sixteen measures of Haydn's C-Major Sonata as a binary form because each eight-measure phrase ends with an HPAC, this formal design is more properly known as a repeated period, a one-part form (see example 4–18c below). The standard repeated period would simply have a repeat sign at the end of the first eight measures; however, since measures 9–16 contain both an altered accompaniment and re-harmonization of the melody, it must be notated a second time. The second eight measures constitutes a written-out repeat, a varied repetition.

Finally, both phrases b and b' contain an identical melodic sequence consisting of a descending figure in the right hand. Phrase b sequences through a voice exchange prolonging two different positions of the tonic between two positions of the dominant serving as a THD/CLT (measures 5–6), whereas phrase b' sequences through a single chord unfolding from V^6 to V^7 (measures 12–14).

A List of Small Forms

This section outlines a few of the ways in which combinations of phrases are brought together to produce small formal designs exhibiting one, two, or three parts. The list presented here is by no means exhaustive, as some compositions may defy classification or yield conflicting interpretations.

Example 4–17a represents a small one-part form (also known as a unipartite form) in which the cadential structure and the thematic design do not produce clear divisions in the form. Usually, such pieces are based upon a single idea that is continuously developed and expanded.

The phrase group, as shown in examples 4–17b through 17i, typically contains three or more phrases with an HPAC concluding the final phrase. All of the internal cadences are open. The group lacks the interdependent structure of the period with its paired arrangement of antecedent and consequent phrases.

It should be noted that there is no universally accepted taxonomy for small forms. Some theoreticians argue that in order to have a phrase group, at least two of the phrases must be related. According to this view, if none of the phrases are related, then the form is identified as a *phrase chain*; thus, 4–17c and 17h would constitute phrase chains. Others hold that a phrase group can only consist of unrelated phrases.

Another interpretation places two of the small forms in 4–17 into a category known as the three phrase period, or asymmetrical period. In this instance, one of the three phrases is repeated to produce either a double consequent or double antecedent group, as in 4–17d (antecedent-consequent-consequent) and 17e (antecedent-antecedent-consequent). A dissenting opinion maintains that two identical (or nearly identical) phrases occurring in succession cannot form a period structure if three or more phrases are involved.

Recognizing that some small forms simply resist classification, we prefer to avoid the conflicting perspectives cited above. If the phrases have only one HPAC and are not symmetrically paired to form a period, we call it a phrase group. The three phrase group, as represented in 7–17b, is later studied in Chopin's Prelude in E Major, Op. 28, No. 9 in Chapter 6 (see below, pp. 145–147).

Example 4–17: one-part form (nonperiod designs)

a. one phrase

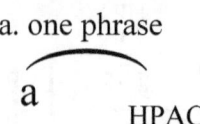

b. three phrase group, varied repetitions

a   a'   a"   HPAC

c. three phrase group, no repetitions

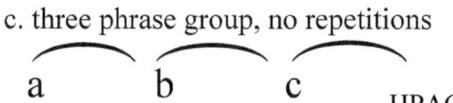
HPAC

d. three phrase group, phrases 2 and 3 parallel

HPAC

e. three phrase group, phrases 1 and 2 parallel

HPAC

f. three phrase group, phrases 1 and 3 parallel

HPAC

g. four phrase group, varied repetitions

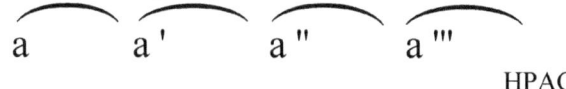
HPAC

h. four phrase group, no repetitions

HPAC

i. five phrase group, phrases 2 and 5 parallel

HPAC

Example 4–18 displays the three basic types of single period: the parallel period, the contrasting period, and the repeated period.

Example 4–18: one-part form (the single period)

a. parallel period

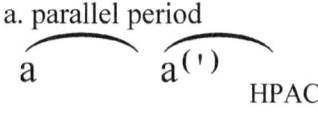
HPAC

b. contrasting period

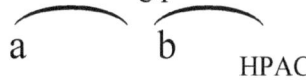
HPAC

c. repeated period versus the varied repetition

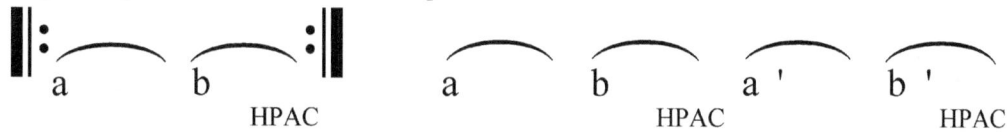
HPAC   HPAC   HPAC

In example 4–19, we have the one-part form known as the double period. As the name suggests, there are two periods within the double period. Consisting of four phrases, with two phrases comprising each period, the double period has the same sense of balance and interdependency as that of the single period.

Broadly stated, all double periods fall into the category of the phrase group. Indeed, some music analysts might describe the four unrelated phrases in 4–19f as a four phrase group (or as a phrase chain). This text recommends the term double period if two conditions are observed:

(1) the four phrases of the group have only one HPAC; and,
(2) these phrases are also symmetrically paired to yield two interdependent period structures.

The double period presents either a parallel or contrasting arrangement between its two periods. If phrases one and three are related to each other, then the double period is parallel (4–19a and 19b). If phrases one and three are not related to each other, then a contrasting double period arises (4–19c through 19f).

Phrases one and two of the double period function as an antecedent period; phrases three and four serve as its consequent. For instance, in 4–19a, phrases a and b form the antecedent period while phrases a' and b' make up the consequent period.

The harmonic organization of the double period consists of the following elements:

(1) the antecedent period typically ends with a half cadence in phrase two (indicated in 4–19 with the ½ sign), usually involving the V;
(2) the consequent period ends with an HPAC in phrase four;
(3) the endings for the first and third phrases consist of open cadences (either half or imperfect authentic cadences).

(The first sixteen measures of Beethoven's Bagatelle No. 1 in G Minor, Op. 119, shown in examples 5–46 and 47 of Chapter 5, is a parallel double period.)

Example 4–19: one-part form (the double period)

a. parallel double period, phrases 1 and 3 parallel (2 and 4 parallel)

```
  a        b        a'       b'
          ½                  HPAC
```

b. parallel double period, phrases 1 and 3 parallel (2 and 4 contrasting)

```
  a        b       a(')      c
          ½                  HPAC
```

c. contrasting double period, phrases 1 and 3 contrasting (2 and 4 parallel)

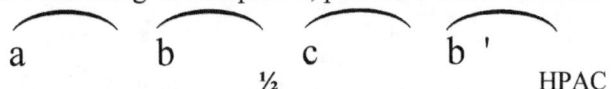

```
  a        b        c        b'
          ½                  HPAC
```

d. contrasting double period, phrases 1 and 3 contrasting

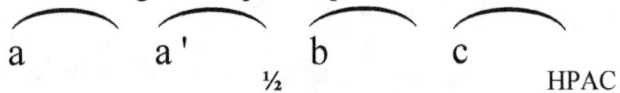

```
  a        a'       b        c
          ½                  HPAC
```

e. contrasting double period, phrases 1 and 3 contrasting

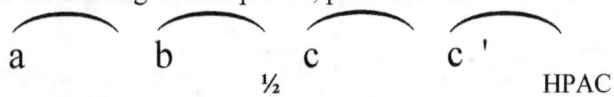

```
  a        b        c        c'
          ½                  HPAC
```

f. contrasting double period, phrases 1 and 3 contrasting (no repetitions)

Together, the antecedent and consequent *periods* project the same question-answer dynamic as that animating the single period. The relationship between the cadences of the antecedent and consequent periods produces the interdependent component of the double period.

Let us compare the interdependent operations of the single and double periods:
(1) In the single period, which has two phrases, the half cadence at the end of the antecedent *phrase* establishes the need for the consequent *phrase*. That is to say, the tonal tension of the antecedent's half cadence is resolved with the appearance of the HPAC in the consequent phrase.
(2) In the double period, which has four phrases, the half cadence at the end of the antecedent *period* establishes the need for the consequent *period*. In other words, the half cadence that ends the antecedent period in phrase two produces a harmonic opening in the form that is closed with the appearance of the HPAC in the consequent period.

Two-part form, or binary form, has an HPAC at the end of each part. Examples 4–20 and 4–21 display a few possibilities for the small binary. Example 4–20 features binary forms consisting of two and four phrases without a restatement of the beginning to round off the form. In a four-phrase binary, the HPAC concludes phrases two and four. (Example 4–21 exhibits the rounded binary.)

Notice that in 4–20d, an HPAC in a lower-level key distinguishes this formal design from that of the repeated period (compare with example 4–18c above). The [HPAC] produces the need for a written return to the main-level key and its HPAC at the end of part two; it also creates the potential for harmonic and contrapuntal modifications that go beyond supporting a simple written-out repeat, or varied repetition.

Example 4–20: two-part form (binary without rounding)

a. binary, two phrases

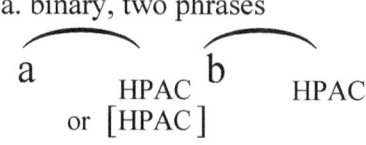

b. binary, four phrases

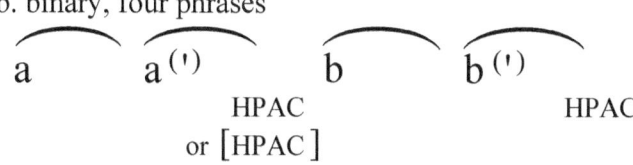

c. binary, four phrases

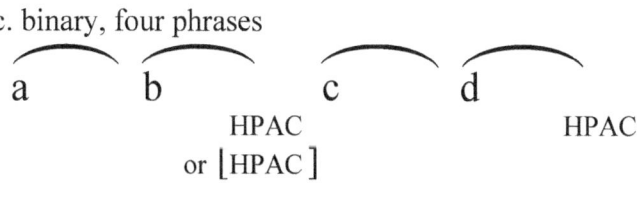

d. binary, four phrases

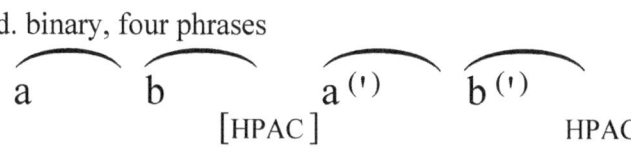

86   Chapter 4 Small Form

Example 4–21: two-part form (the rounded binary)

a. rounded binary, three phrases

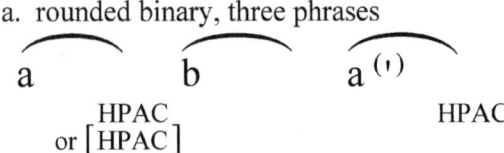

b. rounded binary, four phrases

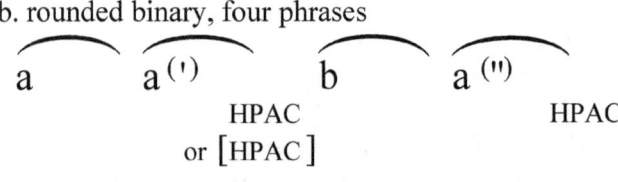

c. rounded binary, six phrases

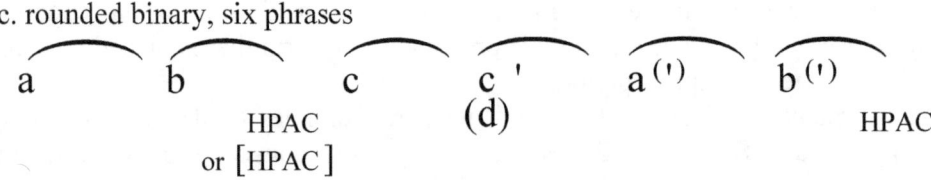

The three-part design of ternary form is based upon the same principle that informs the rounded binary, namely: a statement of music, departure, and restatement of that with which the composition began. Indeed, as mentioned earlier, the rounded binary is sometimes called an incipient ternary. The basic operation of the rounded binary involves a statement of music, departure, and restatement of the beginning. The portion of the rounded binary that marks the departure usually consists of new material supported by excursions into lower-level keys.

In the simplest ternary form, an HPAC concludes each of its three form sections; its three-part design is based upon the presence of a contrasting middle section followed by either an exact or varied repetition of the first section. Ternary form therefore assumes either an A B A or A B A' design. The second section of ternary form, the B section, usually expresses a nontonic key or parallel mode. Because of the move away from the tonic, the second section may contain a retransition to effect a successful return to the tonic in the third part, the A or A' section. Moreover, it is not unusual for the B section to end with an open cadence. The problem is: removing the HPAC from the B section produces what could be viewed as a rounded binary. Let us consider what happens to a ternary form when the second HPAC is omitted.

Example 4–22 demonstrates one typical arrangement for what is sometimes called a *small* ternary. In this instance, all three parts conclude with an HPAC. Phrases a and b constitute the A section of the ternary. Section B consists of phrases c and c' (or d). Phrases a and b (or a' and b') comprise an exact or varied repetition of A. Now, if we remove the HPAC from the B section (phrases c and c'), then the form is virtually the same as the rounded binary. (Compare 4–22a with 4–21c above.)

Example 4–22: three-part form

a. ternary, six phrases

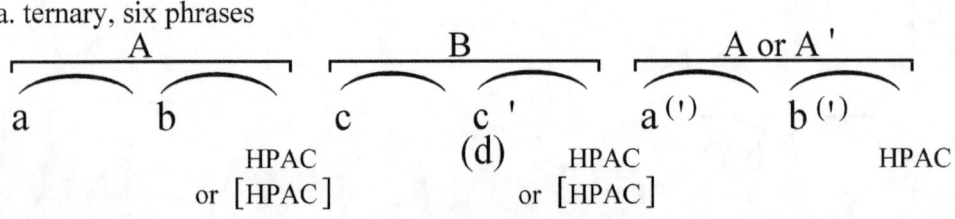

One of the determining factors in distinguishing between binary and ternary form is the presence of a self-contained second section of material unrelated to the first section and closed off with an HPAC. A significant degree of contrast between parts strongly suggests a ternary design. Moreover, having an HPAC at the end of each part produces a *sectional* ternary form.

However, not all ternary forms exhibit a clear sectional design. Indeed, it is quite possible to create a *continuous* three-part composition in which the phrase structure does not coincide with the supporting harmonic and/or contrapuntal progressions in a way that makes the divisions in the form readily apparent.

Establishing a continuous relationship between parts usually involves the presence of a lower-level prolongation across form sections and/or some disruption or delay of the HPAC. For example, the end of one section reaches the dominant which then resolves to the tonic only within the next section. Another strategy delays the *approach* to the cadential tonic until *after* the next section begins. Thus, in both cases, phrase design and harmony overlap.

Obscuring the divisions in the form of a continuous ternary can result in a composition that resists simple classification and leads consequently to conflicting analytic interpretations. Additionally, the terminology used to describe three-part form as either large or small is somewhat problematic. Ternary forms often assume proportions that exceed the limits of what would convincingly be described as small. The point at which the small ternary becomes a large ternary is not always clear. The conventional view of the large ternary, or compound ternary, finds small forms embedded within each of its discernible parts. In other words, each form section may consist of a rounded binary, or a double period, or any other combination of small forms.

Chapter 5   Degree-Inflected Chords (Altered Triads and Sevenths)

This text explores three general forms of chromaticism. Motion into lower-level keys using applied chords is the first form of chromaticism. (We consider primary borrowing to be an extension of diatonicism rather than a distinct form of chromaticism.) The inflection of scale degrees produces a second form of chromaticism and a special class of chords, generally known as "altered chords" or "degree-inflected chords." The third form of chromaticism involves a *secondary* application of borrowing referred to in this book as "secondary borrowing," but usually described as "secondary mixture" and "double mixture." This chapter examines six types of degree-inflected chords. (A review of all six types concludes the chapter.)

Chromatic passing activity constitutes the fundamental operation for producing degree-inflected chords. In example 5–1, we have the chromatic passing tone in both its ascending and descending forms (5–1a and 1b). The ascending chromatic passing tone between scale degrees 1 and 3 is written as ♯2 ("raised two"), the descending chromatic passing tone between scale degrees 3 and 1 as ♭2 ("lowered two"). Scale degree ♭2 is also known as the Phrygian supertonic. (All sharps and flats attached to numbers are generic.)

Example 5–1: the chromatic passing tone

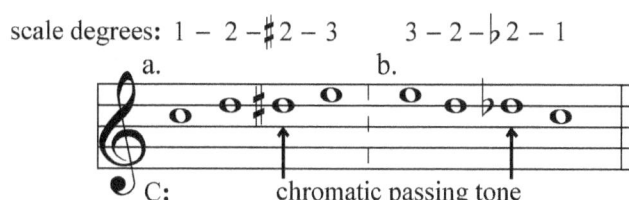

Type I: The Altered Tonal Harmonic Dominant (THD)

Examples 5–2 and 5–3 show how degree inflection alters the chord fifth of the THD. The chord fifth of the THD is scale degree 2 of the mode (C major) and may take either ♯2 or ♭2 (or even both within the same chord). This type of degree inflection raises or lowers the chord fifth by one half step.

Example 5–2a provides the linear origin for the THD with the raised fifth: the ascending chromatic passing tone in the supertonic area (D♯). Ultimately, the ascending chromatic passing tone *replaces* the diatonic chord fifth with a raised fifth. This fifth, scale degree ♯2, intensifies the upward motion to scale degree 3, the chord third of the tonic triad (examples 5–2b through 2e). The omission of the diatonic chord fifth (D) constitutes a skip in the compositional process whereby that which has been established through common practice (here, the passing tone) is shortened, or contracted.

Example 5–2: the THD with the raised chord fifth moving to scale degree 3

The Augmented 6th of the THD

The $V^7_{\sharp 5}$ (examples 5–2d and 2e above and example 5–4a below) has a diminished 3rd between its chord fifth and seventh, which becomes an augmented 6th when the seventh and fifth are inverted. The augmented 6th proceeds to the octave, the diminished 3rd to the unison. The usual resolution of the $V^7_{\sharp 5}$ produces a tonic chord with a doubled third, scale degree 3 of the mode.

It would be well to understand that the THD *triad* with the raised fifth, the $V\sharp 5$, does not produce an augmented 6th within the chord. However, raising the fifth does result in the formation of an augmented triad (G B D♯ in example 5–2 above). (All future references to the augmented 6th are understood to include its inversion, the diminished 3rd).

Example 5–3 illustrates the THD triad and seventh with the lowered chord fifth, which has a diminished 5th between its root and fifth (G/D♭). The diminished 3rd (or d10th) of both the $V\flat 5$ and the $V^7_{\flat 5}$ occurs between the third and fifth (also 5–4c). The diminished 3rd becomes an augmented 6th when the third and fifth are inverted. Together, the third and fifth (and fifth and third) usually resolve to scale degree 1 of the mode.

The $V^7_{\sharp 5}$ and all of the chromatic alterations of the THD in example 5–3 produce chords containing an augmented 6th. These chords fall within the sub-category of degree-inflected chords known as the "augmented 6th chord." We shall encounter other types of augmented 6th chords later in this chapter.

Example 5–3: the THD with the lowered chord fifth moving to scale degree 1

The Degree-Inflected THD and the Whole-Tone Scale

The degree-inflected THD, or altered dominant, is sometimes referred to as a whole-tone dominant because of its formation within the whole-tone scale, which divides the chromatic scale (and octave) into six whole tones. A scale consisting of six major 2nds is completely symmetrical and therefore somewhat limited both melodically and harmonically.

As shown in example 5–4 below, the whole-tone scale is formed on only two pitches of the chromatic scale, C and C♯ (or D♭). That is, the two formations of the whole-tone scale are mutually exclusive. Building the scale on any pitch other than C and C♯ leads to duplications of pitches. Further, any pitch in the whole-tone scale may assume tonic status because its scale structure lacks the important key-defining properties of the leading tone and the intervals of the perfect 5th and 4th.

Examples 5–4a and 5–4c demonstrate the formation of the whole-tone dominant seventh with the raised or lowered fifth. The construction of whole-tone dominants requires enharmonic respellings of A♯ as B♭ (4a) and C♯ as D♭ (4c).

Example 5–4: extracting whole-tone scales from the chromatic scale to produce whole-tone dominants

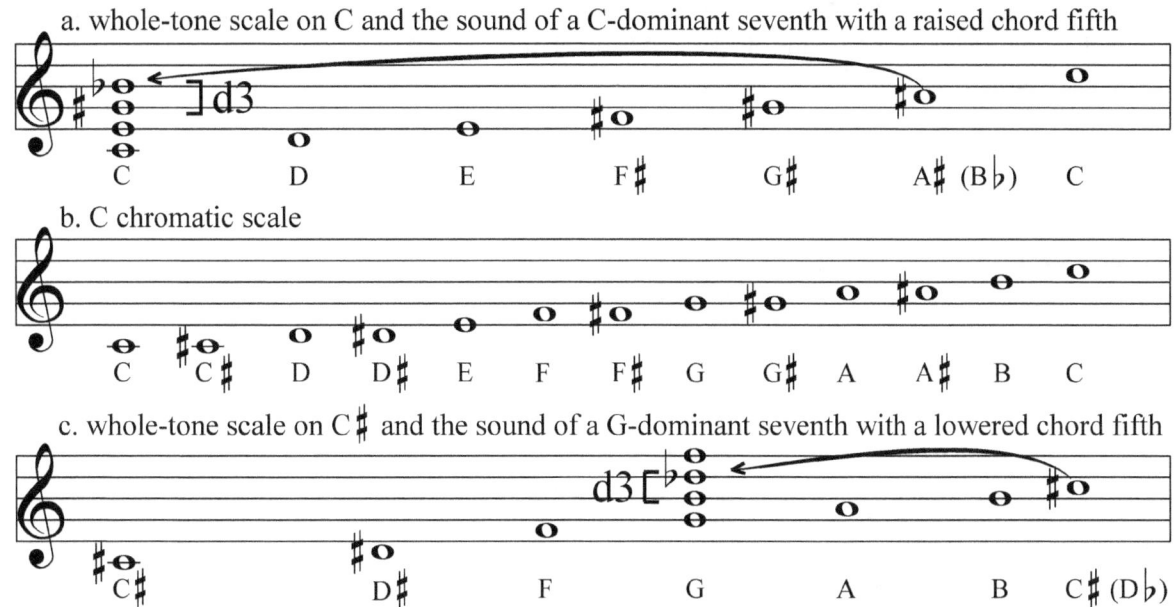

The Degree-Inflected THD in Minor

The $V{}^{7}_{\flat 5}$ in minor presents no voice-leading difficulties (examples 5–5a and 5b). The $V{}^{7}_{\sharp 5}$, however, is problematic (examples 5–5c and 5d). In minor, scale degrees $\sharp 2$ and 3 are identical pitches. Therefore, the intensification of motion between scale degrees $\sharp 2$ and 3 in major cannot be duplicated in minor (see the dotted lines in examples 5–5c and 5d). The raised fifth has nowhere to go, limiting the utility of the chord.

If the chord is used in minor, then the fifth should be correctly misspelled as scale degree 3 (E$\flat$) rather than as $\sharp 2$ (D$\sharp$). The parentheses enclosing $\sharp 5$ in examples 5–5c and 5d is a reminder of the true identity of the misspelled chord fifth. (Placing $\sharp 5$ in parentheses tells us that the chord has a raised fifth, regardless of how it is spelled or configured.)

Example 5–5: the degree-inflected THD in minor

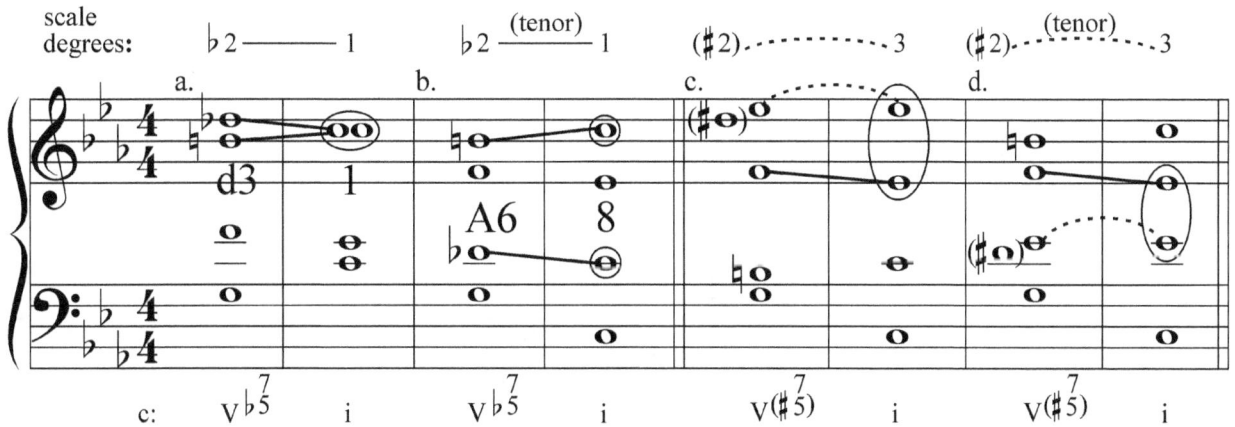

Inversions of the Degree-Inflected THD

When the degree-inflected THD triad is in root position, the best doubling in four voices is the root, as its third is the leading tone, its fifth the altered tone. When the THD triad inverts, both the leading tone and the altered fifth remain unavailable for doubling. When expressed as a seventh chord, there are no doubling options in four voices.

Example 5–6 shows how to retain the generic ♯5 in the notation when the $V^7_{♯5}$ inverts. We enclose ♯5 in parentheses and place the generic sign above the chord's figured bass. The various components in the chord symbol in 5–6b would be read or verbalized as follows: "the dominant seventh, six-five position, raised fifth variety." The other inversions in 5–6 would be expressed the same way. Although not included in our examples, inversions of the V♯5 *triad* use the same parenthetical ♯5 as its seventh-chord counterpart.

Example 5–6: the THD with the raised chord fifth in all positions

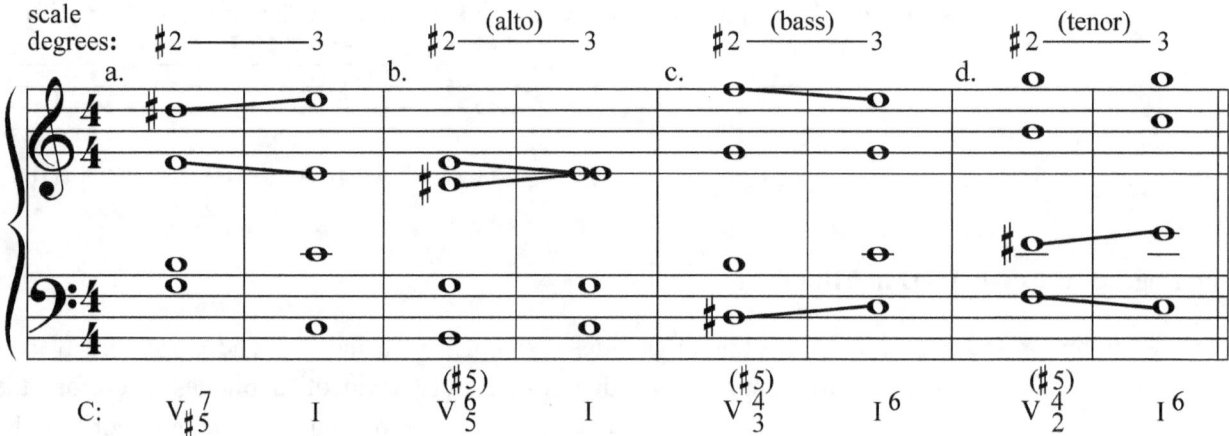

Examples 5–7 and 5–8 show how to preserve the generic ♭5 when the $V^7_{♭5}$ inverts. The ♭5 in parentheses is placed above the chord's figured bass. Reading or verbalizing the chord symbol in 5–7c would be as follows: "the dominant seventh, four-three position, lowered fifth variety." The remaining inversions would be expressed the same way. As in 5–6, inversions of the V♭5 *triad* use the same parenthetical ♭5 as its seventh-chord counterpart.

Example 5–7: the THD with the lowered chord fifth in all positions

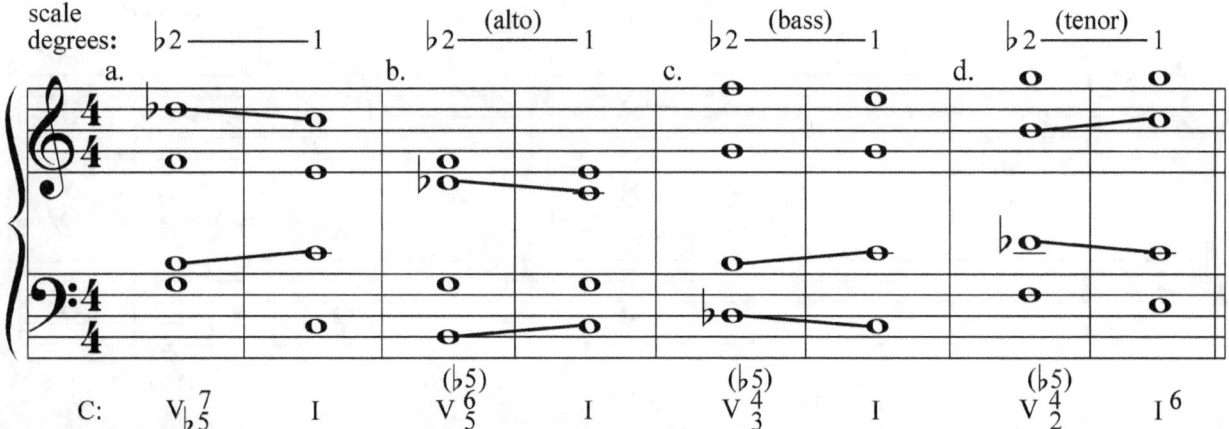

Example 5–8: the THD with the lowered chord fifth in all positions in minor

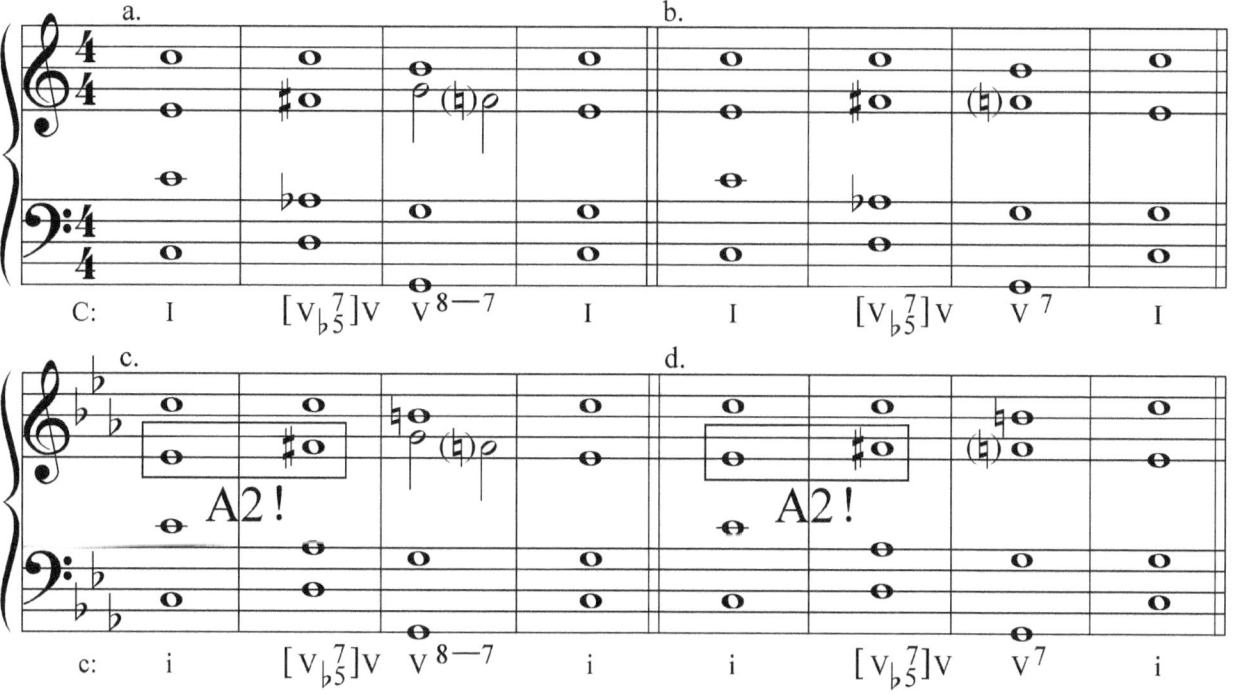

The Applied Degree-Inflected THD

Under certain circumstances, particularly when applied chords are involved, the interval of the augmented 6th (or diminished 3rd) may not resolve to an octave (or unison). Example 5–9a illustrates an 8—7 motion in the alto voice, which is then contracted into a chord seventh of the dominant in 5–9b, denying the expected resolution of the augmented 6th (A♭/F♯ to G/G). (It would be instructive to play examples 5–9a and 9b with F♯ and A♭ and then without them. The voice leading is the same either way.)

Additionally, voice-leading problems may arise when using the degree-inflected THD. As demonstrated in examples 5–9c and 9d, moving in c minor from scale degree 3 (E♭) to scale degree ♯4 (F♯), the chord third of the applied dominant, produces an undesirable augmented 2nd.

Example 5–9: contraction from an octave to a 7th

Type II: The Neapolitan 6th Chord

The Neapolitan 6th chord is so-named for its association with a group of opera composers located in Naples during the eighteenth century, though the chord is also found in the works of composers from areas outside of Naples during the second half of the seventeenth century and in other countries outside of Italy through the nineteenth century.

When the Neapolitan 6th is in first inversion, the traditional symbol for its notation is N^6. The figured bass identifies the chord's most common position before the nineteenth century. Some theory books show a preference for a chord symbol consisting of a flat in front of the Roman numeral with figured bass attached: ♭II, ♭II^6, and ♭II$^6_4$. The flat in front of the II indicates scale degree ♭2 as the root of the chord.

In c minor, the Neapolitan 6th chord in root position is spelled D♭ F A♭. The Neapolitan 6th is often called the Phrygian supertonic because the distance from the Phrygian tonic to scale degree 2 is a half step. Thus, in C Phrygian, scale degree 2 is D♭. The triad quality of the Phrygian supertonic is major.

One reason for using the Phrygian supertonic in the minor mode is the weakness of the supertonic that occurs diatonically, which is often a diminished triad. Bringing scale degree ♭2 into major or minor from a parallel mode outside of the major-minor tonal system constitutes an operation falling within the purview of secondary borrowing. (Secondary borrowing is discussed in Chapter 6.)

The second inversion of the Phrygian supertonic is less common than either its root position or first inversion. Generally, the ♭II$^6_4$ is a contrapuntal chord whose fifth, variable ♭6 in minor, seeks to move down to scale degree 5. In four-voice texture, doubling the chord fifth (variable ♭6) may result in parallel octaves when moving directly to the dominant (as shown in example 5–20b). The voice leading from the ♭II$^6_4$ to the dominant is improved when chords such as the subdominant in first inversion and/or the tonal melodic dominant in third inversion are placed between them (see example 5–21).

Chord Symbols

Following convention, and leaving aside the Phrygian origin of the Neapolitan 6th, this text retains the N^6 description when the chord third is the lowest pitch of the musical texture. However, when the chord is in either root position or second inversion, we use ♭II and ♭II$^6_4$ to underscore its identity as a chord of secondary borrowing (indicated in the examples with an asterisk located directly above the Roman numeral).

When referenced in this chapter and then later in Chapter 6, ♭II and ♭II$^6_4$ are understood clearly within the context of secondary borrowing involving the Phrygian supertonic. Therefore, without minimizing the chord's Phrygian origin, we use the conventional symbol N^6 when the Neapolitan 6th is in first inversion to telegraph its status as a degree-inflected chord involving scale degree ♭2 (example 5–10b). Additionally, the fifth of the Neapolitan chord is variable ♭6 in minor and (♭6) in major.

Example 5–10: the diminished supertonic and the Neapolitan 6th chord

The X-Chord Function of the Neapolitan 6th

The optimal doubling in four voices for the N^6 is the chord third, which emphasizes scale degree 4, the subdominant. The N^6 addressing the THD has the same X-chord function as that of the subdominant. But despite its function, the N^6 remains a supertonic harmony. As such, the N^6 supports a version of scale degree 2 in the top melodic voice (albeit ♭2), whereas the subdominant does not. The only choice to be made between the harmonic progressions in examples 5–10a and 10b above involves which version of scale degree 2 to use in the soprano, 2 or ♭2, D or D♭ (the latter is the root of the N^6 chord). The two progressions are otherwise identical.

The c-minor passage in 5–10b is a secondary harmonic progression (SHP) with a melodic descent from scale degrees 3 to 1 (E♭–D♭–B♮–C) with the leading tone, variable ♯7, serving as a substitute for scale degree 2. A diminished 3rd occurs between ♭2 and ♯7, which in *other* circumstances would be an unacceptable melodic interval. It is notable that the N^6 appears more readily in minor than in major, as the latter has an augmented 2nd between scale degrees 3 and ♭2 (see below, p. 102).

Filling in the Diminished 3rd

Although the diminished 3rd between scale degrees ♭2 and ♯7 is the preferred voicing when proceeding from the N^6 to the dominant, it may be desirable to fill in the melodic interval (D♭ to B♮ in c minor) with a chord-supported passing tone (on C). Examples 5–11 and 5–12 show how to fill in the interval between scale degrees ♭2 and ♯7. (In the major mode, voicing the melodic line above the N^6 presents the additional complication of the augmented 2nd between scale degrees 3 and ♭2.)

In measure 2 of example 5–11a, an apparent chord of the subdominant, formed within the complex of the N^6, supports an unaccented passing tone (P). The passing tone connects ♭2 to ♯7 (D♭ to B♮). The THD is expressed as an incomplete dominant seventh with the chord fifth omitted.

Example 5–11b has an accented passing tone (P) on the first part of the cadential $^6_4$. The dominant is once again left incomplete (G G F B), as the 6th above the bass in the alto voice moves upwards to form the chord seventh of the THD (E♭ to F).

As shown in 5–14 below, the succession from scale degrees ♭2 to 2 (D♭ to D♮ in c minor) should be avoided when all chord tones of the *root-position* dominant are present; for this disposition produces an augmented 2nd between variable ♭6 and ♯7 (A♭ and B♮) in another voice. (The apparent cross relation, mentioned earlier in Chapter 3, provides a successful way to move from scale degrees ♭2 to 2 when connecting the N^6 to the dominant chord. Examples 5–17, 20, 22, and 23 illustrate the succession between chromatic and diatonic versions of the same pitch in the same voice, scale degrees ♭2 and 2.)

Example 5–11: adding a chord-supported passing tone between scale degrees ♭2 and ♯7

As in measure 2 of 5–11a above, example 5–12a contains an instance of the unaccented passing tone (P), which here becomes a consonant preparation for the 4—3 suspension in measure 3. The chord seventh of the THD in measure 3 comes as a result of a suspension from the third of the preceding N^6. Both suspensions are untied (that is, re-articulated). Two chords support the passing tone C, the apparent subdominant (F A♭ C) and the THD (G G C–B F).

In the bass of examples 5–12b and 5–12c, we have an intensification of the motion between F and G by means of a chromatic passing tone on F♯. In both examples, the passing tone occurs within its own chord of prolongation, an applied CLT chord. The A♮ in the tenor voice occurs within the context of G major rather than as variable ♯6 in c minor. Another factor to observe is the cross relation between the D♭ in the N^6 (soprano) and the D♮ in the V chord (alto), an acceptable usage of this relationship.

In 5–12b, the applied CLT chord resolves to a dominant triad; subsequently, the fifth unfolds into the seventh (D to F). In 5–12c, the resolution of the CLT chord takes place within the cadential $^6_4$.

Example 5–12: passing from the N^6 to the V

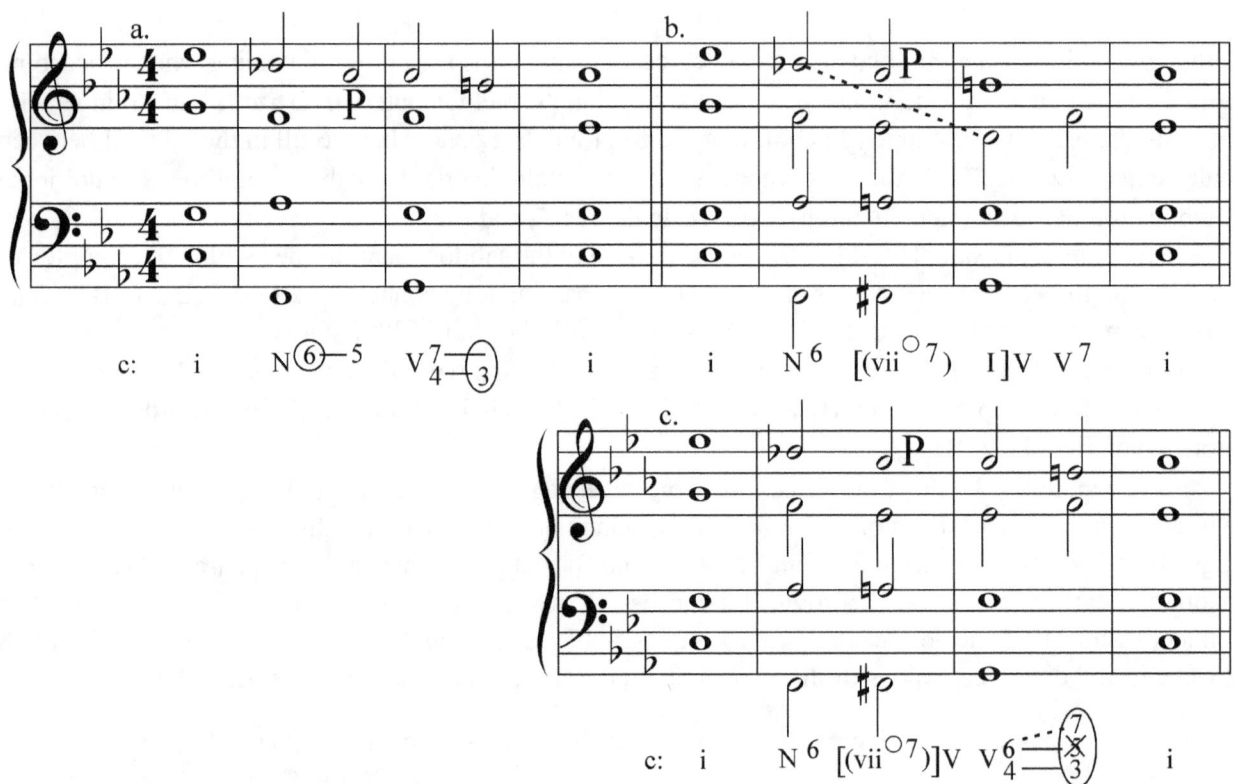

The acceptable use of the cross relation between the N^6 and V chords is demonstrated in 5–13a. As we observed in Chapter 3, another way to weaken the effect of the cross relation involves inserting either a passing tone or chord between the conflicting pitches in order to separate them, as an intervening passing tone or chord prevents the harmonic clash from continuing (as in examples 5–12b and 5–12c above). Example 1–13b uses the cadential $^6_4$ to support the passing tone.

Example 5–13: the cross relation between the N^6 and the V

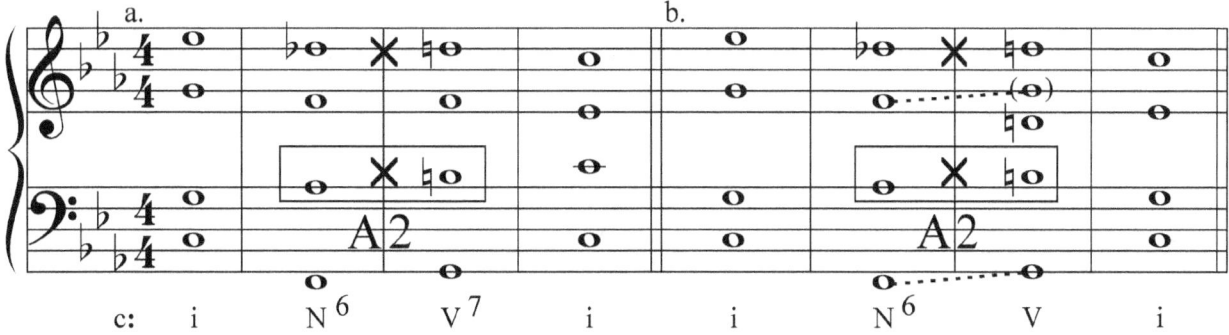

Example 5–14 confirms the peril of maintaining diatonic and chromatic versions of the same pitch in the same voice when the N^6 is involved. Here, the problem is between scale degrees $\flat 2$ and 2 (D$\flat$ to D$\natural$ in c minor). In other circumstances, the succession between different versions of the same pitch should remain in the same voice. However, when proceeding from the N^6 to the V, place the two pitches in different voices and retain the diminished 3rd in the same voice.

Failing to preserve the motion from $\flat 2$ to the leading tone yields an augmented 2nd in one of the other voices. Additionally, if the THD is a triad instead of a seventh chord, as in 5–14b, then potential parallel octaves arise. Doubling the fifth of the THD (D) instead of the root (G) averts the faulty parallel motion but the augmented 2nd remains.

Example 5–14: avoid diatonic and chromatic versions of the same pitch in the same voice with the N^6

The Phrygian Supertonic Itself

When the Neapolitan chord is in either root position or second inversion, we recognize its true identify as a supertonic chord, the Phrygian supertonic. As stated earlier, bringing scale degree $\flat 2$ into major or minor from a parallel mode outside of the major-minor tonal system constitutes an operation known as secondary borrowing.

Although reserved for Chapter 6, the topic of secondary borrowing must be addressed here in order to introduce our notation for this operation. When using the chord in first inversion, retaining the traditional N^6 places more emphasis on its service as a subdominant X-chord. However, both the chord's root position and second inversion are understood in this text as the Phrygian supertonic (itself), a chord of secondary borrowing.

When the Phrygian supertonic version of the chord is expressed, the notation is ♭II or ♭II$^6_4$. Throughout this text (in the examples), the Phrygian supertonic is marked as a chord of secondary borrowing with an asterisk located directly above the Roman numeral, as in example 5–15. If the Phrygian supertonic appears in major, then the chord symbol is also enclosed in parentheses to account for the primary borrowing of the lowered submediant, scale degree (♭6).

Example 5–15: the Phrygian supertonic

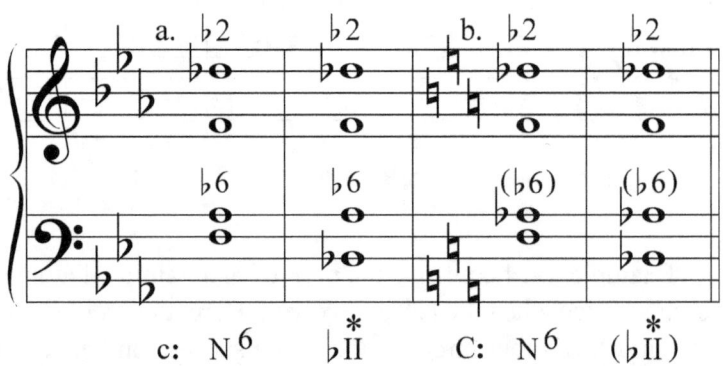

Example 5–16a displays an SHP with a melodic descent from scale degree 5. The X-chord is ♭II supporting scale degree 4. The only circumstance in which the tritone should be used melodically is when it occurs in the bass, as in measures 2–3. The usual doubling for the ♭II is the root; however, notice the direct 5th between the bass and alto in measures 1–2 (which can be averted by omitting the fifth and doubling the *third* of ♭II or by inserting iv between i^6 and ♭II). The diminished 3rd is filled in with the cadential $^6_4$ supporting the passing C in the tenor voice. When the THD completes itself in the second half of the cadential $^6_4$, it is possible to replace the diatonic chord fifth with the lowered variety, that is, D♭ instead of D♮ in c minor (soprano voice, measure 3).

In 5–16b, we have a two-progression framework with a melodic descent from scale degree 5. Progression 1 is an SHP with ♭II as the X-chord. Progression 2 is a basic harmonic progression (BHP). (Again, the lowered fifth is an option for the THD.)

Example 5–16: the ♭II as the X-chord of an SHP with a melodic descent from scale degree 5

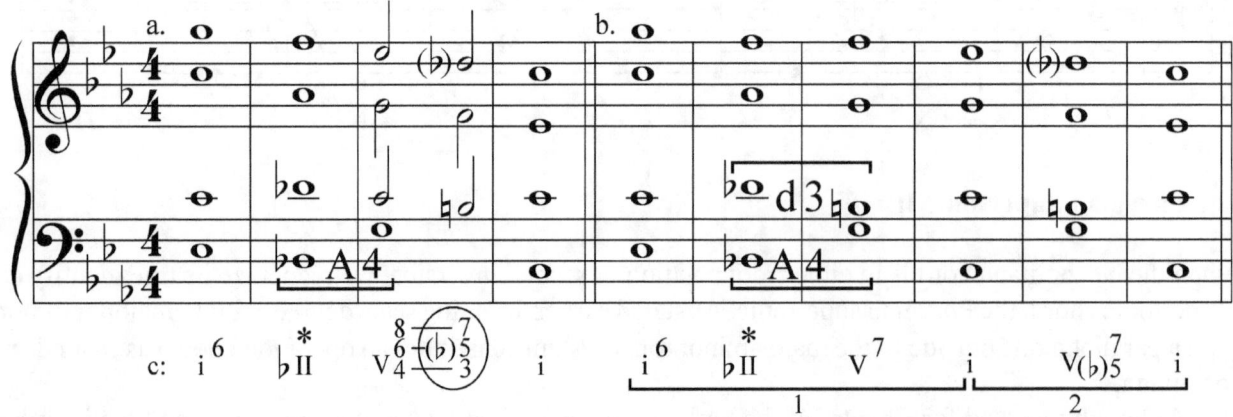

In example 5–17, a melodic descent from scale degree 5 is supported by a two-progression framework. The first progression is a secondary contrapuntal progression (SCP), the second a BHP. In progression 1, notice the immediate succession of D♭ to D♮. Normally, this is not the recommended voice leading for connecting the Phrygian supertonic to the dominant.

The voice leading recalls the apparent cross relation introduced in example 3–3 (Chapter 3). When another voice duplicates one of the two pitches of the cross relation, the clash of tones in different voices is acceptable provided the succession between chromatic and diatonic versions of the same pitch remain in the same voice (D♭ in the bass against D♭ to D♮ in the tenor).

Notably, in this instance, a *chromatic* duplication (D♭) rather than a diatonic one (D♮) moves to another tone (B♮) in order to mitigate the harmonic conflict. (In 3–3, the opposite condition takes place: a *diatonic* duplication moves to another tone to lessen the clash between pitches.) In the voice opposing the succession of chromatic and diatonic activity, stepwise motion away from the duplicated pitch is best; however, a departure by leap also works, as in 5–17 (D♭ down to B♮ in the bass).

Example 5–17: the apparent cross relation involving the ♭II

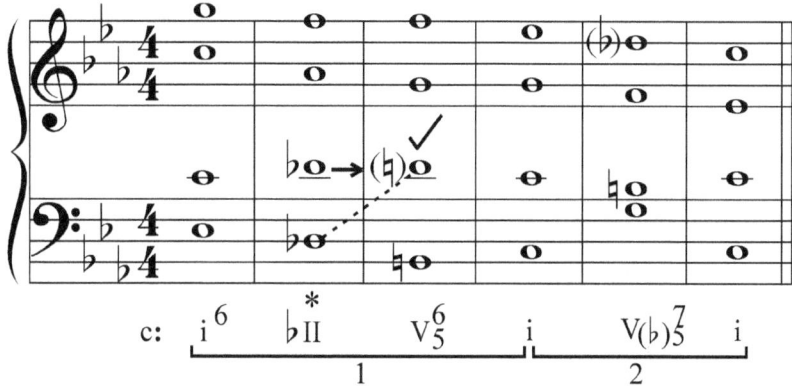

Using the Submediant before the Neapolitan 6th

The major triad of the lowered submediant stands in a falling 5th (or rising 4th) root relationship to the Neapolitan chord. When two chords share a harmonic root relationship of a falling 5th (or rising 4th) and the approach chord is a major triad resolving to another major or minor triad, the approach chord becomes an applied dominant to the succeeding chord. In example 5–18, the ♭VI serves as an applied dominant of the N⁶ and as an extended passing chord between the tonic and the N⁶.

The strength of the ♭VI as an applied chord depends on its connection to the N⁶, in other words, its voice leading. Examples 5–18 and 5–19 demonstrate how to connect the two chords *without* resolving the applied leading-tone C to its D♭-tonic. (Example 5–20 below improves the connection between chords.)

Example 5–18: preceding the N⁶ with the ♭VI

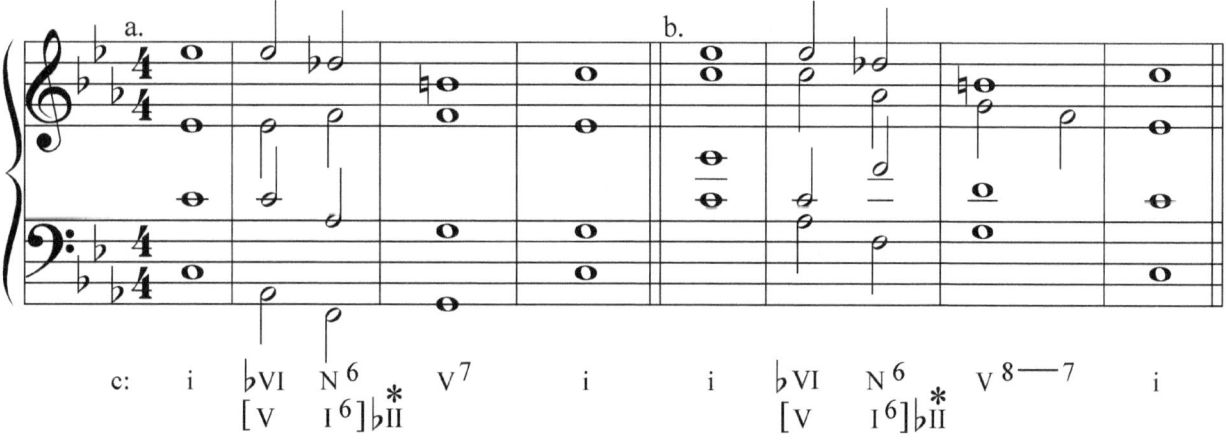

Example 5–19: preceding the N ^{6} with the $\flat$VI

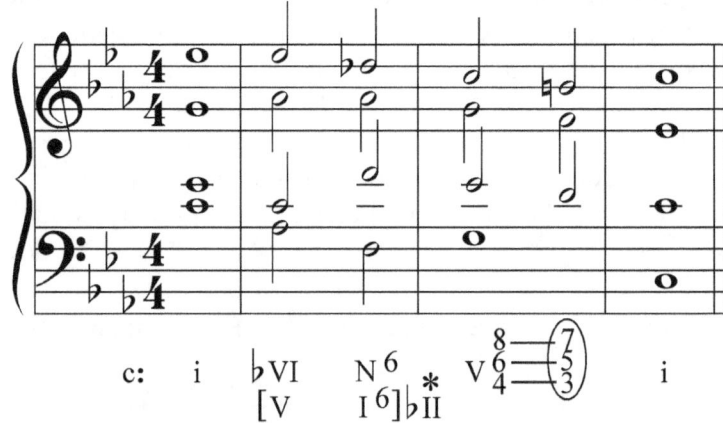

Example 5–20 presents two versions of the Neapolitan chord: the Neapolitan 6th as a chord of degree inflection; and, the Phrygian supertonic in second inversion as a chord of secondary borrowing. (The asterisk attached to the top of the descriptive chord symbol in the example reminds us that the chord arises from secondary borrowing.)

In example 5–20, we see a more emphatic connection between the two chords than that demonstrated in examples 5–18 and 5–19. In 5–20 (tenor), the D$\flat$-root of the N ^{6} is preceded by its own leading tone (C), the chord third of the $\flat$VI. Maintaining chromatic and diatonic versions of the same pitch in the same voice (D$\flat$ and D$\natural$) while resolving the leading tone to its D$\flat$-tonic engenders an apparent cross relation with the main-level THD that follows (measure 3).

In 5–20b, the strength of the applied dominant is increased with the addition of a passing 7th on G$\flat$, an operation that creates a dominant seventh chord, an applied THD ^{7} of the $\flat$II $^6_4$. The A$\flat$-bass moves down by half step to G, the root of the THD.

Notice the doubling of the Phrygian supertonic's root (5–20b, soprano and tenor). If we fail to take the downward resolution of the G$\flat$ to the F in measure 2 (alto) and instead double the chord fifth (A$\flat$) of the Phrygian supertonic, parallel octaves occur when proceeding to the THD. (See the octaves from A$\flat$ to G between the alto and bass). Moreover, in four-part texture, there is no voice left for the chord third (F).

Example 5–20: motion into the chord

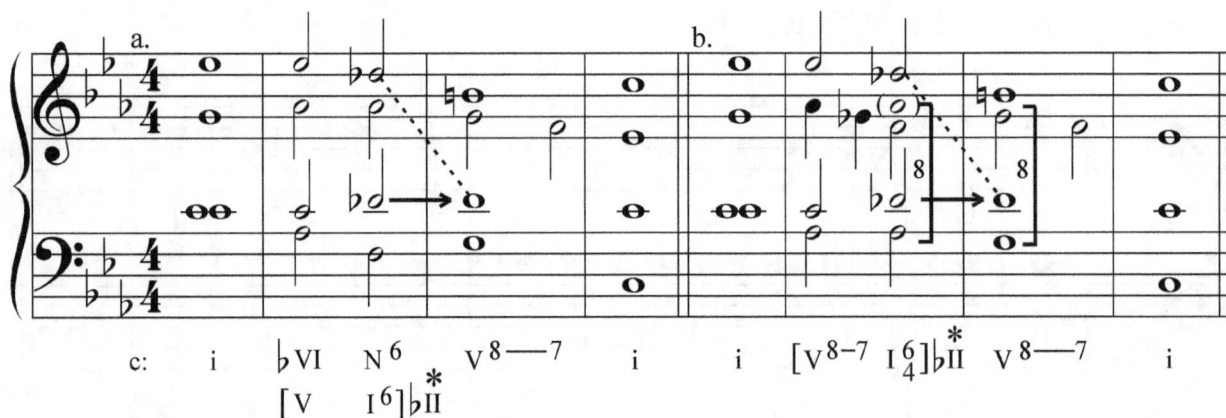

The second inversion of the Phrygian supertonic is less common than either its root position or first inversion. As indicated above in 5–20b, doubling the chord fifth of the ♭II$^6_4$ may not be the best choice when moving directly to the THD. The voice leading from the ♭II$^6_4$ to the dominant is improved when chords of the subdominant and/or leading tone are placed between them (example 5–21). However, when proceeding from the ♭II$^6_4$ to the iv^6, exercise caution; for doubling the chord fifth of the Phrygian supertonic (A♭) can lead to a direct 5th with the subdominant (see the dotted lines in 5–21a, measure 2, soprano and tenor).

In example 5–21b, the direct 5th is averted by doubling the chord third (A♭) of the iv^6, scale degree ♭6. Since ♭6 in minor and (♭6) in major are active tones, we usually do not double them. But in this context, doubling the chord fifth of the ♭II$^6_4$ prepares ♭6 in the next chord, the iv^6.

Normally, second inversion triads are unstable and apparent; they exist primarily in association with other chords more stable and real. Within the framework of the progression exhibited in 5–21, the ♭II$^6_4$ assumes additional significance as an upper neighbor chord to the THD (scale degree 5) and in its support of scale degree ♭2 in the top voice.

Both examples 5–21a and 21b show a descending contrapuntal bass in which the ♭II$^6_4$ functions as an X-chord, albeit an unusual one. The chord seventh (B♭) of the tonic initiates the stepwise descent in the bass. The iv^6 and the ♯vii°$^4_2$ are passing chords that smooth out the voice leading between the ♭II$^6_4$ and the THD.

The A♭ of the Phrygian supertonic is maintained as a common tone in the bass through the iv^6 and the ♯vii°$^4_2$. Ultimately, the A♭ initiates a conversion dominant as it descends by half step to G, the root of the THD. (When playing these examples on the keyboard, notice the option for using D♭, the lowered fifth in the THD, a selection that adds a pungent quality to the chord. For an additional contrast in the modal color of the progression, use the Picardy third, E♮, for the cadential tonic.)

Example 5–21: voice-leading the ♭II$^6_4$ to the iv^6

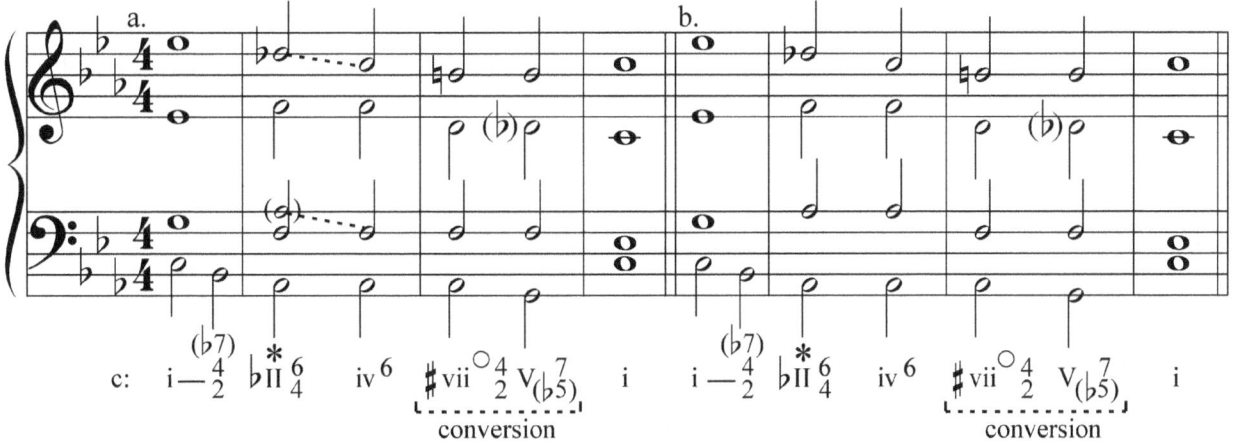

Example 5–22 below revisits the SHP displayed in example 5–20 above. In 5–22, the N^6 is addressed by it own applied dominant in third inversion. The contrapuntal bass fills in a descending-3rd motion (C–A♭–F) with passing tones. The passing tones, B♭ and G♭, are the chord sevenths for the tonic minor seventh and the applied dominant of the N^6 respectively.

On beat 3 of measure 2 (5–22a), notice the motion between the bass and the tenor: F/D♭ proceeds without difficulty to G/D, a minor 6th to a perfect 5th. However, the D♭ is enharmonically C♯, which combined with the F produces an "augmented 5th" moving to a perfect 5th, an apparent succession of unequal 5ths. Although acceptable, particularly when an inner voice is involved, the cadential $^6_4$ in 5–22b provides a better connection and breaks up the "5ths."

Example 5–22: [V$^4_2$ I^6]♭II

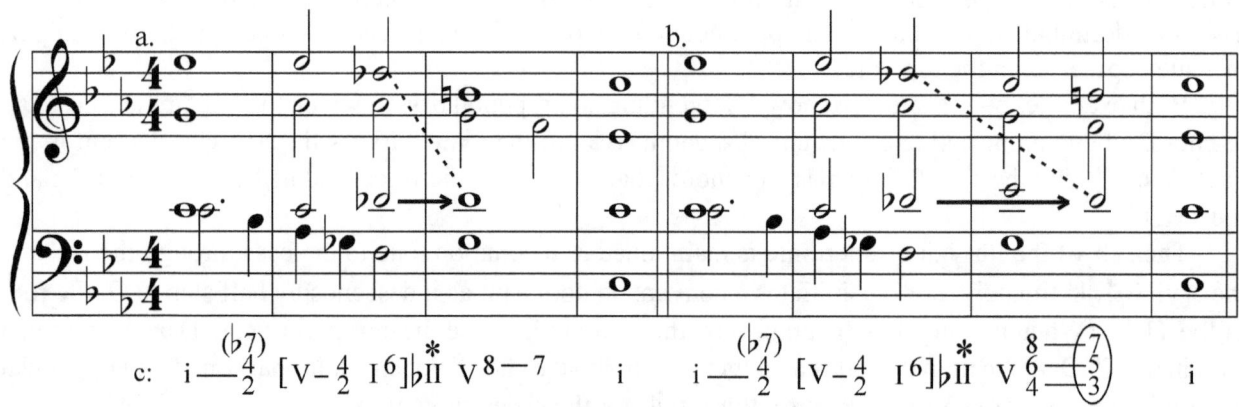

The Neapolitan 6th and the Phrygian Supertonic in Major

In the major mode, using (♭VI) makes the melodic descent from scale degree 3 practicable by avoiding the augmented 2nd between scale degrees 3 and ♭2. As illustrated in example 5–23, the melodic descent from scale degree 3 is E–E♭–D♭–B–C. (The E♭ is supported by the submediant chord acting as an applied dominant.) As mentioned earlier, the submediant also serves as an extended passing chord between the tonic and the N^6. The E♭ contained within (♭VI) infuses the progression with minor, making the final C-major triad sound somewhat like a Picardy third.

Example 5–23: preceding the N^6 with the (♭VI) in major

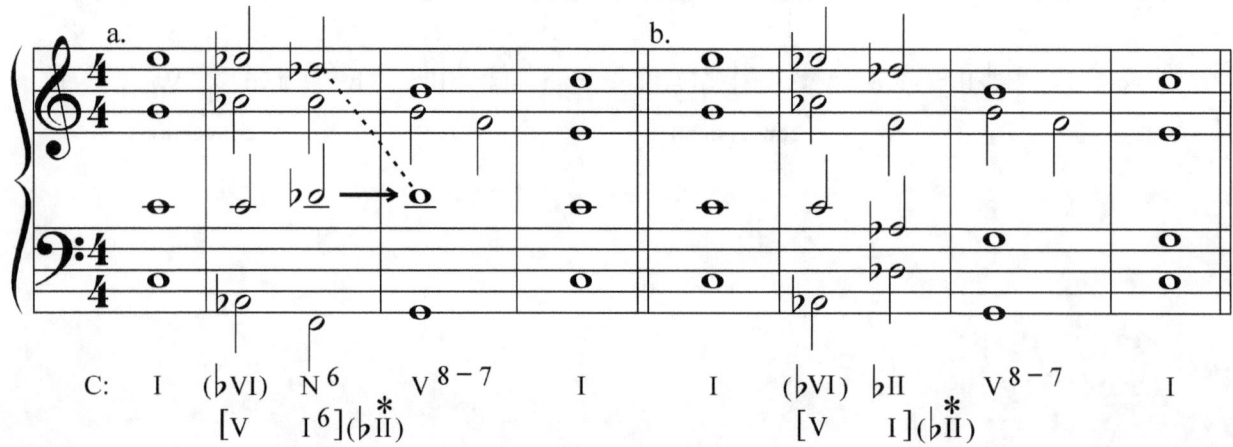

Type III: Common-Tone Fully Diminished Seventh Chords

This section explores the operation of the fully diminished seventh chord serving a non-dominant function. We use two interchangeable terms to describe this chord (but with a decided preference for the latter): the "non-CLT o7" and the "non-TMD o7." The chord is built on scale degrees ♯2 and ♯6 and is usually attached to a genuine major triad of the tonic or dominant. (The non-TMD o7 occurs less frequently in the minor mode.)

Example 5–24 illustrates the use of scale degrees ♯2 and ♯6 as chromatic passing tones intensifying the motion between diatonic scale degrees. As shown in measure 3 of examples 5–25a and 25b, the non-TMD o7 standing on scale degrees ♯2 and ♯6 grows out of chromatic linear activity. The chord yields three basic types of contrapuntal prolongation: passing (as in example 5–25), neighboring (as in examples 5–28b and 28c), and pedal embellishing (as in example 5–29).

The non-TMD o7 is expressed with the chord symbols ♯ii o7 and ♯vi o7. The chord typically appears in unaccented circumstances; however, sometimes it assumes an appoggiatura function, occurring on the primary accent of the measure and preceding the formation of the real chord, the chord to which the non-TMD o7 is attached (as in example 5–31, measure 3).

The intervallic relationship of the augmented 2nd (enharmonically a minor 3rd) between scale degrees 1 and ♯2 (C/D♯ in C major) is duplicated between scale degrees 5 and ♯6 (G/A♯ in C major). That is, the relationship between the ♯vi o7 and the dominant corresponds to that between the ♯ii o7 and the tonic. Therefore, the same voice-leading options are available for both chords.

Example 5–24: scale degrees ♯2 and ♯6

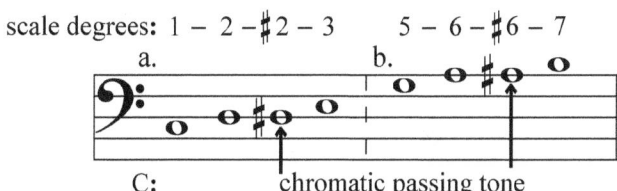

The Common Tone

The ♯ii o7 consists of scale degrees ♯2, ♯4, 6, and 1. The seventh of the raised supertonic is the root of the tonic chord. In example 5–25a, the common tone between these two chords is C. The voice leading in measures 3 and 4 of 5–25a is: ♯2 to 3, ♯4 to 5, and 6 to 5. Scale degree 1 (C) does not move.

The ♯vi o7 consists of scale degrees ♯6, ♯1, 3, and 5. The seventh of the ♯vi o7 is the root of the dominant chord. The common tone between these two chords in example 5–25b is G, the dominant scale degree. The voice leading in measures 3 and 4 of 5–25b is: ♯6 to 7, ♯1 to 2, and 3 to 4. Scale degree 5 (G) does not move.

Example 5–25: scale degrees 1 and 5 as common tones

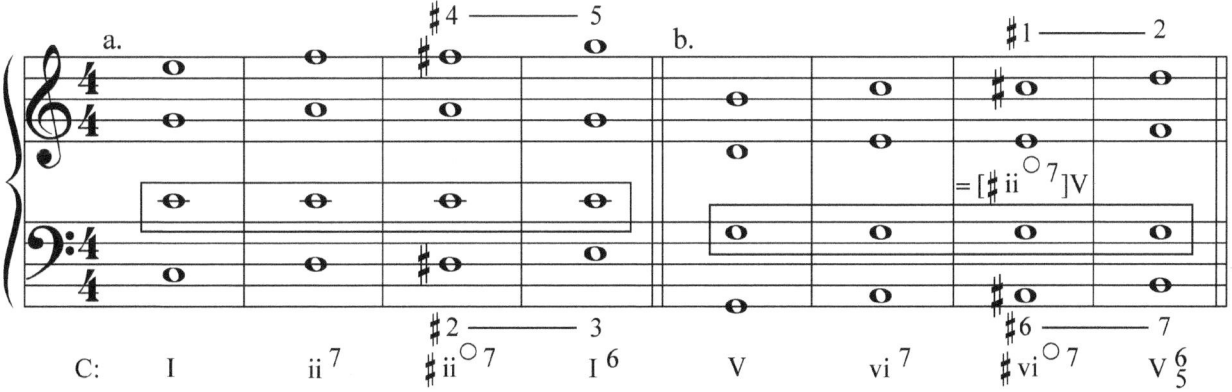

The Common-Tone Fully Diminished Seventh in Minor

There are few factors to consider when using the non-TMD $°^7$ in minor, as demonstrated in examples 5–26a and 26b. First, the root of the $\sharp$ii $°^7$ is enharmonically scale degree 3 of the mode. In c minor (5–26a), scale degree $\sharp$2 is D$\sharp$ while scale 3 is E$\flat$. Therefore, when the $\sharp$ii $°^7$ occurs in minor, its root should be correctly misspelled as scale degree 3.

The raised supertonic in 5–26a proceeds to a minor tonic triad and shares two common tones with the chord of resolution; in c minor, the common tones are C and E$\flat$ (D$\sharp$). In measures 3 and 4, one of the common tones is in the bass (E$\flat$), making the alternative representation of the $\sharp$ii $°^7$ as an apparent chord possible. For ultimately, the non-TMD $°^7$ in both major and minor is an apparent chord. (We shall revisit the notation of the non-TMD $°^7$ as an apparent chord over a stationary bass in examples 5–29, 30, 31, and 33.)

Additionally, variable $\sharp$6 moves *down* to scale degree 5, an irregular voice leading for the raised submediant in minor. The seventh chord built on scale degree $\sharp$6 in minor, $\sharp$vi$\varnothing^7$, is a half-diminished seventh. The submediant scale degree *above* $\sharp$6 in minor is referred to in this text as the "raised-raised submediant" and indicated as $\substack{\sharp \\ \sharp}$vi $°^7$ (5–26b). Leaving aside this notational complication, the chord fifth of the $\substack{\sharp \\ \sharp}$vi $°^7$ is scale degree 3 of the parallel major (see the circled E in 5–26b), which suggests a mixture of major and minor modes.

Example 5–26: using the common-tone fully diminished seventh in minor

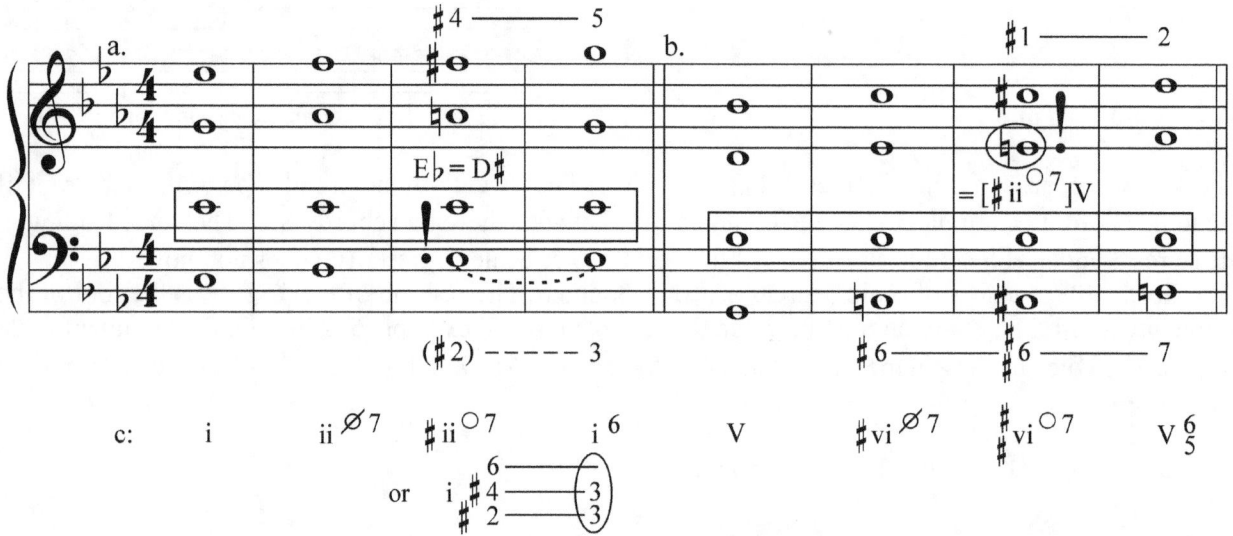

Using Exact Accidentals in Front of the Roman Numeral Instead of Generic Accidentals

As indicated in the heading of this section and in example 5–27, an alternative method for representing the non-TMD ^{o}^{7} reads the exact accidental found in the music for the root of the chord and then places that accidental in front of the Roman numeral chord symbol. The application of this literal approach produces an inconsistent representation of the chord, one that might vary depending on the pitch content of the key signature (as in 5–27b and 27c).

On the other hand, the generic accidental that precedes the Roman numeral requires the *understanding* that the diatonic scale degree is raised to provide the appropriate chromatic tone and root for either non-TMD ^{o}^{7} : the ♯ii ^{o}^{7} or the ♯vi ^{o}^{7}. In order to read the generic symbol, you must be able to locate the pitch in question based upon your *knowledge* of the music's key signature.

Example 5–27: adding the literal accidental to the chord description

Example 5–28 presents another way to consider the generic descriptors ♯ii ^{o}^{7} and ♯vi ^{o}^{7}. A fully diminished seventh on B appears in three different major modes (C, A♭, and D♭). Ultimately, one fully diminished seventh is displayed within three different tonal contexts. A half step separates the ^{o}^{7} from its destination chord. The voice leading depends on the chord's status as either a TMD ^{o}^{7} (5–28a) or a non-TMD ^{o}^{7} (5–28b and 28c). In 5–28a, the chord seventh, (♭6), resolves to chord fifth of the tonic. However, in 5–28b, the chord seventh remains as the root of the tonic; in 5–28c, the chord seventh remains as the root of the dominant.

Example 5–28: three different resolutions for a fully diminished seventh on B

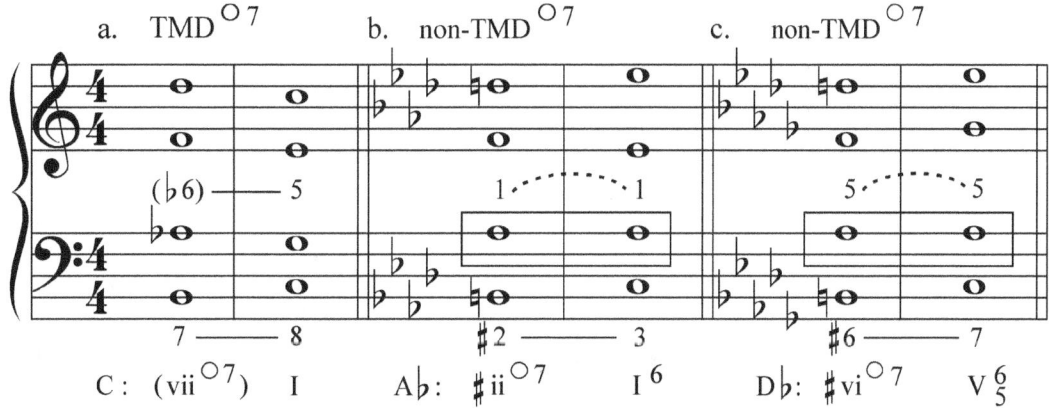

The Common-Tone Fully Diminished Seventh as a Pedal Embellishing Chord

As displayed in example 5–29, the apparent nature of the non-TMD $°^7$ is most evident when it becomes a pedal embellishing chord. Here, the chord seventh is placed in the bass to prolong the root of the tonic and dominant chords. Below the line of conventional chord symbols, the alternative notation representing the apparent ♯ii $°^7$ and ♯vi $°^7$ shows the motion of the upper voices above the stationary bass. In examples 5–29b and 29d, the chord fifth is omitted and the seventh doubled for both the ♯ii $°^7$ and the ♯vi $°^7$. That such an irregular doubling is even possible *and* desirable underscores the apparent identity of the chord.

Example 5–29: the apparent non-TMD $°^7$ above a stationary bass

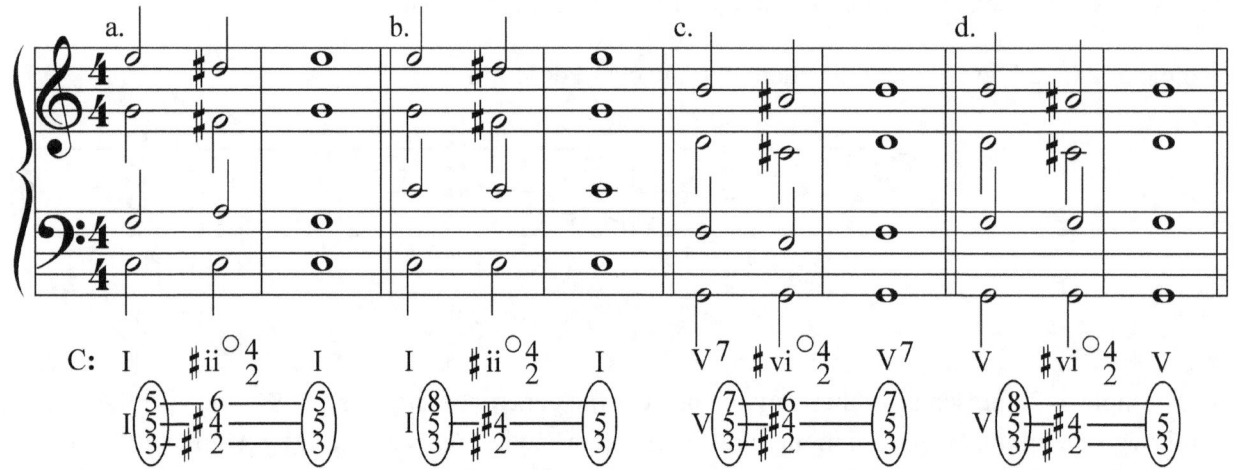

Example 5–30 revisits an excerpt from Chapter 4, the first four measures of Mozart's Sonata No. 16 in C Major (K. 545), II. Recognition of the non-TMD $°^7$ affords us the opportunity to amend our initial interpretation of the chordal activity in measure 3. The tones G A♯ C♯ E on beat 3 form a ♯ii $°^4_2$. There are three possible interpretations: stay with the analysis from Chapter 4, add ♯ii $°^4_2$, or read the measure as a tonic G in the bass over which an apparent pedal embellishing $^6_4$ proceeds to an apparent ♯ii $°^4_2$. The tonic chord in root position completes itself in measure 4.

Example 5–30: Mozart, Sonata No. 16 in C Major (K. 545), II, measures 1–4

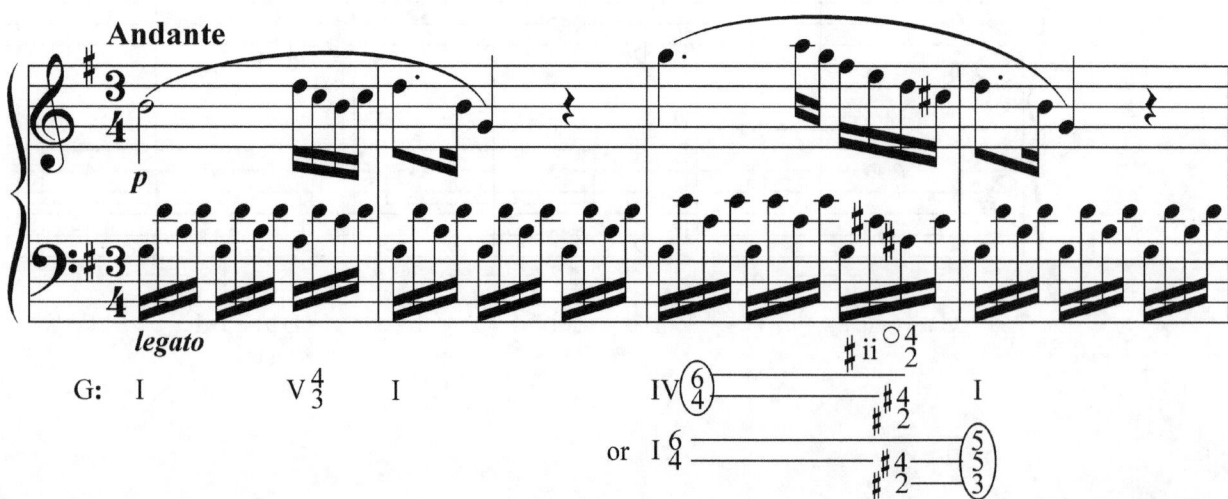

Chapter 5 Degree-Inflected Chords   107

The placement of the non-TMD o⁷ in examples 5–29 and 5–30 above is unaccented in relation to the real chord, which occurs in a metrically stronger position. In example 5–31, the non-TMD o⁷ becomes an appoggiatura chord, appearing on the primary accent of the measure.

Example 5–31 illustrates two types of chord-supported structural melody: a *tone-embellishing melodic succession*, abbreviated as TEMB, and a *basic melodic progression*, abbreviated as BMP. A TEMB is melodic activity involving either neighbor motion above or below a tone, or repetitions of a tone (inverted pedal embellishment), or combinations of neighbor tones and repeated tones (in 5–31a: E–F–E–D–D♯–E). A BMP is a melodic descent to scale degree 1 from either scale degree 5 or 3 (in 5–31b: E–D–C).

Example 5–31: the SHP/TEMB and SHP/BMP with the non-TMD o⁷ as an appoggiatura chord

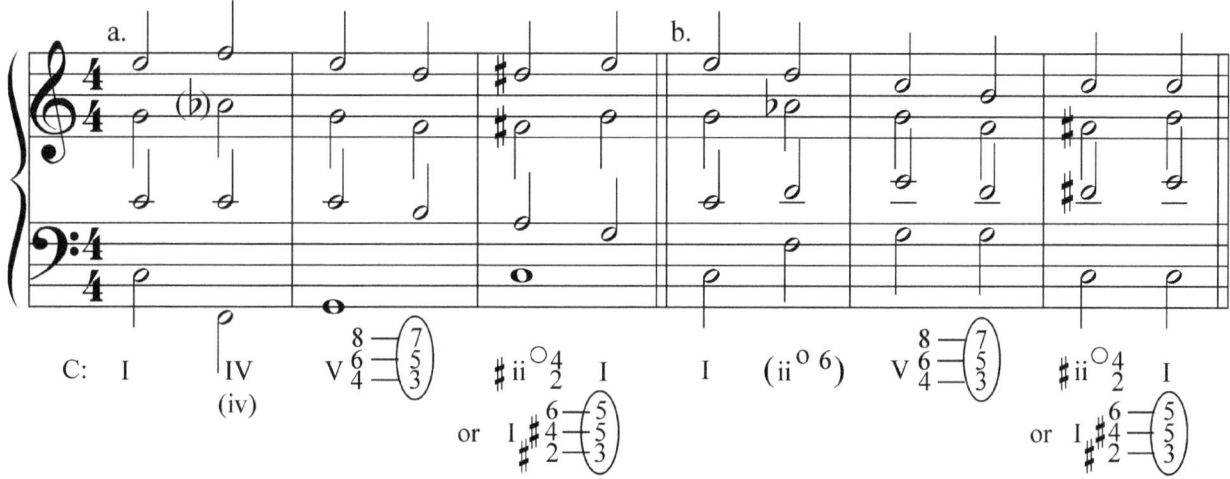

Voicing the Fully Diminished Seventh Chord

When a fully diminished seventh on scale degree ♯4 approaches the cadential $^6_4$ (the first part of which is an apparent major triad), two interpretations for the same pitch content are possible. However, each interpretation requires a different understanding of the voice leading, description of the chord, and spelling of pitches. In 5–32a, the chord is an applied (vii o⁷) of the dominant, a lower-level CLT o⁷ chord. Although there are common tones between the [(vii o⁷)]V and the first part of the cadential $^6_4$, the completion of the root-position dominant is seen as the chord of resolution. There are no common tones with the dominant chord. In 5–32b, the same chord is described and spelled as ♯ii o $^6_5$; the common tone is C.

Example 5–32: addressing the cadential $^6_4$ with scale degree ♯4 in the bass projecting a o⁷ chord

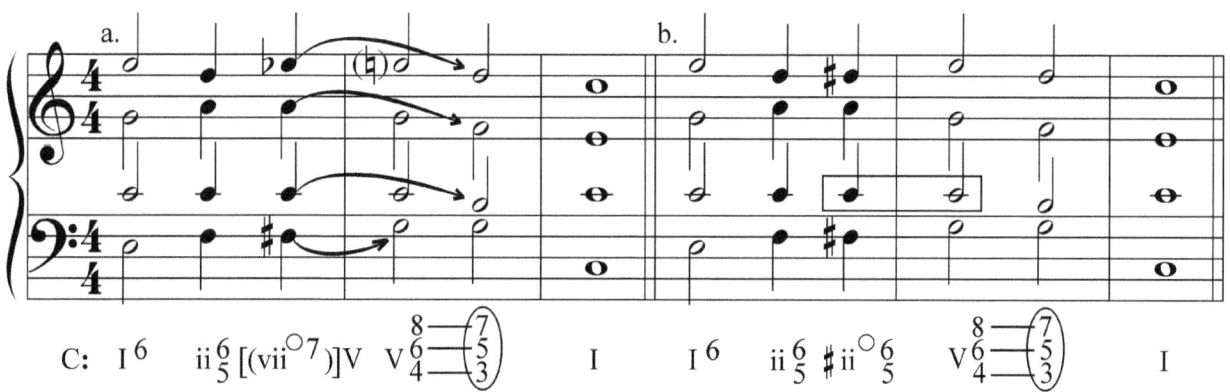

Example 5–33 illustrates the contrapuntal function of the non-TMD $°^7$. The ascending passing motion in the bass produces a contrapuntal prolongation of the way from I to V (measures 1–4). Above the chromatic bass, the $\sharp$vi $°^7$ appears twice, the $\sharp$ii $°^7$ once. Both root-position chords resolve to inverted chords.

Measure 5 contains a $\sharp$ii$°^4_2$ as an appoggiatura chord attached to the cadential tonic. The chord on the first beat of measure 6 is part of a complex that includes the raised supertonic (on the second quarter) assuming appoggiatura status *after* the formation of an unusual chord. That is, the complete disposition of the $\sharp$ii$°^4_2$ occurs only after the statement of a *diminished triad on C with a major 7th*. The major 7th is between the C bass and the B soprano, enharmonically from the chord root to the seventh. This is an exceptional apparent chord. (The chord was displayed earlier in examples 2–4 and 5, p. 21.)

Spelled enharmonically from the bass as C E♭ G♭ B, this diminished triad/major 7th becomes a fully diminished seventh only when the apparent major 7th over C moves down from B to A (measure 6, beats 1–2). Ultimately, the final measure is a modified restatement of measure 5. The modifications include a voice exchange between the tenor and soprano (A/F$\sharp$ becomes F$\sharp$/A). The diminished triad/major 7th further elaborates the previous measure.

Example 5–33: the non-TMD $°^7$ as a passing chord within an ascending contrapuntal bass

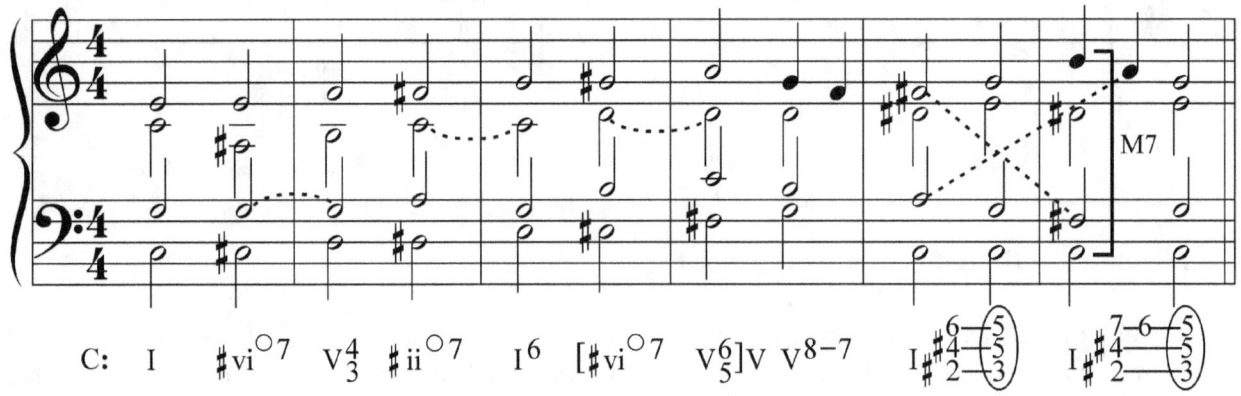

Fully Diminished Seventh Chords in Succession

The examples in this section demonstrate the two principal ways in which fully diminished sevenths in succession usually occur. Both techniques have the potential to destabilize the main-level key if extended into a series of paired chords. The $°^7$ produces a sense of tension because of its symmetrical structure (minor 3rds) and dissonance, which comes from the two interlocking tritones embedded within the chord's design. (Two such tritones are in the applied $\sharp$vi $°^7$ of example 5–34: E$\sharp$-B and D-G$\sharp$).

When two or more $°^7$ chords appear in succession, the direction of the bass line and its intervallic content helps us to understand the operation. A very important step in the inquiry is to find the real chord to which the succession of $°^7$ chords finally resolve. The approach to the chord of resolution in the bass is either from above or below by either whole or half step.

A succession of fully diminished seventh chords is problematic when the bass line ascends because the chord seventh cannot move down. In a succession of ascending $°^7$ chords, all of the voices move in the same direction. An ascending succession becomes possible because the diminished 7th from the root to the seventh is more of a contextual dissonance that an acoustical one. Independent of the key, the contextual dissonance of the diminished 7th sounds like a major 6th. To be sure, we want a downward resolution for both the contextual and acoustical interval of the 7th, *if the tone of resolution is available in the next chord.* In any case, an ascending conjunct succession of fully diminished sevenths carries a relatively low level of dissonance between the chord root and seventh, as illustrated in 5–34.

Example 5–34 displays motion between two fully diminished seventh chords in which the bass ascends by half steps: [♯vi o 7 (vii o 7)]V.

Example 5–34: o 7 chords ascending by half step

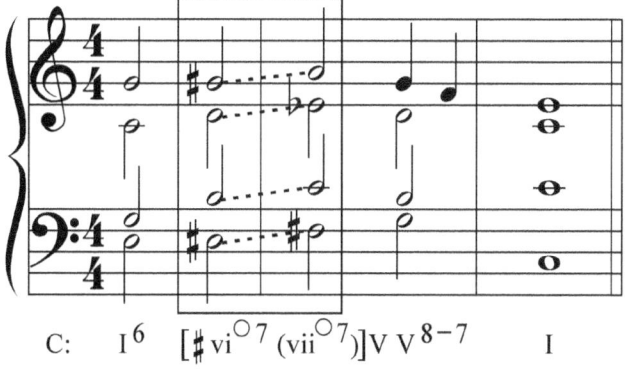

Example 5–35 posits one interpretation for the succession of fully diminished sevenths shown in 5–34 above. The succession begins initially in C major as a paired succession of raised submediant and leading-tone o 7 chords attached to the tonic and then to the supertonic: an upward motion of a whole step (C–D). In 5–35, each pair of fully diminished seventh chords points to a tonal center one whole step above the previous tonal center, starting on C major and continuing with d minor.

If we followed the succession beyond d minor, the tones addressed by each pair of o 7 chords would become part of an ascending series of whole steps (C–D–E–F♯–G♯–A♯–C) moving far away from the starting key before returning to it. The potential for modulation is secured by the strength of the underlying dominant harmony supporting this two-chord pattern. In 5–35, this support *and* confirmation of key is implicit, as the resolution to the real chord is omitted (see the X), the harmonic motion contracted to produce a succession of four fully diminished seventh chords ascending by half step: A♯, B, B♯, C♯. (The succession of alternating ♯vi o 7 and TMD o 7 chords can also be expressed in a descending succession of whole steps.)

Example 5–35 supplies the roots (G and A in parentheses) of implied THD ♭$^9_7$ chords below each TMD o 7. The chord seventh of the fully diminished seventh constitutes a lowered 9th above the implied root. Ultimately, if used instead of the TMD o 7, this dominant ninth (or dominant seventh) would be the chord of resolution for the raised submediant. The inherent relationship between the raised submediant and the dominant helps to hold this succession of fully diminished sevenths together.

Example 5–35: four o 7 chords ascending by half step

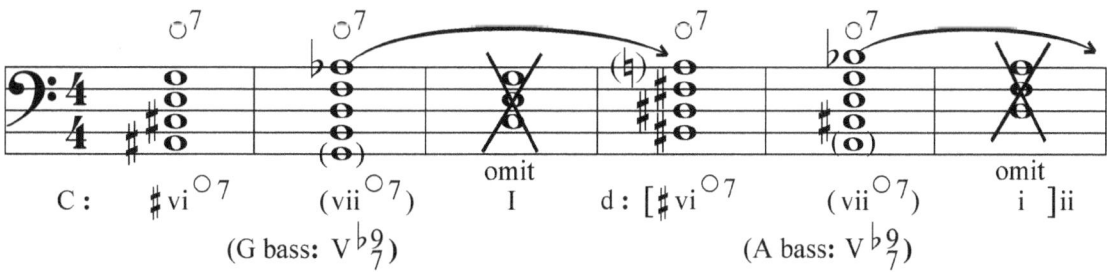

Example 5–36 presents a different operation, based on the descending 5th sequence. Here, we have four o⁷ chords descending by half step: B♭, A, A♭, G. (The succession of TMD o⁷ chords can also be expressed in an ascending succession of whole steps.) When fully diminished sevenths appear in a descending succession, the chord seventh may take a downward resolution (see the solid descending lines in 5–36). In the example, the first chord of each pair is inverted to better illustrate the action of the chord seventh.

The descending 5th sequence is realized by providing the roots of implied dominant ninth chords below each TMD o⁷: C–F–B♭–E♭. As with the o⁷ chords ascending by half step, the o⁷ chords descending by half step generate harmonic tension by destabilizing the main-level key and/or modulating from it.

Although an effective technique for moving from one key to another or for weakening the gravitational pull of the central tonality, using the fully diminished seventh in a series is not without its limitations: there are only three versions of the chord. As shown in both examples 5–35 and 36, three successive statements of o⁷ chords separated by half steps utilize all twelve available tones. The fourth statement duplicates the pitch content of the first chord (compare the pitch content of measures 1 and 5 of 5–35 and measures 1 and 4 of 5–36).

Example 5–36: four o⁷ chords descending by half step (with implied descending 5th bass motion)

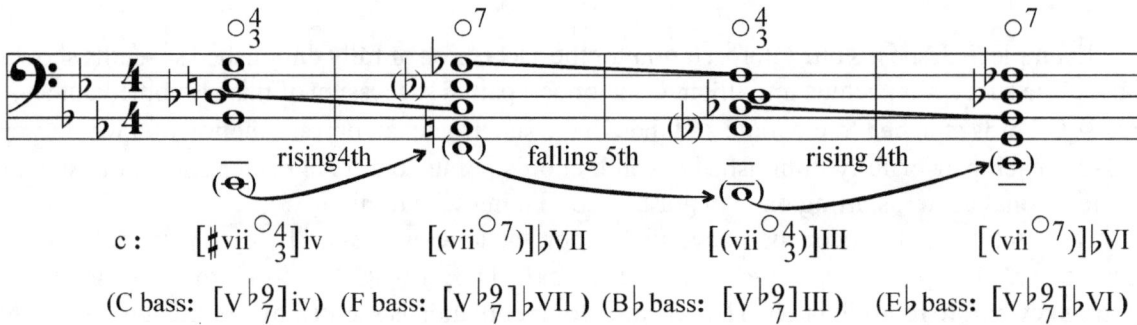

Type IV: Augmented 6th Chords of the Tonal Melodic Dominant (TMD) Family (Triads)

Augmented 6th chords of the TMD family all contain within their respective chord structures a lowered or raised third. The altered third is the result of inflecting scale degree 2 of the mode. Altering the chord third of any TMD triad determines the voice leading for scale degree 2 when the chord resolves to the tonic.

Although the altered third changes the basic structure of the diminished triad, the only possible position for the TMD triad remains its first inversion. (As we have learned, adding a major or minor 3rd above the chord fifth of the TMD triad produces either a ø⁷ or a o⁷. The addition of the chord seventh softens the tritone dissonance of the triad, enabling the TMD ø⁷ and TMD o⁷ to be used in all four positions.)

Raising or lowering the third of the TMD triad (or seventh) produces an augmented 6th or diminished 3rd within the chord structure. In both its triad and seventh-chord dispositions, the intervals of the augmented 6th or diminished 3rd contained within the altered TMD seek to expand or contract into the root or third of the tonic triad (scale degrees 1 and 3). In other terms, scale degree ♭2 moves to 1; scale degree ♯2 proceeds to 3.

Example 5–37 outlines the basic voice leading and disposition for the altered TMD triad. For voicing the chord with four parts, double the fifth (scale degree 4) and avoid doubling the root (scale degree 7) or third (scale degree ♭2 or ♯2). When the altered TMD triad (or seventh) addresses the tonic triad, both the augmented 6th and diminished 10th resolve to the octave while the diminished 3rd moves to the unison.

Examples 5–37a and 37c instance the "doubly diminished" TMD in first inversion, formed by lowering scale degree 2, the chord third. Examples 5–37c and 37d are in the parallel minor. Examples 5–37b and 37d illustrate the "raised diminished" triad, created by raising scale degree 2. (Parentheses around d10 and ♯2 in 5–37d remind us that the true interval between the chord third and fifth is D♯/F rather than the notated E♭/F.)

Example 5–37: ♭2 to 1 and ♯2 to 3

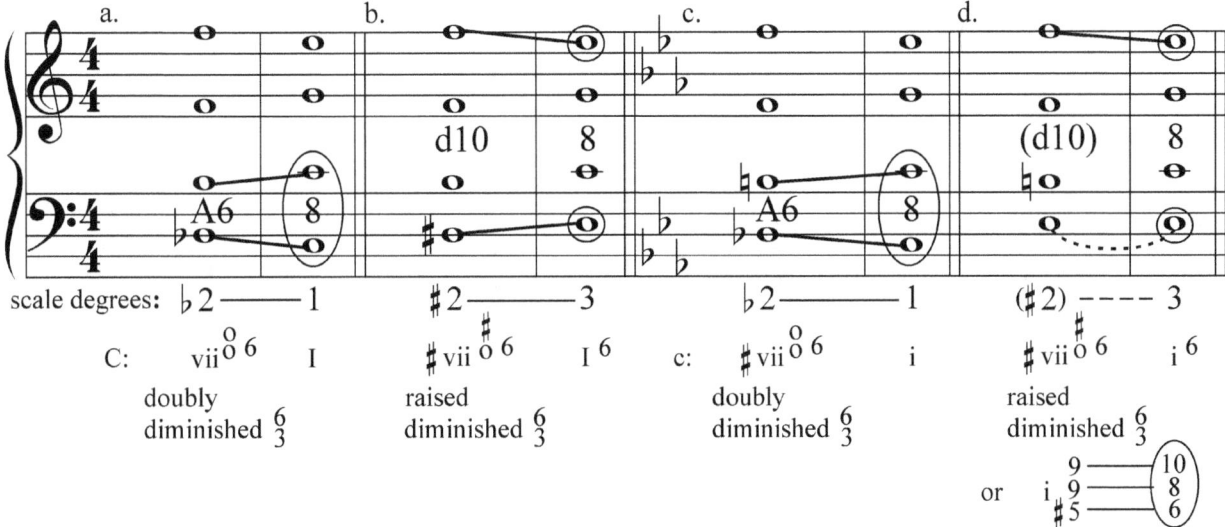

For the chord symbol, we use a composite sign to represent the quality of the altered diminished triad (or seventh). The lower part of the composite sign represents the chord in its original form as either a
(1) diminished triad (example 5–37),
(2) half-diminished seventh (examples 5–38, 39, 40), or,
(3) fully diminished seventh (examples 5–41, 42, 43, 44).

The upper part of the sign indicates the alteration of the chord third, which is either
(1) lowered (in examples 5–37a and 37c, a superscript circle above a superscript circle), or,
(2) raised (in examples 5–37b and 37d, a superscript *sharp* above a superscript circle).

The alteration of the TMD chord intensifies the approach to the tonic, the chord of resolution. In example 5–37b, the diminished 10th within the raised diminished TMD resolves to an octave, resulting in a tonic triad with a doubled third.

Notice that in the minor mode, as shown in 5–37d, scale degrees ♯2 and 3 are enharmonic equivalents. This equivalency renders the raised diminished TMD triad less effective in minor than in major because its chord third is also scale degree 3.

However, if the raised diminished TMD triad is used minor, then its chord third should be correctly misspelled as scale degree 3. For example, in c minor, scale degree ♯2 is D♯, whereas scale 3 is E♭. Hence, the chord third of the raised diminished TMD is spelled as E♭ rather than as D♯.

Since both the raised diminished TMD triad and the tonic express the same chord third in the bass, it becomes possible to use apparent chord terminology (5–37d). Here, the B♮ and F above the E♭ bass are nonharmonic tones resolving to those of the real chord, the tonic triad.

Augmented 6th Chords of the Tonal Melodic Dominant (TMD) Family (Seventh Chords)

The next seven examples demonstrate different types of altered half-diminished and fully diminished seventh chords, all of which have either lowered or raised chord thirds, and all of which contain either doubly diminished or raised diminished triads.

In example 5–38, we have the doubly half-diminished TMD in all four chord positions in C major. Within each expression of the chord, the diminished 10th contracts to the octave and the augmented 6th expands to the octave. (The diminished 3rd contracts to the unison.) Scale degree ♭2 resolves to 1.

In terms of voice leading, the third inversion of the chord in 5–38d stands apart from the other three positions. The doubly half-diminished TMD resolves to a $\genfrac{}{}{0pt}{}{6}{4}$ chord, an apparent tonic. The voice leading produces an incorrect doubling of the root (scale degree 1) in the chord of resolution. However, *any chord, approached correctly, can add subsequently the preferred doubling before proceeding to the next chord.* Example 5–38d works around the problem by taking a chordal skip down to scale degree 5 (G) in the alto voice, forming the doubled chord fifth for the second-inversion tonic.

Example 5–38: ♭2 to 1

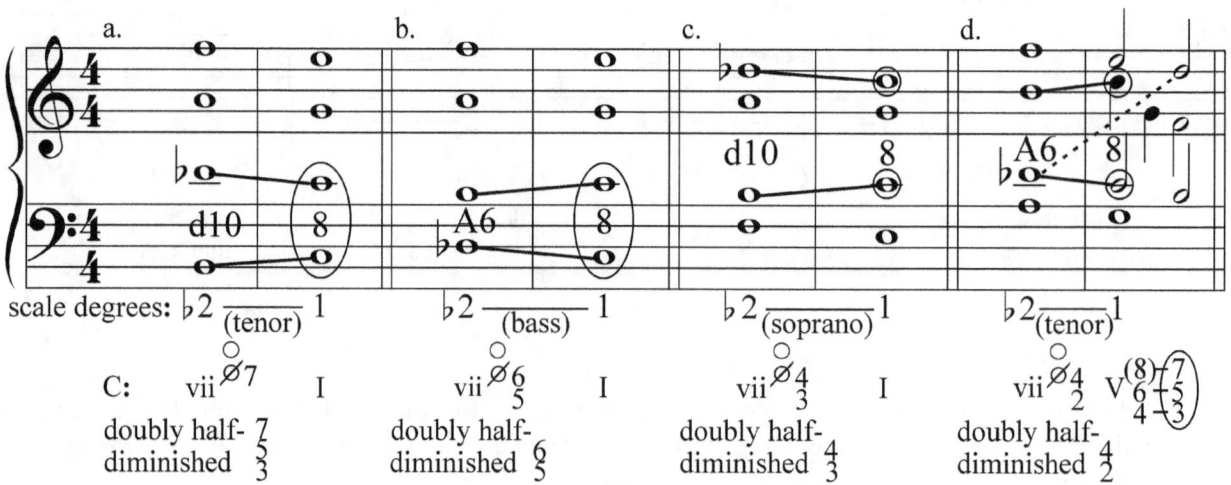

Example 5–39: ♭2 to 1

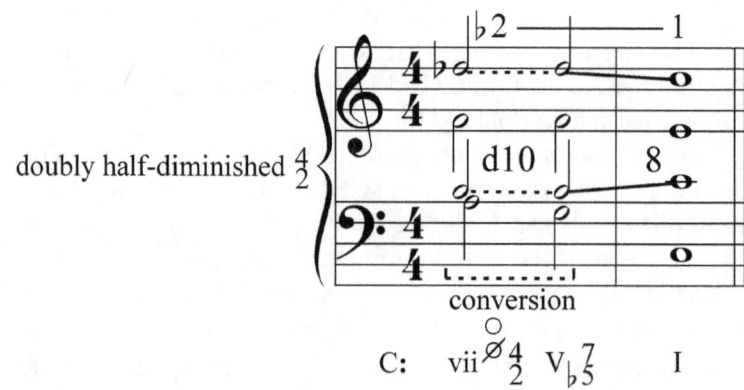

Example 5–39 above places the doubly half-diminished TMD within the context of a conversion dominant as an alternative to voice leading the third inversion of the doubly half-diminished TMD into an apparent tonic $^6_4$, as in 5–38d. For the conversion dominant in 5–39, the bass drops down one whole step (A to G) to form the chord of the dominant seventh, root position, lowered fifth variety (G B D♭ F). Ultimately, scale degree ♭2 moves to 1 and the diminished 10th contracts to the octave.

Examples 5–40 through 44 exhibit the voice-leading procedures outlined in examples 5–38 and 39 above within the context of the half-diminished TMD with a raised third, the fully diminished TMD with a lowered third, and the fully diminished TMD with a raised third.

Examples 5–40, 42, and 44 show the altered TMD with the raised third resolving to scale degree 3 (scale degrees ♯2 to 3); examples 5–41 and 43 display the altered TMD with the lowered third resolving to scale degree 1 (scale degrees ♭2 to 1). (In minor, the half-diminished TMD is not used because it contains variable ♯6 as its chord seventh. Altering the third of the TMD ⌀7 does not make the chord more practicable.)

Example 5–40: ♯2 to 3

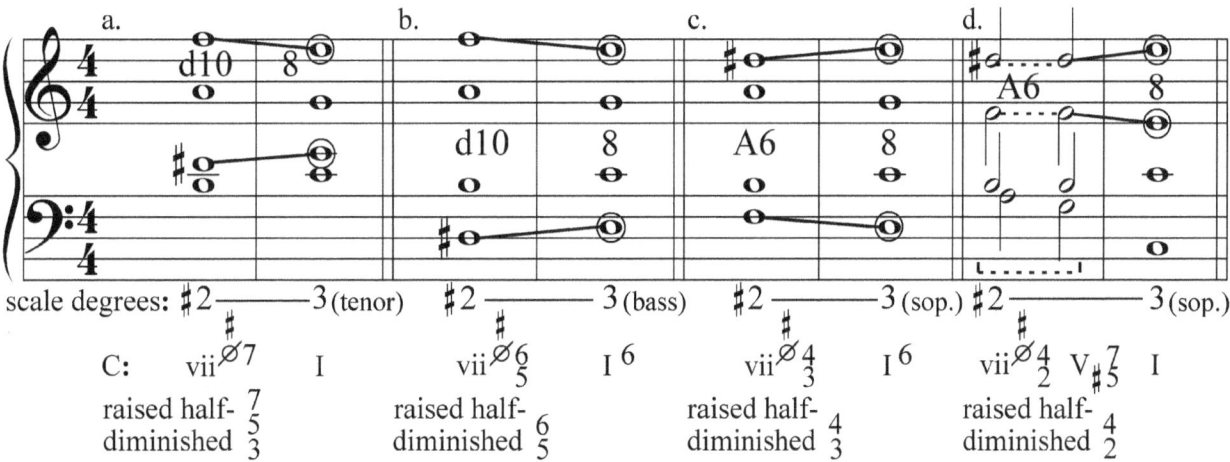

In example 5–41, the lowered third of the doubly fully diminished TMD proceeds to scale degree 1. The basic chord is borrowed from the parallel minor.

Example 5–41: ♭2 to 1

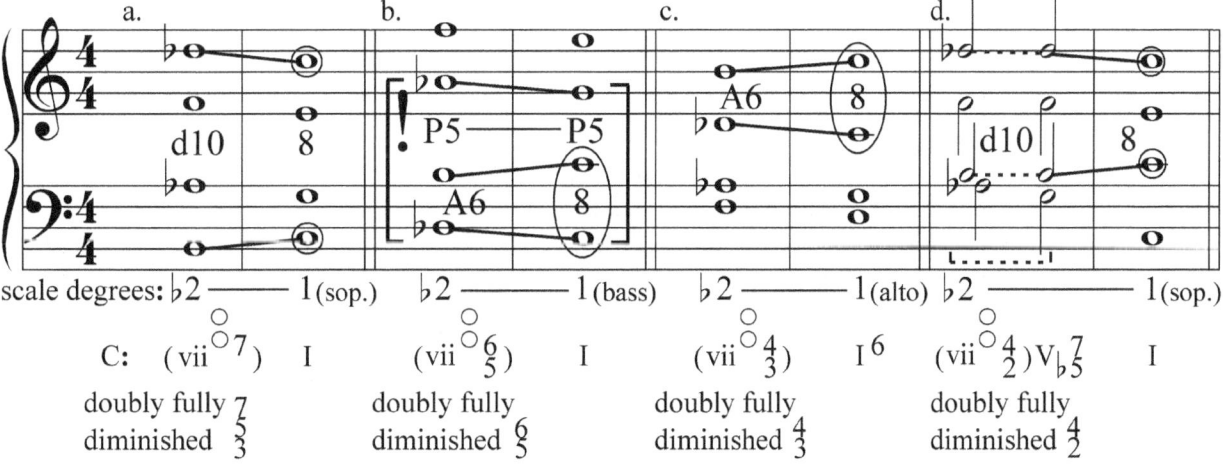

114   Chapter 5   Degree-Inflected Chords

Notice the parallel 5ths between the bass and alto voices in example 5–41b above (and in example 5–43b below). Usually such 5ths can be avoided by inverting the disposition of the 5th (producing a perfect 4th, as in examples 5–41a, 41c, and 41d). However, in this instance, the bottom note of the 5th is in the bass. The most acceptable way to use the first inversion of this chord is to bury the upper note of the 5th in one of the inner voices, as in 5–41b (and 5–43b). This strategy covers the 5ths with 10ths in the outer voices (D♭/F to C/E or C/E♭).

Examples 5–42 presents the raised fully diminished seventh. The principal voice leading for the chord takes scale degree ♯2 up to 3 (D♯ to E), a motion displayed earlier in example 5–40 above. We shall soon see why this chord is rarely used in the parallel minor (example 5–44). Both the diminished 10th and the augmented 6th of the altered TMD move to an octave on E, producing a doubled chord third for the C-major tonic.

Example 5–42: ♯2 to 3

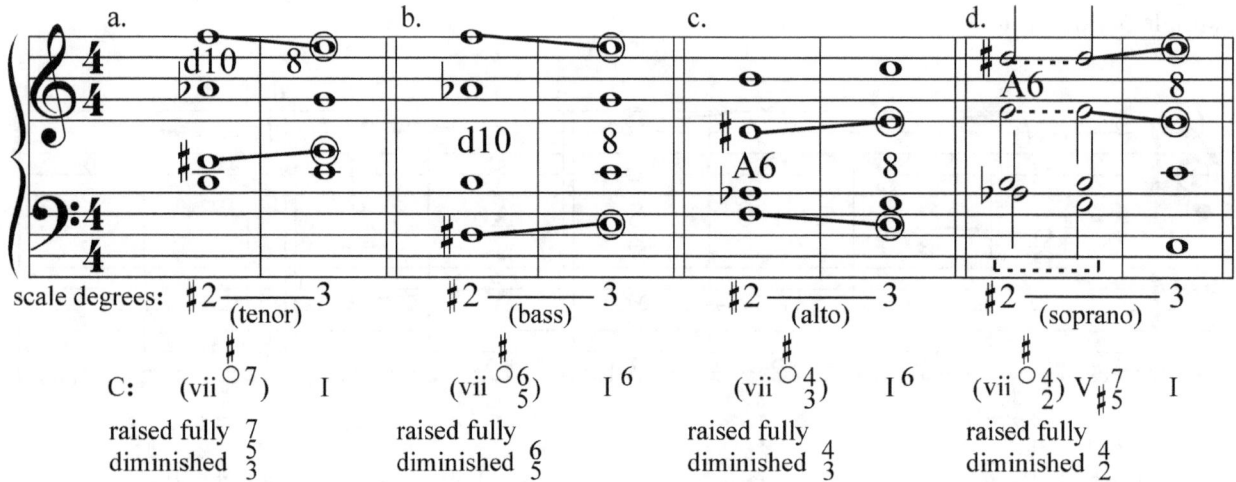

Example 5–43 gives us the doubly fully diminished TMD in c minor. The parallel 5ths seen in 5–41b above are duplicated below in 5–43b. Ultimately, a perfect 5th above scale degree ♭2 is formed when using either (♭6) in major or variable ♭6 in minor as the chord seventh of the doubly diminished TMD.

Example 5–43: ♭2 to 1

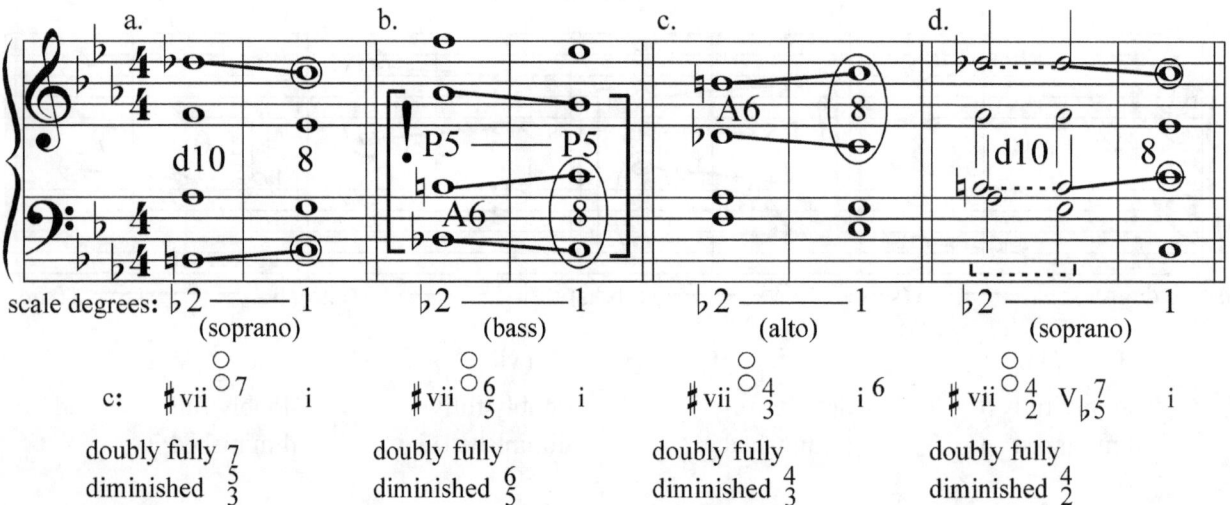

Earlier, example 5–37d illustrated the questionable use of the raised diminished TMD triad in minor. The inherent difficulties of the triad in minor are also found its seventh-chord counterpart: the raised fully diminished TMD.

As we have observed, scale degrees ♯2 and 3 are enharmonic equivalents. (In c minor, D♯ is spelled as E♭.) This equivalency renders the underlying leading-tone triad less effective in minor than in major because its raised third is also scale degree 3. Adding a seventh to the triad cannot erase the basic weakness of the chord. (However, the unequal 5ths between the alto and tenor in 5–37 can be eliminated by placing the chord seventh, A♭, in the alto voice. Examples 5–44a and 44b below take the chord seventh in the alto.)

In any case, if the seventh-chord version is used in minor, then its third should be correctly misspelled as scale degree 3. As in example 5–44, the chord third of the raised fully diminished TMD is spelled as E♭ rather than as D♯ because the chord third of the tonic C-minor triad is E♭, scale degree 3.

Example 5–44: uncommon in minor

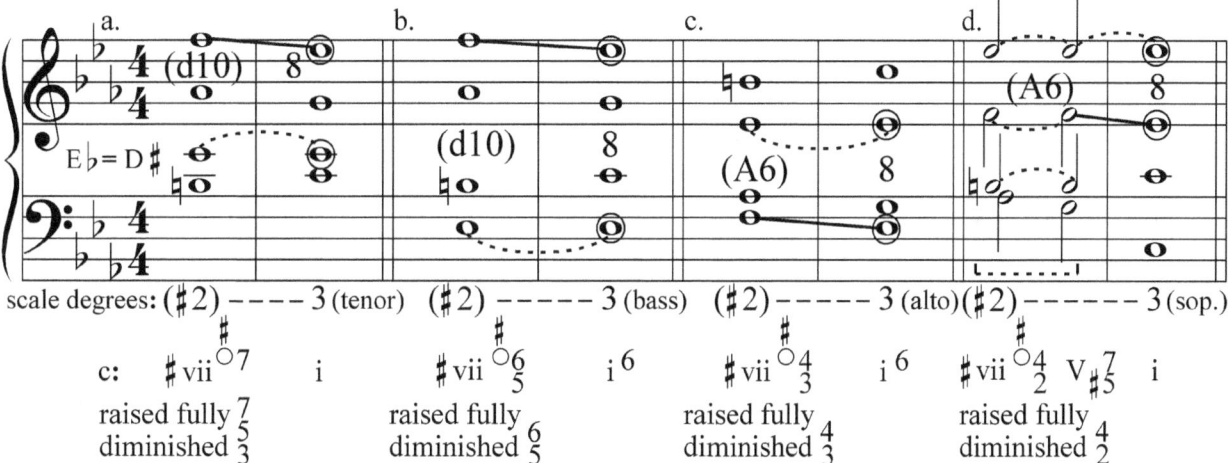

Type V: The "Ethnic" Augmented 6th Chord

This section examines a type of augmented 6th chord that *sounds* like some form of dominant seventh in root position. Marked by the status of its fifth, there are four configurations of the chord: either the fifth is omitted, unaltered, lowered, or raised. The various dispositions of the chord are most commonly named after the countries of Italy, Germany, and France, despite the fact that "the Italian 6th," "the German 6th," and "the French 6th" are not unique to these nationalities. Nor do they exhibit Italian, German, or French characteristics. We shall refer to these chords as ethnic augmented 6ths to distinguish them from other degree-inflected chords that also contain the augmented 6th. (Occasionally, the German 6th is referred to as "the Swiss 6th" when the chord resolves to a major tonic in $^6_4$ position. See below, p. 121.)

The ethnic augmented 6th chord intensifies the way to the dominant or to the cadential $^6_4$; it may also proceed to a passing tonic $^6_4$. All ethnic augmented 6ths contain scale degrees 1, ♭6 or (♭6), and ♯4. The interval of the augmented 6th (or diminished 3rd) resolves to scale degree 5, either as the root of the dominant or as the chord fifth of the tonic. As we shall see in examples 5–46 and 5–47, when approaching a half cadence, the augmented 6th is often understood as an altered CLT chord (measures 3 and 11, beat 3).

Traditionally, the ethnic augmented 6th is identified from its *written* rather than sounding root. The written root is associated with scale degrees of the supertonic and subdominant. Each chord symbol carries an inverted figured-bass description according to which element of the written chord appears in the bass. Depending on the location of the written root, Italian, German, and French augmented 6ths are regarded as altered versions of IV$^6_3$, IV$^6_5$, and II$^4_3$ respectively.

116   Chapter 5 Degree-Inflected Chords

Musicians find the geographical names easier to use than the names expressing chord roots on II and IV. And yet, the common practice of theoreticians is to draw the figured bass from the written position and attach it to the geographical names, resulting in the following notational compromise: the Italian $^6_3$, the German $^6_5$, and the French $^4_3$. (The countries are typically abbreviated as It., Ger., and Fr.)

Later in this chapter, example 5–59 compares our notation for representing the ethnic augmented 6th to both the traditional approach that combines Roman numerals II and IV with the figured bass drawn from the written position and the compromise that combines the geographical names with the traditional figured bass.

The Contrapuntal Origin of the Ethnic Augmented 6th

As we observed in Chapter 3, scale degree ♯4 can be a chord member of either an applied THD/CLT or TMD/CLT chord. In example 5–45a, an applied THD/CLT chord on beat 1 of measure 2 is supported by ♯4 in the bass, the leading tone of the dominant. The introduction of ♯4 intensifies the upward motion in the bass from ii$^6_5$ to V. The resolution from scale degrees ♯4 to 5 is by half step (from F♯ to G).

Example 5–45b displays the Phrygian cadence. Supporting a subdominant triad, scale degree ♭6 (A♭) intensifies the downward approach to V, the THD. Again, we have a half-step resolution to scale degree 5 (from A♭ to G). (The Phrygian cadence is discussed in *Finding The Right Pitch II*, Chapter 6, pp. 130–131.)

Example 5–45c illustrates the result of combining the contrapuntal passing motions of examples 5–45a and 45b. The chord is called the Italian augmented 6th (IA6). The traditional description of the chord identifies scale degree ♯4 (F♯) as the written root and presents accordingly the following combination of symbols: ♯IV$^6_3$.

This text starts from the premise that the structure of any ethnic augmented 6th chord stands upon the *sounding* rather than written root of the chord, namely, ♭6 or (♭6). As stated above, the ethnic augmented 6th chord sounds like a root-position dominant seventh yielding four possible configurations: either with an omitted fifth, an unaltered fifth, a lowered fifth, or a raised fifth. All versions of the chord are built on scale degree ♭6 or (♭6). (For instance, in c minor, the sounding root of any ethnic augmented 6th is A♭.)

When the sounding position of the chord inverts, combining the geographical names with traditional figured bass drawn from the written position adds an unnecessary level of complexity to the chord symbol. Our study of the ethnic augmented 6th avoids confusing complications in the terminology whenever practicable while providing a few refinements to the traditional and geographical descriptions.

Example 5–45c displays the IA6 as an X-chord of an SHP supporting a tone-embellishing melodic succession, a TEMB. The IA6 can also be interpreted as an altered CLT chord.

Example 5–45: the SHP/TEMB with the IA6 as an X-chord

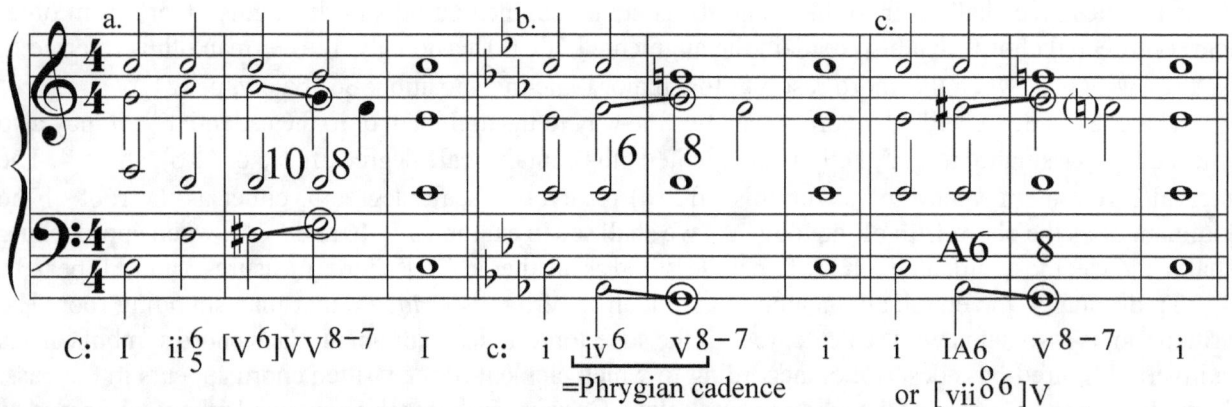

The Italian Augmented 6th (IA6)

In 5–45c above, the sounding root of the Italian augmented 6th (IA6) is A♭. Since the IA6 does not have a chord fifth, doubling the third (scale degree 1) is the best option in four voices. Avoid doubling ♭6 and ♯4, as they are both chromatically active tones. The augmented 6th of the chord takes the expected resolution to scale degree 5, the doubled root of the dominant.

As mentioned above, the chord can also be considered an altered CLT chord, specifically: a doubly diminished TMD in first inversion applied to V. One of the principal functions for the augmented 6th chord is to strengthen the cadences at the ends of phrases or form sections.

Serving as an applied CLT chord, the IA6 in examples 5–46, and 47 produces a cadence *in* V rather than on V. Examples 5–46 and 47 show Beethoven's use of the IA6 in the Bagatelle No. 1 in G Minor, Op. 119. The opening 16-measures constitutes a parallel double period with three contrapuntal half cadences in V. Phrases one and three are parallel, as are phrases two and four.

The antecedent period (measures 1–8), which contains an interruption of its melodic and harmonic framework, shows an incomplete basic melodic progression, a BMP from scale degrees 5 (D) to 7 (F♯). A prolongation of the dominant supports the juncture between phrases a and b (measures 4–5). In measure 8, the leading tone substitutes for scale degree 2 (A in parentheses), the missing chord fifth of the interrupting V. The descent from D becomes D–C–B–A–F♯ instead of D–C–B–A–A. The structural value of the D in the top voice at the beginning of phrase a is retained into the beginning of phrase b, despite its absence from measures 2 and 3. (D remains in an inner voice throughout phrase a.)

Notice that the IA6 in measure 4 has the same contrapuntal prolonging function as that of the [V^6]V in measure 7. The augmented 6th of the IA6 at the end of phrase a (E♭/C♯) expands to a D octave, whereas the diminished 5th of the [V^6]V at the end of phrase b (C♯/G) contracts to a 3rd. Beethoven animates the rhythm in phrase b with eighth notes and uses dissonant and consonant suspensions to drive the harmony to the interruption in measure 8.

Example 5–46: Beethoven, Bagatelle No. 1 in G Minor, Op. 119, measures 1–8

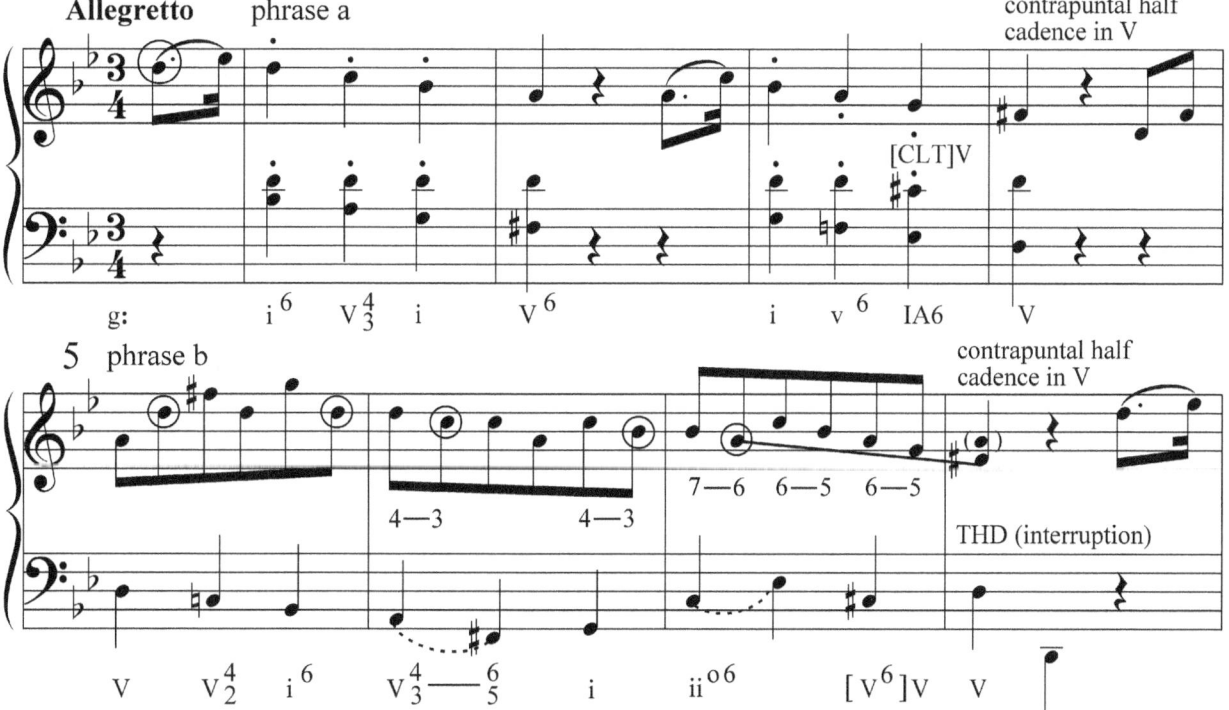

118   Chapter 5 Degree-Inflected Chords

The consequent period (5–47, measures 9–16) is a modified repeat of the antecedent with only two differences: the ornamental figure on beat 3 of measure 10 and the placement of the THD on beat 2 of measure 15. The corresponding place in measure 7 situates the [V^6]V on beat 3, which allows the interrupting V to fall on beat 1 of the next measure. In measure 15, the main-level THD is moved forward one quarter and held for two quarters to slow down the harmonic rhythm and to set up the full cadence in measure 16. The double period ends with a harmonic perfect authentic cadence.

As in the antecedent period, the consequent shows a stepwise melodic descent (circled notes) from scale degrees 5 (D) to 7 (F♯). Once again, the leading tone substitutes for scale degree 2 (A in parentheses), the missing chord fifth of the main-level THD. However, since the double period closes in the tonic, the melodic structure pushes onward to scale degree 1 (G), bringing the BMP to completion.

Ultimately, the first sixteen measures of the Bagatelle No. 1 consists of descending contrapuntal motions in the bass between tonic and dominant chords. The X-chord in both the antecedent and consequent periods, ii^{o6}, supports scale degree 2 on beat 1 of measures 7 and 15. Within each period, a six-measure tonic prolongation of a higher order (measures 1–6 and 9–14) precedes the arrival of the X-chord. Although the cadential dominants are in root position (measures 4, 8, 12, and 15), the internal dominants within each phrase are all expressed as CLT chords prolonging the tonic.

In each period, the motion from the first-inversion tonic to the root-position tonic (measures 1–6 and 9–14) supports a melodic descent from scale degrees 5 to 3. An incomplete SHP supports the antecedent period: i–ii^{o6}–[V^6]V–V (as interruption). A complete SHP supports the consequent period: i–ii^{o6}–V–I.

The placement of the IA6 in the G-minor Bagatelle effects the first and third contrapuntal half cadences in V, each instance functioning as an altered TMD in first inversion (E♭ G C♯) applied to V (D). The motion into V prolongs the chord across the a and b phrase of each period. The prolonged V, however, takes place within the larger context of a contrapuntal prolongation of the way from i^6 to i($^5_3$) (measures 1–6 and 9–14).

Example 5–47: Beethoven, Bagatelle No. 1 in G Minor, Op. 119, measures 9–16

Example 5–48 shows some of the other contrapuntal circumstances in which the IA6 occurs. Most commonly, the IA6 follows the expression of the subdominant chord, which is why the traditional view interprets the chord as some type of chromatic subdominant rooted on scale degree ♯4 (F♯).

The IA6 often follows either IV^6 or iv^6, as in 5–48. The bass proceeds from the subdominant to (♭6) in major or ♭6 in minor. When the triad of the subdominant is minor, its chord third prepares the root of the IA6 as a common tone (A♭ in 5–48d). In the alto voice, the motion from scale degrees 4 to 5 is intensified with the introduction of ♯4, a chromatic passing tone forming the augmented 6th above (♭6) or ♭6 (A♭/F♯). Scale degree ♯4 moves up to scale degree 5: F♯ proceeds to G.

Example 5–48a displays a descending chromatic bass (C–B–B♭–A–A♭–G) supporting four passing chords that prolong the way from I to V: V$^6_5$–[(vii°$^4_3$)]IV–IV^6–IV6–IA6. The IA6, which grows out of the IV^6, effects the half-step resolution down to V: A♭ proceeds to G. Thus, the augmented 6th, A♭/F♯, expands to an octave on G. The [(vii°$^4_3$)]IV provides chromatic passing tones for the soprano and bass. Ultimately, the outer voices descend in parallel 10ths while the inner voices move upwards.

Example 5–48b omits the first two passing chords of 5–48a, an omission that alters the status of the remaining IV^6 and IA6, which now become *extended* passing chords between I and the cadential $^6_4$. In examples 5–48b and 48d, the IV^6 assumes status as the X-chord of an SHP supporting a tone-embellishing melodic succession, a TEMB (C–C–C–C–B–C). However, in examples 5–48a and 48c, there is no X-chord. A contrapuntal prolongation of the dominant from its first inversion to root position sustains a prolongation of the way from scale degrees 2 to 7 in the top voice. Therefore, a BHP (I–V–I in 48a and i–V–i in 48c) supports a melodic descent from scale degrees 3 to 1, a BMP.

Example 5–48: contrapuntal contexts for the IA6

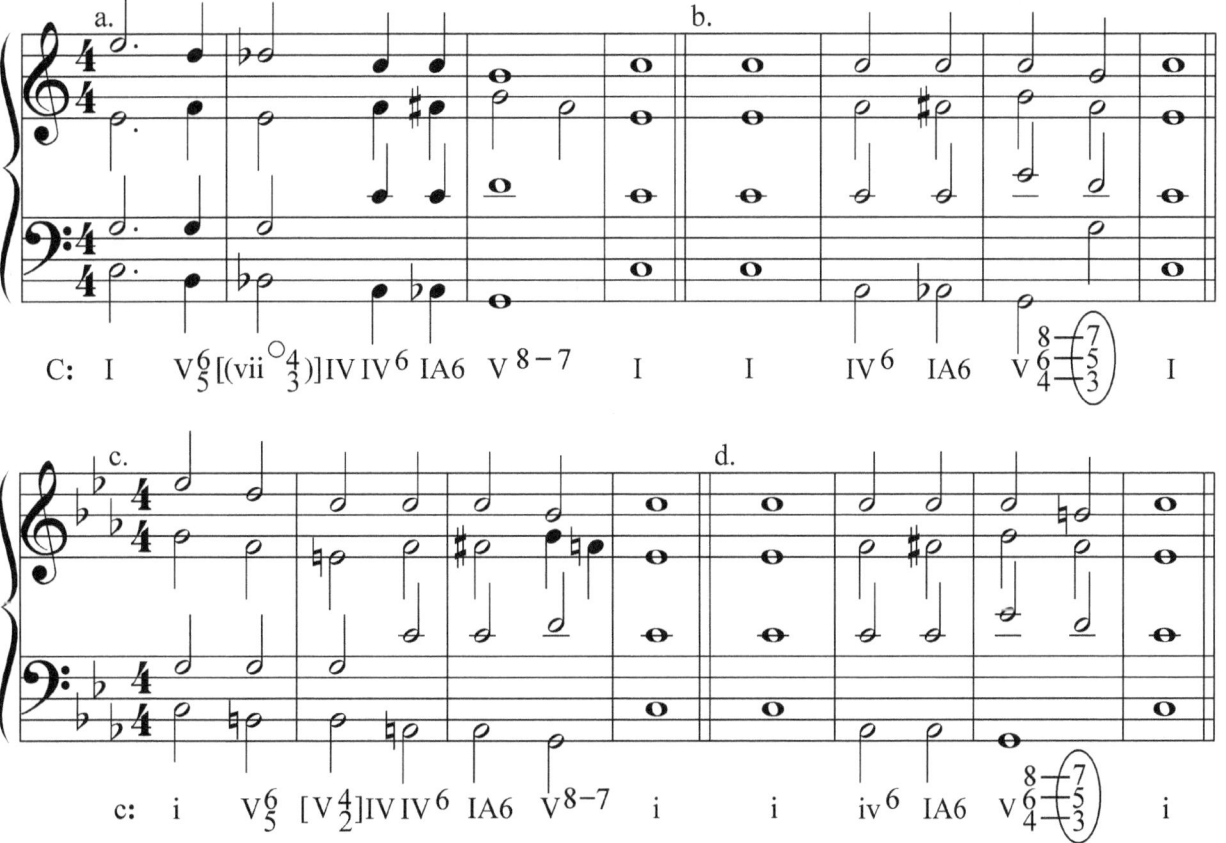

The leading tone in measure 3 (B) of examples 5–48a and 48c above is significant because it substitutes for scale degree 2 (D). Only after the arrival of the substitute leading tone can the C bring closure to the progression by assuming its place within the melodic structure as part of the tonic chord (5–48a and 48c). The earlier C supported by the IV^6 and IA6 is not part of that melodic structure; rather, its sole function is to prolong the motion between two different dispositions of the dominant, namely, V$^6_5$ and V$^{8-7}$.

The German Augmented 6th and the German Doubly Augmented 6th (GA6 and GDA6)

Both the German augmented 6th (GA6) and its enharmonic respelling as the German doubly augmented 6th (GDA6) sound exactly like a dominant seventh with all chord tones present, that is: a major triad with a minor 7th from root to seventh. The chord fifth is scale degree (♭3) in major and 3 in minor.

In c minor, the interval from ♭6 to ♯4, A♭ to F♯, is an augmented 6th, which is enharmonically a minor 7th, A♭ to G♭. Spelled as a dominant seventh, the tones A♭ C E♭ G♭ can be interpreted as V^7 of D♭, the Phrygian supertonic of C major or c minor. (This possibility was discussed earlier, pp. 99–102.)

In example 5–49, this sounding dominant seventh becomes the GA6 by simply respelling the G♭ as F♯. The GA6 is frequently prepared by a chord of the subdominant or supertonic. As shown in examples 5–49a and 49c, the GA6 may yield parallel 5ths when resolving directly to V. These 5ths are permissible when involving one of the inner voices and usually avoided when placed between the outer voices. Connecting the GA6 to the cadential $^6_4$ breaks up the parallel 5ths (examples 5–49d) but also produces a notational issue when the chord resolves to a major tonic.

Example 5–49: the GA6 and the GDA6

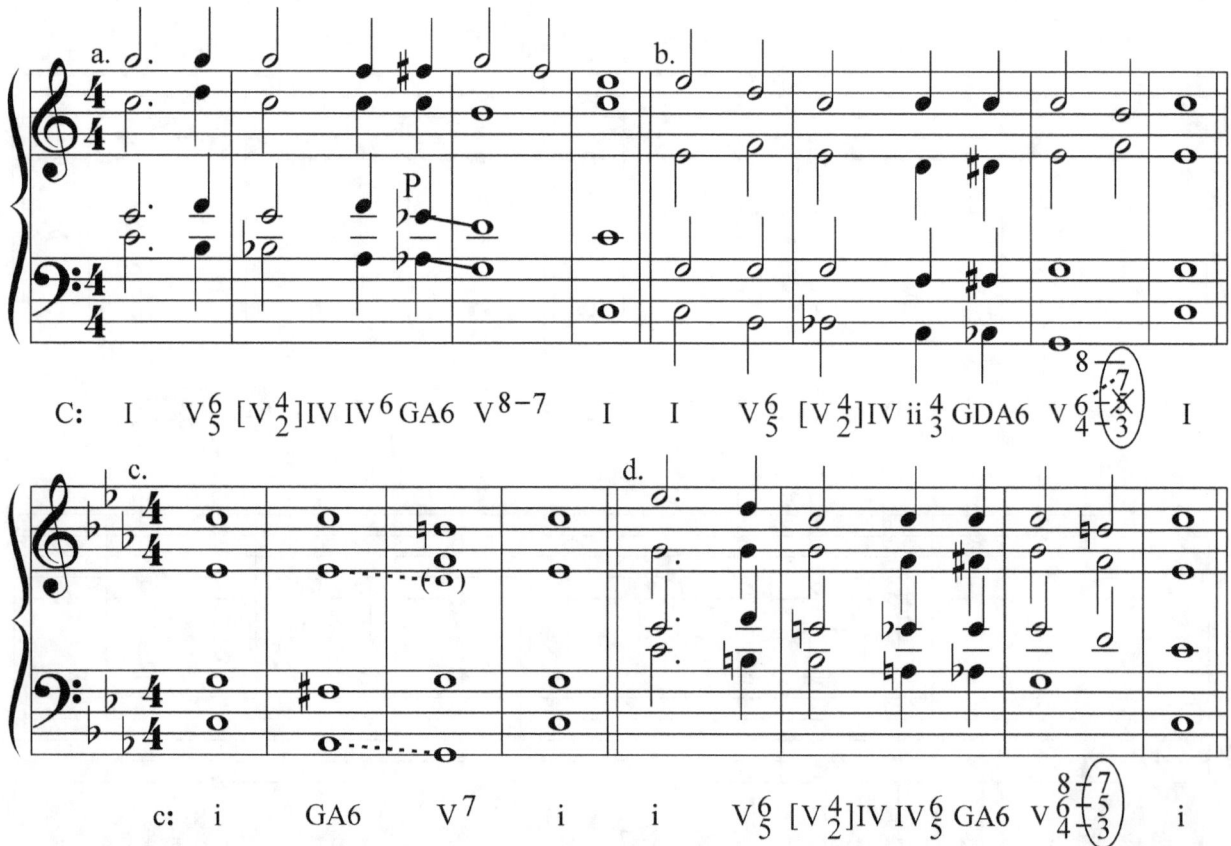

If the GA6 leads to a major triad of the tonic, as in 5–49b above, then the chord fifth is often respelled one pitch name lower to produce a doubly augmented 4th above the root. In other words, the chord fifth, scale degree (♭3), is written as ♯2. Thus, in C major, E♭ becomes D♯, a doubly augmented 4th above A♭. Respelling (♭3) as ♯2 produces an ascending chromatic resolution from D♯ to E, intensifies the motion to the major tonic, and avoids the awkward succession from E♭ to E♮. The chord is often referred to as the "augmented 6th with the doubly augmented 4th" and occasionally as the "Swiss 6th."

We prefer the name German doubly augmented 6th, the GDA6. When the GA6 proceeds to a minor tonic, the chord is not respelled as a GDA6 because it shares a common tone with the chord of resolution: the chord fifth of the GA6 becomes the third of the minor tonic. In c minor, the fifth of the GA6, E♭, is also the third of the tonic triad.

The traditional view of the GDA6 interprets the chord as a chromatic version of the supertonic seventh in second inversion: in C major, D♯ F♯ A♭ C, with A♭ in the bass. However, for us, the chord is A♭ C D♯ F♯; its operational interval resolves to scale degree 5 as the chord fifth of the major tonic.

The French Augmented 6th (FA6)

The French augmented 6th sounds like a dominant seventh chord with a lowered fifth, that is, a whole-tone dominant. Spelled as a degree-inflected dominant seventh, the tones A♭ C E♭♭ G♭ can be interpreted as the $V^7_{♭5}$ of D♭. As an altered THD with a lowered fifth, the chord intensifies the motion to scale degree 1 (D♭). In example 5–50, this sounding dominant seventh becomes the FA6 by respelling the G♭ as F♯ and E♭♭ as D. The FA6 intensifies the motion to scale degree 5 of the main-level key.

Example 5–50: the FA6

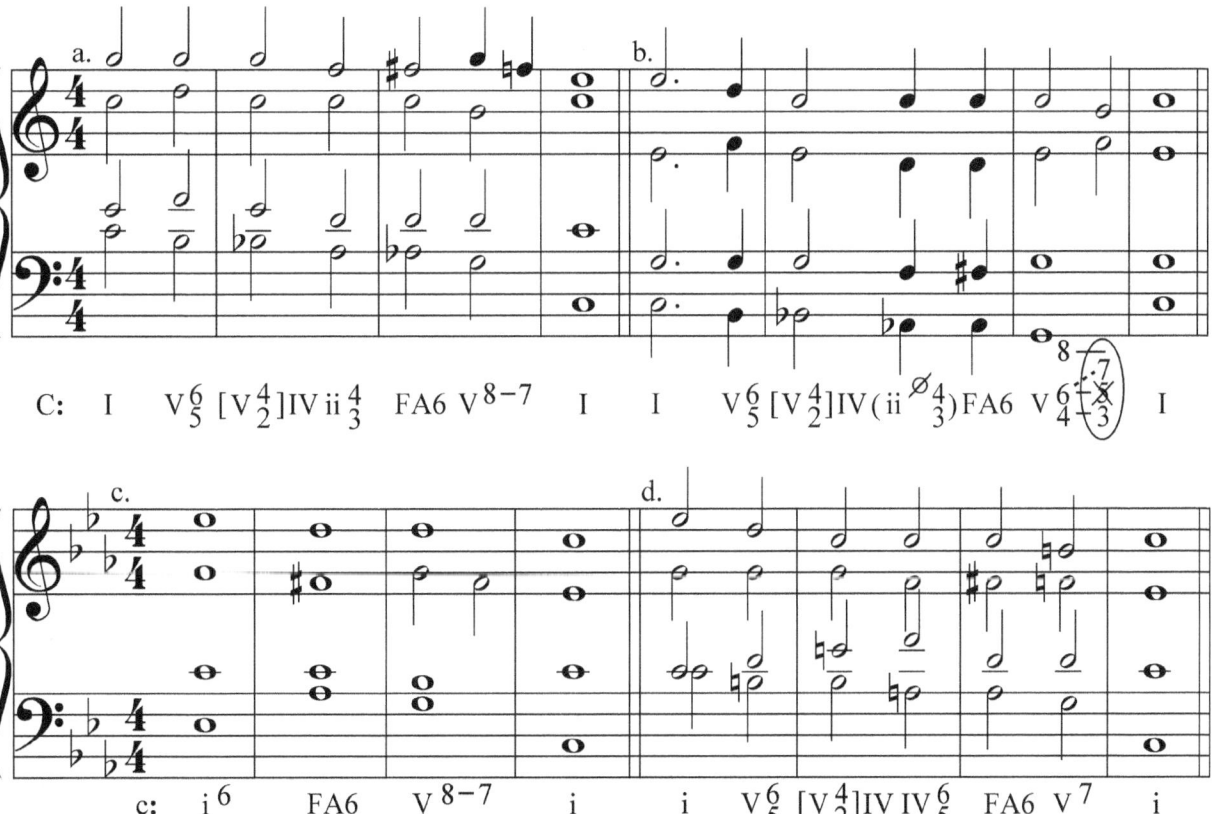

As with the GDA6, the traditional view of the FA6 interprets the chord as a chromatic version of the supertonic in second inversion: in C major, D F♯ A♭ C (with A♭ in the bass). For us, the chord is A♭ C D F♯; its operational interval resolves to scale degree 5 as either the root of the dominant or chord fifth of the tonic. The FA6 connects easily to the V because the two chords share a common tone: scale degree 2 is the chord fifth of both the FA6 and the dominant.

Example 5–50 above presents various dispositions and uses of the FA6. As in examples 5–48 and 5–49, 5–50a, 50b, and 50d display descending chromatic basses prolonging the way from I to V. The FA6 is frequently prepared by a chord of the subdominant or supertonic. In 5–50c, the FA6 proceeds directly from i^6 and functions as an X-chord supporting scale degree 2 in the top voice. An SHP supports a BMP from scale degree 3. (Both the IA6 in 5–45c and the GA6 in 5–49c serve as X-chords supporting a TEMB in the top voice, that is, C–C–B–C.) In 5–50d, the FA6 resolves to V^7 instead of V^{8-7}, contracting the resolution of the augmented 6th from an octave to a 7th: A♭/F♯ resolves to G/F♮ instead of G/G.

The Exceptional Augmented 6th (EA6)

The least common ethnic augmented 6th sounds like a dominant seventh chord with a raised fifth, that is, a whole-tone dominant. Spelled as a degree-inflected dominant seventh, as in example 5–51a, A♭ C E G♭ can be interpreted as the $V^7_{\sharp 5}$ of D♭. As an altered THD, the chord of resolution takes a doubled third, intensifying the motion to scale degree 3 of the mode. Example 5–51b transforms this altered dominant seventh into an ethnic augmented 6th by respelling the G♭ as F♯; so configured, the chord intensifies the motion to scale degree 5.

Example 5–51: the EA6

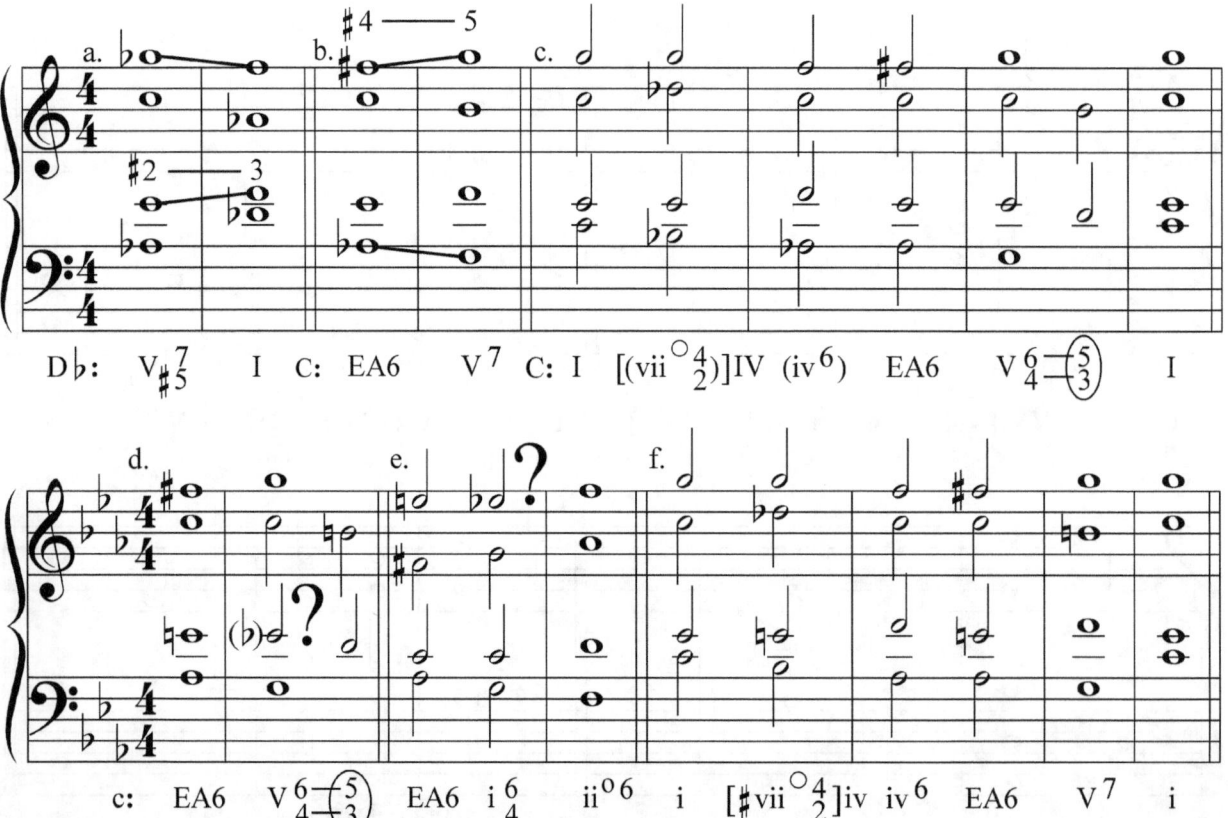

The tone of resolution distinguishes the altered chords of the dominant family from those of the ethnic augmented 6th. The interval of the augmented 6th (or diminished 3rd) in the altered formations of both the THD and TMD moves to either scale degree 1 or 3 (the root or third of the tonic triad), whereas the same interval in the ethnic augmented 6th proceeds to scale degree 5 (the root of the THD or fifth of the tonic).

Since there is no generally accepted name for the ethnic augmented 6th with a raised fifth and because of its limited presence in both the theoretical and musical literature, the term "exceptional" augmented 6th (EA6) seems appropriate. At the very least, our terminology avoids assigning a descriptor of nationality.

As shown in 5–51b above, the EA6 connects easily to a V^7 with an omitted fifth. Examples 5–51c and 51f place the EA6 within the context of a descending bass. In both examples, the EA6 is preceded by iv$^6_4$, yielding two common tones between the two chords (bass and alto).

Resolving the EA6 to the cadential $^6_4$ presents no problems in major (5–51c); however, connecting the chord to a minor tonic in $^6_4$ position is dubious. Examples 5–51d and 51e demonstrate the EA6 resolving to the tonic $^6_4$ in c minor. The chord fifth of the EA6 is E♮; the third of the tonic is E♭. In 5–51d, moving from E♮ back to E♭ is melodically unproductive, although it does impart a mixture of major and minor modes. In 5–51e, the operation is pointless.

Inversions

Earlier in this chapter, we learned that the traditional understanding of the ethnic augmented 6th starts from the premise that the figured-bass description is based upon the location of the written root. Accordingly, the various formations of the chord are interpreted as altered versions of IV$^6_3$, IV$^6_5$, or II$^4_3$. When the chord inverts, the interval of the augmented 6th becomes a diminished 3rd. Some theoreticians refer to these inversions as "diminished 3rd chords" and change the figured bass to reflect which chord tone is in the bass *in relation to the written root*.

For instance, in example 5–52e, the F♯ of the GA6 in C major is in the bass. As the written root, F♯ stands a diminished 3rd below the written third, A♭. From the written root, the chord is F♯ A♭ C E♭. The traditional view interprets the GA6 in 5–52a as a Ger$^6_5$ or ♯IV$^6_5$ (A♭ C E♭ F♯). Therefore, when the chord inverts, as in 5–52e, it would be described as a Ger7, Ger$^{\circ}$3, or ♯IV^7 (F♯ A♭ C E♭).

Since we recognize the sounding root of the chord as A♭, the sounding position in 5–52d is that of a dominant seventh in $^4_2$ position. The diminished 3rd between F♯ and A♭ sounds like a major 2nd (that is, G♭ to A♭); the upper note of a sounding major 2nd suggests the root of a seventh chord with a minor 7th from its root to seventh (A♭ to G♭). Thus, the F♯ constitutes the sounding seventh of the chord. Our description of the chord places the sounding figured bass in parentheses and attaches it to the chord symbol.

Example 5–52: the sounding positions of the GA6

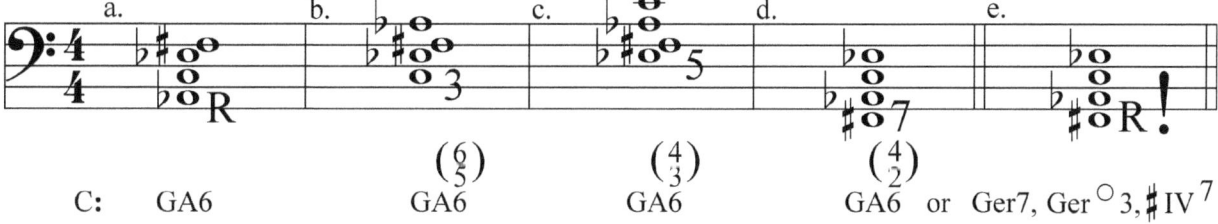

As we have seen in previous examples (5–45c, 49c, and 50c), it is possible for the ethnic augmented 6th to function as an X-chord *if its sounding root is in the bass*. However, we also know that when approaching a half cadence, the ethnic augmented 6th is often understood as an altered CLT chord applied to the cadential chord, usually the V.

Example 5–53 illustrates the alternative descriptions for the ethnic augmented 6th chord in its role as an altered CLT chord. We shall see that when the ethnic augmented 6th appears in *sounding* inversions (as in 5–52b, 52c, and 52d), the chord serves the function of contrapuntal prolongation and is unlikely to be an X-chord. (Those who follow the theories of Heinrich Schenker and Felix Salzer argue correctly that a contrapuntal chord supporting a structural melodic tone may become a contrapuntal-prolonging chord with added structural significance.)

Example 5–53: reinterpreting the ethnic augmented 6th as an altered CLT chord applied to V

The Augmented 6th as an Applied CLT Chord

Examples 5–54 and 55 are in C major and include a chord with an augmented 6th consisting of the tones A♭ C E♭ F♯ (or A♭ C D♯ F♯). In 5–54, the tones form the third inversion of the GA6 and GDA6. The GA6 is a chromatic passing chord between scale degrees 4 and 5 in the bass. But the chord can also be a doubly diminished TMD of V in root position, an applied chord. More importantly, beyond either interpretation, it is a chord of prolongation addressing the V within an SHP supporting

(1) a TEMB prolonging scale degree 5 (G–A♭–A♭–G–G) in 5–54a; and,
(2) a combination of a TEMB prolonging scale degree 3 (E–D–D♯–E) and a BMP moving through scale degrees 3, 2, 1 (E–D–C) in 5–54b.

The X-chord is the half-diminished supertonic (in first inversion) borrowed from the parallel minor.

Example 5–54: the GA6 in third inversion as a doubly diminished TMD applied to V

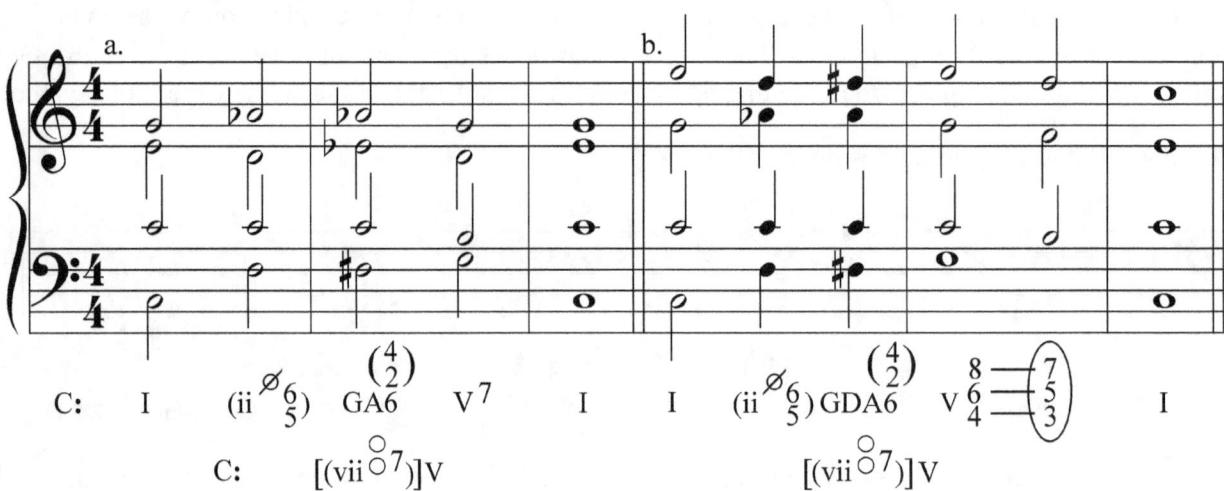

Based upon the progression in 5–54a, example 5–55 displays an SCP supporting
(1) a TEMB (G–A–A♭–G) prolonging scale degree 5;
(2) an incomplete BMP descending through scale degrees 5, 4, 3 (G–F–E). The progression is contrapuntal because the THD assumes the form of a CLT chord. (Remember, whenever the THD is inverted, a CLT chord is produced above either the leading tone, scale degree 2, or scale degree 4 in the bass.) An additional harmonic or contrapuntal progression is required to complete the melodic progression down from scale degree 3 to scale degree 1.

Although the tones of the GA6 are all present (A♭ C E♭ F♯), we describe the chord here as a doubly diminished TMD in second inversion applied to the V. The X-chord is the supertonic triad in first inversion.

Example 5–55: the SCP/TEMB-BMP

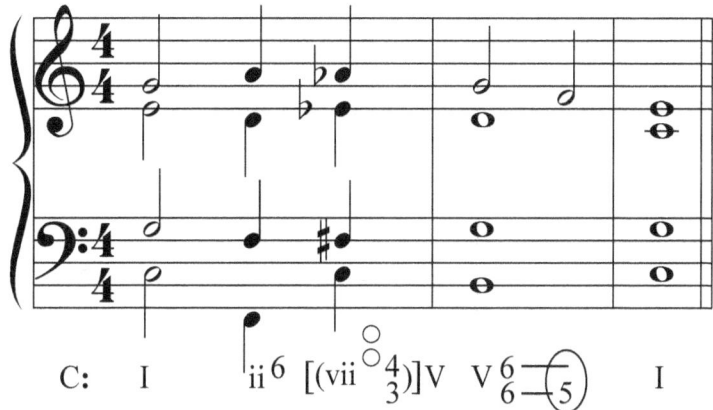

The Augmented 6th as a Pedal Embellishing Chord

As demonstrated in example 5–56, it is possible for the sounding first inversion of the GA6 (or the GDA6) to assume the status of an apparent chord prolonging the tonic through pedal embellishment. (The spelling of the GA6 and the GDA6 engenders a generic figured bass that contradicts the sounding position of the chord.)

Example 5–56: the apparent GA6 (GDA6) above a stationary bass

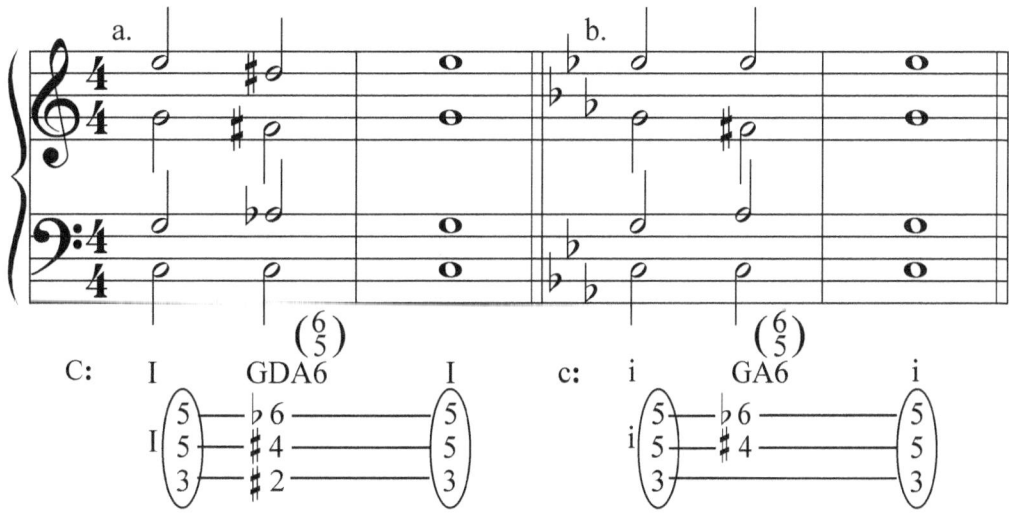

The Augmented 6th as a Mediant Embellishing Chord

Examples 5–57a and 57b illustrate the close relationship between the $\sharp\text{ii}^{\circ}{}^{4}_{2}$ and the GDA6 ($^{6}_{5}$). Indeed, the traditional view interprets the latter chord as a chromatic version of the supertonic seventh in second inversion, as some kind of II^{4}_{3}: in C major, D$\sharp$ F$\sharp$ A$\flat$ C (with A$\flat$ in the bass). As we have seen in examples 5–29 and 5–56 above, both the raised supertonic and the GA6 (and GDA6) can serve as apparent chords prolonging a stationary bass. Changing the A in 5–57a to A$\flat$ in 5–57b transforms the apparent raised supertonic $^{4}_{2}$ into the apparent GDA6 in its sounding $^{6}_{5}$ position.

The voice leading in 5–57c produces a contrapuntal chord that takes the stationary bass of examples 57a and 57b and transfers it to the soprano, producing an inverted pedal embellishing tonic. From the bass, the GDA6 (A$\flat$ C D$\sharp$ F$\sharp$) functions as a "mediant embellishing chord" (MEMB) producing a contrapuntal prolongation of the tonic by means of an extended lower neighbor tone and chord. We describe the motion in the bass as extended and as mediant embellishing because the neighbor tone stands in a 3rd relationship to scale degree 1.

The dotted lines attached to the generic figured bass in 5–57c indicate that the operation is based upon the technique of pedal embellishment, albeit inverted. Since the root of the tonic is doubled instead of its chord fifth (as in 5–57a and 57b), the implied generic bass (Arabic numbers with dotted lines) cannot account for the A$\flat$ because the A$\flat$ should have appeared above the bass and taken a resolution to scale degree 5.

The 3rd relationship between the tonic and its apparent chord constitutes an adaptation of the pedal embellishing activity in 5–57b. Indeed, the strength of the inverted pedal enables the apparent GDA6 to form a mediant relationship with the tonic. Apart from A$\flat$ not seeking its expected resolution, scale degrees $\sharp 2$ and $\sharp 4$ proceed to scale degrees 3 and 5 respectively. The basic identity of the operation is thereby secured. Thus, *once a certain usage of a chord is established through common practice, that chord may then lend itself to a related contrapuntal function.* According to this interpretation, the bass is understood as C, despite the actual presence of A$\flat$.

Example 5–57: origins of the GDA6 as a MEMB chord

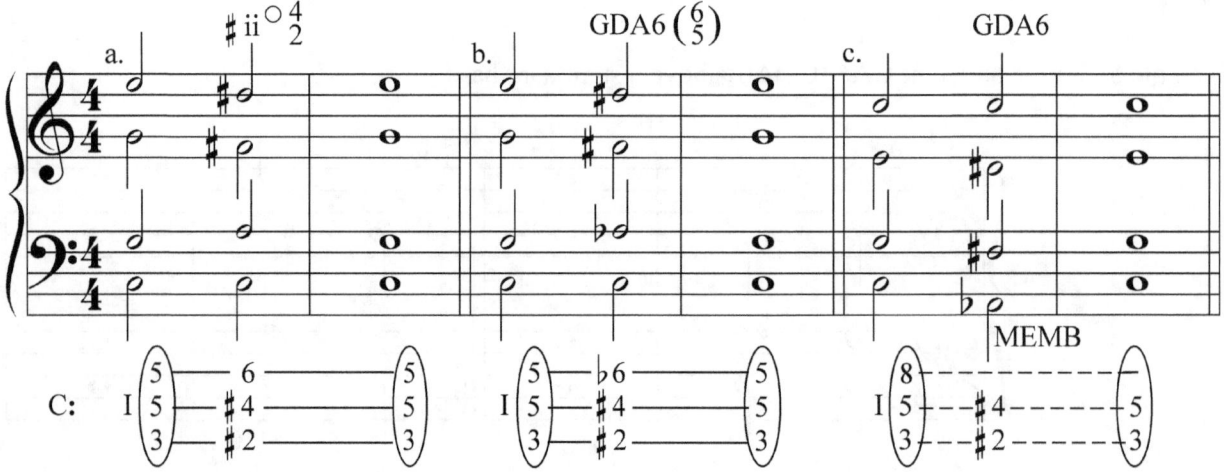

Disjunct Resolutions

Not all resolutions of the ethnic augmented 6th are conjunct, as example 5–57c suggests. We know that as long as at least two or three chord tones of the augmented 6th in four voices fulfill their linear tendencies, then the fourth voice may well leap.

Example 5–58 illustrates the two most common disjunct resolutions for the ethnic augmented 6th. The first possibility, displayed in 5–58a as a GA6, takes the sounding root, third, and seventh of the augmented 6th to their expected tones of resolution. As we have seen, however, the GA6 may yield parallel 5ths when it proceeds directly to V.

The resultant parallel 5ths are acceptable unless they appear in the outer voices. The dotted lines in examples 5–58a and 58b suggest how an alternative voicing could have produced parallel 5ths, which in 58a shows the outer voices carrying the faulty motion (A♭/E♭ to G/D). Again, these parallel 5ths are too exposed and should be avoided.

Notice the resolution of the soprano of 5–58a. The line jumps up from the sounding chord fifth to the root of the V (E♭–G). The bass, tenor, and alto fulfill their linear tendencies. The soprano is therefore free to leap in this manner, up a 3rd. Example 5–58b exchanges the previous soprano and tenor parts; the disjunct resolution of the ascending melodic 3rd is shifted to the tenor. Regardless of its voicing, the disjunct connection from the augmented 6th to the V puts emphasis the latter's root, scale degree 5: the goal of all ethnic augmented 6th chords.

Examples 5–58c and 58d exhibit the second type of disjunct resolution: the disjunct connection is made between the sounding chord third of the IA6 and the root of the V. As three of the four voices resolve according to their linear tendencies, the fourth voice becomes available to release a strong articulation of the melody by leaping upwards a perfect 5th to scale degree 5.

Placing the disjunct resolution in the uppermost voice of the texture is sure to give additional prominence to the tone of resolution. In four voices, however, the leap may put too much emphasis on the direct octaves shown in examples 5–58a and 58c.

Examples 5–58b and 58d offer an alternative that avoids the direct octave on scale degree 5.

Example 5–58: resolutions involving leaps of 3rds and 5ths

Alternative Descriptions for the Ethnic Augmented 6th Chord

Before we continue with another type of degree-inflected chord, let us examine the three general ways in which to represent the ethnic augmented 6th with chord symbols. This text recommends the method closest to the staff in example 5–59 (IA6, GA6, GDA6, FA6, and EA6).

In the traditional approach the ethnic augmented 6th is identified from its written rather than sounding root. The written root is associated with scale degrees of the supertonic and subdominant. Each chord symbol carries an inverted figured-bass description according to which element of the written chord appears in the bass. Depending on the location of the written root, Italian, German, and French augmented 6ths are regarded as altered versions of IV_3^6, IV_5^6, and II_3^4 respectively.

The traditional method of chord representation is displayed in 5–59 as a row of Roman numerals enclosed in circles. Although the circles are never included in the traditional description, we use the circles here as a generalized type of chord symbol that, without describing the specific chord quality, nonetheless indicates the scale degree of the mode upon which a triad or seventh chord may be formed. As a generalized type of chord symbol, there is no distinction between chord qualities. (All of the Roman numerals are expressed in uppercase). Nor is an altered root reflected in the chord symbol, such as attaching a generic sharp in front of the Roman numeral IV to signify that the root is scale degree ♯4: ♯IV.

Since the traditional method is based upon recognizing the written root rather than the sounding root, the circled Roman numeral provides limited information, indicating that the written root stands on either scale degree 2 or 4 of the mode. As in examples 5–59a through 59e, the traditional figured bass reflects the location of the written root and position of the chord. According to this application, the exceptional augmented 6th (EA6), which has no universally accepted name, might be described as either IV_5^6, or more specifically as $\sharp IV_5^6$.

Frequently, the attached figured bass also contains inflections to account for the altered scale degrees and intervals, as in the GDA6 shown in example 5–59f. The Roman numeral is inflected to account for the root carrying a sharp (scale degree ♯2). The intervals of the 6th and 4th above the A♭ bass both take sharps (D♯ and F♯).

When the GDA6 inverts, the inflected figured bass must be modified to reflect chord's new disposition, as in 5–59g. Intervals of the 6th, 4th, and 2nd above the bass take accidentals (A♭, D♯, and F♯). The 6th in the written second inversion has a sharp (59f), whereas the 6th in written third inversion has a flat (59g). Thus, using traditional figured bass drawn from the written position produces notational inconsistencies that add an unnecessary level of complexity to the chord symbol.

Examples 5–59a through 59d combine the geographical names with the traditional figured bass drawn from the written position, resulting in the following notational compromise: It.$_3^6$, Ger.$_5^6$, and Fr.$_3^4$.

Example 5–59: ways to describe the ethnic augmented 6th chord

Type VI: Raising and Lowering the Third of Diminished Chords Other Than the TMD

Earlier in this chapter, we encountered chords of the TMD family that contain within their respective chord structures a lowered or raised third, involving scale degrees ♭2 or ♯2 respectively. Raising or lowering the third of the TMD triad (or seventh) produces an augmented 6th or diminished 3rd within the chord structure. In both its triad and seventh-chord dispositions, the intervals of the augmented 6th or diminished 3rd contained within the altered TMD seek to resolve to either the root or third of the tonic triad (see example 5–37 above, p. 111). Scale degree ♭2 moves to 1; scale degree ♯2 proceeds to 3.

If it is possible to alter the chord third of the TMD, then diminished triads and sevenths occurring in the areas of the supertonic and submediant may also undergo degree inflection. *Altered supertonic and submediant chords do not resolve to scale degree 5*, the goal of the ethnic augmented 6th chord. In the examples that follow, some of the chord formations presented function as altered chords of the dominant family or as ethnic augmented 6th chords rather than as true supertonic or submediant chords. Other altered chords built on diatonic and chromatic versions of scale degrees 2 and 6 are simply not practicable.

Example 5–60 introduces us to degree-inflected chords of the supertonic. Although inflecting the chord third alters the basic structure of the diminished triad, the preferred position remains its first inversion, as in 5–60a.

Although put forward here in C major, the succession from doubly diminished triad of the supertonic to the tonic requires primary borrowing for both chords. Therefore, this usage, as well as that of the doubly half-diminished seventh shown in 5–60b, is more likely to occur in minor. The goal of the augmented 6th in the (ii$_0^{o6}$) is scale degree (♭3) in major and scale degree 3 in minor. (When using the chord symbol in minor, the ii$_0^o$ chord is expressed without parentheses.)

The tone of resolution for the (ii$_0^{o6}$) in 5–60a is the chord third of the minor tonic. The doubly half-diminished seventh of the supertonic takes the same resolution (5–60b). (Remember that adding a 3rd above the fifth of the diminished triad makes chords of the diminished seventh acceptable in all four positions.)

In 5–60c, notice what happens to the half-diminished seventh when its chord third is raised. The augmented 6th or diminished 3rd formed between the chord's third and fifth *resolves to scale degree 5* while the pitch content of the chord produces the sound of a dominant seventh with a lowered fifth. As such, two interpretations are possible: either the chord is the FA6 of the main-level key in third inversion; or, it is a dominant seventh with a lowered fifth in first inversion serving as an applied CLT chord of V. Examples 5–60d and 60e demonstrate the chords of 5–60b and 60c in c minor.

Example 5–60: the effects of raising and lowering the third of the diminished supertonic

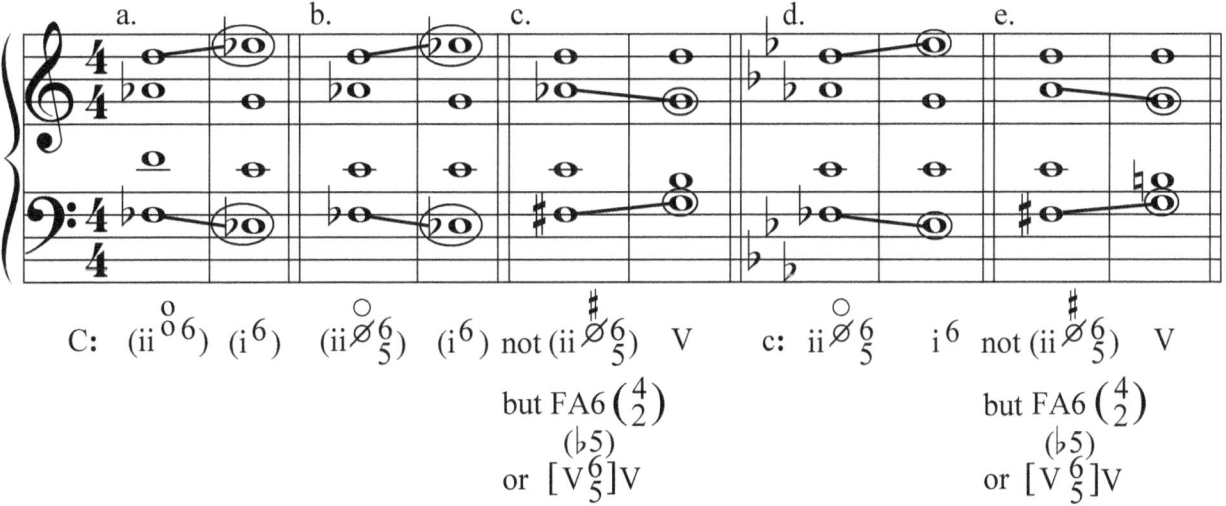

130   Chapter 5 Degree-Inflected Chords

In example 5–61a, the doubly diminished triad of the submediant is formed by degree inflection (C♭) and primary borrowing (E♭), producing the tones A C♭ E♭ (C♭ bass). The augmented 6th (C♭/A) contained within the (vi$_o^{o6}$) resolves to scale degree ♭7 (B♭), a tone that is unavailable in major. Although the doubly diminished triad and doubly half-diminished seventh of the submediant are used more readily in the minor mode, the pitch content of both chords suggests alternative interpretations.

Example 5–61c indicates that despite its resolution to variable ♭7, the ♯vi$_o^{o6}$ chord can also be recognized as [vii$_o^{o6}$]♭VII. The doubly half-diminished seventh of the submediant has the same potential function and ambiguity. (Lowering the chord third of (vi$_o^{o6}$) or ♯vi$_o^{o6}$ by one half step transforms scale degree 1 into the enharmonic equivalent of the leading tone, which undermines the chord's viability as a submediant.)

Again, the degree-inflected submediant cannot be classified as an ethnic augmented 6th because its operational interval does not resolve to scale degree 5. In all of the submediant chords displayed in 5–61, the augmented 6th (or diminished 3rd) contained within the each submediant resolves to either scale degree 2 in major and minor (D) or variable ♭7 in minor (B♭). In 5–61d, variable ♭7, the tone of resolution becomes the chord third of the minor dominant in the minor mode.

Examples 5–61b and 61e show the half-diminished seventh of the submediant with a raised third resolving to ii, first in major and then in minor. The tones A C♯ E♭ G (C♯ bass) may well constitute a raised half-diminished seventh built on scale degree 6 in major and ♯6 in minor; however, the chord is also an applied V with a lowered fifth in first inversion addressing ii (5–61b and 61e).

Although the context for the altered chord may be ambiguous, the most important action for the harmonic operation is the proper resolution of the augmented 6th (or diminished 3rd). In examples 5–61b and 61e, the tone of resolution is scale degree 2 (D), either as the chord fifth of V, the root of ii, or the third of ♭VII in minor. In both examples, scale degree 2 projects a D-minor triad, the ii chord.

Adding F♯ to the D-minor supertonic in examples 5–61b and 61e transforms the chord into an applied dominant: the supertonic becomes [V]V. The D-major triad, [V]V, receives a contrapuntal approach from the applied V with the lowered fifth, A C♯ E♭ G (C♯ bass).

Example 5–61: the effects of raising and lowering the third of the diminished submediant

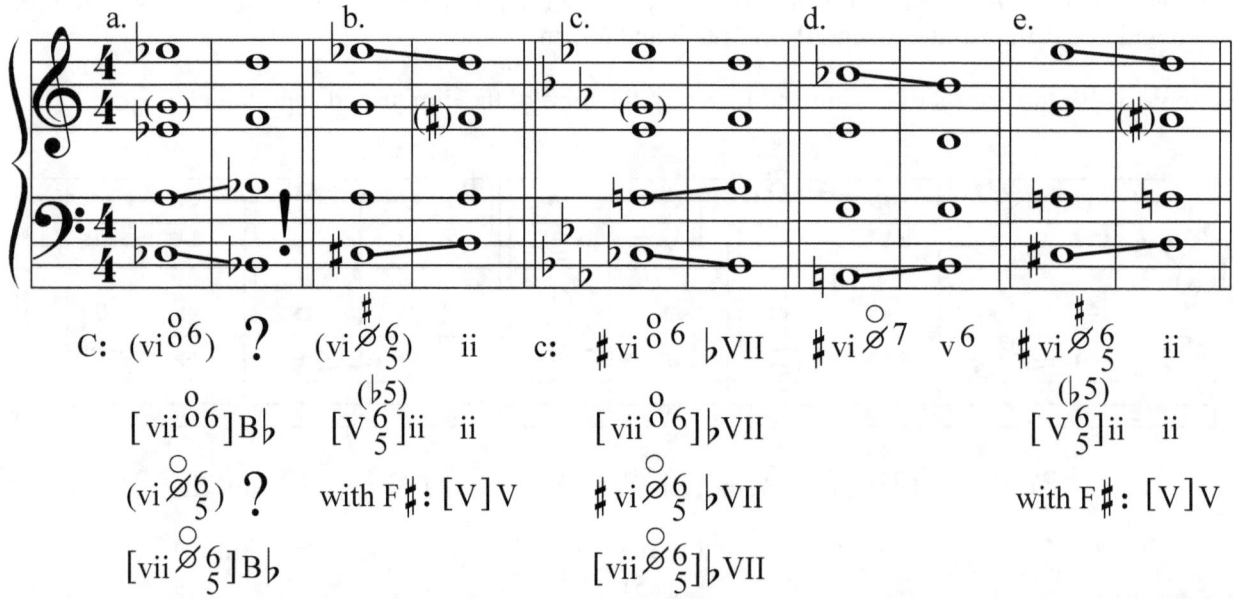

On the other hand, the diminished 3rd (C♯/E♭) contained in the chord (examples 5–61b and 61e above) could also resolve to scale degree 2 (D) as the fifth of V or as the third of ♭VII. In any case, the main thing to remember here is to observe how the operational interval resolves: *the function of the augmented 6th chord is determined by what scale degree and element of the chord constitutes the tone of resolution.* We know that if the tone of resolution is scale degree 5 as either the root of the dominant or fifth of the tonic, then the chord is an ethnic augmented 6th.

Raising and Lowering the Third of the Common-Tone Fully Diminished Seventh

The common-tone fully diminished seventh is built on scale degrees ♯2 and ♯6 (or ♯6 in minor); it is attached to a chord of the tonic or dominant. In the ♯ii○7, ♯2 and ♯4 resolve to scale degrees 3 and 5 (example 5–62a). In the ♯vi○7 (or the ♯vi○7 in minor), ♯6 (or ♯6) and ♯1 resolve to scale degrees 7 (or ♯7) and 2 respectively (example 5–64a). We shall find that raising and lowering the thirds of these chords changes the resolution, produces an augmented 6th chord, and renders most of them impractical.

The ♯ii○7 in root position in 5–62b resolves to I 6; however, the chord sounds like a dominant seventh in third inversion with F (scale degree 4) as its root (the E♭ chord seventh is misspelled as D♯). If we reinterpret the root as F, then the dominant seventh could be used as a pivot chord serving as either the THD of B♭ or as the GA6 in the key of A. The ♯ii○7 becomes either a diatonic or chromatic chord in the new key, the THD of the subtonic in minor or the GA6 of the submediant in major.

Despite the ambiguous implications of this chord, its augmented 6th (or diminished 3rd) resolves correctly to scale degree 3 as the chord third of the tonic; hence, the basic function of the raised supertonic remains undisturbed when its third is lowered. Notably, the relationship between the doubly fully diminished seventh of the raised supertonic and the tonic triad in 5–62b is weakened in minor because the two chords share two common tones (E♭ and C in 5–62d). Another application of this chord, also associated with the tonic, is explored in example 5–63.

Raising the third of the ♯ii○7, as in examples 5–62c and 62e, is questionable. The augmented 6th within the chord resolves to scale degree ♯5 within the complex of an augmented triad. Apart from creating an unusual harmonic effect, there is little reason to use the chord. And so, in the supertonic area of common-tone sevenths, the ♯ii○7 chord is the best option for carrying the augmented 6th. However, as noted above, the chord remains open to alternative interpretations and uses.

Example 5–62: alterations of the ♯ii○7

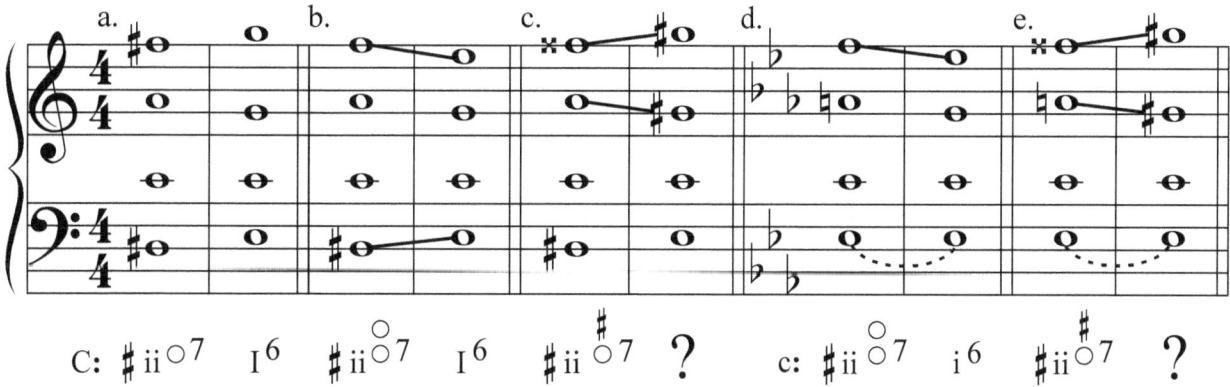

Earlier in this chapter, example 5–57c illustrated a 3rd relationship between the tonic and the GDA6. Example 5–63a reproduces 5–57c to facilitate comparison with 5–63b. (Remember that the traditional view of this chord interprets the GDA6 in root position as some kind of chromatic version of the II$^4_3$ chord: in C major, D♯ F♯ A♭ C, with A♭ in the bass.)

The strength of the inverted pedal embellishing tone in 5–63a enables the GDA6 to stand firmly in a mediant relationship with the tonic. In this context, the GDA6 becomes a mediant embellishing chord prolonging the tonic (C–A♭–C in the bass). Moreover, the voice leading between the chords in the voices above the bass proceeds as expected.

In 5–63a, scale degrees ♯2 and ♯4 move to scale degrees 3 and 5 respectively while an inverted pedal maintains scale degree 1 in the soprano. The stability of the voice leading in the upper parts enables the bass to follow its inclination to leap. The basic identity of the operation remains secure as established through common practice. *And once a certain usage of a chord becomes conventional, that chord may then lend itself to a related contrapuntal function.* (The dotted lines attached to the generic figured bass in 5–63 indicate an implied stationary bass that has been transferred to one of the upper voices as an inverted pedal.)

Example 5–63b presents an interesting adaptation of the voice leading for the GDA6. The augmented 6th chord in 5–63b, ♯ii$^{o\,6}_{o\,5}$, serves as a harmonic embellishing chord (HEMB). As with the application of the GDA6 in 5–63a, the voice leading for the ♯ii$^{o\,6}_{o\,5}$ consists of conjunct motion above a disjunct bass. The leap of the 4th in the bass constitutes a harmonic interval. The lowered third (F) of the ♯ii$^{o\,6}_{o\,5}$, which denies its resolution to scale degree 3 (E) and takes a downwards leap of a 4th to scale degree 1 (C–F–C in the bass), is free to leap because of the strength of the voice leading in the upper parts.

The alto carries the inverted pedal embellishing tone, sustaining the tonic note. Scale degree 6 (A) descends to scale degree 5 (G) while ♯2 ascends to scale degree 3 (E). Thus, the latter operation (♯2 to 3) gives us *half* of the correct resolution for the apparent chord's augmented 6th (D♯ to E). As we have observed, the lowered third of the ♯ii$^{o\,6}_{o\,5}$, F, assumes the function of harmonic embellishment by denying a melodic resolution to E in favor of a harmonic leap to C.

Resolving the augmented 6th in one voice rather than in both is always acceptable when the chord moves directly to V^7 instead of V$^{8-7}$, a contraction from an octave to a 7th (see example 5–9b above, p. 93). Therefore, when an apparent augmented 6th chord fulfills the role of mediant or harmonic embellishment of a chord, the operational interval does not have to resolve in *both* voices.

Example 5–63: the ♯ii$^{o\,6}_{o\,5}$ as an HEMB chord

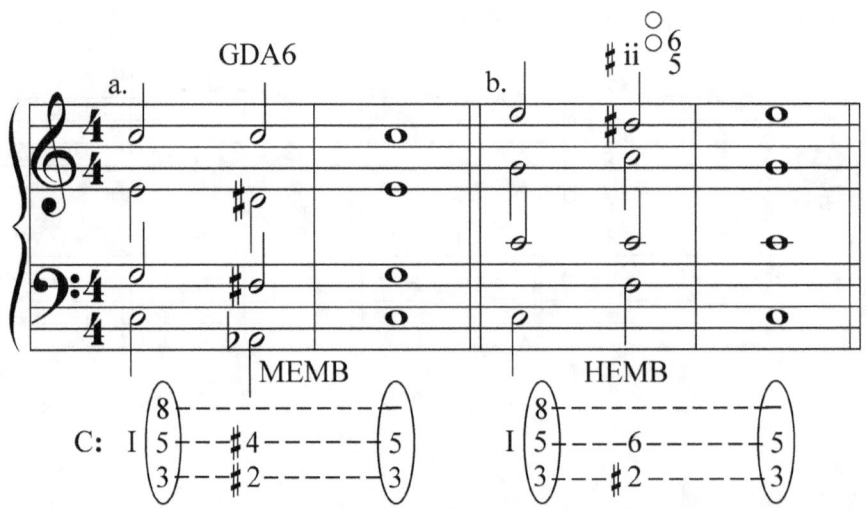

As shown in example 5–64a, the ♯vi○⁷ (♯vi○⁷ in minor) moves to the V⁶. Scale degrees ♯6 (♯6) and ♯1 proceed to the leading tone and scale degree 2 respectively. Lowering the third of the chord, as in 5–64b, produces a diminished 3rd and changes thereby the resolution to V⁶. In this instance, the diminished 3rd contracts to the leading tone in *both* voices, an undesirable doubling of a highly sensitive scale degree. (Example 5–64d reproduces the same problem in minor.)

An important feature of the ♯vi₀○⁷ is its sound, which is that of a dominant seventh in third inversion with C (scale degree 1) as its root (the B♭ chord seventh is misspelled as A♯). If we reinterpret the root as C instead of as A♯ (♯6), then the chord could function as the THD of the subdominant in major and minor or serve as the GA6 of the mediant in major. The ambiguous implications of the chord and its resolution to the leading tone present significant issues for using ♯vi₀○⁷ as a submediant chord.

Raising the third of the ♯vi○⁷, as in examples 5–64c and 64e, is doubtful. The augmented 6th within the chord resolves to scale degree ♯2 within the complex of an augmented triad. (We saw the same unusual resolution in examples 5–62c and 62e.)

And so, the common-tone fully diminished seventh with the lowered or raised third tends to lose its identity as a supertonic or submediant chord. To be sure, this loss of identity might be useful if the musical context requires a pivot chord, such as the aforementioned reinterpretation of the ♯vi₀○⁷ as either a diatonic or chromatic chord in the new key.

As we have said, since the ♯vi₀○⁷ sounds like a dominant seventh, at least two pivot-chord options are available: it becomes the diatonic THD of the new key; or, it becomes the chromatic GA6 of the new key. But beyond the harmonic potentialities of these chords or their limitations, the tone of resolution remains the main factor to observe when attempting to understand the operations of the augmented 6th and its potential functions.

Example 5–64: alterations of the ♯vi○⁷ (♯vi○⁷ in minor)

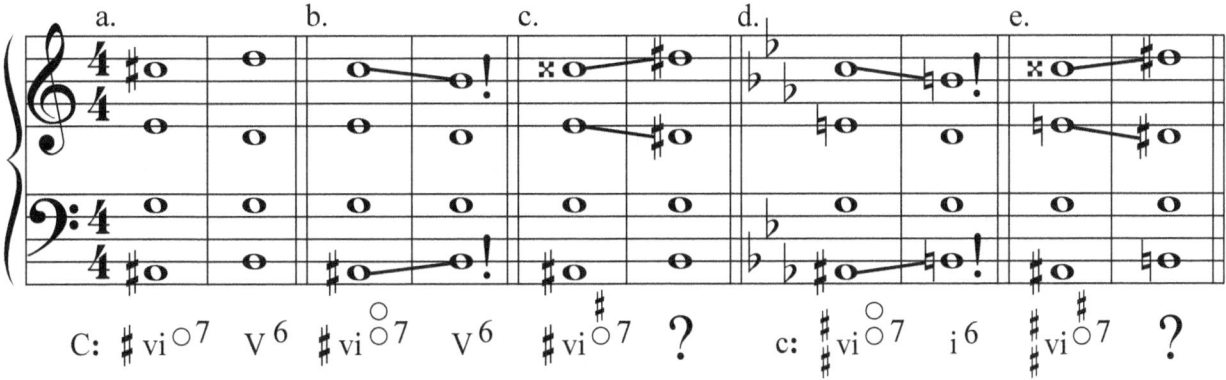

A Review of the Six Types of Degree-Inflected Chords

Type I: The Altered Tonal Harmonic Dominant (THD) (pp. 89–93, examples 5–2 and 5–3 above)

(1) The chord of resolution is usually the tonic.
(2) The root of the chord is scale degree 5.
(3) The degree-inflected tone is the chord fifth and scale degree 2, which becomes either ♯2 or ♭2. The degree inflection resolves to either scale degree 1 or 3, the root or third of the tonic triad.
(4) Double the root, scale degree 5, if needed.
(5) All triads and sevenths of Type-I degree inflection contain an augmented 6th (or diminished 3rd) within their chord structures except for the triad with a raised fifth, the V♯5.

Type II: The Neapolitan 6th Chord (pp. 94–102, example 5–13 above)

(1) Often serves as an X-chord. (In C major, the chord in first inversion is F A♭ D♭.)
(2) The degree-inflected tone is the root of the chord, scale degree ♭2.
(3) The chord fifth is scale degree (♭6) in major and variable ♭6 in minor
(4) The chord usually appears in first inversion, expressed as N^6. The root position of the chord begins to appear in the nineteenth century.
(5) In root position, it becomes a chord of secondary borrowing (see Chapter 6).
(6) In first inversion, double the third, scale degree 4; in any other position, double either the root, scale degree ♭2, or the chord third. The fifth, scale degree (♭6) in major and variable ♭6 in minor, is the least preferable doubling.
(7) Chords of Type-II degree inflection do not contain an augmented 6th.

Type III: Common-Tone Fully Diminished Seventh Chords (pp. 103–110, example 5–25 above)

(1) The root of the chord is either scale degree ♯2 in major and 3 in minor (♯2 correctly misspelled) or ♯6 in major and variable ♯6 in minor.
(2) The ♯ii°^{7} consists of scale degrees ♯2, ♯4, 6, and 1 (in C major: D♯ F♯ A C).
   (a) The chord of resolution is usually the tonic.
   (b) The voice leading from the raised supertonic to the tonic is ♯2 to 3, ♯4 to 5, and 6 to 5.
   (c) The common tone, scale degree 1, does not move between chords.
   (d) In four voices, the raised supertonic in third inversion may omit the fifth and double its chord seventh (scale degree 1).
(3) The ♯vi°^{7} consists of scale degrees ♯6, ♯1, 3, and 5 (in C major: A♯ C♯ E G).
   (a) The chord of resolution is usually the dominant.
   (b) The voice leading from the raised submediant to the dominant is ♯6 to 7, ♯1 to 2, and 3 to 4 (or 2.)
   (c) The common tone, scale degree 5, does not move between chords.
   (d) In four voices, the raised submediant in third inversion may omit the fifth and double its chord seventh (scale degree 5).
(4) Chords of Type-III degree inflection do not contain an augmented 6th.

Type IV: Augmented 6th Chords of the Tonal Melodic Dominant (TMD) Family (pp. 110–115, example 5–37 above)

(1) The chord of resolution is usually the tonic triad.
(2) The root of the altered TMD is scale degree 7 in major and variable ♯7 in minor.
(3) The degree-inflected tone is the chord third, scale degree 2, which becomes either ♯2 or ♭2. The degree inflection resolves to either scale degree 1 or 3, the root or third of the tonic triad.
(4) In minor, if the chord third is ♯2, then it may be correctly misspelled as scale degree 3.
(5) The voice leading from the altered TMD to the tonic is ♭2 to 1 and ♯2 to 3.
(6) For voicing the chord with four parts, double the fifth (scale degree 4) if needed; avoid doubling anything else in the chord.
(7) In minor, both the altered and diatonic versions of the half-diminished TMD do not exist because it contains ♯6 as its chord seventh.
(8) All chords of Type-IV degree inflection contain an augmented 6th (or diminished 3rd) within their chord structures.

Type V: The Ethnic Augmented 6th Chord (pp. 115–128, examples 5–48 through 5–51 above)

(1) The sounding root of the chord is scale degree (♭6) in major and variable ♭6 in minor.
(2) In its sounding root position, the ethnic augmented 6th may serve as an X-chord.
(3) The chord of resolution is either the dominant, the cadential $^6_4$, or the passing tonic $^6_4$.
(4) The interval of the augmented 6th (or diminished 3rd) resolves to scale degree 5, either as the root of the dominant or as the chord fifth of the tonic.
(5) All ethnic augmented 6ths contain scale degrees 1, ♭6 or (♭6), and ♯4; the chord third is the tonic.
(6) When approaching a half cadence, the augmented 6th is often interpreted as an altered CLT chord.
(7) The ethnic augmented 6th can be interpreted as an applied dominant of the Phrygian supertonic.
(8) There are four different configurations of the ethnic augmented 6th:
   (a) The Italian augmented 6th (IA6) has no chord fifth; in four voices, double the chord third (in C major: A♭ C F♯).
   (b) The German augmented 6th (GA6) sounds like a dominant seventh with all chord tones present.
      i) Its sounding chord fifth is (♭3) in major and scale degree 3 in minor.
      ii) When the GA6 leads to a major triad, the sounding chord fifth is spelled one pitch name lower and the chord is called the German doubly augmented 6th (GDA6) because of the doubly augmented 4th produced between the sounding root (♭6) and the correctly misspelled fifth (♯2). In major, the chord fifth of the GDA6, scale degree (♭3) is respelled as ♯2. (In C major: A♭ C E♭ F♯, the GA6, becomes A♭ C D♯ F♯, the GDA6.)
   (c) The French augmented 6th (FA6) sounds like a whole-tone dominant (with a lowered fifth).
      i) Located one half step *below* the fifth of the GA6, the lowered fifth of the FA6 is scale degree 2.
      ii) The chord fifth takes the pitch name associated with scale degree 2 and is therefore correctly misspelled. (In C major: A♭ C E♭♭ F♯ becomes A♭ C D F♯.)
   (d) The exceptional augmented 6th (EA6) sounds like a whole-tone dominant (with a raised fifth).
      i) Located one half step *above* the fifth of the GA6, the raised fifth of the EA6 is scale degree 3 in major (in C major: A♭ C E F♯).
      ii) The normal resolution of the EA6 produces an incomplete V^7 (doubled root, omitted fifth). Resolving the EA6 to a minor tonic in $^6_4$ position yields a poor result.
(9) All chords of Type-V degree inflection contain an augmented 6th (or diminished 3rd) within their chord structures.

Type VI: Raising and Lowering the Third of Diminished Chords Other Than the TMD

(1) The diminished triad or half-diminished seventh rooted on scale degree 2 or 6 and variable ♯6 in minor (pp. 129–131, examples 5–60 and 61 above).
   (a) Raising or lowering the third of the supertonic and submediant triads and sevenths produces an augmented 6th (or diminished 3rd) within their chord structures.
   (b) The augmented 6th (or diminished 3rd) within the altered supertonic usually resolves to either scale degree (♭3), 3 (in minor), or 5 (!).
      i) The augmented 6th contained within the supertonic triad or seventh with a lowered third resolves to scale degree (♭3) or 3 (examples 5–60a, 60b, and 60d). Both chords are used more readily in the minor mode.
      ii) The supertonic triad or seventh with a raised third does not function as a chord built on scale degree 2 because its augmented 6th interval resolves to scale degree 5 as the root of the dominant (5–60c and 60e). This operation is indicative of the chord functioning as either an ethnic augmented 6th or an applied dominant rather than as a main-level supertonic.
   (c) The augmented 6th (or diminished 3rd) within the altered submediant usually resolves to either scale degree 2 or ♭7 (in minor). Lowering the third of the submediant one half step transforms scale degree 1 into the leading tone, which undermines the chord's viability as a submediant.
      i) The augmented 6th contained within the submediant triad or seventh with a lowered third resolves to scale degree ♭7, a tone unavailable in major (examples 5–61a, 61c, and 61d). Therefore, both the doubly diminished triad and doubly half-diminished seventh of the submediant are used more readily in the minor mode.
      ii) The submediant triad or seventh with a raised third resolves to scale degree 2, either as the chord fifth of V, the root of ii (5–61b and 61e), or the third of ♭VII in minor.
(2) The fully diminished seventh rooted on scale degree ♯2 or ♯6 and variable ♯♯6 in minor (pp. 131–133, examples 5–62 and 64 above).
   (a) The common-tone fully diminished seventh with a lowered or raised third tends to lose its identity as a supertonic or submediant chord.
   (b) The raised supertonic with a lowered third sounds like a dominant seventh. So constituted, the chord can serve as a pivot to a lower-level key as either a THD or as an ethnic augmented 6th.
   (c) The raised submediant with a lowered third sounds like a dominant seventh. So constituted, the chord can serve as a pivot to a lower-level key as either a THD or as an ethnic augmented 6th.
   (d) The raised supertonic with a raised third resolves to an augmented triad, rendering its use in the main-level key unlikely.
   (d) The raised submediant with a raised third resolves to an augmented triad, rendering its use in the main-level key unlikely.
(3) All chords of Type-VI degree inflection contain an augmented 6th (or diminished 3rd) within their chord structures.

We conclude this chapter by recalling the ambiguous nature of the doubly fully diminished seventh of the raised supertonic (example 5–62b), a chord whose identity is obscured in the main-level key. The raised supertonic seventh with a lowered third may be used not only as an applied THD of the subtonic in minor but also as an ethnic augmented 6th chord pivoting towards the submediant in major.

Any chord of the main-level key sounding like a dominant seventh, with or without an altered fifth, contains a minor 7th within its structure. The minor 7th can stand as a minor 7th *or* be reinterpreted as an augmented 6th. If the tone of resolution is not scale degree 5 of the starting key, then it may assume status as scale degree 5 in the new key, a lower-level key. Functioning as an ethnic augmented 6th, the chord pivots to the new key by targeting that key's dominant scale degree. We shall learn more about the potentialities of pivot-chord modulation in Chapter 8.

Chapter 6 Secondary Borrowing

Secondary borrowing is the third form of chromaticism in tonal music. There are three types of operations for producing chords of secondary borrowing:
  (1) the complete interchangeability of the extended major mode with the parallel extended minor mode;
  (2) the complete interchangeability of the extended major mode with parallel non-major-minor modes (that is, the church modes); and,
  (3) sonoric substitution (chord substitution).

(Remember that primary borrowing brings scale degrees 3 and ♭6 into major from the parallel minor. Therefore, any chord of secondary borrowing in major that contains a tone of primary borrowing takes parentheses in its chord description. Additionally, all chords and elements of secondary borrowing displayed in the examples of this text are marked with an asterisk directly above the Roman numeral.)

Type I: Complete Interchangeability of the Extended Major with the Parallel Extended Minor

As shown in example 6–1, the first operation of secondary borrowing completes the extended-diatonic major-minor system. In type I, we have the total interchangeability of parallel major and minor modes, incorporating variable ♭7 into major and scale degree 3 from major into minor. (The latter yields the Picardy third.)

The first type of secondary borrowing eliminates the differences in pitch content between extended major and minor. All tones of primary and secondary borrowing in major are treated as they are in minor. Within the context of the extended diatonic system, the melodic minor is both understood and configured as a nine-tone ascending scale. As illustrated in 6–1b, placing scale degree 3 of major (E♮) into the extended minor transforms the nine-tone scale into a ten-tone scale. (Filled-in note heads indicate either primary or secondary borrowing.)

Example 6–1: the completion of the extended-diatonic major-minor system

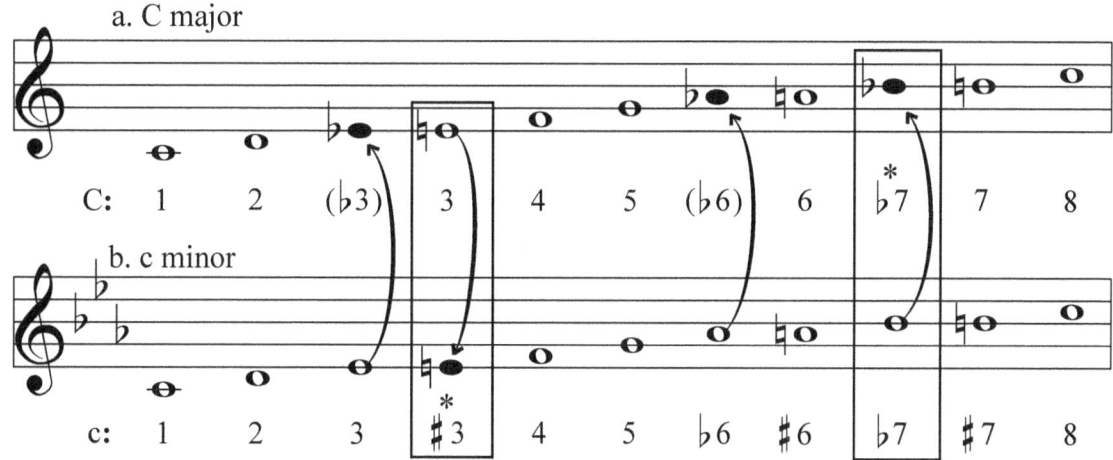

137

Bringing ♭7 into major from the parallel minor produces a major triad of the lowered mediant, a minor triad of the dominant, and a major triad of the subtonic (example 6–2a). As we have seen, if elements of primary borrowing are present in a chord of secondary borrowing, then parentheses are attached to the chord symbol in major.

The root of the first chord in example 6–2a is scale degree (♭3), E♭. In 6–2b, the minor mode borrows scale degree 3 from major and forms thereby a minor triad on scale degrees ♯3 (E♮) and ♯6 (A♮). Scale degree ♯3 forms the root of the first chord, which also has ♯7 as its chord fifth (B♮). The secondary borrowing of ♯3 as the fifth of the raised submediant engenders the second minor triad (6–2b).

Example 6–2: type-I triads

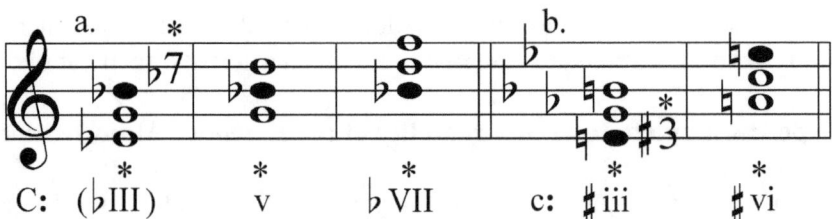

Type II: Complete Interchangeability of the Extended Major with Parallel Non-Major-Minor Modes

A complete interchange of properties between extended major and non-major-minor modes produces a variety of chordal possibilities, the most likely of which come from the Lydian and Phrygian modes. In example 6–3, triads from the parallel Lydian and Phrygian modes are brought into the extended major and minor.

Examples 6–3a and 3d begin with a major triad of the supertonic borrowed from the Lydian mode. In the *second* chord of examples 6–3a and 3d, we have a major triad of the Phrygian supertonic. Although examples 6–3b and 3e confirm the potential formation of a diminished triad on scale degree 5 in both major and minor, expressing the chord as a half-diminished seventh softens the effect of the tritone from the root to the chord fifth. (Claude Debussy uses the half-diminished seventh of the dominant in *Beau Soir* in 1880; Samuel Barber uses it in his *Adagio For Strings* in 1936.) In any case, secondary borrowing produces minor triads of the subtonic and leading tone in both major and minor (examples 6–3c and 3f, first and second chords respectively).

Example 6–3: type-II triads (and one seventh)

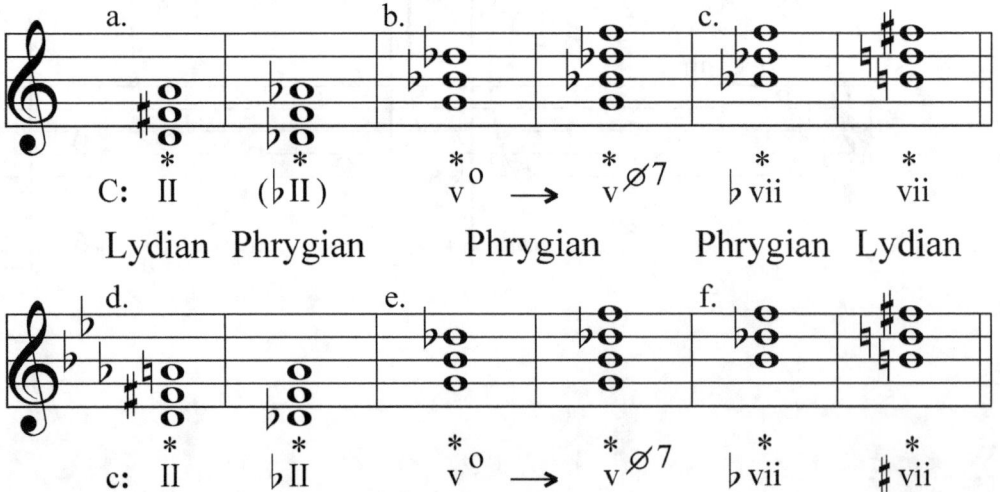

Type III: Sonoric Substitution (Chord Substitution)

The third type of secondary borrowing, as presented in example 6–4, involves major and minor chords whose roots occur most commonly in the areas of the supertonic, mediant, submediant, and leading tone. Type-III chords cannot be placed into the first or second categories of secondary borrowing because they are not derived from a parallel mode. Rather, the triads of type III are produced by altering chords that otherwise exist as a result of primary borrowing, the interchangeability of parallel major and minor modes (type I), or the mixture of elements from extended major with those of non-major-minor modes (type II).

Let us consider the chords of the supertonic and the leading tone. We know that in type II, the Phrygian supertonic is a major triad (examples 6–3a and 3d above, second chord). The Phrygian supertonic assumes type-III status when secondary borrowing transforms the chord into a minor triad (examples 6–4a and 4e). In type II, the chord and key area of the leading tone is a minor triad (examples 6–3c and 3f above, second chord). In type III, the chord of the leading-tone area becomes a major triad (examples 6–4d and 4h).

In examples 6–4b and 4f, type-III major and minor triads of the mediant have chord thirds involving either scale degree ♯5 or ♭5 (that is, G♯ or G♭). Mediant chords are formed on two different versions of scale degree 3. The first triads in examples 6–4b and 4f have diatonic roots; the root of the second triad in 6–4b is (♭3) while its chord fifth is ♭7, a tone of type-I borrowing. The root of second triad in 6–4f is ♯3, also a type-I tone.

In examples 6–4c and 4g, type-III major and minor triads of the submediant have chord thirds involving either scale degree ♯1 or ♭1 (that is, C♯ or C♭). Submediant chords are formed on two different versions of scale degree 6. The first triads in examples 6–4c and 4g have roots on scale degrees 6 and variable ♭6 respectively. The root of the second triad in 6–4c is (♭6) while its chord fifth is (♭3), both tones of primary borrowing. The root of the second triad in 6–4g is variable ♯6; its chord fifth is ♯3, a tone of type-I borrowing.

Example 6–4: type-III triads

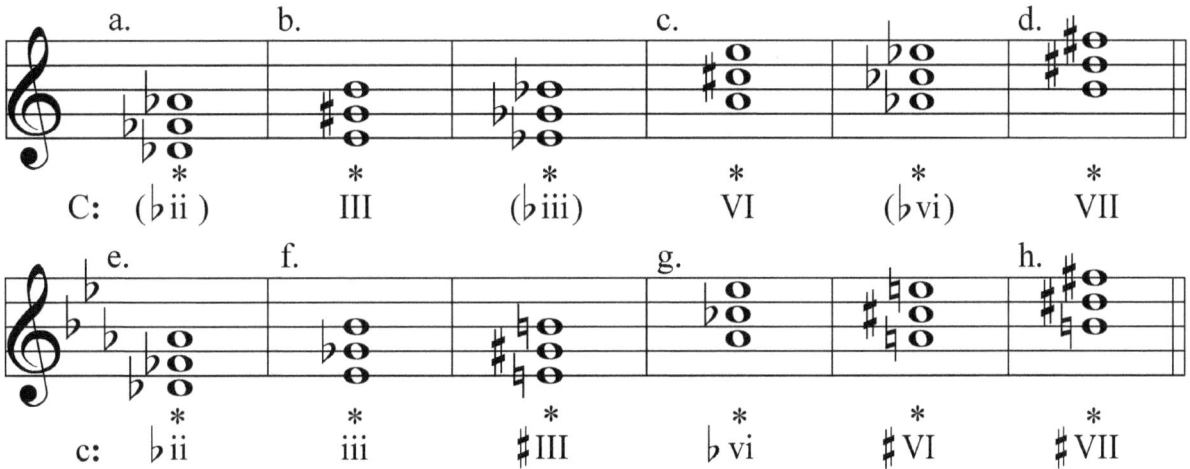

Interpreting Major Triads of Secondary Borrowing As Applied Dominants

Some of the major triads of secondary borrowing stand in a falling perfect 5th (or rising perfect 4th) root relationship to major or minor triads formed on scale degrees (♭6), 5, 6, 2, and 3, functioning potentially as applied dominants of (♭VI), V, vi, ii, and iii (example 6–5).

We find such triads among all three types of secondary borrowing. Type I is represented in example 6–1a as [V](♭VI), an E♭-major triad addressing A♭, (♭6). Type II occurs in both major and minor as [V]V in examples 6–5b and 5d, a D-major triad prolonging G, scale degree 5.

In examples 6–5c and 5e, we have four type-III triads, each serving as a chord of harmonic prolongation. In 6–5c, major triads on E, A, and B stand in a rising perfect 4th relationship to scale degrees 6, 2, and 3 respectively, becoming [V]vi, [V]ii, and [V]iii. In 6–5e, an A-major triad also appears in c minor as [V]ii. The identity of major triads on scale degrees (♭3), 2, 3, 6, and 7 in major and 2 and ♯6 in minor as chords of secondary borrowing is bolstered by the potential use of these harmonies as applied dominants, the first *real* form of chromaticism (as maintained in this text).

Example 6–5: chords of secondary borrowing as harmonic prolonging chords

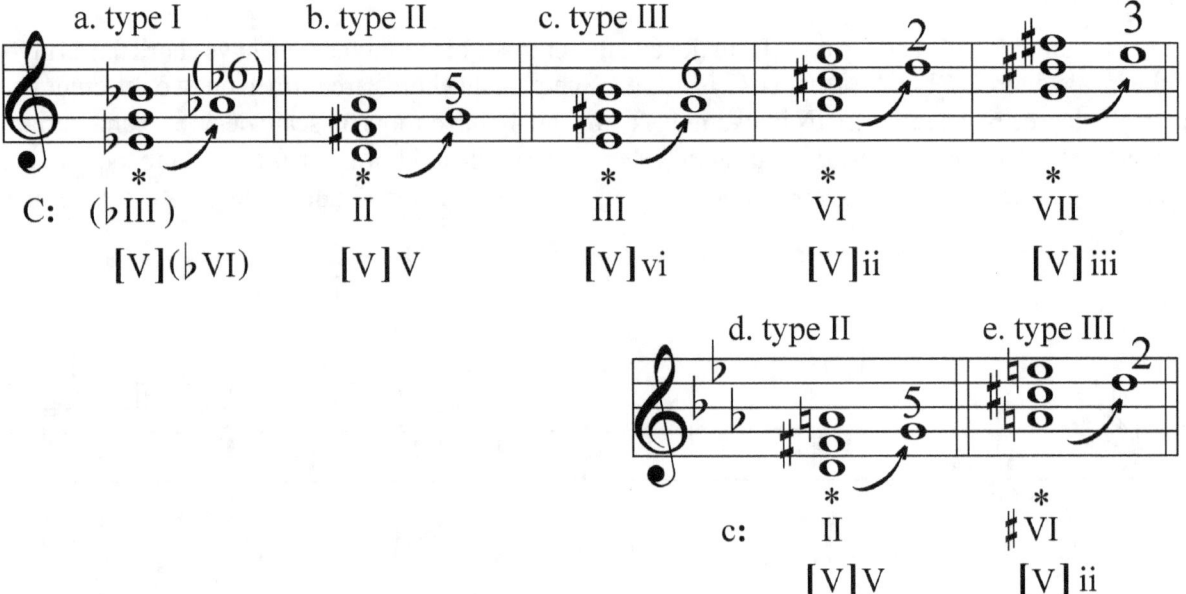

General Uses for Chords of Secondary Borrowing

Chords of secondary borrowing may be used in contrapuntal circumstances to embellish other chords or to effect passing motion between chords; and most importantly, they may also serve as X-chords. Indeed, extended prolongations of lower-level keys representing chords of secondary borrowing constitute a significant step forward in the development of tonality and harmony in the early 1800s. Composers at the dawn of the Romantic period began to write more adventurous excursions into keys of secondary borrowing, particularly in the areas of the mediant and submediant.

In the first movement of the Beethoven Piano Sonata No. 21 in C Major, Op. 53 (*"Waldstein"*), composed 1803–1804, the first theme is in the main-level key of C major, the second theme is in the lower-level key of E major. Later, when the second theme returns, it begins in the lower-level key of A major. Within the context of the main-level key, both E major and A major are type-III tonalities of secondary borrowing, III and VI.

Mediant Embellishing Chords of Secondary Borrowing

The chords shown in example 6–6 demonstrate contrapuntal prolongations of the tonic chord by chords of the mediant and submediant. Prolongations such as those in 6–6 are effected by neighbor-embellishing operations. A triad whose root is located a 2nd above or below the tonic note (and chord) serves as a chord of melodic prolongation, a *melodic embellishing chord* (as in examples 6–10 and 6–11 below). Expanding the 2nd to a 3rd produces a chord of mediant prolongation, a *mediant embellishing chord.*

All of the mediant and submediant chords in examples 6–6 and 6–7 are formed through secondary borrowing. Most of these chords constitute type-III formations, except for 6–6b, 6–7c and 6–7f, which are of the type-I variety.

There is one important consideration when using mediant root-related chords: the chords share common tones. This commonality of tones is one of the reasons why it can be difficult to hear a motion between chords whose roots are a 3rd apart.

In both examples 6–6 and 6–7, the tonic and its prolonging chord have common tones that are chromatic variants of each other. Observe the linear operations in examples 6–6a, 6b, and 6c: G becomes G♯ in the tenor; E moves to E♭ in the alto; G proceeds to G♭ in the tenor while E shifts simultaneously to E♭ in the alto. The chromatic differences help us to hear the chords as separate harmonies. As displayed in both examples 6–6 and 6–7, chromatic common tones also occur between tonic and submediant chords.

Using chords of secondary borrowing may produce some unusual voice leading. For instance, in examples 6–7e and 7f, variable ♯6 defies its normal tendency to move upwards to scale degrees ♯7 and 8 (A♮–B♮–C), moving instead down to scale degree 5 (A♮–G).

Example 6–6: in major (the soprano proceeds from scale degree 1)

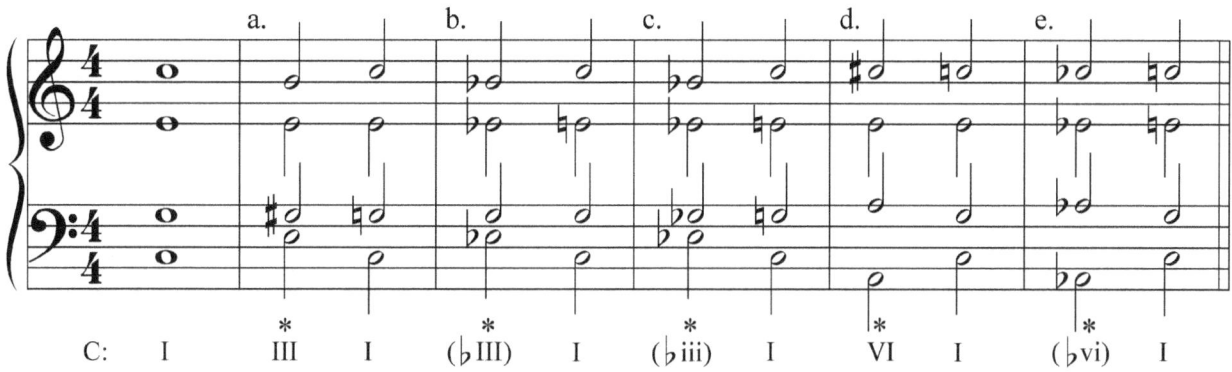

Example 6–7: in minor (the soprano proceeds from scale degree 1)

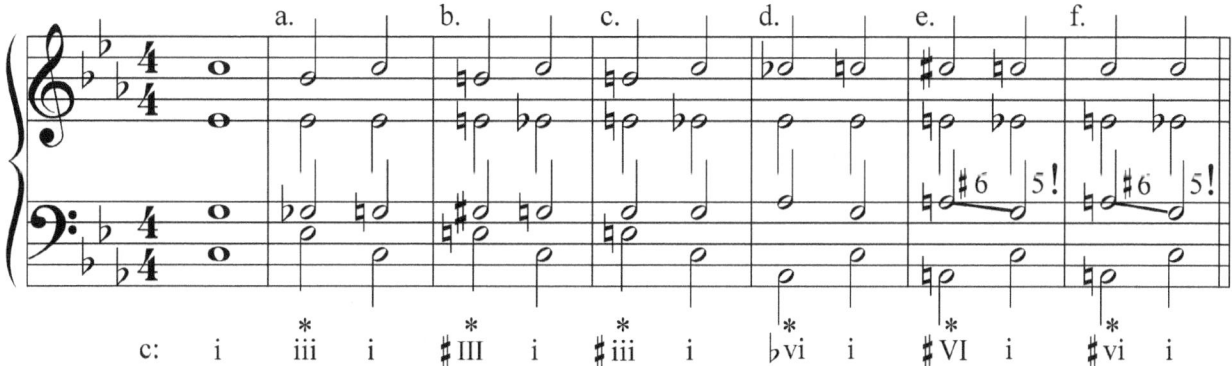

Examples 6–8 and 6–9 present mediant embellishing chords with an alternative disposition: the tonic third, scale degree 3, is carried in the soprano. Although the spacing of the chords in the present example differs from that of the chords in examples 6–6 and 6–7 above, the respective voice leading remains essentially the same.

Example 6–8: in major (the soprano proceeds from scale degree 3)

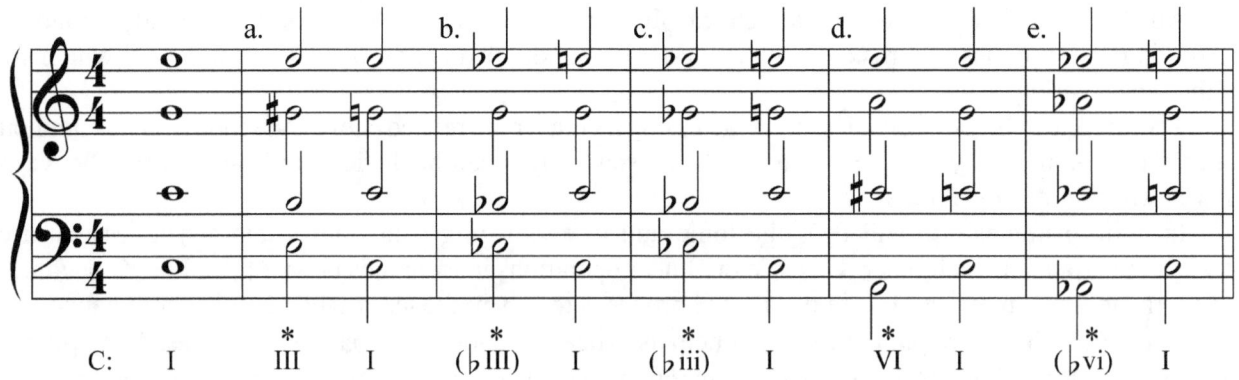

Example 6–9: in minor (the soprano proceeds from scale degree 3)

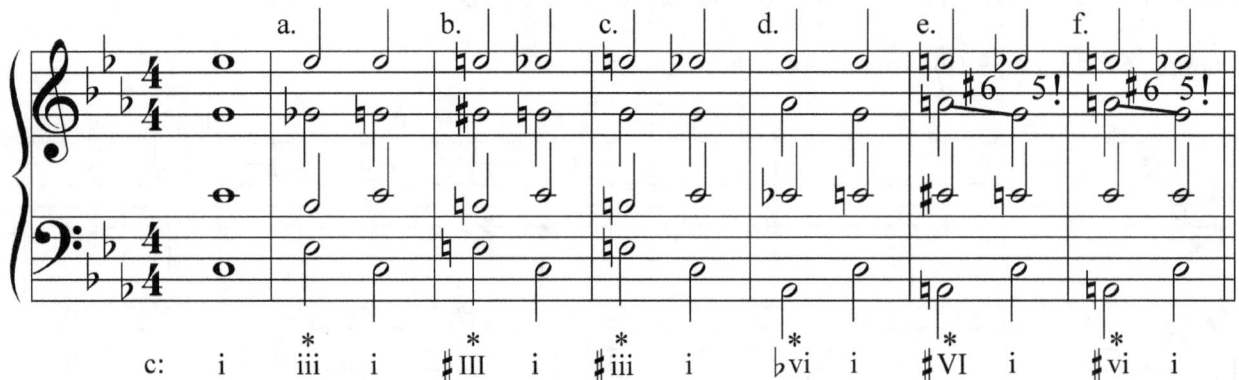

Melodic Embellishing Chords of Secondary Borrowing

As we shall see in examples 6–10 and 6–11, using melodic embellishing chords within the context of four-part texture is not without its challenges. When chords stand in a root relationship of a 2nd to each other, faulty motion is easily accomplished, particularly when triads are used as prolonging chords. The addition of the chord seventh can be helpful in establishing connections between chords. Seventh chords also provide more interpretative possibilites.

Enharmonic respelling produces the chord third of the melodic embellishing chord in 6–10a, a minor triad of the Phrygian supertonic prolonging the tonic chord. The chord third of the tonic, E, becomes F♭, the chord third of the Phrygian supertonic. Caution should be exercised when voicing this chord as a root-position melodic embellishing chord. (Notice, for example, the awkward succession of perfect 4th to diminished 3rd in the alto and tenor of example 6–10a.) The disposition of the voices and the tones of primary and secondary borrowing in 6–10a (A♭ and D♭ respectively) provide sufficient contrast between the two chords. The contrast is further darkened when the relationship occurs in minor, as in 6–11a. In any case, watch the voice leading with chords whose roots are a 2nd apart.

Chapter 6 Secondary Borrowing   143

In examples 6–10b and 6–11b, the cross-relation tritone (C and F♯) creates a strong contrast between the two chords, the tonic and its prolongation. The question becomes: how much contrast is too much contrast? And therefore: if the contrast is very strong, are there ways to lessen the intensity of the harmonic clash from the chromaticism of secondary borrowing? Can elements of secondary borrowing be made to sound as if they are appropriate to the tonal context? Ultimately, these concerns count among the problems through which composers of the early Romantic era worked.

Chords of secondary borrowing may be employed to prolong other chords or to serve as members of chord progressions, that is, as X-chords (some uses are shown below in examples 6–12, 13, and 14). As we have said, composers from the Romantic period forward began to write passages or sections of their compositions in keys of secondary borrowing, as demonstrated in examples 6–15 and 16 (Chopin's Prelude in E Major, Op. 28, No. 9).

Examples 6–10c and 6–11c present the Phrygian supertonic with a minor 7th (D♭/C♭) spelled as an augmented 6th (D♭/B). The addition of the seventh renders the function and context of the chord ambiguous. The augmented 6th resolves to a C octave. Thus, the chord may be heard as an Italian augmented 6th resolving to a C-major triad as V of the subdominant (F). Indeed, transforming the C-major triad into a dominant seventh with the addition of B♭ takes the chord's resolution to F. On the other hand, the chord could also be a doubly diminished TMD triad in first inversion. (The D♭ becomes the lowered chord third of the TMD.) The subtonic (6–10d), though less likely to occur as a melodic embellishing chord in minor, presents both a strong contrast to the tonic triad and a real seventh resolution in major (the chord seventh of the subtonic moves to the chord fifth of the tonic).

Example 6–10: in major

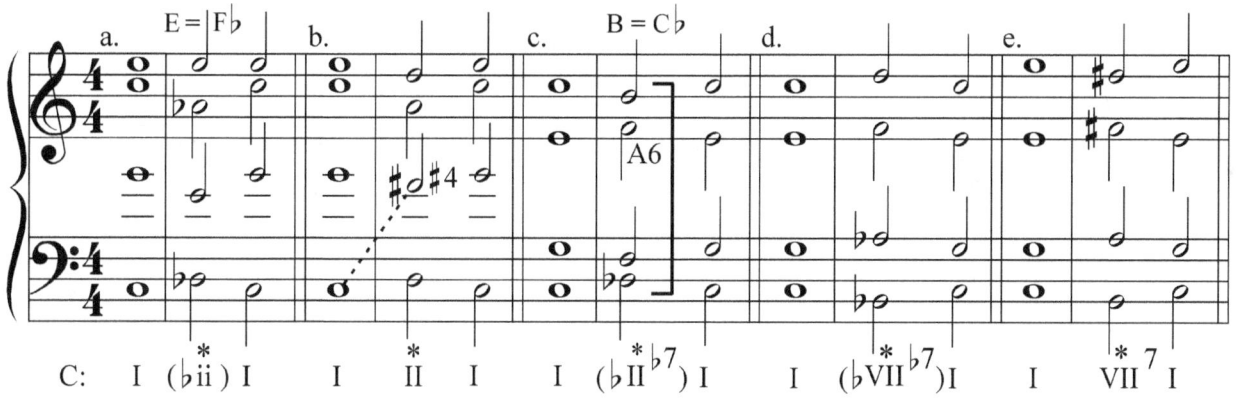

Example 6–11: in minor

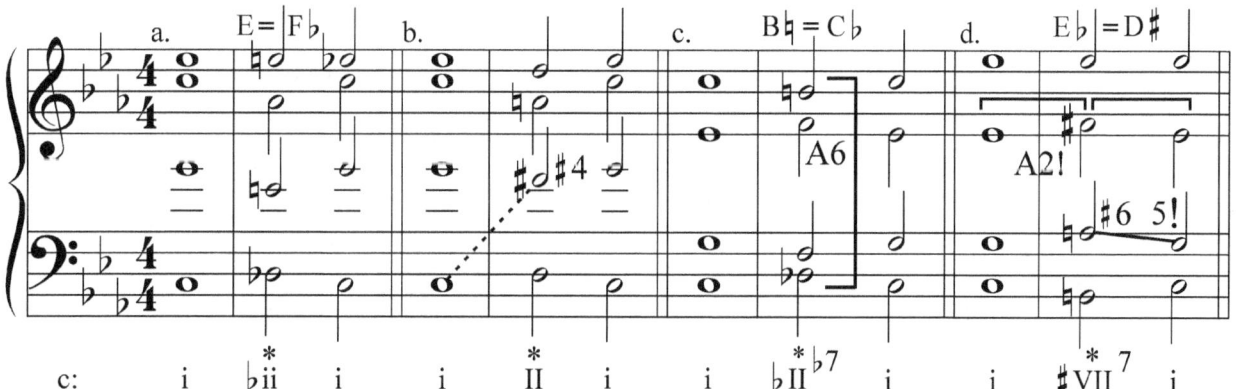

Chapter 6 Secondary Borrowing

The dominant seventh formed on the leading tone in examples 6–10e and 6–11d is more convincing in major (6–10e) than in minor (6–11d) because of the augmented 2nd between the third (E♭) of the minor tonic and the fifth (F♯) of the embellishing chord. In both major and minor, the chord takes a real seventh resolution (the seventh of the first chord proceeds to the fifth of the second).

In 6–11d, as seen in previous examples, variable ♯6 defies its normal tendency to move upwards to scale degrees ♯7 and 8 (A♮–B♮–C), moving instead down to scale degree 5 (A♮–G). Additionally, the third of the melodic embellishing chord, D♯, is enharmonically equivalent to scale degree 3, E♭.

The Mediant as an X-Chord of Secondary Borrowing

There are limitations in the voice leading when using diatonic triads of the mediant as X-chords. As we have said, a commonality of tones can make it difficult to hear a motion between chords whose roots are a 3rd apart. For instance, the minor mediant in C major (E G B), as displayed in 6–12a, has two tones in common with the tonic and dominant triads: the third and fifth of the tonic (E and G) and the root and third of the dominant (G and B). When the minor mediant follows the major tonic in a chord progression, the mediant is usually heard as an elaboration of the preceding tonic. Thus, in major, the mediant occurs infrequently as an X-chord. (The instability of the augmented mediant in minor discourages its use as an intermediary harmony. Additionally, the chord's fifth anticipates the third of the dominant, the leading tone.)

Example 6–12b demonstrates how the addition of a passing chord between the mediant and the dominant improves the voicing leading between the iii and the V. Further, the passing supertonic breaks up the common tones (B and G) between the two chords. In the soprano, the leading tone within the V serves as a substitute for scale degree 2 in measure 4 (see the D in parentheses).

Example 6–12: improving the voice leading between iii and V in major

Example 6–13: the major mediant of secondary borrowing in major

Example 6–13 above illustrates the major mediant in C major, a type-III chord of secondary borrowing. In the alto, the chord third (G♯) of the mediant provides a significant element of contrast with the fifth of the tonic and the root of the dominant (G♮). An 8—7 motion smooths out the connection from the mediant's chromatic third to the seventh (F) of the V. In 6–13b, the chord fifth (A) of the passing ii⁶ provides a tone of resolution for the third of the mediant (G♯).

In example 6–14, an E♭-major triad of type-I secondary borrowing stands on (♭3). Serving as an X-chord of the mediant, the E♭-major triad produces a high level of contrast with the initial tonic. In both examples 6–14a and 14b, the passing chord is given as either a diminished supertonic or Neapolitan 6th.

The E♭ and B♭ contained within the mediant X-chord as well as the A♭ in both the supertonic and the Neapolitan 6th infuses the progression with minor characteristics, making the final C-major triad sound like a Picardy third. In example 6–14b, the alto line is chromatically altered with the introduction of the G♭, the chord third of the minor mediant of secondary borrowing.

The THD in measure 4 of both examples 6–14a and 14b projects the variant leading tone in the soprano as a substitute for scale degree 2 (see the D in parentheses). It would be well to remember that when moving from the Neapolitan 6th to the THD, the preferred voice leading takes scale degree ♭2 down a diminished 3rd to the leading tone, either with or without passing tones.

Example 6–14: other mediants of secondary borrowing in major and minor

$$\text{C: I (♭III) (ii}^{o6}\text{) or N}^6\text{ V}^7\text{ I} \qquad \text{c: i iii ii}^{o6}\text{ or N}^6\text{ V}^7\text{ i}$$

The Chopin Prelude in E Major, Op. 28, No. 9

In 6–13a, we saw how the mediant X-chord of secondary borrowing (E G♯ B) presents a higher degree of contrast with the subsequent THD (G B D) than that provided by the diatonic iii (E G♮ B), shown previously in 6–12a.

Although the addition of a passing chord after the mediant X-chord (and before the THD) usually improves the voice leading, a mediant X-chord of secondary borrowing may proceed more readily to the dominant without an intervening passing chord, as Chopin's Prelude in E Major, Op. 28, No. 9, confirms (examples 6–15 and 16 below; in particular, measures 8 and 11).

The Prelude in E Major is a small one-part form, represented as: a a' a", with a harmonic perfect authentic cadence at the end (measure 12). More specifically, we have a three phrase group with two varied repetitions of the first four measures, phrases a and a' ending with contrapuntal half cadences in measures 4 and 8 respectively.

The top voice of each phrase begins on B, a tone which maintains its structural value until the arrival of a" (measure 9). For nine measures, inner voices rise above the structural B, prolonged by upper neighbors C (or B♯) and C♯ (example 6–23, measures 6–8). Finally, in measure 10, the melodic structure takes an unusual turn: instead of making a final descent to complete the progression, the governing 5 moves upwards to reach scale degree 1 (B–C–D–D♯–E, example 6–20).

146 Chapter 6 Secondary Borrowing

The first phrase (measures 1–4) is supported by an incomplete SHP with the half cadence on the dominant (example 6–15). An X-chord of the supertonic occurs in measure 2, beat 1. Serving as a voice-leading chord (VL), the subdominant on beat 4 of measure 1 breaks up the parallel 5ths between the tonic and the supertonic (E/B–F♯/C♯). A supertonic voice-leading chord prevents parallel 5ths in measure 3 (C♯/G♯–B/F♯). The THD is prolonged from beat 3 of measure 2 through measure 4. A voice exchange between the outer voices spans the prolongation of the dominant (B/D♯, D♯/B).

The parallel 5ths between measures 3 and 4 involve one of the inner voices (B/F♯–C♯/G♯) and occur within the larger context of the dominant prolongation and its attendant voice exchange. (On the fourth beats of measures 9–10, voice-leading chords avert parallel 5ths between E/B, F/C, F/C, and G/D.)

Example 6–15: Chopin, Prelude in E Major, Op. 28, No. 9, measures 1–6

Phrase a' begins with an E-major triad prolonged retroactively by V on beat 2 of measure 5. Beat 3 begins an excursion into the lower-level key of F major, the Phrygian supertonic. The first two measures of phrase a' contain root-position dominant triads moving to their respective chord sevenths on the last thirty-second note of each measure, producing a motion from the root position to the third inversion of the chord. In measures 1–2, this operation breaks up the parallel 5ths between the initial tonic and the supertonic

X-chord. In all instances, the third inversion resolves to either a root-position or first-inversion triad. Note for later consideration the root-position chord of resolution in measure 7 (example 6–16): an A-major passing triad on the primary accent of the measure. It occurs within an intriguing complex of interlocking voice exchanges between inner and outer voices extending across measures 6–7.

The prolongation of F-major begins in the fifth measure with [V$^{5}_{3}$–$^{4}_{2}$–I^{6}] of C, the dominant. A G-minor passing $^{6}_{4}$ leads to V^{7}–$^{4}_{2}$ in F major. The second V$^{4}_{2}$ should proceed to the main-level I^{6}; however, the resolution to F major is denied (see the crossed-out I^{6} in 6–15, measure 6) in favor of a more important harmonic destination at the end of phrase a', namely, G♯ major (spelled A♭ in example 6–16, measure 8).

Ultimately, the G♯ major triad constitutes a major mediant in a major key, a chord of secondary borrowing. Since G♯ major presents the reader with an excessive number of sharps, we are grateful to Chopin for writing the passage in A♭ major.

Example 6–16: Chopin, Prelude in E Major, Op. 28, No. 9, measures 7–12

148   Chapter 6   Secondary Borrowing

The cadences for the first two phrases (a and a') involve elaborations of the dominant chord. As stated earlier, phrase a is an incomplete SHP: I – ii – V, ending in measure 4 with an elaborating V^6_5 (example 6–17). Phrase a' also forms an incomplete SHP: I – III – V^7, concluding in measure 8 on the dominant of E major. The B-dominant seventh is preceded by an applied cadential $^6_4$ that extends the articulation of the A♭-major X-chord (that is, G♯ major) across three beats.

The gesture in F major after the retroactive dominant in measure 5 provides an effective harmonic transition to the subsequent entry of A♭ major, as F major eliminates the four sharps of E major and adds B♭, the first flat of A♭ major. The network of interlocking voice exchanges in measures 6–7 moves through the tones C, E, G, and B♭, all pitches for the THD of F major.

The resolution to F major is withheld, however, as the C-dominant seventh begins (or perhaps continues) a crucial harmonic transformation. Indeed, the very function and identity of this chord changes with the harmony of measure 7. The upper components of the chord (E, G, B♭) assume an important role in establishing the key of A♭ major (G♯ major). As we shall see, the root (C) becomes something else entirely.

Example 6–17: Chopin, Prelude in E Major, Op. 28, No. 9, measures 4–9

Harmonic Transformation and Reinterpretation

Instead of the V$^4_2$ of F major (measure 6, beat 4) resolving as expected, the chord proceeds to an A-major triad in root position (measure 7), a passing chord within the third voice exchange (B♭/G, G/B♭). The most important component of the A-major triad is its chord third, C♯. It is only with the arrival of the C♯ within the A-major triad that the significance of the tones C, E, G, and B♭ can be understood.

The C-dominant seventh is a gradual enharmonic respelling of a fully diminished seventh rooted on F𝑥, the leading tone of G♯ major: F𝑥 A♯ C♯ E. The fully diminished seventh forms the (vii o^7) of G♯ major (A♭ major). In effect, Chopin stretches out the formation of the applied TMD by using the C-dominant seventh to point first to F major and then by taking the C of that chord to its real destination, C♯, the chord fifth of the F𝑥-fully diminished seventh.

The meaning of the tone C is determined by its forward direction, the C functions like a B♯ leading to C♯. Ultimately, the duty of the A-major passing chord is to introduce the C♯, the missing chord fifth for G♯'s (vii o^7). The third and fourth voice exchanges move through the root, third, and seventh of (vii o^7), but not its chord fifth: F𝑥 A♯ E is spelled as G B♭ E (or F♭).

A passing ii$^6_4$ chord on beat 3 (measure 7) leads to (vii o$^4_2$) on beat 4, written as: F♭ G B♭ D♭ (in G♯ major: E F𝑥 A♯ C♯). The (vii o$^4_2$) proceeds to the cadential $^6_4$ of G♯ major in measure 8, forming a conversion dominant as the bass descends from F♭ to E♭ (E to D♯ in G♯ major).

Both passing chords in measure 7 (beats 1 and 3) have supertonic roots within the written context of A♭ major. The root of the ii$^6_4$ on beat 3 is B♭ (A♯ in G♯ major). The root of the supertonic on beat 1 is B♭♭ in A♭ major, misspelled, fortunately, as A (A in G♯ major). In any case, regardless of its spelling, the A-major triad is (♭II) of G♯ major.

Now, in order to summarize what we understand about phrase a', let us revisit its harmony. Two important questions arise:

(1) Is the C chord in measure 6 (example 6–17) real or apparent?

The C chord is apparent. As we have observed, it contains the root (F𝑥), third (A♯), and seventh (E) of a fully diminished seventh whose fifth (C♯) is missing. The chord fifth is added only after the arrival of the A-major triad in measure 7. First, Chopin points towards F major with the tones C E G B♭; but then, he turns in a different direction by treating the C as a placeholder for C♯. Instead of C E G B♭ taking us to F major, the C turns into C♯; the chord is reinterpreted as F𝑥 A♯ C♯ E and we are thus led to the (vii o^7) of G♯ major.

(2) How do we describe the chord over the B♭ on beat 4 of measure 6?

The task is to represent the formation of a first-inversion fully diminished seventh whose chord fifth, C♯, is denied. Spelled in A♭ major and standing a major 2nd above a B♭ bass, the tone C remains frozen. It produces what sounds like a dominant seventh (of F major). Since the C♯ does not yet appear within the fully diminished seventh, the interval of the 2nd above B♭ cannot be represented in the generic figured bass as proceeding to the interval of the 3rd (which would be a B♯ moving to C♯, assuming an A♯ bass).

Therefore, as in 6–17 above, the 3 of the generic figured bass is crossed out in order to avoid the indication that the C♯ has actually occurred within the chord (with the understanding that the B♭ is really A♯). The figured bass and crossed-out 3 tell us that the apparent chord does not move to the real chord. Instead, we get the C♯ within the A-major triad. A complete statement of G♯'s (vii o^7) occurs only after the A-major triad has introduced the C♯.

In the top voice of the first two phrases (a and a ′), the most important tone for the melodic structure is B, scale degree 5 of the main-level key. Both phrases begin and end on B with a stepwise ascending motion towards E (moving beyond E in the second phrase). In the first phrase, the E is reached within a prolongation of the dominant and therefore does not serve as a melodic goal of arrival (example 6–15, measure 3, beat 1). In the second phrase (example 6–17, measure 6), E becomes part of the harmonic transformation that ultimately yields the (vii$°^7$) of G♯ major (F𝄪 A♯ C♯ E).

The E belongs to the complex of voice exchanges in measures 6–7. Spelled as F♭ in measure 7 (example 6–18), E ends up in the bass moving down to E♭ (E to D♯ in G♯ major) while the top voice continues upwards to A♭. Ultimately, the E bass (F♭) leads the (vii$°^4_2$) to the cadential $^6_4$ of G♯ major. And so, E is not a melodic goal of arrival in phrase a ′, though it is part of the conversion dominant that heralds the arrival of G♯ major.

The structural value of B is retained throughout phrases a and a ′. As the top voice ascends, B moves into the inner voice. In the first phrase, the inner voices rise above the B. In measure 6 (6–17), the second phrase gains B♭ and loses B♮, which despite its conspicuous absence from the melody maintains its superiority as the primary melodic tone. The B returns at the end of phrase a ′ with the arrival of the dominant. As we have indicated, the introduction of the B♭ facilitates the spelling of G♯ major as A♭ major.

The Secondary Melodic Progression (SMP): Ascending Melodic Structure

In Chapter 5, we cited two types of chord-supported structural melody: a tone-embellishing melodic succession, abbreviated as TEMB, and a basic melodic progression, abbreviated as BMP. A TEMB is melodic activity involving either neighbor motion above or below a tone, or repetitions of a tone (inverted pedal embellishment), or combinations of neighbor tones and repeated tones. A BMP is a melodic descent to scale degree 1 from either scale degree 5 or 3.

A third type of chord-supported structural melody has a stepwise ascent from scale degree 5 to scale degree 1; we call this melodic structure a secondary melodic progression, abbreviated as SMP. The SMP is supported by an SHP and is far less common than either the BMP or TEMB (less common at the highest structural level, or background, as referenced in the next section). The third phrase of the Prelude in E Major contains an SMP supported by an SHP.

Thus, it is only with the third phrase, a ″ (6–18), that the melodic structure begins to move away from the B. The Prelude in E Major shows an *ascending* melodic progression to the tonic, E (B–C–D–D♯–E); this ascent completes the melodic structure of the composition.

As shown in measures 10–11 (example 6–18), two chords of secondary borrowing occur between the E-major tonic and the dominant: the Phrygian supertonic (F A C) and the mediant X-chord (G B D). Both chords support ascending tones in the melodic structure (C and D).

Two voice-leading chords (VL) facilitate the connections between I, (♭II), and (♭III). Borrowed from the parallel minor, E major's minor subdominant (A C E) prevents faulty motion (E/B–F/C) between the tonic and Phrygian supertonic in measures 9–10. An applied subdominant (B♭ D F) of the Phrygian supertonic breaks up parallel 5ths (F/C–G/D) between (♭II) and (♭III) in measures 10–11.

The respective thirds of both voice-leading chords become the fifths of the chords they precede (a reduction of this operation is shown in example 6–19): the C of the A-minor triad is the fifth of the following F-major triad; the D of the B♭-major triad is the fifth of the following G-major triad.

Over the tonic triad in measure 9 (beat 3), an ascending 5—6 motion (E/B–C) becomes 5—3 (E/B–A/C), as the E bass moves to A instead of remaining stationary. The A bass on beat 4 forms an octave with one of the inner voices and then proceeds to F in measure 10, producing an 8—10 motion (A/A–F/A). (Measure 1 is almost identical to measure 9 and uses the same 8—10 motion on beat 4.)

Measure 10 continues sequentially: over the Phrygian supertonic (beat 3), the 5—6 motion (F/C–D) becomes 5—3 (F/C–B♭/D), as the F bass proceeds to B♭. The B♭ bass forms an octave with the inner voice and then moves to G, sequencing the 8—10 motion of the previous measure (B♭/B♭–G/B♭).

Example 6–18: Chopin, Prelude in E Major, Op. 28, No. 9, measures 7–12

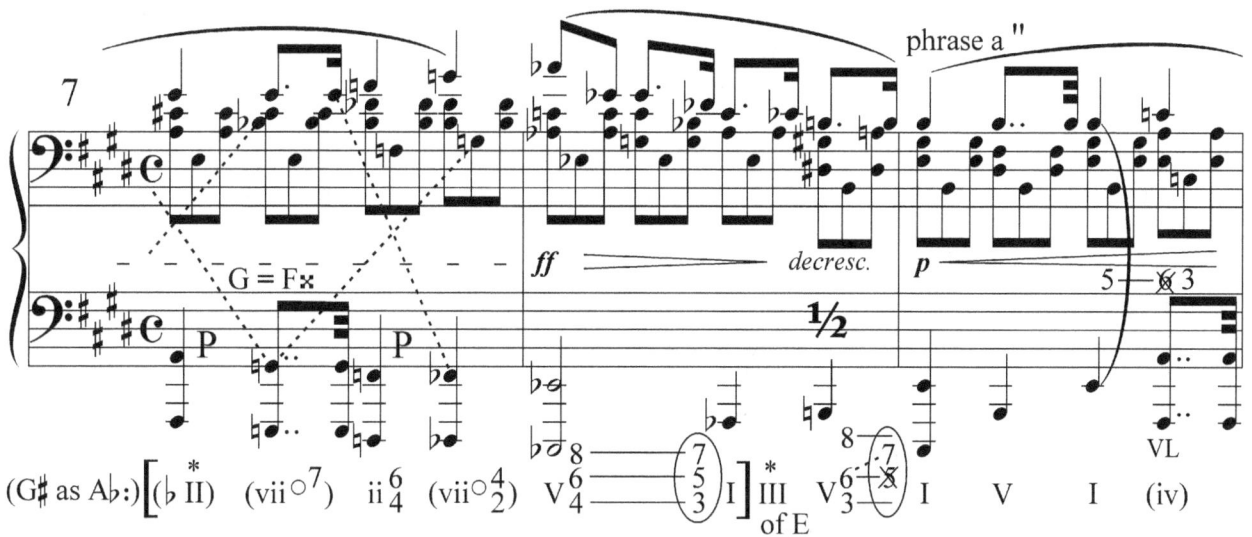

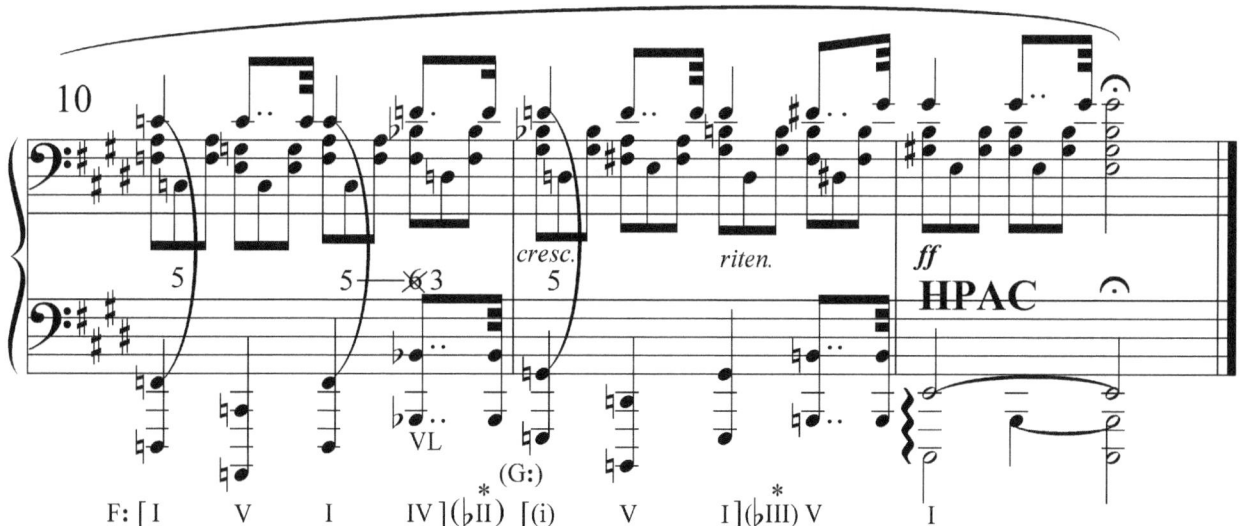

Example 6–19: the ascending 5—6

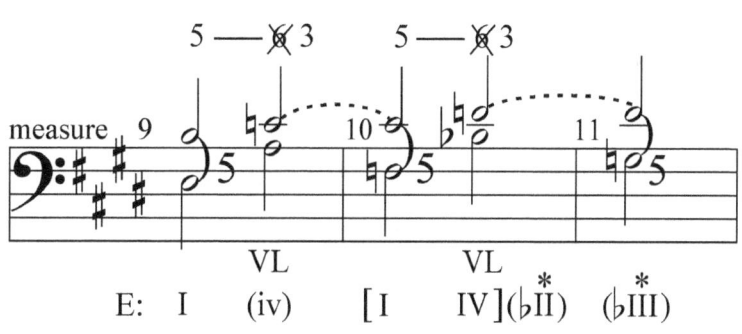

The Late Middleground of Chopin's Prelude in E Major, Op. 28, No. 9

Up to this point in our studies of both diatonic and chromatic harmony, we have given the reader the opportunity to focus more on harmonic principles and less on the symbols and jargon associated with the great analytic tradition of Heinrich Schenker and his foremost disciple, Felix Salzer. To be sure, we have introduced important concepts associated with structural analysis in that tradition.

With Chopin, however, we find a form of musical expression that should be considered from a structuralist perspective even by those who might not otherwise want to delve deeply into the analytic insights of Schenker. Indeed, entire volumes are devoted exclusively to teaching Schenkerian analysis. This is not our objective here, as we would prefer a text devoted entirely to the concepts of structure and prolongation.

Still, the E-Major Prelude tempts us with its unusual melodic structure, its chords of secondary borrowing, and its voice leading. The SMP that exists within this composition is not a typical structure of the highest rank, what Schenkerians call "the background." Such structures, the bare bones of the musical work, rarely exhibit an ascending structural progression. The SMP is not typically an operation of the background, which usually contains a descending melodic structure (scale degrees 5 or 3 down to 1). (As discussed later in this chapter, the SMP is but one type of "linear melodic progression," or LMP.)

Using Schenkerian carets (∧) over Arabic numbers to represent melodic scale degrees of the highest structural rank, example 6–20 presents what would be described as a late middleground voice-leading graph for the E-Major Prelude. In Schenkerian notation, notes of higher structural significance are assigned longer note values; accordingly, unfilled note heads represent the events of the background, whereas prolongational elements of the middleground take filled-in note heads.

We have the retained B from measures 1–9 after which the melodic voice takes a partial chromatic ascent to E, the tonic. The ascending line contains tones of primary (C) and secondary (D) borrowing. Two incomplete progressions of the middleground (in phrases a and a ') prolong the tonic chord across the first nine measures.

Example 6–20: structural framework of Chopin's Prelude in E Major, Op. 28, No. 9 (SHP/SMP)

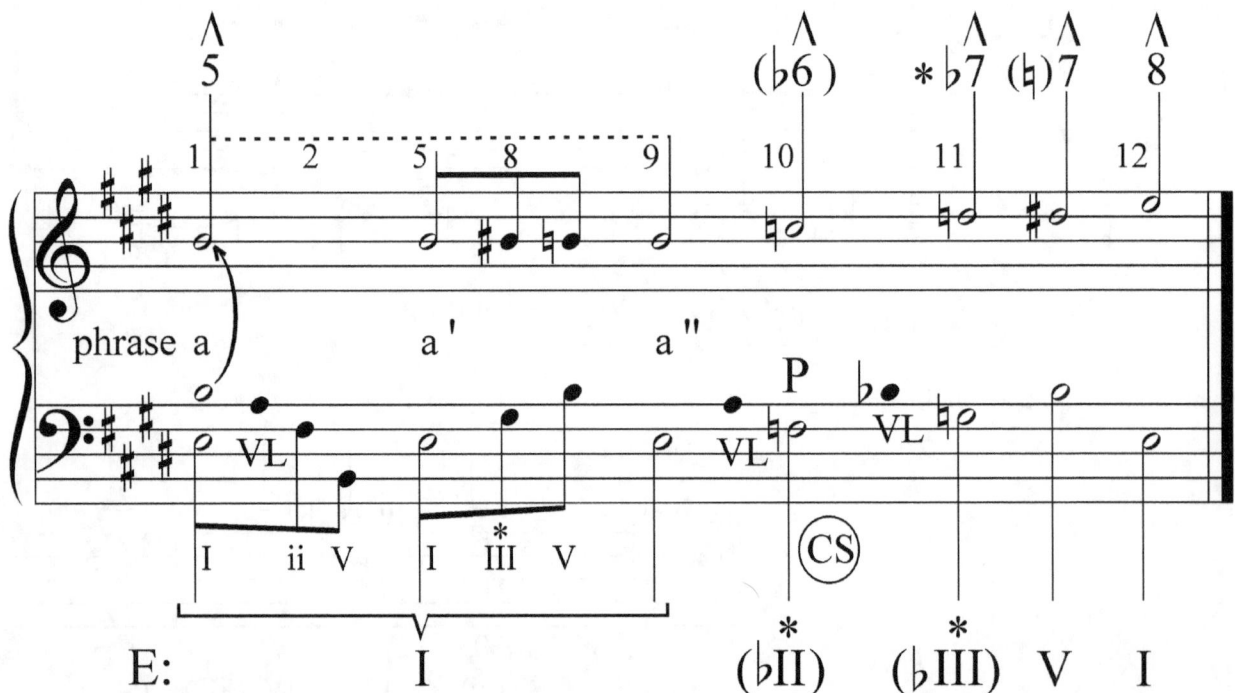

The Contrapuntal-Structural Chord

In *Structural Hearing: Tonal Coherence In Music* (New York: Boni, 1952), Felix Salzer puts forward the term "contrapuntal-structural chord" to describe an operation in which a chord serving a contrapuntal function (such as a passing chord or neighbor chord) also supports a tone of the melodic structure.

In *Finding The Right Pitch III*, we understand the contrapuntal-structural chord as a harmony which in any other circumstance would fulfill the function of contrapuntal prolongation at the middleground rank; however, in its new role of supporting a structural melodic tone, this contrapuntal chord is elevated to the rank of middleground or background structural progression, becoming thereby a contrapuntal-prolonging chord with added structural significance.

Usually, the X-chord is some type of supertonic, mediant, subdominant, or submediant harmony that supports the melodic structure. In its support of the top voice, the contrapuntal-structural chord adds another potential X-chord type to the progression. (Note carefully: mediant chords always take precedence over all other chords as the intermediary harmony of rank.)

The Phrygian supertonic in example 6–20 above is both a passing chord (P) and contrapuntal-structural chord (CS), as it supports the structural melodic C, scale degree (♭6). The mediant X-chord supports D, a tone of secondary borrowing, indicated as ♭7. Since the next melodic tone is D♯, the mediant X-chord prevents an augmented 2nd in the top voice (C–D♯) by filling in the undesirable interval with D♮.

The generic natural in parentheses (6–20) indicates that the leading tone, D♯, follows an altered tone. In this instance, the reinstatement of diatonic scale degree 7 is represented with the generic natural. The natural tells us that the inflected voice returns to the tone that would have otherwise occurred within the diatonic framework of the key and mode. When ♭7 comes into major as a result of secondary borrowing and then proceeds to the leading tone, the description of the operation remains essentially the same as that used in the parallel minor. (Example 2–8 demonstrates the application of the generic natural in minor when variable ♯7 is preceded by variable ♭7.)

Example 6–21 displays a few possibilities for the contrapuntal-structural chord (CS). In 6–21a and 21b, we have CLT chords addressing the tonic: a vii^7 chord of secondary borrowing and the V$^6_5$, both lower neighbor chords. Examples 6–21c and 21d have descents from scale degree 5 supported by two-progression frameworks (numbered 1 and 2 in brackets). Example 21c uses two CLT dominants to support scale degrees 4 and 2 in the top voice; the first is an upper neighbor chord, the second a passing chord. Example 21d shows three successive CS chords, including I^6 as a passing chord.

Example 6–21: uses for the contrapuntal-structural chord

The Acclimation of Secondary Borrowing

The third phrase, a″, consists of three I–V–I progressions: in E, F, and G major respectively (example 6–22). The latter progression, [(i) V I] (♭III), proceeds from a G-minor triad to a G-major triad, a chord of secondary borrowing. As we have observed, over the tonic triad in measure 9 (beat 3), the voices move upwards within an ascending 5—6 sequence (E/B–C) that becomes 5—3 (E/B–A/C) as the E bass moves to A instead of remaining stationary. Measure 10 continues the ascent. Over the Phrygian supertonic (beat 3), the 5—6 motion (F/C–D) becomes 5—3 (F/C–B♭/D), as the F bass proceeds to B♭.

Chopin acclimates the listener to the chromatic shock of G major by moving first to a G-minor triad, which contains a B♭ as its chord third. The B♭ occurs previously in F major as the root of IV and as part of the 8—10 motion initiated on beat 4 of measure 10 (B♭/B♭–G/B♭). The G-minor triad, a ii chord in F major, provides a convincing link to G major as the motion from B♭ to B♮ transforms the quality of the chord from minor to major. Ultimately, the B♮ becomes the goal of arrival for a chromatic ascent that begins in the inner voice on G♯ in measure 9, that is: G♯–A–A♯(B♭)–B♮.

Example 6–22: Chopin, Prelude in E Major, Op. 28, No. 9, third phrase (a″)

Earlier, in example 6–5, we saw how a triad of secondary borrowing can be interpreted as an applied dominant of diatonic scale degrees. Using an applied THD or TMD is an effective way to introduce a chord of secondary borrowing into the tonal framework. For example, in C major, the key (or chord) of A major could be established with its own dominant. Although A major is not diatonically related C major, using an E-dominant seventh encourages the listener to anticipate and accept its appearance.

As we have seen, a complete statement of the (vii○^{7}) of G♯ major (F× A♯ C♯ E) occurs only after the A-major triad in measure 7 has introduced the C♯. Subsequently, C♯ (D♭) becomes the chord third of the passing ii$^6_4$ of G♯ major (A♭) on beat 3 (A♯ is spelled as B♭). The ii$^6_4$ is located within the network of interlocking voice exchanges from which (vii○^{7}) of G♯ major emerges. Notably, the chord seventh of G♯'s eventual V is C♯ (D♯ F× A♯ C♯).

Throughout the inner voice of measure 7, the C♯ (D♭) provides an element of pitch continuity between the harmonic transformation and the cadence in G♯ major (A♭). All of the chords in measure 7 contain the C♯, the tone so conspicuously withheld in measure 6 just as the harmonic transformation commences.

An Early Middleground of Chopin's Prelude in E Major, Op. 28, No. 9, Measures 5–8

Example 6–23 displays an early middleground voice-leading graph of measures 5–8 of the E-Major Prelude, that is, phrase a'. (The harmonic framework of the III chord of secondary borrowing is spelled in G♯ major.) In measure 6, the C-major triad presents itself as both (♭VI^6) of E major and as V of F major. The bass unfolds through the chord seventh, third, and root of G♯'s (vii○^{7}): E–A♯–F×–E.

As the harmonic transformation ensues, the (vii○^{7}) of G♯ major moves across the network of interlocking voice exchanges. Subsequently, the conversion dominant and its elaboration prepares the arrival of the mediant X-chord. (As in example 6–20 above, only the unfilled note heads represent the events of the background, whereas prolongational elements of the middleground take filled-in note heads.)

Example 6–23: Chopin, Prelude in E Major, Op. 28, No. 9, measures 5–8

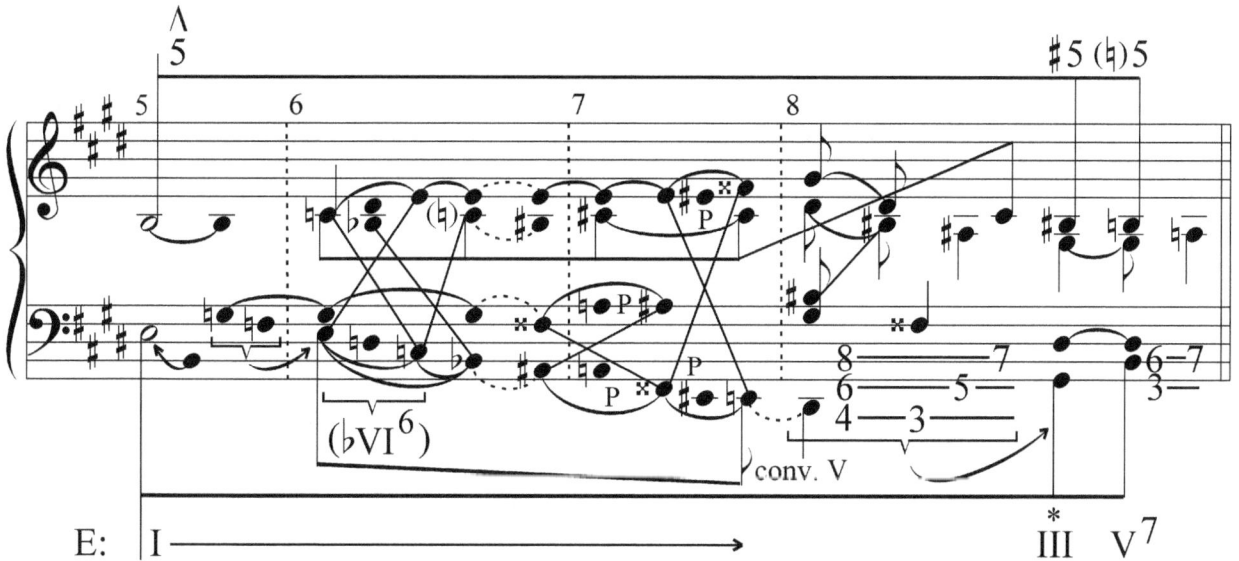

The Linear Melodic Progression (LMP)

Melodic-harmonic structures and melodic-contrapuntal structures of the middleground rank occur in both the main-level key and lower-level keys. These operations constitute prolongation-structures of internal elements (that is, smaller formal units) contained within a large-scale composition. The melodic aspect of prolongation-structures projects what we call the linear melodic progression, or LMP.

The LMP is an upward or downward stepwise expression of a melodic interval or chord, fully harmonized, and appearing in the main-level key and in lower-level keys. LMPs constitute middleground melodic activities prolonging either a single chord or the way between chords. The governing tone of the LMP and its prolongation are connected to the background framework or even to the melodic structure of the later middleground.

The SMP in Chopin's Prelude in E Major is but one type of LMP, an ascending LMP that proceeds upwards from scale degrees 5 to 1. When the melodic structure takes an ascent from scale degrees 5 to 1, it is supported by a one-progression framework, an SHP.

As we have seen in the E-Major Prelude, the SMP may sometimes be encountered as a typical background structure for a composition that is notably short but nonetheless complete. In other words, we may find the SMP serving as the structural framework for a short composition.

Example 6–24 is a later middleground graph for the first ten measures of Beethoven's Violin Sonata No. 5 in F Major, Op. 24, the "Spring" Sonata. (Example 6–25 displays the music for this passage.) An ascending LMP spanning a minor 3rd from scale degrees 3 to 5 extends across measures 1–8. The LMP is supported by an SHP in F major: I – ii – V – I^6.

This progression also occurs as an SHP of the background rank for measures 1–10: I – ii^6 – V^7 – I. In the top voice, scale degree 3 retains its structural value through the first eight measures, reaching scale degree 2 in measure 9. Subsequently, the leading tone serves as a substitute for the supertonic.

Example 6–24: later middleground of Beethoven's Violin Sonata No. 5 in F Major, Op. 24 (Allegro)

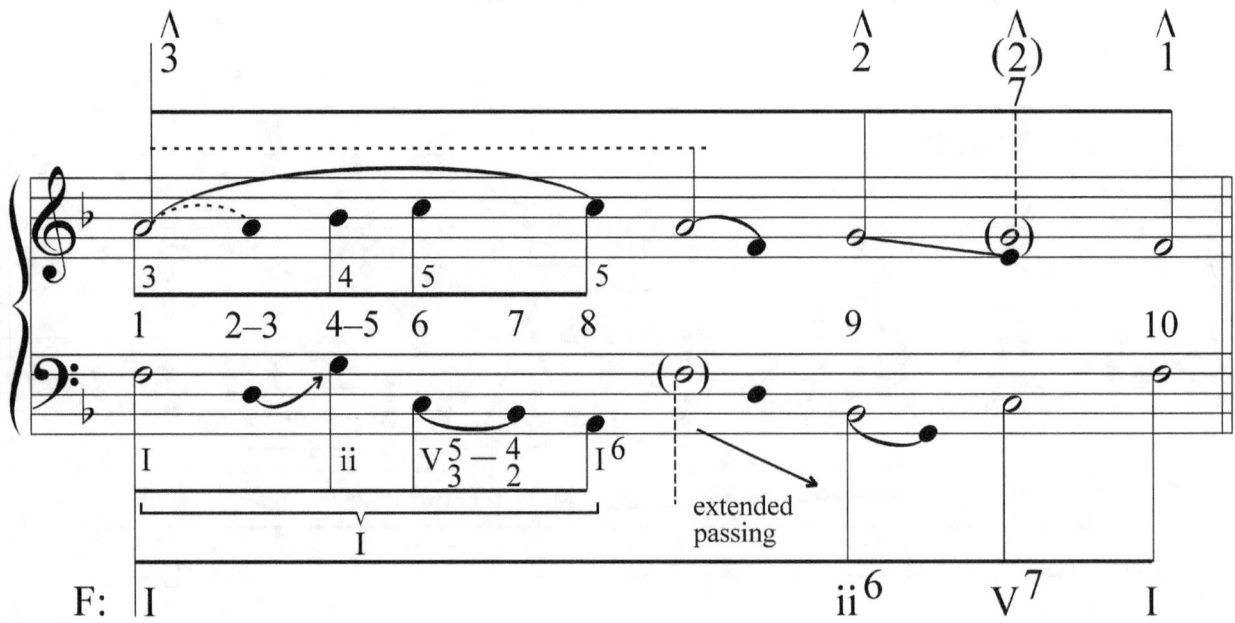

Example 6–25: Beethoven, Violin Sonata No. 5 in F Major, Op. 24 (Allegro, measures 1–10)

As we have indicated, the LMP is harmonized linear expression of a vertical interval or chord. It occurs in both the main-level key and in lower-level keys. LMPs constitute middleground melodic activities prolonging either a single chord or the way between chords. The following list identifies the other properties of the LMP. The LMP is

(1) a line the individual notes of which are supported by chords of succession, chords of harmonic or contrapuntal progression, or chords of sequential succession;

(2) a line in which the linear interval formed by the head note with its final note must vertically belong to the chord of arrival, be it identical to or different from the chord supporting the head note. An LMP is a false LMP when the interval formed by the head note with its final note does not fit the chord of arrival;

(3) a line in which non-harmonic tone activity as well as interval unfolding(s) may additionally elaborate any or all of its tones. In fact, such elaborated lines are far more common than the unelaborated ones, particularly when the interval spanned is a 4th or more;

(4) a line which may appear in its totality either in the principal voice or in a secondary voice; further, elements of the line may occasionally share two voices;

(5) a line in which the interval formed by the head note with its final note will span a major or minor 3rd (as in example 6–24 above, measures 1–8) through a major or minor 6th, never a 2nd and rarely a 7th;

(6) a line in which the governing tone (of the LMP) may be either the first or last tone or neither; in the latter instance, the motion from the head note to the final note constitutes an unfolding from one inner voice to another;

(7) a line which may involve "variant" harmonizations. A variant harmonization occurs when any two successive notes belong to a *single* chord, as opposed to the standard harmonization whereby each note belongs to a *different* chord. Thus, variant harmonizations commonly consist of melodic activities above a single chord derived from contrapuntal operations involving passing motion (for instance: 8—7, 6—5, 5—6) and suspensions (for example: 4—3, 7—6, 9—8).

Double-Function Chords

The concept of the double-function chord was introduced in *Structural Hearing: Tonal Coherence In Music* by Felix Salzer. Double-function chords are chords of harmony, standing in a harmonic root relationship to the chords they address and prolong. In *Finding The Right Pitch III*, we discern two types of double-function chords:

(1) The first type (DF) is a chord which, in any other circumstances, would fulfill the function of harmonic prolongation at the middleground rank; however, in a new role of supporting a structural melodic tone, this harmonic chord is elevated to the rank of middleground or background structural progression, becoming thereby a harmonic-prolonging chord with added structural significance.

(2) The second type (X-DF) is a chord which normally fulfills the function of a regular X-chord member of a middleground or background harmonic or contrapuntal progression; however, in a new role of supporting a prolonging-embellishing tone (i.e., a complete or incomplete upper or lower neighbor, which has replaced an expected structural melodic tone), this otherwise intermediate chord of harmony assumes a hybrid status—it becomes a chord of weakened harmonic influence supporting a decorating tone.

Example 6–26a shows an applied dominant of V serving as a DF chord. The structural melody (soprano) moves down from scale degrees 3 to 1. Since the applied dominant in 6–26a supports scale degree 2 in the top voice, the chord is elevated to the rank of background.

However, it would be well to understand that background progressions such as the ones in 6–26 yield a multitude of prolongation-structures for smaller formal units of the middleground rank. For instance, the background progression for the first ten measures of the Beethoven Violin Sonata No. 5 in F Major (example 6–24 above), I – ii ^{6} – V ^{7} – I, is duplicated at an earlier middleground as I – ii – V – I ^{6} (measures 1-8). Were either of these supertonic X-chords transformed into a major triad or dominant seventh, they would function as applied dominants supporting the structural melodic tones of their respective background and middleground ranks. In other words, they would become DF chords.

Examples 6–26b and 26c display a few other possibilities. In measure 1 of 6–26b, a harmonic embellishing chord of the subdominant supports scale degree 4 in the top voice; the IV is a DF chord. In measure 2, the IV occupies the X-chord position but does not support a structural melodic tone. Rather, the IV takes an incomplete upper neighbor in the soprano (inc UN), a prolonging-embellishing tone. This subdominant is an X-DF chord. (The direct 5th between the tenor and alto, A/F–G/D, is avoided with the cadential $^6_4$.)

In 6–26c, the harmonic prolongation is retroactive. The B♭-major triad relates back to the mediant X-chord while the F-minor triad prolongs the subtonic. Therefore, two DF chords appear in succession. Each chord of this SHP supports a BMP of the background (or an LMP of the middleground) with a descent from scale degree 5: G–G–F–F–E♭–D–C. (Remember: mediant chords always take precedence over all other chords as the intermediary harmony of rank.)

Example 6–26: uses for the double-function chord

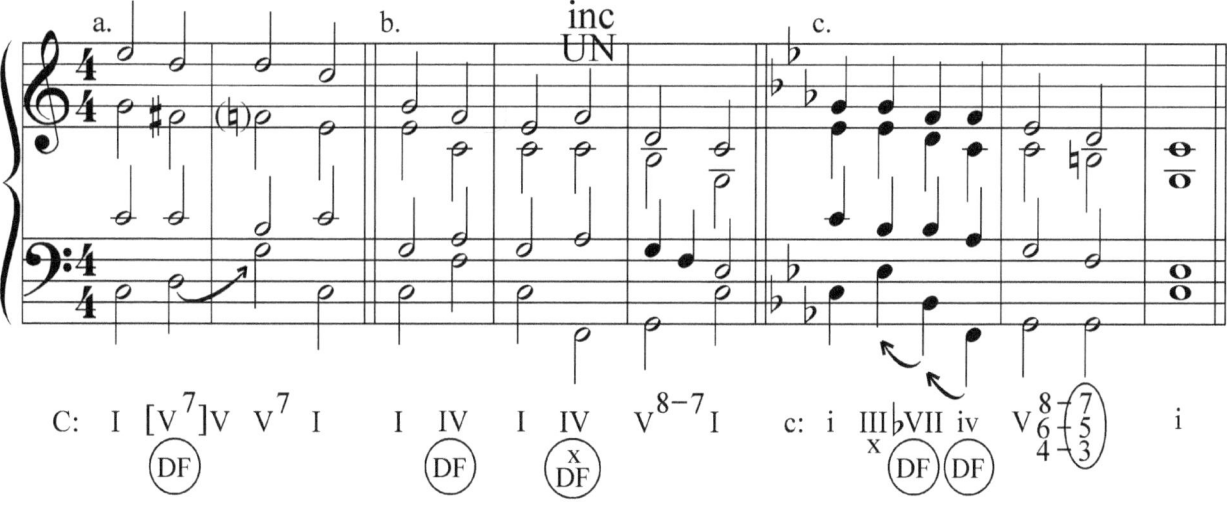

Chapter 7   The Sequence

One of the most important functions of the sequence is to serve as an expansion, or transition, either between unlike chords or different positions of the same chord. In this chapter, we will examine several types of sequences within both diatonic and chromatic frameworks and discover a variety of harmonic and contrapuntal techniques for effecting these expansions. The chords of these sequences are displayed first as triads and then as sevenths or as combinations of triads and sevenths (examples 7–1 through 7–12 feature sevenths only). The figured bass symbols between the clefs and staves at the beginning of each example represent the first two chord positions of the sequence. (In the first twelve examples, the lines adjoining the numbers, either curved or with arrows, indicate voice leading.)

Our study of each pattern of intervals within the sequence exceeds the scope of what usually occurs in music literature. In practice, more than three repetitions of any sequential pattern may prove to be excessive, as the examples below confirm. Of particular interest in the sequence is the pattern of intervals in the outer voices, which are the most exposed voices. In the examples, we identify this outer-voice interval-pattern with the abbreviation "OVIP."

Many of the examples from 7–13 forward demonstrate the potential appearance of the diminished triad in root position, which composers sometimes avoid when writing harmonic sequences. However, as we observed in the descending 5th sequence of examples 3–32 and 3–33 above, there are sequences in which the diminished triad in root position may occur. Indeed, the compelling forward momentum of the descending 5th shifts the focus away from the dissonant tritone above the root of the chord. In the present chapter, our exploration of the diminished triad's appearance within the various types of sequences will help us understand when this chord might be used and when it should be avoided.

The Descending 5th: Root-Position Seventh Chords (Harmonic Bass)

In Chapter 3, we presented the descending 5th sequence as an interlocking pattern of seventh chords. This pattern may be expressed with either harmonic or contrapuntal bass lines and may occur in both diatonic and chromatic settings. Modal dominants are "in the key" (example 7–1) whereas applied dominants are "out of (the) key" (example 7–2).

Example 7–1 displays a series (or chain) of root-position *modal* dominant sevenths. The voice leading corresponds to that shown in example 3–14 above, which illustrates the overlapping resolutions of interlocking sevenths using applied dominants. One chord finishes a 7 3 motion in one voice (C down to B, measure 2, soprano) while simultaneously initiating a 7 3 motion with the next chord in a different voice (F down to E, measures 2–3, alto). (Remember that with applied dominants, a stationary seventh occurs.)

Example 7–1: OVIP 7 3 (in the key, sevenths, harmonic bass)

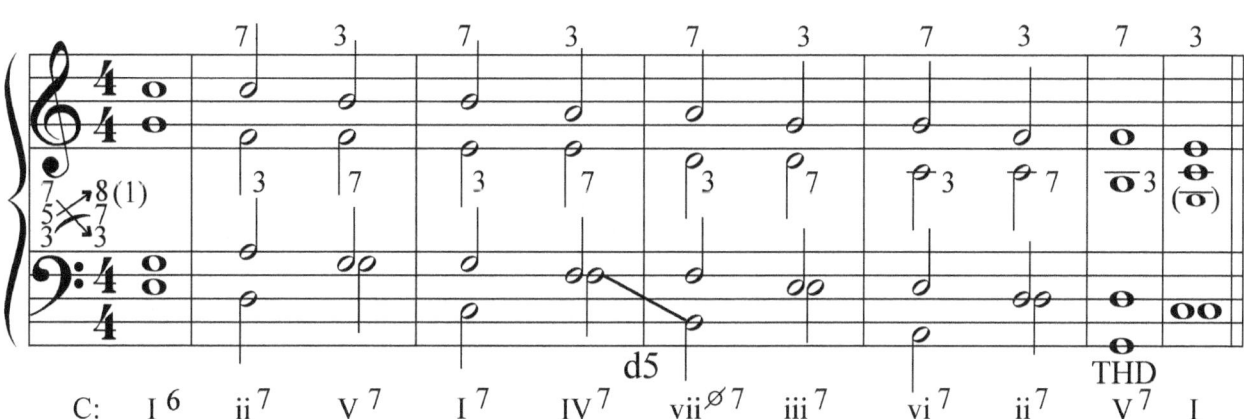

162   Chapter 7 The Sequence

Ultimately, the sequence of modal dominants shown above constitutes a harmonic prolongation of the way from the I^6 to the THD, with a stepwise descent in the bass on the primary accent of each measure, from E to G: E–D–C–B–A–G. The second chord of each chord pair breaks up the parallel 5ths that would otherwise occur on the primary accents between the bass and tenor (measures 2–6).

The sequence in 7–1 draws to a close with the arrival of ii^7, the X-chord. In addition to averting the parallel 5ths between vi^7 and V^7, the supertonic thereby constitutes both the end of the sequence and beginning of the cadential structure (X – V – I).

Throughout this chapter, the sequences are presented first in C major and then in c minor, starting here with various expressions of the descending 5th using interlocking sevenths. Subsequently, we consider the following sequences, using combinations of triads and sevenths: the ascending 5—6, the ascending 5th, and the descending 5—6 (in that order). Within these sequences, there are diatonic and chromatic variants that merit our attention as well.

The Tritone and the Descending 5th

Every diatonic mode contains a tritone between two of its scale degrees (B–F in example 7–1). The tritone prevents the succession of chords from leading away from the main-level key, as the root movement would otherwise proceed through a succession of falling perfect 5ths and rising perfect 4ths (or rising perfect 4ths and falling perfect 5ths); for example: C–F–B–E–A–D–G would become C–F–B♭–E♭–A♭–D♭–G♭.

As we saw in Chapter 3, however, the tritone presents certain difficulties in major between scale degrees 4 and 7 and in minor between scale degrees 2 and ♭6. When using *applied* dominants on these scale degrees, the seventh of the first chord does not move down because the tone is enharmonically equivalent to the third of the next chord, resulting in the stationary seventh. (See 7–2 below, measures 3–4; the stationary seventh on E♭ is re-interpreted as D♯.)

In major, scale degree 7 supports a diminished triad, a chord that cannot be tonicized. Moreover, the tritone between scale degrees 4 and 7 in major and 2 and ♭6 in minor prevents a true applied dominant relationship from developing between the chords on these scale degrees. For this relationship can be established only when the distance between the two chords is that of a rising perfect 4th or falling perfect 5th. (In 7–2, the exclamation mark attached to the bracket underscores the problematic nature of the tritone area in the sequence of applied dominants. To review the presence of the tritone and the stationary seventh when using applied dominants on scale degrees 4 and 7 in major and 2 and ♭6 in minor, see Chapter 3, pp. 44–47.)

Example 7–2: OVIP 7   3 (out of key, sevenths, harmonic bass)

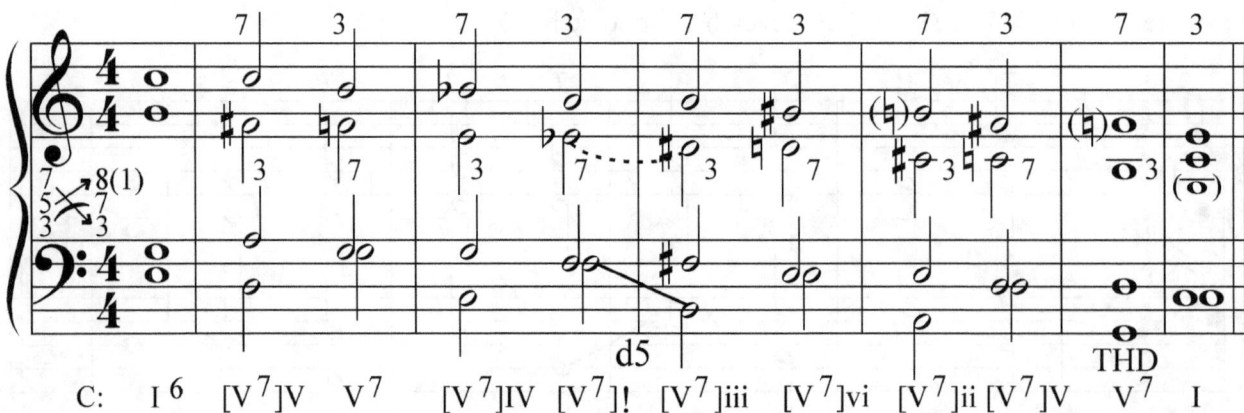

The Descending 5th: First and Third Inversions (Contrapuntal Bass)

In example 7–1, we saw a stepwise descent in the bass on the primary accent of each measure, from E to G (E–D–C–B–A–G), that is, from the tonic I ^{6} to the V ^{7}. It constitutes a secondary line. But despite the contrapuntal nature of this secondary line, the primary bass motion for the modal dominants in 7–1 is harmonic. Indeed, as observed above, the second chord of each chord pair prevents parallel 5ths.

The overlapping resolutions of interlocking sevenths in the descending 5th remain the same with both harmonic and contrapuntal basses: the seventh of the first chord moves to the third of the second chord while the third of the first chord becomes the seventh of the second chord.

The modal dominant sevenths in example 7–3 take a contrapuntal bass in which *both* chords of the two-chord pattern are inverted. In 7–3, the first-inversion dominant in measure 6 assumes root position to effect a harmonic cadence. The potential for parallel 5ths is lost in the example, as 5ths become 4ths upon inversion (for example, D/A becomes A/D). Inverting the chords also produces the cross-relation tritone between F and B (see the dotted line). The contrapuntal bass in 7–3 is effected by alternating seventh chords in $^6_5$ and $^4_2$ positions.

Example 7–3: OVIP 6   6 (in the key, sevenths)

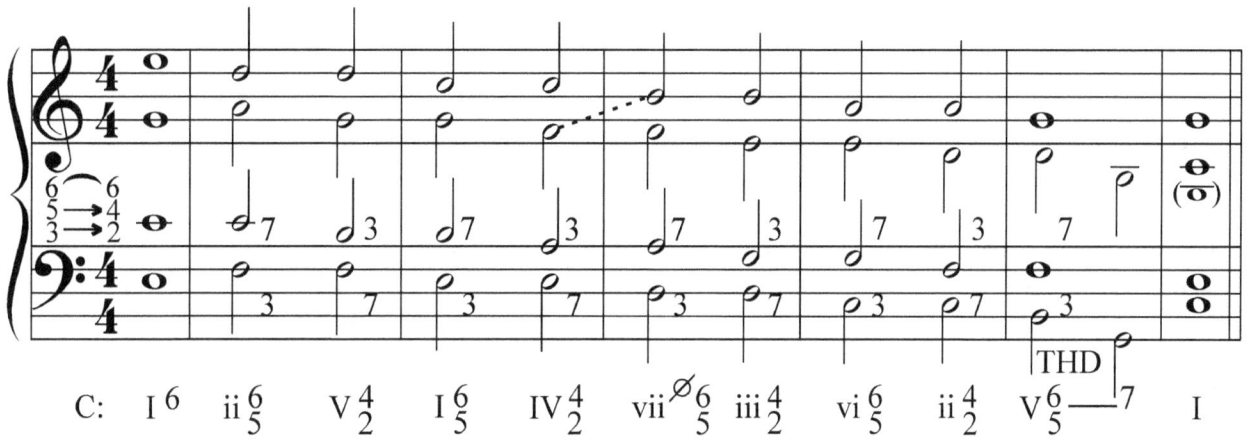

Example 7–4 alternates $^4_2$ and $^6_5$ positions. Here, the sequence proceeds from a root-position tonic to a root-position dominant, the THD. Compare the figured bass signs between the clefs and staves of examples 7–3 and 7–4. In example 7–3, the interval of the 6th holds, the 5th moves to the 4th, the 3rd to the 2nd. In example 7–4, the interval of the 6th holds, the 4th proceeds to the 5th, the 2nd to the 3rd.

In both examples 7–3 and 7–4, as well as in all of the other examples throughout this chapter, the initial pattern between the two chords of the chord pair and its duplications exhibit consistent intervallic relationships in all the voices above the bass. This consistency is retained when the sequences are expressed in minor.

Example 7–4: OVIP 9 10 (in the key, sevenths)

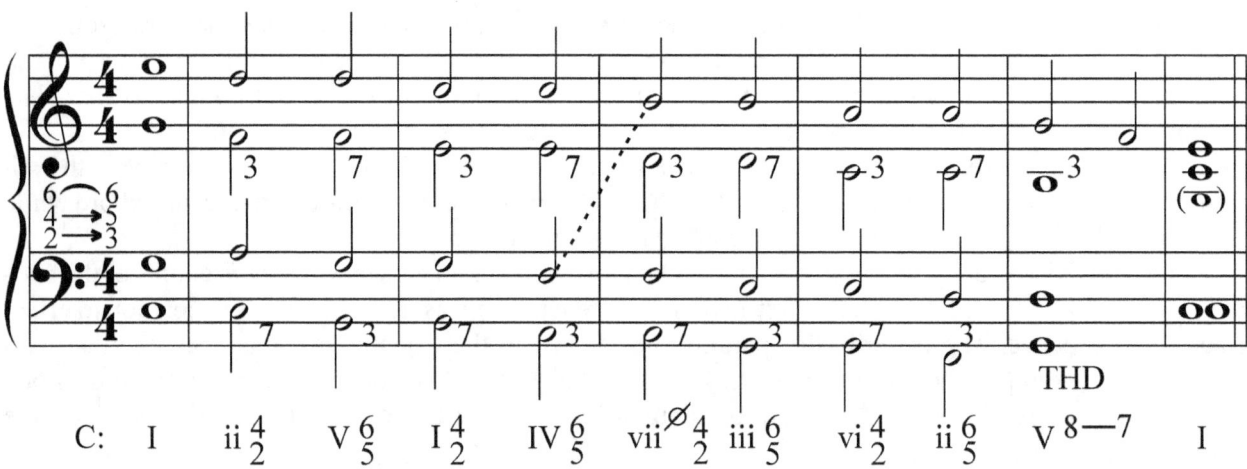

Examples 7–5 and 7–6 place examples 7–3 and 7–4 within the context of the parallel minor. Since these examples are in minor, the tritone falls between scale degrees 2 and ♭6; thus, in c minor, the cross-relation tritone consists of A♭ and D (see the dotted lines). In 7–5, the contrapuntal bass is effected by alternating seventh chords in $\frac{6}{5}$ and $\frac{4}{2}$ positions; in 7–6, the bass projects $\frac{4}{2}$ and $\frac{6}{5}$ positions.

The descending form of the melodic minor provides the pitch content for the vocabulary of seventh chords in the sequence. As we have seen, seventh chords of the tonic and subtonic require some refinements in their respective chord descriptions. Thus, when either the i ♭7 or the ♭VII ♭7 inverts, we indicate the quality of the seventh by placing the symbol for lowered 7 in parentheses (♭7) above the traditional figured bass, identifying the position of the chord and designating it to be of the "lowered variety." Thus, in measure 3 of 7–5, we have a tonic minor seventh, six-five position, lowered (seventh) variety.

Example 7–5: OVIP 6 6 (in the key, minor, sevenths)

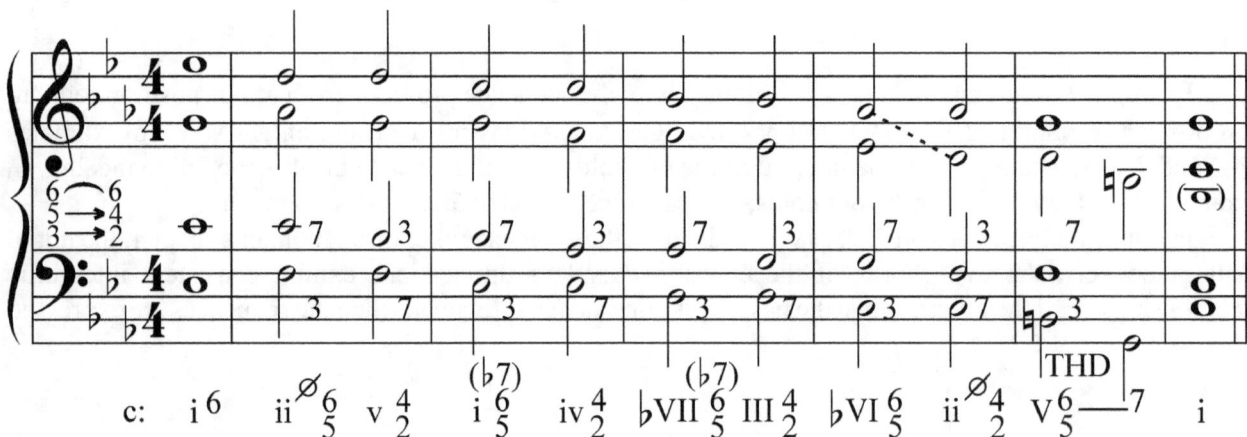

The succession of $^4_2$ and $^6_5$ positions in 7–6 produces a stepwise descent in the bass from the tonic to V^{8-7}. As in 7–5, the cross-relation tritone in 7–6 falls between the chords of the submediant and supertonic (measure 5). The descending melodic minor yields stepwise motion from scale degrees 1 to 5 in the bass, with $\flat 7$ (B$\flat$) and $\flat 6$ (A$\flat$) providing the chord thirds for the minor sevenths of the dominant and subdominant (measures 2–3) respectively.

Example 7–6: OVIP 9 10 (in the key, minor, sevenths)

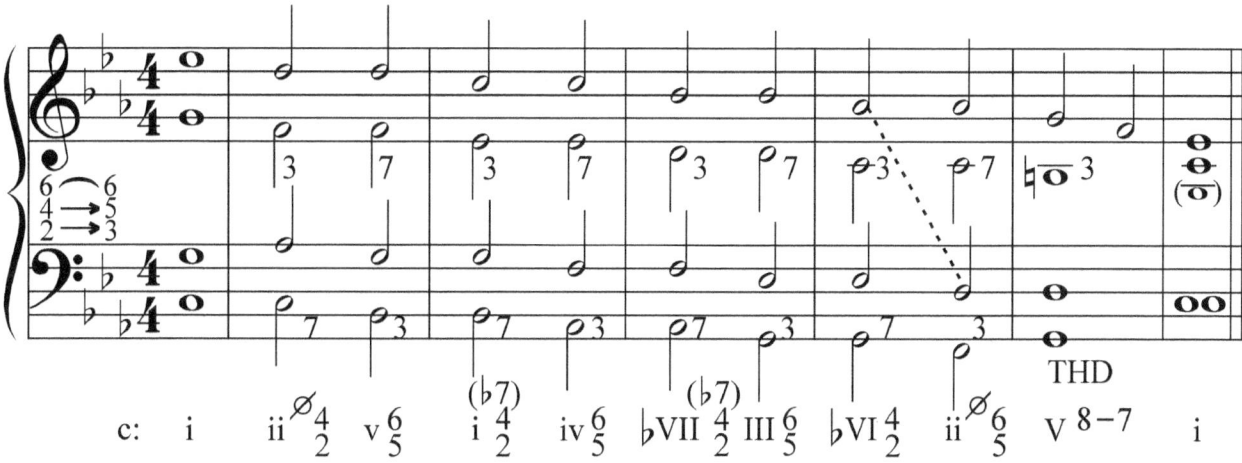

The Descending 5th: First and Third Inversions (Contrapuntal Bass, Out of Key)

This section transforms the diatonic chords of the previous section into chromatic chords. The contrapuntal bass in examples 7–3 through 7–6 above supports a diatonic expansion of the motion from the tonic to the dominant by using a progression of modal dominants. In examples 7–7 through 7–10 below, the bass effects a chromatic expansion of the way from the tonic to the dominant, that is, a progression of applied THD/CLT seventh chords. Each example has the stationary seventh and the cross-relation tritone.

Example 7–7: OVIP 6 6 (out of key, sevenths)

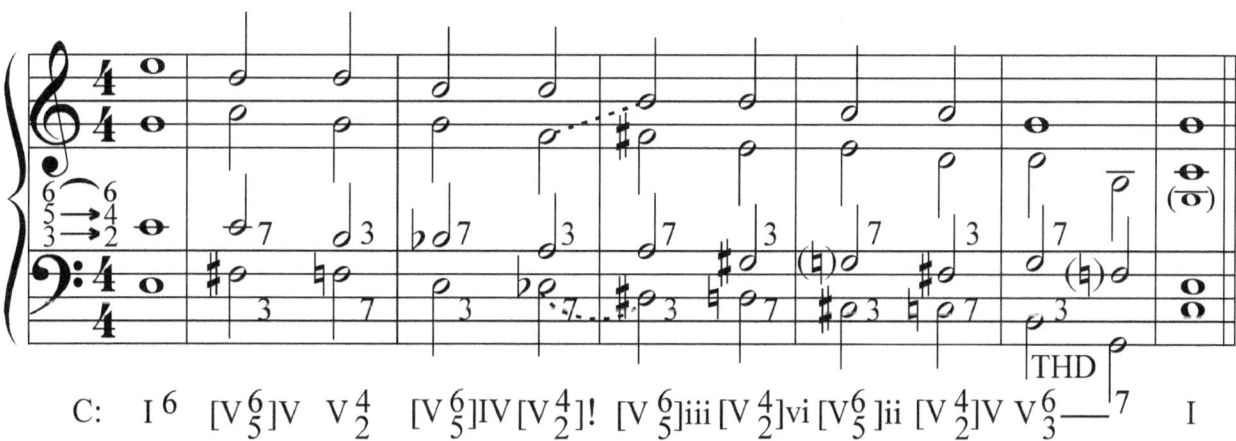

Chapter 7 The Sequence

Example 7–8: OVIP 9 10 (out of key, sevenths)

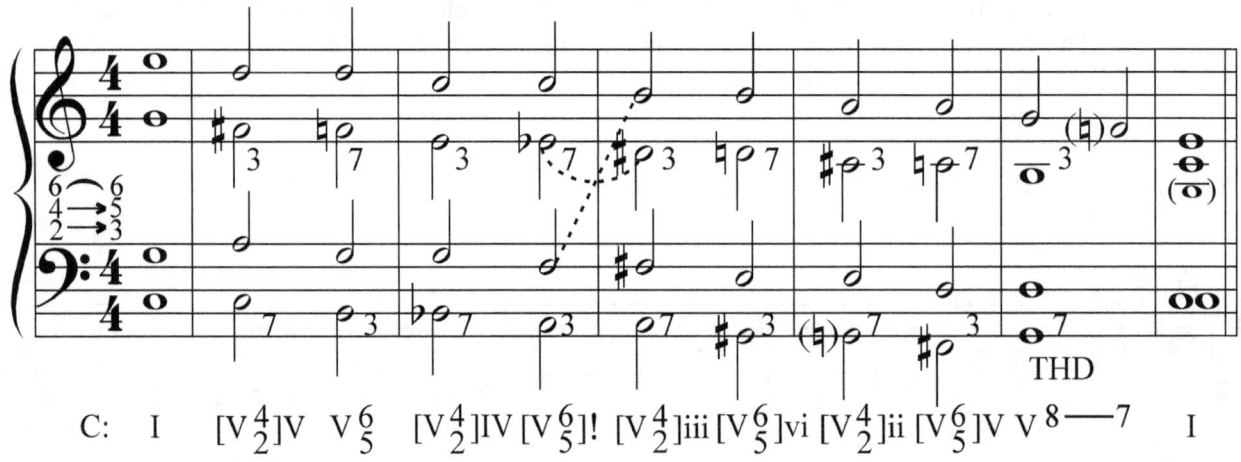

Example 7–9: OVIP 6 6 (out of key, minor, sevenths)

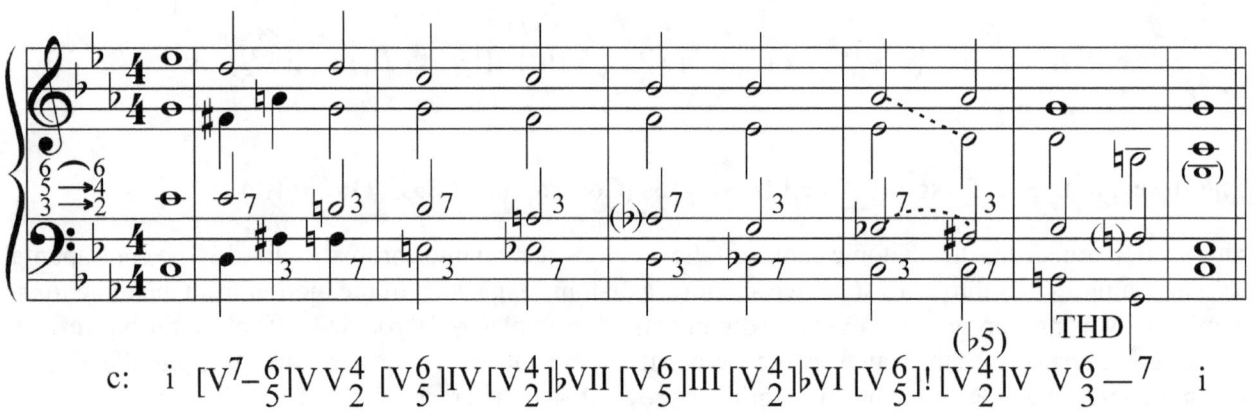

Example 7–10: OVIP 9 10 (out of key, minor, sevenths)

In examples 7–9 and 7–10 above, the last applied dominant becomes a degree-inflected THD/CLT, a contrapuntal expression of $V_{\flat 5}^7$. Thus, in measure 5 of 7–9, we have an applied dominant seventh, four-two position, lowered fifth variety (C D F♯ A♭). Inflecting the fifth of the chord (retaining the A♭ from the previous chord) avoids the succession of ♭6 to ♯6 to 5 (A♭ to A♮ to G).

On the other hand, the uninflected dominant, with A♮, provides a better sense of movement between chords. Indeed, with the lowered fifth in the chord (A♭), the altered dominant shares three common tones with the preceding applied dominant; only the chord fifth of the latter (E♭) moves to the root of the altered dominant (D).

Transferring the Resolution in the Descending 5th: (Rising 2nd-Falling 3rd)

In examples 7–11 and 7–12, we have the descending 5th sequence expressed as a contrapuntal bass supporting seventh chords in first inversion and root position. This disposition produces a bass consisting of rising 2nds and falling 3rds.

As we saw in Chapter 3, it is possible with the descending 5th to transfer the resolution of the chord seventh to another voice. In examples 7–11a and 7–12 (measures 2–6), the resolution of the chord seventh for each V^7 moves from the alto to the bass of the ensuing V^6_5, forming the bass pattern of rising 2nds and falling 3rds (measure 6 transfers the resolution to a first inversion triad). In example 7–11b, the transferred resolution is avoided by omitting the seventh from the root-position dominant.

Example 7–11: OVIP 6 5 (out of key, sevenths, rising 2nd-falling 3rd)

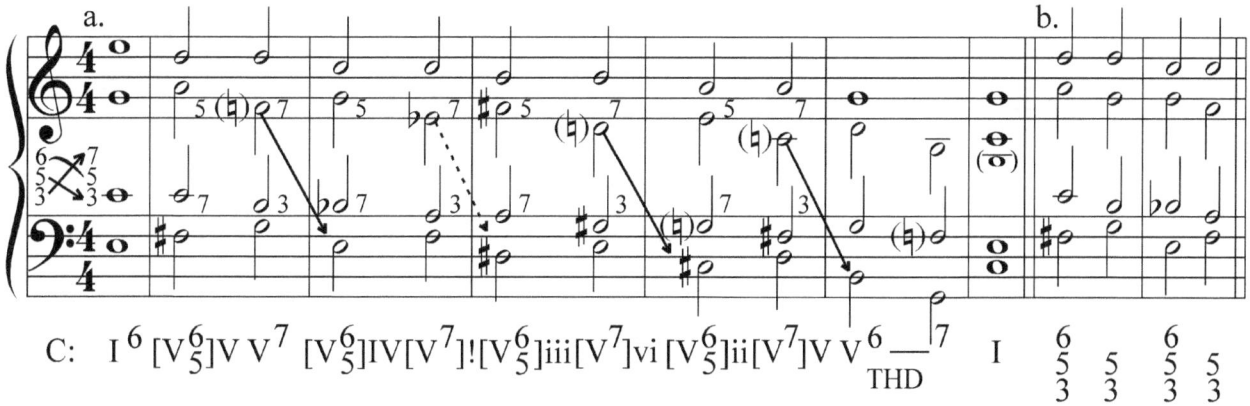

Example 7–12: OVIP 6 5 (out of key, minor, sevenths, rising 2nd-falling 3rd)

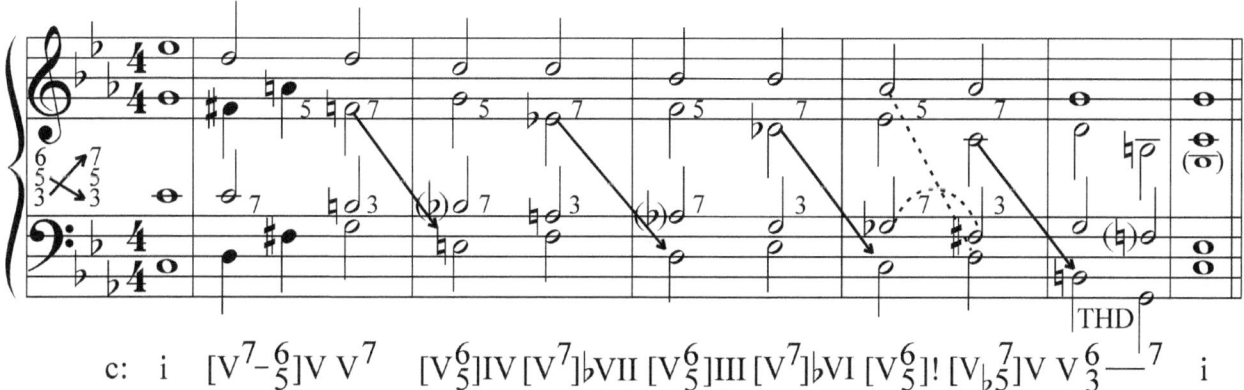

Root-Position and First-Inversion Chords (Descending 5th): Falling 3rd-Rising 2nd

Example 7–13 demonstrates alternating $\frac{5}{3}$ and $\frac{6}{3}$ triads. The bass line of the sequence proceeds through a pattern of falling 3rds and rising 2nds, leading from the tonic to the X-chord of the SHP (I – ii^6 – V – I). The diminished triad of the leading tone appears in root position with its tritone 5th in the outer voices, the worst possible disposition for this chord.

However, the offending interval is part an alternating OVIP of 5ths and 6ths repeated within the compelling harmonic framework of the descending 5th. The strong sense of momentum provided by the harmonic root relationship between the chords of the sequence helps to cover the harsh effect of the tritone dissonance. Additionally, the chord's inconspicuous location, standing far enough from both the beginning and the end of the sequence, renders its presence more acceptable.

The second chord of each chord pair in the descending 5th facilitates the voice leading by averting parallel 5ths and octaves between the bass and soprano, the soprano and alto, and the alto and bass (in this disposition of the sequential pattern). Without the voice-leading chord, this succession would be very problematic; but even with the intervening chord, the texture remains stark.

Example 7–13: OVIP 5   6 (in the key, falling 3rd-rising 2nd)

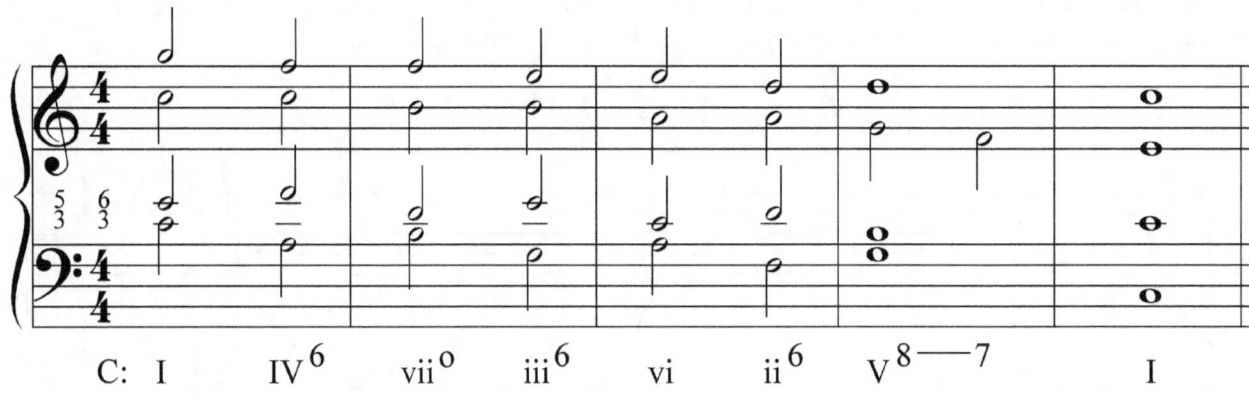

The minor version of 7–13, shown in example 7–14, presents no voice-leading difficulties, as the diminished supertonic appears in $\frac{6}{3}$ position.

Example 7–14: OVIP 5   6 (in the key, minor, falling 3rd-rising 2nd)

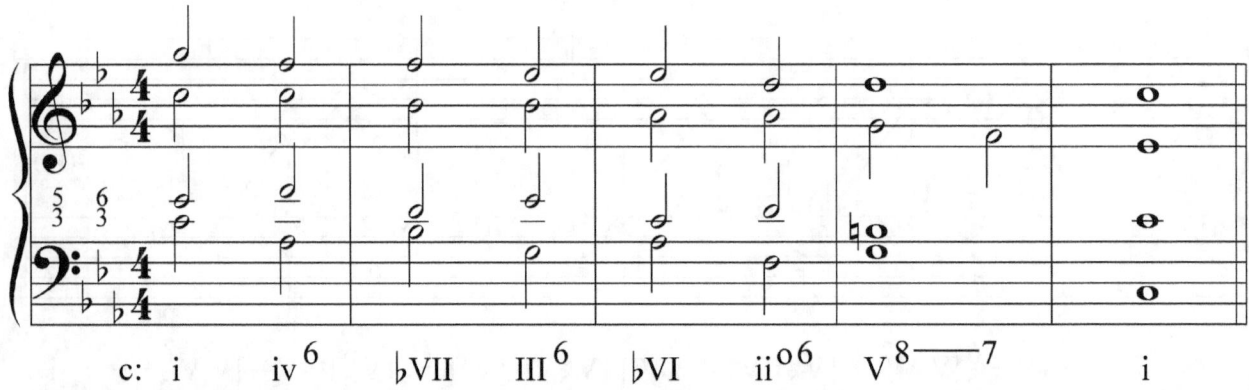

Based upon the falling 3rd-rising 2nd sequence of examples 7–13 and 7–14 above, examples 7–15 and 7–16 add the chord seventh to the tenor of the second chord (measures 1–3). In both examples, the seventh of each voice-leading chord resolves to the third of the next chord on the primary accent of each measure (descending in the tenor from scale degrees 3 to 1: E♮ or E♭–D–C–B–C). The addition of the dissonant seventh helps to animate the progression (despite, as we have seen, the use of vii° in major).

Example 7–15: OVIP 5 6 (in the key, sevenths, falling 3rd-rising 2nd)

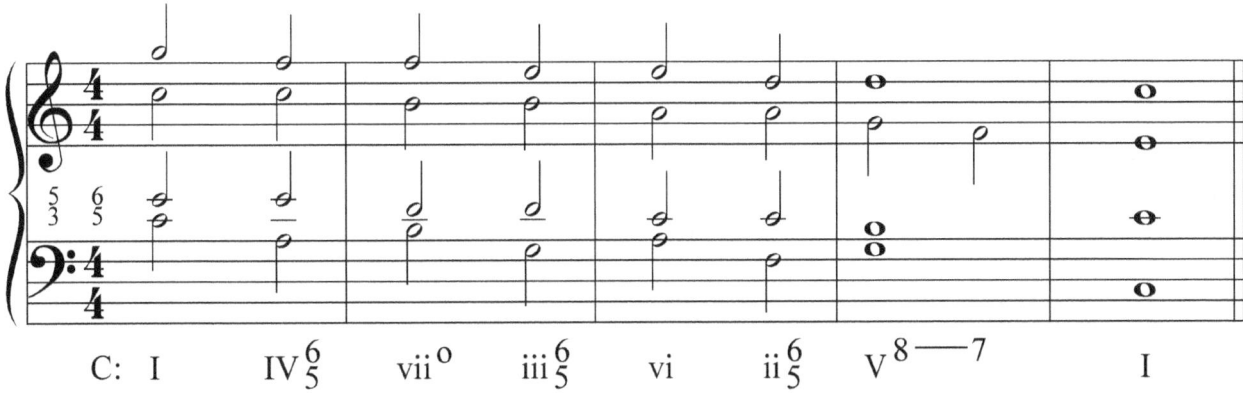

Corresponding to 7–14 above but with the addition of the chord seventh, 7–16 becomes a stronger progression. The weak diminished triad of 7–15 is replaced in 7–16 with a root-position major triad of the subtonic; that is to say, vii° in major becomes ♭VII in minor.

In major, the IV$^6_5$ moves to vii°; thus, a diminished triad forms the resolution for the major seventh of the subdominant. As we shall see in examples 7–48 and 7–52, proceeding from a major seventh chord to a diminished triad in root position often yields an unsatisfactory resolution. Here, the corresponding motion in minor produces a more euphonous sonority (that is, ♭VII, a major triad).

The minor seventh of the mediant, iii$^6_5$ in 7–15, becomes a major seventh in 7–16, the III$^6_5$, which subsequently addresses ♭VI. Adding the dissonant seventh to the supertonic results in a half-diminished seventh, a compelling approach chord for the THD.

Example 7–16: OVIP 5 6 (in the key, minor, sevenths, falling 3rd-rising 2nd)

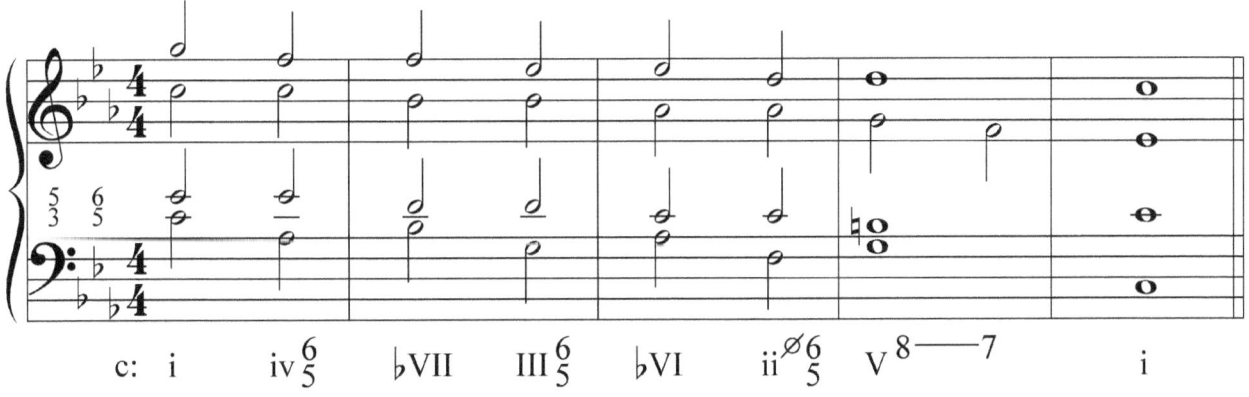

Root-Position and First-Inversion Chords (Descending 5th): Falling 3rd-Rising 2nd (Out of Key)

Examples 7–17 and 7–18 place the sequence of the previous examples 7–15 and 7–16 within a chromatic context, transforming modal dominants into applied dominants. In measure 1 of example 7–17, we avoid the problematic application of a dominant seventh chord to the area of the leading tone, opting instead for a modal dominant, IV$^6_5$, to address scale degree 7.

Example 7–17: OVIP 5 6 (out of key, sevenths, falling 3rd-rising 2nd)

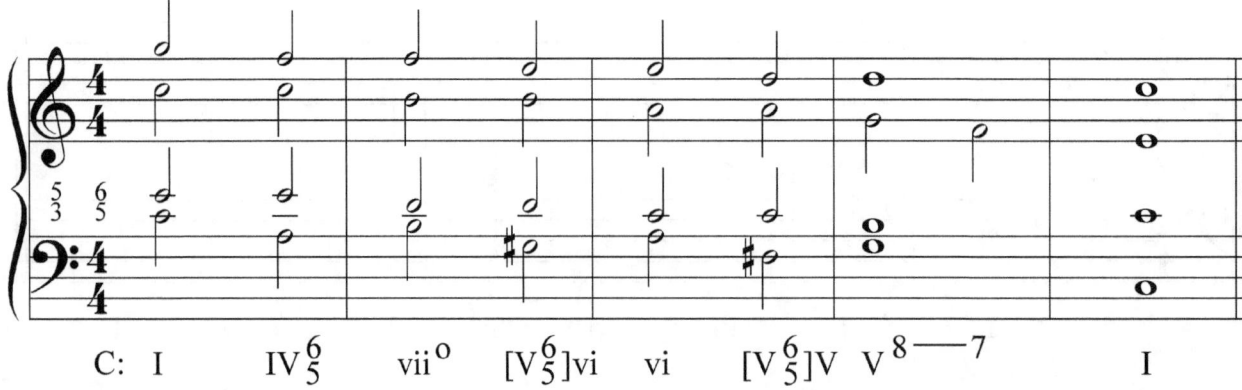

In measure 1 of example 7–18, an applied dominant seventh approaches the area of the subtonic. Scale degree ♭7 provides a strong rising perfect 4th (or falling perfect 5th) resolution to a major triad (B♭ D F instead of ♯7's B♮ D F). As we have seen, the uninflected dominant in measure 3 produces ♭6 to ♯6 to 5 (A♭ to A♮ to G).

In minor, the sequence may, under certain conditions, deny the normal selection of its variable scale degrees according to the mode's ascending and descending tendencies. One such condition is chromaticism, a state in which the diatonic usage has been interrupted, producing characteristics that are peculiar to the minor mode. We shall refer to these exceptional instances as "idiomatic usages of the minor mode."

When applied dominants are used, as in 7–18, it is possible to have a raised variable proceed to scale degree 5 instead of continuing upwards in the direction of the tonic. The motion from ♯6 to 5 constitutes an idiomatic instance of the ascending melodic minor *descending*.

Example 7–18: OVIP 5 6 (out of key, minor, sevenths, falling 3rd-rising 2nd)

First-Inversion and Root-Position Chords (Descending 5th): Rising 2nd-Falling 3rd

This section explores the descending 5th sequence with alternating $\frac{6}{3}$ and $\frac{5}{3}$ triads, a combination of chords that produces a contrapuntal bass consisting of rising 2nds and falling 3rds.

In major, as shown in example 7–19, the diminished triad of the leading tone is in first inversion, a perfectly acceptable disposition of the chord. The principal difficulty with the same progression in minor, as in example 7–20, is the root-position diminished supertonic triad at the end of the sequence. However, as we have observed, the forward momentum provided by the harmonic root relationship between the chords of the descending 5th sequence helps to mitigate the harsh effect of the tritone dissonance. Additionally, the chord occurs within the context of the sequential pattern, forming both the end of the sequence and the beginning of the cadential structure.

To be sure, adding a seventh would make the diminished triad in root position less objectionable; but one of the best options, and one that composers have used, is simply to skip the chord altogether. Indeed, successful progressions are possible without including the diminished triad in root position. As we shall see, a common solution is to use portions of the sequence that do not involve this troublesome chord.

Example 7–19: OVIP 6   5 (in the key, rising 2nd-falling 3rd)

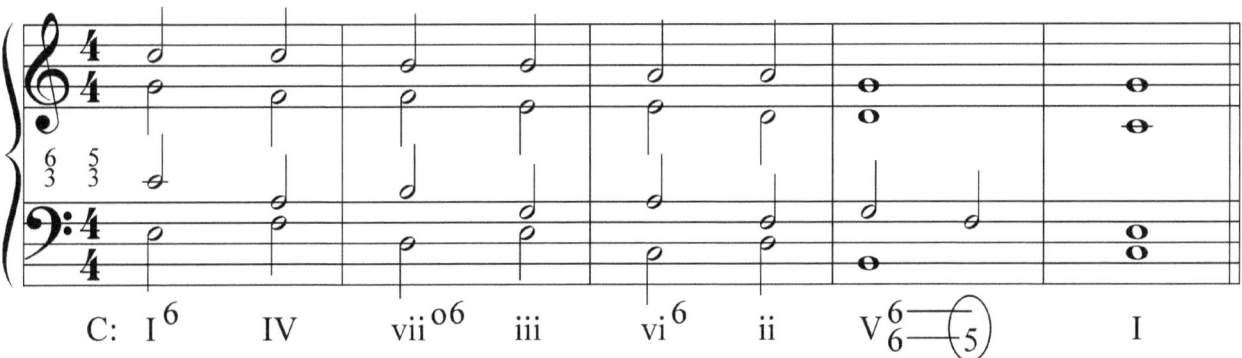

Example 7–20: OVIP 6   5 (in the key, minor, rising 2nd-falling 3rd)

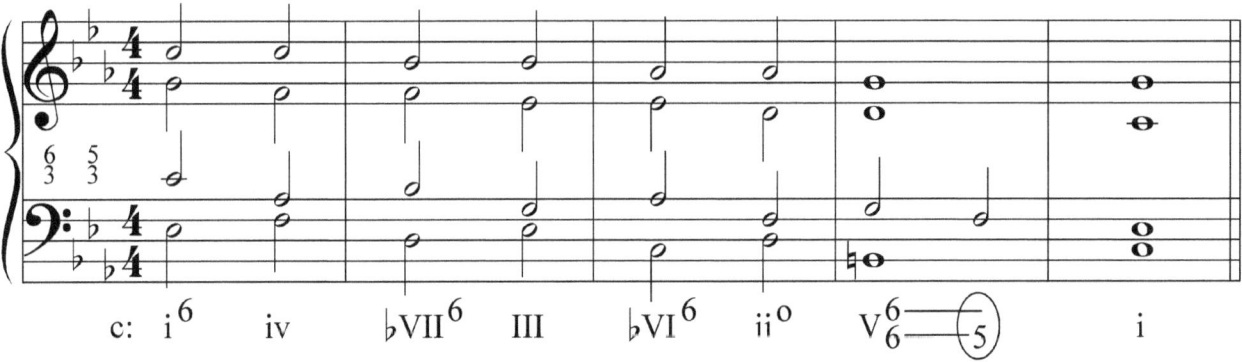

172 Chapter 7 The Sequence

Adding the seventh to the first-inversion triads in examples 7–21 and 7–22 produces alternating $^6_5$ and $^5_3$ chords. As we have observed, the inclusion of the dissonant seventh and the rising 4th-falling 5th root relationship between the chords help to carry the progression forward.

Example 7–21: OVIP 6 5 (in the key, sevenths, rising 2nd-falling 3rd)

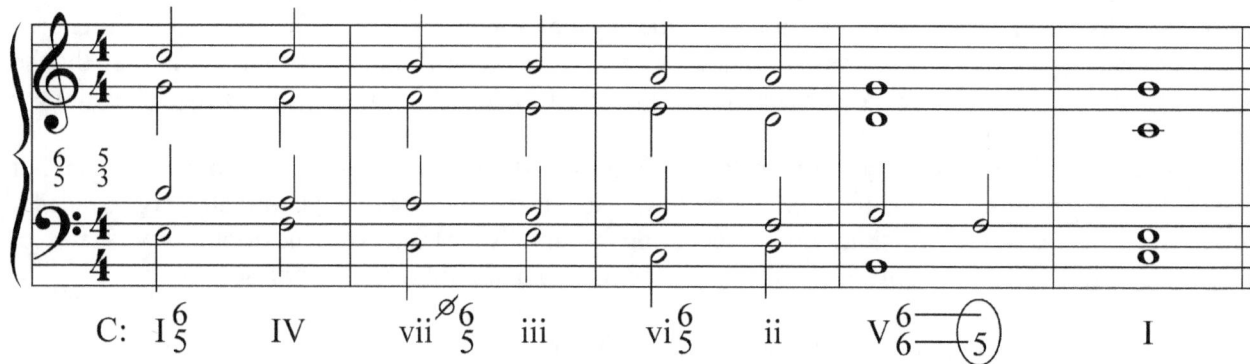

In minor, the inclusion of the seventh results in the formation of a dominant seventh on the subtonic, effecting an applied dominant relationship to III, the chord and key area the minor mode most commonly seeks when moving from the tonic.

Example 7–22: OVIP 6 5 (in the key, minor, sevenths, rising 2nd-falling 3rd)

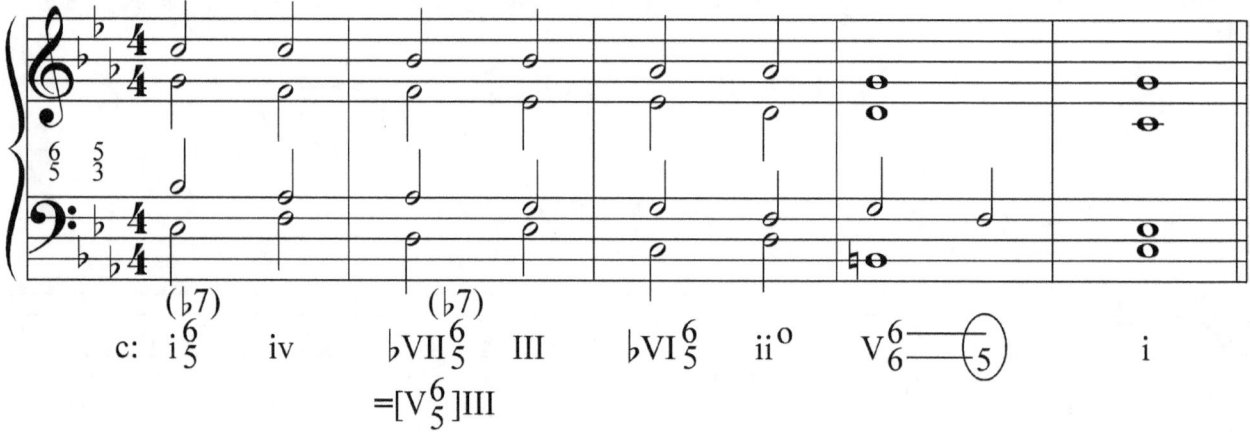

First-Inversion and Root-Position Chords (Descending 5th): Rising 2nd-Falling 3rd (Out of Key)

In example 7–23, applied THD/CLT chords address the IV, iii, and ii. As in the previous section, the contrapuntal bass proceeds by rising 2nds and falling 3rds. The supertonic in example 7–24 takes a modal dominant because the diminished triad cannot be tonicized. Although the diminished supertonic in root position constitutes the weakest component of the progression, it remains an option within the framework of the descending 5th sequence.

Example 7–23: OVIP 6   5 (out of key, sevenths, rising 2nd-falling 3rd)

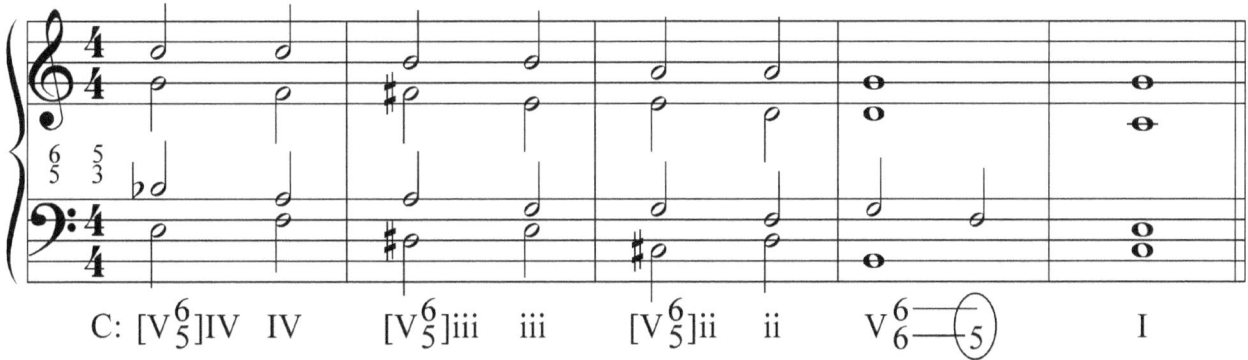

Example 7–24: OVIP 6   5 (out of key, minor, sevenths, rising 2nd-falling 3rd)

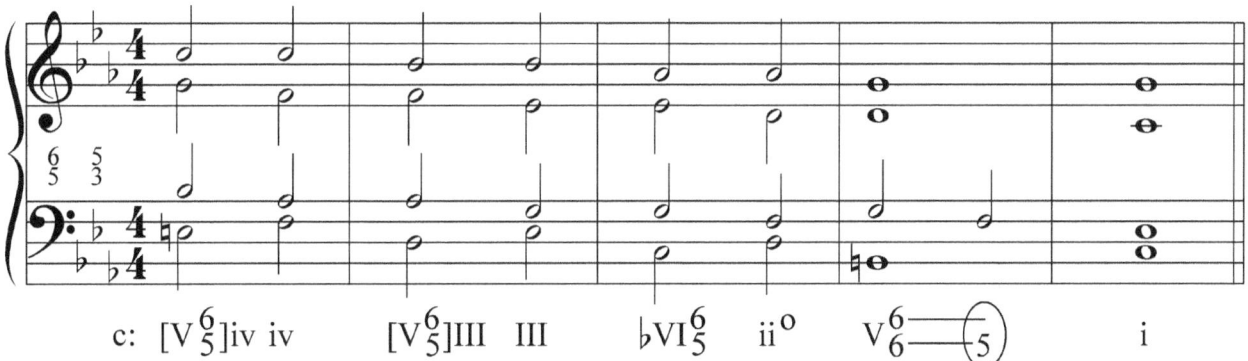

The Ascending 5—6

In broad terms, the ascending 5—6 and its variants in examples 7–25 to 7–60 have an ascending top voice supported by various contrapuntal bass lines (though some of the root-position variants include a mixture of harmonic and contrapuntal basses). The ascending 5—6 alternates 5ths and 6ths. Parallel 5ths and octaves are averted by intervening 6th chords; hence, the second chord of each pair corrects the voice leading. The variants of this sequence modify the basic OVIP (outer-voice interval-pattern). (Later in this study, we examine variants with the following OVIPs: 12—7, 5—8, and 5—10.)

Example 7–25 illustrates an ascent from scale degrees 5 to 2, concluding with a harmonic perfect authentic cadence (HPAC). When the bass of the ascending 5—6 is completely contrapuntal, each sequence is shown within the framework of two separate though related progressions. The first progression (7–25) consists of the tonic chord, the sequence, and the cadence.

Example 7–25: OVIP 5 6 (in the key)

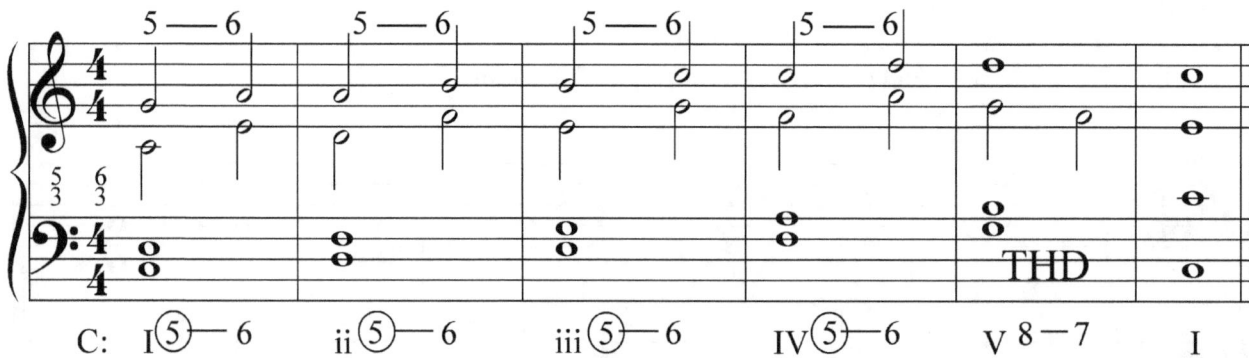

The second progression, shown in example 7–26, expands the first with the addition of an extended passing chord of the submediant. The extended passing chord separates the ascending 5—6 from the succeeding X-chord. Used exclusively for examples 7–44 to 7–60, the second progression reaffirms the tonic key with the cadential $^6_4$. Ultimately, the expansion shores up the progression.

Notice also that the ascent from scale degrees 5 to 2 in the soprano continues upwards to scale degree 3 (E) and beyond. The sequence, which supports the ascent in the top voice, becomes part of a larger descending motion spanning scale degrees 5–4–3–2–1 (G–F–E–D–C), a basic melodic progression (BMP). However, instead of moving down a major 2nd from scale degrees 5 to 4 (G–F), the melodic ascent inverts the interval to a minor 7th, scale degrees 5–6–7–1–2–3–4 (G–A–B–C–D–E–F). Thus, the sequence, extended passing chord, and X-chord all support the melodic inversion.

Example 7–26: OVIP 5 6 (in the key, with extended passing, X-chord, and cadential $^6_4$)

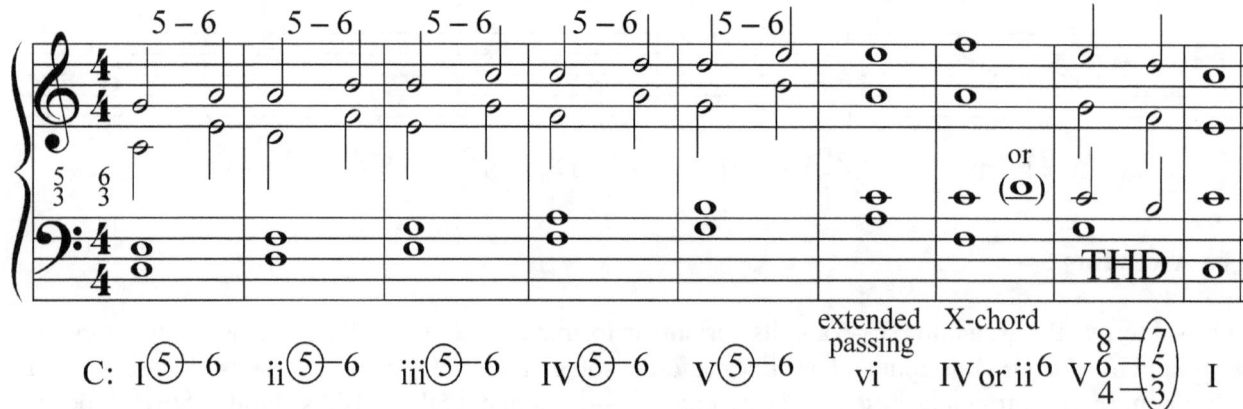

In example 7–27, we have the unelaborated progression: the tonic chord, the sequence, and the cadence. The progression ends with ♭VII – V$^6_5$ – i. This combination of chords produces a chromatic ascent in the bass. Using both variables ♭7 and ♯7 in succession is less common in minor; the usual succession is ♭7 to ♭6 descending and ♯6 to ♯7 ascending.

Since ♭VII often precedes III, moving to a dominant-functioning chord instead of approaching the mediant is an unexpected though successful turn in the harmony. As ♭7 proceeds to ♯7, an unusual harmonic conversion occurs in which the subtonic is transformed into a CLT chord of the dominant family.

The diminished triad of the supertonic in root position makes an interesting appearance in the minor mode. Although it is better to avoid the root position of this chord (measure 2), it forms vii° of III; moreover, the apparent chord that follows constitutes V⁶ of III. As part of an applied conversion dominant, then, the diminished supertonic becomes possible in its alternative role as a contrapuntal prolonging chord finding its resolution in the mediant, a goal of motion in minor. The relationship of the diminished triad to the mediant chord thus provides the former with a context convincing enough to justify its presence. The apparent 6th chords throughout the sequence facilitate the voice leading.

The ascending 5—6 in examples 7–27 and 7–28 demonstrates another significant idiomatic usage of the minor mode: the descending variables ascending, that is, the upward movement of ♭6 and ♭7 (A♭ and B♭).

As in 7–26, the descending major 2nd in example 7–28 (scale degrees 5 to 4) inverts to become an ascending minor 7th (scale degrees 5–♭6–♭7–1–2–3–4), yielding thereby a BMP with a melodic descent from scale degrees 5 to 1 (G–F–E♭–D–C), 4 proceeding to 3 in measures 10–11.

Example 7–27: OVIP 5 6 (in the key, minor)

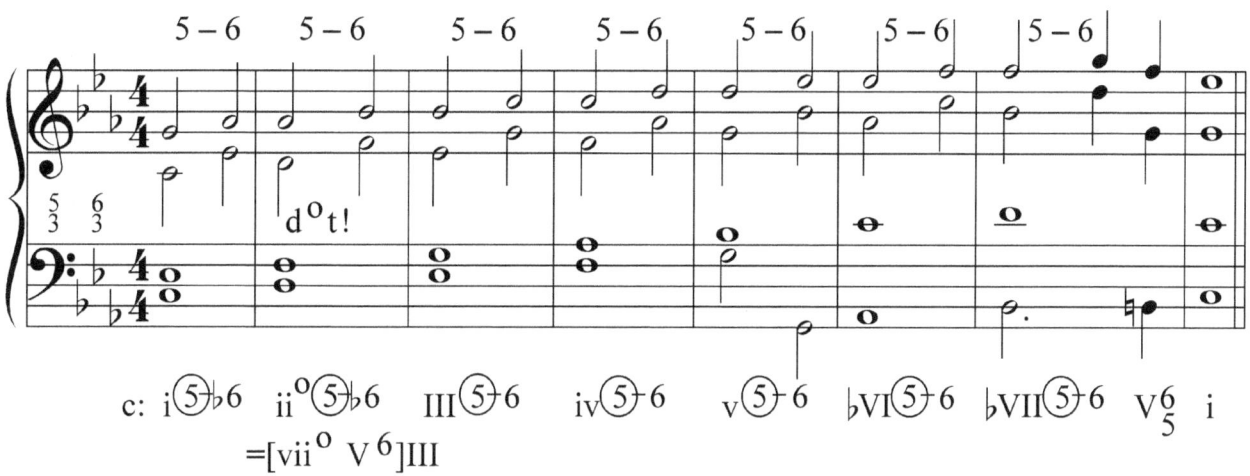

Example 7–28: OVIP 5 6 (in the key, minor, with extended passing, X-chord, and cadential $^6_4$)

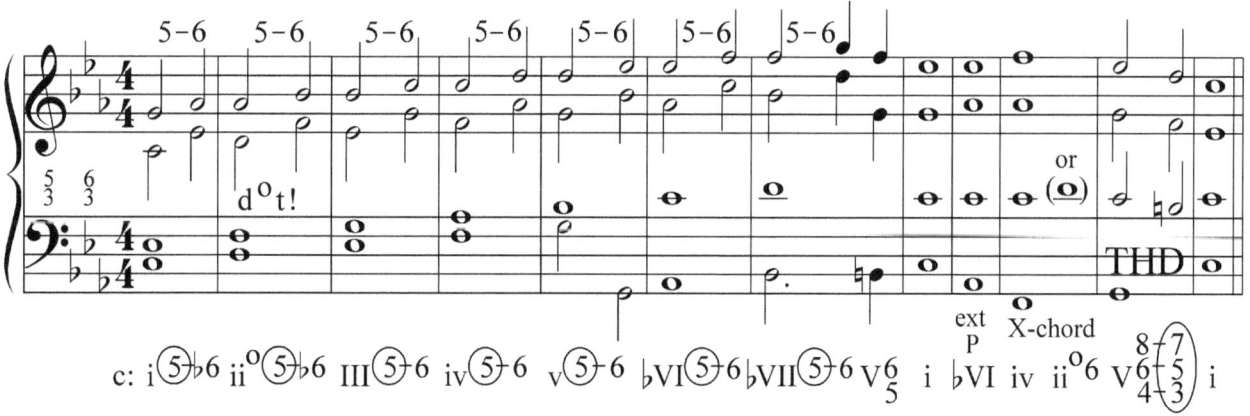

176   Chapter 7 The Sequence

In examples 7–29 and 7–30, the sevenths on beat 1 of each measure in the sequence are based upon the corresponding triads in examples 7–25 and 7–26. The progression in 7–29 has the tonic chord, the sequence, and the cadence. The progression in 7–30 adds the extended passing chord, X-chord, and cadential $^6_4$.

The sevenths start with the initial tonic. The alto takes the third of each chord, resulting in parallel 3rds with the bass. Driving the progression forward, the dissonant 7th moves down to the root of the apparent chord on beat 3. The 5—6 motion in the soprano breaks up the parallel 5ths with the bass.

Continuing the seventh resolutions into the final tonic, the chord fifth of the THD in 7–29 leaps into the seventh (tenor). Had the bass continued upwards to A, the seventh would have prevented parallel 5ths between the bass and the tenor (that is, G/D to A/E).

Since the motion between chord tones (D to F) produces a dissonance rather than a consonance, the motion between the pitches ought not to be described as a chordal or consonant skip. Still, the seventh remains part of a dominant complex—the motion is within a single chord. Notably, all of the sevenths in the sequence are approached by leap as well (except for the tonic seventh); however, the jump into the seventh is from an unlike chord (measures 1–4).

Example 7–29: OVIP 5 6 (in the key, sevenths)

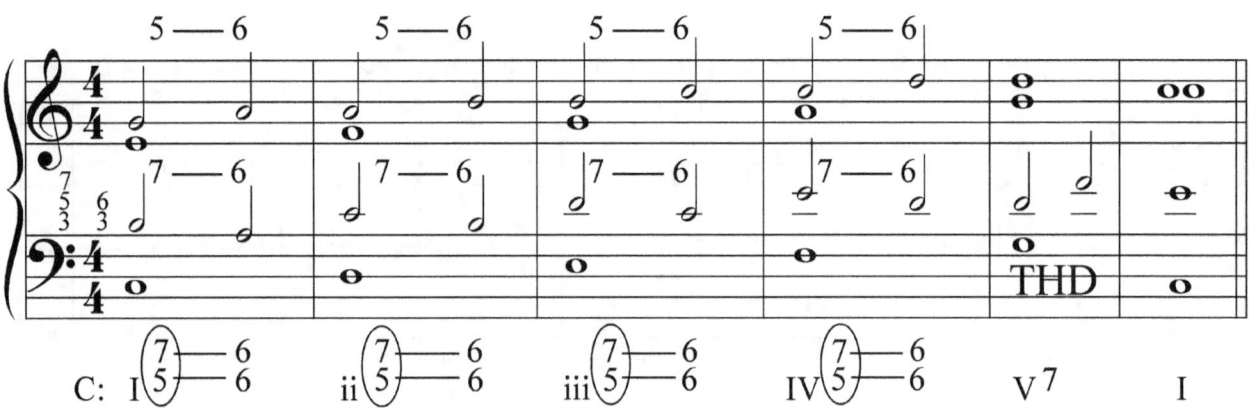

Example 7–30: OVIP 5 6 (in the key, sevenths, with extended passing, X-chord, and cadential $^6_4$)

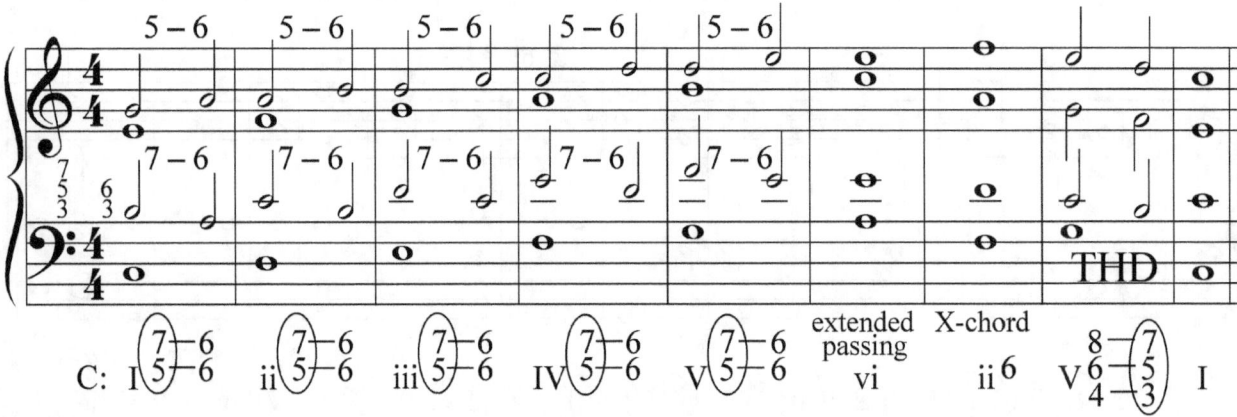

Chapter 7 The Sequence   177

The move into the seventh (7–29) might be called an *apparent* chordal skip. The seventh of the THD forms an incomplete upper neighbor to the chord third of the tonic, serving therefore as a cambiata tone to scale degree 3. (For a discussion of the cambiata tone, see *Finding The Right Pitch II: A Guide To The Study Of Basic Harmony*, Chapter 9.)

In example 7–30, with scale degree 4 (F) in the top voice, the supertonic X-chord supports the interval inversion from scale degree 5 (G). Subsequently, the progression proceeds to the cadence and the completion of the melodic structure (scale degree 1).

Examples 7–31 and 7–32 place the two preceding examples within the context of the minor mode. The progression in 7–31 contains the tonic chord, the sequence, and the cadence. This cadence transforms the subtonic into a CLT chord: $\flat\text{VII} - \text{V}^6_5 - \text{i}$.

Example 7–31: OVIP 5 6 (in the key, minor, sevenths)

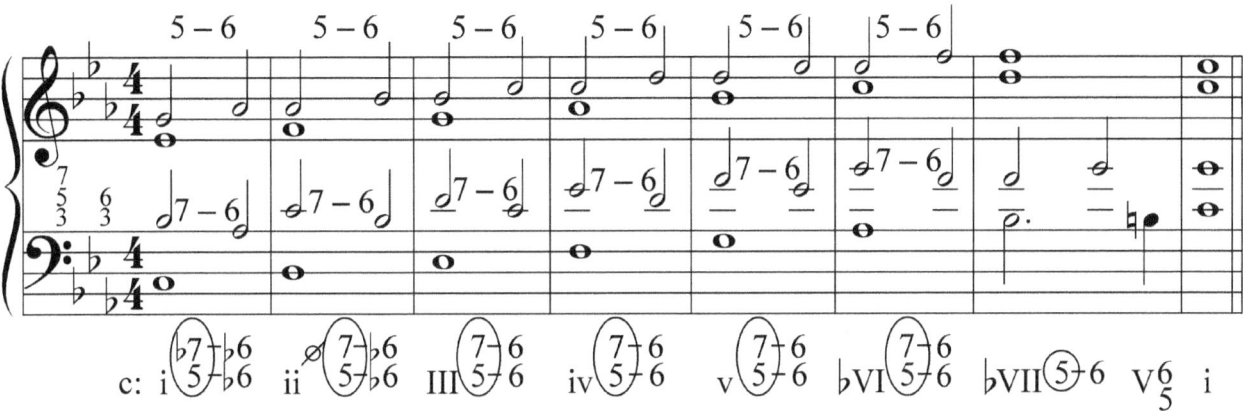

Example 7–32 includes the extended passing chord, X-chord, and cadential $^6_4$, as well as the conversion from subtonic to CLT chord. (These elements also inform the progressions in examples 7–28 above and 7–36, 7–40, and 7–44 below.) Once again in the soprano voice, we have an ascent involving scale degrees 5–$\flat$6–$\flat$7–1–2–3–4. In measure 7, the top voice reaches scale degree 4, which is prolonged by scale degree 3 as a lower neighbor (E$\flat$) before its return in measure 10, supported there by the X-chord.

Example 7–32: OVIP 5 6 (in the key, minor, sevenths, with extended passing, X-chord, and cadential $^6_4$)

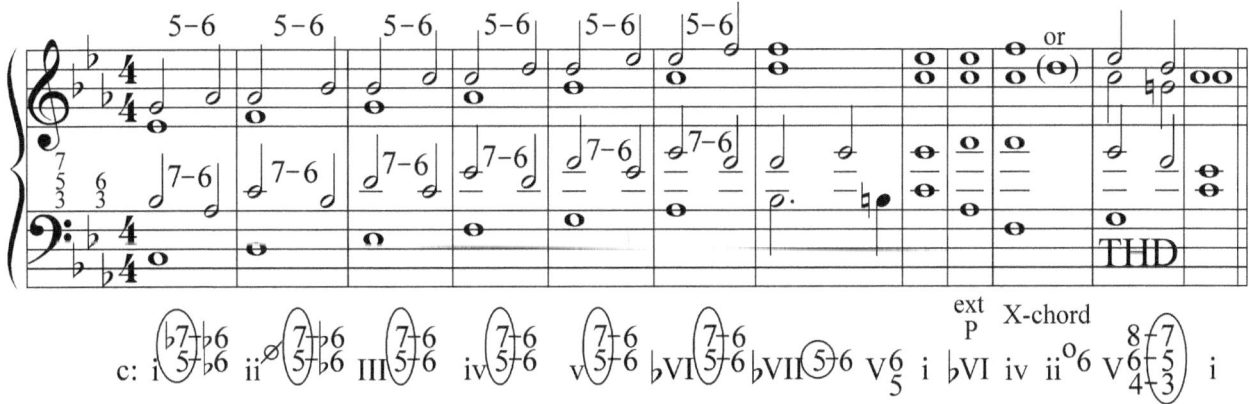

The Ascending 5—6 (Chromatic Bass)

Examples 7–27, 28, 31, and 32 above demonstrate a chromatic approach to the tonic chord using the conversion from the subtonic to a CLT chord of the dominant family: $\flat\text{VII} - \text{V}^6_5 - \text{i}$. Chromatic motion in the bass may be duplicated on every scale degree in both major and minor, except in those places where diatonic half steps already exist. The chromatic passing tone between diatonic pitches intensifies the motion upwards to the next scale degree.

The mediant in major cannot take a chromatic passing tone because it already stands a minor 2nd below the subdominant. Thus, in example 7–33, scale degree 3 does not move up a half step to scale degree 4 until after it becomes the third of an applied CLT dominant: $[\text{V}^6]$ IV. Breaking the exact intervallic pattern of the sequence preserves the diatonic half step of the mode, a necessary adjustment in the pattern. As we shall see, the profile of half steps in minor yields other options for the chromatic passing tone.

In example 7–34, elaborating the basic progression (7–33) with the extended passing chord, X-chord, and cadential $^6_4$ allows the chromatic bass to reach beyond scale degree 5, which moves chromatically to scale degree 6. The elaborated progression provides a more convincing conclusion in C major after the flurry of half steps. Indeed, it would be well to remember that more than two or three statements of any sequential pattern is usually unproductive.

Example 7–33: OVIP 5 6 (out of key)

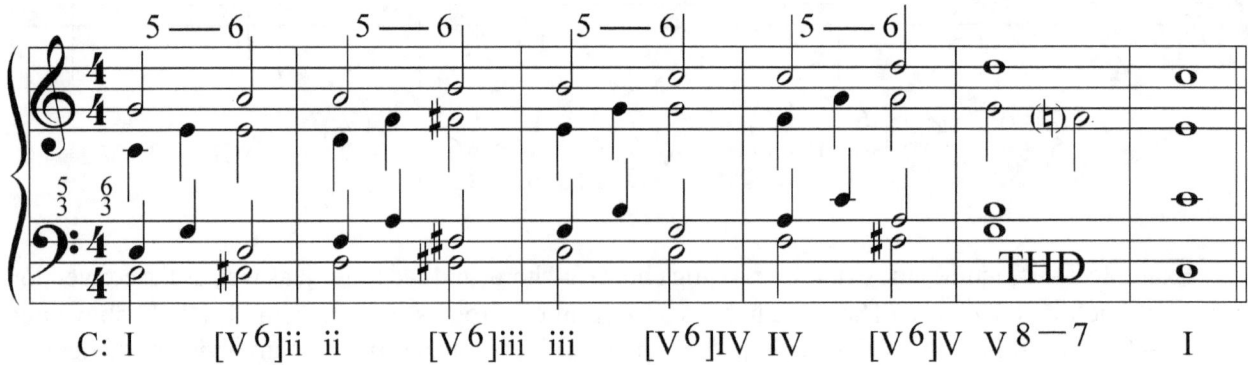

Example 7–34: OVIP 5 6 (out of key, extended passing, X-chord, and cadential $^6_4$)

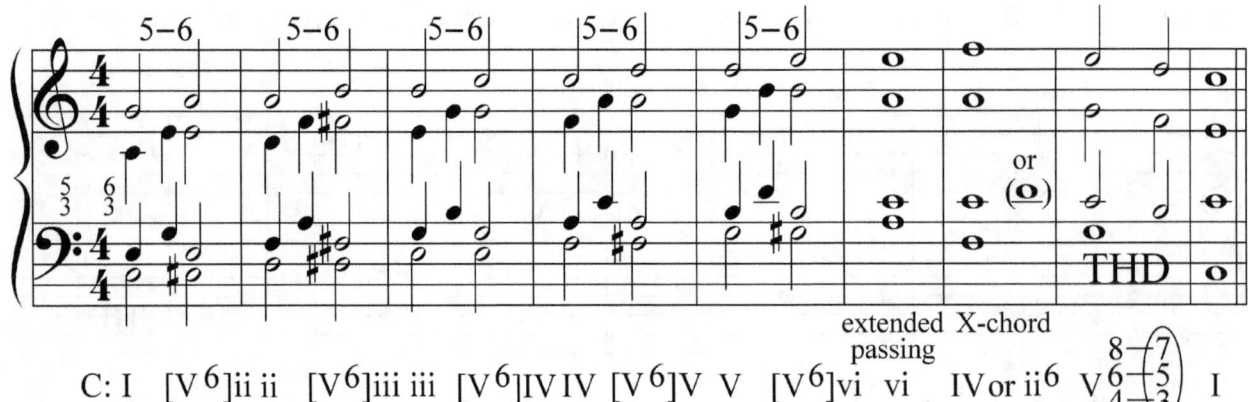

Chapter 7 The Sequence   179

In minor, we avoid the chromatic passing tone and its attendant applied dominant between scale degrees 1 and 2 because the chord of resolution would be the diminished supertonic, which cannot be tonicized. Since the sequence occurs in minor, scale degree 3 may be chromaticized (E♭ to E♮).

If the supertonic in example 7–35 is included in the sequence (again, merely an option), it stands reinterpreted as [vii°] III proceeding to [V^6] III, part of an applied conversion dominant. Scale degree 5 does not move to variable ♭6 until after it becomes the chord third of an applied CLT dominant: [V^6] ♭VI.

Example 7–35: OVIP 5   6 (out of key, minor)

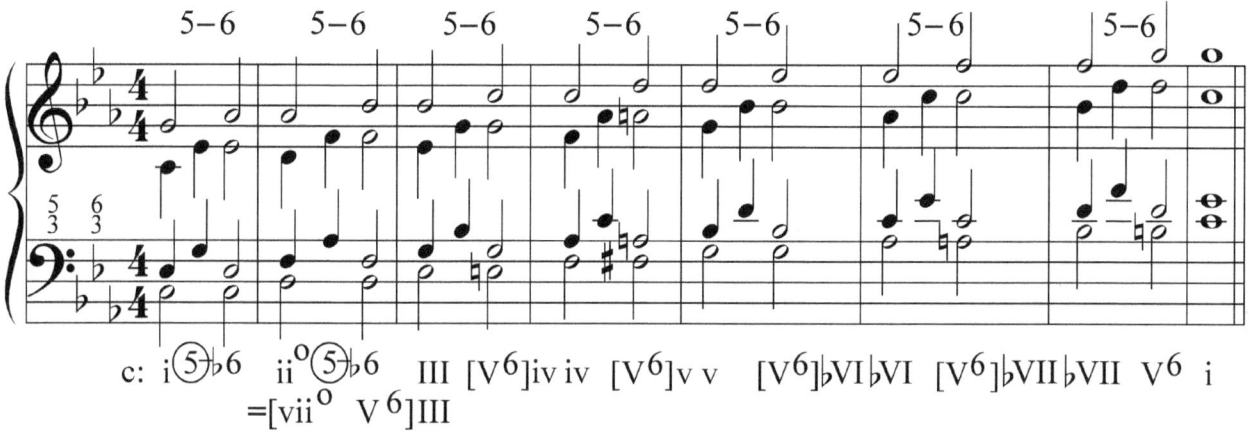

Example 7–36: OVIP 5   6 (out of key, minor, extended passing, X-chord, and cadential $^6_4$)

Examples 7–37 and 7–38 demonstrate the addition of the seventh to the applied CLT dominants in first inversion. Standing above the chromatic passing tones in the bass, [V$^6_5$] addresses ii, iii, IV, and V (and vi in 7–38). As we have seen, scale degree 3 cannot be chromaticized in major. In example 7–38, the chromatic bass continues upwards to scale degree 6.

In the tenor of both examples, the fifth of the first chord of each chord pair prepares the seventh of the second, the applied CLT. In turn, the seventh moves down by step to become the third of the following root-position triad.

Example 7–37: OVIP 5 6 (out of key, sevenths)

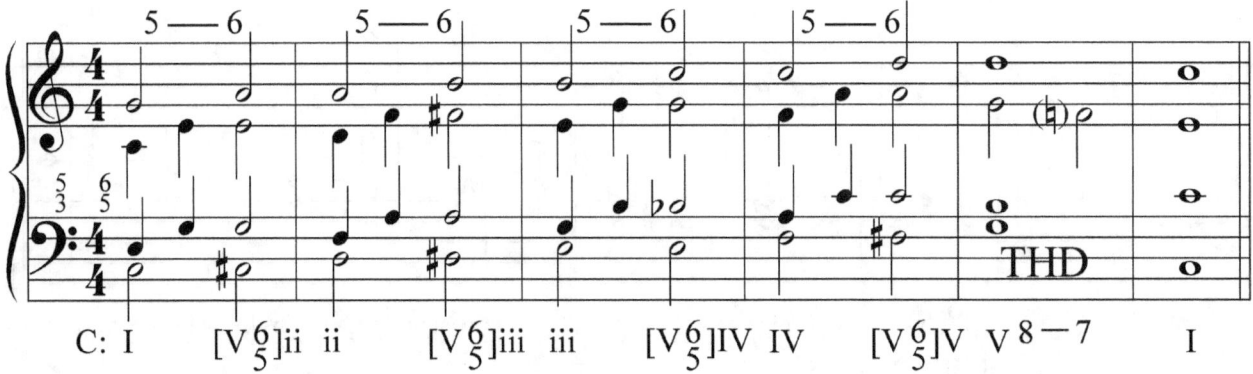

Example 7–38: OVIP 5 6 (out of key, sevenths, extended passing, X-chord, and cadential $^6_4$)

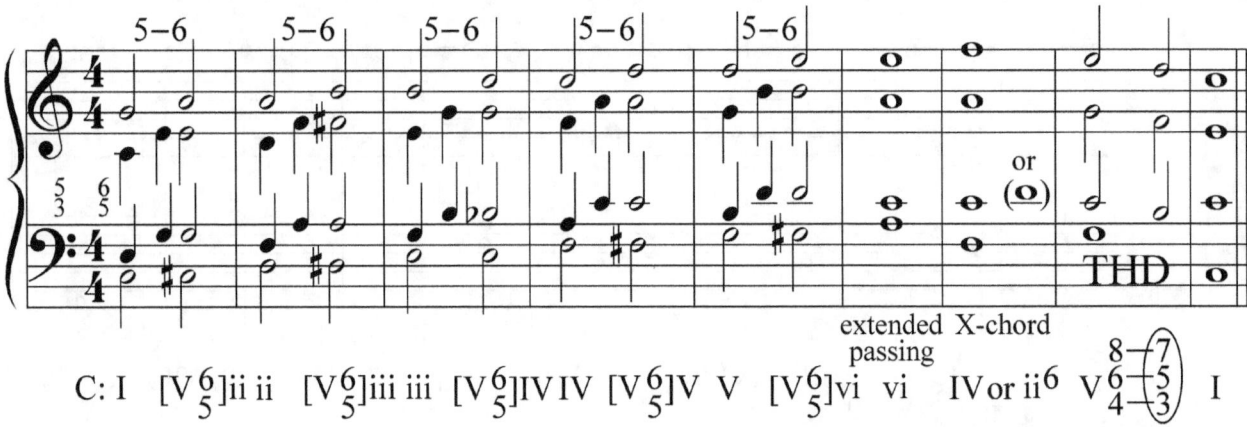

The chromatic version of the ascending 5—6 in both major and minor yields opportunities for excursions into keys of a lower order. The motion into these lower-level keys enhances, expands, and enriches the expression of the main-level key and its chords. Ultimately, the chromatic operations of the sequence constitutes one of the most common ways to produce a momentary or extended departure from the tonic.

As we have observed throughout this study, the tendency in minor is to move to the mediant chord, the key area of the relative major (see above, p. 36). The diminished supertonic and subtonic chords, shown in examples 7–39 and 7–40 below, may also belong to the relative major as its TMD and THD respectively. Again, the main-level key's ii° is also [vii°] III. The apparent subtonic seventh that follows the diminished supertonic in both examples becomes [V$^6_5$] III.

Using the diminished supertonic and the subtonic as dominant-family chords in the new key is a direct way to shift from the minor mode to its relative major. The presence of [vii° and/or V$^6_5$ – I] III gives momentary emphasis to the mediant chord. But following this operation with [X – V – I] III establishes the event (that is, the new key) as a potential modulation.

Example 7–39: OVIP 5   6 (out of key, minor, sevenths)

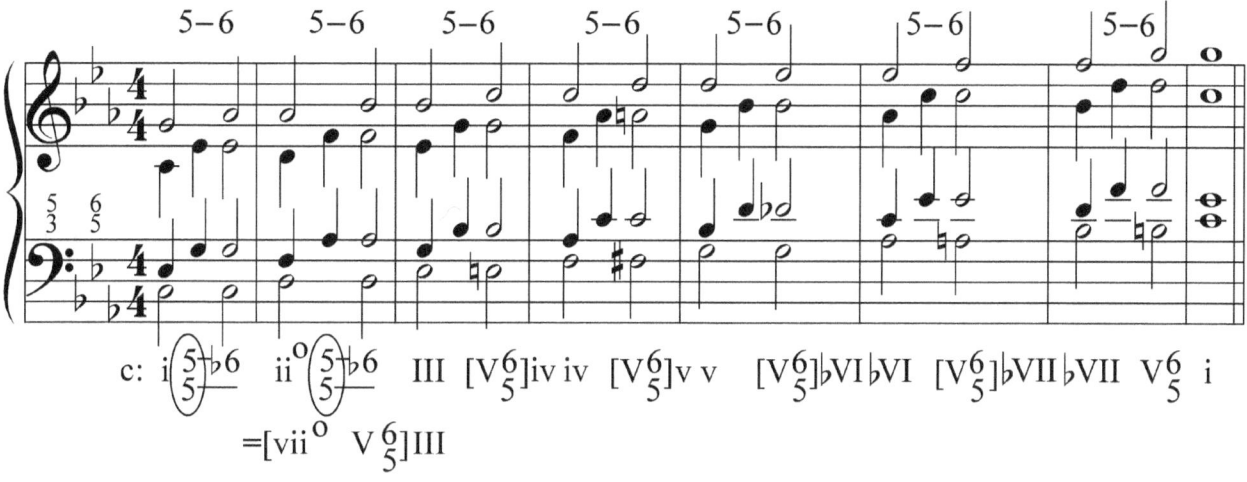

Example 7–40: OVIP 5   6 (out of key, minor, sevenths, extended passing, X-chord, and cadential $^6_4$)

One result of the ascending 5—6 (or of any sequence) may be an excursion into a lower-level key, as the possibility for moving away from the tonic readily occurs on each of its scale degrees. For example, in the ascending 5—6, a key change can be initiated from any scale degree upon on which a major or minor triad may be formed.

As we shall see in Chapter 8, establishing an X-chord in the new key as a common chord between both keys—a pivot chord—and then continuing the progression with a harmonic cadence in the new key constitutes a more convincing technique for modulation than simply invoking an applied dominant to effect the operation. Indeed, the lower-level SHP counts among the most effective devices for moving decisively away from the tonic, with or without the additional presence of a sequence.

Root-Position Variants of the Ascending 5—6 (becoming 12—7): the Applied TMD/CLT

The foregoing examples of the ascending 5—6 sequence show the second chord in first inversion breaking up faulty parallel motion above the contrapuntal bass. In the next five sections, both chords appear in root position, with the second maintaining its role as a voice-leading chord.

One variant for the ascending 5—6 with the chromatic bass replaces the applied THD/CLTs with the TMD as a fully diminished seventh in root position. In examples 7–41 through 7–44, the disposition of the chords presents an alternating OVIP of 12ths and 7ths, each 7th resolving to a 5th (12th) in the next chord. The chord seventh of each [TMD] breaks up the parallel 5ths and octaves between the outer and inner voices respectively.

Example 7–41: OVIP 12 7 (out of key, sevenths)

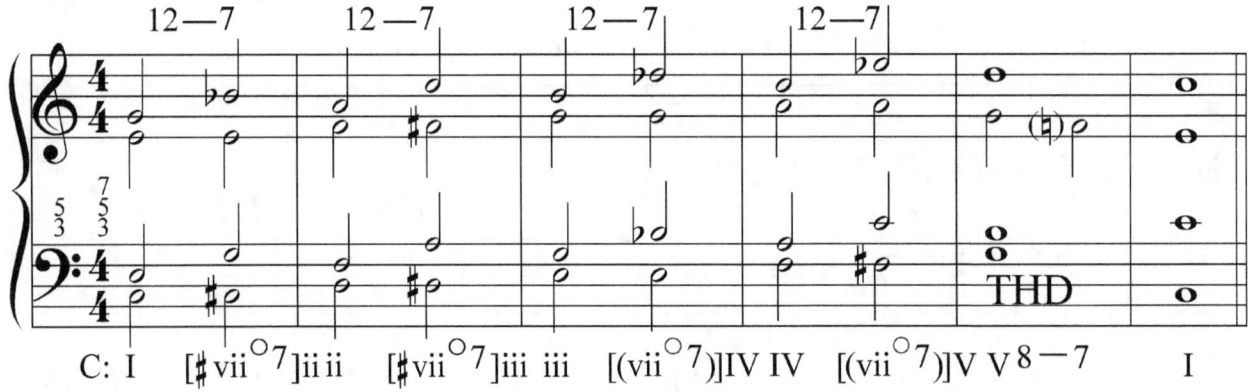

Example 7–42: OVIP 12 7 (out of key, sevenths, extended passing, X-chord, and cadential $^6_4$)

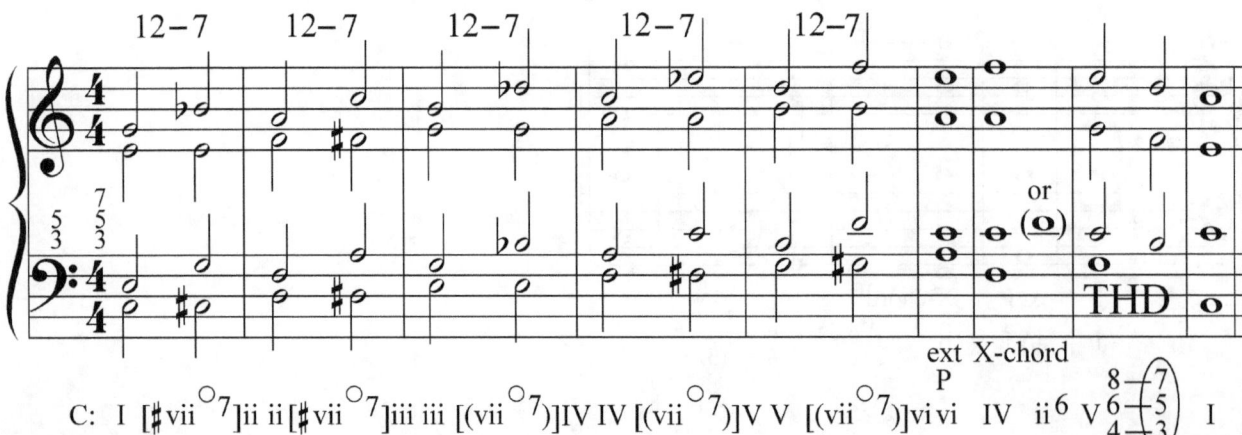

In sequences that ascend in minor, there is always the potential problem of the diminished supertonic in root position. In both examples 7–43 and 7–44, the diminished supertonic makes its appearance in measure 2. As we have seen, the best way to use the diminished supertonic is to associate it with the mediant as an applied chord.

Notice that the disposition of the voices in the examples below takes the soprano slightly beyond the top of its range, were this to be sung. However, the immediate objective here is to demonstrate the operations of this ascending 5—6 variant, its voice-leading, and hazards.

Example 7–43: OVIP 12 7 (out of key, minor, sevenths)

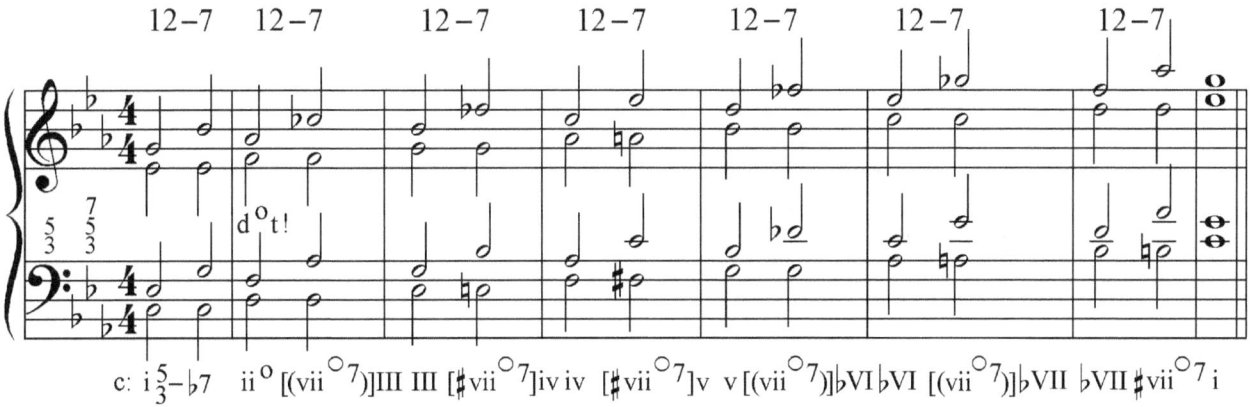

Example 7–44: OVIP 12 7 (out of key, minor, sevenths, extended passing, X-chord, and cadential $^6_4$)

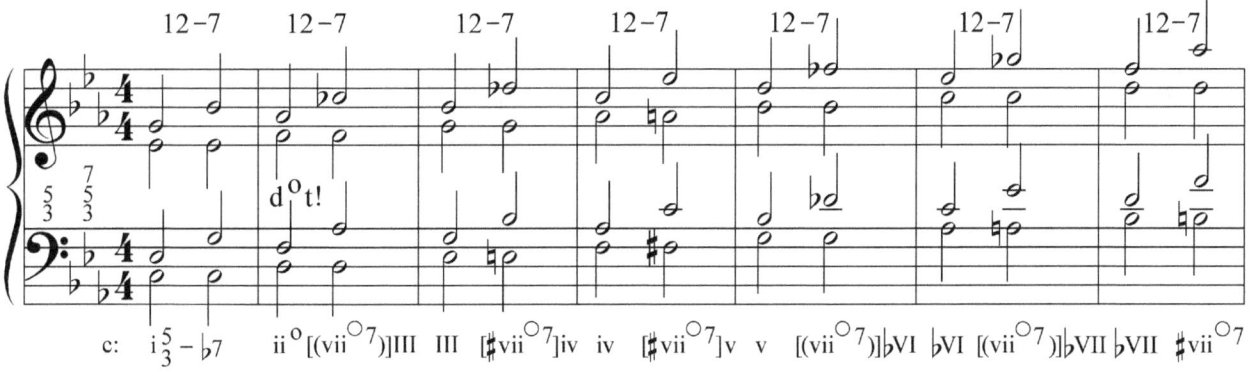

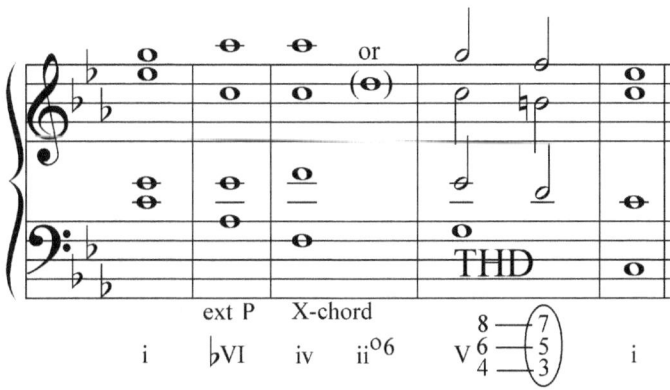

Root-Position Variants of the Ascending 5—6 (becoming 5—8): Falling 3rd-Rising 4th

The following four sections contain variants of the ascending 5—6 in which the 6th is replaced with either an octave or 10th. Both chords of each chord pair are in root position with an alternating OVIP of 5ths and octaves or 5ths and 10ths.

The bass line consists of various combinations of 3rds and 4ths. On the primary accents of examples 7–45 and 7–46, the bass line of the sequence takes a stepwise ascent from the tonic up to the submediant chord. The second chord continues to prevent parallel 5ths and octaves while serving as a modal dominant to the first sequential chord of each measure.

The most obvious weakness of this variant is the diminished triad in root position, vii° in major and ii° in minor. However, within the context of this variant of the sequence, the diminished triad may occur. Proceeding from the tonic, the diminished triad stands within the sequence as the fourth chord in major and as the third chord in minor. Adding a seventh to the chord stabilizes the sonority. (The seventh is added to the leading-tone triad in example 7–47 and to the supertonic triad in examples 7–48 and 7–56.)

Although vii° does not resolve directly to the tonic in 7–45 (usually the best option), the chord remains covered within the sequence as an internal event while addressing the mediant as a modal dominant (and voice-leading chord). In 7–46, both ii° and ♭VII are associated with the mediant as [vii° – V] III. In its second appearance, ii° becomes a modal dominant to v.

Example 7–45: OVIP 5 8 (in the key, falling 3rd-rising 4th)

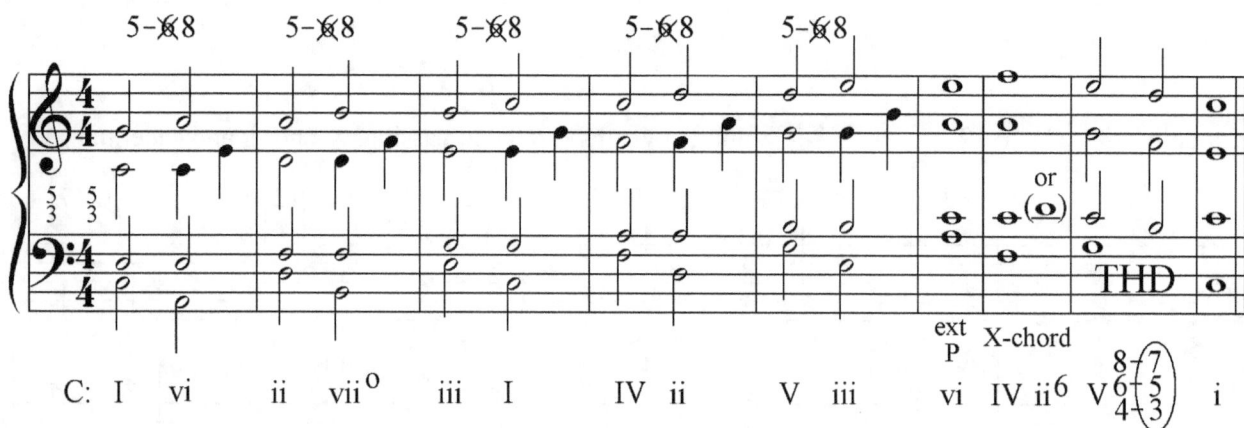

Example 7–46: OVIP 5 8 (in the key, minor, falling 3rd-rising 4th)

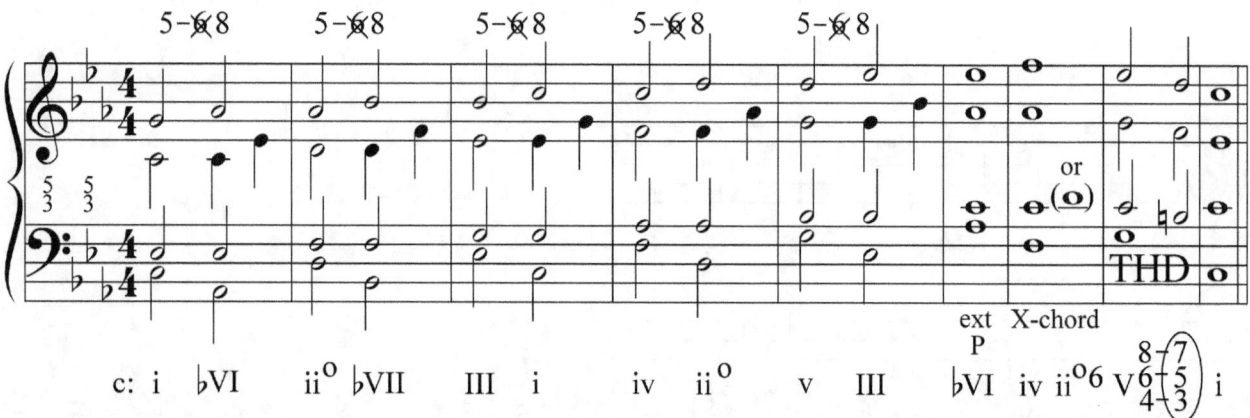

The static tenor in the second chord of examples 7–45 and 7–46 takes the chord seventh in examples 7–47 and 7–48, adding both dissonance and momentum to the progression and to each successive modal dominant. The problem with the diminished triad of the leading-tone in root position is solved when the chord becomes a half-diminished seventh.

Example 7–47: OVIP 5 8 (in the key, sevenths, falling 3rd-rising 4th)

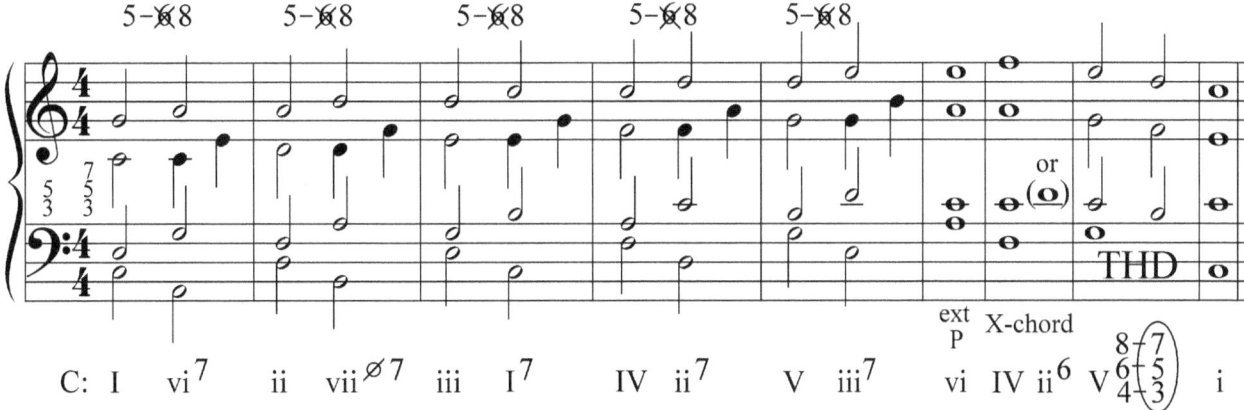

In 7–48, near the beginning of the sequence, ♭VI⁷ to ii° generates a distracting level of dissonance: a less than ideal succession between chords in which a major seventh resolves to a diminished triad in root position. Since more than two or three repetitions of any pattern may prove excessive, it would be well to avoid beginning this sequence with the tonic and then passing through its weakest area. The mediant is a better place to start the ascent. In measure 4, the sonority of the supertonic is much improved as a half-diminished seventh.

Example 7–48: OVIP 5 8 (in the key, minor, sevenths, falling 3rd-rising 4th)

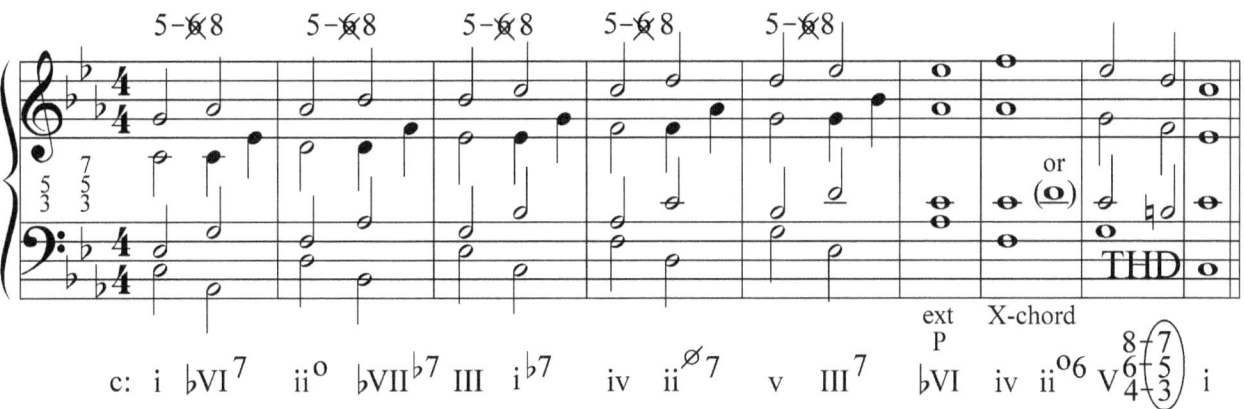

Root-Position Variants of the Ascending 5—6 (becoming 5—8): Falling 3rd-Rising 4th (Out of Key)

The second chord of the variant in examples 7–45 and 7–46 above becomes an applied dominant in examples 7–49 and 7–50 below. The out-of-key setting engenders an ascending chromatic line in the alto of 7–49. The chromaticism assumes the root and third of the two sequential chords. (Compare the chromatic bass of examples 7–34 and 7–38 to the half-step activity in the alto of 7–49.)

In 7–50, a modal dominant rather than an applied dominant addresses ii°, eliminating a portion of the chromaticism in the alto. However, as we have observed with the succession of ♭VI⁷ to ii°, ascending from the tonic in minor takes the sequential pattern through the diminished triad in root position. Though possible, ii° remains the weakest area of the sequence. The mediant serves as a better starting point for this variant; here, it is addressed by ♭VII, the naturally-occurring V of III in minor.

Example 7–49: OVIP 5 8 (out of key, falling 3rd-rising 4th)

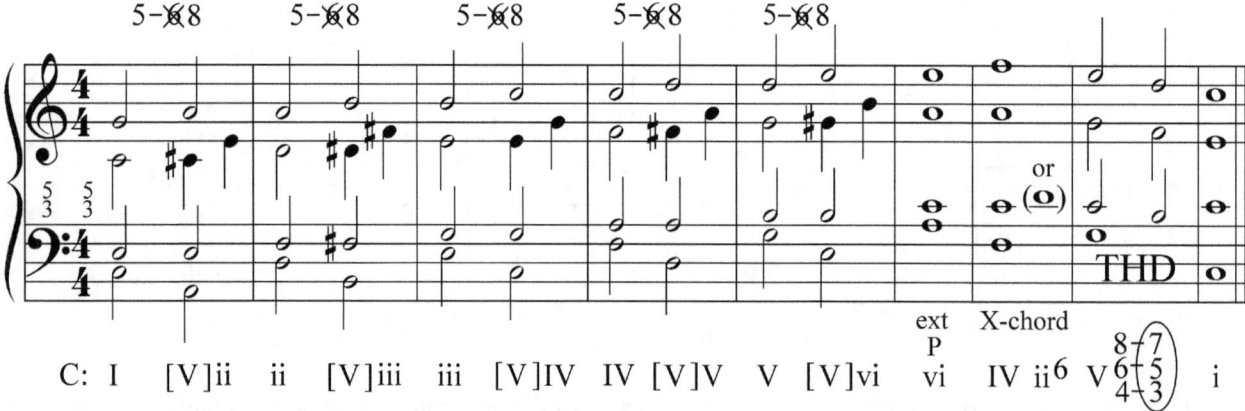

Example 7–50: OVIP 5 8 (out of key, minor, falling 3rd-rising 4th)

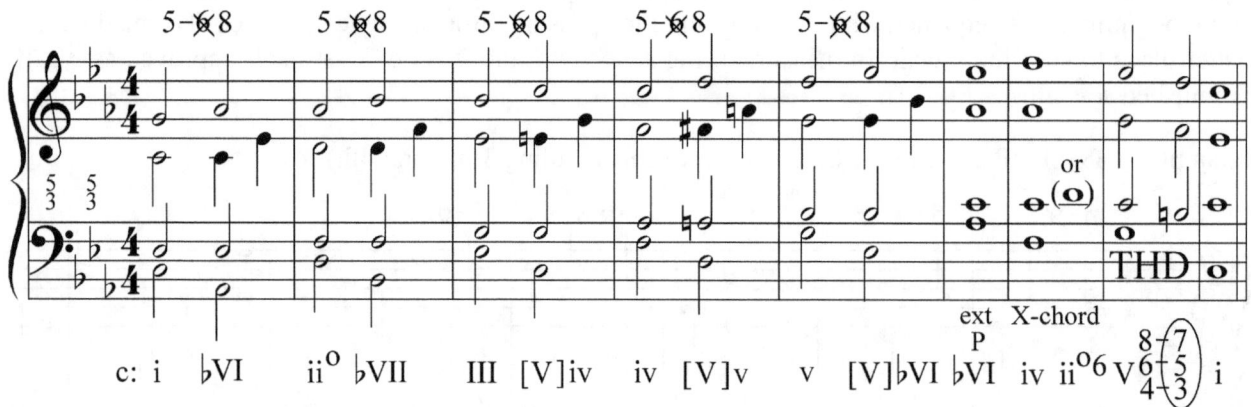

Examples 7–51 and 7–52 add sevenths to the second chord, the applied dominants, leaving the first chord as a the root-position triad, including the supertonic. Thus, as in 7–48 above, the questionable succession of ♭VI⁷ to ii° remains. The motion to the mediant, however, is both strengthened and intensified with the formation of a dominant seventh on the subtonic, becoming [V⁷]III, a key-defining operation which continues with iv, v, and ♭VI.

As with the other root-position variants of the ascending 5—6 (becoming 5—8), both examples 7–51 and 7–52 demonstrate an ascent from scale degrees 5 to 4. Supporting the ascent, the sequence becomes part of a larger descending motion spanning scale degrees 5–4–3–2–1 (G–F–E–D–C or G–F–E♭–D–C), a BMP. However, as we have seen, instead of moving down a major 2nd from scale degrees 5 to 4 (G–F), the melodic ascent inverts the interval to a minor 7th (G up to F). The sequence, extended passing chord, and X-chord all support the melodic inversion.

Example 7–51: OVIP: 5 8 (out of key, sevenths, falling 3rd-rising 4th)

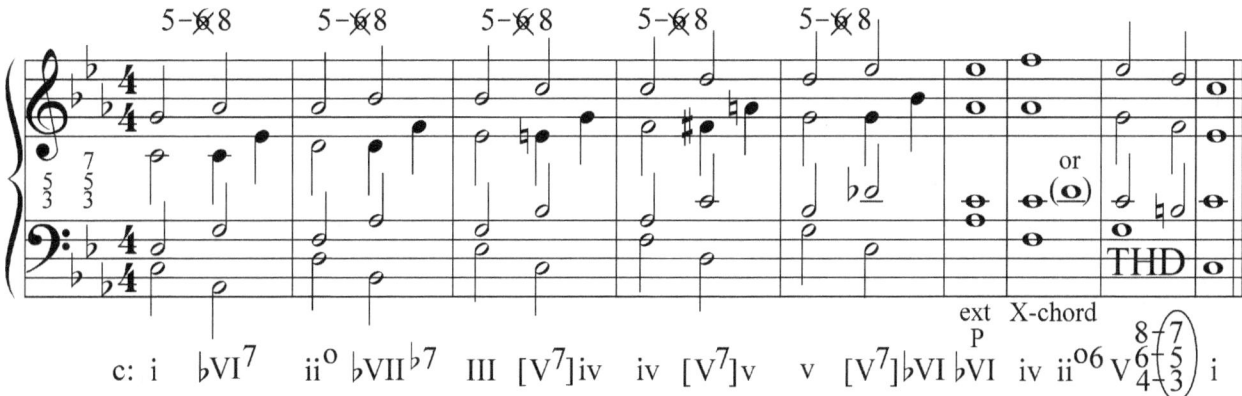

Example 7–52: OVIP 5 8 (out of key, minor, sevenths, falling 3rd-rising 4th)

Root-Position Variants of the Ascending 5—6 (becoming 5—10): Rising 4th-Falling 3rd

In this section, the second chord replaces the 6th with a 10th, producing an alternating OVIP of 5ths and 10ths. The first chord stands in a modal dominant relationship to the second, the voice-leading chord; together, they support the 5—10 motion. The emphasis the second chord receives is noteworthy, as it breaks up parallel octaves in the lower voices and parallel 5ths between the bass and alto while providing strong harmonic support for the 10th in the outer voices.

As we have suggested, one potential result of any sequence may be a lower-level progression, as the possibility for moving away from the tonic readily occurs on each of its diatonic scale degrees: a key change can be initiated from any scale degree upon on which a major or minor triad may be formed.

Our preference for the elaborated progression (for examples 7–44 through 7–60 exclusively), with its capacity to shore up the main-level key, underscores the ease with which the sequence can move away from the tonic. This is particularly evident in the ascending 5—6 becoming 5—10, as it provides harmonic emphasis to the second chord. Examples 7–57 through 7–60 present the first chord as an applied dominant to the second chord, the first becoming a chord of harmonic prolongation. The first chord as [V or V^7] articulates the key areas of the subdominant, dominant, and submediant.

Either a complete or incomplete progression, harmonic or contrapuntal, may effect the excursion into the lower-level key. However, if the intention is to firmly reestablish the tonic, then its arrival in measure 5 of the examples below should be followed by an elaboration of the progression in the main-level key, submitted here with the extended passing chord, X-chord, and cadential $^6_4$.

This variant of the ascending 5—6, shown in example 7–53, presents no difficulties in major. However, when the progression is expressed in minor, as in example 7–54, we encounter the root-position diminished supertonic as the first chord of the two-chord pattern (measure 2). Ultimately, in both major and minor versions of the ascending 5—6, the supertonic is part of an ascending line of root-position triads from scale degrees 1 to 5 (and sometimes beyond) while the second chord breaks up parallel 5ths and octaves.

As we have seen with the variant of the ascending 5—6 becoming 5—8, if the sequence begins with the tonic in minor, then it proceeds to ii°, which is approached by a leap in the bass. The leap places strong emphasis on the tritone between the root and fifth of the chord. Still, ii°'s presence may be justified within context of the sequential pattern and as a chord of harmonic prolongation addressing v as a modal dominant.

Example 7–53: OVIP 5 10 (in the key, rising 4th-falling 3rd)

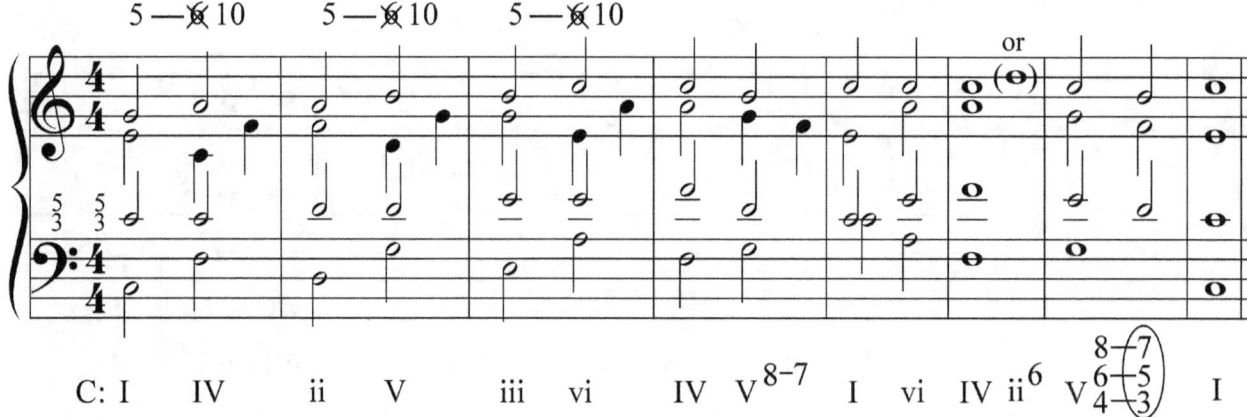

Example 7–54: OVIP 5 10 (in the key, minor, rising 4th-falling 3rd)

The addition of the chord seventh, illustrated below in examples 7–55 and 7–56, provides a dissonant component to the first chord, which in turn demands resolution to the second. The seventh also transforms ii° into the more acceptable half-diminished seventh; indeed, its presence in the sonority telegraphs the role of the supertonic as a chord of prolongation. Notice also the unusual doubling of scale degree 7 in major and of scale degrees ♭6 and ♭7 in minor.

In the top voice of both examples, there is an ascent from scale degrees 5 to 1, with the tonic C as the goal (scale degrees 5–6–7–1 or 5–♭6–♭7–1). The C is reached first with vi and then with IV ^{7}. The cadential framework of X – V – I (or i), with the subdominant seventh as the X-chord, brings the sequential pattern to a close.

The initial chord of this SHP is the first tonic seventh, which kicks off the sequence. At the end of the sequence, the cadential structure asserts the main-level key (measures 4–5); its elaboration, or expansion, follows (measures 5–8).

Example 7–55: OVIP 5 10 (in the key, sevenths, rising 4th-falling 3rd)

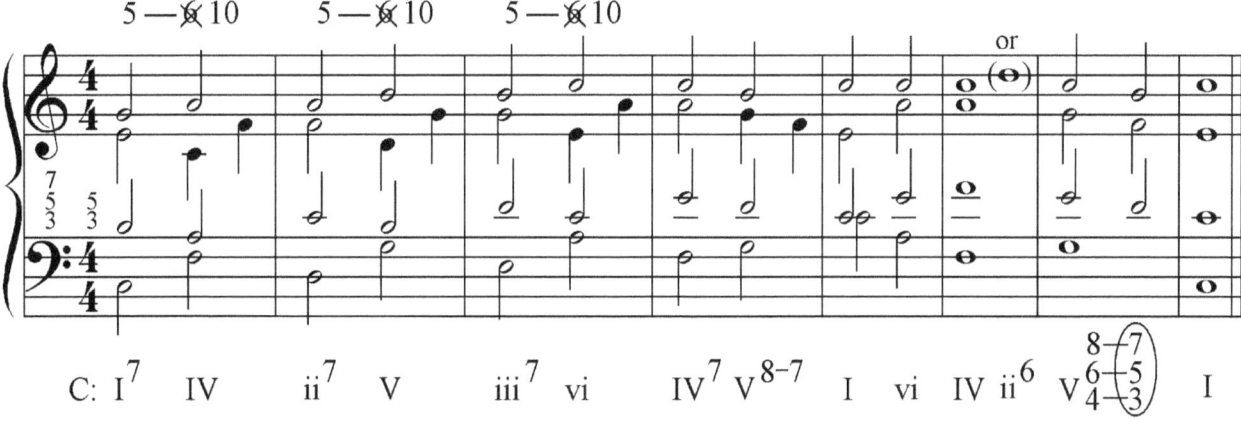

Example 7–56 OVIP: 5 10 (in the key, minor, sevenths, rising 4th-falling 3rd)

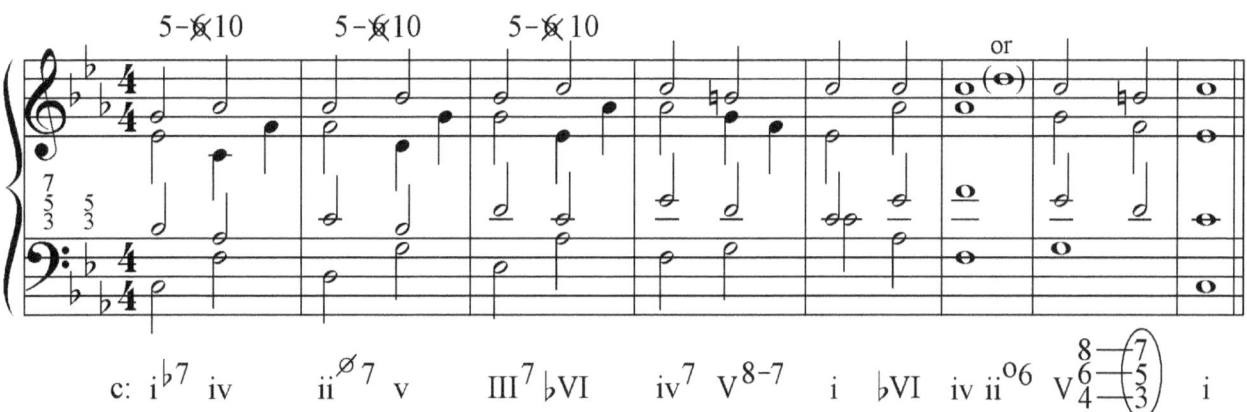

Root-Position Variants of the Ascending 5—6 (becoming 5—10): Rising 4th-Falling 3rd (Out of Key)

In this section, examples 7–57 through 7–60 place the sequential patterns of 7–53 through 7–56 within a chromatic context, transforming the first chord of each chord pair into an applied dominant triad or seventh. The articulation of the second chord is strongest when it is addressed by an applied dominant, particularly an applied dominant seventh. When the tonic chord becomes [V ^{7}]IV, as in example 7–59 below, it may serve as a substitute for the tonic.

190   Chapter 7 The Sequence

Example 7–57: OVIP 5 10 (out of key, rising 4th-falling 3rd)

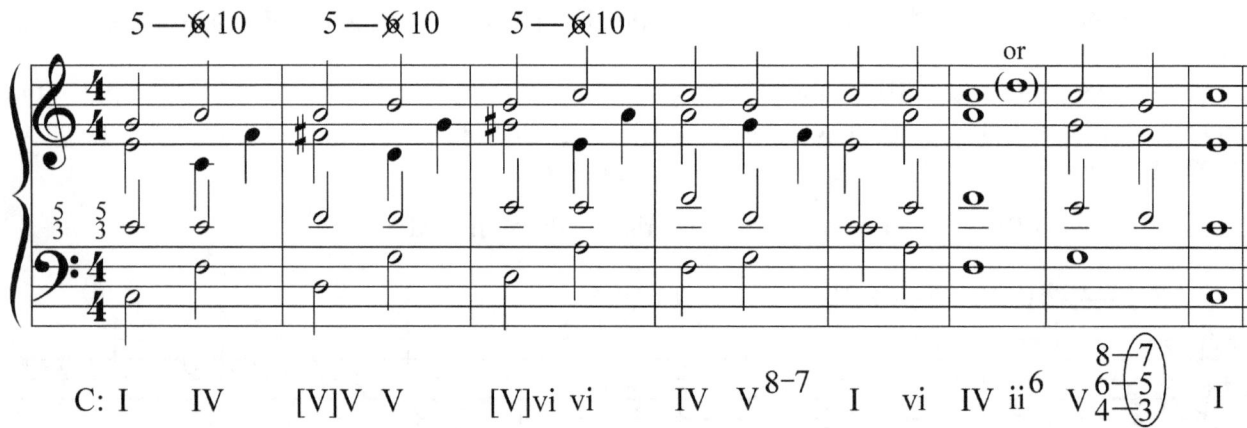

Example 7–58: OVIP 5 10 (out of key, minor, rising 4th-falling 3rd)

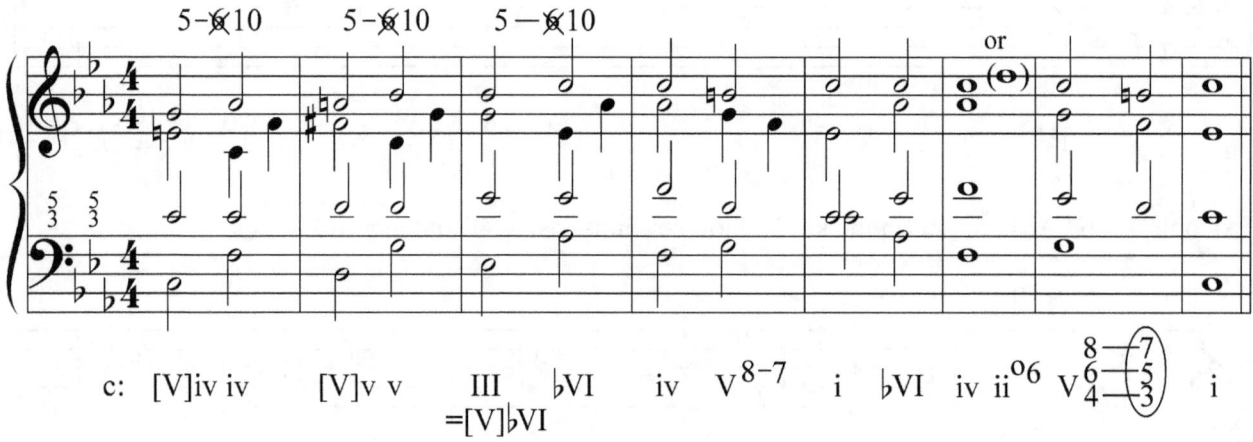

Example 7–59: OVIP 5 10 (out of key, sevenths, rising 4th-falling 3rd)

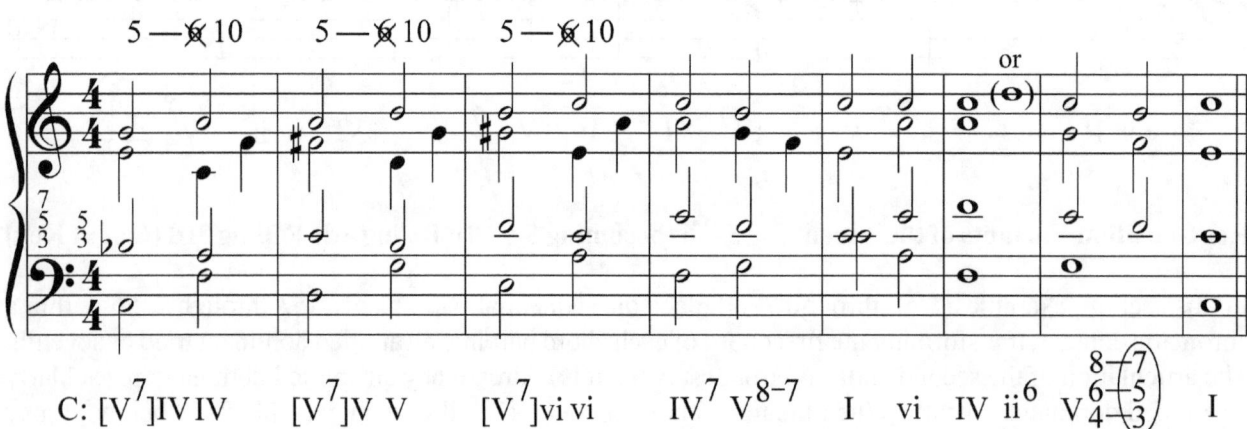

Example 7–60: OVIP 5 10 (out of key, minor, sevenths, rising 4th-falling 3rd)

c: [V⁷]iv iv [V⁷]v v [V⁷]♭VI ♭VI iv⁷ V⁸⁻⁷ i ♭VI iv ii°⁶ V⁶⁴⁽⁸⁻⁷⁵⁻₃⁾ i

The Ascending 5th

The rising 4th-falling 5th relationship between the chords of the descending 5th sequence produces a compelling sense of forward motion. Conversely, the rising 5th-falling 4th root activity of the ascending 5th sequence strengthens the retroactive (back-relating) function of the second chord; for the second chord seeks to return the one that preceded it.

As illustrated in example 7–61, the complete succession of chords for the ascending 5th does not lead directly to a dominant cadence before the return of the tonic. Hence, a full statement of this sequence is not likely to occur.

The most practicable portion of the ascending 5th sequence (identified with brackets in examples 7–61 through 7–70) is I – V – ii – vi – iii in major and III – ♭VII – iv – i – V in minor. The ascending 5th, as presented in this chapter, takes the unelaborated progression, that is: the tonic chord, the sequence, and the cadence. (Notice that the tenor works its way up to B prime, which is beyond the practical register for the tenor voice, though certainly possible.)

Example 7–61: OVIP 8 12 (in the key)

C: I V ii vi iii vii° IV I V⁸⁻⁷ I

In both examples 7–61 and 7–62, the root-position diminished triad should be avoided. For without the propulsive quality of the descending 5th sequence to drive the progression forward, the sequential patterns cannot overshadow the inherent dissonance of the chord. Moreover, even when its sonority is improved as a half-diminished seventh, as in example 7–63, the root position remains too strident for this progression.

192   Chapter 7 The Sequence

Example 7–62: OVIP 8 12 (in the key, minor)

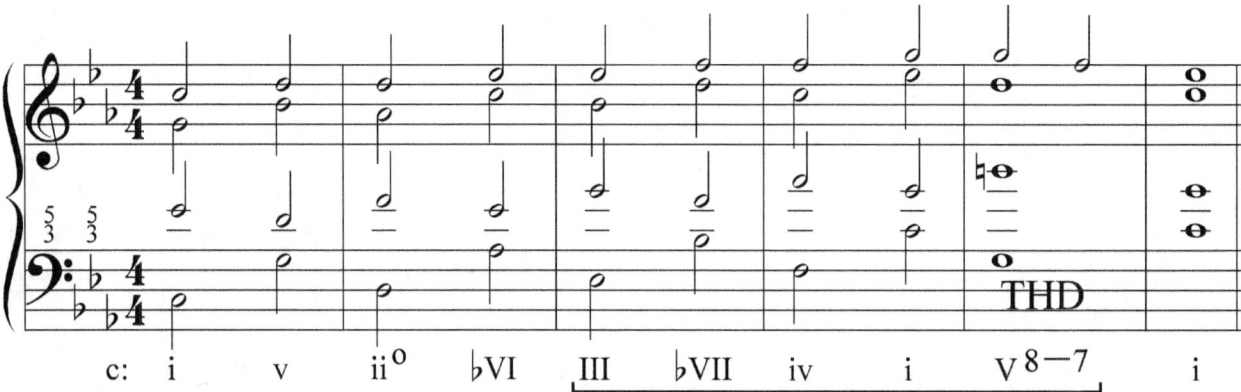

As we have seen with the ascending 5—6, the first chord of the ascending 5th projects a conjunct line of root-position triads from scale degrees 1 to 5 while the second chord corrects faulty motion. The tonic at the end of the sequence (before the THD) retains its status as a chord of voice leading and prolongation.

In major, the most useful portion of the sequence ends with the mediant and never reaches the voice-leading tonic. However, in minor, it appears near the end of the best part of the sequence and leads directly to the THD.

Example 7–63: OVIP 8 12 (in the key, sevenths)

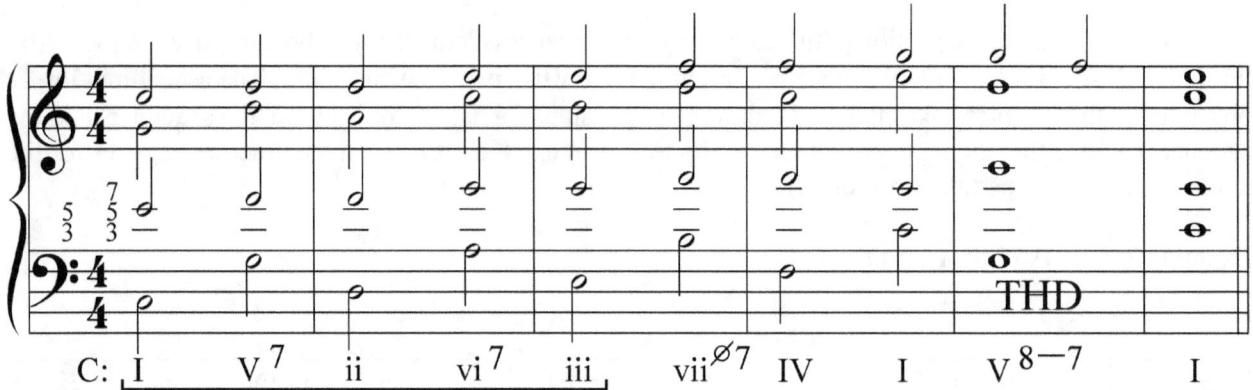

Example 7–64: OVIP 8 12 (in the key, minor, sevenths)

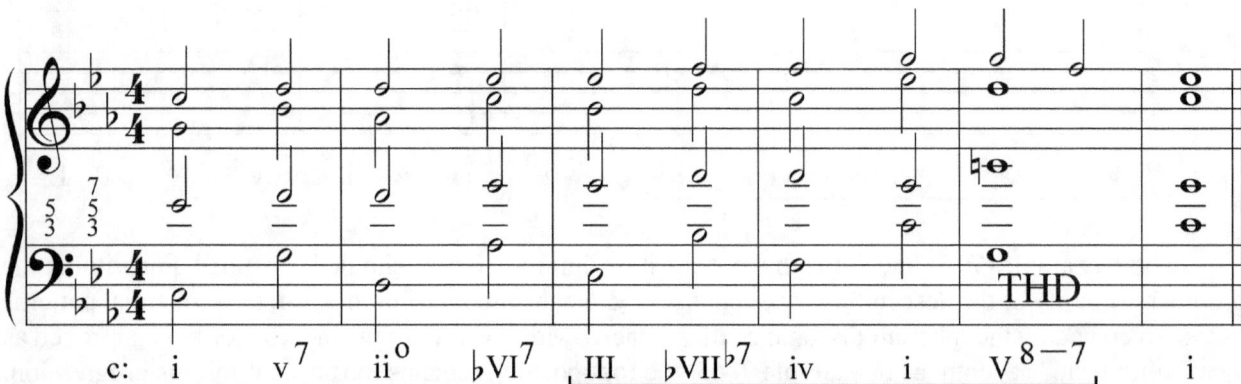

The Ascending 5th (Out of Key)

Using applied dominants with the ascending 5th strengthens the back-relating tendency of the second chord while also giving rise to a melodic augmented 2nd (examples 7–65 through 7–68, alto voice). Although the augmented 2nd might be acceptable within the framework of the sequential pattern, the problematic interval shows up in the weakest portion of the progression.

As we have suggested, the ascending 5th is most convincing when confined to the chordal areas of I through iii in major and of III through V in minor. (The brackets in the examples identify the best areas of the sequence.)

In example 7–65, a retroactive applied dominant, [V]ii, replaces the submediant in major (measure 2, beat 3). In example 7–66, the subtonic constitutes the naturally-occurring V of III in minor (measure 3, beat 3). The [V]iv in minor is also the tonic triad expressed as a Picardy third (measure 4, beat 3).

Example 7–65: OVIP 8 12 (out of key)

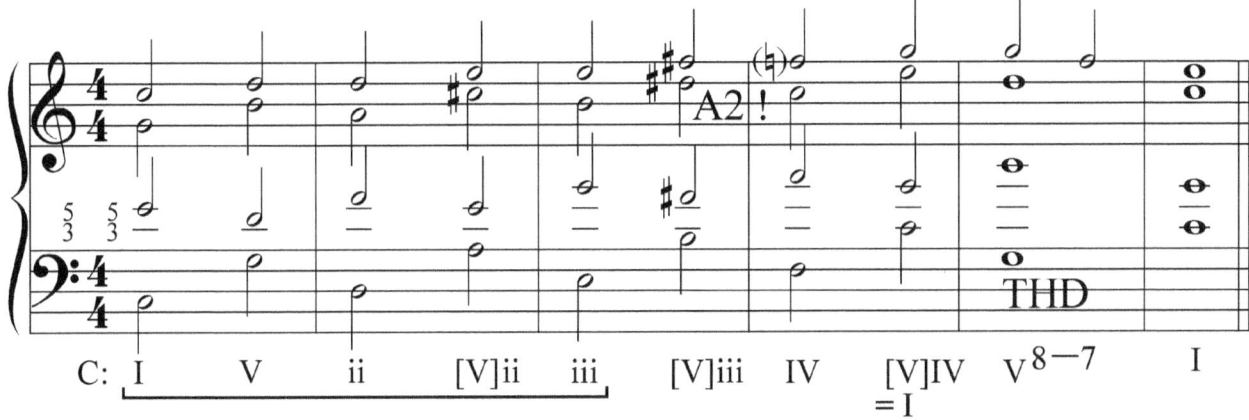

Example 7–66: OVIP 8 12 (out of key, minor)

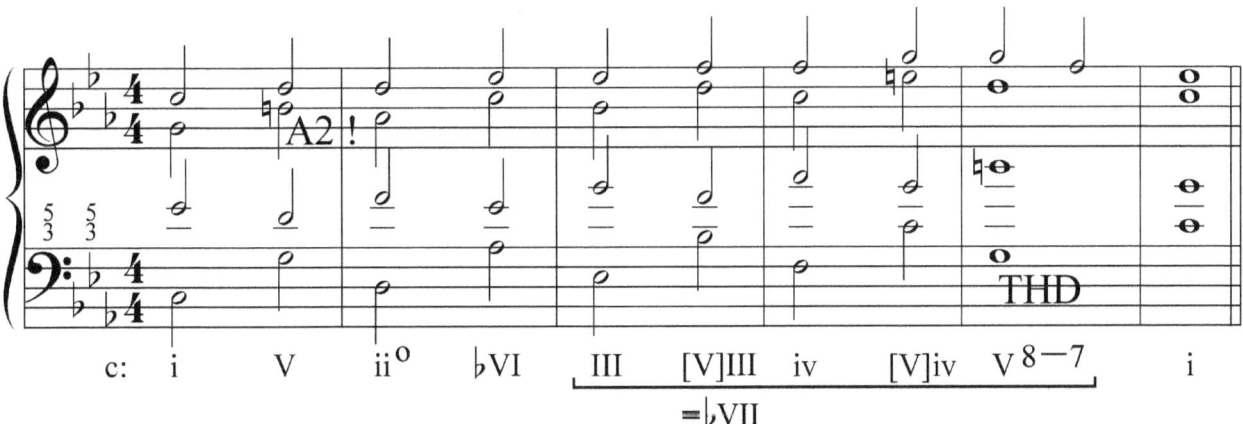

Examples 7–67 and 7–68 add the seventh to the second chord of the ascending 5th. The sevenths, however, do not take a downward resolution and are therefore apparent. The dissonant seventh in each applied V^7 becomes the chord third of the succeeding supertonic, mediant, and subdominant triads, producing a smooth though unproductive connection between chords. As a consequence, the second chord of the ascending 5th sequence usually appears as a triad rather than as a seventh chord.

In its alternative role as a retroactive dominant of IV in major and of iv in minor, the tonic at the end of the sequence does not take a seventh (measure 4, beat 3) in order to avoid having two pitch names in common with the dominant (THD). For including the seventh would obscure the chord change and weaken the arrival of the THD. The omission also averts the peculiar succession of two different versions of the same pitch, revolving upwards from a dissonance, from B♭ to B♮. (The seventh is also withheld from the prolonging tonic in examples 7–63 and 7–64 above in order to strengthen the entry of the THD.)

Example 7–67: OVIP 8 12 (out of key, sevenths)

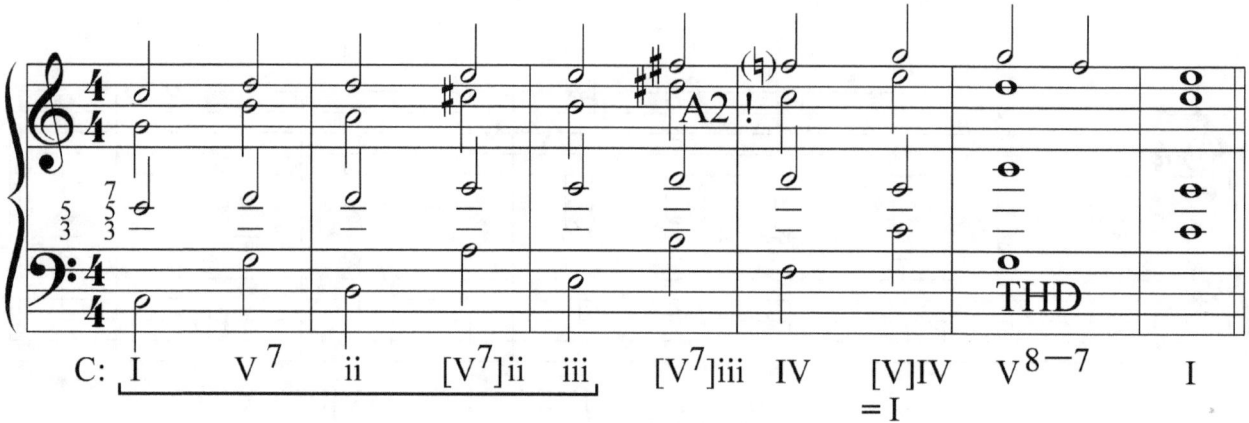

Example 7–68: OVIP 8 12 (out of key, minor, sevenths)

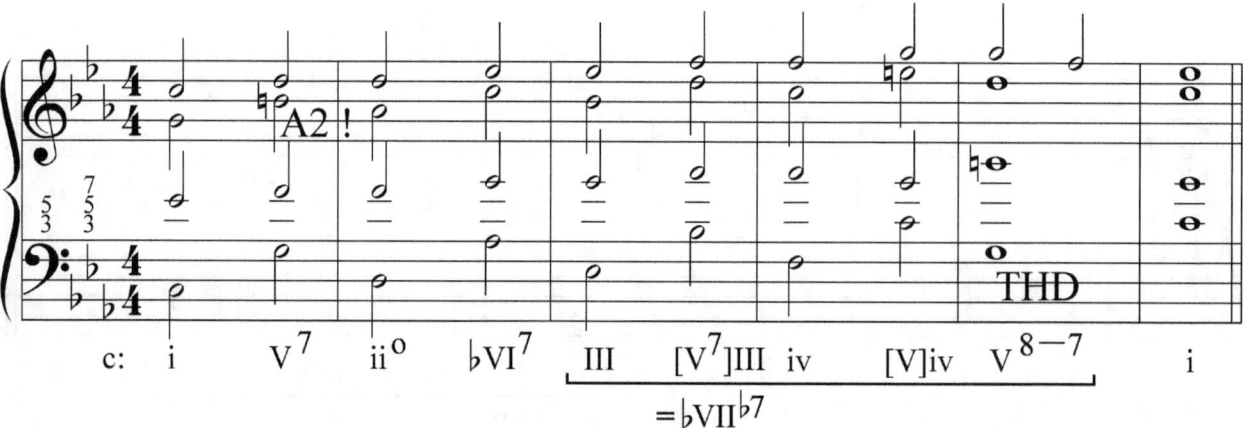

Avoiding the Problems of the Ascending 5th

Examples 7–69 and 7–70 use only the best segment of the ascending 5th in major and in minor. Displayed in the main-level key, the triads in examples 7–69a and 7–70a illustrate an alternative voicing of the previous examples of the sequence while examples 7–69b and 7–70b retain the earlier voicing, which takes the tenor to the top of its register.

Example 7–69: OVIP 10   5 (in the key, major)

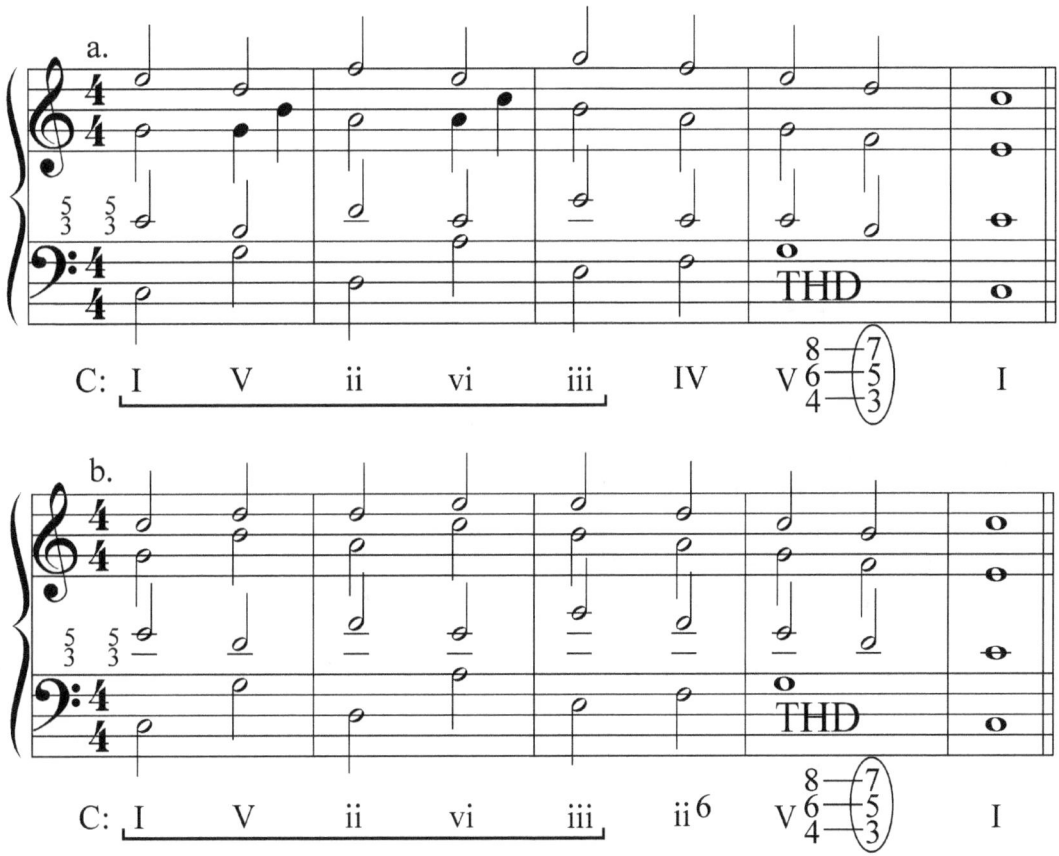

Example 7–70: OVIP 8   5 (in the key, minor)

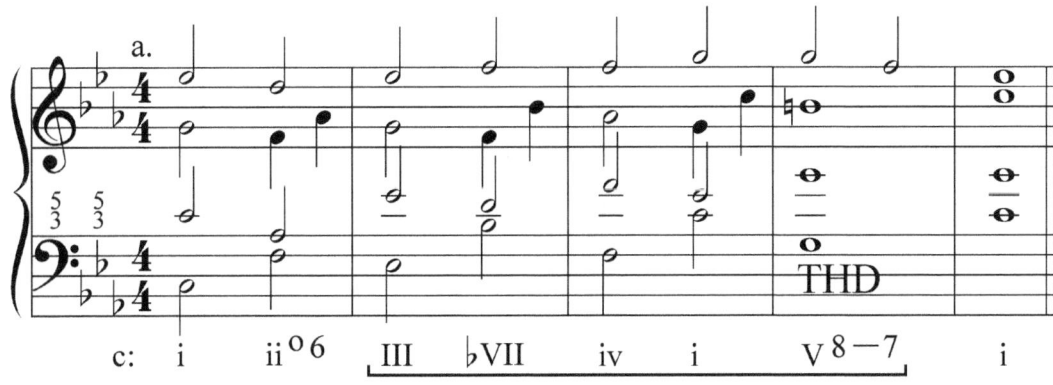

Example 7–70 (continued): OVIP 8 5 (in the key, minor)

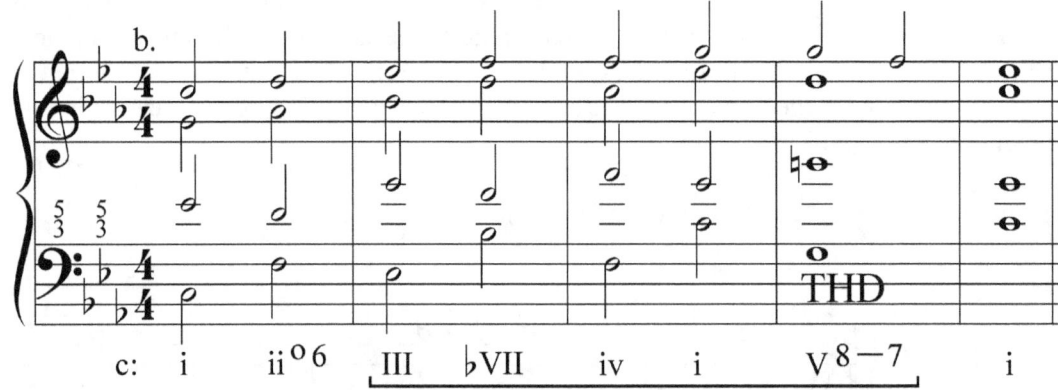

Root-Position and First-Inversion Chords (Ascending 5th): Falling 2nd-Rising 3rd

Placing the second chord in first inversion transforms the harmonic bass of the ascending 5th into a contrapuntal bass of falling 2nds and rising 3rds. The TMD triad in measure 3 of example 7–71(beat 3) is more acceptable in first inversion though it appears just beyond the preferred segment of the sequence.

In measures 1–4 of examples 7–71 and 7–72 (beats 3–4), the alto voice in the second chord proceeds from fifth to root, producing in measure 3 a melodic tritone. In the upper voices, the tritone should be avoided between unlike chords; however, in this instance, the interval is expressed within the same chord. Only the bass may take a melodic augmented 4th or diminished 5th between unlike chords.

In the tenor voice of examples 7–71 through 7–74 (measures 1–4, beats 3–4), the second chord takes a chordal skip from root to third to avoid a potential direct 5th between the bass and tenor of the succeeding triad. In examples 7–75 through 7–78, a nonharmonic tone corrects the faulty motion.

Example 7–71: OVIP 8 10 (in the key, falling 2nd-rising 3rd)

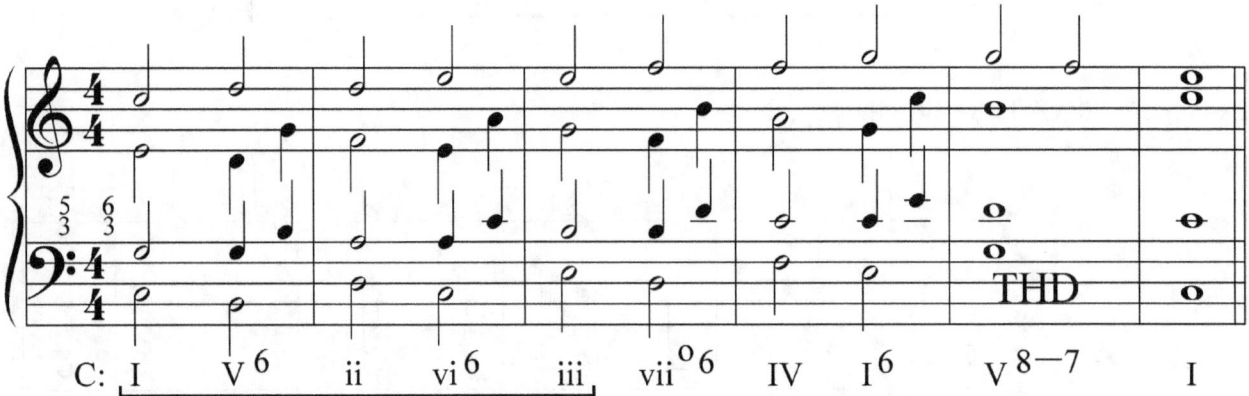

Chapter 7 The Sequence   197

Example 7–72: OVIP 8   10 (in the key, minor, falling 2nd-rising 3rd)

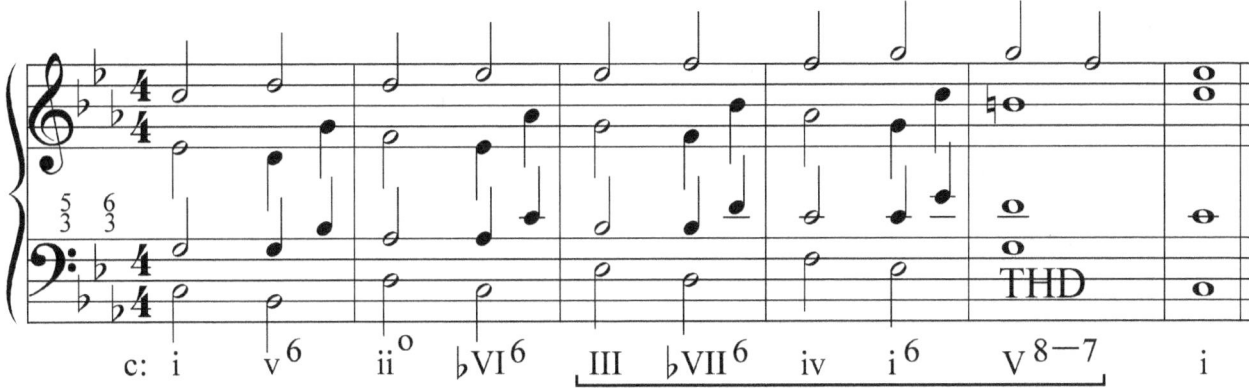

In measures 1–4 of examples 7–73 and 7–74 (alto, beats 3–4), the apparent seventh in the second chord is more animated than the previous usage, as it unfolds upwards into the root of the sonority. However, the unfolding of tones within the same chord, the second chord, is too insignificant an event to avert the unproductive course of the seventh as it becomes the chord third of the following triad. In minor, ii° remains outside the best portion of the sequence.

Example 7–73: OVIP 8   10 (in the key, sevenths, falling 2nd-rising 3rd)

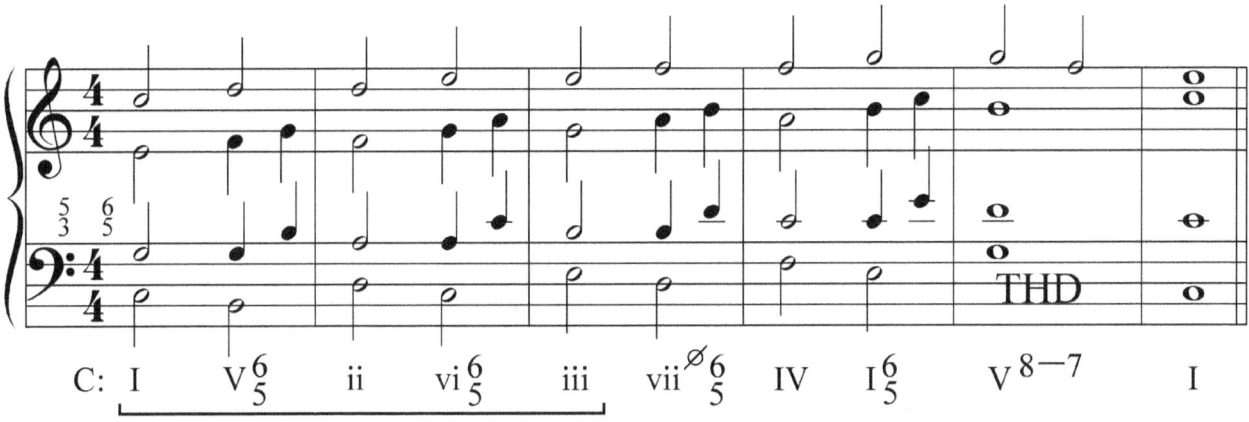

Example 7–74: OVIP 8   10 (in the key, minor, sevenths, falling 2nd-rising 3rd)

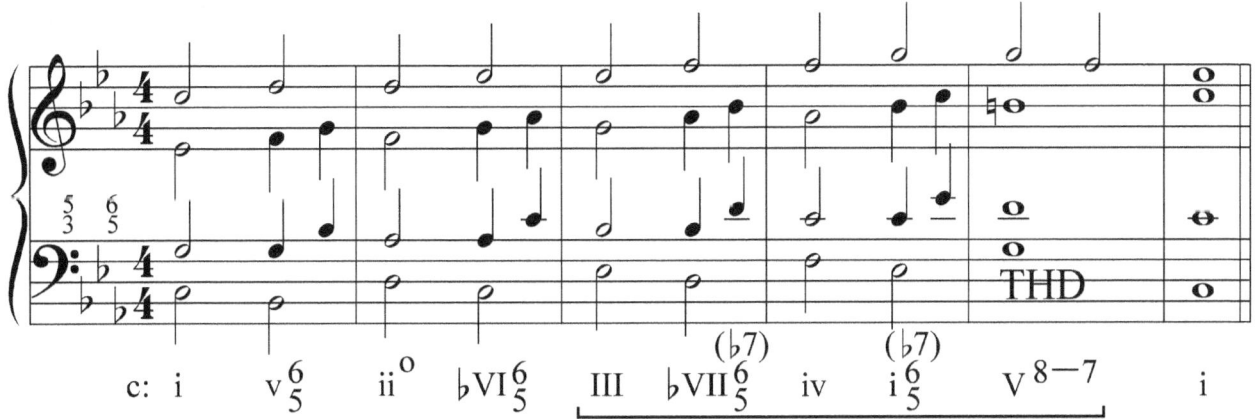

Root-Position and First-Inversion Chords (Ascending 5th): Falling 2nd-Rising 3rd (Out of Key)

In examples 7–75 through 7–78, the second chord becomes a retroactive applied dominant expressed in the examples as a CLT chord, either a major triad or a dominant seventh in first inversion. As we have seen, when applied dominants are used in the ascending 5th sequence, the chromaticism may give rise to unusual intervals, such as the augmented 2nd.

In 7–75, a diminished 3rd appears in the bass after the most effective segment of the sequence has run its course. Here, in measure 3, the harmony struggles to remain convincing within the framework of the sequence. Indeed, the tritone root relationship between [V^6]iii and IV yields a strident succession.

Example 7–75: OVIP 8 10 (out of key, falling 2nd-rising 3rd)

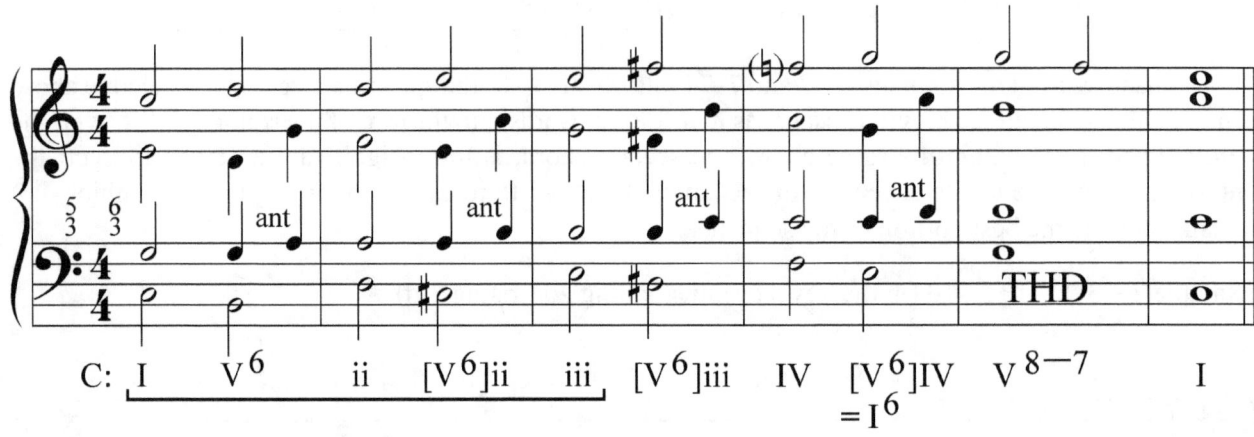

Example 7–76: OVIP 8 10 (out of key, minor, falling 2nd-rising 3rd)

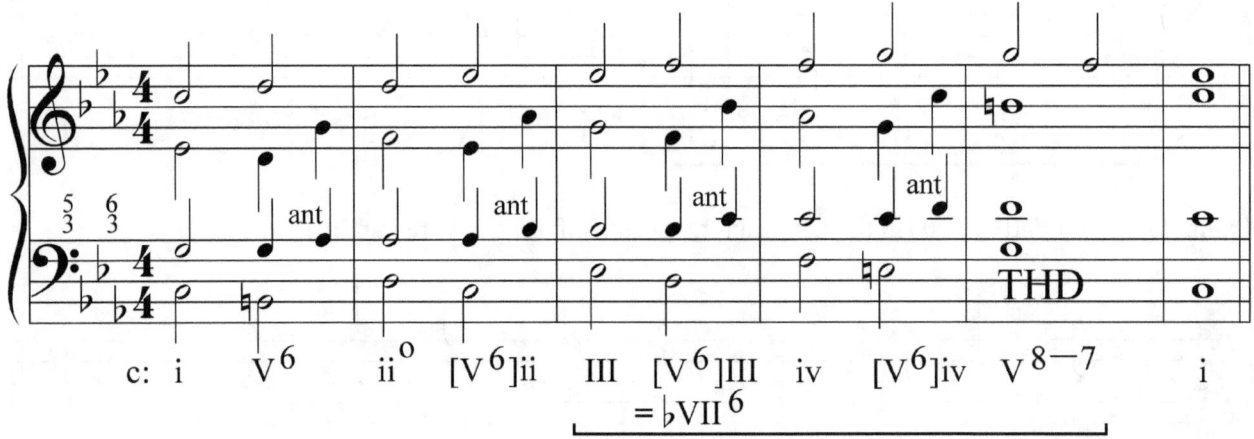

Examples 7–75 through 7–78 show an alternative strategy for avoiding the direct 5th between the bass and tenor (measures 1–4, from beat 4 forward): the anticipation tone (ant). The tenor anticipates the fifth of the first chord, creating a dissonant 7th with the alto voice. (In any case, some theoreticians allow the direct 5th here because it involves an inner voice and remains somewhat inconspicuous.)

The 7th so positioned sounds particularly harsh when its quality is major, as in measure 3 of examples 7–75 and 7–77 (beat 4) and measure 1 of examples 7–76 and 7–78 (beat 4); moreover, the latter instance proceeds to ii°. Both appearances of the major 7th occur in the weakest portions of the ascending 5th in major and in minor and should be skipped.

Example 7–77: OVIP 8   10 (out of key, sevenths, falling 2nd-rising 3rd)

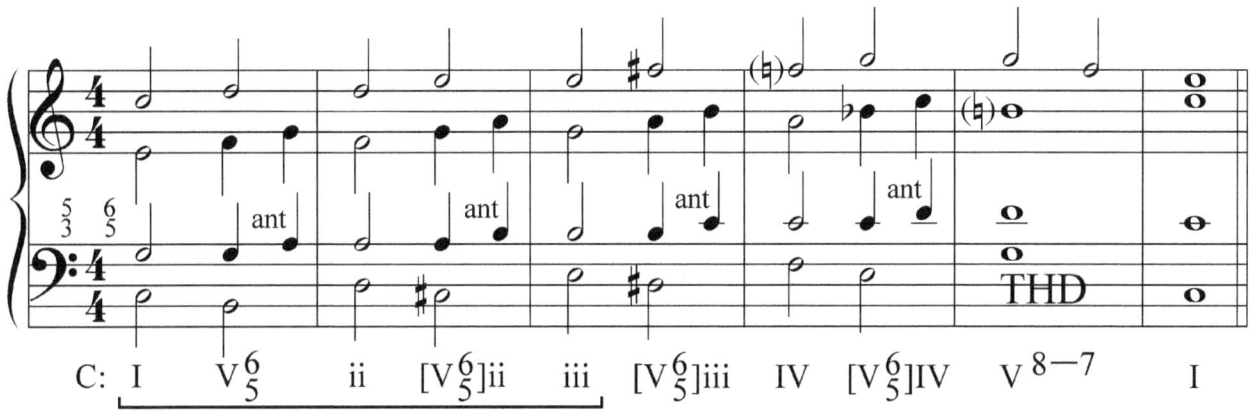

Example 7–78: OVIP 8   10 (out of key, minor, sevenths, falling 2nd-rising 3rd)

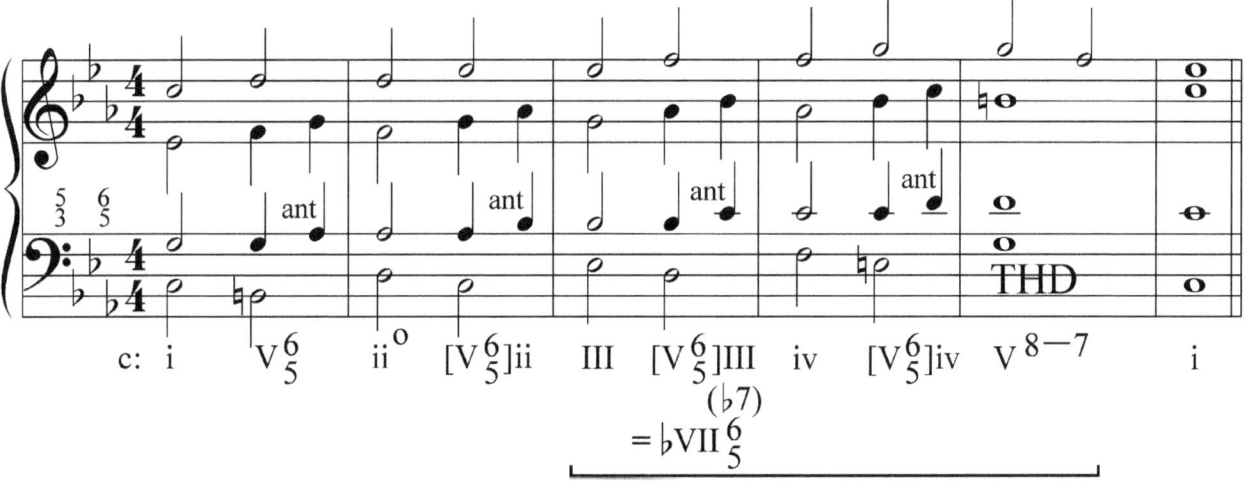

The Descending 5—6

In the foregoing examination of the ascending 5th sequence, we observed the potential back-relating, or retroactive, function of the second chord of each chord pair. The voice leading that produces the retroactive dominant was demonstrated earlier in Chapter 4 (examples 4–11 and 4–12).

In the fourth chapter, we linked the retroactive dominant to the operations of the descending 5—6 sequence, which projects another pattern of alternating 5ths and 6ths. The numbers representing the motion of the 5th proceeding to the 6th takes a dash because one voice is stationary. Situated above the moving voice, the stationary voice serves as an inverted pedal embellishing tone (the stationary tone is located in an upper voice).

As we have seen, one of the problems of the sequence in general and of the descending 5—6 here is that somewhere in the course of the progression, a diminished 5th occurs. Sometimes, the best solution is to avoid the interval both melodically and harmonically.

Example 4–11 above introduces the descending 5—6 sequence with two pairs of skipped chords, namely (in D major): vii° – IV⁶ after V⁶ and V – ii⁶ after iii⁶. The root-position chords of the leading tone and the dominant are omitted from the sequence. The first-inversion triads paired with the omitted chords are removed as well.

As a consequence of these omissions, which are continued in examples 7–79 through 7–88 below, a pattern of descending 3rds in the bass emerges. That is, each subsequent chord pair for the descending 5—6 (and each 5—6 succession of intervals) begins a 3rd below the one that preceded it. The descending 3rd action in the bass becomes an integral component of the descending 5—6.

Example 7–79: OVIP 10   10 (in the key)

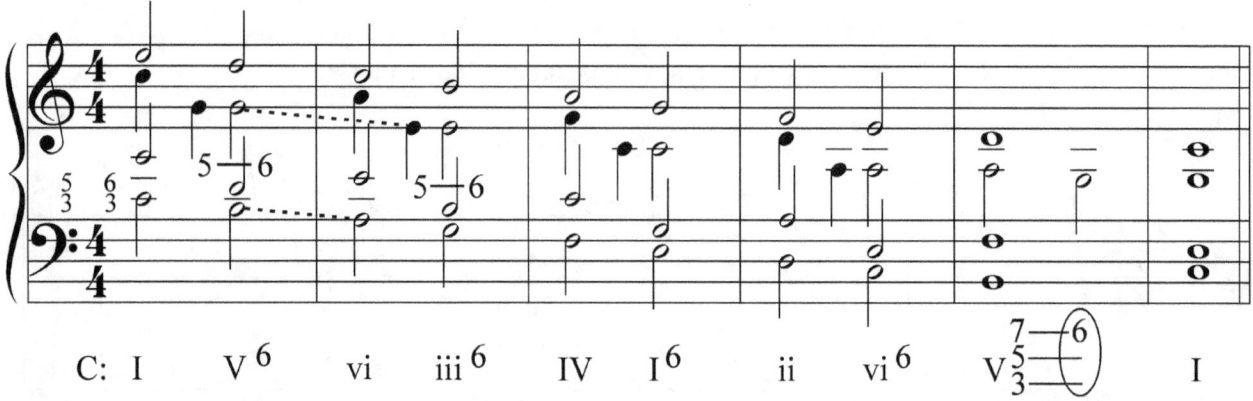

Example 7–80: OVIP 10   10 (in the key, minor)

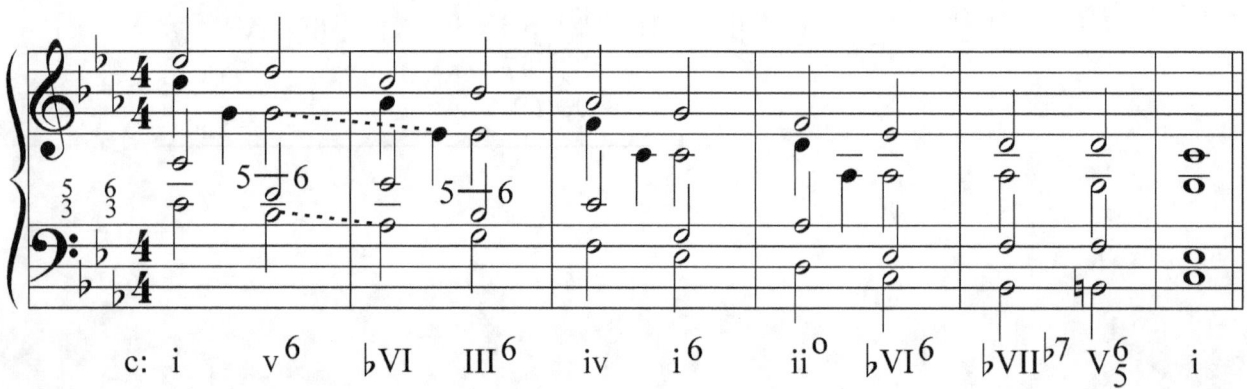

As in other sequences, the potential for faulty motion presents itself with the descending 5—6. Alternating 5ths and 6ths avert the parallels. However, examples 7–79 and 7–80 illustrate a possible direct (or hidden) 5th between the second and first chords (see the dotted lines in measures 1–2).

Examples 7–81 and 7–82 add the seventh element to the second chord, which creates another complication. Notice that as the dissonant seventh in the second chord resolves to the fifth of the next chord, parallel 5ths are produced.

Whenever a seventh chord stands in a rising 2nd root relationship to another chord, there is always a possibility of parallel 5ths when the dissonance resolves, particularly if the seventh chord is in first inversion. In four voices, such parallels can be disguised somewhat (as attempted in 7–81a and 7–82a) but the result usually remains poor. However, when these chords are transformed into applied dominant sevenths, the 5ths become unequal, yielding a more acceptable operation (see examples 7–85 and 7–86). Another solution effects a 6—5 motion above the bass with each iteration of the first chord (examples 7–81b and 7–82b).

Ultimately, the descending 5—6, as demonstrated in this section, progresses from the tonic to a contrapuntal cadence and takes three repetitions. However, a full statement of this sequence should not be presented, as it is most effective when limited to no more than one or two repetitions of the pattern. In measure 4 of examples 7–82, 84, 90, and 92, the ii ° is usually skipped, unless it forms part of the cadential structure.

Example 7–81: OVIP 5 6 (in the key, sevenths)

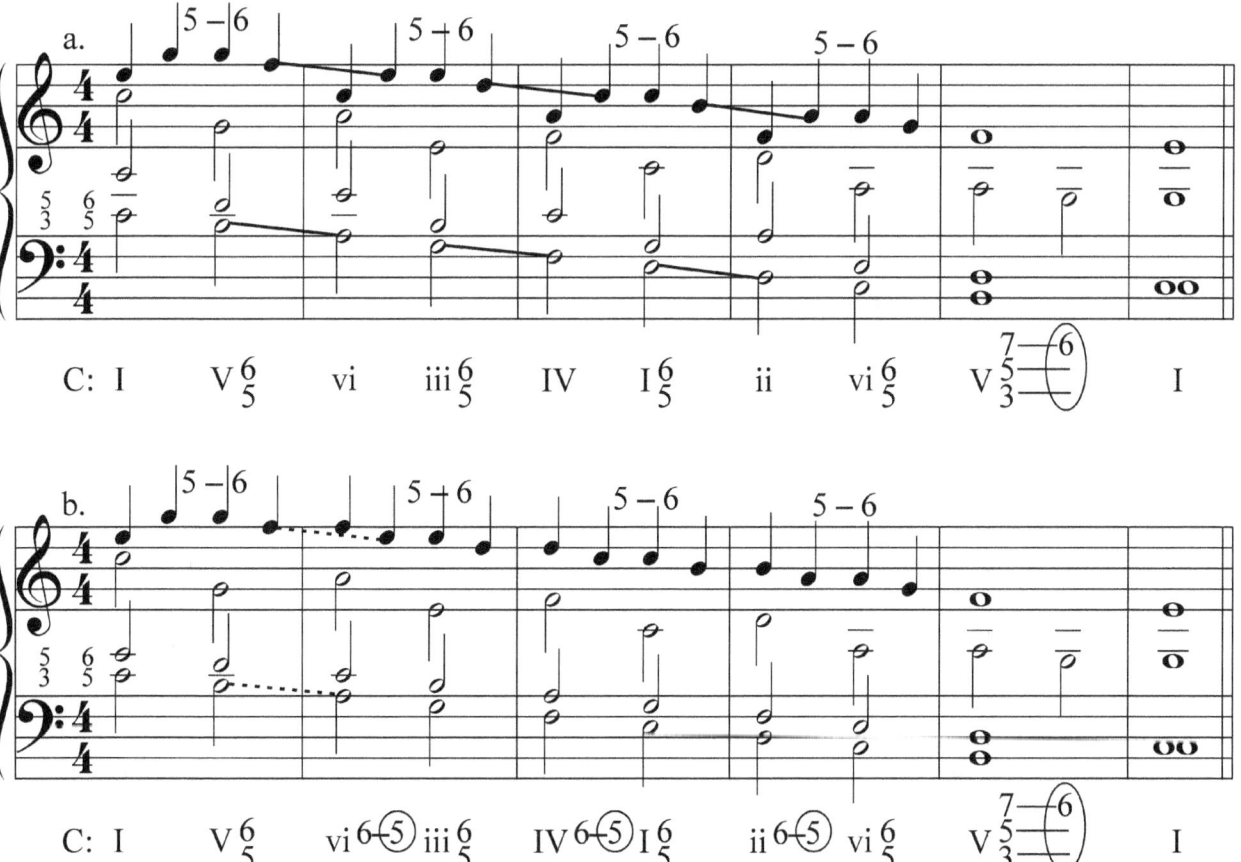

Example 7–82: OVIP 5 6 (in the key, minor, sevenths)

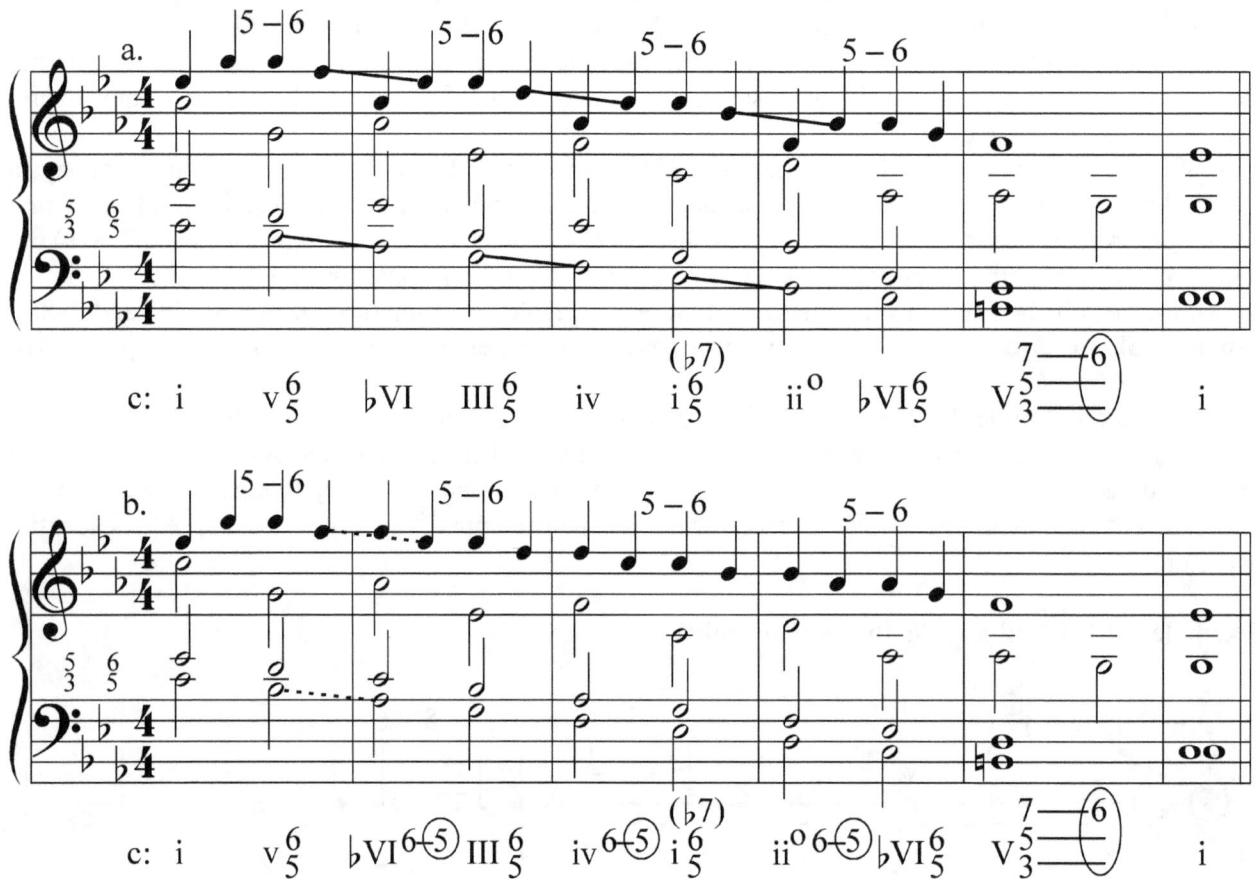

The Descending 5—6 (Out of Key)

We know that when applied dominants are used in sequences, the chromaticism may give rise to unusual intervals, such as the augmented 2nd. Examples 7–83 through 7–86 illustrate the appearance of the augmented 2nd in the descending 5—6; it shows up while maintaining the stepwise descent in the bass from the tonic to the THD/CLT. The appearance of an unacceptable interval often becomes less problematic when it occurs within the repetitive framework of a sequence. One option for avoiding the augmented 2nd uses variable ♭7 to form the chord third of the minor dominant, which leads smoothly to the root-position submediant (in example 7–88a: i – v⁶ – ♭VI – III⁶ – iv – i⁶).

The descending 5—6 often stops when the bass reaches scale degree 3 as the third of either the tonic in first inversion or an applied dominant of the subdominant (as indicated in 7–83, measure 3). In examples 7–87a and 7–88a, the sequence expands the tonic triad downwards from its root position to first inversion. In examples 7–87b and 7–88b, the sequence prolongs the way from the initial tonic to the X-chord (IV or iv). Thus, in both examples, the two basic functions of the sequence are demonstrated: the prolongation of a single chord and the prolongation of the way between chords.

Example 7–83: OVIP 10 10 (out of key)

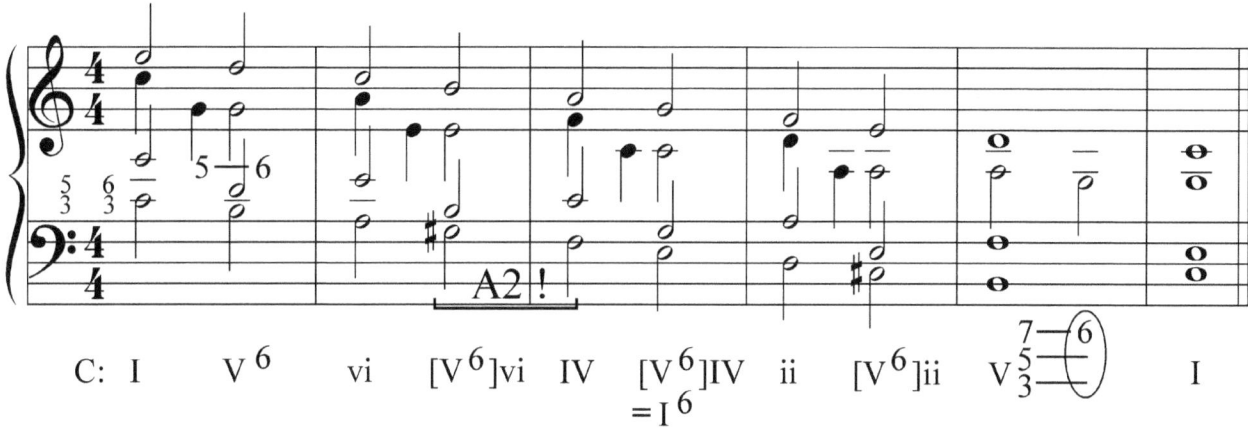

Example 7–84: OVIP 10 10 (out of key, minor)

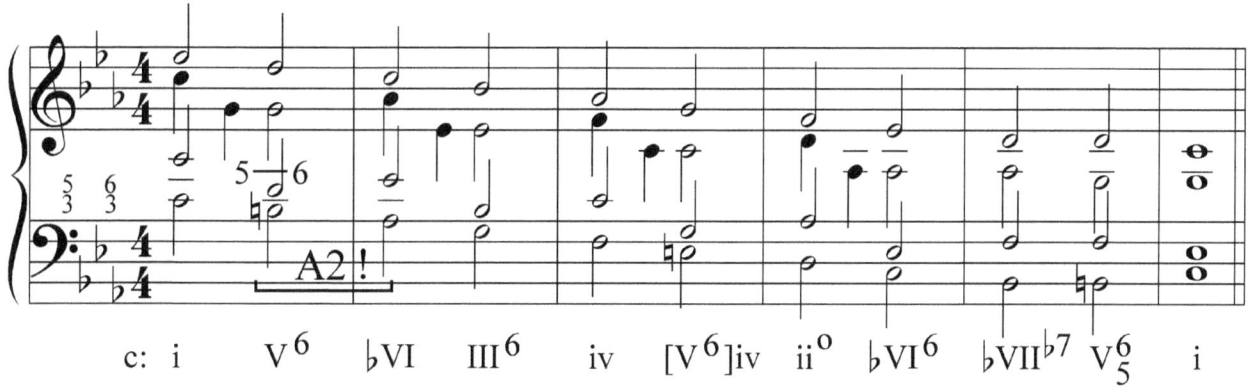

As stated earlier, when the second chord of the descending 5—6 carries a seventh and is in first inversion, parallel 5ths may occur; however, when these seventh chords are transformed into applied dominants, the 5ths become unequal and acceptable. It is even possible to find parallel diminished 5ths, used more successfully in example 7–85 than in 7–86, as the latter instance involves ii°.

Example 7–85: OVIP 10 10 (out of key, sevenths)

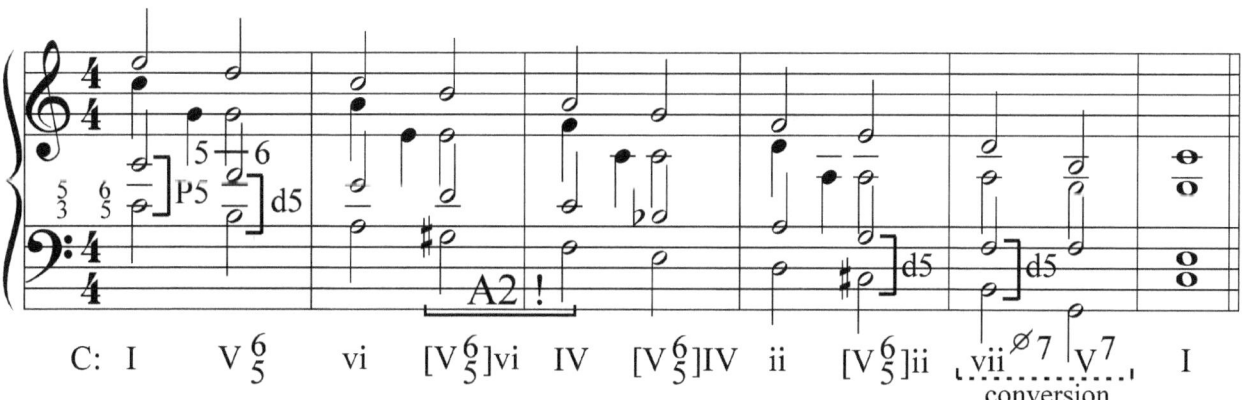

Example 7–86: OVIP 10 10 (out of key, minor, sevenths)

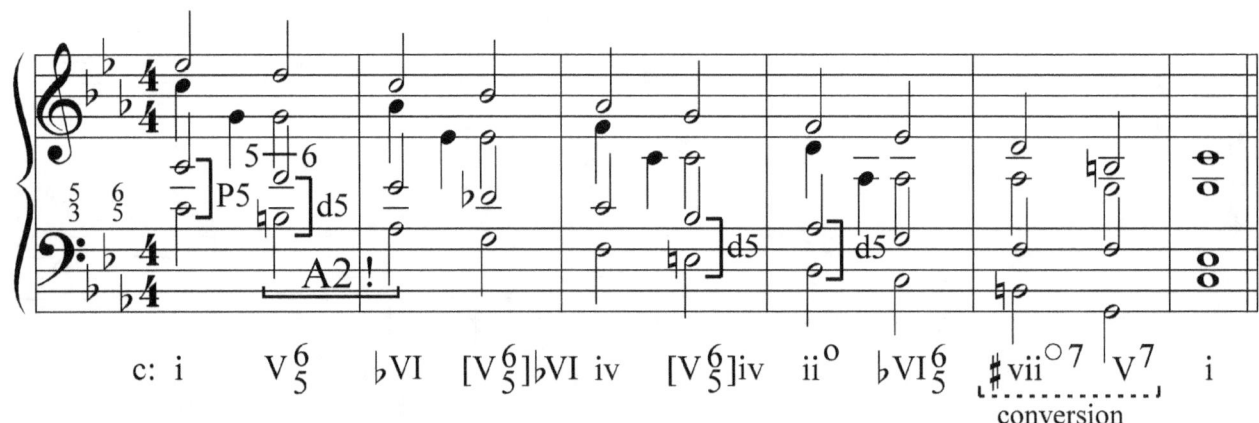

Avoiding the Problems of the Descending 5—6

Examples 7–87 and 7–88 utilize the best portion of the descending 5—6 while avoiding the first-inversion seventh for the second chord both in and out of key. To be sure, when the second chord consists of [V $^6_5$], the procession of 5ths is unequal, alternating perfect and diminished qualities. Sometimes, however, the descending 5—6 proves most successful in its simplest form. Here, we see the descending 3rds of the sequence: C – A (or A♭) – F, with B (or B♭) and G supporting the second chord.

Example 7–87: OVIP 10 10 (in the key)

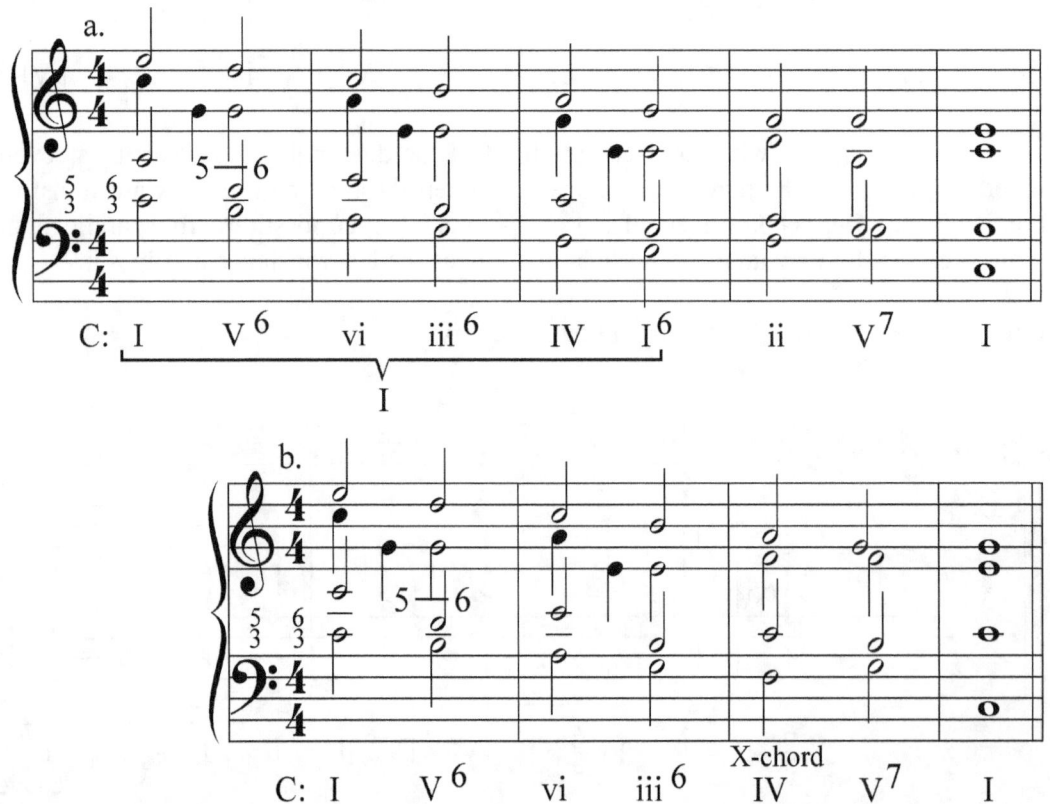

As explained earlier, examples 7–87 and 7–88 illustrate the two basic functions of the sequence: the prolongation of a single chord and the prolongation of the way from one chord to another. The a versions of the examples present the former, the b versions the latter. The a versions contain two repetitions of the two-chord pattern, the b versions one. The X-chord in the b versions is the subdominant; however, the supertonic in first inversion may also serve as the intermediary harmony (as in the a versions but with a different voicing).

From these and the other examples throughout this chapter, we see that the function of the sequence is to prolong—to support and elaborate (or expand) the structural progression, ultimately of the highest rank: the BHP, SHP, BCP, or SCP. Examples 7–87 and 7–88 constitute five-measure prolongations of a tonic chord with a supporting SHP, presumably, of lower rank.

Since there is no stepwise motion from either scale degree 3 or 5 down to 1 in the top voice, these examples do not represent progressions of the background rank. (Scale degree 1 in measure 2 of the soprano serves as a passing tone within the sequence and is not structural.) Indeed, both versions a and b start with scale degree 3 in the soprano and proceed downwards to either 3 or 5. In version a, the progression takes the soprano down an octave.

There are several potential interpretations for the progressions in examples 7–87 and 7–88; let us consider two possible scenarios. Perhaps the a versions exhibit an SHP of the middleground supporting scale degree 3 in the top voice. Were this sequence part of a larger composition, scale degree 3 could end up as a governing tone of the background. With respect to the b versions, we might well imagine that an SHP of the middleground initially supports scale degree 3 leading to scale degree 5 as the true governing tone.

Example 7–88: OVIP 10 10 (in the key, minor)

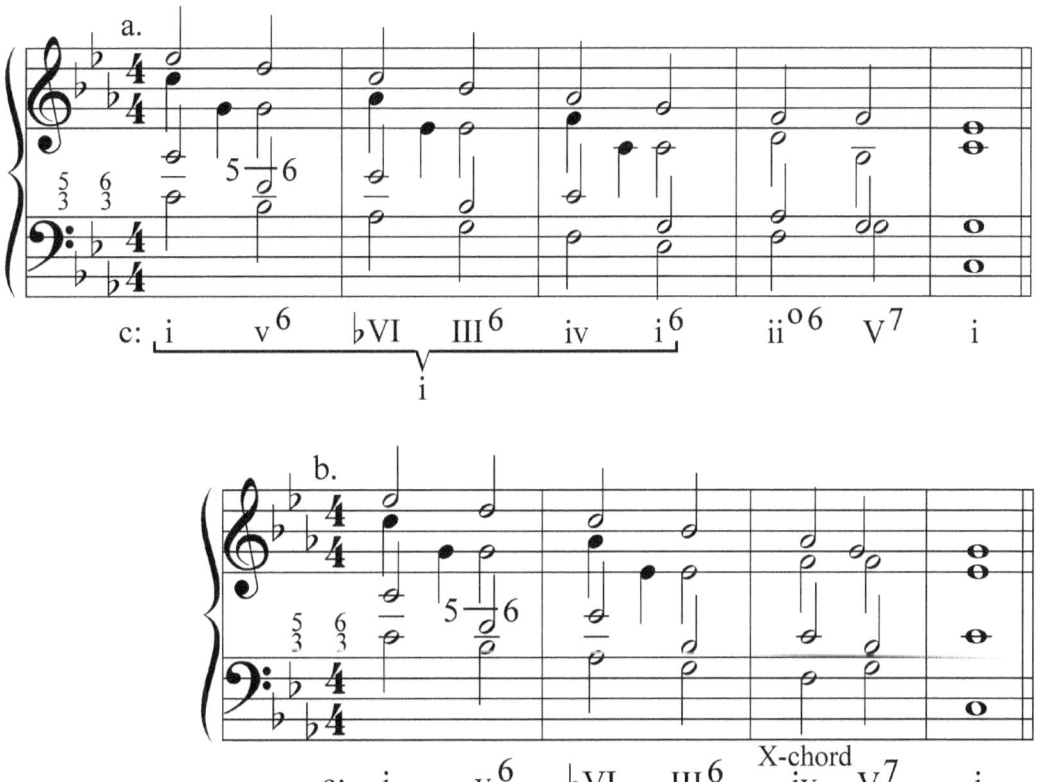

Root-Position Variants of the Descending 5—6: Falling 4th-Rising 2nd

The most common variant of the descending 5—6 sets the second chord of the pattern in root position, transforming the 6th into the octave and producing a pattern of falling 4ths and rising 2nds. In the bass of examples 7–89 and 7–90, the root replaces the third of the second chord (see the X in the bass clef of measures 1–4). The numbers between the staves represent the action of the variant: 6 is crossed out and replaced by 8. The leap of the falling 4th from the first chord to the second helps to bring out the pattern of descending 3rds in the bass: C – A (or A♭) – F – D – B (or B♭ moving to B♮).

The bass proceeds with root-position chords, alternating triads and sevenths. We know that when a seventh chord stands in a rising 2nd root relationship to another chord, parallel 5ths may ensue when the dissonance resolves. In the second chord, passing motion in the tenor takes the seventh to the fifth of the next chord, a 7—5 resolution. Adding the seventh to the second chord enhances the sense of forward momentum and improves the voice leading.

However, despite the welcome appearance of the dissonant seventh, it fails to overshadow the arrival of the root-position supertonic in measure 4 of 7–90, which can be avoided by breaking off the sequence before or with the return of the tonic (for instance, in measure 3) after no more than two repetitions of the pattern. Following the sequence with ii○6, as in 7–88 above, provides a strong X-chord for the cadential structure.

Example 7–89: OVIP 10   12 (in the key, sevenths)

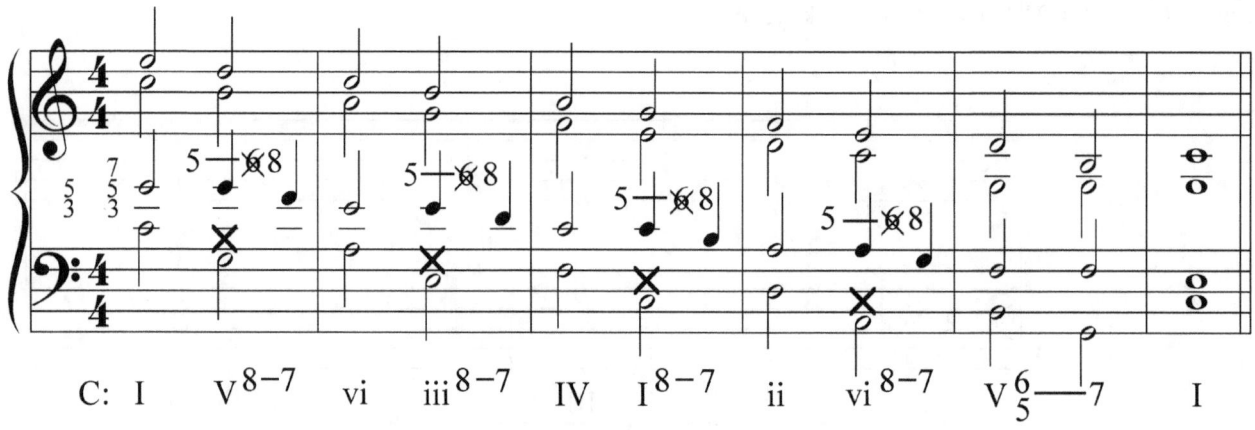

Example 7–90: OVIP 10   12 (in the key, minor, sevenths)

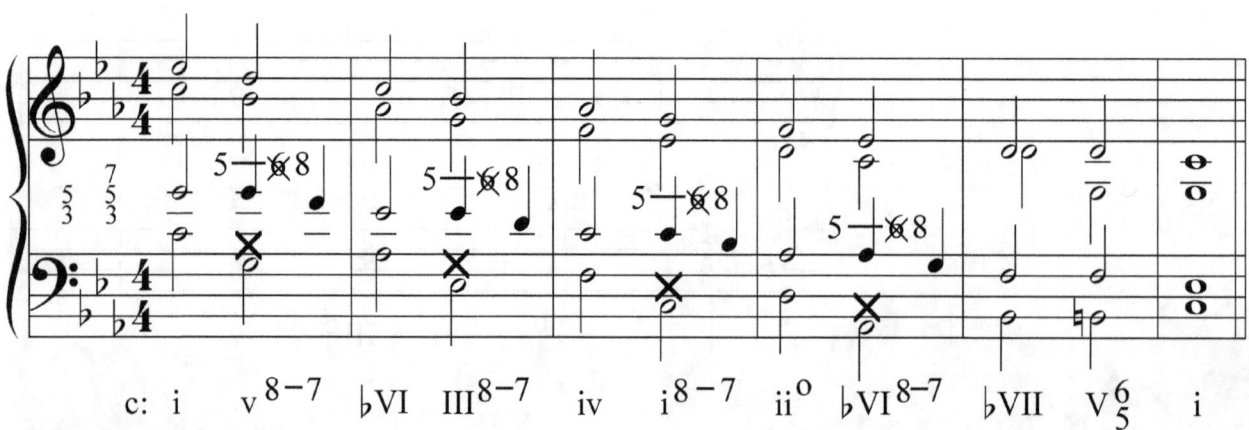

Finally, it should be noted that the root-position variant of the descending 5—6 is also found without the addition of the seventh to the second chord. Thus, an alternative reading of examples 7–89 and 7–90 proceeds with triads (omitting the seventh on beat 4).

Root-Position Variants of the Descending 5—6: Falling 4th-Rising 2nd (Out of Key)

As illustrated in the alto of examples 7–91 and 7–92 below, when the root-position variant of the descending 5—6 uses applied retroactive dominants for the second chord, a melodic augmented 2nd occurs between vi and IV in major and between V and ♭VI in minor. The out-of-key variant of the descending 5—6 in minor also contains the root-position supertonic (7–92, measure 4). Although this variant improves the voice leading of the descending 5—6 in some respects, more than two repetitions of the sequential pattern generally produces an unattractive result.

Example 7–91: OVIP 10   12 (out of key, sevenths)

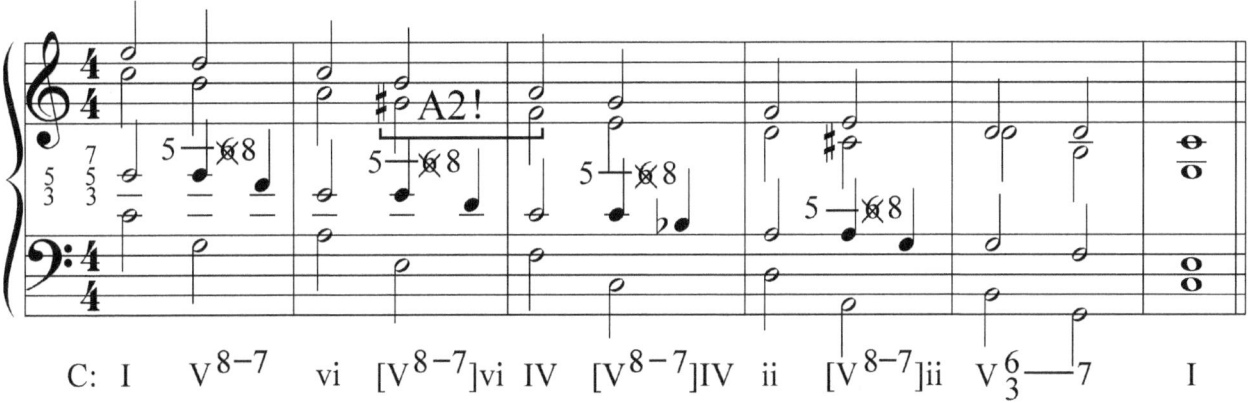

Example 7–92: OVIP 10   12 (out of key, minor, sevenths)

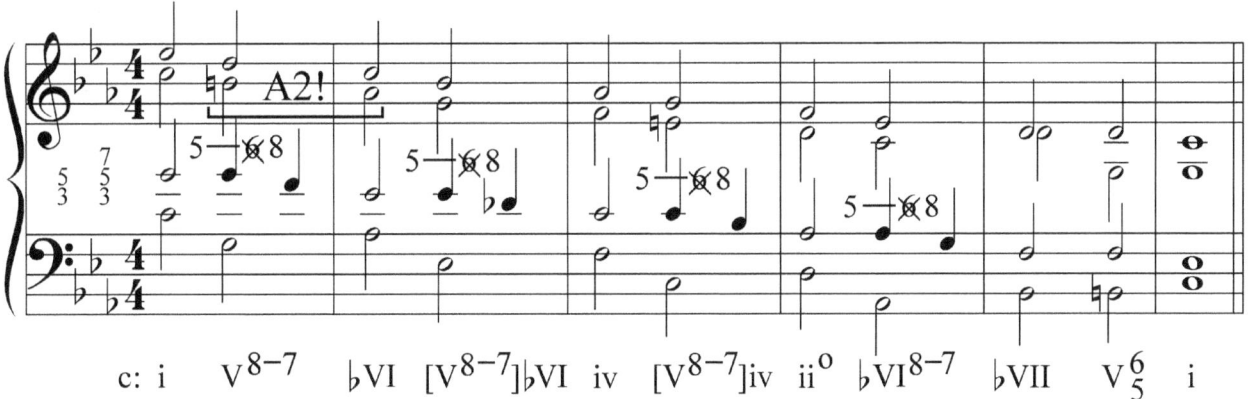

The Three-Chord Pattern (Out of Key)

While most harmonic sequences might be based upon repetitions of two-chord patterns, extending (or expanding) these patterns produces additional techniques for prolongation and ultimately, modulation.

For instance, we can use the ascending 5—6 pattern with the chromatic bass (see above, examples 7–33 through 7–44) as the basis for constructing a three-chord pattern by harmonizing the chromatic bass with two dominant sevenths in succession, the first in root position, the second in first inversion.

In examples 7–93 and 7–94, this adaptation of the ascending 5—6 with the chromatic bass yields an OVIP succession of 7ths, 6ths, and 5ths. The basic approach demonstrated is derived from the techniques displayed previously in examples 7–38 and 7–40.

Here, each diatonic scale degree takes an applied dominant seventh in root position as the first chord of the pattern. The first chord addresses a potential lower-level tonic whose appearance is withheld in order to harmonize the chromatic passing tone in the bass. The chromatic bass interrupts the resolution of the first dominant seventh and becomes instead the third of the second applied dominant, the second chord of the pattern.

And so, the root-position dominant sevenths standing on each diatonic scale degree seek to resolve to a chord standing a rising perfect 4th above or falling perfect 5th below it (tritone root relationships in major and minor remain a problem). The first dominant seventh is denied its traditional resolution and transformed into a dominant seventh in first inversion, assuming status as an applied THD/CLT of the next diatonic scale degree (in 7–93: ii, iii, IV, V, and vi).

Example 7–93: OVIP 7 6 5 (out of key, sevenths)

The three-chord pattern suffers from some of the same afflictions as the two-chord pattern. In 7–94, the tonic chord is not converted into a root-position dominant seventh because the second chord in the pattern cannot tonicize ii°, the third chord. Hence, the best option is to skip the supertonic.

In measure 7, we have the familiar problem of the tritone between scale degrees 4 and ♯7, as the applied dominant seventh on scale degree 4 cannot tonicize the leading-tone triad (the resolution is evaded by the chromatic passing tone and its chord).

A similar difficulty with the tritone is averted in measure 11; here, the root of the applied dominant is ♭6 (A♭), which is denied its impracticable resolution to scale degree 2 (D). Instead, the first dominant seventh becomes an applied dominant in first inversion to the subtonic. (The disposition of the voices in 7–94 takes the soprano slightly beyond the top of its comfortable range to A♭.)

Example 7–94: OVIP 7 6 5 (out of key, minor, sevenths)

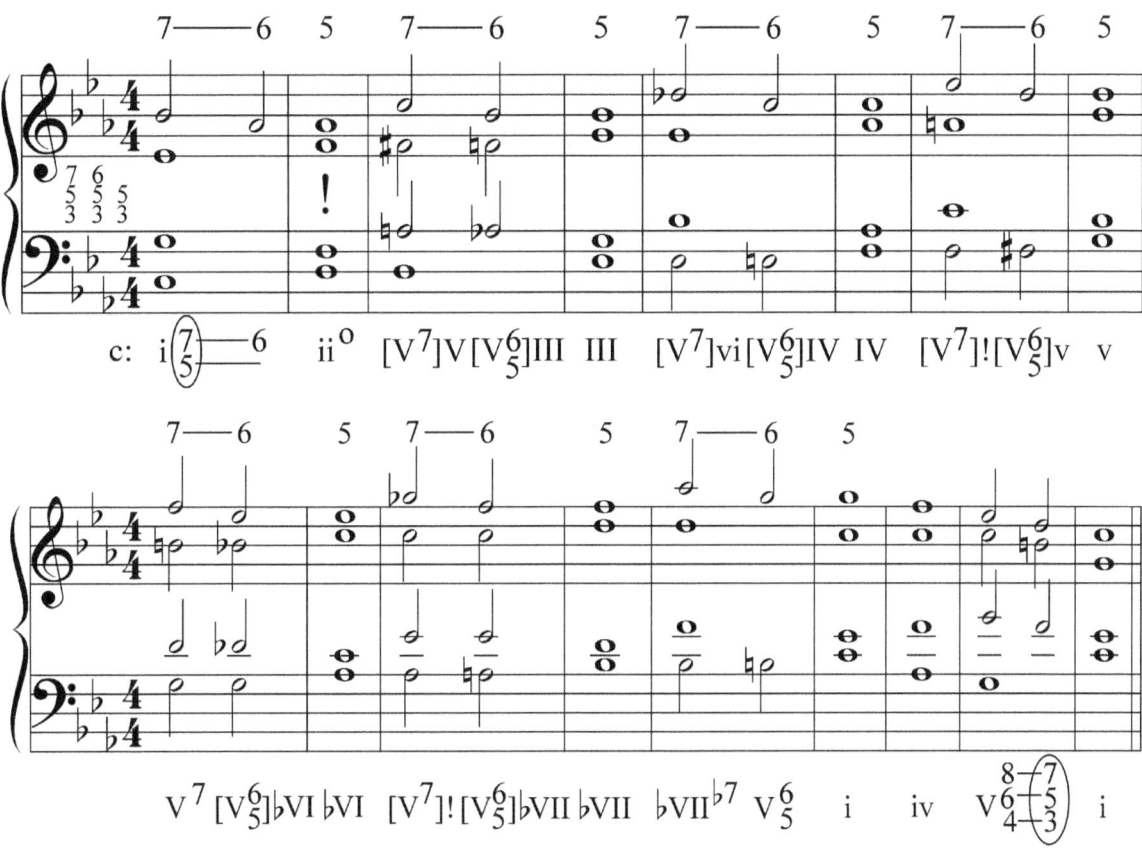

Invention Number 13 in A Minor

We close this chapter with a work by one of the foremost practitioners of the sequence, J. S. Bach. The Invention Number 13 in A Minor is a keyboard composition with a contrapuntal texture in two parts, one for each hand. In addition to the usual chord symbols, examples 7–95 through 7–100 identify some of the more significant harmonic and contrapuntal operations. Examples 7–101 through 7–103 offer additional analysis of the voice leading in the tradition of Schenker and Salzer.

In the music of Bach, we have the shoring up of the major-minor tonal system with a harmonic structure generated from the bass. On the surface, the texture of Bach's Invention appears quite linear, but the underlying conception is harmonic. The linear elements present chordal skips, nonharmonic tones, and suspensions. Imitation between the hands (the parts) occurs within the framework of sequential activity.

In measure 1 of example 7–95, Bach presents the initial idea, theme 1, in sixteenth notes, which is subsequently repeated in measure 2. Theme 1 is imitated in the small register and passed between the hands. In measure 3, a sequence accompanies a second idea, theme 2, which also proceeds in imitation.

As we shall see later in example 7–96, there is one particularly notable technique that Bach often uses in imitative textures, both sequential and non-sequential. For now, suffice it to say that this compositional strategy enables Bach to obtain a 100 per cent return on his musical investment of ideas.

Essential and Nonessential Melodic Tones

Underlying most foreground melodies are fundamental segments of pitches, or shapes—tones that govern the line but that are not necessarily elements of the structural melodic progression of the highest rank, the BMP (though such tones might also form components of or support the BMP). The structural melody of theme 1 is circled in 7–95: A – B – C – G♯ – A – B – C.

When theme 1 is imitated in the lower voice amidst the flurry of sixteenth notes, recognizing what is fundamental to the top line helps us evaluate the bass line and distinguish between its essential and nonessential elements. (The point of imitation for each initial statement of the first idea is marked with double lines in the examples for measures 1–18.)

Two voice exchanges prolong the initial tonic (see the dotted lines in measures 1–2). Within these voice exchanges, the leading tone, G♯, serves as a passing element between the tonic's root position and first inversion. (Notice that in minor, the distance from scale degree 3 down to ♯7 is a diminished 4th.) Moreover, the inclusion of G♯ (measure 1, beat 4) helps to define the contour of the melody; G♯ substitutes for B, which would otherwise proceed conjunctly from C down to A. B retains its significance as a bass tone supporting the substitute G♯. (The line moves C – G♯ – A instead of C – B – A. This motion is demonstrated below in example 7–96, measures 1–2.)

Modulation to III

A descending 5th sequence in measures 3–5 takes theme 2 to the relative major, C major. The sequence first alternates $^6_3$ and $^5_3$ chords and then continues in root position for both chords, reducing the harmonic rhythm from half notes to quarters.

The sequence ends with ♭VII addressing III in measure 5 (beats 3–4). An SHP in C major establishes the lower-level tonic: [I – IV – V – I]III. (Note: A curved arrow sign either below or in the bass clef is an indication of harmonic or contrapuntal prolongation of the chord the arrow addresses. Usually, the prolonging chord is a CLT chord, a modal dominant, or an applied dominant, the context determining which function the arrow signifies.)

J. S. Bach is well-known for using one melodic line to suggest, or imply, two melodic lines, a technique known as *polyphonic melody*. Whenever there is extensive chord unfolding (linear motion between chord tones), as in the Invention in A Minor, the melody may move from one register to another in a way that suggests a secondary line.

In measures 5–6, Bach's polyphonic melody produces three *implied suspensions*: 9—8, 7—6, and 4—3 (the dissonant portion of each suspension is given in parentheses). These implied dissonances provide momentum to the progression just as the harmonic rhythm is reduced from half notes to quarters. Bach gives us an exciting harmonic transition to III, the relative major.

Example 7–95: J.S. Bach, Invention Number 13 in A Minor, measures 1–6

Exchanging the Parts: Invertible Counterpoint

From the beginning of Bach's Invention in A Minor, he displays one of his characteristic compositional strategies, referred to variously as invertible counterpoint, double counterpoint, or interchangeable counterpoint, a technique for getting the most out of his ideas in contrapuntal works (see below, example 7–96).

When composers use invertible counterpoint, there is an exchange of parts, with each part serving in the role previously occupied by the other. Upon inversion, the bass line must also work as a good upper melody while the upper voice must be capable of serving as a convincing bass line. Invertible counterpoint may be non-sequential (as in measures 1–2) or sequential (as in measures 3–4); it may also involve more than two parts.

The most common type of invertible counterpoint occurs at the interval of the octave (or the 15th) and moves one or both voices by at least one octave. Invertible counterpoint at the octave is the most successful type because when the lines are exchanged, the inverted intervals retain their quantitative and qualitative identities, following the natural principles of interval inversion. The only problem is with the 5th, since upon inversion it becomes a dissonant 4th. Thus, in the original version, the 5th must be treated as a dissonance because when the parts invert at the octave, a dissonance is formed.

Invertible counterpoints at the 10th and 12th are less common. Invertible counterpoint at the 10th is particularly rare because parallel 3rds become parallel octaves and parallel 6ths become parallel 5ths. At the 12th, the 6th becomes the 7th and therefore must be treated as a dissonance in its original position.

The following table summarizes the intervals for invertible counterpoint at the octave, 12th, and 10th; the squared numbers identify problematic inversions for each type: 5ths at the octave, 6ths at the 12th, 3rds and 6ths at the 10th.

invertible counterpoint at the octave (most used)

original   1 2 3 4 |5| 6 7 8
inversion   8 7 6 5 |4| 3 2 1

invertible counterpoint at the 12th

original   1 2 3 4 5 |6| 7 8 9 10 11 12
inversion   12 11 10 9 8 |7| 6 5 4 3 2 1

invertible counterpoint at the 10th (least used)

original   1 2 |3| 4 5 |6| 7 8 9 10
inversion   10 9 |8| 7 6 |5| 4 3 2 1

Example 7–96a isolates some of the essential intervals from themes 1 and 2 in order to determine if the two parts are inverted at the octave. It should be noted that with invertible counterpoint, when voices exchange places, adjustments in the intervals of the original idea may occur in order to produce a certain chord position, to form a better line, or to adhere to the requirements of the key and mode.

The combination of intervals identified in measures 1–4 of examples 7–96a and 96b indicates invertible counterpoint at the octave. In measure 1, theme 1 is imitated one octave below in the small register, an action described as imitation at the octave. On beats 3 and 4 of the first measure, the melody presents a 10th (A/C) and a 6th (B/G♯). On beats 1 and 2 of the second measure, the 10th becomes a 6th (C/A) and the 6th becomes a 10th (G♯/B). Here, the invertible counterpoint at the octave is easily recognizable because the theme is imitated at the octave and is not transposed through sequential activity.

However, in measure 3, theme 2 imitates at the 12th below and is sequenced in measure 4. Still, we can determine if the theme is inverted by focusing on the important intervals. Notice, for example, that the D in the bass on beat 3 (7–96b) is an adjusted tone (the root of iv) and should not be used to confirm the distance of the inversion. The intervals occurring above F, D, and A in the bass of theme 2 form a 10th, 15th, and 6th; on beats 1 and 2 of measure 4, they become a 6th, octave, and 3rd. Therefore, we have another instance of invertible counterpoint at the octave.

Example 7–96: invertible counterpoint at the octave in Invention Number 13 in A Minor, measures 1–4

The Prolongation of the Mediant

After the SHP in C major (I – IV – V – I) establishes III (the relative major) in measures 5–6, theme 1 passes between the hands as the harmony alternates between tonic and dominant chords (example 7–97). In the ninth measure, a descending 5th sequence of seventh chords supports an exchange of parts involving theme 2, with the harmonies changing at the level of the half note.

The sequence supports a motion in 10ths in the bass and soprano; the 10ths constitute the resolutions of dissonant 7ths heard in the top voice (measures 9–13). In measures 11–13, the pace of the sequence accelerates to the level of the quarter note. As in measures 5–7, the increase in the harmonic rhythm is accompanied by a polyphonic melody that fragments the first portion of theme 2 (though all of the sixteenth-note figures in themes 1 and 2 exhibit similar intervallic characteristics).

Ultimately, the sequence becomes a prolongation of the way from the initial expression of the lower-level C-major tonic (measures 5–8) to the mediant X-chord of a secondary contrapuntal progression (SCP) spanning measures 5–16, that is: [I – descending 5th sequence – iii – V$^6_5$ – I]III.

Example 7–103 below shows the position of this SCP within the larger framework of a minor. Notice that the SCP in C major duplicates an SCP of a higher middleground rank in the main-level key, extending from measures 1–23: i – III – V$^6_5$ – i.

Example 7–97: J.S. Bach, Invention Number 13 in A Minor, measures 7–12

In measure 13, the descending 5th sequence ends as the harmony moves towards a B-major triad, an applied dominant of e minor, iii of C major. Throughout this extended sequence of sevenths *and beyond*, Bach maintains a consistent motion in 10ths in the bass and soprano. Ultimately, the 10ths connect all of the surface events to the prolongation of the structural tonic through its first twenty-three measures.

As observed earlier, this prolongation of the initial structural tonic is effected by an SCP consisting of i – III – V$^6_5$ – i (in a minor). III is prolonged by its own SCP, I – iii – V$^6_5$ – I (in C major). This contrapuntal progression in III consumes nearly half of the entire composition (measures 5–16).

In measure 14, just after the arrival of C-major's iii chord, a melodic figure drawn from theme 2 is treated sequentially. The 10ths stop with return of both the governing tonic and theme 1 in measure 18. Following the iii chord (e minor), an applied CLT chord addresses ii (d minor). This contrapuntal motion is sequenced both in the final articulation of C major (measure 16) and in the return of a minor (measure 18).

Example 7–98: J.S. Bach, Invention Number 13 in A Minor, measures 13–18

And so, the sequence in measures 14–18 takes the thematic idea down by step from scale degrees 5 to 1 in the bass, E – D – C – B – A. Above the descending bass, a broad motion in parallel 10ths bridges the span between the iii chord of C major and the appearance of theme 1 in a minor (see below, example 7–101, measures 14–18).

The Return of A Minor

Following the return of the main-level tonic, theme 1 leads to a continuation of the melodic figure heard in the previous sequence; this continuation extends the basic melodic shape heard initially in measures 1–2: A – B – C – G♯ – A – B – C (see the circled notes in measures 19–23 of examples 7–99 and 7–100).

In measures 18–23, voice exchanges and passing dominants prolong the tonic chord. CLT chords, both applied and main-level, emphasize dominant and tonic chords. With the tonic reestablished, a final sequence leads to the completion of the melodic and harmonic structure.

Example 7–99: J.S. Bach, Invention Number 13 in A Minor, measures 19–21

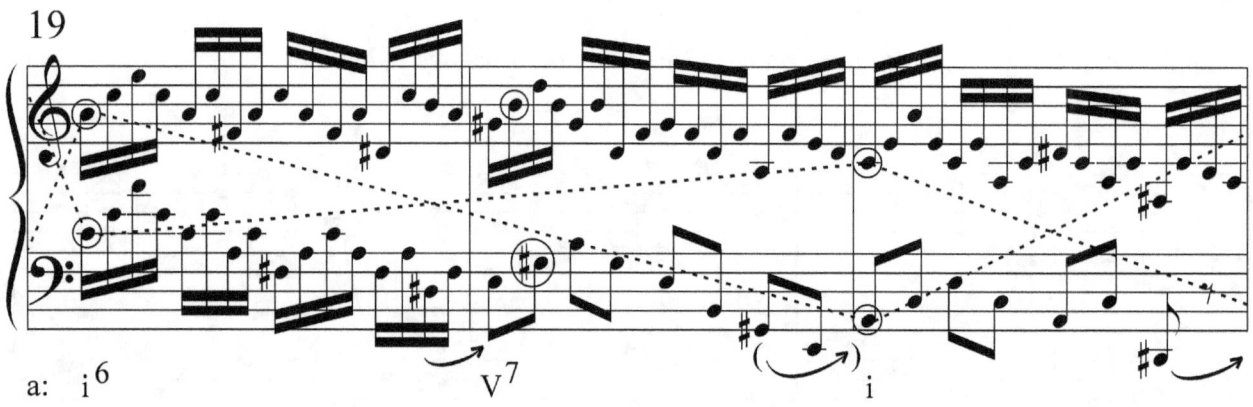

In measure 23, Bach uses a polyphonic melody in the left hand to suggest an ascending 5—6 sequence. (In example 7–100, implied 5ths are indicated in parentheses.) Parallel 10ths between the bass and soprano occur on each downbeat of measures 23–24. The rising line and chord change on every quarter increases the level of excitement in the closing measures.

In this version of the ascending 5—6, the raised variables are used to provide linear emphasis to the main-level key before the completion of the melodic and harmonic structure in measures 24–25. Notice that in the top voice (measure 23), the descending form of minor provides the pitches that move away from and towards scale degree 5. On the last sixteenth of each beat, the top line moves through E – F – G before returning to E (a passing tone leading downwards to D, scale degree 4.) Thus, we have both the ascending and descending forms of minor operating simultaneously in accordance with their respective voice-leading requirements.

Variable ♯7, G♯, becomes an important tone in measure 24 as the root of the fully diminished seventh chord of the leading tone, arpeggiated downwards in the bass (G♯ – F – D – B – G♯). Employing both linear and harmonic resources, the ascending 5—6 in measure 23 prepares the tonality for the structural progression of the highest order, the background: i – ii○6 – CS – V – i (see below, examples 7–100, measures 24–25, and 7–103).

The sequence moves the tonic chord from root position to first inversion, taking the bass upwards to scale degree 4, D, a tone that becomes the chord third of the subsequent X-chord, ii○6. Here, on the second half of beat 4 (measure 23), scale degree 4 makes its first appearance as the next governing melodic tone of the background. The ii○6 that ultimately supports the D does not assume its full disposition until the fourth beat of the following measure.

Initially, the D in the top voice is supported by B♭ in the left hand, resulting in an apparent B♭-major triad. The B♭ is a chromatic upper neighbor to A, which retains its significance as a prolonged tone until the arrival of the X-chord in measure 24. The D is also the chord fifth of the leading-tone seventh, arpeggiated in the bass and prolonged by voice exchange on beats 1 and 2.

In measure 24, both voices shift registers by an octave: the soprano rising from b prime to b double prime and the bass unfolding from small g♯ to great G♯. The 10th between G♯ and B leads to A, the root of the tonic chord, functioning on the second half of beat 3 as a harmonic embellishing chord (HEMB) prolonging ii○6. A voice exchange prolongs the X-chord and supports the governing scale degree 4 in the soprano.

In measure 25, Bach exploits the common pitch content between ii○6 and ♯vii○7 : the chord tones of the former correspond to the third, fifth, and seventh of the latter; hence, the X-chord emerges from a complex of tones associated with the dominant family of chords.

With the subsequent appearance of the contrapuntal-structural chord (CS), the melodic structure moves to C, scale degree 3. The D♯ in the bass passes from the D bass of ii○6 upwards to E, the root of the THD, V^{4-3}. As explained earlier in Chapter 6, the contrapuntal-structural chord functions as a chord of contrapuntal prolongation while also supporting a governing melodic tone. So constituted, the sonority on D♯ (which is heard with C and A) functions as an applied CLT chord addressing V^{4-3} while supporting the structural melody (C). The CS chord thereby serves as a type of X-chord. (The chord also addresses the dominant in measures 19 and 21, beat 4.)

Example 7–100: J.S. Bach, Invention Number 13 in A Minor, measures 22–25

218   Chapter 7   The Sequence

The Middleground

Examples 7–101 and 7–102 present a middleground reading of Invention Number 13, measures 1–25. Example 7–103 shows a later middleground, closer to the background, the former indicated with filled-in note heads (both with and without stems), the latter with half notes. As suggested earlier, the totality of structure is an SCP consisting of two X-chord types that support scale degrees 4 and 3 respectively of a BMP descending from scale degree 5: i – ii°^{6} – CS – V – i (see below, 7–103).

Example 7–101: J.S. Bach, Invention Number 13 in A Minor, middleground, measures 1–23

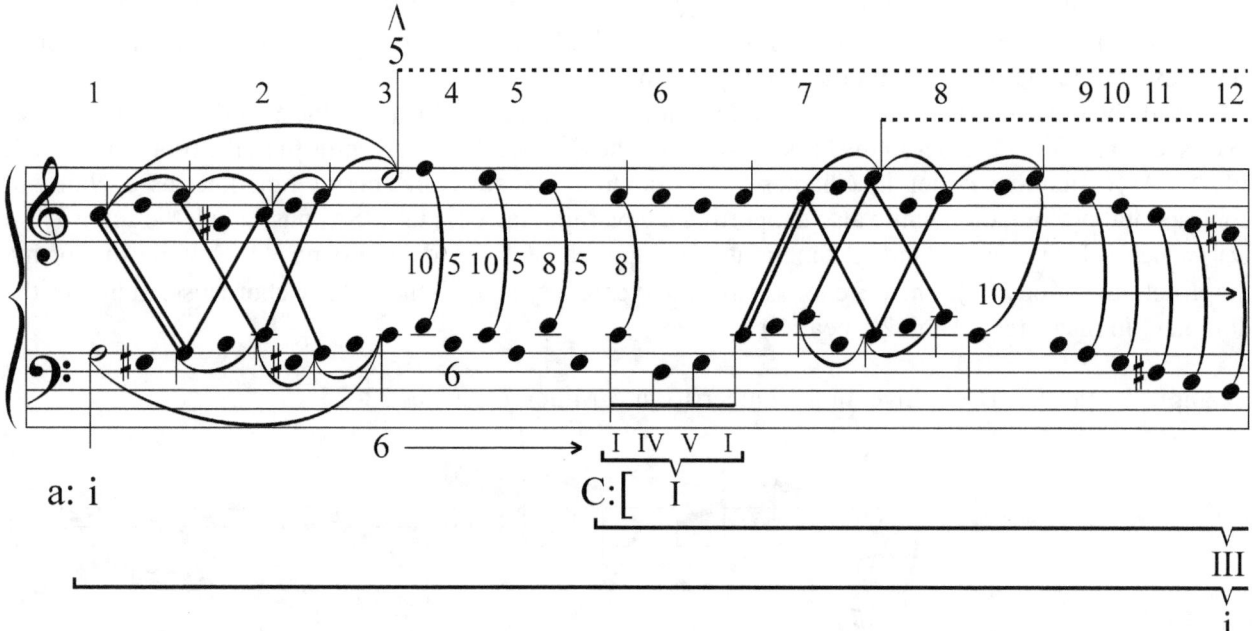

There is an initial ascent in the top voice from the tonic to the governing scale degree 5 in measure 3 (7–101). The governing 5 is retained throughout most of the composition by motion into and out of inner voices (filled-in note heads), voice exchange, and sequential activity. The sequences provide the connections between important events of the middleground and background.

The descending 5th sequence of measures 3–5 prolongs the way to the relative major, C major, which in turn is prolonged by its own descending 5th sequence (measures 9–13). The sequential motion beginning in measure 14 proceeds through the completion of the SCP in C major and ends with the return of the tonic in measure 18.

After the return of theme 1 in a minor, the material from the previous sequence (measures 14–17) continues in measures 19–21 with alternating tonic and dominant chords (each addressed by CLT chords). In measure 23, the ascending 5—6 projects a linear melodic progression (LMP) spanning a major 3rd upwards from scale degrees 3 to 5 (a case could be made for recognizing the start of the LMP on scale degree 1 in measure 22, beat 3). (To review the properties of the LMP, see above, pp. 156–158.)

With the structural return of scale degree 5 in measure 23, the governing top voice moves to the first appearance of scale degree 4 (7–102); the bass leads to D, the third of the X-chord, ii° 6. After all of the elements of the X-chord are heard on beat 4 of measure 24, the melodic and harmonic structure completes itself in measure 25.

Example 7–101: measures 12–23 (continued)

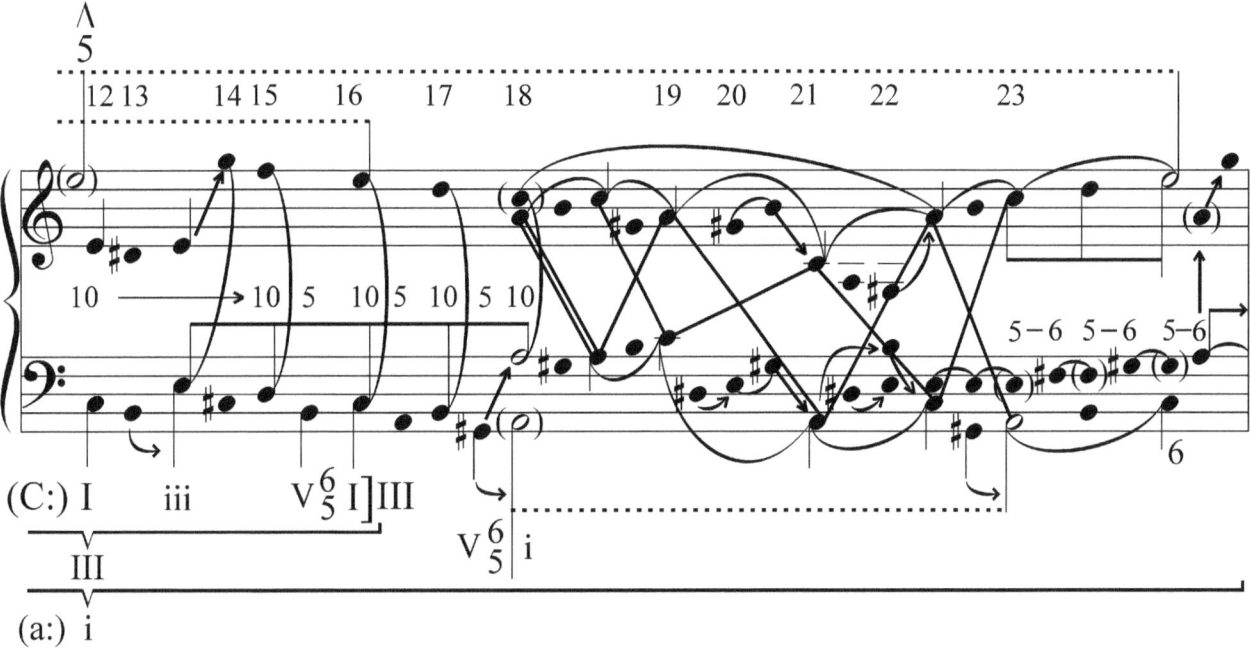

Example 7–102: J.S. Bach, Invention Number 13 in A Minor, middleground, measures 23–25

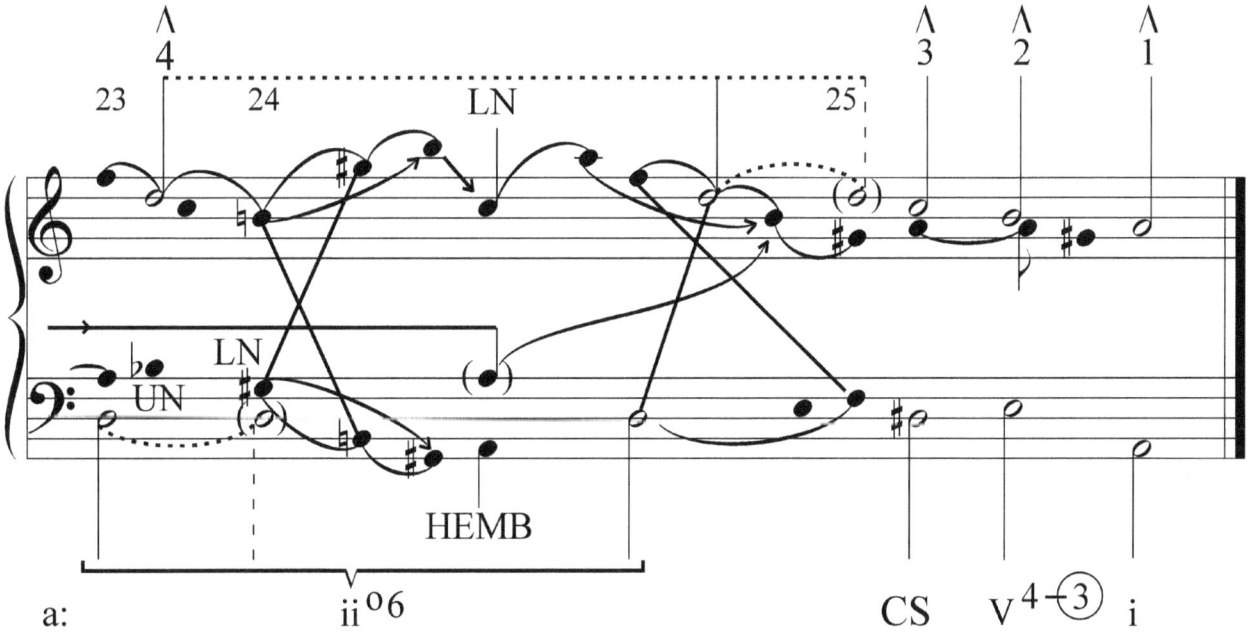

Example 7–103: J.S. Bach, Invention Number 13 in A Minor, later middleground, measures 1–25

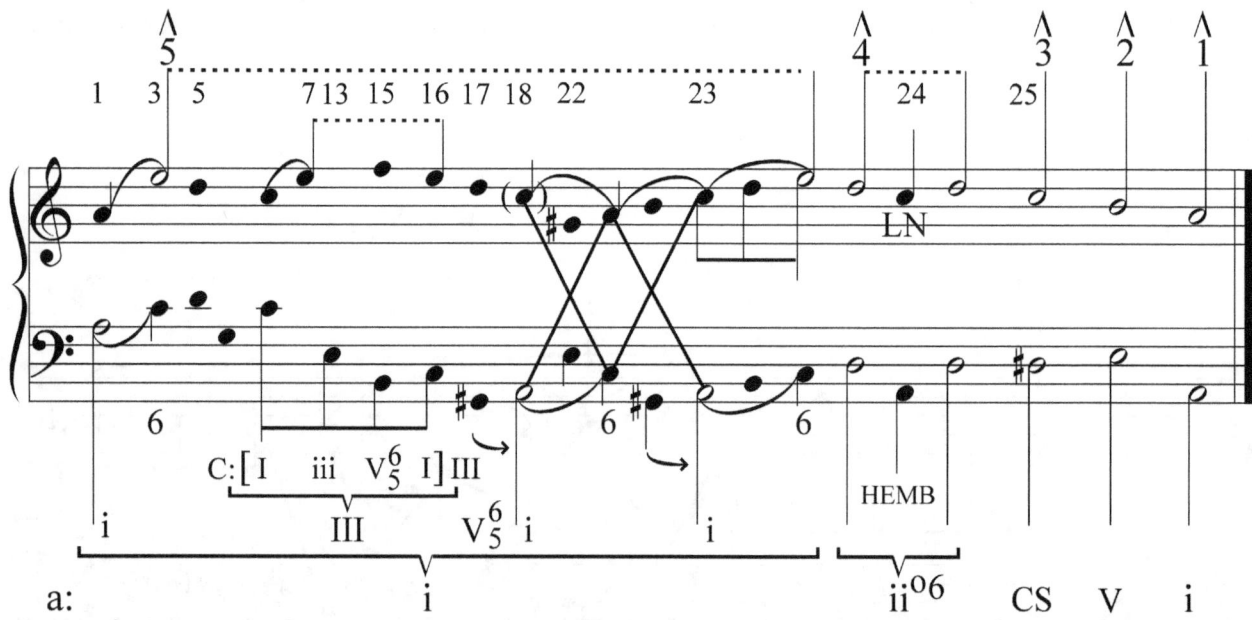

Leaving Home

In this chapter, we have seen how connections are made between chords in some of the most common sequential operations in tonal music, both harmonic and contrapuntal. Each sequence has its own characteristic features, advantages, and limitations.

Sequences are useful devices for leaving the main-level key, the home key. From the very beginning of the common practice period, the sequence was employed to facilitate excursions into lower-level keys. One of the most immediate considerations for us in moving away from the main-level key is effecting the arrival of the new key in a way that is convincing within the context of the harmonic framework. With that consideration, the next chapter explores the means by which harmonic relationships between keys are established and how successful modulation from one key to another is achieved.

Chapter 8   Modulation

Changing the key in tonal music is traditionally referred to as modulation. Occurring as long or short segments of music within the harmonic framework, each modulation constitutes an instance of middleground prolongation. A change of key that does not continue beyond its initial gesture is usually called a transient modulation, a brief excursion away from the main-level key.

One issue often raised involves those situations in which the key has apparently changed without a cadence effecting or confirming that change. In such cases, it could be argued whether a modulation has truly taken place, despite what may have been a flirtation with another key.

Certainly, we can agree that a modulation has occurred if there is a strong authentic cadence in the new key. Therefore, anytime we have a cadence in a lower-level key, a modulation has been effected, regardless of whether the musical context in which the cadence appears constitutes a long or short period of time.

Moreover, irrespective of the terminology used to describe changing the key, when there is a motion away from the main-level key, either with or without a harmonic authentic cadence in the new key, the action prolongs a chord—*a modulation is a prolongation of something*.

Some discussions of modulation make no distinction between main-level and lower-level keys. The process is simply viewed as a string (or series) of key changes: a change from the old key to the new key, with each new key in turn awaiting the next key change. No attempt is made to discover how the operation prolongs the progression of the highest structural rank (the BHP, SHP, BCP, or SCP). Modulation involves motion into a chord other than the tonic, motion into a lower-level key. From the standpoint of the middleground, there is no modulation, just chord prolongation.

And so, starting from the premise that modulation is chord prolongation, we explore this process by reviewing some traditional concepts as well as finding applications for the taxonomy of chromaticism put forward throughout this text. Our primary focus is on two fundamental factors associated with changing keys:
(1)   the basic techniques of modulation, that is, the types of modulation, and,
(2)   the relationship between the old key and the new key, identified as the distance of modulation.

Techniques of Modulation: Pivot, Sequential, and Abrupt Modulation

In Chapters 3, 4, and 5, we considered the utility of the pivot chord for moving from one key to another. The strength of the pivot chord lies in its potential for harmonic reinterpretation. Also called common-chord modulation, pivot-chord modulation occurs when a harmony may be used convincingly in both the old key and the new key. However, since the tonal context for the chord changes, the function of that chord also changes. As a common component of both keys, the pivot chord provides a harmonic bridge between the old key and the new key. The pivot chord prepares the new key through a prior relationship with the old key.

Another technique for changing keys uses a single common tone to establish a connection between two keys, an operation known as common-tone or pivot-tone modulation. A pivot-tone modulation is usually accomplished by selecting a chord tone from the old key's tonic triad for placement within the new key, where the pitch assumes a different identity and possibly *a different spelling*. What we have is a transformation of one scale degree from the old key into another scale degree in the new key.

The pivot-tone modulation involves two keys a 3rd apart (up or down), a mediant modulation using a common tone. Frequently, when this type of modulation is employed, the tonic of the old key and the tonic of the new key project major triads. As shown in example 8–1 below, when pairing two mediant-related triads that contain properties of primary and/or secondary borrowing, one of the chord tones of the old tonic takes a chromatic inflection in the new tonic (see the boxed pitches: G to G♯, C to C♯, and E to E♭).

Typically, the pivot-tone modulation produces a motion away from the main-level tonic to either its mediant or submediant chord. One of the chord tones of the old tonic triad seeks a new tonic chord (the mediant or submediant of the old key) in which to embed itself. Within that chord, which stands a 3rd above or below the old tonic, the common tone assumes its new identity as the root, third, or fifth of the new tonic. As suggested above, these mediant and submediant keys of a lower level may also contain elements of primary and/or secondary borrowing.

Example 8–1 displays a few possible chord pairs representing mediant-related keys. In 8–1a, the third of the tonic becomes the root of the secondarily-borrowed mediant. In 8–1b, the third of the tonic triad is reinterpreted as the fifth of the submediant. Example 8–1c demonstrates both primary and secondary borrowing, with the fifth of the tonic becoming the third of the mediant. Example 8–1d shows the root of the tonic assuming the third of the borrowed submediant.

Example 8–1: pairs of mediant-related major triads of modulation linked by a common tone

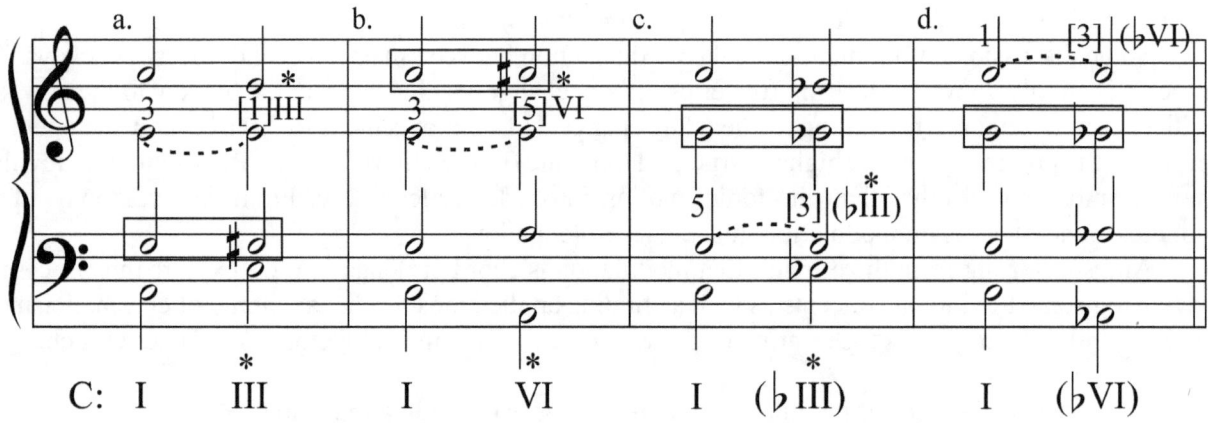

The preferred usage for the common tone is to feature it prominently in the musical texture in order to provide a convincing and audible link; for without a clear relationship between the old key and the new key, the shift in tonality could sound rather abrupt, an acceptable result if intended. Thus, when the motion between keys is abrupt, the shift often occurs at a point where one musical thought ends and the next one begins. The sudden change in tonality articulates the succeeding gesture.

The Brahms Intermezzo in A Major, discussed later in this chapter, demonstrates the operation of the pivot tone. A large ternary with an A B A¹ design, its middle section is in f♯, the relative minor. C♯, the chord third of the main-level tonic, becomes the fifth of the submediant.

The third type of modulation is sequential. In Chapter 7, the sequence was shown to be an effective way to move from one key to another. Unlike the pivot function, which effects a modulation within a relatively short period of time, a sequential modulation is a more gradual process. While pivot modulation prepares the new key through a prior relationship with the old key, the preparation for a sequential modulation is time. Repeated at different pitch levels over time, the intervallic patterns of the modulating sequence shift all of the voices of the texture upwards or downwards, as the operation moves towards its goal.

In the fourth type of modulation, the abrupt modulation (also referred to variously as jumped, skipped, or sudden), there is no preparation for the new key; there is no time. The shift is more immediate and pronounced. The whole purpose of the pivot action is to change the key smoothly. Removing the pivot (and any other function associated with the pivot, such as an applied dominant of the new key) can produce an abrupt modulation.

The Distance of Modulation

There are a number of ways to identify the distance of modulation with respect to the old key and the new key. This chapter examines two. The first type of distance measures the interval between the respective tonics of the old and new keys. The second distance is between the keys themselves, measured according to the difference between their respective key signatures, that is, their relative position within the circle of 5ths. An accurate assessment of both distances of modulation often requires an enharmonic reinterpretation of one of the keys.

As we address the question of distance, remember that regardless of the descriptive terminology employed for assessing the relationship between two keys, a shift to a parallel mode does not constitute a modulation because the action preserves the original tonic note. We do not measure a parallel mode for distance.

The Root Relationship Between Tonics: Melodic, Mediant, Tonal, and Tritone Modulations

The only true intervallic relationships between the tonics of the old and new keys consist of major and minor 2nds, major and minor 3rds, perfect 4ths and 5ths, and tritones. All other intervals are enharmonic equivalents of these and should be respelled to identify the actual distance of the modulation. We will describe the root relationship between old and new tonics in the following terms:

(1) A melodic modulation spans a major or minor 2nd between tonics. For example,
  (a) a modulation from c minor to D♭ major is a melodic modulation;
  (b) a modulation from c♯ minor to b minor is a melodic modulation.
(2) A mediant modulation spans a major or minor 3rd between tonics. For example,
  (a) a modulation from C major to E♭ major is a mediant modulation;
  (b) a modulation from c minor to A♭ major is a mediant modulation; however, notice that
  (c) a modulation from F major to g♯ minor is also a mediant modulation because the G♯ should be respelled as A♭ to properly assess the distance as a minor 3rd.
(3) A tonal modulation spans a perfect 4th or 5th between tonics. For example,
  (a) a modulation from C major to g minor is a tonal modulation;
  (b) a modulation from c minor to F major is a tonal modulation; however, notice that
  (c) a modulation from G♭ major to B major is also a tonal modulation because the B should be respelled as C♭ to properly assess the distance as a perfect 4th (or G♭ becomes F♯).
(4) Finally, a tritone modulation spans an augmented 4th or a diminished 5th between tonics. For example,
  (a) a modulation from C to f♯ is a tritone modulation;
  (b) a modulation from C to G♭ is a tritone modulation.

The Distance Between the Key Signatures: Degrees of Relationship Between the Two Tonics

The other important factor to consider when identifying the distance of modulation measures the degree of the relationship between the old and new tonics according to the content of their respective key signatures. Most commonly, theoreticians discern only two degrees of relationship, namely, keys that are related and keys that are distant (also described variously as foreign, remote, or removed).

If there is no change of accidentals from the old key to the new key or if the change is limited to one sharp or flat of difference from the original tonic, then the modulation (from the standpoint of the old key) is to a diatonically *related* key. Rather than placing all other modulations into the category of distant, the present inquiry recognizes two additional degrees of relationship between the old and new tonics: modulation to a diatonically *remote* key and modulation to a diatonically *distant* key.

In a modulation to a diatonically remote key (alternatively referred to as a removed modulation), there are two to four sharps or flats of difference between the old and new tonics. As suggested above, theoreticians often classify remote (or removed) modulations as distant and avoid the former term altogether. However, if the keys differ by five or more accidentals, we describe the distance as *modulation to a diatonically distant key*.

Determining the Distance Between Key Signatures: Modulation to a Related, Remote, or Distant Key

Determining the distance between the two key areas tells us whether the modulation is related, remote, or distant. The answer can be very simple and straightforward; or finding it may involve a slight detour, an enharmonic adjustment. Ultimately, any distance between tonics that is spelled as an augmented or diminished interval *other than the tritone* must be respelled to the determine the true degree of relationship.

The key signatures of the two key areas, old and new, may be all sharps, all flats, or a combination of both. If the root relationship between the two tonics is *not* that of a major or minor 2nd or 3rd, perfect 4th or 5th, or tritone, then the first step is to respell one of the tonics in order to identify accurately the modulation as melodic, mediant, tonal, or tritone.

We start with the root relationship between tonics. Subsequently, upon completion of any enharmonic step, the key signatures of the two tonics can be assessed. Let us consider a few examples of diatonically related, remote, and distant keys:

(1) For two key areas with same type of accidental, all sharps or flats, subtract the smaller number of accidentals from the larger number for the difference between them.
  (a) a modulation from E♭ major to A♭ major is a difference of one flat (subtract three flats from four flats), a tonal modulation to a diatonically *related* key;
  (b) a modulation from G major to a minor is a difference of one sharp, a melodic modulation to a diatonically *related* key (subtract the key signature for a minor from G major);
  (c) a modulation from g minor to E♭ major is a difference of one flat, a mediant modulation to a diatonically *related* key.
  (d) a modulation from E major to G major is a difference of three sharps, a mediant modulation to a diatonically *remote* key;
  (e) a modulation from C major to B♭ major is a difference of two flats, a melodic modulation to a diatonically *remote* key (subtract the key signature for C major from B♭ major);
  (f) a modulation from B major to f♯ minor is a difference of two sharps, a tonal modulation to a diatonically *remote* key.
  (g) a modulation from f minor to B♭ major is a difference of two flats, a tonal modulation to a diatonically *remote* key.
  (h) a modulation from D major to C♯ major is a difference of five sharps, a melodic modulation to a diatonically *distant* key.
  (i) a modulation from F major to a♭ minor is a difference of six flats, a mediant modulation to a diatonically *distant* key.

(2) For two key areas which do not share the same type of accidental, add them together, unless the relationship between tonics appears to be enharmonically based. In other words, if the root relationship between tonics yields an augmented or diminished interval (*other than the tritone*), then an enharmonic adjustment must be made in order to determine the true degree of relationship. Indeed, there will be times when adding the key signatures together fails to reveal the actual distance between tonics. Here are a few more examples:
   (a) a modulation from D major to B♭ major constitutes a change of four accidentals (two sharps plus 2 flats), a mediant modulation to a diatonically *remote* key;
   (b) a modulation from d minor to A major constitutes a change of four accidentals (one flat plus three sharps), a tonal modulation to a diatonically *remote* key;
   (c) a modulation from A♭ major to D major constitutes a change of six accidentals (four flats plus two sharps), a tritone modulation to a diatonically *distant* key;
   (d) a modulation from f minor to C♯ major requires an enharmonic adjustment of the interval between tonics. C♯ converts to D♭. A modulation from f minor to D♭ major is a difference of one flat (subtract four flats from five flats), a mediant modulation to a diatonically *related* key;
   (e) a modulation from C♯ major to A♭ major requires an enharmonic adjustment of the interval, a conversion of one of the key signatures. C♯ becomes D♭ or A♭ becomes G♯ (adding seven sharps to G major produces G♯ major's eight sharps). Either way (subtract four flats from five flats or seven sharps from eight sharps), there is a difference of one accidental, a tonal modulation to a diatonically *related* key;
   (f) a modulation from E major to e♭ minor requires an enharmonic adjustment of the interval, a conversion of one of the key signatures. E converts to F♭ (adding seven flats to F major yields F♭ major's eight flats) or e♭ converts to d♯. Either way (subtract four sharps from six sharps or six flats from eight flats), there is a difference of two accidentals, a melodic modulation to a diatonically *remote* key;
   (g) a modulation from b minor to A♭ major constitutes a change of six accidentals (two sharps plus four flats). Although this calculation is accurate, adding two different key signatures together, may not always work. Converting one of the key signatures confirms the degree of relationship. In this instance, b becomes c♭ (c♭ minor's ten flats are produced by adding seven flats to c minor) or A♭ becomes G♯. Either way (subtract four flats from ten flats or two sharps from eight sharps), there is a difference of six accidentals, a mediant modulation to a diatonically *distant* key.
   (h) Let us consider a modulation from e♭ minor to B major. Six flats (e♭) plus five sharps (B) produces eleven accidentals. It would appear that this is a distant modulation; however, it is not.
   Converting e♭ minor to d♯ minor (or B major to C♭ major) allows us to determine the true degree of relationship. Six sharps (d♯) minus five sharps (B) is a difference of one sharp, a mediant modulation to a diatonically *related* key. Why use e♭ minor at all? Choosing e♭ minor instead of d♯ minor avoids the C𝑥 leading tone of the latter.

As we continue with our study of modulation with a brief return to the topic of the sequence, it would be well to outline the foregoing explication of technique and distance in modulation; for these principles underlie the remainder of the chapter.
   (1) techniques (or types) of modulation (all of which may have enharmonic adjustments)
      (a) sequential modulation
      (b) pivot modulation (pivot-chord and pivot-tone modulation)
      (c) abrupt modulation

(2) distances of modulation
  (a) root relationship between tonics (may have enharmonic adjustments in either key; and additionally, any enharmonic equivalents of the following distances of modulation should be converted into one of the root relationships listed here):
      (i) melodic modulation: major or minor 2nds between tonics
      (ii) mediant modulation: major or minor 3rds between tonics
      (iii) tonal modulation: perfect 4ths or perfect 5ths
      (iv) tritone modulation: augmented 4ths or diminished 5ths
  (b) distances between key signatures
      (i) related modulation: either no change of accidental(s) or a difference of no more than one flat or sharp more or less between the old key and the new key
      (ii) remote (or removed) modulation: a change of two to four sharps or flats more or less between the old key and the new key
      (iii) distant modulation: a change of five or more sharps or flats more or less between the old key and the new key

Sequential Modulation Revisited

Example 8–2 illustrates a descending 5th motion from C major to B♭ major, a melodic modulation to a remote key (a change of two accidentals). The move away from the old key becomes evident in measure 4, with the appearance of B♭ in the bass. From that point forward, the bass and chords associated with that motion are *directed* towards the harmonic perfect authentic cadence in B♭.

And yet, notice that the chords of measures 4–5 arise from primary and secondary borrowing from the standpoint of the old tonic, C major. The optional B♭ in the tenor (measure 3) provides a hint of the new key before its appearance in the bass, a *preparation* for the two flats of the new key signature.

The area enclosed by the box is that place in the prolongation of the way from C major to B♭ major where the key fluctuates somewhat if the B♭ is invoked. (Introducing the B♭ one half note earlier in the tenor hastens the departure from C major.) The temptation would be to then place an E♭ in the soprano in measure 3. This action takes us more directly to the new key (the addition of E♭ transforms the major seventh on F into an applied THD of the ensuing B♭ tonic). However, the E♭ is not needed until it appears on beat 3 of measure 4. Unless a more immediate modulation is intended, gradual changes are preferred.

Example 8–2: C major to B♭ major

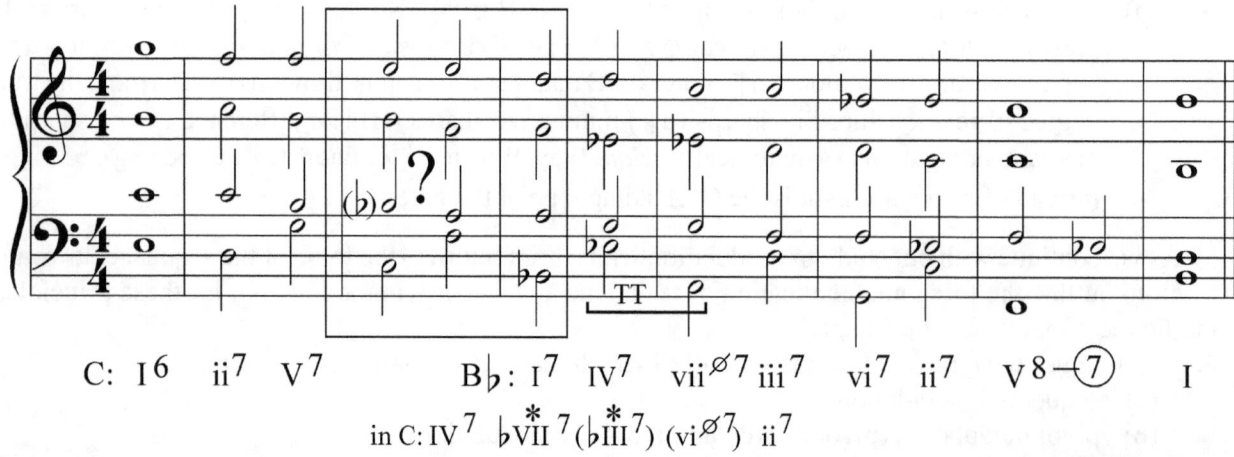

A similar move from c minor to the remote key of b♭ minor is shown in example 8–3. The sequence begins with a succession of modal dominants in measure 2, without any chord in the series serving as an applied dominant until the progression reaches the subtonic, the naturally-occurring [THD] of III in the minor mode, expressed here as [♭VII ♭7 III 7] b♭.

On the primary accents of measures 4–7, the bass takes a stepwise descent in b♭ minor from scale degrees 1 to 5, through variables ♭7 and ♭6: B♭–A♭–G♭–F. (The outer voices of both examples 8–2 and 8–3 consist of parallel 10ths on the primary accents, a secure framework for the prolongation of the way from the old tonic to the new.)

The key signature starts to change in measure 4 with the appearance of D♭ in the soprano, followed by G♭ in the tenor. D♭ and G♭ form the roots of III 7 and ♭VI 7 respectively; both pitches, which take the bass in measures 5–6, move the progression decisively towards b♭ minor in measures 5–6. (Note: the diminished supertonic in measure 6 is so marked because another voicing would include the chord fifth, variable ♭6, G♭.)

Example 8–3: c minor to b♭ minor

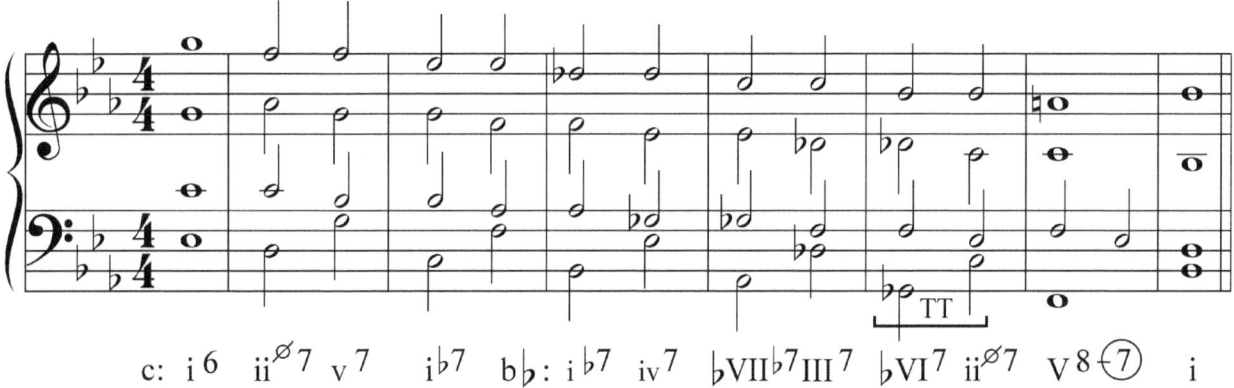

Pivot-Chord Modulation

Both the sequence and the pivot chord produce successful modulations, changes of key that sound logical and unobtrusive. As stated earlier, a sequential modulation reaches its destination over time, whereas pivot modulation prepares the arrival of the new key through a prior relationship with the old key.

With pivot modulation, a convincing change of key depends on this previous relationship; in other words, it depends on finding a good pivot chord. Indeed, this is the first challenge confronting the student of modulation. In pivot-chord modulation, a chord belonging to the old key is restated in the new key as either an X-chord or as a chord *applied* to the X-chord. The latter usage constitutes an extension of the pivot principle in which the chord common to both keys is an applied chord in the new progression. (We know that a major triad can address any major or minor triad as an applied dominant except when the root relationship between the chords involves the tritone. For example, a tonic on B cannot be tonicized by a dominant seventh on F.)

And so, although it may be associated with a component of the harmonic or contrapuntal progression, the pivot chord does not have to be an X-chord in the old key. The pivot could be the THD, the tonic, or even an extended passing chord in the old key and still facilitate the connection between tonics (as we shall see in example 8–4).

228   Chapter 8   Modulation

The Status of the Pivot within the Tonal Contexts of the Old and New Keys

In terms of its status within both keys, the pivot chord can be diatonic or chromatic. That is to say, there are four basic combinations for the pivot chord within the tonal contexts of the old and new keys. The pivot is
  (1) diatonic in the old key and diatonic in the new key,
  (2) chromatic in the old key and diatonic in the new key,
  (3) diatonic in the old key and chromatic in the new key, or
  (4) chromatic in the old key and chromatic in the new key.
Understand that it may not always be possible to use a pivot that is diatonic in both the old and new keys. In fact, distant modulations rarely yield diatonic pivots. Rather, when the keys are distant, the pivot tends to be chromatic in both keys.

Finding and Using the Right Pivot

As we have suggested, finding the right pivot is the first challenge to meet when modulating. A good starting point is to consider the chords on scale degrees 2, 4, and 6 in the new key while avoiding chords on scale degrees 1 and 5. (In this section, we are not concerned with modulations that simply establish the new tonic with an applied dominant because the operation avoids X-chords and any chords associated with them altogether. Excluding the service of the X-chord from the process often results in an abrupt modulation rather than a smooth, or less tenuous, connection between tonics.)

In the next several examples, we shall study a few successful ways to use the pivot chord while also examining strategies for finding them, starting with a familiar excerpt from Chapter 4, which demonstrates a tonal modulation to a diatonically related key: D major to A major.

Example 8–4: pivot from D major to A major in Mozart, Sonata No. 6 (K. 284), III, measures 1–8

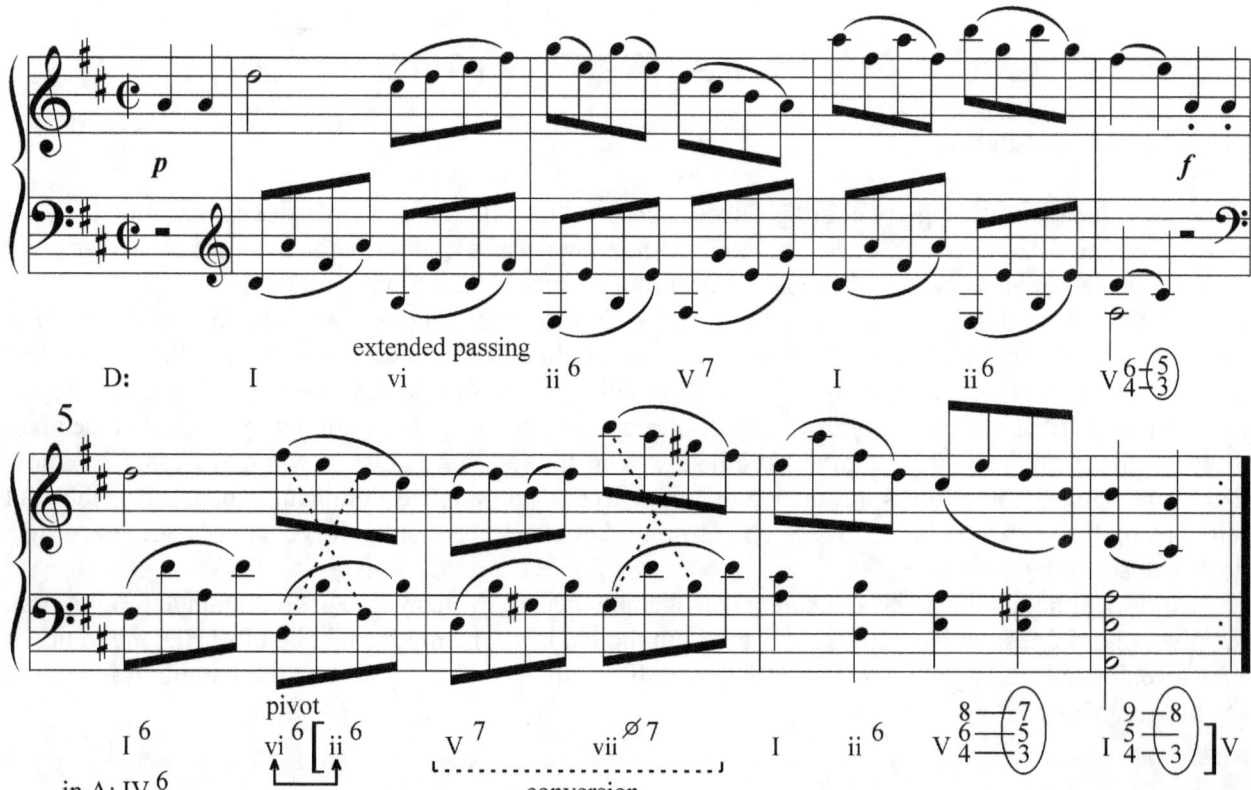

In example 8–4, Mozart transforms the extended passing chord in D major into a supertonic in A major (measure 5). Subsequently, the supertonic becomes part of the cadential structure (measure 7). Additionally, the D-major tonic is the subdominant in the new key. Thus, a modulation may reference more than one pivot.

Let us consider the triads that exist on scale degrees 2, 4, and 6 in A major. As indicated below (example 8–5), the supertonic, subdominant, and submediant areas of A major project ii, (ii°), IV, (iv), vi, and (♭VI+). The augmented submediant is an impractical choice for the pivot; appearing as (♭III+) in D major, it cannot serve as an X-chord.

Example 8–5: potential pivots from D major to A major on scale degrees 2, 4, and 6 of the new key

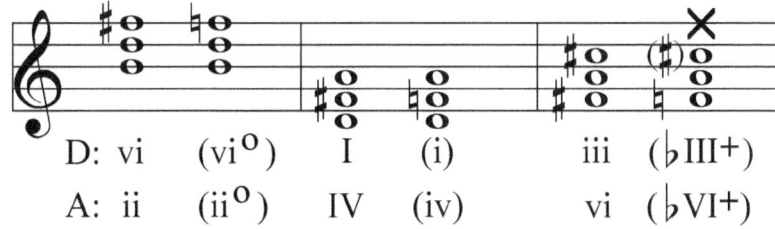

D: vi   (vi°)   I   (i)   iii   (♭III+)
A: ii   (ii°)   IV   (iv)   vi   (♭VI+)

Another way to find pivot chords is to use the chord-area formats for triads (or sevenths) introduced in Chapter 1. If we are considering the potentiality of a B-minor triad for pivot modulation, then the format displayed in example 8–6 provides some insight into the chord's transportability between certain keys, either major and minor.

Notice that the B-minor triad shows up as a submediant in D major and a supertonic in A major (Mozart's choice in K. 284, III). The chord is a subdominant in F♯ major and minor, a minor (prolonging) dominant in e minor, and a mediant in G major. Knowing these chord-area formats for all triad qualities and sevenths enable us to find within moments a number of immediate possibilities for the selection of a pivot.

Example 8–6: chord-area format for the B-minor triad

Minor Triad (B D F♯)	
Major	Minor
B : (i)	b : i
A : ii	a : ii
G : iii	f♯ : iv
F♯ : (iv)	e : v
D : vi	

Example 8–7 illustrates a tonal modulation to a diatonically related key: A major to E major. Once again, the pivot is the submediant in the old key and the supertonic in the new key. In the present instance, the pivot chord effects a deceptive resolution for the complete SHP in the old key (ending on vi as a substitute for I, that is: I–ii–V^7–vi for I) while also serving as the X-chord for the incomplete SHP in the new key.

As the cadential chord of the first progression, the pivot establishes an immediate connection between the keys, whereas in 8–4 above, the pivot chord appears first as an extended passing chord and then as an X-chord. In both examples, the pivot is diatonic in the old key and diatonic in the new. The change of key in 8–7 is accomplished with dispatch. The cadential $^6_4$ follows easily from the pivot, directing the motion towards E major.

Example 8–7: pivot from A major to E major (diatonic in the old key, diatonic in the new key)

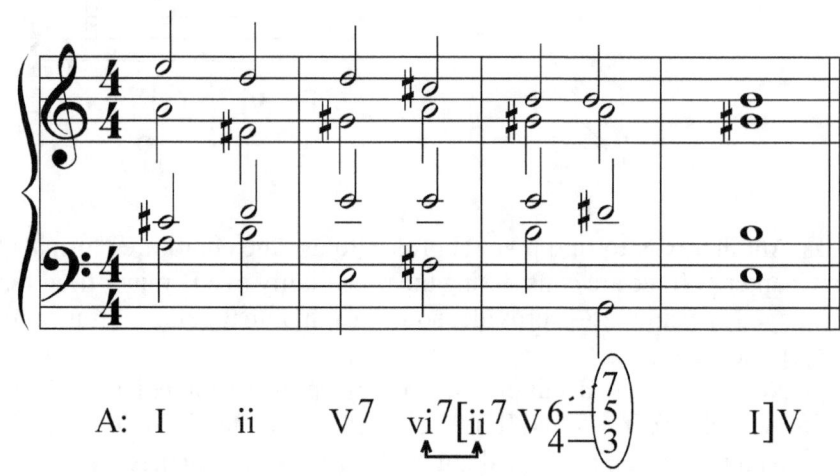

Example 8–6 above showed the location for a B-minor triad in various keys in both major and minor. The chord-area formats for triads (or sevenths) is a basic starting point for finding common connections between keys. A word of caution regarding the chord-area formats, however: some of the chords are produced through the process of primary borrowing.

Although we categorize primary borrowing as a form of diatonicism (extended diatonicism), the traditional view regards borrowed chords as chromatic. Thus, when using the chord-area formats to select triads and sevenths for pivot modulation, any chords of primary borrowing are likely to be considered chromatic beyond this text.

Extended diatonicism, as put forward here, yields three possibilities for the pivot chord within the tonal contexts of the old and new keys:

(1) old key, diatonic; new key, diatonic (possible primary borrowing in both keys),
(2) old key, diatonic; new key, chromatic (possible primary borrowing in the old key), or,
(3) old key, chromatic; new key, diatonic (possible primary borrowing in the new key).

Example 8–8 investigates some basic possibilities for a C-major triad, which stands as a tonic chord but also appears as a subdominant in G major and g minor, a dominant in F major and f minor, a submediant in E major (primary borrowing) and e minor, a mediant in a minor, and a subtonic in d minor. Again, knowing the chord-area formats for all triad qualities and sevenths facilitates the recognition of certain common chords between keys.

Example 8–8: chord-area format for the C-major triad

Major Triad (C E G)			
Major		Minor	
C	: I	a	: III
G	: IV	g	: IV
F	: V	f	: V
E	: (♭VI)	e	: ♭VI
		d	: ♭VII

As we have seen, the subtonic triad in d minor may serve as the naturally-occurring [THD] of III, F major. That is, the tonic of the old key, C major, assumes the role of the subtonic in d-minor and addresses its III chord (F major) as an applied dominant. Example 8–9 illustrates how ♭VII^6 forms a relationship with III, the X-chord of the new key.

Although the pivot serves as a THD/CLT of III, the absence of the chord seventh (B♭) prevents the subtonic from pointing decisively towards F major. Indeed, when the B♭ appears as the chord fifth of the E-diminished triad in measure 3, it relates back to F major as its TMD and forward to d minor as a passing chord between the X-chord and the cadential $^6_4$. (Alternatively, the progression could continue in F major by employing its tonic triad on beat 1 of measure 4.) Though the preparation for d minor is subtle, using the subtonic to provide harmonic emphasis to the new key's mediant (the old key's subdominant) ultimately makes the move to d minor practicable.

Example 8–9: pivot from C major to d minor (diatonic in the old key, diatonic in the new key)

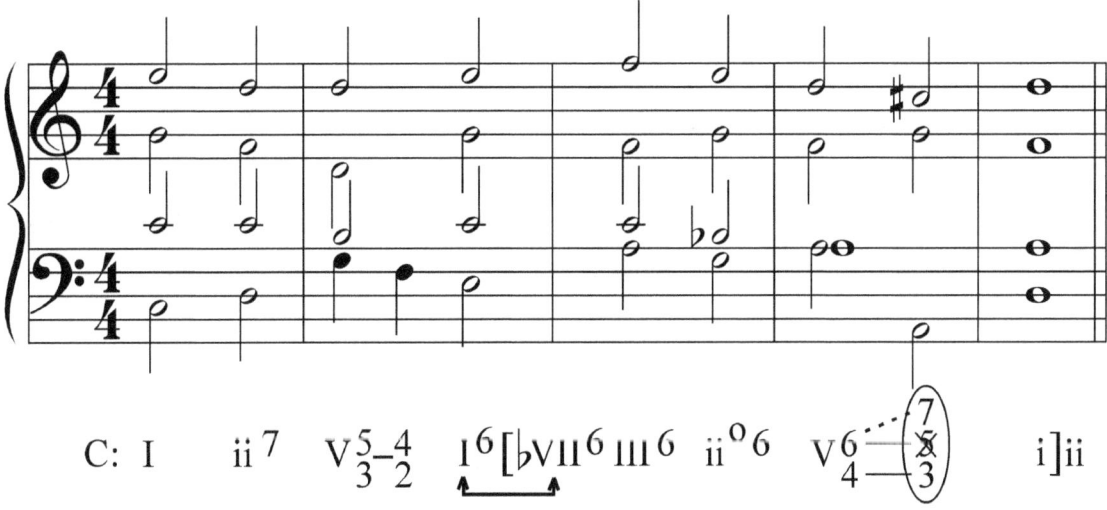

Example 8–10 displays five pivots for modulating from b minor to A♭ (G♯) major, the first of which (8–10a) is diatonic in both keys (the C♯-minor triad is formable through primary borrowing in the new key and would be respelled as D♭). The remaining four chords, however, are chromatic pivots. From the conventional perspective, all of the pivots, including 8–10a, are chromatic.

Example 8–10: potential pivots from b minor to A♭ major

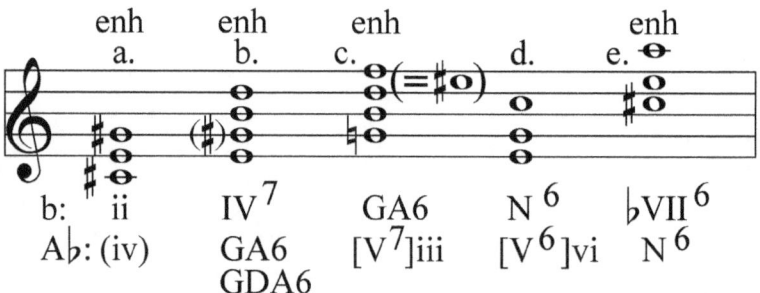

Examples 8–11 and 12 demonstrate a diatonic pivot in b minor becoming a chromatic one in A♭ (G♯) major, an enharmonic mediant modulation to a diatonically distant key (see above, p. 225). The contrapuntal bass motion (G–G♯–A♯) in 8–11, which leads to the cadence in b minor (measure 3), incorporates variable ♯6 into the subdominant chord.

In the voicing of 8–11, placing ♯6 (G♯) in the bass produces an inverted dominant seventh chord resolving directly to V (of b minor), the latter expressed in $^6_3$ and $^5_3$ positions. The imperfect authentic cadence in b minor shores up the old key before proceeding to the new. Though chromatic pivots engender a bolder shift in tonality, when the relationship between keys is distant, they often remain the best option; in this instance, IV^7 of b minor becomes the GDA6 of A♭ major.

Example 8–11: pivot from b minor to A♭ (G♯) major (diatonic in the old key, chromatic in the new key)

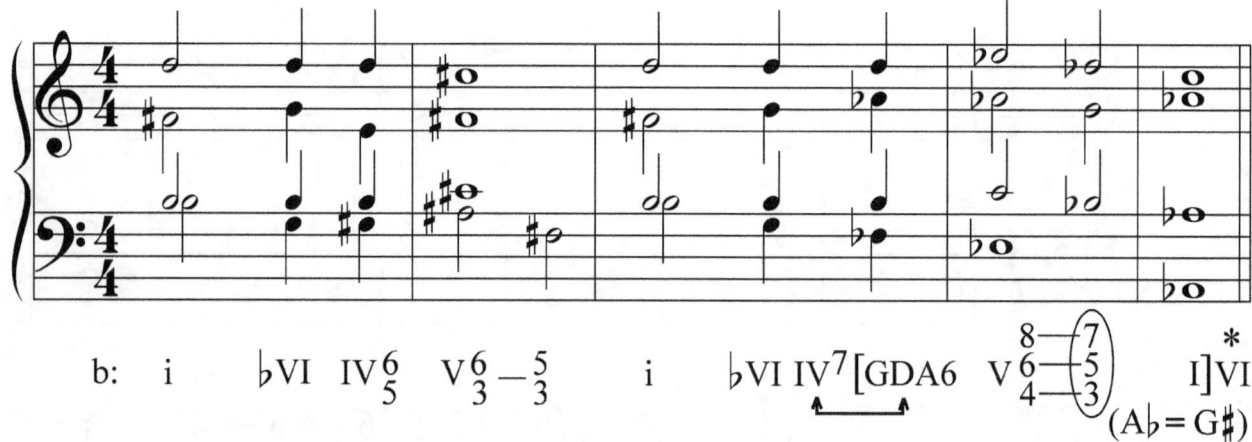

In example 8–12, notice the parallel perfect 5ths between the N^6 and the cadential $^6_4$ in the tenor and alto of measures 4–5. It would be well to recall that the first part of the cadential $^6_4$ is an apparent chord; so constituted, the second 5th (A♭/E♭) is a nonessential interval, consisting of nonharmonic tones seeking resolution to an unequal though "real" 5th (G/D♭). (Further, the A♭ in the tenor is a dissonant passing tone.) A chromatic chord in the new key, the N^6, effects the modulation.

Example 8–12: pivot from b minor to A♭ (G♯) major (diatonic in the old key, chromatic in the new key)

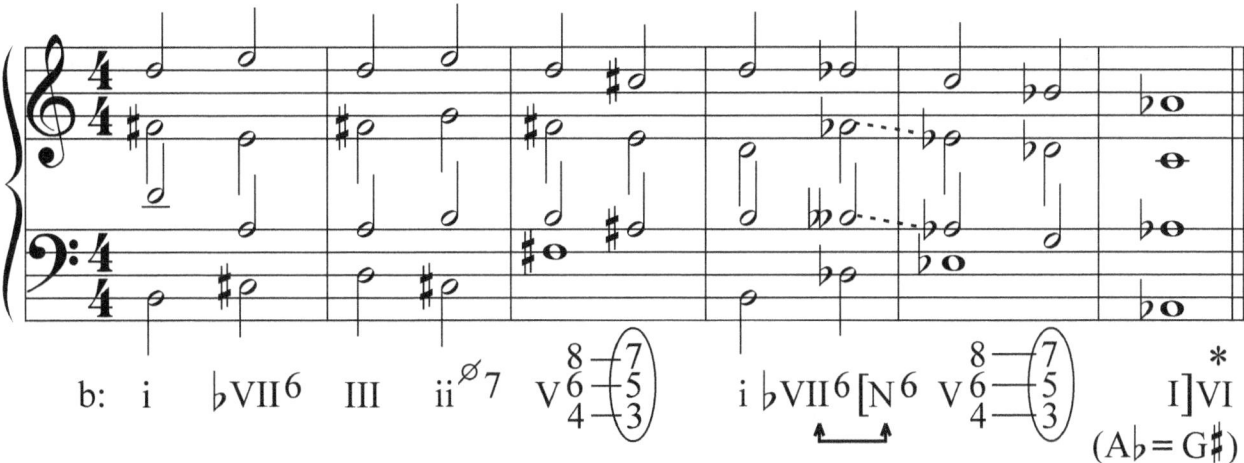

Comparing the Diatonic Pitch Content of the Two Keys

Perhaps the best starting point for finding the right diatonic (or extended-diatonic) pivot compares the pitch content of the two keys. As illustrated in examples 8–13 and 8–14 below, the disparity of pitches between distant keys, such as b minor and A♭ major, limits the number of available diatonic pivots. When only a small number of common tones can be established between keys, there are fewer common chords available as well. Ultimately, then, *distant modulations produce more chromatic pivots.*

As we have observed, look for scale degrees 1 and 5 of the new key and dismiss them; thus, in example 8–13, eliminate A♭ and E♭. Scale degrees 3 and 6 of the new key, C and F, are not diatonically related to b minor and should be excluded as well. The remaining five pitches form common connections: A♯/B♭, B/C♭, C♯/D♭, E/F♭, and G/G.

In b minor, G (variable ♭6) supports ♭VI, whereas in A♭ major, G supports vii°. Although ♭VI in b minor could serve as an applied dominant of the new key's mediant, the current objective is to find diatonic pivots. In the old key, A is ♭7; in the new key, it is ♭2 (B♭♭), a chromatic scale degree (see above, 8–10e). (Additionally, remember to avoid G♯/A♭, the tonic of the new key.)

Example 8–13: common pitch content between b minor and A♭ (G♯) major

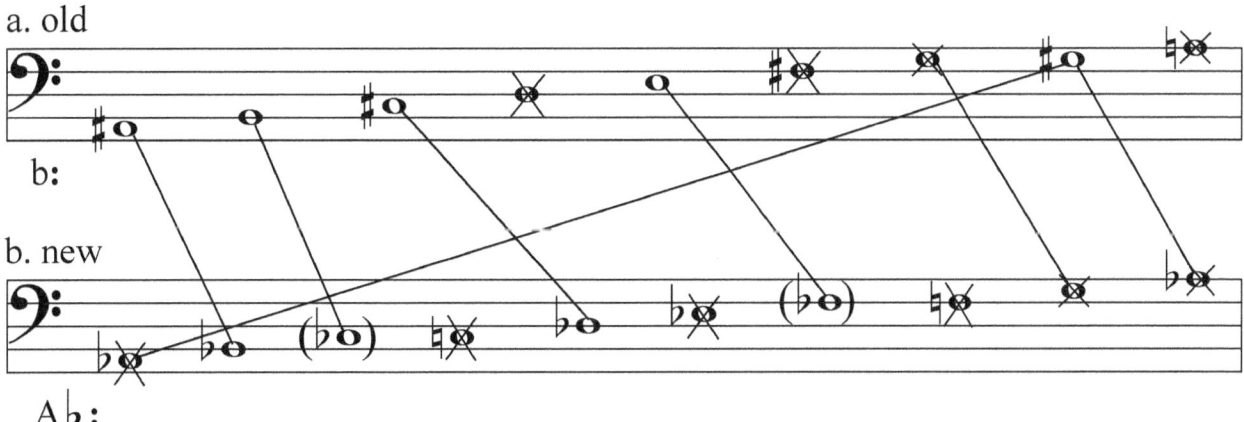

234   Chapter 8   Modulation

The next step is to find the pivot chords produced from the pitches that exist in both b minor and A♭ major. Example 8–14 confirms our earlier assertion that distant modulations tend to produce more chromatic pivots between the old and new keys.

Sharing five pitches, b minor and A♭ major yield only three possible pivot chords, all of which are diatonic in the old key and extended-diatonic in the new. The crossed-out chords cannot be placed in both keys. Earlier, in examples 8–10a and 10b, we cited the availability of b minor's supertonic and subdominant chords as pivots to A♭ major. Example 8–14 shows one additional pivot: the ♯vii° of b minor becomes (ii°), a potential X-chord in the new key.

Example 8–14: common diatonic chords between b minor and A♭ (G♯) major

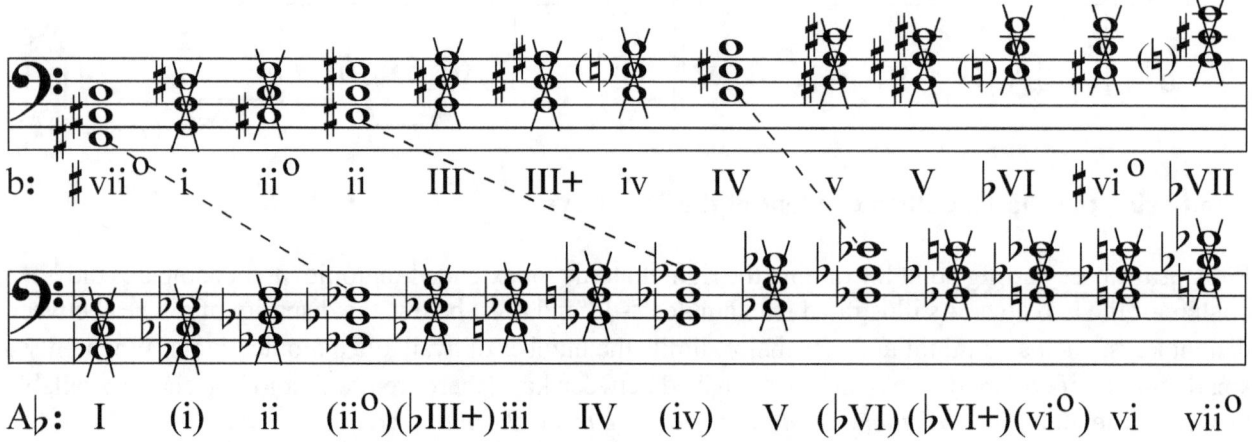

The Brahms Intermezzo in A Major, Op. 118, No. 2

At the conclusion of Chapter 4, we noted that large-scale tonal compositions are produced from combinations of smaller formal units. Each form section of a tonal work usually presents an internal design consisting of groups of phrases and/or period structures. A variety of open and closed cadential structures articulate the individual phrases.

The Brahms Intermezzo in A Major consists of 116 measures of great music; it is a large ternary, assuming the traditional A B A¹ design. Section B is in the relative minor, f♯. While an extended study of the entire work is beyond the limits of this volume, a brief look at the Intermezzo's formal design and later an examination of its harmonic structure will help us understand the broader context in which the pivot chord operates. (For optimal use of the following analysis, access to the complete score of Brahms's A-Major Intermezzo is recommended.)

In Chapter 4, we observed that large ternary forms often assume proportions exceeding the limits of what can be described as small. The large ternary contains small forms embedded within each of its discernible parts. Each form section of the Intermezzo in A Major contains either a small two- or three-part form. The phrases listed below are keyed to the measures in which they begin. (The measure numbers appear in parentheses after each phrase designation. In section A, measures 8–16 constitute a varied repetition of measures 1–8; in section B, measures 49–56 take repeat signs.)

A: a (1)   a' (4)   a (8)   a' (12)   b (16)   a" (24)   a'" (34)   b' (38)   2 parts

B: a (49)   a' (53)   b (57)   b' (61)   a" (65)   a'" (69)   3 parts

A¹: a (76)   a' (80)   b (84)   a" (92)   a'" (102) b' (106)   2 parts

Our present focus is on Brahms's use of a pivot chord to move from f♯ minor to C♯ major, near the beginning of section B. The pivot occurs in measure 54, within an eight-measure segment (example 8–15, measures 49–56. The plus sign indicates a nonharmonic tone). Section B has a small three-part form; the cadences involve dominant chords and remain open. Most notably, at the end of the B section, in measure 76, there is a division of the melodic and harmonic structure at the background rank.

After the onset of the B section, f♯ minor proceeds to C♯ major, a prolongation spanning some thirteen measures (see below, example 8–18, measures 52–64). Within the tonal context of C♯, f♯ minor serves as a subdominant. Subsequently, Brahms reestablishes f♯ minor as the main prolongation (8–18, measure 65).

Brahms uses a chord that is diatonic in the old key and chromatic in the new key: the lowered submediant of the old key becomes the Phrygian supertonic of secondary borrowing, and subsequently, the N ^{6}. Both phrases a and a ' end with a C♯-dominant seventh, V ^{7} of f♯ minor, with the second iteration articulated by the N ^{6} and the cadential $^6_4$ of C♯ major (measures 54–56).

Example 8–15: pivot from f♯ minor to C♯ major in Brahms, Intermezzo in A Major, measures 49–56

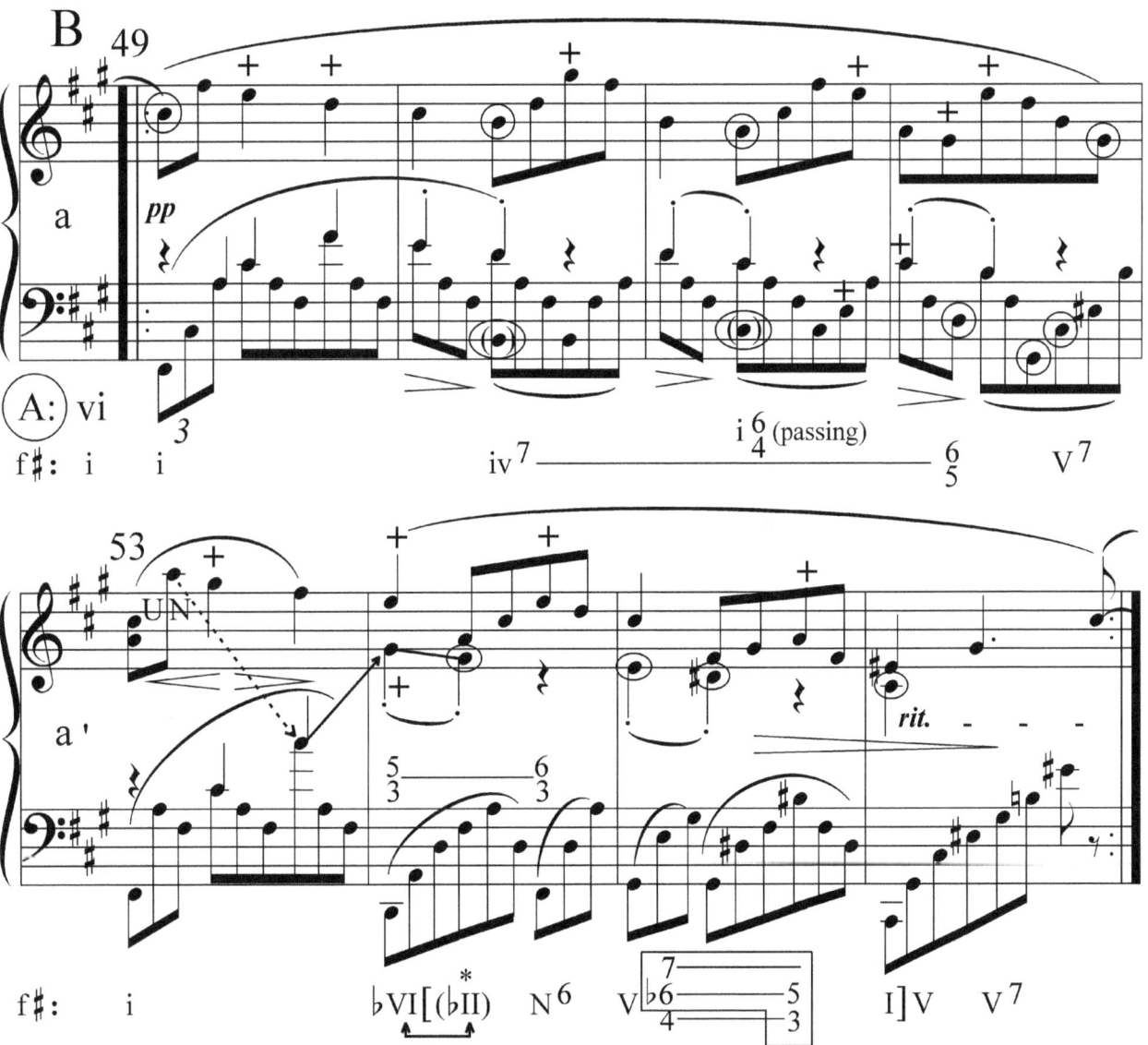

Example 8–16 displays a middleground reading of measures 49–56. The top melodic structure shows an octave transfer of C♯, scale degree 3 and the primary melodic tone (retained until measure 76). The transfer is accomplished by two linear melodic progressions (LMP).

The first LMP descends C♯–B–A–G♯ (see the circled notes in measures 49–52 of 8–15); the G♯ is where the octave transfer divides, supported by f♯ minor's V chord, the C♯-dominant seventh (measure 52). Thus, an incomplete SHP with the subdominant as the X-chord supports the first LMP. (As shown in 8–16, two vertical bars identify the technique of interruption. An uppercase D in parentheses attached to the Roman numeral V further underscores the function of the chord as a divider, as a dividing dominant.)

Example 8–16: Brahms, Intermezzo in A Major, middleground, measures 49–56

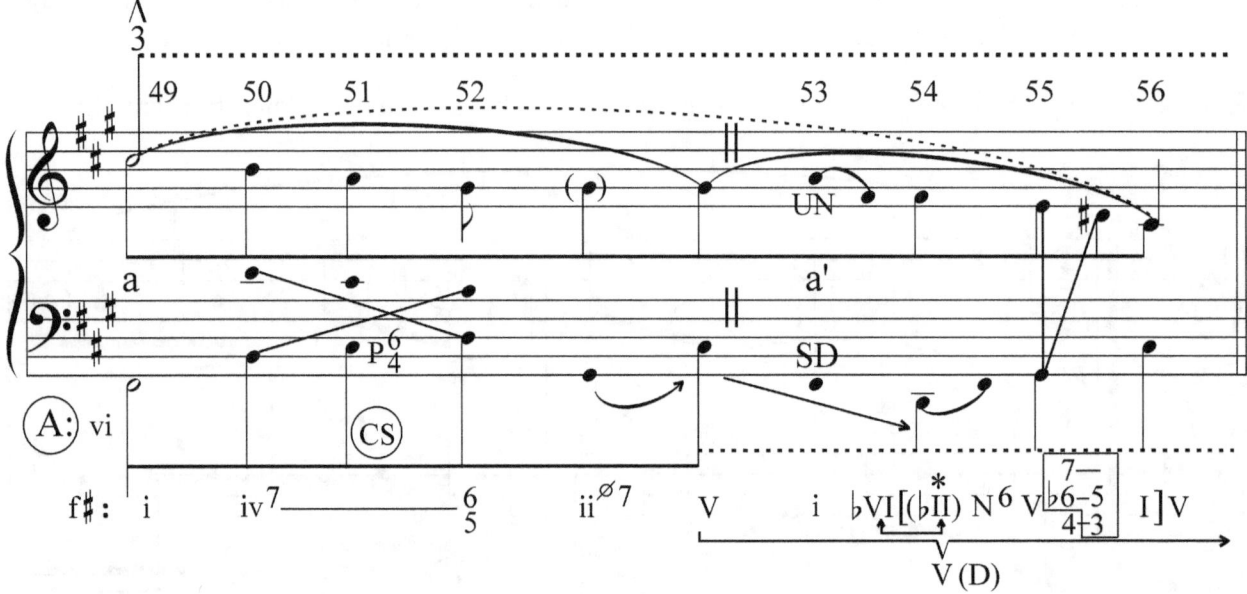

Though an F♯-minor triad appears in measure 53, its function is to prolong the way from the dividing V in measure 52 to the pivot chord in measure 54. The F♯-minor triad is an extended passing chord, and, C♯ major's subdominant (of primary borrowing), another pivot relationship.

In the top voice (measure 53), the second LMP (G♯–F♯–E–D♯–C♯) proceeds away from the dividing G♯ to an upper-neighbor tone on A, which then passes to the bass clef (see the arrow signs in 8–15). This sleight of hand takes the line into the inner voice A, where the LMP reaches its goal tone, C♯, in measure 56. The second progression (containing the pivot) initiates a prolongation of f♯ minor's dividing dominant.

Within the broader context of f♯ minor, the C♯-dominant seventh in measure 52 divides both the melodic and harmonic framework. However, the operation does not yield a *full interruption* in which there is a repetition of the melodic progression from the initial primary tone, using either of the following successions of scale degrees: 5–4–3–2 || 5–4–3–2–1 or 3–2 || 3–2–1.

In other words, the melodic progression in measure 52 does not stop on scale degree 2, and then start over from scale degree 5 of f♯ minor with the support of a second harmonic progression. (Example 8–17 demonstrates a full interruption from scale degree 3.) Rather, the line continues downwards through the second LMP, whose goal is C♯ major, not f♯ minor.

In measure 53, the F♯-minor triad is of a lower order; it constitutes a subdividing chord within the larger framework of C♯. The f♯ minor of measure 49 carries more structural value than the f♯ minor of measure 53; the former is an X-chord of the background rank (8–17), the latter, a chord prolonging the way from the C♯-divider to the D-major pivot (an X-chord).

And so, the a' phrase moves to the C♯-dominant seventh, which is addressed by its own N^6 and cadential $^6_4$ (8–15, measures 54–55). In measure 55, the dominant of C♯ major supports both scale degrees (♭3) and 2 of the second LMP, moving ♭6—5 above the bass (E–D♯). After a melodic sequence, the C♯-chord takes its root on the last eighth note (measure 56, right hand), a tone that ultimately serves as a common connection to a wonderful passage in F♯ major.

As example 8–18 indicates (measures 57–64), F♯ major grows out of f♯-minor's Picardy third. The shift from minor to major facilitates the subsequent move to a♯ minor, the X-chord of the progression. Ultimately, F♯ major serves as a harmonic embellishing chord (HEMB) prolonging f♯-minor's dominant. Although the F♯-major chord occurs within the prolongation of the C♯ divider, notice that in relation to A major, F♯ major is a submediant of secondary borrowing: VI. Brahms transforms the minor triad on scale degree 6 into a major triad by using A♯, scale degree ♯1. (For a review of secondary borrowing on scale degree 6 in major, see above, p. 139.)

Brahms prolongs the C♯ chord for thirteen measures, retaining scale degree 3 as the primary tone throughout the first half of section B. Measure 65 (8–18) marks the return of f♯ minor, the X-chord of the background. The LMPs leading from C♯ and G♯ and their harmonic frameworks support the prolongation of the governing C♯ until the structure divides and begins its repetition in measure 76, shown below in example 8–17.

Interruption divides the melodic and harmonic structure into two (not necessarily equal) parts. In *Structural Hearing* (p. 146), Salzer refers to these two sections as the "pre-interruption and post-interruption period[s]." The two sections become unequal if chord prolongation delays the interruption (or if the interruption itself is prolonged). As we shall see presently, under certain conditions, three-part forms become projections of the harmonic framework and its sustaining operations.

In 8–17, a prolongation of the X-chord (f♯ minor) supports the middle section of the Brahms Intermezzo (measures 49–76). A three-part form is produced when prolongations of the tonic and of the X-chord expand the pre-interruption segment of the harmonic structure into two discernable parts, sections A and B. Thus, the initial tonic prolongation supports the first form section (A), the X-chord the second (B). The post-interruption constitutes the third section of the form (A¹).

Example 8–17: Brahms, Intermezzo in A Major, large ternary, background

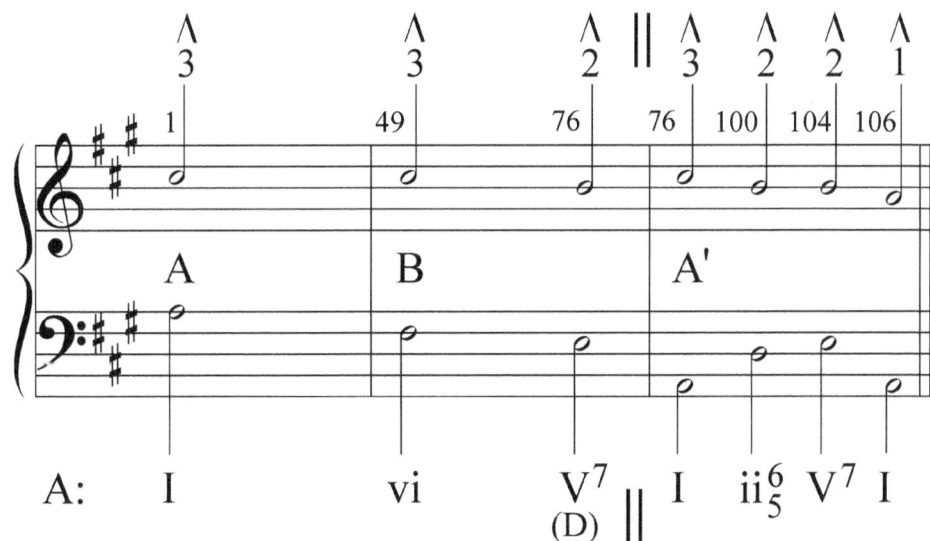

238 Chapter 8 Modulation

The first section of the Intermezzo closes in the tonic with an HPAC, producing a clear subdivision in the formal design. The completion of the structure in measure 106 corresponds to the cadential tonic in measure 38, which is prolonged for 10 measures in both instances. (Compare measures 38 and 106 in example 8–18 below.) Brahms connects section A to section B by reinterpreting C♯, the chord third of the main-level tonic, as the fifth of the submediant: a pivot-tone modulation. (See the C♯ in the right hand of measure 49 in 8–15 and in the soprano of 8–18, measures 48–49.)

The dividing dominant in measure 76, which eventually becomes an E-dominant seventh, contains three nonharmonic tones that reach their respective goals only after the bass has proceeded to the A tonic (8–18, measures 75–76). Brahms withholds the chord third and seventh of the dividing dominant until the expression of the tonic triad and onset of A¹, producing a subtle (and elegant) overlap between the two form sections (B and A¹).

Example 8–18: Brahms, Intermezzo in A Major, later middleground

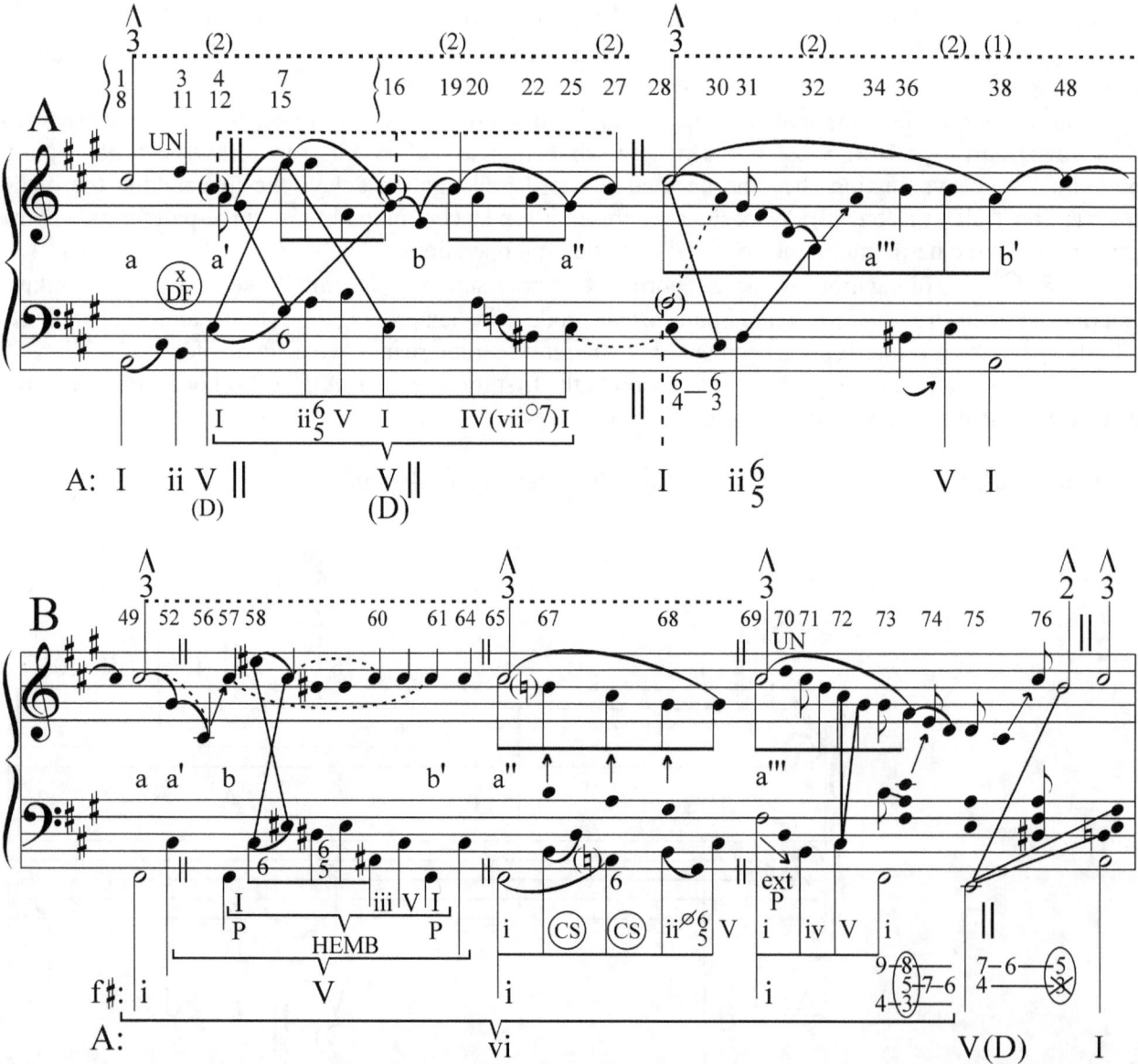

Example 8–18 (continued): Brahms, Intermezzo in A Major, later middleground

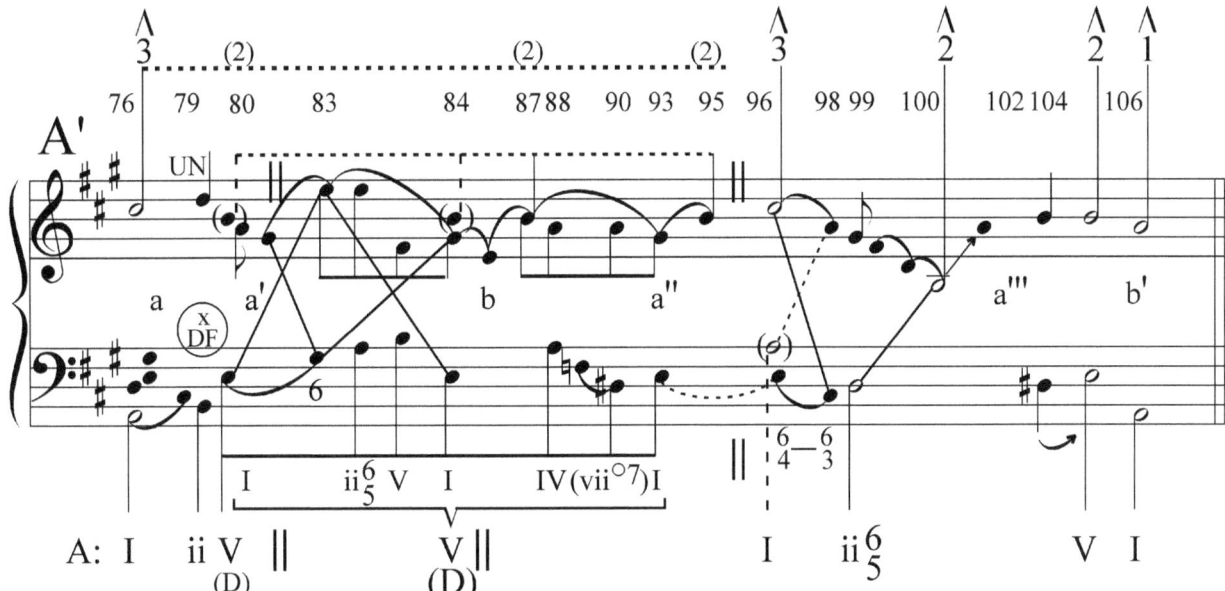

In the first and third sections of the Intermezzo, the tonic triad in $^6_4$ position produces a harmonic overlap between the prolonged dividing dominant of the middleground and the structural tonic (measures 28 and 96 in 8–18). Scale degree 5 (E) is held in the bass while elements of A major are invoked, resulting in the formation of the tonic $^6_4$. Except for the modified restatement of measures 1–8 (measures 9–16), Brahms avoids a root-position expression of the A-major triad as a tonic chord until the respective closes of sections A and A^1.

With the introduction of the opening theme in section A, the top voice retains the governing C♯ as the harmony moves to a subdominant $^6_4$ to support the melody (example 8–19 below, measure 1). The early association of the subdominant $^6_4$ with the initial idea makes the subsequent use of the tonic $^6_4$ in measures 28 and 96 more convincing as a chord of harmony. In fact, the subdominant does not resolve to a $^5_3$ position over the A bass (that is, IV $^{6-5}_{4-3}$). Rather, it moves to its root position in measure 2 (8–19). Ultimately, the initial gesture with the $^6_4$ chord and harmonic overlap become integral components of the work.

The first 27 measures of section A show a descent from the governing scale degree 3 (C♯) to scale degree 2 (B) of the middleground. The division and repetition of the melodic structure (returning to C♯ in the top voice) occurs *within* the presentation of a" (8–18, measures 27–28), rather than coinciding with its onset or conclusion.

Two LMPs in E major, one ascending (E–E–F♯–G♯) and the other descending (B–A–A–G♯), support the retention of the scale degree 2 in the top voice. The progression underlying the second LMP contains a TMD/CLT (of primary borrowing) whose chord third appears initially in the bass as a lowered tone (F♮, measure 21). The lowered third produces an augmented 6th chord, doubling as the GA6 of the dominant (F♮ A C D♯ moves to D♯ F♯ A C).

As indicated by the brackets in examples 8–19 and 8–20 below, the first phrase of the Intermezzo begins with a six-note motive (X): C–B–D–C–B–A. (Initially, note 6 drops down an octave to a prime, extending the motive to seven notes.) In measures 28 and 96, as the a" phrase continues, a slightly modified version of the motive marks the completion of the middleground division, the return of the governing tone (C♯), and the harmonic overlap between the prolonging V and the tonic $^6_4$ (the latter shown in 8–18).

It would be well to understand that in tonal music, the onset and completion of foreground events (rhythmic and/or melodic motives, phrases, and themes) may not always coincide with the actions of the structural framework. As we observed in measures 27–28, the division of the melodic structure and subsequent rearticulation of the primary governing tone both occur after the a" phrase has begun its journey and before it runs through nearly four measures of extension.

At the beginning of all three form sections, Brahms takes the a' phrase of each respective section to the dominant key. In section B, the dominant is of f♯ minor, whereas in section A, the dominant is of A major. Both modulations involve pivot chords that are diatonic in the old key and chromatic in the new key.

The pivot in section A (and A¹) is a chord of secondary borrowing, the subtonic of e minor, used here in E major. In measure 5 of 8–19, an A-major triad in $^6_4$ position appears as the subdominant of E, providing a second link between the keys of the tonic and dominant. (As demonstrated earlier in Mozart's Sonata No. 6 in D Major, example 4–6, the main-level tonic may serve as the subdominant of the dominant.)

Example 8–19: Brahms, Intermezzo in A Major, measures 1–8

During the statement of the a ' phrase, Brahms changes the underlying harmony of the motive. Modulating to E major, the motive passes through an applied CLT of the D-major pivot, the A-major $^6_4$ as a second pivot, and an inverted dominant seventh of the new key. A network of interlocking voice exchanges prolong the dominant (examples 8–19 and 8–20, measures 4–8).

Example 8–20: Brahms, Intermezzo in A Major, middleground, measures 1–8

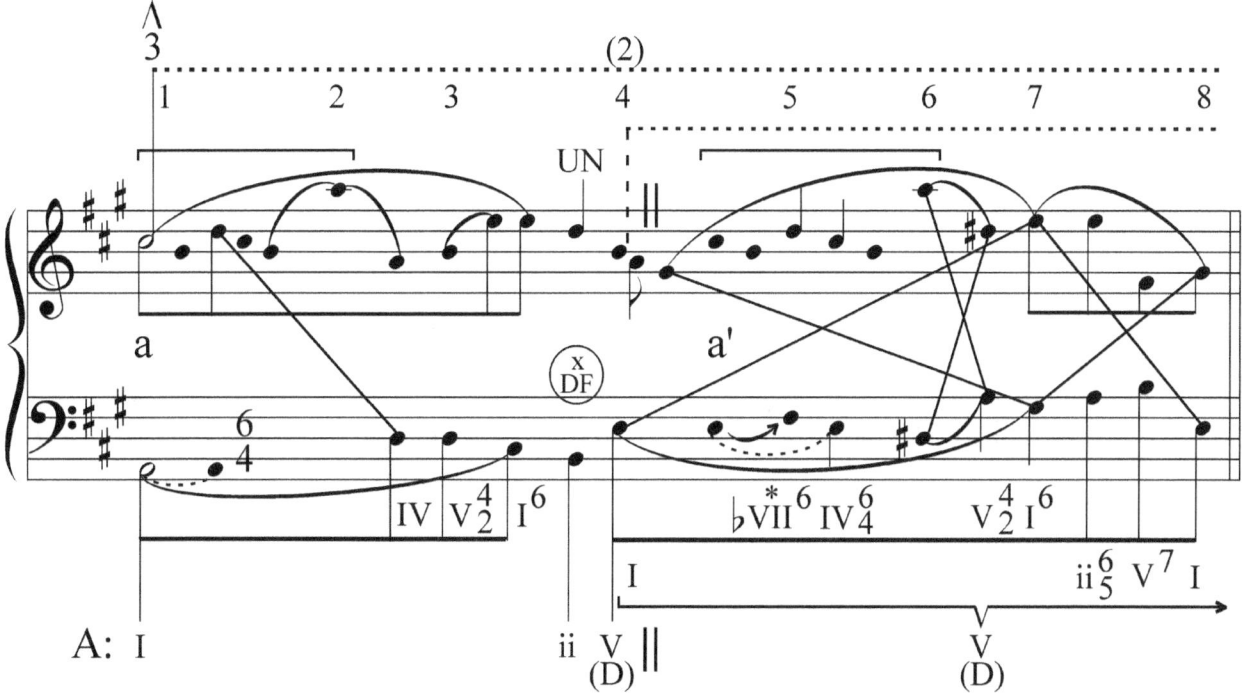

Using the Picardy Third to Produce Chords of Secondary Borrowing

Example 8–21 below demonstrates sequential motion from b♭ minor to C major, a change of five accidentals and therefore a melodic modulation to a diatonically distant key. In this section, we examine how the move away from b♭ minor is accomplished, as the action employs a few of the operations discussed previously.

A pivot chord, chromatic in the old key (GA6) and diatonic in the new (♭VII$^{♭7}$), initiates a three-chord pattern: ♭VII$^{♭7}$ – V$^6_5$ – I. The progression is stated three times and resolves in turn to A♭ major, B♭ major, and C major. Each tonic is subsequently transformed into a dominant seventh whose root is variable ♭7 of the next key. The transformation produces the first chord of the three-chord pattern.

If the mode of the key to which the progression is directed is minor, then the dominant seventh on the subtonic constitutes a diatonic chord; however, if the mode is major, then the chord of the subtonic is the result of secondary borrowing. In the first resolution to A♭ major, which is the subtonic key area of b♭ minor, ♭VII$^{♭7}$ is a chord of secondary borrowing: G♭ B♭ D♭ F♭ (see the asterisk above the subtonic chord symbol in 8–21, measure 2). The latter two keys, B♭ major and C major, use the Picardy third to generate major tonics. Through a simple shift of mode, the third statement of the progression, which ends in C major, becomes motion into a chord of secondary borrowing, as b♭ minor's supertonic is otherwise minor (C E♭ G).

Example 8–21

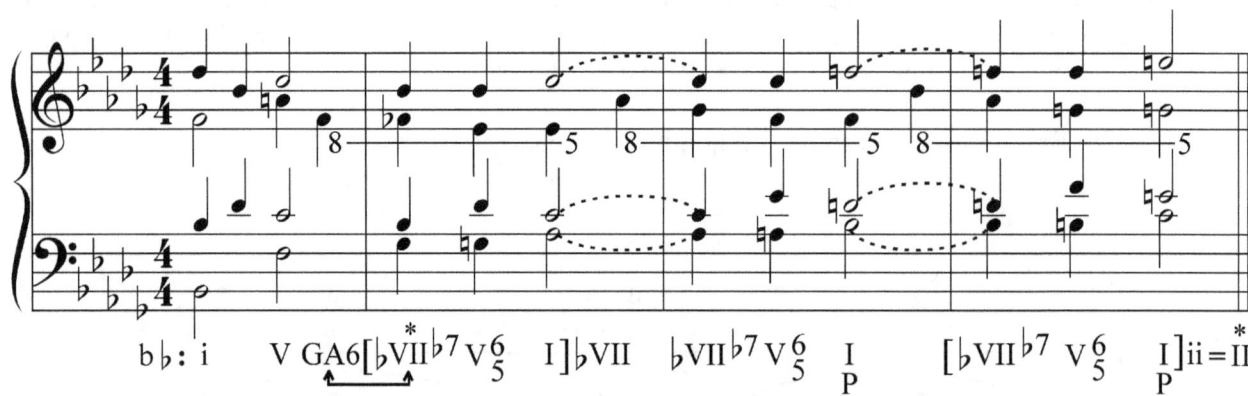

A word of caution regarding the harmonic rhythm in 8–21: notice that the A♭-major triad on beat 3 of measure 2 becomes an A♭-dominant seventh on beat 1 of measure 3. Usually, retaining the same harmony from a weak beat to a strong beat hinders the sense of forward motion. Most of the time, the root of the chord *should* change when proceeding from a weak beat to a strong beat because the harmonic action reflects and supports the natural movement within the meter between the primary and secondary accents.

Example 8–21, however, displays an exceptional usage in which a chord is repeated from weak to strong beats: the A♭-rooted chord in measures 2–3 occurs within the context of a *repeated pattern* and constitutes the goal tonic of the progression, the completion of a musical thought treated sequentially. Moreover, when the same underlying A♭-major triad is carried into the primary accent of measure 3, adding a dissonant chord seventh (G♭) marks the sequential repetition of the pattern. The treatment of the chord seventh in the first two chords of the pattern, ♭VII$^{♭7}$ – V$^6_5$, drives the progression forward.

In addition to sequential or repeated segments of music, there is one additional exception to common practice: if the *initial* tonic of a progression (or composition) is repeated from a weak beat to a strong beat, then it reinforces the key and thus becomes an acceptable option. (Later in this chapter, we will consider the first twelve measures of the third movement of Prokofiev's Classical Symphony, Op. 25. The pickup measure of the movement, shown below in example 8–44, consists of the tones B–A–G♯–A. The harmony for this melodic gesture would be a D-major triad, the tonic chord. Subsequently, the first complete measure begins with the tonic. Hence, we have an implicit repetition of the same harmony from weak beat to strong.)

Repeating a chord from a strong beat to a weak beat is permissible because the change of chord occurs consequently on successive strong beats. (It would be well to acknowledge that composers such as Brahms routinely manipulate the natural properties of the meter with operations involving syncopation, displacement of accents, and hemiola—all of which in turn produce changes in the harmonic rhythm.)

The third statement of the pattern takes the B♭-major triad across the bar line, from beat 3 of measure 3 to beat 1 of measure 4, producing in effect a subtonic of secondary borrowing applied to C major (the Picardy third shifts c minor to its parallel major). Adding the chord seventh, A♭, animates the progression and initializes the next repetition of the pattern.

The procedure outlined above could continue beyond C major to another key area; however, more than two or three repetitions of any pattern (melodic and/or rhythmic) may prove to be excessive. Alternatively, the progression shown in 8–21, ♭VII$^{♭7}$ – V$^6_5$ – I, might start with a key area other than the one given in the example (A♭ major) or be used in a different or related way. In Chapter 7, the progression effected a contrapuntal cadence at the end of a different sequential pattern, also contrapuntal.

Enharmonic Reinterpretation, Chromatic Voice Exchange, and the "Omnibus" Principle

We have encountered numerous instances of pivot chords, chords whose status within the tonal framework is reinterpreted as the key changes. *The pivot chord prepares the new key through a prior relationship with the old key.* Heretofore, the pivot chord actually addressed a chord of the new key, a relationship was established and confirmed.

Before investigating the possibility of modulation without a pivot, *abrupt modulation*, let us explore the technique of enharmonic reinterpretation a bit further by addressing the following questions: what if the pivot is directed to an apparent chord or perhaps to a chord that is present by implication only? When the pivot relationship to the new key is not established explicitly, what is the nature of this action?

A consideration of these issues leads ultimately to the understanding that some applied chords may not reach their real destinations. In other words, the articulation of the real chord is withheld (usually through a process of contraction or elision of the real chord) and the lower-level key to which the applied chord points becomes an implication rather than a goal of arrival.

As we have seen, some chords are *merely* by-products of voice leading, of linear motion. The *linear dimension* of tonal music provides much of the magic and mystery that emerges from the creation of a great musical artwork, a dimension from which apparent chords and the implications associated with them are formed. In fact, traditional chord descriptions often fail to reveal the contrapuntal circumstances that produce great music. And so, in this section, we shall investigate what happens when a chord is applied to an apparent chord within the context of two operations of chord prolongation: voice exchange and what has been described as the "omnibus" principle.

The omnibus consists of a voice exchange with chromatic passing tones prolonging the dominant chord. Within this framework, as shown in example 8–22 (its most commonly used form), the voice leading of the omnibus produces a striking (and attractive) moment of tonal ambiguity against an otherwise stable prolongation of a chord. (Numerous variants of the omnibus progression containing additional chords or alternatives to the ones demonstrated in examples 8–22, 23, and 24 are found throughout the literature.)

In 8–22, our familiar subtonic dominant seventh assumes the identity of a GA6 applied to the key of the supertonic, d minor. In this version of the omnibus, the GA6 moves to a $\genfrac{}{}{0pt}{}{6}{4}$ chord, which sounds momentarily like an appearance of the cadential $\genfrac{}{}{0pt}{}{6}{4}$ seeking resolution to the lower-level tonic of d minor. (An elision of the root-position dominant forestalls d minor.) But even before the d-minor $\genfrac{}{}{0pt}{}{6}{4}$, the initial appearance of ♭VII♭7 suggests a resolution to c minor's mediant, E♭ major, as [V 7] III.

Example 8–22: V^6_5 to V^7 (closed omnibus prolonging a single chord)

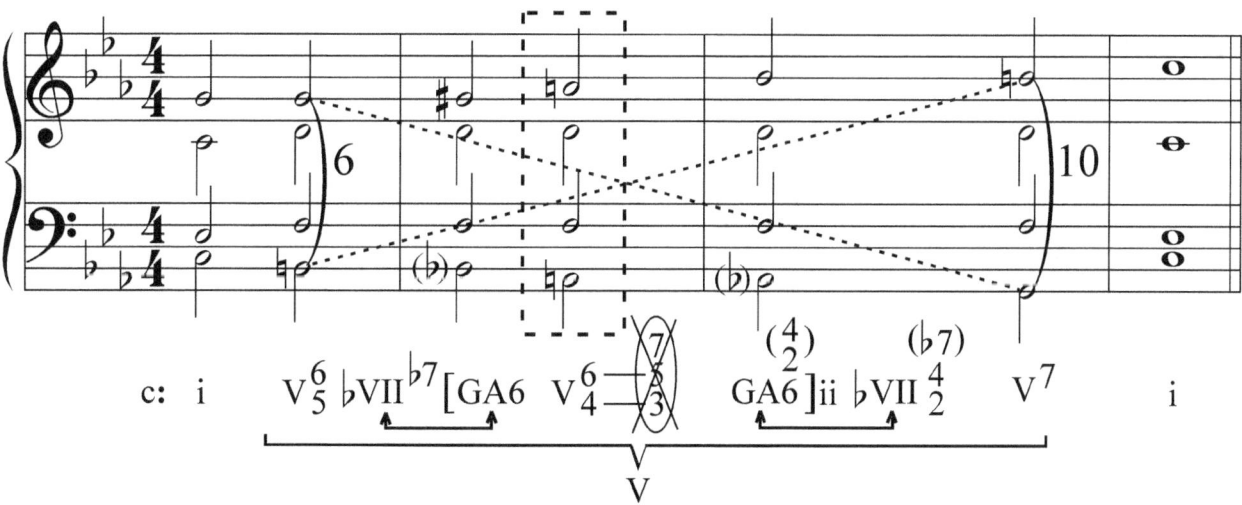

Ultimately, the ambiguities of this progression emerge from the chromatic passing tones in the outer voices: G♯, A♮, B♭ in the soprano and B♭, A♮, A♭ in the bass (the alto and tenor voices of this complex remain stationary). The outer-voice interval-pattern (OVIP) of the dominant prolongation moves from a 6th to a 10th. The top voice ascends from scale degree 5 to the leading tone while the bass proceeds from the leading tone to scale degree 5, *a first-inversion THD unfolding into its root position*.

As shown in example 8–23, *the omnibus progression may also begin with the THD in root position unfolding into its first inversion*. Here, the OVIP for the prolongation of the dominant starts with the 10th and ends with the 6th. Thus, with this disposition of the progression, the top voice descends from the leading tone to scale degree 5 while the bass ascends from scale degree 5 to the leading tone. This form produces a contrapuntal cadence in 8–23.

Notice that in either configuration of the omnibus (6th to 10th or 10th to 6th), the central chord is an apparent triad in second inversion, suggesting the onset of a cadential $^6_4$. When the omnibus moves between two positions of a single chord, we describe the operation as closed, that is, an action that is non-modulating.

The closing position of the chord supporting the voice exchange *frames* the operation and stabilizes the chromatic setting. As we shall see in the next section, reinterpreting the dominant seventh as an augmented 6th chord transforms the omnibus into a device for modulation.

Example 8–23: V^7 to V^6_5 (closed omnibus prolonging a single chord)

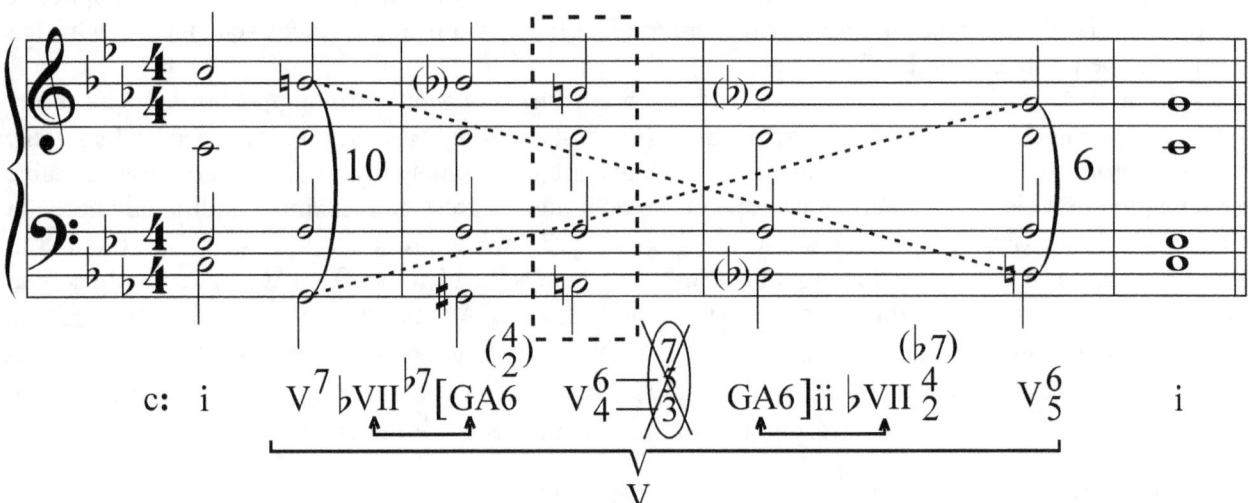

Opening Up the Omnibus

In this text, we reference the term omnibus within the context of a more generalized harmonic-contrapuntal process that places the identity of the main-level key in question. The tonal instability of the omnibus is limited, however, by the closure its framing chord achieves. The operation described in this section opens up the omnibus by denying applied chords resolution to their target chords and/or keys.

If we expand the omnibus beyond the prolongation of a single chord (typically, the dominant), then the device becomes a vehicle for modulation using repeated chord patterns in succession to find the new key. In the course of the tonal journey, the confirmation of the new key is denied, opening up the action for sequential treatment, and potentially, producing parallel chord streams seeking a destination of a lower (tonal) order.

Example 8–24 is an expansion of the harmonic pattern shown above in 8–22, which moves from V$^6_5$ to V^7, a closed omnibus prolonging the dominant. (In 8–24, the pattern exceeds the practical range for the bass voice.) The V^7 on G at the beginning of 8–24 corresponds to the framing V^7 in measure 3 of 8–22, beat 3. In 8–22, the subtonic of c minor is reinterpreted as the GA6 of the supertonic, d minor. The motion continues to d minor's cadential $^6_4$, the resolution denied through contraction (the crossed-out real chord).

In 8–24, reinterpreting the dominant as an augmented 6th chord opens up the omnibus. Proceeding away from the key of C, the harmony points first to A major, and then to F♯ major. The voice exchanges migrate between the voices as the pattern repeats (bass and tenor, bass and alto).

Were the pattern to continue downwards in minor 3rds, it would go to D♯(or E♭). The dominant sevenths on G, E, and C♯(or D♭) constitute V^7 chords for the keys of C, A, and F♯ (or G♭) and subtonic seventh chords of secondary borrowing for the keys of A, F♯, and D♯(or E♭) major respectively.

The completion of the cadential $^6_4$ denied and the confirmation of the lower-level supertonic withheld, the descending motion in 3rds results in a series of prolonged references to the individual components of a fully diminished seventh (in 8–24: C–A–F♯–and implicitly, D♯ or E♭). And with each iteration of the harmonic pattern, a dominant seventh is reinterpreted as a GA6, addressing an apparent cadential $^6_4$.

Example 8–24: open omnibus (modulating)

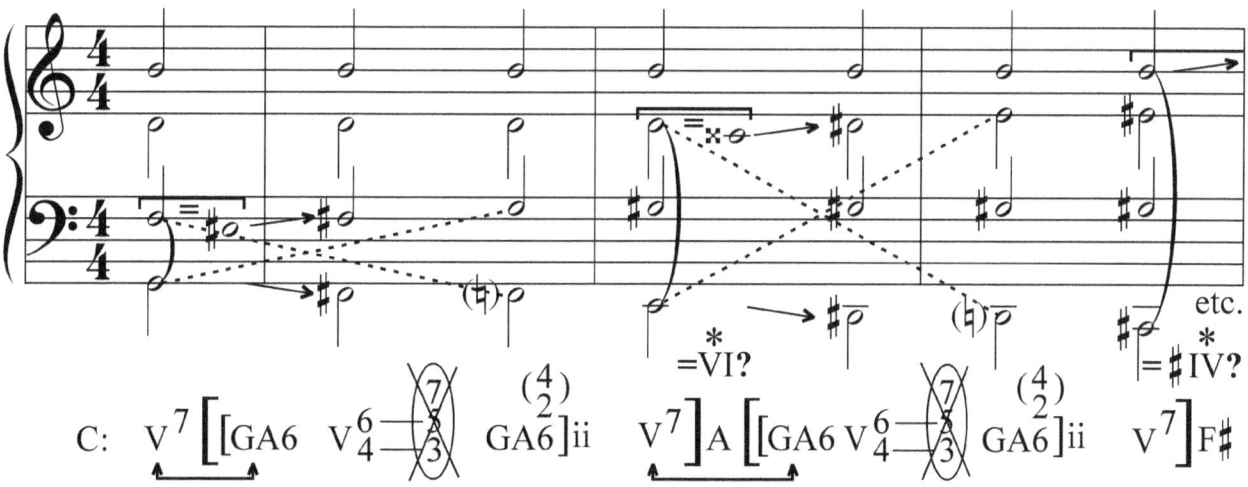

There are many variations of the omnibus, particularly when the device is used to modulate. Ultimately, the omnibus is an act of prolongation serving the compositional middleground. As such, the omnibus is but part of a more general application of enharmonic reinterpretation deployed to either change the key or destabilize it.

The chords of the omnibus (both apparent and real), and its related techniques, grow out of chromatic linear activities and may result in segments of music whose tonal context is open to more than one interpretation. Moreover, as we continue to explore harmonic-contrapuntal operations involving denied resolutions and unconfirmed tonics, it would be well to expect a few local peculiarities in the connections between chords. (For additional study of the omnibus progression and its variants, see Robert Wason, *Viennese Harmonic Theory from Albrechtsberger to Schenker and Schoenberg* (Ann Arbor: UMI Press, 1985), pp. 16–19, and Paula J. Telesco, "Enharmonicism and the Omnibus Progression in Classical-Era Music," Music Theory Spectrum, Vol. 20, No. 2. [Autumn, 1998], pp. 242-279.)

Consecutive Parallel Dominant Sevenths

Now, the foregoing examples illustrate the GA6 addressing the cadential $^6_4$, with the resolution to the root-position dominant withheld. In example 8–25a, the augmented 6th proceeds to an apparent *major* tonic in $^6_4$ position and is therefore spelled as a GDA6. Again, the real chord is denied. In 8–25b, however, the augmented 6th moves directly to the unelaborated dominant, resulting in consecutive dominant sevenths and potential parallel 5ths. (The parallels can be avoided, as in 8–25b, or, by using either the FA6 or the fifthless IA6 instead of the GA6.)

Example 8–25: successive dominant sevenths moving from the ethnic augmented 6th to the V^7

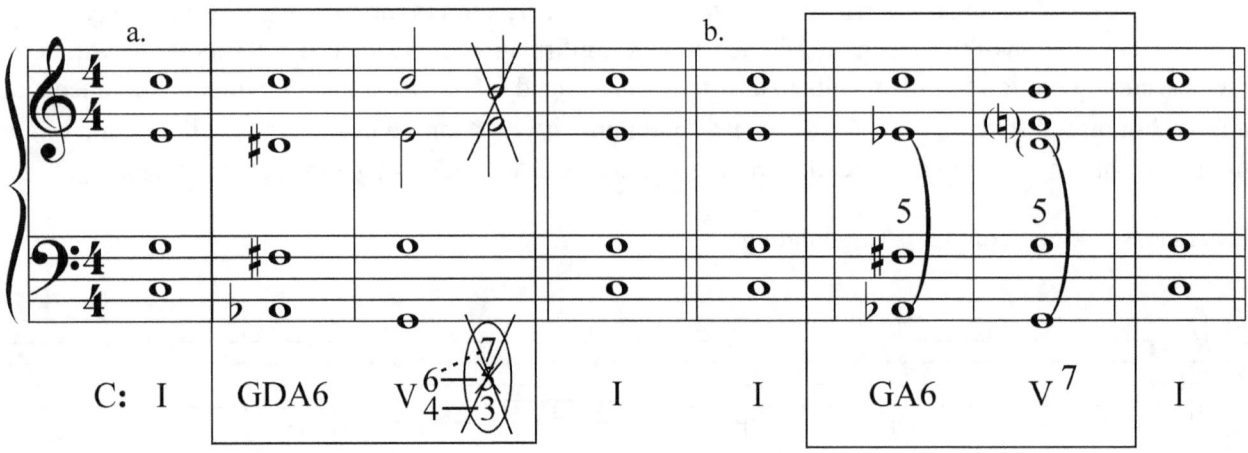

Example 8–26

Examples 8–26 and 27 illustrate the parallel 5ths between the bass and tenor. In 8–26, the interval of the augmented 6th expands to the octave, producing an 8—7 motion above the bass. Each pair of chords, the pivot V (reinterpreted as GA6) and the subsequent THD to which it resolves, points towards an elided key. The elision yields a succession of implied lower-level tonics, descending by whole steps: F♯, E, D, C, etc. The parallel 5ths occur above a chromatic bass.

Example 8–26 contains options for stopping the pattern on C or continuing the descent in the bass. As we have suggested, such chord streams, if implemented, should be treated carefully. Indeed, the upper components of the 5ths within each chord pair are better placed in one of the inner voices to conceal the effect of their sonority.

Removing the 8—7 from the top voice by contraction, as demonstrated in example 8–27, produces a parallel stream of dominant seventh chords in root position. The augmented 6th in the first chord of the two-chord pattern (an acoustical minor 7th) slides into the chord seventh of the ensuing THD ^{7}.

Another way of interpreting the first chord of the pattern is to assume that the bass tone is the lowered third of an applied TMD, a doubly fully diminished seventh in first inversion. The respective destinations of these TMD chords are elided as the chord stream continues its chromatic descent.

Now, if the progression contains a dominant-functioning TMD, then the it also implicitly projects the harmonic identity of an applied THD chord, a chord whose uppermost component becomes a lowered 9th (that is, ♭9). The lowest stave in 8–27 shows the implied root of each THD in parentheses (which also carries a lowered 5th). Thus, the first chord in measure 2 contains B♯, D, F♯, and A, below which an implied G♯ stands to address the key of C♯, the root of the next dominant seventh.

Example 8–27

248   Chapter 8   Modulation

Adding an X-chord, as in example 8–28, helps to stabilize the voice leading by providing the dissonant 7th with a consonant resolution (7—6) and by reinforcing the motion into each lower-level key with an incomplete harmonic progression: $[(iv^6) - V^7]$. A direct octave is covered in the alto voice and by the resolution of the 7th (the octave joins the 6ths above the bass in breaking up the parallel 7ths). The chord symbols at the bottom of 8–28 shows the progression, with its X-chord, as an expansion of $[A^6 - V^7]$. (Designated generically here as A^6, remember that the chord fifth of the ethnic augmented 6th chord may be either altered or omitted altogether.)

Example 8–28

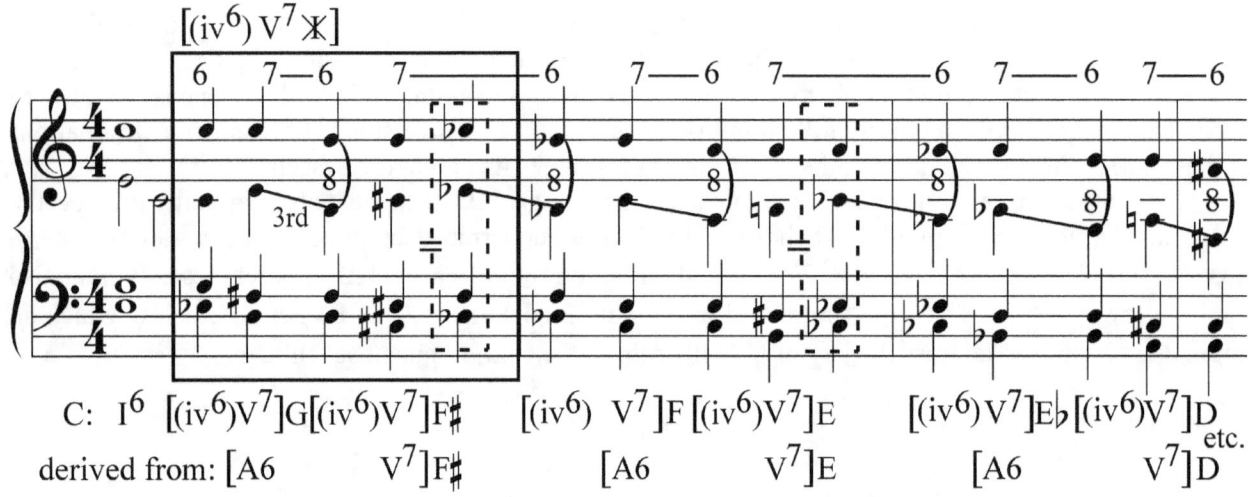

As demonstrated in the keyboard settings of examples 8–29, 30, and 31 below, the peculiarities of the voice leading in the progressions of examples 8–26, 27, and 28 are concealed more easily when using a texture other than our didactic SATB format, though the same basic principles of motion within the tonal framework still apply.

Example 8–29

Example 8–30

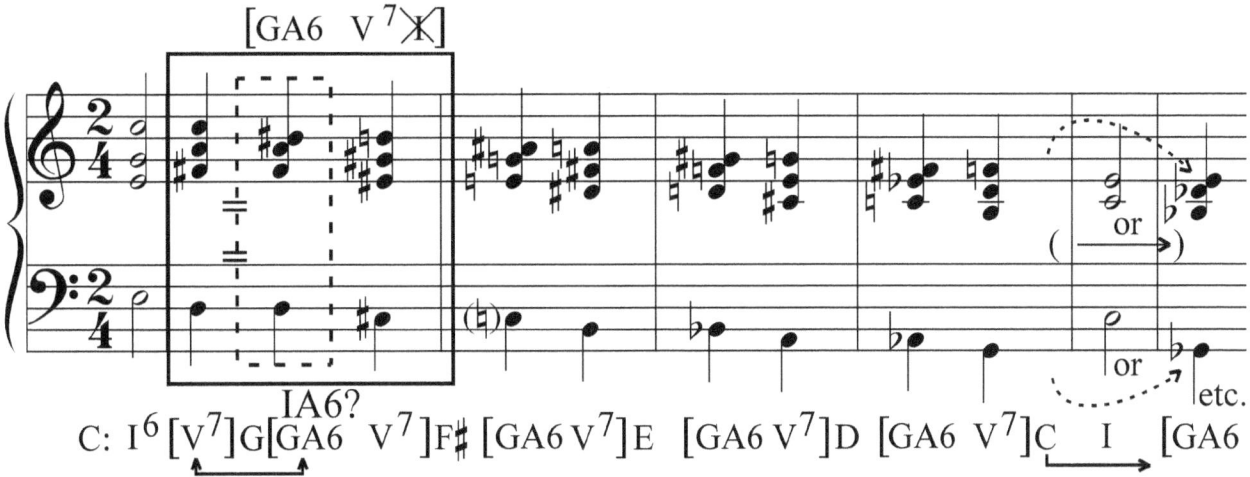

Example 8–31

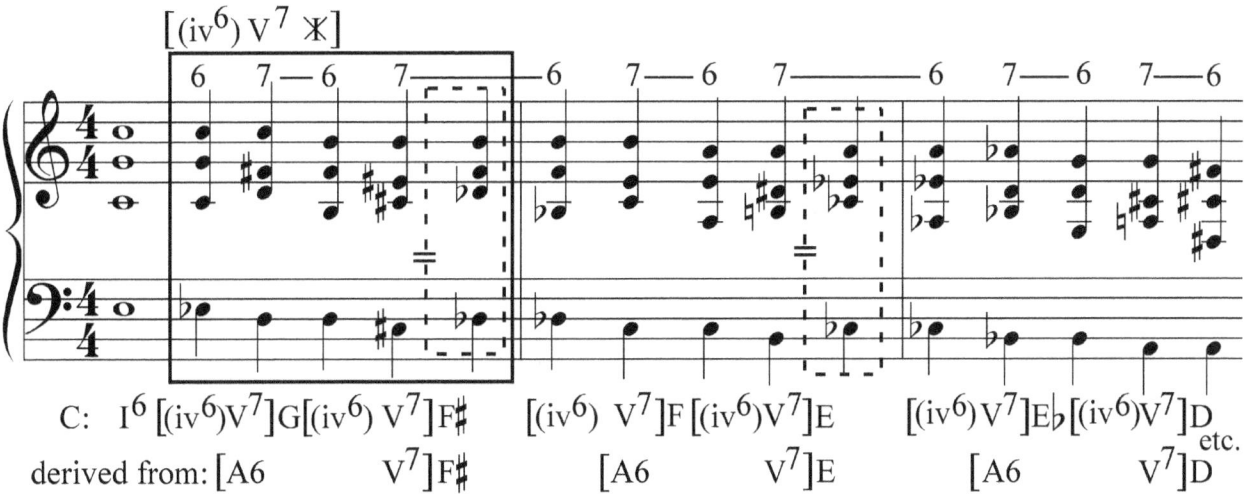

Modulating with the Fully Diminished Seventh

In this section, we shall consider briefly the scope of the fully diminished seventh and its versatility. The fully diminished seventh is a symmetrical sonority (like the augmented triad) that serves either a dominant or non-dominant function. In the literature, the fully diminished seventh often has more than one possible spelling of one or more of its chord tones (like the augmented triad).

Within the fully diminished seventh, if one of the chord tones moves down by one half step, then the action transforms the chord from the TMD $°^7$ to the THD ^{7}. As shown below in example 8–32, a move of one half step is all it takes for the chord to be part of a *conversion dominant* pointing in the direction of a key whose tonic is either major or minor. (However, once the conversion has effected the formation of a dominant seventh sonority, that chord can also take an unexpected turn and be reinterpreted to serve as an augmented 6th chord.)

In 8–32a, the TMD o^7 appears within the context of c minor. Upon conversion in 8–32b, 32c, and 32d, the dominant seventh (inverted) addresses three different lower-level tonics, both major and minor. In 8–32, each conversion dominant effects a contrapuntal approach to a different goal tonic. If the progression of dominant-family chords proceeds from THD^7 to TMD o^7, or if the THD^7 is omitted, then the TMD o^7 addresses the tonic directly without the intervening dominant and the voice leading between the two chords remains unchanged. (In 8–32, the leading tone is abbreviated as LT; the accompanying arrow indicates its resolution to a lower-level tonic.)

Example 8–32

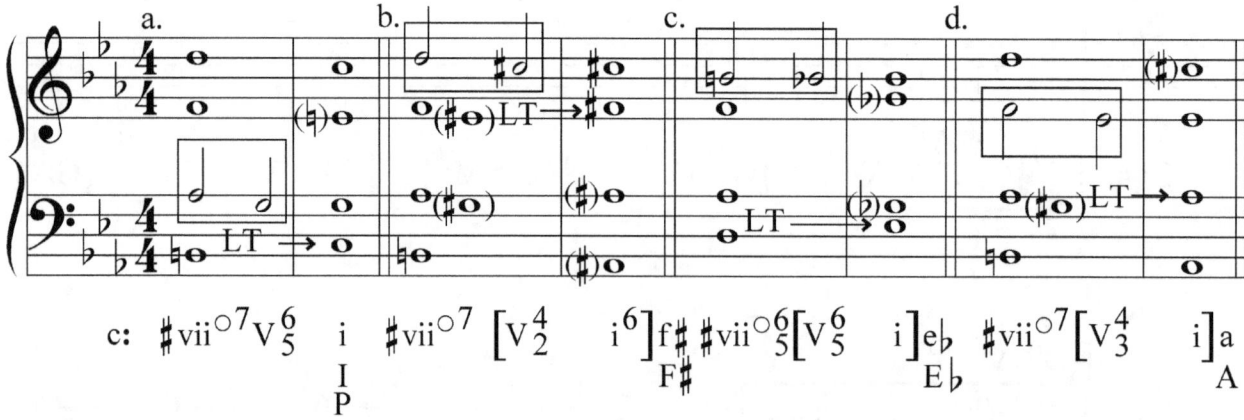

Thus, when the sonority is interpreted as a dominant-family chord whose root is the leading tone, a move of one half step is all it takes to modulate to either a major or minor triad of a lower order. There is a major and minor target key (and mode) for each of the fully diminished seventh's four pitches, in other words, eight destinations.

If the chord functions as a TMD o^7 and addresses a major triad, then that triad might serve as the THD of some destination key, or be transformed into a THD^7. (For example, the fifth of C major's TMD o^7 could be interpreted as E♯ instead of F, the leading tone of an F♯-dominant seventh; in turn, the F♯ dominant might address B as a THD^7, or perhaps B♭ as a GA6.)

In Chapter 5, we learned that the fully diminished seventh can also embellish another chord through a common-tone connection, a non-dominant function. Through enharmonic reinterpretation, any of its chord tones may be interpreted as either scale degrees ♯2 or ♯6 of some potential key.

Example 8–33, which reproduces 5–28 for convenience, compares the voice leading for the TMD o^7 and the non-TMD o^7. The first example identifies the root of the fully diminished seventh, B, as the leading tone of C major (or c minor). In examples 8–33b and 33c, B is scale degree ♯2 of A♭ major and scale degree ♯6 of D♭ major respectively. Notice that A♭, the chord seventh of the fully diminished sonority, is scale degree 1 of A♭ major and scale degree 5 of D♭ major, components of ♯ii o^7 and ♯vi o^7.

In Example 8–34, some of the tones of our reference sonority (B D F A♭) are respelled and attached as non-TMD o^7 chords to three different keys. Thus, 8–34a shows the fully diminished seventh as ♯ii o^7 attached to the tonic F major. The connection with the original chord is its seventh, A♭, reinterpreted here as G♯, the root. Example 8–34b associates the sonority with E major. The chord third of the original, D, becomes C𝄪, the root of ♯vi o^7. Example 8–34c reinterprets F, the fifth of the original, as an E♯ root.

Given the symmetrical structure of the fully diminished seventh (as well as its possible spellings), the sonority's ability to serve as a dominant or as a non-dominant embellishing chord affords a variety of opportunities for both its use and its overuse. In any case, in music literature the fully diminished seventh may not be spelled in a way that clearly reflects its function.

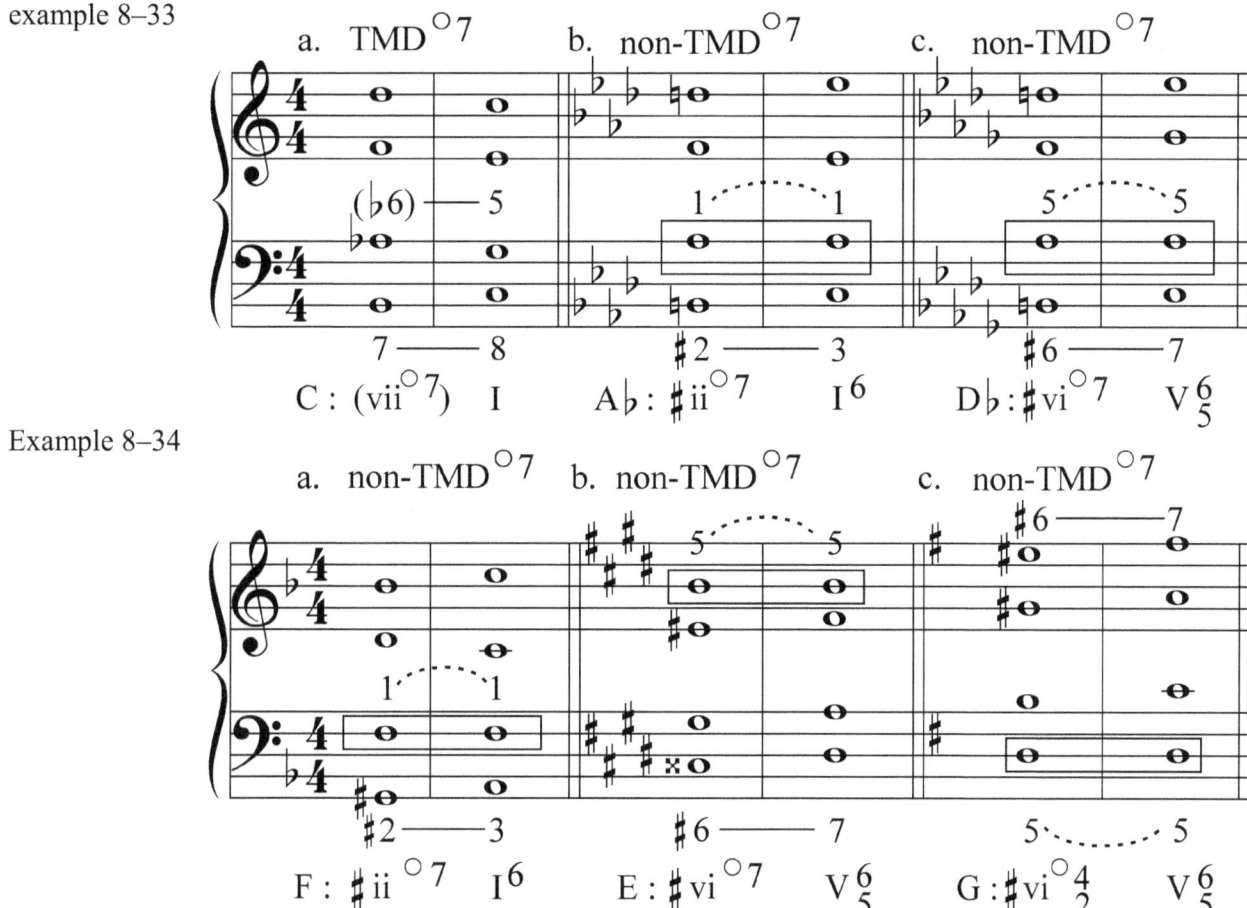

Abrupt Modulation

In the previous sections of this text, we identified some of the most effective ways for preparing the new key through a prior relationship with the old key. Reinterpreting tones and chords enharmonically facilitates the connection between the two keys.

If, however, no prior relationship exists with the old key, then the new key appears without preparation. There is a sudden jump or skip in the tonality, an abrupt modulation (perhaps little more than a hiccup or maybe an expression of something more significant). Simply removing the common connection between the keys, the pivot, produces a sudden and unprepared modulation.

Now, the duration of that modulation is another issue, a matter of time rather than of a specific compositional strategy effecting change in the music. Abrupt modulations occur with increasing frequency in the course of the nineteenth century. As the linear framework becomes more and more chromatic, the harmony becomes less predictable, and our expectations of what might happen next are often *defeated*.

Sudden changes in tonality may be associated with elisions and contractions of local harmony, as well as deceptive cadences and resolutions. These devices appear throughout the art music of the nineteenth century. For during the Romantic period, cadences, particularly authentic cadences, no longer constitute the primary compositional strategy for articulating phrases and segments of music. Indeed, phrase articulation itself is but one of many options rather than the most noticeable characteristic of the musical surface, as it is in the music of the Classic era. At the foreground, nineteenth-century musical forms tend to be more continuous and less cadential in their conception.

The Chopin Prelude in E Minor, Op. 28, No. 4

Chopin's Prelude in E Minor contains sudden shifts in key, as well as elisions of lower-level tonics. The type of key change employed in this work is sometimes described as a jumped or skipped modulation. But regardless of the terminology, the Prelude's chromatic chords and harmonic ambiguities are by-products of linear motion, notably evident in the setting of its chordal foreground and persistent 7—6 suspensions.

The Prelude is also cited as an exemplar for "linear" modulation because the key changes occur within a contrapuntal framework: in this instance, the 7—6 pattern. But while the surface texture is both linear and stepwise, suggesting a smooth and gradual transition between harmonic actions, the counterpoint produces sharp turns in the direction of the key, abrupt modulations.

As illustrated in example 8–35, Chopin wastes no time in plunging us into a world of tonal uncertainty. A parallel period (a a ') dividing melodically and harmonically in measure 12 with a contrapuntal half cadence on V, the Prelude projects an overall sense of descending, conjunct motion supporting a static melody whose repetitions nonetheless become ever more expressive with each tonal surprise.

In measure 2, the dominant of e minor appears, initially in apparent form and subsequently as a real chord with its D♯ third (spelled as E♭). The bass moves to F♮ in measure 3 and the dominant retains its $^4_3$ position but takes a lowered fifth. However, by the time measure 3 arrives, the V has also assumed all of the characteristics of e minor's FA6 in its sounding root position. But is this the only possible interpretation?

In 8–35, the chord formation in measure 3 points towards e minor's subdominant, a minor. The V in measure 2 is back-relating, a retroactive dominant, serving additionally as a passing chord. There is, in measure 3, a unprepared move away from the main-level key and towards a minor.

Example 8–35: Chopin, Prelude in E Minor, Op. 28, No. 4, phrase a, measures 1–3

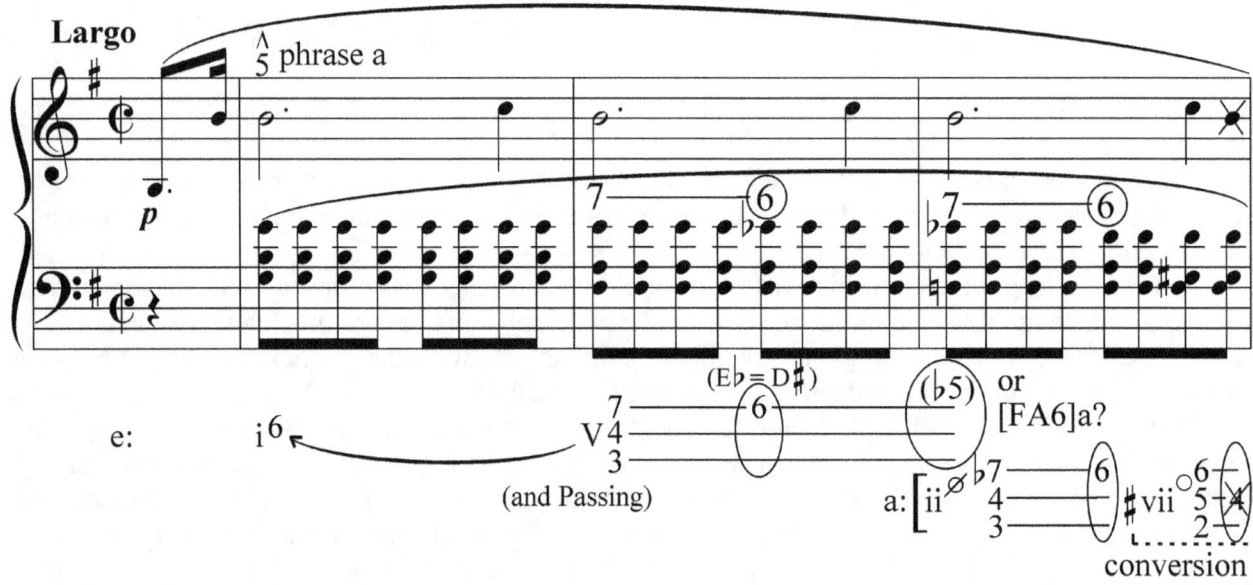

The dominant of e minor, B D♯ F♯ A, is not found in a minor and the chord that ultimately forms on the third quarter of measure 3, B D♮ F♮ A, has no place in e minor. The apparent chord formation on beat 1 makes the shift to a minor no less abrupt. Indeed, its harmonic ambiguity (as e minor's V $^4_3$ with a lowered fifth and as a minor's apparent FA6) does little to establish a convincing pivot between the keys.

Chapter 8 Modulation 253

And so, from the third measure forward, Chopin takes us from one harmonic elision to another. Measures 3–7 contain three conversion dominants, all of which are denied their lower-level destinations. At the end of measure 3 (8–35), the TMD portion of the conversion is suspended in place with an apparent disposition of the chord. Through the process of contraction, the chord third (the crossed-out B in 8–35) is withheld until the formation of a minor's THD on beat 1 of measure 4 (example 8–36)—and then instead of completing the motion to a minor, the X-chord for the first phrase and pre-interruption segment of the Prelude, Chopin proceeds in the direction of G major's dominant, D major. Ultimately, G major occurs as ♭VII within the larger context of a-minor; its reference delays shoring up of the X-chord by three measures.

That delay is effected by the dominant conversions of measures 4–7. The first, surrounded by submediant and supertonic chords of G major, is a contracted conversion. Unlike the initial conversion of measures 3–4, which does not contain a complete formation of its TMD before proceeding to its THD, the contracted conversion simply lacks its second chord, which would have required the pitches A and C♯ sounding together within the same chord (see the crossed-out A in 8–36). Chopin takes the A with C♮ instead. As with the previous two conversions, the third does not reach its goal tonic (G major).

Example 8–36: Chopin, Prelude in E Minor, Op. 28, No. 4, phrase a, measures 4–11

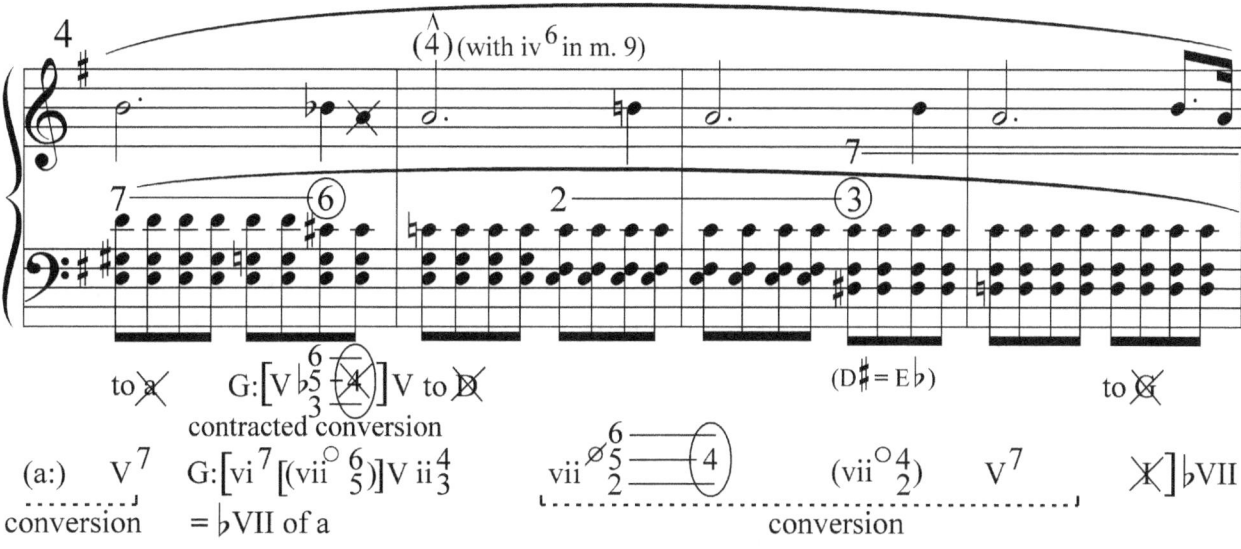

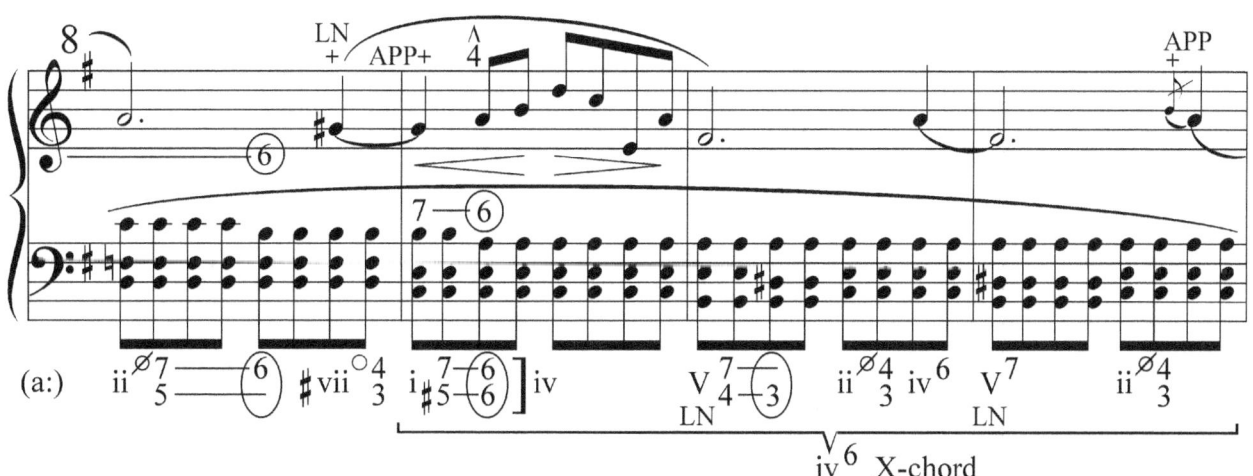

After the harmonic ambiguities and linear chromaticism of the first eight measures, a minor is achieved through an incomplete contrapuntal progression (ii $\varnothing_5^6$ – ♯vii $\circ_3^4$ – i ^{6}); its lower-level tonic appears in measure 9 (8–36). From measures 9–11, a minor (e minor's iv^6) assumes X-chord status at the background rank (for the pre-interruption segment) and is prolonged subsequently by V^7 (as a lower-neighbor) and by ii $\varnothing_3^4$ (as a pedal embellishing chord). At the conclusion of the first phrase in measure 12, the melodic and harmonic structure divides (example 8–37).

In the post-interruption segment of the Prelude (a', measures 13–25), the apparent chord formations and harmonic elisions are escalated, though the foreground texture remains largely unchanged, despite some increased activity in the right hand. As we shall see, beginning with example 8–39, the first phrase contains a BMP with a clear descent from scale degree 5 (B); the melodic structure divides on scale degree 2 (F♯).

In the second phrase, the inner voice rises above the structural soprano and creates a new outer-voice soprano. The operation is usually referred to as "superposition of the inner voice," resulting in what we term here a *superposed embellishing melody*. The procedure renders much of the melodic structure, which starts again from scale degree 5, less obvious.

On the third quarter of measure 15 (8–37), a confluence of operations, anticipation (ANT) and suspension (SUS), produce an apparent E-dominant seventh. We could certainly place the chord within the context of a minor; indeed, in measure 4, the E dominant relates to a minor, the X-chord for the first phrase.

But also in measure 4, Chopin immediately moves in the direction of G major instead of a minor. As we have observed, the X-chord (a minor) arrives only after three conversion dominants (the first of which involves the E-dominant seventh of measure 4). Finally, when the iv^6 appears in measure 9, it supports governing scale degree 4 (A) in the top voice. (Governing 4 occurs earlier in measure 5 with the supertonic of G major, an A-minor seventh; its appearance immediately follows the conversion of G major's V.)

The formation of the apparent E dominant in measure 15 is set up in the previous measure by using the bass (F♮) to anticipate one of the chord tones of the ensuing applied TMD/CLT of F♯ major. Interpreting F♮ as E♯, F♯ major's leading tone, the chord consists of E♯ G♯ B D♯–D♮ (first half of measure 15).

The E in the bass anticipates the chord formation on the second quarter of measure 16; its presence in the second half of measure 15, along with the suspended D from the previous chord produces the apparent dominant seventh on E. Ultimately, the E dominant elides the resolution to F♯ major (crossed out in 8–37).

The E eventually comprises the chord fifth of B major's TMD/CLT (A♯ C♯ E G), unfolding in the bass from its third inversion to its second. The appearance of ii $\varnothing_3^4$, the X-chord of the background for the second phrase, elides the resolution to B major (crossed out in 8–37). (Later, we shall see that it is at this point in the second phrase where changes in register transfer the melodic structure into an *inner voice*.)

The anticipations in the bass (starting in measure 14) intensify the approach to the X-chord. F♯, the root of ii $\varnothing_3^4$, is prepared by implication in the first half of measure 16, where the TMD/CLT of B major (A♯ C♯ E G) serves as a contrapuntal substitute for the THD, whose root would be F♯ (see the whole notes in parentheses in 8–37). The implied F♯ is preceded by an implied C♯ in the bass of measure 15; this missing root underlies the TMD/CLT of F♯ major (E♯ G♯ B D♯–D♮).

And so, regardless of how we reference the E-dominant seventh in measures 15–16, its presence in the texture is part of a larger motion that is driven harmonically (though constructed contrapuntally) and directed towards the X-chord and first appearance of governing scale degree 4 in the post-interruption. Moreover, the prior elisions of F♯ major and B major, two goal tonics of a lower order, help to drive the motion forward to the X-chord.

As we have suggested, scale degree 4 takes an inner voice (see 8–37) with the arrival of the X-chord in measure 16. Serving as a passing chord, the tonic $_4^6$ (measure 17) moves the X-chord into its structural position, ii $\varnothing_5^6$ (measure 18). Initially, the tonic carries a 7th and a 9th; and just before its second inversion is reached, an augmented-major seventh chord appears on the third quarter.

It is tempting to dismiss G B D♯ F♯ as III +^{7} in e minor. To be sure, its chord fifth (variable ♯7) belongs to the key and mode. However, this putative III +^{7} is the by-product of linear activities operating within the unstable complex of tones that animate the passing $^6_4$ in measure 17. Though the foreground at this point in the second phrase may be dramatic and expressive, its role within the compositional middleground is to pass between two positions of the structural X-chord.

Ultimately, the passing $^6_4$ produces a harmonic "upbeat" to the ensuing articulation of the X-chord's structural first inversion. Immediately thereafter, contracted dominants functioning as passing and lower-neighbor chords prolong the second inversion of the X-chord through measure 19. (Notice that the contracted dominants could also be interpreted as contracted tonics. In either case, the function of this "surface" sonority is prolongation.)

Example 8–37: Chopin, Prelude in E Minor, Op. 28, No. 4, phrase a', measures 12–19

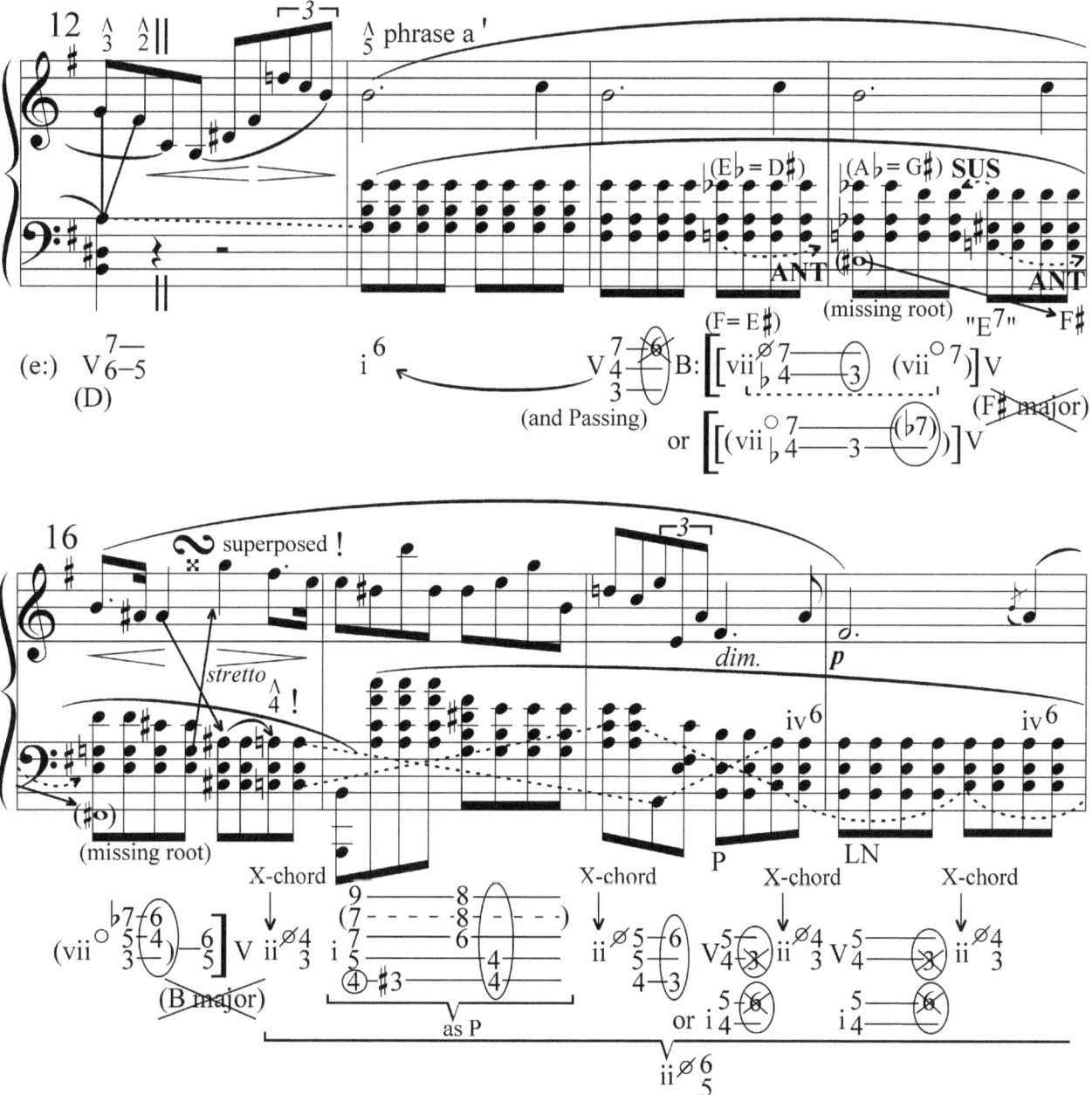

As the Prelude approaches its conclusion, the contracted dominants of measures 18–19 form a complete dominant seventh in measure 20 with both 8—7 and 4—3 motions above the harmonic bass (example 8–38). With what appears to be a clear progression from the X-chord to the dominant in measure 20, Chopin points strongly in the direction of e minor. And with the melody reaching scale degree 2 in the top voice above V, the question becomes: is the dominant in measure 20 a chord of structure or prolongation?

Chopin gives us the answer to our query with a (another) surprise: as shown in measure 21 of example 8–38, the dominant finds a deceptive cadence (or perhaps, deceptive resolution) with the move to ♭VI. On the second half of the measure, we have the sound of e minor's GA6; the augmented 6th is spelled as B♭ instead of A♯. However, on the last quarter of that measure, the X- chord, ii$\varnothing^4_3$, *returns*, confirming the function of the preceding dominant as a chord of prolongation.

Example 8–38: Chopin, Prelude in E Minor, Op. 28, No. 4, phrase a', measures 20–25

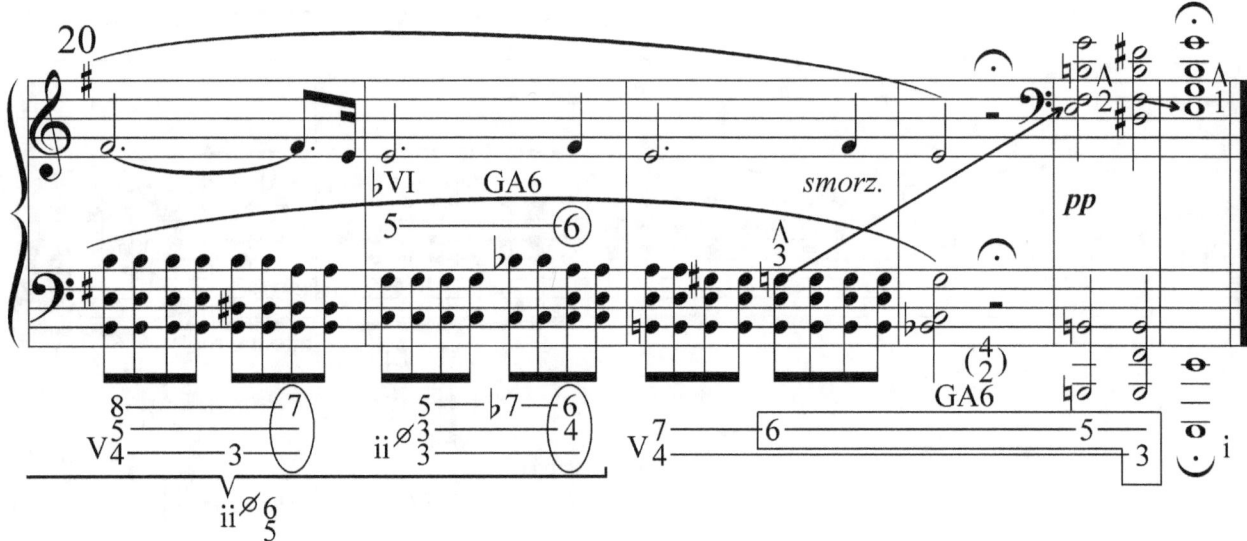

Further, the initial chord succession in measure 21, ♭VI – GA6, constitutes an apparent formation that conveys the effect of a deceptive cadence, but that leads ultimately to the return of the X-chord. Here, in its final appearance, ii$\varnothing^4_3$ improves the voice leading by effecting oblique motion between minor 7ths in the left hand (C/B♭ and B♮/A). The tenor B♭, central to the identity of the GA6, comes from G in the same voice; it is an incomplete upper neighbor to A♮ and part of a 5—6 motion above the prolonged C bass.

And so, from the perspective of the very early middleground, the deceptive cadence is truly false, a musical pun. Subsequently, an apparent GA6 (over the C bass) supports the prolongation of the X-chord. As we have suggested, the V^7 of measure 20 turns out to be a prolonging dominant, *not* a chord of harmony. The deceptive cadence occurs within the final expression of the X-chord, *before* the melodic and harmonic structure moves. The THD arrives in measure 22 and is prolonged through measure 24 by suspensions, and most notably, the GA6 in its sounding third inversion (functioning as a lower-neighbor chord and spelled once again with B♭).

Although each tone of the melody becomes more compelling with each successive chord change, the events of the structure in the second phrase are taking place within the inner voice. Remember, the melody in the right hand constitutes a superposition of an inner voice, a superposed embellishing melody.

From measures 16–21, governing scale degree 4 (A) is prolonged below the top voice. Thus, as the melodic structure moves into the inner voice, the embellishing melody is created in the outer-voice soprano. And once governing 4 (A) takes the inner voice (measure 16), the BMP of the background pursues its goal tonic there, covered by superposed melodic activity. Receiving consonant support from V $^{6-5}$ (measures 22–24), scale degree 3 (G) continues the structural descent of the BMP. Example 8–38 shows the close of the melodic and harmonic structure in the inner voice.

Structure and Prolongation in Chopin's Prelude in E Minor

In the foregoing sections, we cited many similarities between the two phrases of the E-Minor Prelude: the same basic foreground texture, sudden shifts in tonality, harmonic ambiguities, elisions or contractions of chords, a BMP descending from scale degree 5, and the X-chord in first inversion supporting scale degree 4. We also noted that the post-interruption segment presents some significant differences in the disposition of the progression's melodic structure. As illustrated in example 8–39, a different X-chord populates the pre- and post-interruption segments. Each phrase begins with a first-inversion tonic and reaches its X-chord through a prolongation of the way from one structural chord to the next.

The harmonic jolts of the Prelude's musical surface unfold across a clear background. However, the register changes in the second phrase suggest a thickening of the texture to five or perhaps even six voices. Accordingly, discerning the relationship between the structure and its prolongations presents less of a challenge in the first phrase than in the second.

In 8–39, the first phrase of the Prelude takes a melodic descent from scale degree 5 in the governing soprano, supported by an incomplete SHP, within which the 7—6 suspensions discussed earlier proceed (though not shown in 8–39). The suspensions continue in the second phrase, along with various pairings of apparent and real chords, two instances of which are contracted. However, in measure 16, the focus shifts to the change in registers and the resultant submersion of the governing melodic structure and first appearance of scale degree 4 in the post-interruption (demonstrated later in this chapter).

In both phrases, scale degrees 3 and 2 occur within the THD, moving 6—5 above the bass. Notably, the dividing THD also carries the chord seventh, A. After the interruption, the A finds G in the bass within the tonic. But remember, the tonic chord in measure 13 is not the completion of the first progression, but rather, the beginning of the *second*. For here, the structure repeats, albeit with some unusual changes. (The arrows in 8–39 indicate the prolongation of the way between structural chords.)

Example 8–39: Chopin, Prelude in E Minor, Op. 28, No. 4, background, measures 1–25

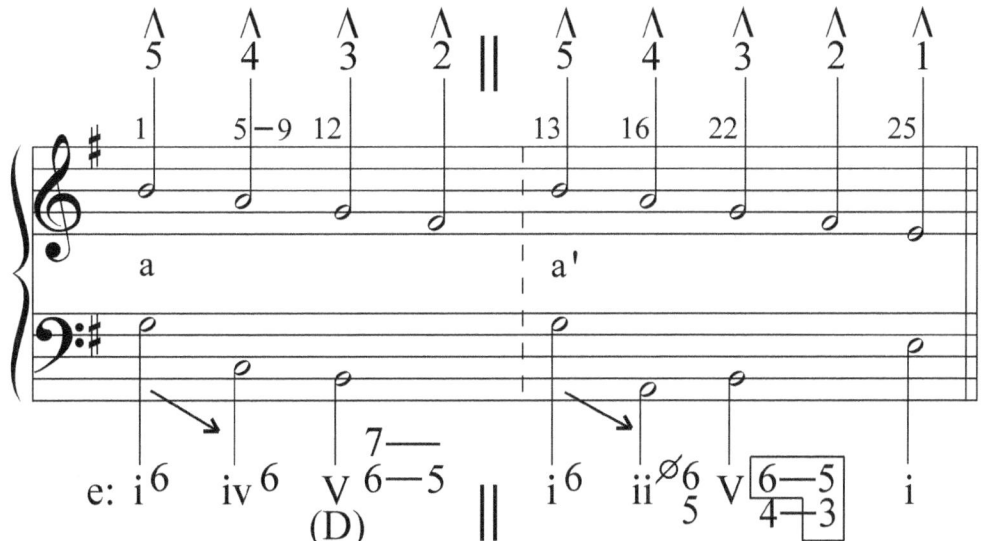

Example 8–40 is a middleground reading of the first phrase. A passing motion in the bass leads from i^6 to the contrapuntal half cadence in measure 12 (G – F♯ – F♮ – E – E♭ – D – C – B). As indicated, the first appearance of governing scale degree 4 in the pre-interruption occurs in measure 5, four measures before the arrival of the structural iv^6. The A-minor seventh in measure 5 occurs within the context of G major as a ii^4_3 passing chord.

The ii^4_3 stands within a series of 7—6 suspensions (2—3 and 7—6 suspensions interlock in measure 7). In the soprano, a chromatic passing tone (B♭) delays the articulation of scale degree 4 (producing the apparent fully diminished seventh). Ultimately, G major's supertonic, the A-minor seventh, effects the contraction of the conversion dominant in measure 5. In other words, the conversion is directed towards D major but denied its resolution by the deployment of the ii^4_3, a chord of elision supporting governing 4 (A).

Finally, in measure 9, the X-chord catches up to the melodic structure as the 7—6 series takes its last resolution. With the upward resolution of the accented nonharmonic G♯, a retardation tone, the top voice finds governing A, supported by its iv^6. In measure 12, after a three-measure prolongation of the X-chord, the structure moves, the melodic and harmonic framework divides.

Example 8–40: Chopin, Prelude in E Minor, Op. 28, No. 4, middleground, measures 1–12

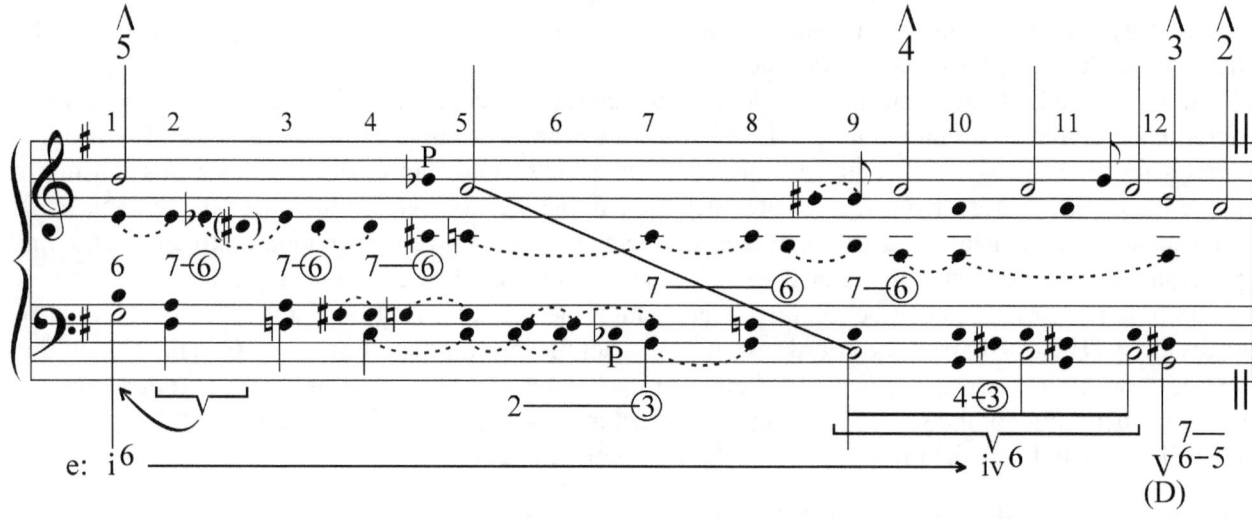

The harmony of measure 13 and half of 14, displayed in example 8–41 (and in 8–37 above), corresponds to the beginning of the first phrase. In terms of structure, the onset of the post-interruption is the same as the pre-interruption. However, as we have observed, governing scale degree 4 of the BMP moves into the inner voice (measure 16). Chopin withholds resolutions to F♯ major and B major in measures 15 and 16 respectively.

In measure 15, a combination of anticipation in the bass and suspension in the inner voice produces an apparent E-dominant seventh. Its E bass is approached from above by F♮, interpreted as E♯, the leading tone of F♯ major. The E^7 elides the resolution to F♯ major. The first appearance of $ii\emptyset^4_3$ at the end of measure 16 elides the resolution to B major. The E-dominant seventh occurs within the larger context of these elisions.

Chopin places the F♮ in the bass (measure 14) one half note earlier than in the corresponding place in the first phrase (measure 3), intensifying the chromatic drive to the X-chord. With the elision of B major and arrival of $ii\emptyset^4_3$, the melodic structure shifts to the inner voice and the superposed embellishing melody takes the soprano.

Chapter 8 Modulation 259

Example 8–41: Chopin, Prelude in E Minor, Op. 28, No. 4, middleground, measures 13–16

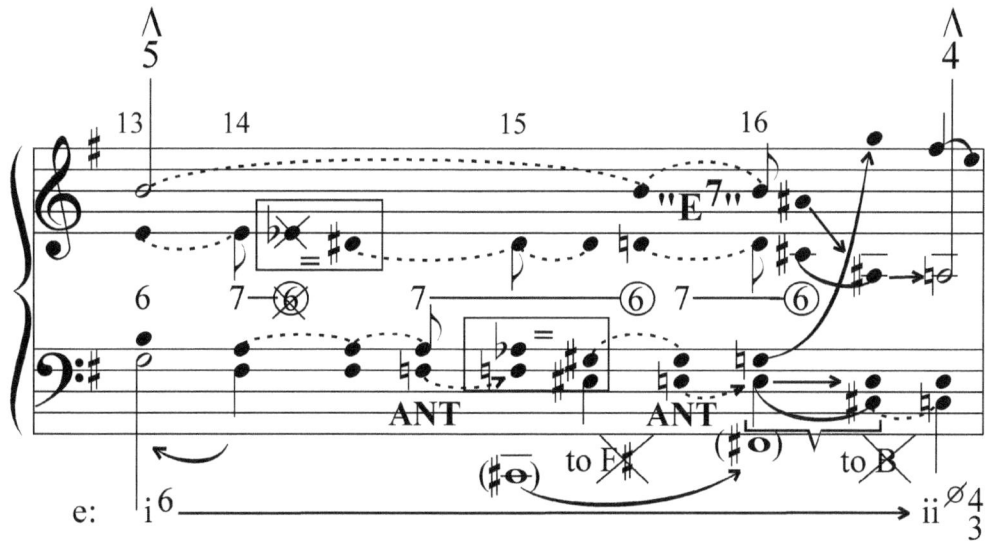

Example 8–42 shows how the register changes in the second phrase suggest a thickening of the texture to five or more voices. A re-voicing of the prolonging position of the X-chord, ii$\emptyset{}^4_3$, is withheld (see the crossed-out chord in 8–42) to effect the superposed embellishing melody, creating unprepared multiple suspensions over the passing tonic ${}^6_4$.

Example 8–42: addressing the passing tonic ${}^6_4$ with multiple unprepared suspensions

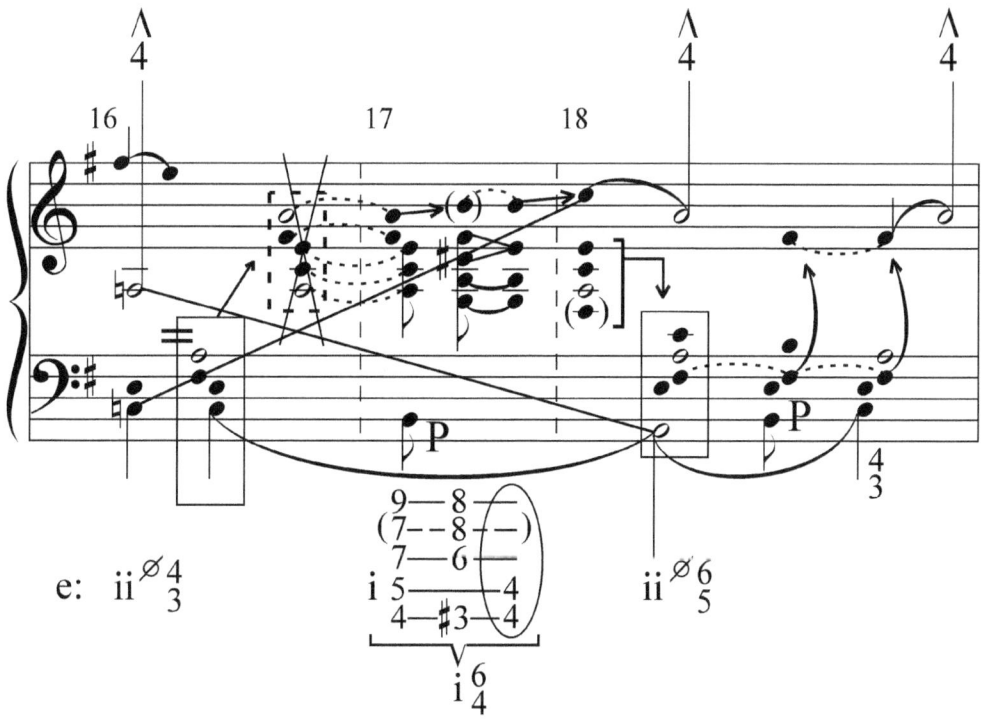

260　Chapter 8　Modulation

The expansion of the texture is indicated with split alto and tenor voices in example 8–43. On the third quarter of measure 16, the embellishing melody begins its superposition in the double prime register. In the course of the melody's descending trajectory, it runs through the chord tones of the passing tonic, finding D♯ and D♮ as nonharmonic tones. F♯, the governing tone for the nonstructural soprano, takes an octave transfer, reaching the prime register in the second half of measure 18.

F♯ moves down within the framework of two voice exchanges that prolong the X-chord between the bass and the structural inner voice. The arrival of F♯ in the prime register echoes the close of the first phrase; it also helps to shore up the prolongation of the X-chord and to prepare for the next structural move, namely, the entry of the THD, which provides consonant support for both scale degrees 3 and 2 of the background.

Example 8–43: Chopin, Prelude in E Minor, Op. 28, No. 4, middleground, measures 17–25

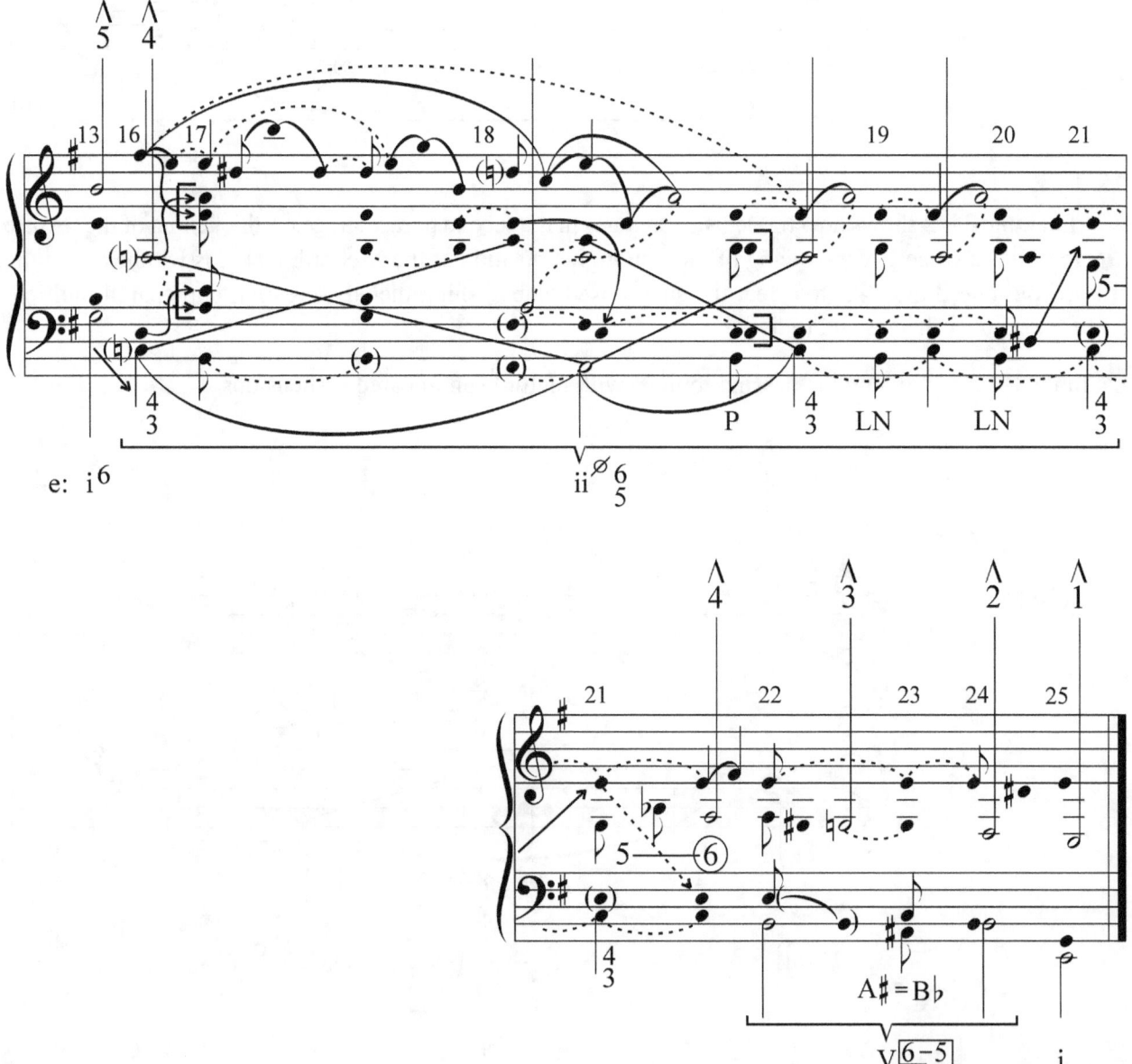

In measure 23, we have the GA6 in its sounding third inversion. Showing the B♭ bass as A♯, 8–43 telegraphs both the identity of the chord as an augmented 6th type (expressed here as a diminished 3rd, A♯/C) and its function as a lower-neighbor to the THD. The melodic structure continues within the inner voice, closing below the superposed soprano, which doubles governing scale degree 1.

Local Harmony and Structure in Prokofiev's "Classical Symphony," Op. 25, III

The first twelve measures of the third movement of Prokofiev's Classical Symphony, entitled Gavotta: Non troppo allegro, demonstrate an abrupt shift between keys, harmonic elisions producing deceptive cadences and resolutions, and some elegant uses of pivot chords. Consisting of three related phrases, a a ' a ", the opening section is closed off by an HPAC in measure 12, resulting in a three phrase group. Although Prokofiev's harmonic language is decidedly modern (within the confines of its tonal framework), the general types of compositional strategies cited above are not unlike those practiced by Joseph Haydn, the Russian composer's self-acknowledged inspiration for the Classical Symphony.

As shown in the reduction below (example 8–44), the G-major chord in measure 4 appears as the cadential chord for the first phrase, which ends with a contrapuntal half-cadence. Ultimately, the G-major triad constitutes a harmonic embellishing chord underlying scale degree 4 of the melodic structure.

In measure 1, Prokofiev plunges immediately into a distant key of secondary borrowing, B major. But not only is the resolution to B major withheld, as illustrated in 8–44, there is no preparation for its potential arrival, no prior relationship with the old key, D major. Rather, the composer moves from a D-major triad to a C-major triad. The latter becomes N^6 of B major, the X-chord for the progression in measures 1–4.

The cadential $^6_4$ on F♯ in measure 2 both confirms and intensifies the motion to B major. The gesture is denied its resolution by a deceptive cadence (DC) involving the G-major triad, (♭VI) of B major and IV of D major. The chord forming the contrapuntal cadence for the first phrase thus serves as a pivot back to the tonic triad (D). The ascending parallel 6ths leading to the cadence are prepared melodically with the outlined 6th in measure 2 (F♯ up to D♯), which is then repeated with the (supporting) harmonic 6ths in measure 3 (C♯ up to A♯).

Example 8–44: Prokofiev, Classical Symphony, Op. 25, III, measures 1–4, phrase a (reduction)

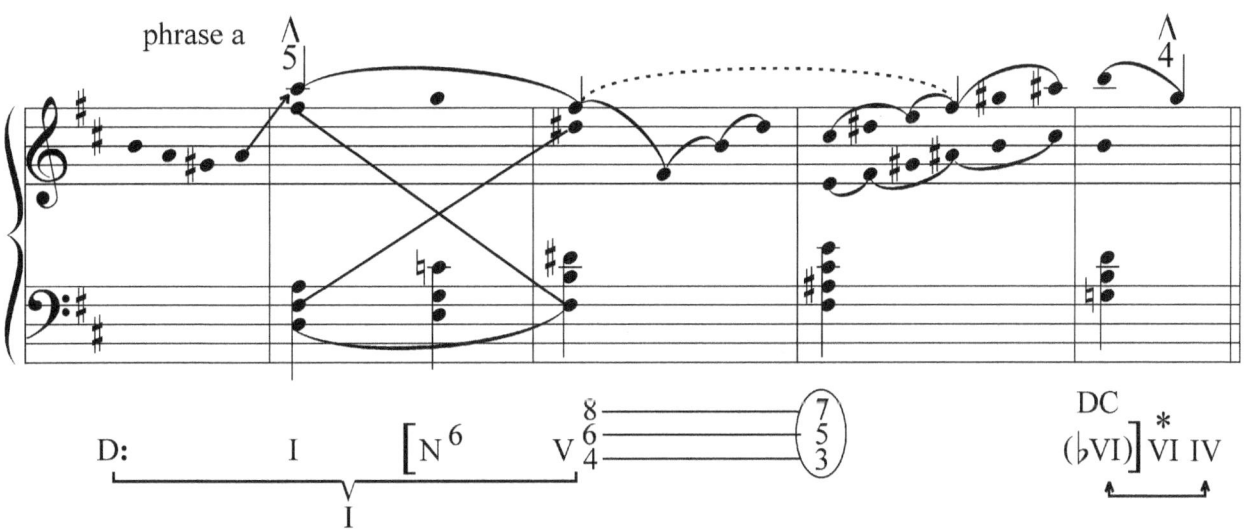

The Chord Scale and the Mode Scale

Phrases a and a' exhibit two different types of scale formation and prolongation. The first type is found within the cadential $^6_4$ of phrase a, whereas the second begins phrase a'. As seen in example 8–45 below (and in 8–44 above), an ascending stepwise melody moves through the tones of the completed cadential $^6_4$. The plus signs identify three nonharmonic tones that pass between the chordal elements of the F♯-dominant seventh: D♯, G♯, and B.

The stepwise collection of tones making up this melodic complex demonstrate two *partial* scales unfolding in parallel 6ths: C♯–D♯–E–F♯–G♯–A♯ and E–F♯–G♯–A♯–B–C♯. Extending each scale to its upper octave (see the pitches in parentheses) produces a complete profile of half steps and whole steps for the Dorian and Lydian modes respectively. However, it should be noted that these scales have nothing to do with either non-major-minor mode. Rather, each melodic gesture prolongs the F♯-dominant seventh as a *chord-unfolding scale*, which in this text is termed a "chord scale."

Example 8–45: the chord scale in Prokofiev, Op. 25, III

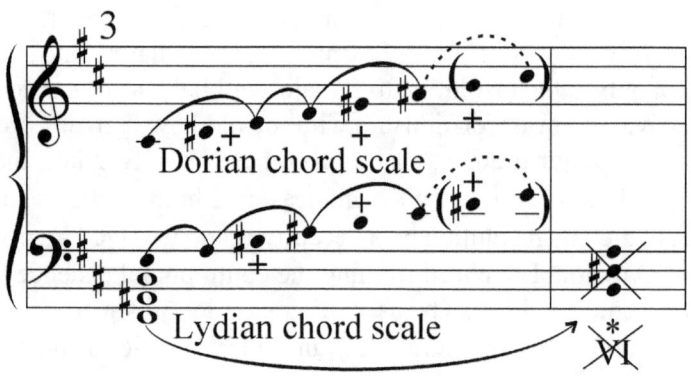

A chord scale is a stepwise assemblage of pitches consisting of tones belonging to a single chord and tones which function as *nonessential* elements, that is, nonharmonic tones passing between members of the prolonged chord. A chord scale, therefore, projects one and one chord *only*; it may be partial, with fewer than seven tones. Moreover, the chord scale does it have to begin with the keynote.

A "mode scale," on the other hand, is a melodic expression exhibiting a stepwise assemblage of diatonic pitches appropriate to the mode, beginning on the keynote and *implicitly* projecting the chord qualities in the seven different areas of the mode. Both triads and sevenths formed in these areas are demonstrated in Chapter 1.

As we shall see later in this chapter, the second phrase of the third movement begins with a mode scale prolonging the tonic chord (example 8–47). The scale unfolds over a sequenced progression containing the tonic triad, a retroactive dominant, and a deceptive resolution (DR). (In 8–47, the D-major mode scale begins on the keynote as the fifth of the G-major triad. Subsequently, the scale proceeds to the tonic in measure 5.)

The Harmonic Minor Chord Scale

In the foregoing section, we observed an F♯-dominant seventh prolonged with a chord-unfolding succession of tones (in parallel 6ths) having nothing to do with the modes the intervallic patterns mimic. Pausing our exploration of local harmony and structure in the Prokofiev, but staying with the topic of the chord scale, let us consider one additional scale emerging from this prolongational technique. In the present instance, the content of the chord scale exhibits the single most distinctive characteristic of the harmonic minor: an augmented 2nd between variables ♭6 and ♯7.

In minor, if a raised or lowered variable scale degree is contained within the chord, then its quality is determined by the selection of the appropriate tone according to the ascending and descending operations of the *melodic minor*. There is always one variable-determining voice while the other voices are non-variable-determining. Moreover, the melody is not always the variable-determining voice, for this important function can also be in any secondary voice. In other words, the principal melodic voice may surrender the variable-determining function to a secondary voice. (Realize that the bass can also be a secondary voice.)

Now, in Chapter 7, we learned that some operations such as the sequence may result in certain idiomatic usages in minor that conflict with the normal tendency of raised variables to ascend and lowered variables to descend. It is possible to find a raised variable descending and a lowered variable ascending. In the sequence, both the prolongation of the way from one chord to another and the prolongation of a single chord have the potential to produce exceptional practices in minor.

Chord-unfolding (prolongation) within a single chord can lead to one very significant idiomatic usage in minor. If the quality of the chord depends on a variable-determining voice, then the melodic expression of that chord may include an augmented 2nd between variables ♭6 and ♯7, the harmonic minor's most noticeable property.

As shown in 8–46, the quality of the subdominant as a minor triad is determined by the use of ♭6 (A♭) as an upper neighbor to scale degree 5. So fixed, variable 7 assumes the status of a nonessential (non-chord) tone and may take the *raised* form (B♮) as a melodic intensifier leading upwards to scale degree 1 (8).

The major triad quality of the dominant is determined by the selection of ♯7 as a lower neighbor to the tonic. Variable 6 is rendered nonessential and may therefore select its *lowered* form as a melodic intensifier to scale degree 5. Either chord configuration, whose quality has been established by the variable-determining voice, produces a partial harmonic minor scale unfolding within either a single subdominant or dominant chord.

Example 8–46: the harmonic minor chord scale

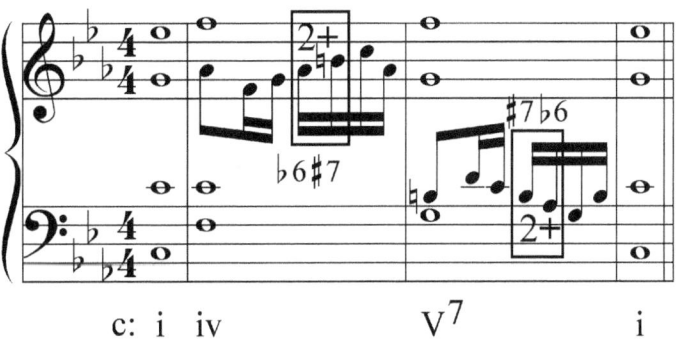

And so, in terms of the characteristic features and patterns of the minor mode, the intervallic profile of the "harmonic" minor grows out of *melodic* (linear) necessities. In other words, the harmonic minor is a melodic-unfolding scale; its harmonic component is drawn from another source: the melodic minor.

The "melodic" minor draws its pitch content from the combination of harmonic and contrapuntal techniques informing the music of the common practice period. The melodic minor is where we find the harmony.

Local Harmony and Structure in Prokofiev's "Classical Symphony," Op. 25, III (Return)

As shown in example 8–47, Prokofiev initiates the second phrase (measures 5–9) of the third movement with a mode scale descending from D and supported by a melodic and harmonic pattern treated sequentially. The D scale reaches its lower octave on the first quarter of measure 6. The cadential G-major triad at the end of the first phrase continues its prolongation with the pick up to measure 5 in the second (phrase).

Ultimately, the second phrase prolongs the tonic. The G major triad in measure 4, which produces both the deceptive cadence and the pivot back to D major, assumes status as a harmonic embellishing chord providing a chordal link between phrases a and a'. The D-major triad in measure 5 supports the first appearance of governing scale degree 3 (F♯).

The second half of the phrase ends with a deceptive cadence on the first quarter of measure 8 (DC). A mode scale moves through the key of F♯ until its tonic becomes the third of a D-major triad: ♭VI of f♯ minor and I of the main-level key. In the first two phrases, then, Prokofiev uses the submediant chord to effect the deceptive cadence: (♭VI) of B major (a key of secondary borrowing) and ♭VI of f♯ minor (the mediant key area of D major).

Example 8–47: Prokofiev, Classical Symphony, Op. 25, III, measures 5–8, phrase a' (reduction)

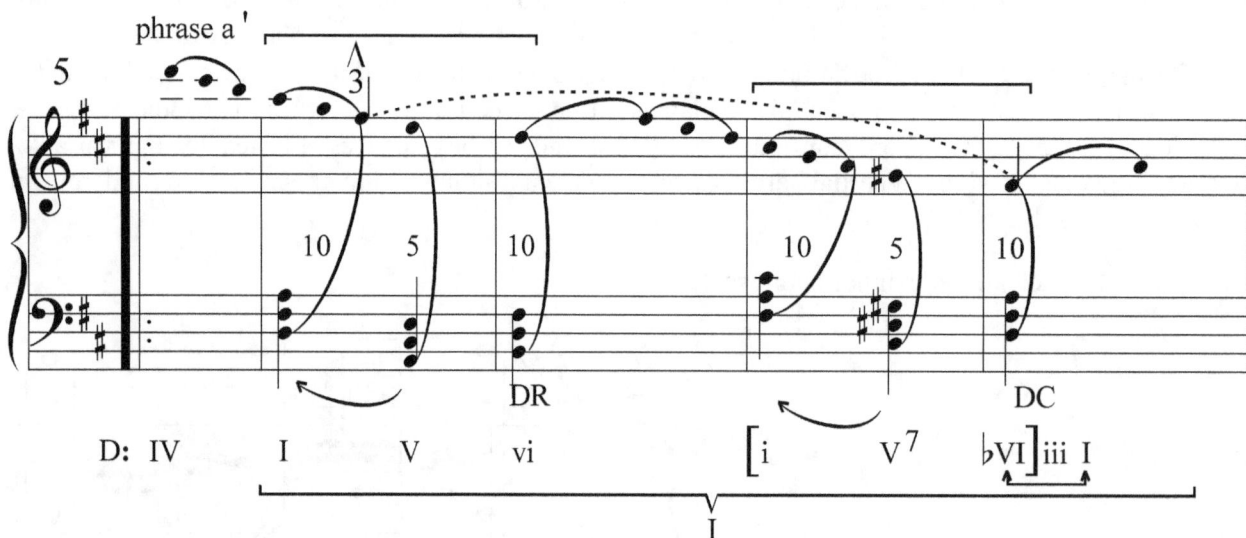

The three-chord pattern in measures 5–6 and its sequential treatment in measures 7–8 effect octave transfers from D and F♯ in the top voice (see 8–47). The pattern of the falling 4th-rising 2nd, which supports a 10–5–10 motion in the outer voices, is derived from the descending 5—6 sequence discussed earlier in Chapters 4 and 7 (see above, pp. 77–79, and p. 206 in particular, example 7–89).

As we have observed, the retroactive dominant grows out of this progression. The lower tone of the 6th of the descending 5—6 is replaced by the octave, forming consequently a triad in root position. Assuming its harmonic configuration as a root-position variant of the descending 5—6, each retroactive dominant proceeds subsequently to a chord whose root is one third below the chord that preceded the retroactive dominant.

The descending 3rd action in the bass becomes an integral component of the descending 5—6. Moreover, the harmonic leap of the falling 4th from the first chord to the retroactive dominant (the second chord of the pattern) helps to bring out the respective roots upon which the descending 3rds stand. (The slurs in the bass clef of example 8–48a mark the descending 3rds.)

Now, the first chord of the pattern is the D-major tonic (example 8–48a). In order to reach the D-major triad as the first chord of the pattern a second time, the sequence and its descending-3rd motion must run through two complete cycles of the octave. Since the D major chord is a retroactive dominant (the second chord of the pattern) when the cycle reaches the first octave, Prokofiev takes a less tedious course, withholding five repetitions of the progression so that D major returns not as a retroactive dominant but as the first chord of the pattern. The contraction of the descending 3rds is effected by the downward leap of a 4th in the bass to F♯, which would have been the next bass note in the sequence even without the omission (8–48a).

In example 8–48a, the brackets identify the pattern of falling 4ths and rising 2nds in the bass. The box enclosing the roots of the sequential chords indicates the omitted octave. The solid slurs outline the motions of the 3rd and 4th.

Example 8–48: Prokofiev, Classical Symphony, Op. 25, III, measures 5–8, middleground

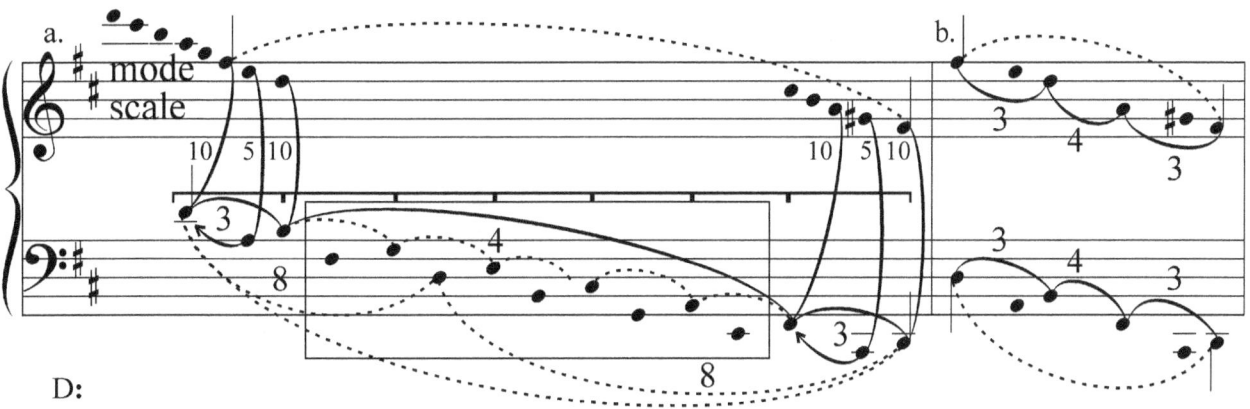

In 8–48b, a succession of 10ths in the outer voices (D/F♯, B/D, F♯/A, D/F♯) underlies the sequence in the second phrase and the prolongation of the D-major tonic. The bass unfolds through a 3rd, 4th, and 3rd (D–B–F♯–D) while the soprano moves through the same intervallic pattern (F♯–D–A–F♯).

The third phrase, shown in example 8–49, begins as a continuation of the D-major tonic supporting F♯ in the top voice. Prokofiev deceives us once again by directing the motion towards the tonic's leading-tone key area, C♯ major, a diatonically distant key with a difference of five accidentals. Within this brief framework of tonal ambiguity, a deceptive resolution (DR) and subsequent HPAC in the main-level key brings this three phrase group to a close.

The THD⁷ of D major (an A-dominant seventh) becomes an augmented 6th chord addressing the cadential $^6_4$ of C♯ major (8–49, measure 9, beat 4). Since the augmented 6th resolves to a major tonic, we refer to the chord as a German doubly augmented 6th (GDA6). In the key and mode of C♯ major, the actual spelling of the GDA6 is A C♯ D × F ×. At first, the GDA6 serves as a pivot to C♯; but after the completion of the cadential $^6_4$, it forms a deceptive resolution while also becoming the approach chord (the THD⁷) for the HPAC of the main-level key.

In the soprano, the cadence for the third phrase contains the leading tone (C♯) substituting for scale degree 2 (E) which takes the inner-voice. The cadential $^6_4$ of C♯ major in measure 11 unfolds through all of the tones of the THD⁷, except for D♯, its chord fifth. Since the second part of the cadential $^6_4$ (G♯ B♯ D♯ F ×) resolves to a chord whose root is one half step above it (that is, the GDA6 of C♯ major and the THD⁷ of D major, spelled as A C♯ E G), there is always the potential for parallel 5ths.

Most of the time, composers avoid parallel 5ths, particularly in the outer voices. Ultimately, omitting D♯ and placing E in the inner voice circumvents the potential problems between the cadential $^6_4$ and the GDA6 of C♯ major. The actual approach to D, governing scale degree 1, comes from the superposed inner-voice C♯. Before completing the melodic structure in measure 12, C♯ forms the goal tone for the deceptive resolution in D-major's leading-tone key area.

Example 8–49: Prokofiev, Classical Symphony, Op. 25, III, measures 9–12, phrase a ʺ (reduction)

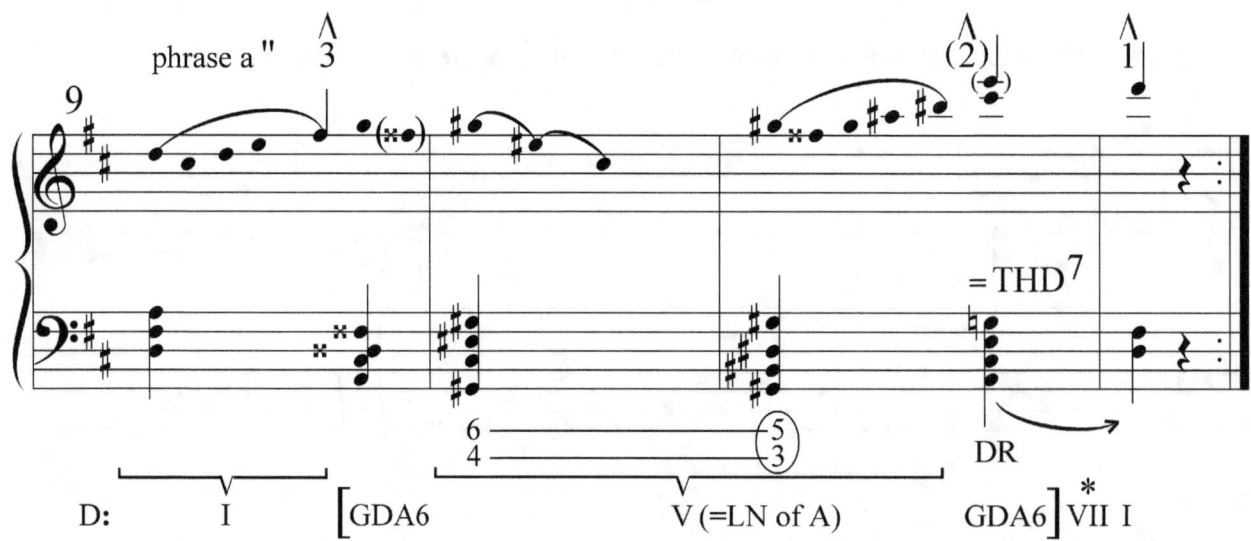

Examples 8–50 and 8–51 below display background and middleground readings for measures 1–12 respectively. The G-major triad in measure 4 is a chord of harmonic prolongation supporting scale degree 4 of the melodic structure, one of two types of double-function chords. Here, the G-major triad constitutes the first type of double-function chord (DF), as defined earlier in Chapter 6. (See above, p. 158.)

The triad in measure 4, in any other circumstance, would fulfill the function of harmonic prolongation at the middleground rank; however, in present role of supporting a governing melodic tone (G), this harmonic chord becomes an important element of the background framework. The G-major triad is elevated to the background rank as a harmonic-prolonging chord with added structural significance.

Example 8–50 shows a BHP supporting a BMP from scale degree 5. The initial tonic is prolonged by the double-function chord. Serving a role similar to that of the contrapuntal-structural chord, this use of double function constitutes a kind of substitution for the X-chord. (It is also possible for the double-function chord to exist as a regular X-chord member of a harmonic or contrapuntal progression. Described in Chapter 6 as an X-DF chord, the harmony supports a top voice whose governing tone has been replaced with a prolonging-embellishing tone. This otherwise intermediate chord of harmony assumes hybrid status as a chord of weakened harmonic influence supporting a decorating tone instead of a structural tone.)

Example 8–50: Prokofiev, Classical Symphony, Op. 25, III, background, measures 1–12

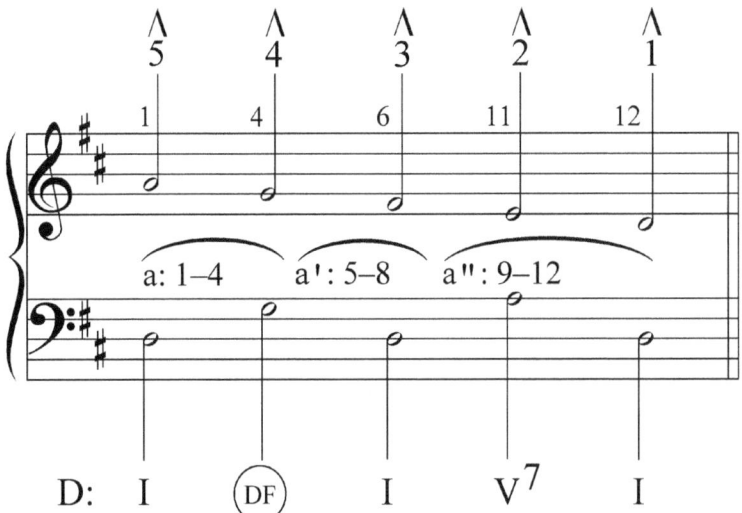

Example 8–51: Prokofiev, Classical Symphony, Op. 25, III, middleground, measures 1–12

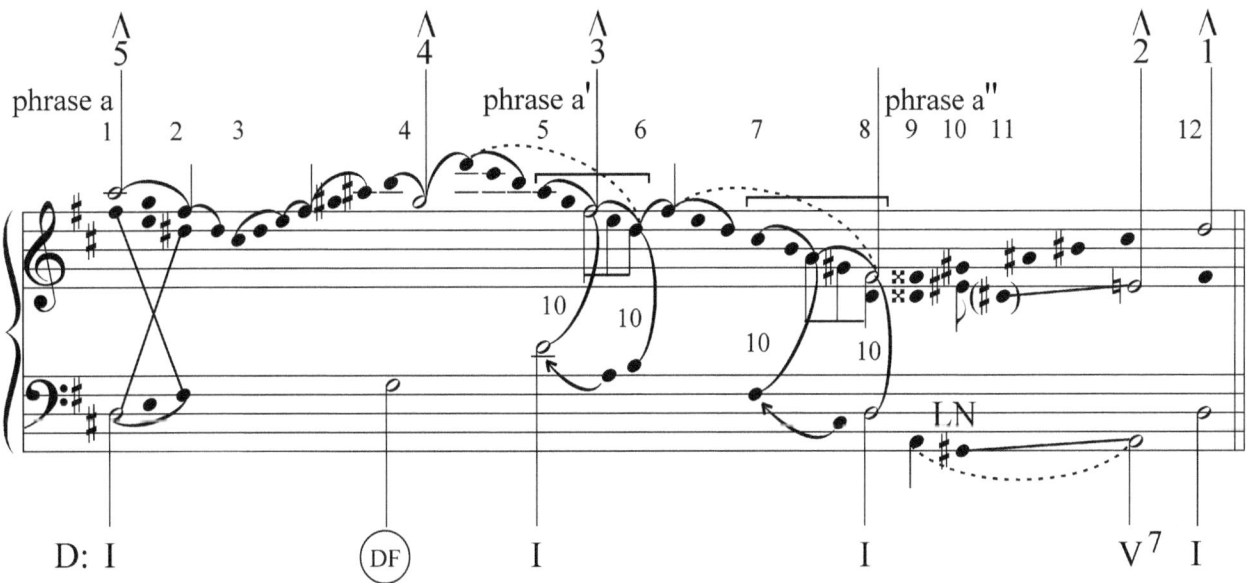

Modulation Is Prolongation

During our discussion of the Brahms Intermezzo, we noted that the onset and completion of foreground events may not always coincide with a tonal composition's structural operations (see above, p. 240). And while key changes may reinforce the harmonic and contrapuntal actions of the background, they serve within the ranks of the foreground and middleground to prolong the progression of the highest order. For regardless of how elaborate the modulations are within a tonal work, they exist primarily if not solely as prolongation.

To be sure, there are notable instances in which structure and prolongation find a convergence in modulation. For example, in the Brahms Intermezzo, the composer connects section A (A major) to section B (f♯ minor) by reinterpreting C♯, the chord third of the main-level tonic, as the fifth of the submediant: a pivot-tone modulation (see above, p. 238). But in addition to its role in effecting the modulation to the relative minor, the C♯ pivot constitutes the primary tone from which the melodic structure proceeds.

Chapter 9   Chords Of "Higher Power"

This chapter examines the additions of the 9th, 11th, and 13th above the root of the triad and its chord seventh. Superimposing 3rds above the fifth of the triad increases the chord's sonority, heightening its dissonance.

The intervals of the 9th and 11th are dissonant with the root and usually seek a downward resolution (or move upwards through linear inflection). The 13th is consonant with the root, but it is dissonant with some of the other chord tones. As we shall see, these higher extensions complicate both the voice leading and the voicing.

The presence of the dissonant 7th in particular can have a significant effect on the behavior of the chord and its application. For example, adding a minor 7th to a major triad produces a strong key-defining dominant seventh and, as a consequence, a variety of options for excursions into lower-level keys via pivot modulation.

It should be noted, however, that any tertian extension beyond the seventh has no effect on the operation of the chord. In other words, regardless of how elaborate the harmony becomes when the chord also carries a ninth, eleventh, and/or thirteenth, the underlying function of the triad and its chord seventh never changes.

Every seventh chord in root position has two components: the basic triad and the interval of the 7th above the root, forming the seventh element. We term the basic triad of the seventh chord the "root triad," consisting of the root, third, and fifth.

The seventh, ninth, eleventh, and/or thirteenth all exist as extensions of "higher power," standing above the identifiers of the triad (its chord tones). To be sure, the chord seventh should be distinguished from the other higher powers because its addition to the root triad has the potential to alter and/or even intensify its identity and function. We therefore refer to the real seventh chord as the "root seventh chord."

General Considerations

There are five ways for extensions of the ninth, eleventh, and/or thirteenth to occur (the first four of which exist as contrapuntal operations):
  (1) as suspended tones or passing tones,
  (2) as nonharmonic tones that resolve,
  (3) as nonharmonic tones that do not resolve (that is, "frozen" nonharmonic tones),
  (4) occasionally, as structural melodic tones,
  (5) and finally, as the result of stacking one or more 3rds above the chord seventh (commonly found in jazz and commercial music, these enriched sonorities are more chordal than contrapuntal in origin).
However, each extension above the root seventh, regardless of its origin,
  (1) must be expressed as a compound interval. In other words, the ninth, eleventh, and thirteenth must stand at the interval of a 9th, 11th, and 13th above the root, and,
  (2) must be supported by the tertian extension immediately below it. In other words, the ninth needs the seventh, the eleventh needs the ninth, and the thirteenth needs the eleventh.

When these two conditions are *not* met, the extra tones in the chord are usually the result of some kind of additive construction rather than from the superimposition of thirds above the root seventh. And so, both the origin and the authenticity of the chord remain as central questions confronting our investigation of these sonorities of higher power.

And if the chord contains one or more *borrowed* tones above its seventh, we do not enclose the Roman numeral in parentheses to represent those pitches. Parentheses are used only when the root triad or seventh is a chord of primary borrowing. If, for example, inflecting a higher extension produces a borrowed tone, do not represent that pitch with parentheses around the chord symbol.

The Governing Ninth Resolving within the Succeeding Chord

The music literature of the nineteenth century (and beyond) demonstrates the use of the ninth chord supporting the melodic structure at the interval of the 9th above the chord's root. In such cases, the structural ninth exists as an upper component of a real seventh chord rather than as part of an apparent sonority.

Now, we know that a chord of harmony may be used to support a dissonant 7th as part of the BMP. Example 9–1 shows a two-progression framework with a descent from scale degree 5 in the top voice. The THD of the first progression supports structural scale degree 4 (F), a dissonant 7th (measure 2, beat 1). (Example 9–2 below illustrates Tchaikovsky's use of the governing ninth.)

The seventh of the subdominant in measure 1 of 9–1 moves down by step to become the fifth of the succeeding dominant in measure 2 (E—D). By contracting the conventional 8—7 motion in the soprano, the ninth component of the subdominant (G) proceeds directly to the chord seventh of the dominant (F) instead of holding on to form an octave above the G bass in measure 2: thus, the 9th dissonance of one chord resolves into the 7th dissonance of the next. Since the resolution of the ninth occurs *within the succeeding chord*, rather than within the same chord, the usage of the higher extension is *real*. A ninth resolving within the same chord (9—8) is either a passing tone, a neighbor tone, or a suspended tone and therefore *apparent*.

Example 9–1: the governing ninth

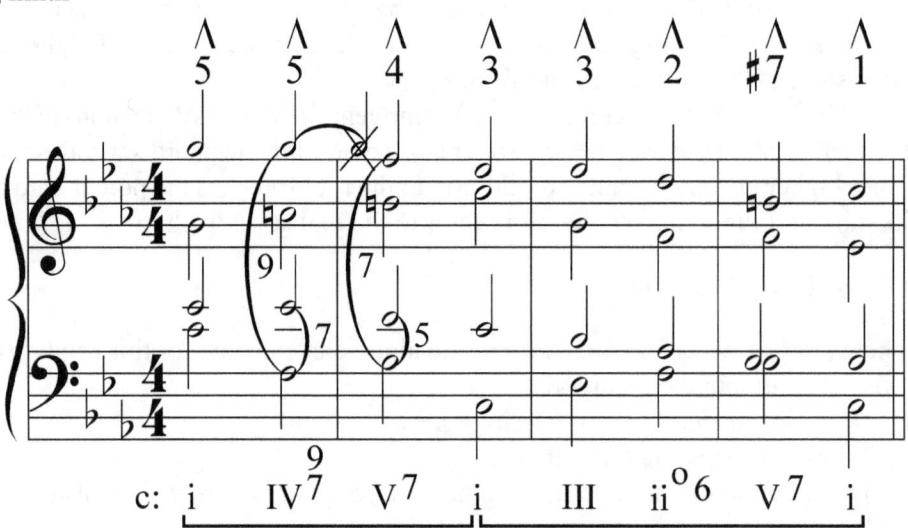

Example 9–2 demonstrates the harmonic framework for the first two phrases of Tchaikovsky's Nutcracker Suite, Op. 71a (a parallel period spanning measures 1–8). Some of the analytical annotations in the score are shown as dotted lines and slurs. The structural events for the excerpt are marked by elongated stems in the outer voices and by carets for scale degrees in the soprano. Tones enclosed in parentheses are implied.

The composition begins with an initial ascent to F, the first structural tone (measure 2, beat 2). The initial ascent also occurs in the second phrase. In the first two measures of both phrases, the soprano unfolds through the tonic chord while pedal-embellishing harmony prolongs B♭ in the bass.

In measure 4, the technique of interruption stops the melodic descent on scale degree 2 (C). An applied ninth, [V$^9_7$]V, addresses the THD in the pre-interruption segment. Scale degree 3 (D) in the top voice (measure 4) forms the ninth of the applied dominant. Most notably, [V$^9_7$]V constitutes a harmonic-prolonging chord with added structural significance, a double-function chord (DF). The ninth takes a *real* resolution within the succeeding dividing dominant. A subdominant DF chord also appears in the post-interruption segment, serving there as a harmonic embellishing chord (HEMB) supporting scale degree 4.

Chapter 9 Chords of Higher Power 271

Example 9–2: Tchaikovsky, Nutcracker Suite, Op. 71a, Overture, measures 1–8

Resolution of the Ninth within the Same Chord

In an excerpt from Gabriel Fauré's art song *Après un rêve*, we examine the operations of five ninths (three of which are in a series). At the outset, it would be well to recognize one particularly challenging aspect of the French language for text setting: its nasal tone quality, an attribute that tends to discourage melismas (an expression of many notes per syllable). Syllabic settings (one note per syllable), on the other hand, are usually more attractive in French.

Although there are some melodic flourishes in *Après un rêve*, the vocal part is mostly syllabic in style and, in terms of the middleground framework, a secondary voice. Thus, the structural activity of the excerpt occurs in the accompaniment rather than in the vocal part (see example 9–6 below).

In measure 17 (9–3), the minor tonic takes a passing 9th on beat 3 in the inner voice (the 9th accompanies a passing 7th). Subsequently, there is a sequence of three applied dominant ninths that point respectively towards the subtonic, mediant, and submediant. The fifth ninth occurs as an upper neighbor to G in measure 22 (9–3).

As stated, after the passing ninth, Fauré deploys a descending 5th sequence consisting of three applied dominants. G, the fifth of the C-minor tonic becomes the first ninth in measure 18, $[V^9_7]\flat VII$. The ninth is apparent, as it resolves to F within the same chord on beat 3 (an F-dominant seventh).

Measure 18 marks the beginning of a series of three interlocking sevenths supporting three suspended ninths. Each 7th interval resolves to a 3rd within the next chord, whereas the first two ninths move to octaves within the same chord:

(1) in the first use of the ninth, $[V^9_7]\flat VII$'s chord seventh (E$\flat$) proceeds to $[V^9_7]III$'s third (D), while

(2) the fifth of $[V^9_7]\flat VII$ (C) is suspended into $[V^9_7]III$, yielding the second ninth in the series: B$\flat$/C. The chord third of $[V^9_7]\flat VII$ moves chromatically to $[V^9_7]III$'s seventh in measure 19, a succession from A$\natural$ to A$\flat$.

Instead of resolving the A$\flat$ to G immediately (the chord third of the next applied dominant, $[V^9_7]\flat VI$), Fauré extends the dissonance by suspending the A$\flat$ into measure 20, producing a 4th above E$\flat$, the root of $[V^9_7]\flat VI$. Hence, the third suspended ninth in the segment is part of a double suspension.

The resolution of the third ninth might have been real were it not for its unusual treatment. Fauré takes the F$\natural$ ninth to F$\flat$ on beat 3 of measure 20 within $[V^9_7]\flat VI$. The F$\flat$ constitutes a lowered ninth above the E$\flat$ chord root ($\flat$9). Enharmonically E$\natural$, the F$\flat$ anticipates the raised fifth above the A$\flat$ root of the next chord, $[V^{\sharp 5}]ii$. Without this anticipation, the ninth would resolve directly to the raised fifth of the succeeding degree-inflected sonority.

On beat 3 of measure 21, Fauré breaks the pattern of applied dominants and drops down a tritone in the bass (instead of a perfect 5th) to the root of the half-diminished supertonic, which serves as a modal dominant to the V^7 of the first progression. Upon reaching the tonic in measure 24, the first progression ends and the second begins (see example 9–6).

Example 9–3: Fauré, *Après un rêve*, measures 17–24

274   Chapter 9 Chords of Higher Power

The second phrase (and progression) moves from a C-minor triad to a B♭-minor triad in first inversion. Ultimately, the latter becomes [iv⁶]iv, f minor being the immediate goal of motion (example 9–4). B♭ minor's chord third and fifth, D♭ and F, are incomplete upper neighbors to the preceding tonic's root and third, C and E♭. F minor, the X-chord key area for the second progression, has its own lower-level incomplete SCP.

And so, while the text is referencing "skies" and "clouds" ("Les cieux pour nous entr'ouvraient leurs nuges..."), the harmony takes a sharp turn away from c minor with the appearance of the B♭-minor triad. This shift is followed by the momentary sound of an augmented triad in measure 26 (at "nuges") consisting of E♮ A♭ C. The formation of f minor's THD/CLT (E G B♭ C) on the second quarter removes the augmented triad as the A♭ proceeds to G, effecting the chord's 4—3 resolution.

As the second progression reaches its THD on beat 3 of measure 27, the leading tone (B♮) serves as a substitute for scale degree 2 (D♮); in the accompaniment, the structural line moves D♭–C–B♮ (examples 9–4 above and 9–6 below).

Example 9–4: Fauré, *Après un rêve*, measures 25–27

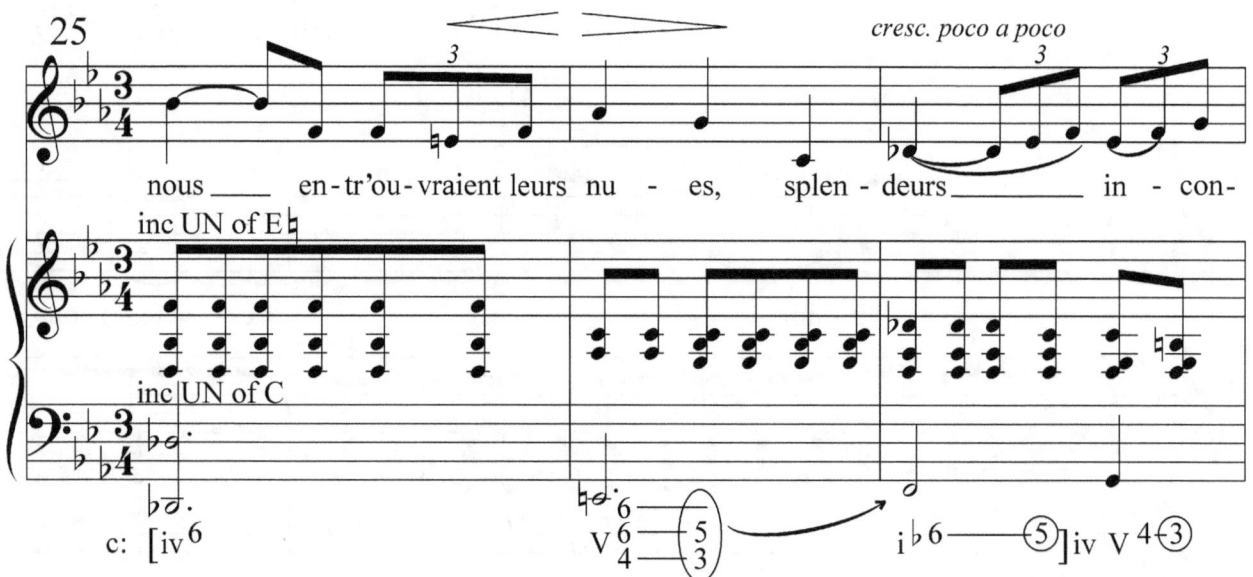

As shown in examples 9–5 and 9–6, the cadential chord for the second progression contains the Picardy third. The subsequent appearance of the Phrygian supertonic in measure 29, expressed as a seventh chord in second inversion, produces an extended passing motion between the tonic and supertonic; the latter sonority forms a harmonic embellishing chord (HEMB) prolonging the major tonic.

Fauré's use of the ninth grows out of passing, neighbor, and suspended tones; in the latter two, the dissonance resolves within the chord. Although the treatment of the sequential ninth is different in its third statement (examples 9–3 and 9–6, measures 20–21), all of the ninths in this excerpt are prolongational within the larger middleground framework.

The next question in our inquiry of these higher extensions above the root triad and seventh becomes: what is the nature of the operation when one or more of these higher powers do not proceed to their expected destinations? In other words, what happens when these tones are frozen, replacing their tones of resolution? (To be sure, the interval of the 13th is not dissonant with its chord root but that 13th is dissonant with the other components of the root triad and seventh.)

Example 9–5: Fauré, *Après un rêve*, measures 28–30

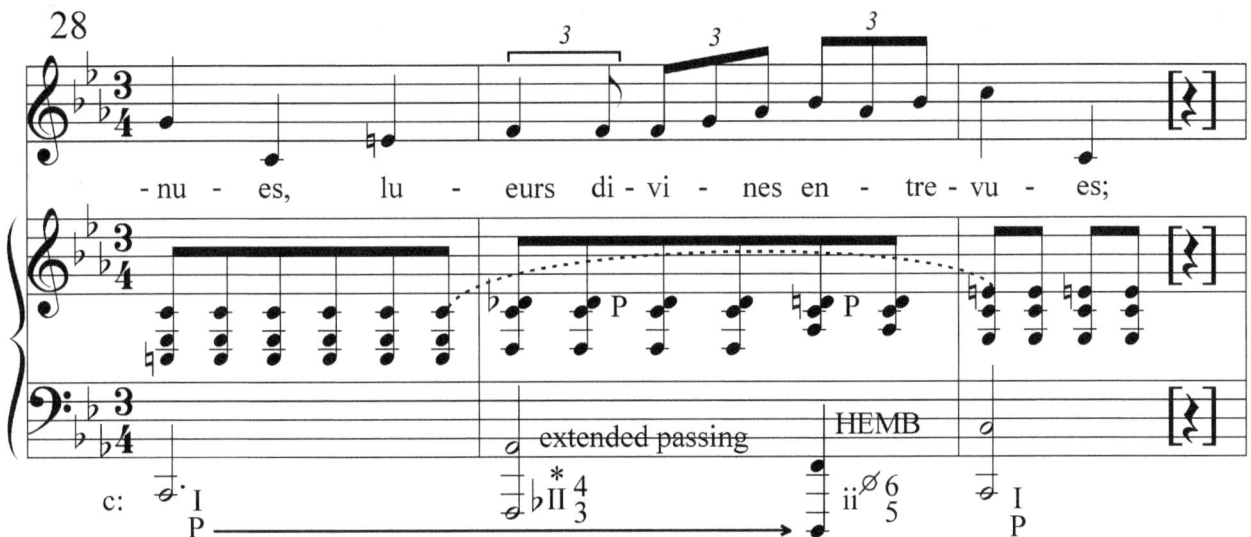

Example 9–6: Fauré,, measures 17–30, middleground

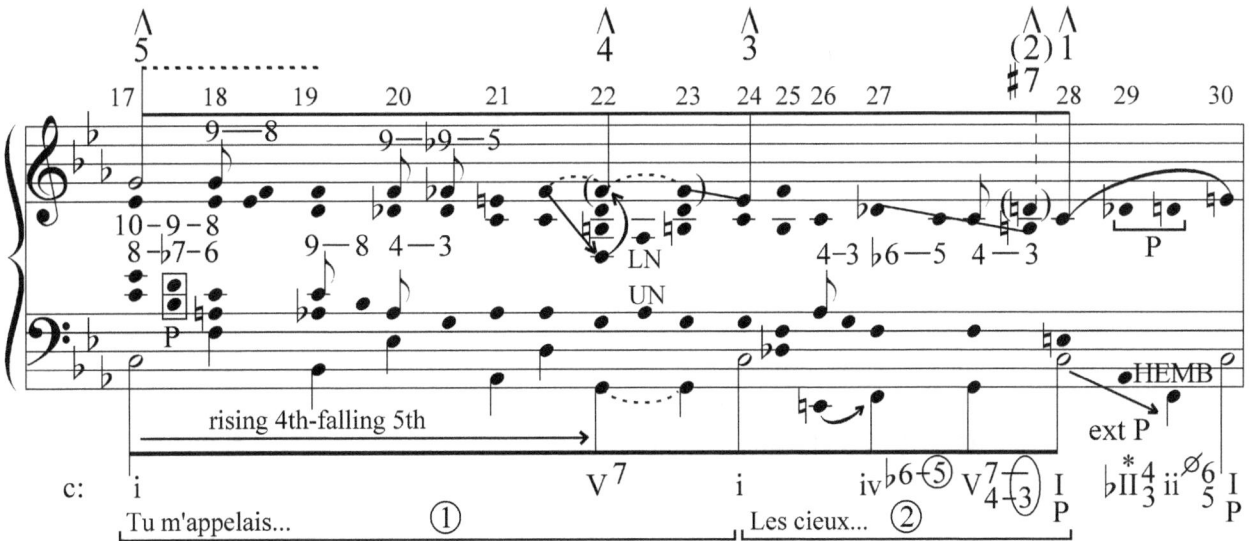

Frozen Nonharmonic Tones

In measure 20 of Fauré's *Après un rêve* (written in the 1870s), we observed a move from F to F♭ (9—♭9) above an E♭ bass that anticipates the raised chord fifth of [V$^{\sharp 5}$]ii (F♭ is reinterpreted as E♮, the fifth of the supertonic's dominant). In addition to carrying the lowered ninth, the sonority in measure 20 has a seventh (D♭) and a 4—3 suspension (A♭—G). The chord third sounds with the seventh and the lowered ninth. Presently, we shall consider a somewhat updated version of this sonority in a composition by Francis Poulenc.

The next example is a reduction of the final cadence for Poulenc's song *Ce doux petit visage* (written in 1939). Example 9–7a shows the basic disposition of the accompaniment (with E♭ spelled as D♯ and the bass dropped into the great register); 9–7b smooths out the voice leading and indicates the omitted tones.

As the piano brings the song to its conclusion, Poulenc uses the chord from *Après un rêve* in measure 27 as part of the cadential structure. However, in Poulenc's twentieth-century version, the sonority also has a thirteenth (C) that does not proceed to the chord fifth (at what would have been a 12th above the root). Rather, the thirteenth is frozen, in effect replacing the fifth (B). Poulenc ends the song with an unresolved ninth (B), replacing the tonic scale degree (A).

Does the sonority in measure 27 qualify as a thirteenth chord or as a seventh chord consisting of an added thirteenth? Without the eleventh, its status as a thirteenth chord is questionable. Moreover, notice that the ninth in the final tonic lacks the support of the chord seventh.

Example 9–7: Poulenc, *Ce doux petit visage*, measures 26–28 (reduction)

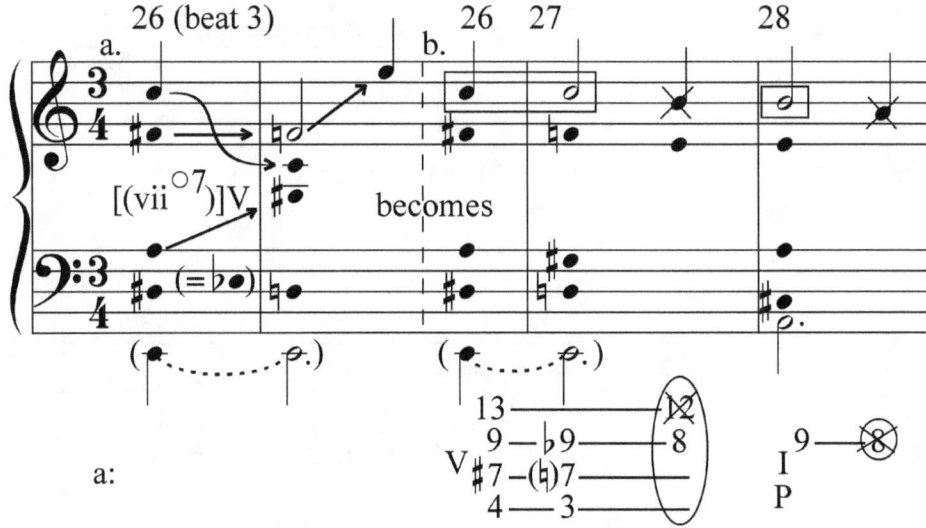

During the twentieth century, replacing chord tones with extensions of higher power becomes increasingly common. As these frozen tones are added to the root triad and seventh, some of the underlying members of the chord may be omitted in order to minimize the dissonance level and improve its sonority. Most notably, the chord third of what would otherwise be a major triad is often withheld if it has a diatonic eleventh attached.

Sometimes the third of the root triad and seventh is withheld by the composer for other reasons. For example, at the conclusion of the first waltz in *Valse nobles et sentimentales*, Maurice Ravel weakens the polarity between the G-major tonic and the dominant by withholding the leading tone (F♯), the chord third of the latter. In the penultimate measure of the waltz (not shown below in example 9–8 but located at *un peu pesant* in the score), Ravel *freezes* a G above the D dominant at the 11th and then carries that extension into the final tonic as its root.

As shown in example 9–8, the same operation occurs earlier in the waltz as part of a cadence in D major, the dominant. Thus, in measures 19–20, Ravel freezes D above A at the 11th, which then becomes the root of the dominant. If C♯ were to sound with the frozen D, the applied dominant of D major would present a considerably greater level of dissonance. Throughout the passage, the higher extensions are introduced into the texture above pedal embellishing harmonies over G, E, and A. Finally, in measures 17–18 in particular, the dominant of D major is extended up to the fifteenth (but without the chord third). (At the end of the waltz, the corresponding eleventh chord on A has C♮ instead of C♯ sounding with D.)

Example 9–8: Ravel, *Valses nobles et sentimentales*, I, measures 5–20

The Basic Anatomy of the Ninth, Eleventh, and Thirteenth

As we continue our study of the operations that produce chords of higher power, analyzing their various dispositions and then examining their actions within the texture, let us make a few general observations regarding the structure of these sonorities. With the potential for as many as seven tones to exist in the chord (a diatonic thirteenth chord yields all seven tones of the key and mode), both the disposition and number of available voices become central issues.

Ninth, eleventh, and thirteenth chords all exceed the range of the octave and therefore usually have their root in the bass, below all of the other tones of the sonority. Since any chord extension above the seventh stands as a compound interval above the root, most tertian-based sonorities of higher power cannot invert successfully. Chords beyond the seventh typically (but *not* invariably) mirror the spacing of the overtone series in which the lower partials of the sonority are closer to the bass and the higher partials are closer to the soprano. To be sure, the composer may generate a comparatively high level of dissonance in the chord by using an unusual position and spacing that does not follow the overtone series.

Occasionally, *chords of the ninth invert*. However, in four voices, their dispositions are restricted to first and third inversions. Second inversion, which has the ninth's fifth in the bass, requires at least five voices because the fifth is the only tone that can be omitted (in four voices). There can be no fourth inversion because the ninth never occurs below the root.

As we have said, the status of these higher extensions as real components of any sonority is based upon the understanding that each higher power also contains the tertian extension immediately below it. For without the support of the underlying extension, the ninth, eleventh, and/or thirteenth in the chord is likely the result of additive construction.

Distinguishing Real and Apparent Chords of Higher Power

Example 9–9 demonstrates three contrapuntal devices producing dissonant 7ths, 9ths, and 11ths above the root triad: the passing tone, the neighbor tone, and the suspended tone. Five voices (with the tenor divided) show the nonharmonic activity within and between each chord (circled tones in the figured bass identify chord members). As we have seen in the examples from the literature, most instances of 9ths, 11ths, and 13ths arise from one of these operations.

In measure 1 of 9–9, a passing tone effects a seventh above the tonic. The chord third suspends into measure 2 to produce a ninth moving to the root on beat 3. A chromatic lower neighbor (C♯) in measure 3 creates a raised eleventh in the soprano sounding with a diatonic and lowered ninth in the alto. The tenor anticipates the tonic's third, which occurs with a $\genfrac{}{}{0pt}{}{9-8}{7-8}$ suspension. Thus, the higher extensions of the ninth and eleventh resolve within their host chords.

Example 9–9

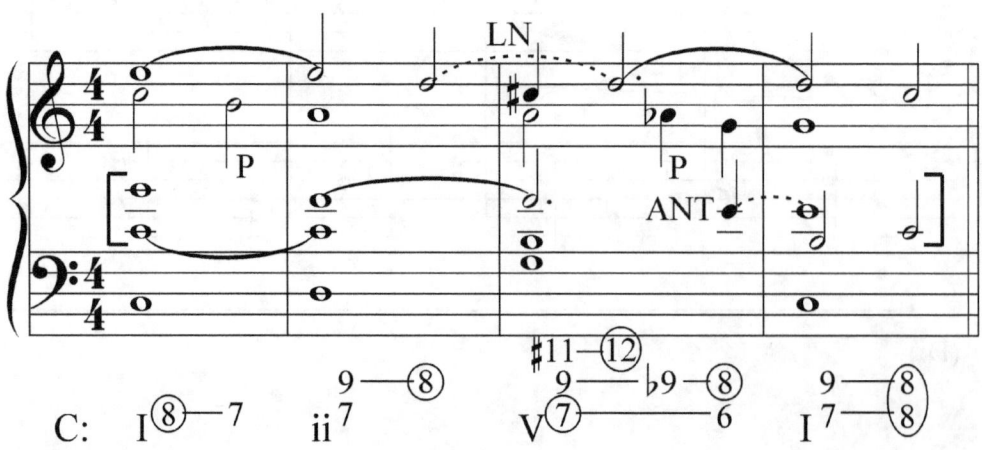

The formation of passing tones and suspended tones is an operation taught in the discipline of counterpoint. The systematic study of counterpoint is organized into five stages of compositional activity, known as species counterpoint, a pedagogical device that directs the student in how to produce melodic independence between voices. In so doing, the student learns how to use the nonharmonic tone. Presently, we are concerned with species two and four.

The passing tone is the principal technique employed in species two counterpoint; the suspension is practiced in species four. The location of the dissonance in each species is different, however. In species two, it occurs on the weak beat, whereas in species four, the dissonance is on the strong beat (the consonant resolution taking place on the subsequent weak beat)

In species two counterpoint, the note ratio between the voices is always 2:1, with one voice having twice as many notes as the other(s). In this species, it is possible to have a dissonance on a weak beat, on the second beat. That dissonance passes upwards or downwards from a weak to a strong beat above or below a stationary voice. Species two is shown in measure 1 of 9–9 above. Here, B fills in the interval of a descending 3rd, passing between C and A in the alto voice over a stationary C in the bass. (It should be noted that the weak beat in species two can also be a consonance.)

Throughout our study of dissonance, we have seen numerous examples in which both the dissonant 7th and 9th take downward resolutions from a strong to a weak beat above a stationary bass (7—6 and 9—8 motions). However, we also know that linear inflection may effect an upward resolution of a dissonance, a retardation resolution. Indeed, measure 4 of 9–9 above shows a re-articulated suspension in the divided tenor ascending 7—8.

Example 9–10 illustrates the difference between real and apparent 7ths and 9ths with various re-articulated suspensions in the soprano, that is, species four counterpoint. (As we have seen, suspended tones can also be tied instead of re-articulated.) Since there are only two voices, the sound is thin, especially in examples 9–10c and 9–10d. A better result requires at least three voices. (Parallel octaves should not occur in two voices, even when they are displaced to a weak beat, as in 9–10c.)

The bass notes in 9–10 imply chordal harmonies. The resolutions over the stationary basses in examples 9–10a and 9–10c are thus within the same chord. The dissonances on the primary accent constitute *apparent* formations resolving to real chords on the second half of the measure: first-inversion chords in 9–10a (moving 7—6), implied root positions in 9–10c (moving 9—8).

Once the bass advances with the resolution, as in examples 9–10b and 9–10d, the dissonance on the primary accent becomes part of a *real* chord formation. The dissonance stands within the host chord until the stationary voice proceeds to the next chord root. Therefore, the active bass forms a new interval with the tone of resolution: in 9–10b, the 3rd replaces the 6th (7—3), in 9–10d, the 5th replaces the octave (9—5). The sense of chord change binds the dissonance to its host; the chordal seventh and ninth serve as *functional* members of the sonority. Thus, the seventh and the ninth in examples 9–10b and 9–10d are *real*.

Example 9–10: real and apparent 7ths and 9ths

Now, withholding the resolution of the higher extensions retains them within the host sonority. They become, as we saw in the Poulenc and Ravel compositions, frozen nonharmonic tones. And, in some cases, perhaps ironically, such tones constitute real components of the chord, "guests" of the host. Certainly, the increasing tendency from the twentieth century forward is for composers to produce chords of sonoric enrichment by stacking one or more thirds above the root triad and allowing these higher extensions to stand unresolved and prolonged within the chord. The repertoires of jazz and commercial music in particular contain the most consistent use of chordal dissonance within the tonal framework: the 4th (or the 11th) replaces the chord third, the 6th (or 13th) the fifth, and the 9th the root.

In any case, not all 7ths and 9ths are forced to resolve downwards or upwards. Example 9–11 shows the passing tone moving *through* the dissonant 7th and 9th in the bass. Instead of resolving, the top voice remains stationary while the bass creates the dissonance and then continues on its way to the next consonance. Therefore, the 7th and 9th exist as incidental passing tones rather than as functional members of a potential chord.

Example 9–11: passing 7ths and 9ths in the bass against a stationary top voice

Sequential Sevenths and Ninths: Descending 5ths

Throughout this volume, particularly in Chapter 7, we have explored the use of sequential sevenths. Fauré's *Après un rêve* gave us a brief demonstration of sequential ninths and sevenths in which the dissonances interlock within a two-chord pattern. To be sure, the interlocking dissonances are obscured somewhat by how Fauré manipulates the counterpoint in the accompaniment, through delay and anticipation of chord tones (see above, 9–3, especially measures 18–21).

Presently, we investigate the interlocking of sevenths and ninths directly, showing the voice leading between chords in five voices; for without five voices, the simultaneous action of dissonance in one voice and resolution in another within the two-chord pattern cannot be achieved with ninths. (The sevenths interlock but ninths do not.) In example 9–12 below, the texture becomes soprano, alto, alto, tenor, and bass (SAATB).

Notice that the upper part of the divided alto in 9–12 is essential to the creation of the chord ninth in the second chord of the pattern. Without the second alto to gain the fifth voice, that ninth cannot resolve to the fifth of the next chord in *that* voice while another ninth forms simultaneously in *another* voice. Removing the upper alto loses the interlocking ninth, though the soprano retains the sequential ninth.

In both examples 9–12 and 9–13, the figured bass symbols between the clefs and staves at the beginning represent the first two chord positions of the sequence. The lines adjoining the numbers, either curved or with arrows, indicate the course of the interlocking intervals above the bass: 9ths and 5ths are combined with 7ths and 3rds. As in Chapter 7, the examples in this section identify and abbreviate the pattern of intervals in the outer voices as OVIP (outer-voice interval-pattern).

Examples 9–12 and 9–13 below show the complete course of the sequence from the tonic to the THD. With the exception of the ninth attached to the cadential dominant in the penultimate measure, which anticipates the tonic's chord fifth, the ninths in the sequence have interlocking resolutions.

Notice the option for a chromatic chord in both examples. First of all, with sequential ninths, as with sequential sevenths, the two chords of the pattern may consist of either applied or modal dominants. Given this possibility, we suggest a stronger ninth chord than the one that would otherwise occur diatonically. For in major, the leading tone normally takes a diminished triad, whereas in minor, the supertonic forms a diminished triad in the mode's descending form. To be sure, attaching a chord seventh in either instance improves the root position of the sonority and allows its appearance within the context of the sequence.

Still, another ninth chord, whose root triad is major (and therefore chromatic and applied) and whose ninth is lowered, is a more common ninth with a comparable level of dissonance. Using this chord removes the tritone between the root and the fifth (and moves it to the fifth and ninth of the sonority). As we have seen, the third and seventh of the first chord interlock with the seventh and third of the second chord.

In the leading-tone area of major and in the supertonic area of minor, the ninth formed above the root is a minor 9th, existing as a diatonic tone within its host chord. Although the examples below demonstrate the normal course of the voices, the choice of sonority remains with the composer. However, regardless of the particular compositional strategy, the ninth is best heard at interval of a 9th (or more) above the root.

Then again, once the higher extensions are invoked, highly dissonant combinations of tones can be formed, producing sonorities that may not even suggest a tertian structure. Such formations might emphasize 2nds and 4ths instead of 3rds. Further, when the texture thickens to the thirteenth power, the melody must employ chromaticism to effect a sense of momentum, as the supporting chord will contain all seven diatonic scale degrees. Thus, the utility of the higher extensions can be limited by their very presence within the sonority: chords with elevenths and thirteenths can topple under their own weight. Composers may take this potential effect into consideration when forming a strategy for the enrichment of their sonorities.

Example 9–12: OVIP 9   5 (in the key, major, interlocking sevenths and ninths, rising 4th-falling 5th)

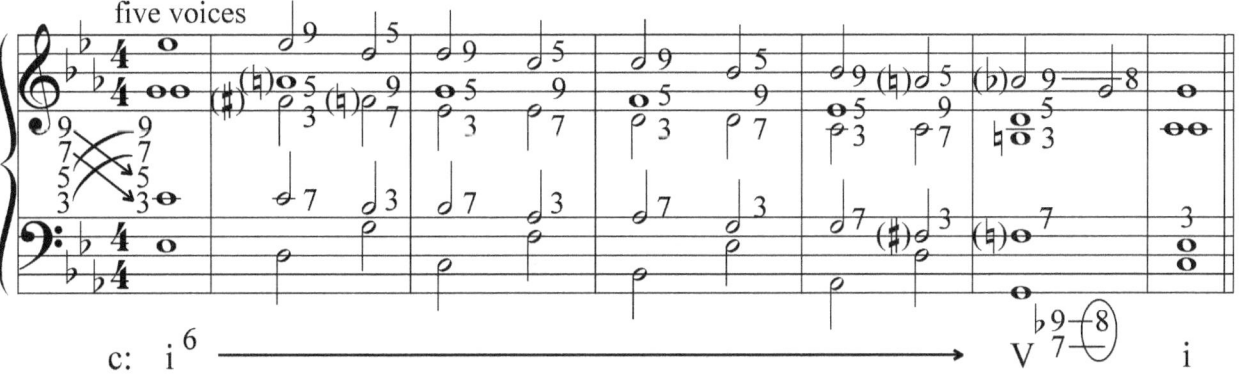

Example 9–13: OVIP 9   5 (in the key, minor, interlocking sevenths and ninths, rising 4th-falling 5th)

282   Chapter 9   Chords of Higher Power

Examples 9–14 and 9–15 transform the SAATB settings of examples 9–12 and 9–13 into a keyboard texture. Example 9–14 exhibits a series of interlocking sevenths expressed as modal dominants in the key and mode of C major; 9–15a adds interlocking ninths (with the applied dominant in measure 4 as a substitute chord).

In *both* examples, the fingering for the right hand is consistent: two fingers hold and two fingers move in alternation. Although the fingering remains unchanged between the examples, retaining the bass line of 9–14 in 9–15a while moving the right hand up a 3rd produces interlocking ninths. After executing an untransposed chain of modal dominant sevenths (in major or minor), use the following steps to transpose the pattern (as demonstrated in examples 9–15b and 9–15c):

(1) move the sequence of sevenths to another pitch level, and then,
(2) shift the right hand up a 3rd to combine and interlock the transposed sevenths with *ninths*.

Example 9–14: OVIP 7 3 (in the key, major, interlocking sevenths, rising 4th-falling 5th)

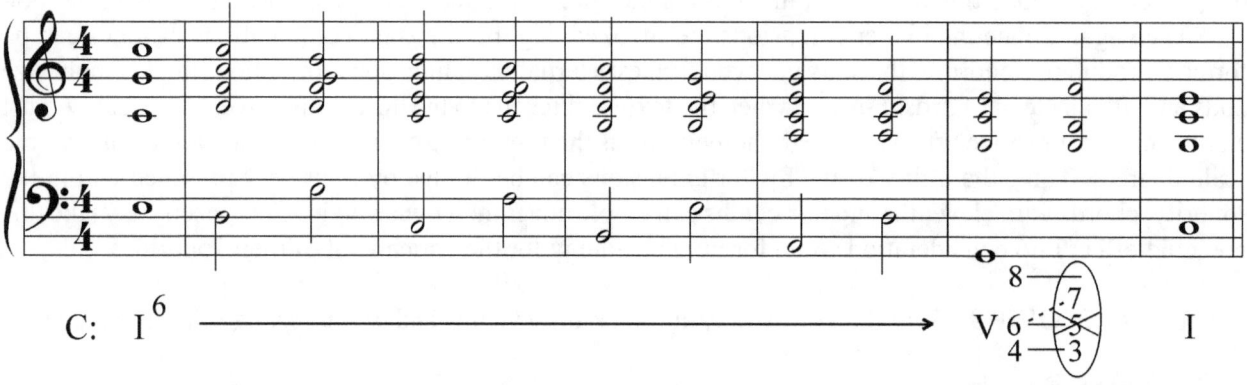

Example 9–15: OVIP 9 5 (in the key, major, interlocking sevenths and ninths, rising 4th-falling 5th)

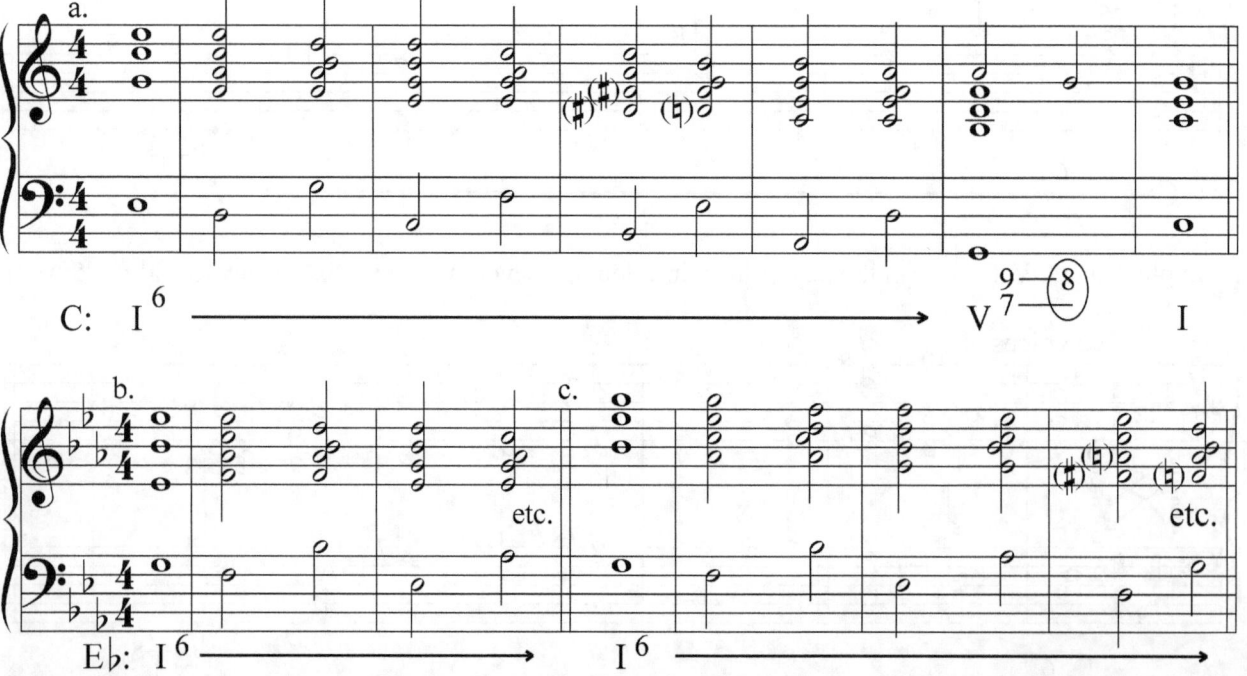

Examples 9–16 and 9–17 demonstrate the sevenths and ninths of examples 9–14 and 9–15 in the parallel minor. As we have observed, in minor, the supertonic forms a diminished triad in the mode's descending form. Thus, 9–17 retains the option for a chord substitution. In the supertonic area of minor, the ninth occurring above the root is minor, existing as a diatonic tone within its host chord. As in example 9–15, when the substitute ninth chord resolves to its successor, the fifth of the first chord forms a major 9th above the root of the second chord.

Example 9–16: OVIP 7 3 (in the key, minor, interlocking sevenths, rising 4th-falling 5th)

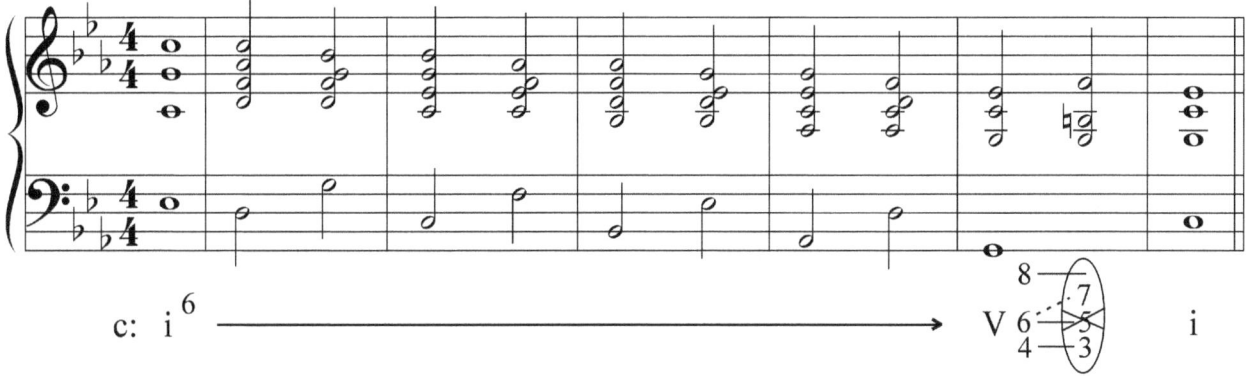

Example 9–17: OVIP 9 5 (in the key, minor, interlocking sevenths and ninths, rising 4th-falling 5th)

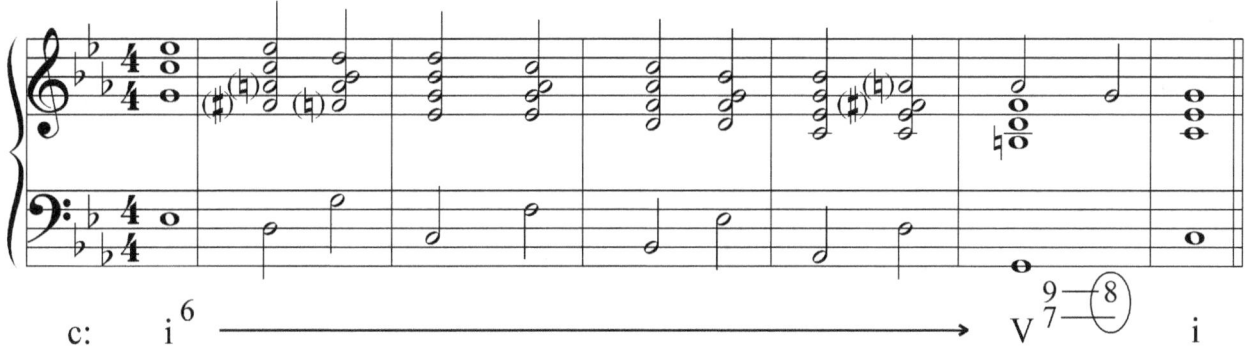

Sequential Sevenths and Ninths: Root-Position Variants of the Ascending 5—6 (becoming 5—8)

In Chapter 7, we looked at numerous sequences with different bass lines and outer-voice interval-patterns, such as the one reviewed in the foregoing section, that is, the descending 5th sequence. The inclusion of the ninth in this series was demonstrated within the context of interlocking dissonances, the 7th and the 9th.

It would be instructive to discover how the ninth operates in *all* of the other sequences explored in Chapter 7, an investigation clearly beyond the scope of this study. However, let us explore one additional possibility with the ninth before drilling down further into some of the nuances of the sonority's structure, inflections, and descriptions.

Examples 9–18 through 9–21 use applied dominant ninths for the variant 5—6 becoming 5—8 (as introduced in Chapter 7, particularly examples 7–48 to 7–52). The bass line consists of the falling 3rd-rising 4th. With one of the upper voices divided to yield five parts (SSATB or SAATB), the 9th placed above the root of each applied chord is minor (indicated as ♭9), positioned most favorably when the interval maintains its compound distance from the root (as in examples 9–18, 19, and 20).

In other words, it is preferable to have the ninth stand at the interval of a 9th above the root of the chord in the upper range of the texture, rather than buried in an inner voice. The most obvious alternative to the minor 9th would be its major counterpart (omit the ♭ from the 9 in the chord description).

Even in such works as Fauré's *Après un rêve*, which has a foreground melody (a secondary voice) above the *suspended* ninth, that higher power is placed in the upper voice of the *accompaniment*. Smashing the ninth against the root (as in 9–20) yields a weaker result.

Example 9–18: OVIP 12 9 (out of key, major, interlocking sevenths and ninths, falling 3rd-rising 4th)

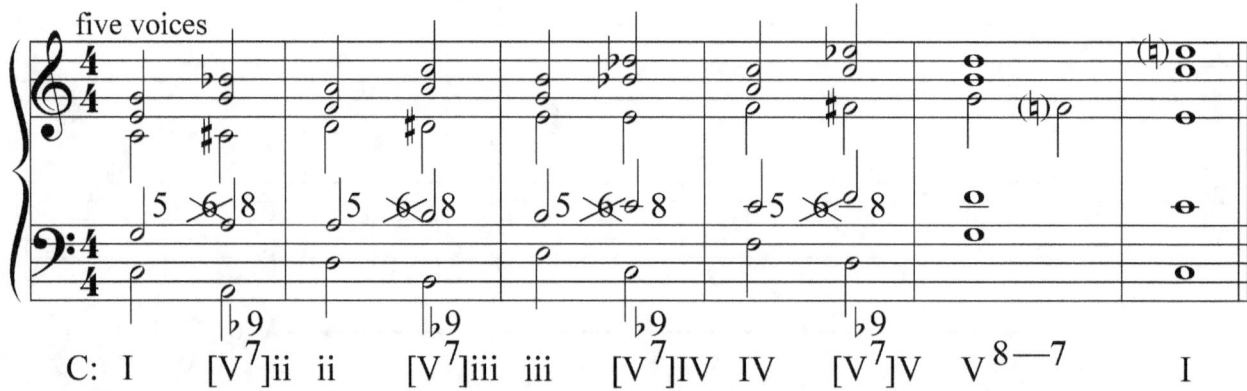

In minor, as in 9–19, the root-position diminished triad in the supertonic area should be avoided. The disposition of the example below assumes five voices after the initial tonic, with the subdominant serving as a substitute for the less-convincing supertonic. Thus, the sequence begins with the mediant.

Example 9–19: OVIP 12 9 (out of key, minor, interlocking sevenths and ninths, falling 3rd-rising 4th)

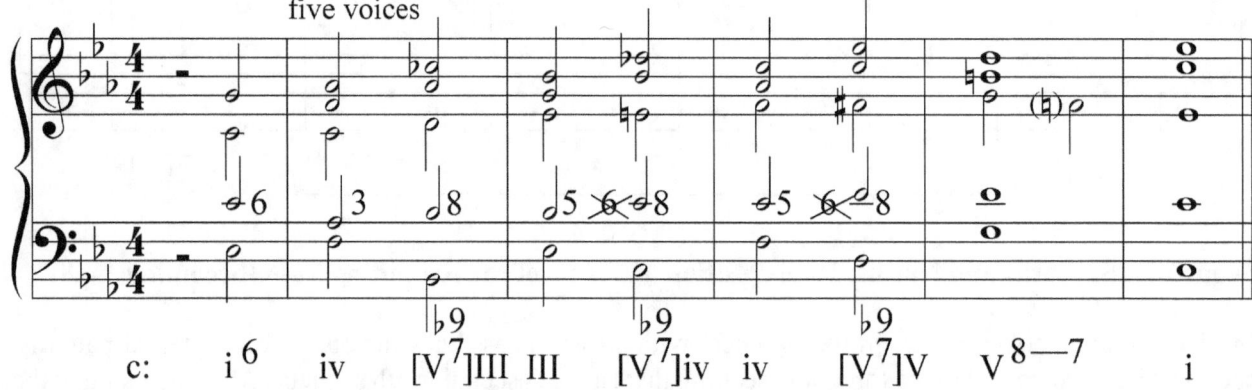

Example 9–20: OVIP 10   7 (out of key, major, interlocking sevenths and ninths, falling 3rd-rising 4th)

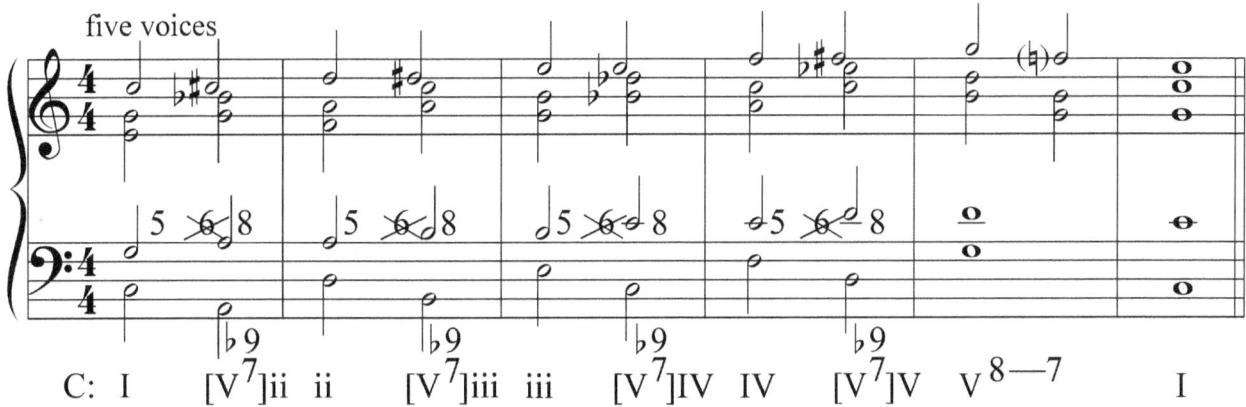

Example 9–21 restores the ninth to its optimal compound distance from the root in the upper portion of the texture, here as the higher of two altos. It would be well to remember that in other dispositions, in which various combinations of the higher extensions are closer to the lower components of the chord, the sonority either loses its tertian identity or acquires an added-note quality.

Example 9–21: OVIP 8   10 (out of key, major, interlocking sevenths and ninths, falling 3rd-rising 4th)

The Chord of the Ninth: Structure, Inflections, and Description

Under certain circumstances, chords of the ninth may invert. However, second inversion in four voices is impossible because the only expendable chord tone, the fifth, is in the bass and cannot be omitted. Fourth inversion is also excluded because this position would have the ninth below the root. Therefore, ninth chords may be set in root position, first inversion, and third inversion, having either the root, third or seventh in the bass. Five voices enable the use of second inversion.

One of the challenges of understanding chords of higher power is determining when these higher extensions constitute real components of the sonority and when the harmony is the result of additive construction. Our guiding principle is based upon the understanding that each higher power also contains the tertian extension immediately below it.

For without the support of the underlying extension, the inclusion of the ninth, eleventh, and/or thirteenth produces a chord of addition. And to be sure, as additives, these extensions may appear as as either simple or compound intervals in relation to the root and/or bass. In other words, the 2nd might be expressed as a 9th, the 4th as an 11th, and the 6th as a 13th. (We return to the expression of these additions as simple intervals in example 9–27.)

The chords in examples 9–22 indicate the correct positioning of the ninth *above* the root. Expressing the ninth at the interval of the 2nd above the root produces a chord of addition, an "added-2nd chord." As we have said, placing the chord fifth in the bass is impracticable in four voices (9–22c). The second chord in examples 9–22b, 9–22c, and 9–22d display the ninth at its proper distance from the root.

There are two options for describing the inversion of the ninth chord with figured bass, the second of which reflects more precisely the arrangement of intervals in the sonority when the ninth is expressed in its true compound form. Although ninths are more common in root position, the inverted disposition of the chord takes either version of figured bass. In any case, chords of the eleventh and thirteenth, if found, exist *only* as root-position sonorities.

As illustrated in examples 9–22e and 9–22f, placing the ninth *below* the root distorts the relationship between the two elements and cannot be used. This arrangement destroys the identity of the higher extension by creating a 7th (or 2nd) instead of the requisite 9th. (Since the chord ninth does not appear in the bass, 9–22e's fourth inversion is not possible.)

Example 9–22: the structure of the ninth chord and its inversions

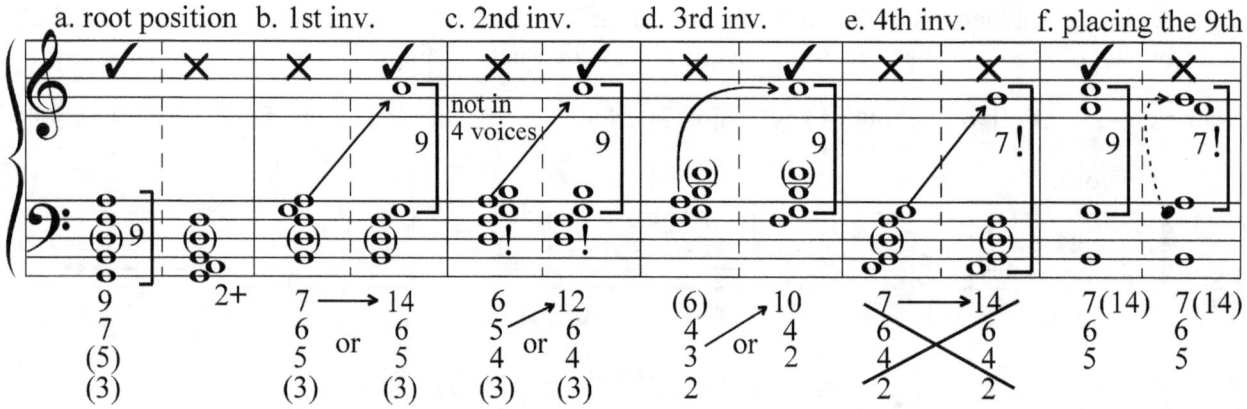

We have a few issues to consider in example 9–23, the first of which involves the improper arrangement of the root and ninth, encountered in 9–22f and repeated in 9–23a for emphasis (the sopranos are divided in the second chord).

With the introduction of the higher powers, the principle of allowing no more than one octave between adjacent voices (except between the tenor and bass) may now be relaxed to include spacing that exceeds the octave between *upper* adjacent voices. Example 9–23b presents two such possibilities. Ultimately, the sound of the chord determines its disposition.

Example 9–23c previews the topic of the next section, namely, the inflection of the higher extensions and their figured-bass description. Notice that the ninth is indicated as raised in the figured bass. It would be well to remember that our use of figured bass requires generic accidentals. The sharp (♯) in front of the number in the examples is a generic symbol; its use does not necessarily mean that the pitch itself carries a sharp, thus: the ninth in 9–23c has a sharp attached to the figured bass because the note is raised, and not because it is written as an A♯.

The figured bass for the third inversion of the chord in 9–23c demonstrates the placement of the generic accidental when the root of the chord is *not* in the bass. In 9–23d, the second chord (in second inversion) needs five voices. This inverted subdominant (9–23d) accounts for its lowered seventh variety with the flat attached to the 7 in parentheses. The generic flat, (♭7), must be retained with the ninth chord's figured bass as a reminder that this is the subdominant seventh in major whose quality is that of a minor seventh, a chord of primary borrowing (taking both A♭ and E♭ from the parallel minor).

Example 9–23: spacing, positioning, and describing the inflected ninth

Inflecting the Higher Extensions

To form a diatonic ninth, eleventh, and/or thirteenth, we must use diatonic pitches. But as we have seen, it is also possible to have chromatic alterations of the higher powers. As in example 9–24a, the lowered ninth and raised ninth each take a generic accidental in the figure bass: either ♭9 or ♯9.

Our discussion of chromatic inflection begins with its potential for compromising the integrity of the root sonority, particularly, the dominant seventh. Generally, it is preferable to have the third of the chord sounding below the ninth. And in the dominant seventh with a raised ninth, the chord third *must* be situated below the ninth.

In example 9–24b, the raised ninth is A♯, which is enharmonically B♭. When the B♭ is placed below B♮ (the third of the root triad), as in the second chord of 9–24b, the disposition changes the basic sound of the dominant seventh; it destroys the dominant quality of the sonority.

An additional complication arises from inflecting the higher extensions: some alterations of the ninth, eleventh, and thirteenth might create enharmonic equivalencies with certain members of the chord. Examples 9–24d and 9–24e show the lowered eleventh duplicating the chord third and the raised thirteenth becoming the chord seventh. Inflections such as these are impracticable.

Example 9–24

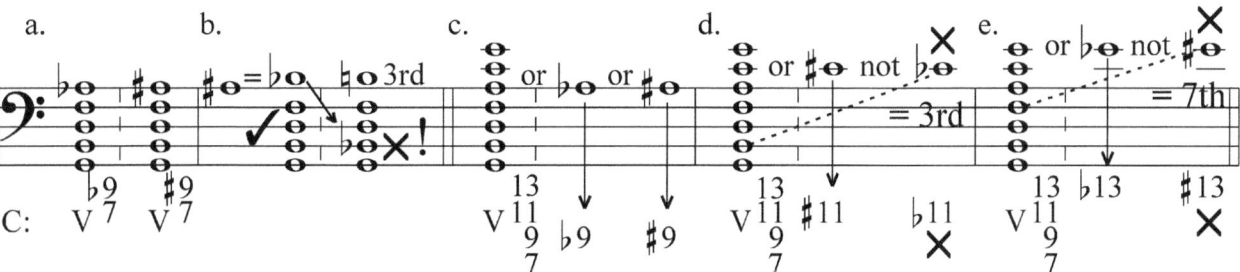

Example 9–25 illustrates additional inflections of the dominant seventh involving the altered fifth and the lowered and diatonic ninth. The first chord of each example displays a root-position ninth while the second chord demonstrates either first or third inversions. In each inversion, the degree-inflected fifth is indicated as either ($\flat$5) or ($\sharp$5).

If the ninth is inflected (examples 9–25b, 25d, and 25e), then a generic flat attaches to the appropriate figured-bass number. (Remember that the figured bass has two options for when the chord inverts, one of which represents the *compound* interval of the 9th above the bass and one that represents all intervals as simple.) In the inverted subtonic of example 9–25e, the lowered seventh variety is accounted for as ($\flat$7) while generic flat for the lowered ninth is attached to the figured bass.

Example 9–25

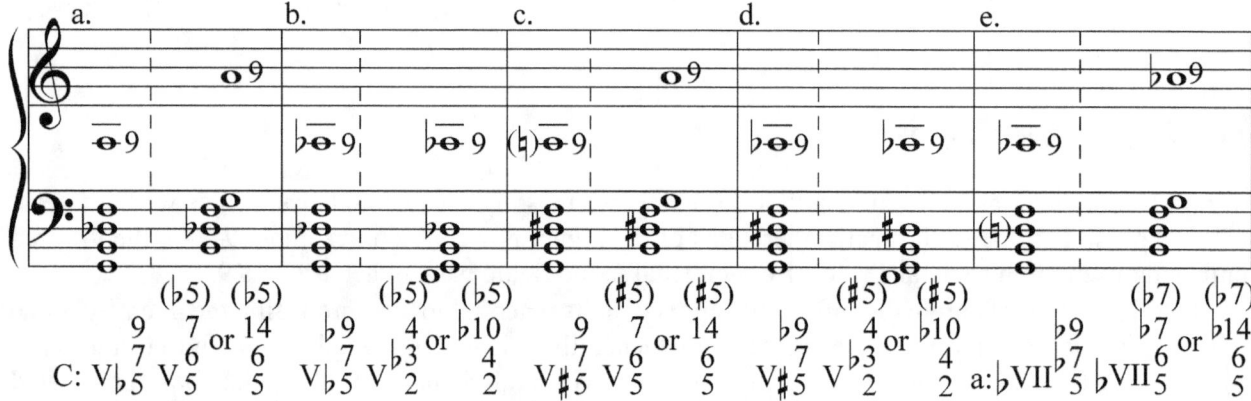

Chords of Addition

Example 9–26a introduces a diatonic thirteenth chord of the subdominant in C major. The subsequent versions of the IV chord illustrate various chords of addition, represented by the plus sign attached to the right of the figured-bass number. Notice that in each instance, the extension immediately below the highest is missing. The added-note chords of examples 9–26c, 9–26d, and 9–26f are missing two extensions below the highest. As we shall see in the next example, it is possible to express chordal additions in simple rather than compound form.

Example 9–26

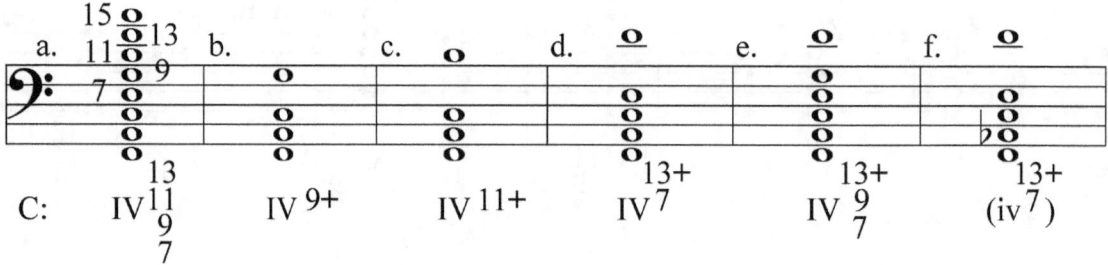

In example 9–27, we interpret the added notes within the span of the octave rather than beyond it. (In 9–27f, the host chord for the added 6th is a ninth, however.) The first three instances show the context for the added 4th. Generally, placing the 4th within the framework of a minor triad at the distance of a major 2nd from the third and fifth works best. Examples 9–27a, 27b, and 27c all provide E♭ as an option.

When the 4th occurs as part of a 4—3 motion, as in 9–27b, both its identity as an added tone and its potential clash with the other members of the chord are lost. Example 9–27c illustrates the process of contraction, whereby the 4th is frozen, denied its resolution (the chord third crossed out).

Example 9–27e transforms the diatonic ninth of 9–27d into an added 2nd, as 2+. The added 2nd is most successful when appearing in a major triad because its distance from both the root and third is that of a major 2nd. The last three instances in 9–27 describe the added note as both a frozen tone (with the resolution crossed out) and as 6+ or 4+. Example 9–27f shows an added 6th with both the chord seventh and ninth (lowered). Examples 9–27g and 9–27h have the 4th occurring with the chord seventh.

Example 9–27

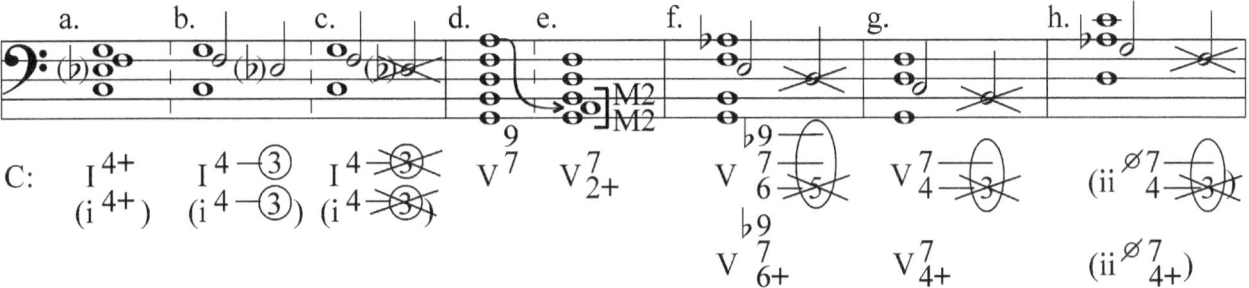

Descriptions of Ninths, Elevenths, and Thirteenths in Commercial Music and Jazz

The third volume of *Finding The Right Pitch* closes with a brief look at ninths, elevenths, and thirteenths as they are described in traditional lead-sheet terminology. Some of the basic principles of lead-sheet terminology differ from what we have been learning throughout this volume. To maintain as much clarity as possible, the present topic has been deferred until now. (The following discussion of the ninth, eleventh, and thirteenth is drawn from the more complete survey of lead-sheet terminology found in David Nivans, *Introduction To Music Fundamentals And Lead-Sheet Terminology*, World Bet Books, 2012.)

Throughout our studies of harmony, we have seen how the higher extensions of the root triad are traditionally resolved and how these elements may operate as components of apparent sonorities, either as frozen nonharmonic tones or as dissonant elements seeking consonant resolution within the host chord.

In commercial music and jazz, the higher extensions may or may not resolve as we expect. Indeed, it is not unusual in popular music in general and in jazz in particular to find unresolved dissonances, even at the end of a composition. Musical traditions that thrive on increasing the sonority of chords also tend to exploit their unresolved formations.

With respect to the action of chromatic alteration, lead-sheet terminology starts from the following premise: *the major 7th is an alteration of the minor 7th* (see example 9–28). We do not view chromatic alteration in this way, as our perspective is shaped by the recognition of a distinction that exists between diatonicism and chromaticism and by the desire to discern their respective operations in a musical work: to understand how the connections between the two are established, the nature of those connections, where the connections between them are the closest and the most remote, and how diatonic and chromatic elements serve the larger concerns, that is, how diatonicism and chromaticism interact throughout the compositional middleground.

Lead-sheet terminology references the foreground. Any changes in key, for example, are never seen as part of something larger, as emanating from a deeper background. The dynamic is to move from one chord to the next and to play the "chart," preferably, on the first attempt with the rest of the ensemble. Even in those works in jazz that might exhibit foreground, middleground, and background relationships, the lead sheet is not used to represent structure and prolongation in such works.

Example 9–28 illustrates one principle of alteration indicated in the lead sheet, mentioned earlier: the basic precept that the major 7th is an alteration of the minor 7th; 9–28b emerges as the "unaltered" version of 9–28a. Within the context of C major, however, the chord with B♭ is a chromatic sonority, and, from that perspective, altered.

The MA symbol in 9–28 indicates that the interval of the major 7th occurs above the root (C up to B). In lead sheet, we interpret the major 7th above the root of the chord as an *alteration* of the minor 7th. For the dominant seventh in root position, the chord name consists of an uppercase letter denoting the quality of the root triad followed by the number 7. The absence of MA indicates an unaltered minor 7th above the root of the chord (C up to B♭).

Example 9–28

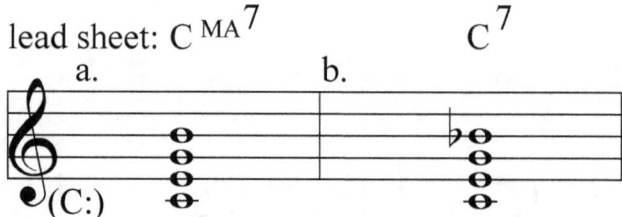

Chords of the Ninth

As stated above, an actual ninth chord should also contain the chord seventh; otherwise, the ninth is simply an added note. Example 9–29 exhibits four chords of the ninth; here, the seventh is included in the chord structure and the uppermost extension of the ninth remains *unaltered*. That is to say, the interval from the root up to the ninth is a major 9th, an *unaltered* ninth. However, if the top note of the ninth is either raised or lowered from its original major quality, then we have an alteration of the highest component of the chord.

The chord in 9–29a is called a *dominant ninth* because its underlying seventh-chord quality is that of a dominant seventh, with a minor 7th from the root to the seventh. The chord in 9–29b is termed a *major ninth* because it contains a major 7th (the MA refers to the seventh) from the root to the seventh. Technically, the major 7th above the root of the major ninth chord is an altered component; therefore, strictly speaking, a ninth chord with an altered seventh is an altered chord. We refer to the chord in 9–29c as a *minor ninth* because the basic triad is minor, with the MI symbol attached to the chord name designating its quality. The 7th is minor as well (C up to B♭).

The MI in 9–29d indicates the quality of the triad as minor while the MA7 in parentheses identifies the 7th as major (an altered 7th): the minor-major ninth. Using the number 9 in the lead-sheet symbol implies a complete chord with both the ninth *and* seventh elements.

Example 9–29: chords of the ninth

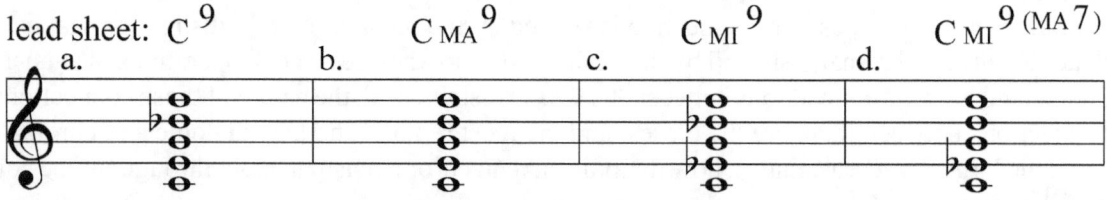

The Altered Fifth and Altered Ninth

In lead-sheet terminology, a flat or sharp appearing in conjunction with numbers such as 5, 9, 11, or 13 indicates an alteration of a chord in which one or more of elements of the chord is either raised or lowered (the eleventh occurs only at the interval of a perfect or augmented 11th above the root of the chord; it cannot be lowered). We prefer enclosing both the accidental and the number in parentheses to represent the alteration.

In earlier examples, we used (♭5) to designate the lowered fifth. Lead sheet employs the sign for both the diminished triad (as a minor triad with a lowered fifth) and the half-diminished seventh (as a minor triad with a lowered fifth and a minor 7th between its root and seventh). Example 9–30 displays the lead sheet for the diminished triad, the half-diminished seventh, and what is termed either the half-diminished ninth or the minor ninth with the flat fifth. Again, the inclusion of the number 9 implies the presence of the seventh element of the chord.

Example 9–30: the lowered-fifth sign with the diminished triad, seventh, and ninth

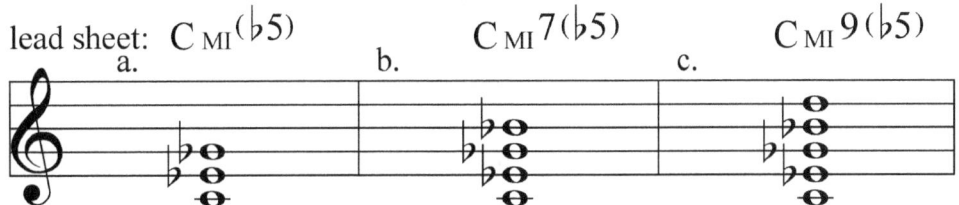

The lowered fifth is referred to variously as the flat fifth, flatted fifth, or flat five. The raised fifth is usually associated with the augmented triad and called the "augmented fifth," "sharp fifth," or "sharp five." The flat fifth is shown below with the major triad (example 9–31a), the dominant seventh (9–31b), and dominant ninth (9–31c). Although it is possible to have altered fifths in chords of the eleventh and thirteenth, *unaltered* fifths are often omitted from the texture in chords above the ninth.

Example 9–31: the major triad, dominant seventh, and dominant ninth (flat fifth)

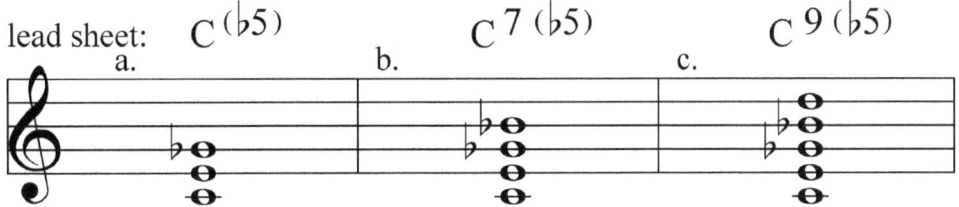

The major triad with the flat fifth (example 9–32a) may also carry a major 7th (9–32b) and a major 9th (9–32c) above its root.

Example 9–32: the major triad, major seventh, and major ninth (flat fifth)

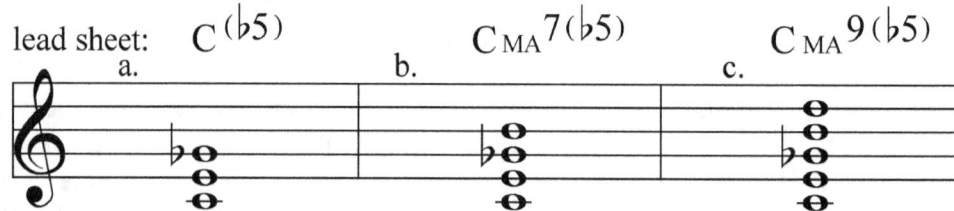

We know that when the fifth of the major triad is raised one half step, the chord becomes an augmented triad. The augmented triad takes a plus sign after the chord name (example 9–33a), the augmented-major seventh adds MA7 in parentheses to its lead-sheet description (9–33b), and the augmented-major ninth places the number 9 between the plus sign and the symbol for the major 7th (9–33c).

Notice that the augmented-major seventh C E G♯ B can be described as an E-major triad with a C bass (E / C). Musicians often recognize the augmented-major ninth C E G♯ B D as an E-dominant seventh with a C bass (9–33c).

Example 9–33: the augmented triad, augmented-major seventh, and the augmented-major ninth

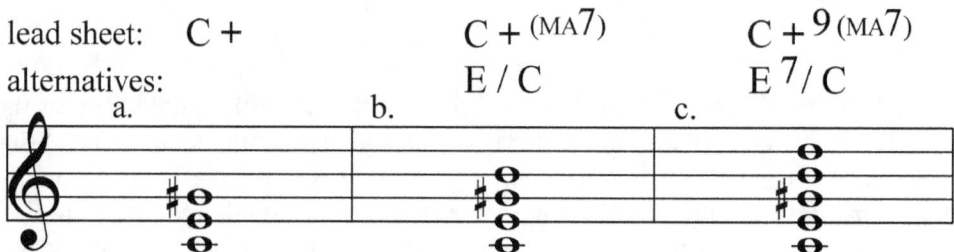

The unaltered ninth stands at the interval of a major 9th above the root of the chord. To alter the ninth, convert the major 9th into either a minor or augmented interval by lowering or raising its pitch one half step. As demonstrated in example 9–34, the chord symbol for altering the ninth involves placing either a flat or a sharp before the number 9 and enclosing both figures in parentheses.

When the ninth is altered, we must show the presence of the seventh element by including the number 7 directly to the right of the chord name. Remember that the MI symbol between the chord name and the number 7 refers to the minor quality of the basic triad (9–34b).

Example 9–34: the dominant ninth (flat ninth), minor ninth (flat ninth), and dominant ninth (sharp ninth)

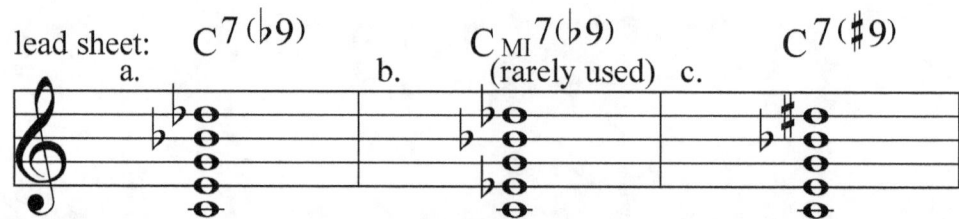

As with the major seventh chord, the altered ninth incorporates the MA symbol into the chord name if the interval between the seventh and the root is a major 7th. Example 9–35 shows the major ninth chord with the sharp ninth, a chord with a relatively high level of dissonance because of the major 7ths between the root and the seventh (C up to B) and between the third and the ninth (E up to D♯).

Example 9–35: the major ninth (sharp ninth)

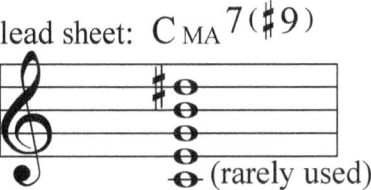

The Altered Fifth and Altered Ninth Together

The raised fifth is often used together with the flat ninth or sharp ninth as altered components of the dominant chord (example 9–36). Since raising the fifth of the major triad produces the augmented triad, it is unnecessary to combine the symbol for the sharp fifth with either of the altered ninth symbols, as the plus sign between the chord name and the number seven accounts for the altered fifth. Still, despite the advantage of having the plus sign available, you will probably encounter some lead sheets that exhibit a preference for the sharp fifth sign (♯5).

Example 9–36: the dominant ninth (sharp fifth, flat ninth or sharp ninth)

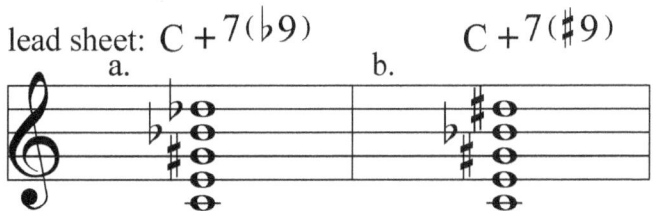

However, if the basic triad of the ninth chord does not have a raised fifth, then the symbols for the altered components are stacked vertically and usually enclosed in a single set of parentheses. As illustrated in example 9–37, place the lowest altered element(s) of the chord below the highest. The first two ninth chords shown below have lowered components, producing the dominant ninth with the flat fifth and flat ninth (9–37a) and the minor ninth with the flat fifth and flat ninth (9–37b). The third ninth chord is a dominant ninth with the flat fifth and sharp ninth (9–37c).

The underlying seventh chord of the second ninth (9–37b) is the half-diminished seventh. Both commercial and jazz musicians would recognize the half-diminished seventh with its chord ninth but nonetheless read the lead-sheet symbol as the minor seventh with the flat fifth (and flat ninth).

Example 9–37: the dominant ninth and minor ninth (flat fifth, flat ninth or sharp ninth)

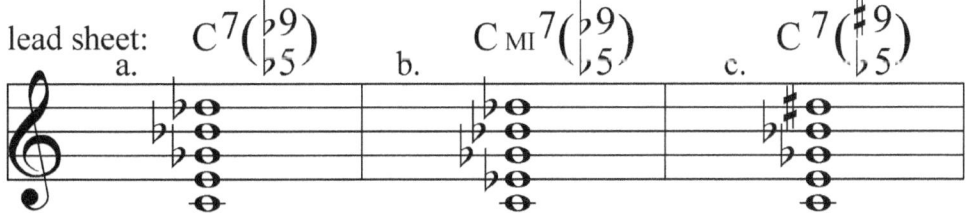

Chords of the Eleventh and Thirteenth

Chords of the eleventh and thirteenth often omit one or more elements of their respective chord structures. This section will show when these omissions are advisable. We shall also encounter some of the most common chromatic alterations to the higher extensions.

The uppermost component of the eleventh chord occurs at the interval of a perfect or augmented 11th above the root. As demonstrated in example 9–38a, the eleventh chord frequently *omits its third* when
(1) the distance from the root to the eleventh is a perfect 11th (that is, an unaltered eleventh), and,
(2) the distance from the root to the third is a major 3rd. This formation produces a minor 9th between the third and the eleventh of the chord, a very dissonant interval (E up to F). The most likely chord to omit the third is the dominant eleventh. In 9–38a: C (E) G B♭ D F (the omitted chord tone is represented as a filled-in note head in parentheses).

On the other hand, 9–38b confirms a different set of options for the minor eleventh chord. Since the major 9th between the third and the eleventh (E♭ up to F) is less dissonant than the minor 9th, the third is usually retained. However, the chord might omit its fifth if that tone is unaltered, in other words, if the distance between the root and the fifth constitutes a perfect 5th, rather than a diminished 5th or augmented 5th: C E♭ (G) B♭ D F.

Example 9–38: the chords of the dominant eleventh and minor eleventh

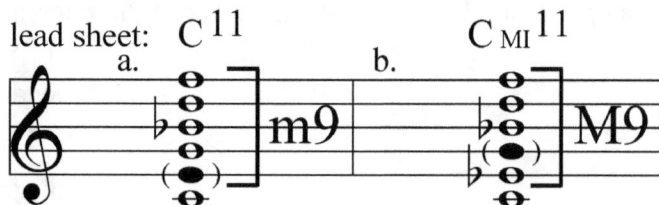

In all instances, we interpret the major 13th of the thirteenth chord as an *unaltered* interval (example 9–39); therefore, a minor 13th or augmented 13th would be considered an altered element of the chord. And if the thirteenth turns out to be an added 6th, then an adjustment to maintain the interval of the major 6th above the root may be necessary to preserve its unaltered form (as in 9–48 below).

Example 9–39a indicates that if the thirteenth chord has a major 3rd between its root and third and a perfect 11th between its root and eleventh (an unaltered eleventh), then a dissonant minor 9th results between the third and the eleventh (E up to F). In this case, the chord is likely to be a dominant thirteenth, a chord that usually *omits the eleventh* rather than the third. (Notably, this option contradicts our contention that the thirteenth chord must have the tertian extension immediately below it.) Since the chord retains the third, we can also omit the fifth, if unaltered: C E (G) B♭ D (F) A.

The minor thirteenth, shown in 9–39b, is usually expressed with all chord tones present; however, an unaltered fifth would be the most expendable tone should you want an incomplete disposition of the chord: C E♭ (G) B♭ D F A.

Example 9–39: the chords of the dominant thirteenth and minor thirteenth

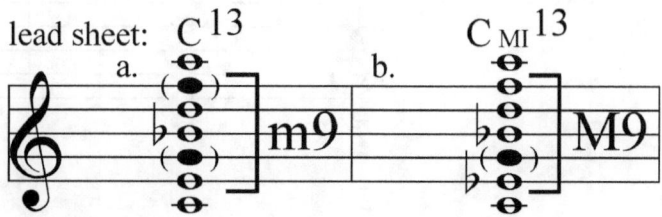

Altered Eleventh and Thirteenth Chords

There are myriad forms of altered chords in the music literature. Some are exceedingly rare, even impractical, while others appear in virtually every popular music or jazz composition. In this section, we draw upon those lead-sheet symbols that most clearly represent the altered chords typically notated and read by those who use this terminology. We begin with some alterations of the dominant seventh with the eleventh as its uppermost extension.

In example 9–40a, the dominant eleventh contains a flat ninth (♭9). Since the eleventh element itself is not altered, the number 11 immediately follows the chord name. With the exception of using the plus sign for representing the augmented fifth of a triad, the most acceptable practice places the altered symbol in parentheses. Thus, we enclose the flat ninth symbol in parentheses and situate it to the right of the number 11. In this disposition of the chord, *the third is omitted* and the unaltered eleventh retained.

Examples 9–40b and 9–40c call for a slightly different approach. In 9–40b, we have a dominant eleventh with an unaltered ninth and a raised eleventh (an augmented 11th above the root of the chord). The number 9 represents the unaltered ninth and is placed after the chord name but before the parentheses, which enclose the altered eleventh. Since the distance from the chord third to the eleventh is a major 9th (E up to F♯), we retain both elements and have the option of leaving out the fifth (G), the most expendable tone. (Notably, the raised eleventh and the flatted fifth are enharmonic equivalents.)

Example 9–40c combines the alterations of 40a and 40b. The ninth is flatted, the eleventh sharped. Both alterations are expressed in parentheses. The seventh, which is unaltered, appears between the chord name and the alterations. Again, the fifth is expendable; its omission will not upset the balance or identity of the chord.

It is notable, however, that without the fifth (G), many musicians will re-interpret the F♯ and E of the chord as G♭ and F♭ respectively and recognize a G♭-dominant seventh over a C bass: G♭ B♭ D♭ F♭ over C. (Musicians could also re-interpret the B♭ and D♭ of the chord as A♯ and C♯ respectively and recognize an F♯-dominant seventh over a C bass: F♯ A♯ C♯ E over C). If we retain the fifth, a very convincing case can be made for a G♭-major triad over a C-major triad. Example 9–40d illustrates the common practice of indicating a "chord over a chord" with one chord name standing directly above the other, both marked and separated by a straight horizontal line. (We shall revisit this sonority for its polychordal implications at the end of the chapter.)

Example 9–40: altered dominant eleventh

(1) 9–40a: C-dominant eleventh, flat ninth
(2) 9–40b: C-dominant ninth, sharp eleventh
(3) 9–40c: C-dominant seventh, sharp eleventh, flat ninth
(4) 9–40d: G♭-major triad over C-major triad

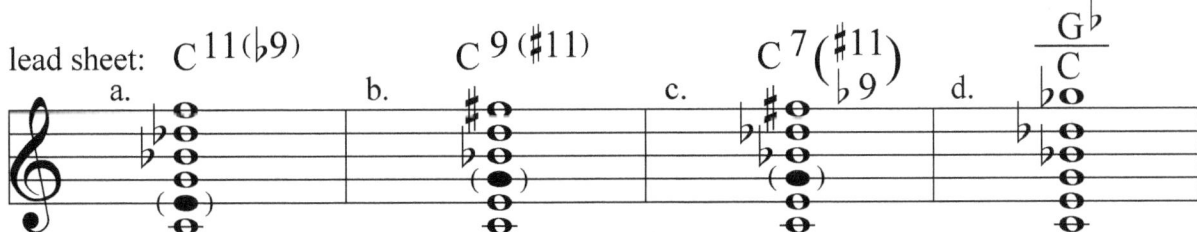

296   Chapter 9   Chords of Higher Power

There are two different ways to indicate the dominant eleventh in example 9–41. Since the two uppermost extensions are altered and appear in parentheses (the ninth and the eleventh), we attach the number 7 to the chord name, instead of 9 or 11. The plus sign represents the raised fifth, which produces an augmented triad. Using the chord over a chord method of notation introduced in example 9–41d, we can re-interpret the F♯ of the chord enharmonically and describe the chord as a G♭-major triad over a C-augmented triad.

Example 9–41: altered dominant eleventh

(1)   9–41a: C-dominant seventh, sharp eleventh, flat ninth, sharp fifth
(2)   9–41b: G♭-major triad over C-augmented triad

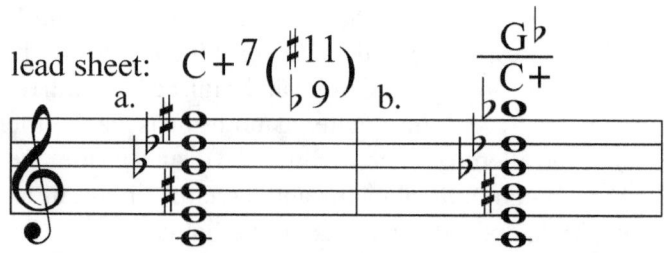

Example 9–42 lists some of the possibilities for the chord of the eleventh with the minor triad as the basic tertian unit. In two instances, the fifth of the minor triad is lowered one half step (examples 9–42a and 9–42b); in the other two, the fifth remains unaltered and therefore constitutes the most expendable chord tone (examples 9–42c and 9–42d).

The only altered tone in 9–42a is the lowered fifth; 9–42b adds a lowered ninth to the chord. Examples 9–42c and 9–42d both contain raised elevenths in their respective chords. The ninth in 9–42c is unaltered, whereas 9–42d shows a lowered ninth.

Example 9–42: altered minor eleventh

(1)   9–42a: C-minor eleventh, flat fifth
(2)   9–42b: C-minor eleventh, flat ninth, flat fifth
(3)   9–42c: C-minor ninth, sharp eleventh
(4)   9–42d: C-minor seventh, sharp eleventh, flat ninth

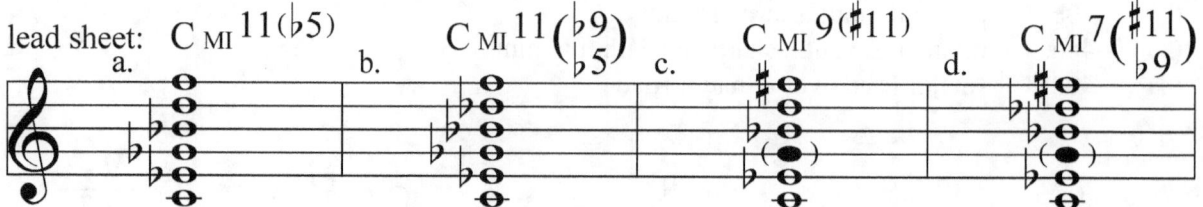

As we have observed, the interval of the major 7th between the root and the seventh of the chord is an alteration of the minor 7th. Accordingly, we refer to the tertian harmony displayed in example 9–43a as an altered eleventh chord because C up to B is a major 7th. Omitting the third of the chord avoids the dissonant minor 9th between the third and the eleventh (E up to F).

In both examples 9–43b and 9–43c, the unaltered fifth is the most expendable tone while the raised eleventh (an augmented 11th above the root) of the chord allows us to retain the third. Additionally, 9–43c raises the ninth. If we chose not to omit the fifth of 9–43c, then using the chord over a chord notation in 9–43d enables us to put forward a simple lead-sheet description that also stipulates a complete disposition of the chord.

Example 9–43: altered major eleventh

(1) 9–43a: C-major eleventh
(2) 9–43b: C-major ninth, sharp eleventh
(3) 9–43c: C-major seventh, sharp eleventh, sharp ninth
(4) 9–43d: B major triad over C-major triad

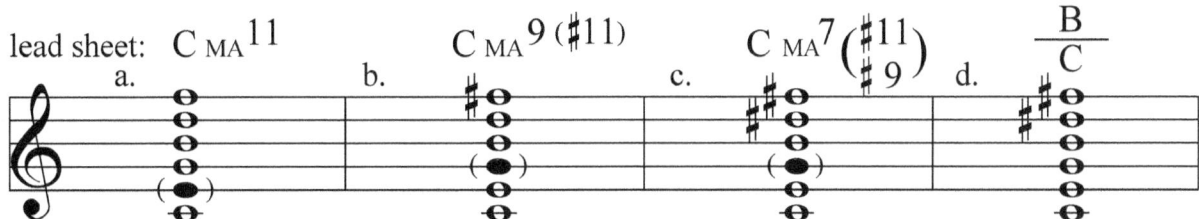

The dominant thirteenth in example 9–44a, which has a lowered ninth, may omit its unaltered fifth and eleventh. However, the dominant thirteenth in 9–44b has an altered (raised) eleventh which is therefore retained in the chord's disposition. We must assume the presence of an unaltered ninth (a major 9th) because there is no indication of an altered ninth in the chord symbol. Example 9–44c combines the lowered ninth and raised eleventh in its chord description, leaving only the fifth as an option for omission. Accounting for all of the elements in each respective version of the altered dominant thirteenth in 9–44 yields the following descriptions:

Example 9–44: altered dominant thirteenth

(1) 9–44a: C-dominant thirteenth, flat ninth
(2) 9–44b: C-dominant thirteenth, sharp eleventh
(3) 9–44c: C-dominant thirteenth, sharp eleventh, flat ninth

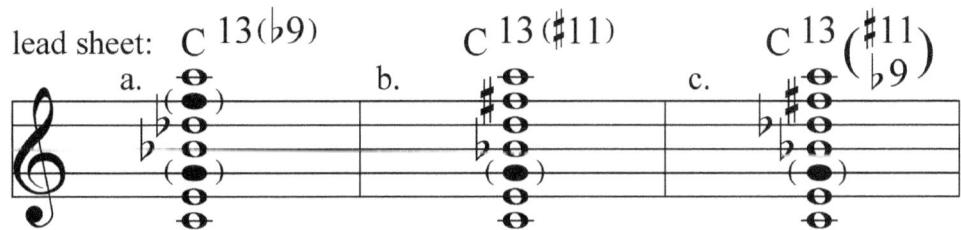

Example 9–45 presents some additional alterations of the dominant thirteenth with the same options for omission as example 9–44. Notice that alterations to the ninth and thirteenth (9–45a) require the chord name to take the number 7. Similarly, alterations to the thirteenth and eleventh (9–45b) require the number 9, while alterations to the eleventh and ninth (9–45c) require the number 13. Regardless of the number attached to the chord name, however, each tertian harmony in the example constitutes a different altered version of the dominant thirteenth. (Notably, the flatted thirteenth and the raised fifth are enharmonic equivalents.)

Example 9–45: altered dominant thirteenth

(1) 9–45a: C-dominant thirteenth, flat thirteenth, flat ninth
(2) 9–45b: C-dominant thirteenth, flat thirteenth, sharp eleventh
(3) 9–45c: C-dominant thirteenth, sharp eleventh, sharp ninth

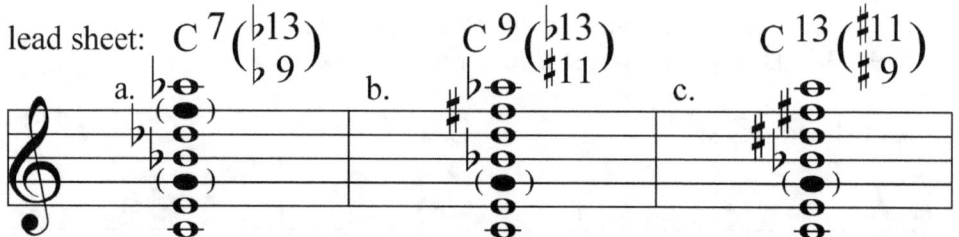

The three major thirteenth chords in example 9–46 all have one or more altered components in their respective dispositions. The fifth in each chord is unaltered and therefore expendable. Example 9–46a has a major 7th from its root to seventh. The thirteenth chord in 9–46b cannot omit its eleventh because it is raised. In 9–46c, the three uppermost extensions are raised; hence, the chord name takes the number 7.

Example 9–46: altered major thirteenth

(1) 9–46a: C-major thirteenth
(2) 9–46b: C-major thirteenth, sharp eleventh
(3) 9–46c: C-major seventh, sharp thirteenth, sharp eleventh, sharp ninth

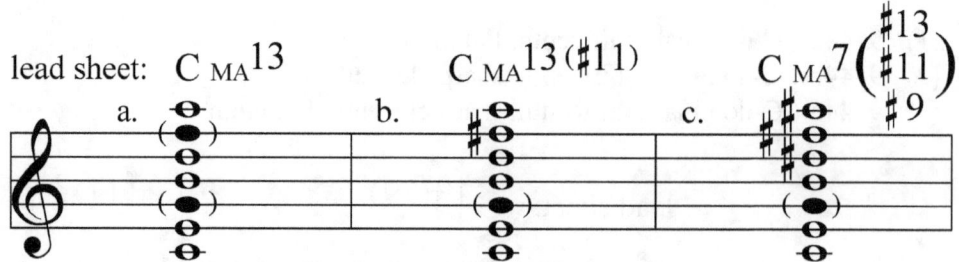

The Added 6th and Added 9th

Examples 9–47a and 9–47c display the minor seventh and half-diminished seventh in root position. Examples 9–47b and 9–47d present what could be interpreted as the first inversion of each chord. This position of the seventh chord, however, projects the sound of a "false triad" upwards from its bass, consisting of the seventh chord's third, fifth, and seventh elements.

Although you hear what sounds like the root, third, and fifth of a triad, the "root" is actually the third, the "third" is actually the fifth, and the "fifth" is actually the seventh. This false triad has a different quality than the actual root triad for each seventh chord.

The third, fifth, and seventh elements of the minor seventh (9–47b) and those of the half-diminished seventh (9–47d) constitute false major and minor triads. Commercial musicians interpret the three lowest pitches of these first-inversion chords as triads with a 6th added above their respective "roots."

In 9–47b, we have an E♭-major triad (E♭ G B♭) with an added 6th (C), and in 9–47d, an E♭-minor triad (E♭ G♭ B♭) with an added 6th (C). The lead sheet for the triad with the added 6th is the number 6 positioned to the right of the chord name. The minor triad (9–47d) also takes the MI symbol to distinguish it from the major triad (9–47b).

Example 9–47: the minor seventh and half-diminished seventh as added-6th chords

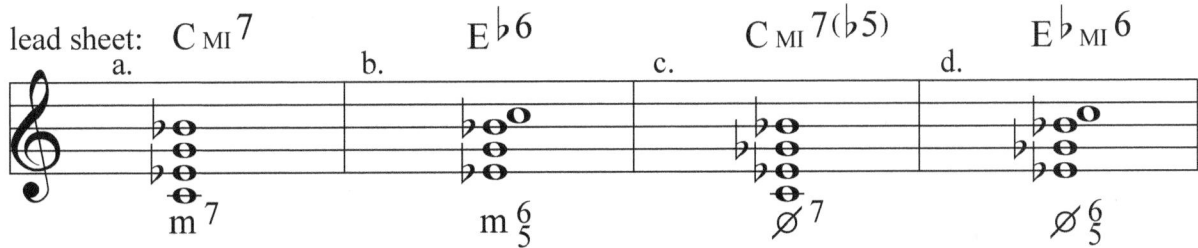

In order to maintain its unaltered form within the context of the key signature (see above, p. 294), the added 6th may have to be adjusted to preserve the major 6th above the root. As demonstrated in example 9–48, which expresses the key and mode of e♭ minor, the added 6th is stipulated as C♮. Studying the intervallic structure of the chords that commonly occur in lead sheets will help you to make the necessary adjustments more easily whenever confronted with a key signature.

Example 9–48: maintaining the major 6th of the added-6th chord when there is a key signature

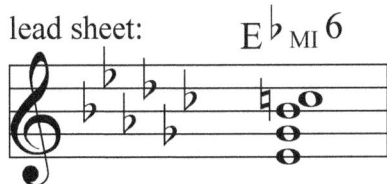

Example 9–49 shows how to notate the added 6th with a seventh chord in root position by placing "ADD6" in parentheses to the right of the number 7.

Example 9–49: adding the 6th to a seventh chord

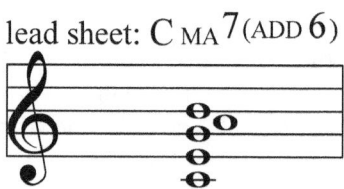

As we have seen throughout this chapter, a tertian harmony consisting of four superimposed 3rds is a chord of the ninth. If, however, the seventh component is not present in a triad that nonetheless has the interval of the 9th above the root, then we refer to the resulting harmony as an added-9th chord rather than as an actual ninth chord. The "ADD9" indication is enclosed in parentheses and attached to the chord name (examples 9–50a and 9–50b). If adding both the 6th and the 9th to the triad, place the numbers 6 and 9 after the chord name to the left and right of the forward slash as follows: 6 / 9 (examples 9–50c and 9–50d).

Example 9–50: adding the 9th or both the 6th and 9th to the major and minor triads

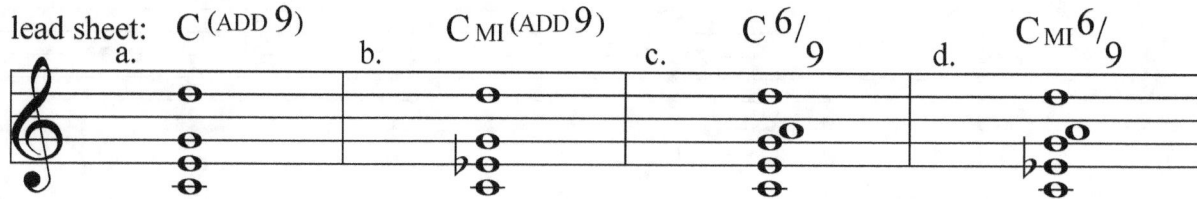

It should be understood that a marking such as "ADD2" means that you place an additional tone in the chord at the interval of a major 2nd above the root, not at the interval of a major 9th. An alternative notation simply includes the number 2 after the chord name (for example: C2 means a major triad with an added 2nd, C D E G). Usually, the third of the chord is retained; however, one way to specify the omission of the third is to write "SUS2" after the chord name. The SUS2 sign directs the musician to suspend a 2nd above the root of the chord and omit the third (for example: C SUS2 indicates C D G).

The Polychordal Potential of the Higher Powers

Though beyond the scope of this chapter, an exhaustive investigation of the potential for drawing one or more additional chords from sonorities beyond the basic triad yields some notable possibilities. To begin with, any seventh chord contains two triads whose roots are a 3rd apart: one from its root and another from its third.

The most obvious example within the context of a single key and mode is the TMD triad standing a 3rd above the THD triad (in C major, B D F standing above G B D, overlapping tones B and D). To be sure, these two chords usually work together in some form of dominant conversion as a diatonic operation. However, adding extensions beyond the seventh produces two results: (1) more triads and sevenths embedded within the overall pitch content of the chord and (2) greater contrasts between sonorities. As we shall see, the latter condition usually requires inflections of the higher extensions.

A ninth chord, for instance, has three triads and two seventh chords. Although it is possible to draw separate chords from the common pitch content of higher-powered sonorities, their recognition as distinct entities depends on how they are handled in terms of register, spacing, tone color and/or instrumentation. Inflecting the higher extensions, particularly above the ninth, enables the composer to draw more easily sharp contrasts between sonorities.

We conclude with the dominant seventh, sharp eleventh, flat ninth, introduced in 9–40c above and reproduced here as 9–51a. Reinterpreting enharmonically the pitches of this sonority in 9–51b creates two major triads whose roots stand a tritone apart. This polychord is found in such works as Ravel's *Jeux d'eau* (1901) and Stravinsky's *Petrushka* (1911). As stated above, how one hears the chord is contingent upon its treatment.

Example 9–51: the dominant seventh, sharp eleventh, flat ninth

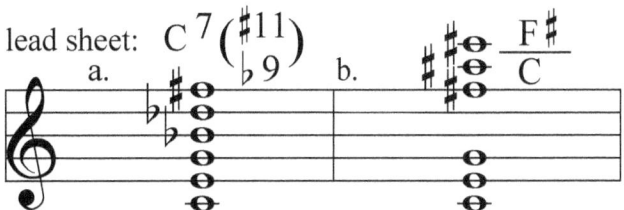

Epilog: Wallace H. Bower, Jr.

Finding The Right Pitch III closes with some personal observations about my teacher, Wallace Henry Bower, Jr., who taught music theory at El Camino College in Torrance, California, from 1968 to 2006. Many will argue justifiably that I should have placed this essay much earlier in the *Finding The Right Pitch* series or at least at the beginning of the present volume. This was, however, an ongoing search for the best way to preserve in book form what was central to Bower's pedagogy based upon a student-teacher relationship that spanned more than three decades.

These reflections could only emerge near the end of a narrative that began for me in the Fall of 1970, in what would become for Bower "the greatest class" he ever had. Subsequently, this class split into two different sections in the second semester, after which he referred to the first class as "one of the two best classes he ever had." It was a highly competitive though affable group, an unusual blend of personalities. I soon took the inherited and perhaps coveted position of page turner for his piano performances and recitals, selected periodically by him from the new arrivals to the music program. I began my individual studies with Bower shortly thereafter.

People who knew Bower invariably referred to him as brilliant *and* funny. Often these descriptions were given in reverse order. Bower was indeed very funny; he loved to laugh. Bower also loved crossword puzzles; he completed the ones in the New York Times in ink. His multilingual vocabulary was impressive. Crossword puzzles and languages were mysteries that had to be solved. And to Bower, music analysis was a puzzle he spent his entire life trying to solve. "The study of harmony is a life long study," he told me when I was eighteen.

His mother was Viennese, his father American. Bower's early comprehension of both English and German led to his passion for languages. He had perfect pitch and knew at least eight languages (English, German, French, Italian, Spanish, Portugese, modern Greek, and Latin). He earned a Bachelor's degree in languages at Ohio Wesleyan University in 1951, deferring the academic study of music for graduate school. Bower began learning piano at a very young age, doubtless encouraged by his mother, who was a stride pianist.

Bower served in the United States Army from 1951 to 1954, attaining the rank of Sergeant and attending both Army Counter-Intelligence School and Army Language School before being sent to Vienna, Austria. There, while continuing his military service, he became a music and language coach for the Vienna State Opera. With his knowledge of German and residency in Vienna, Bower became familiar with Heinrich Schenker's writings before returning to the United States in 1956 and before beginning his graduate studies in composition at UCLA the following year. Bower taught at California State University, Dominguez Hills, from 1966–1967, before assuming a tenured professorship at El Camino College in 1968.

The application of Schenkerian analysis was an integral component of Bower's classroom experience. Bower preferred the approach to structural analysis put forward by Felix Salzer, Schenker's foremost disciple. Although Bower attended a graduate seminar in music theory in Spring 1960 with a visiting professor Salzer (Music 250), he did not study structural analysis with the theorist. In fact, Bower's paper for Salzer was called "Some Speculations Concerning the Larger Meanings of Harmony," a topic to which the former devoted considerable thought throughout his career.

Early on, Bower recognized the disparity between the description of a chord as a member of a given tonality (that is, its chord nomenclature or grammar) and the meaning of that chord within the larger tonal context, in other words: the disparity between chord grammar and chord significance. He searched for ways to improve the inherent limitations of chord symbols to explain linear operations.

In 1960 (and probably before that), Bower set upon a course that would ultimately lead him to find functional descriptions for local harmonic events, particularly those that form apparent sonorities. It is likely that the seminar in music theory with Salzer in the Spring of 1960 helped to shape Bower's development as a theorist. Bower acquired Salzer's book, *Structural Hearing,* no later than 1958, two years before the seminar, and preferred the latter's graphic notation to that of Schenker's.

The principles of structural analysis informed everything Bower believed and taught about tonal music. As early as the second semester of harmony, he would explain the difference between structure and prolongation to his bewildered but engaged students, introducing them to the principles of graphic notation while many were still learning to read music. He routinely sent them to other schools to continue their studies, equipped with a level of understanding of common practice harmony that approached graduate proficiency.

Bower did not use textbooks to supplement his lectures on musical structure; he did, however, reference anthologies for analysis and theory books for discussions of harmony. He understood that anthologies were essential components of any harmony class, regardless of what examples might or might not be included in any given textbook. Bower rarely referred to the anthology by the name of its author or title when making assignments or when using them to demonstrate a musical operation. Rather, a typical instruction from him would be: "for next time, bring the green book because we're going to use it." He subsequently concluded his instructions by selecting which compositions were to be analyzed in advance. As much as any other harmony teacher, Bower had his own preferences, drawing freely from the available literature.

As compelling as Bower's instruction was, the application of structural analysis does not count among his most significant contributions to the pedagogy of music theory, though he applied it to virtually all of his examinations of the musical literature. Musical structuralism was central to his classroom dynamic; students leaving his class had an interest in and appreciation of the "larger concerns." Bower's own approach to describing apparent chord formations emerged from his keen understanding of structural harmony.

Although the classroom experience with Bower is difficult to duplicate in a book, *Finding The Right Pitch III* provides insight into his pedagogy, taxonomy of extended diatonicism and chromaticism, and nomenclature. The latter includes generic chord descriptions for both real and apparent sonorities. These concepts are integrated into the narrative within the context of structural analysis.

During his graduate studies at UCLA, Bower was that one student in the entire music department who knew more than any of the other graduate students. It did not seem to matter how much someone else advanced because Bower advanced at a much faster pace. Ultimately, from his earliest days in high school until he was gone, Bower was a "go to" guy. His colleagues at El Camino referred to him as the "resident genius."

When I met Bower in 1970, his formation of generic chord nomenclature was entering its maturity, while other theory teachers were clinging to conventional, literal descriptions of harmonic and contrapuntal operations, only slightly more informative than those existing in lead-sheet terminology. These literal descriptions invariably altered the accidentals of the figured bass to accommodate the various key signatures. Throughout the course of its development (from the sixties through the early eighties), Bower's generic chord grammar offered a functional nomenclature that always had at its core, a keen understanding of the background and its harmonic and contrapuntal projections.

While the first two books in this series were intended for a somewhat broader audience without direct reference to the Schenkerian tradition, the goal of the present volume is obviously different, not just because the concepts are more advanced and sometimes accompanied by voice-leading graphs, but also because I have deliberately shaped my explanations in a less distilled manner than in volumes one and two in order to more vividly capture the essence of Bower's overall approach to common practice harmony. In *Finding The Right Pitch III*, the focus narrows to more closely reproduce the intensity and rigor of his thinking.

As suggested above, there are limits to what a book can accomplish in meeting the aforementioned objective. A few notable departures from Bower's pedagogy merit comment here. In the first semester of Bower's harmony class, students learning major and minor key signatures were also expected to understand primary borrowing, including its inherent conflicts with the purely diatonic content.

In other words, Bower taught extended diatonicism from the beginning, with the assumption that the modal borrowing was from the parallel *melodic* minor rather than from the harmonic or natural minor. Students also enclosed borrowed triads in parentheses (and, in second semester, sevenths) to identify and mark the borrowed sonorities. He referenced certain chords that only exist in theory, such as the subtonic triad in minor that takes variable ♯7 as its chord seventh (a chord that does not yield a downward resolution). Bower termed the augmented-major seventh chord the "great seventh" and the minor-major seventh the "small seventh." I use the more conventional descriptions cited here. Admittedly, the three books in this series constitute a search to find the right balance between what Bower taught and what he equipped me to believe. Bower would have it no other way.

The first two volumes of *Finding The Right Pitch* are directed towards a general readership seeking a guided study of the basics of music theory, distilling concepts that ultimately become central to the narrative of *Finding The Right Pitch III*, wherein Bower's taxonomy, vocabulary, and general tone are employed more explicitly.

The principle of extended diatonicism and the attendant discussion of mixture between major and minor takes its more traditional place in advanced harmony, in *Finding The Right Pitch III*, rather than in the second volume, *Finding The Right Pitch II: A Guide To The Study Of Basic Harmony*, where it would have followed Bower's practice of introducing primary borrowing in beginning harmony. (An edition replicating precisely Bower's schedule would attract a more focused readership.)

Volumes one and two of *Finding The Right Pitch* deal with the fundamental problems of harmony, using harmonic reductions (often in four-voice texture) and depending on external access to music literature for examples. They are study guides in the purest sense. To be sure, without a connection to music literature, such demonstrations amount to little more than "paper progressions," a term and practice Bower exploited throughout his career, both for his own convenience and as an object of criticism.

In his 1960 seminar paper, Bower maintains that paper progressions encourage students to "think only in terms of rhythmically insipid harmony," accompanied by a certain rigid understanding of what are perceived as *rules* for doubling in chords and the voice leading that ensues between them. He criticized the use of these musical abstractions because they "bear no relation to an actual composition." And yet, he also drew upon them for their one valid purpose: "to demonstrate, by diagram, harmonic movement driving *onward to its final goal*" (also from "Some Speculations Concerning the Larger Meanings of Harmony," emphasis mine).

Finding The Right Pitch III retains the overall tone of the previous guides and continues to use reductive progressions and textures as the primary pedagogical device; however, the third volume also incorporates examples from music literature to demonstrate certain harmonic and contrapuntal operations. A comparison of the harmonic adaptation of Chopin's E-Minor Prelude in example 3–36 with the analysis of the score in Chapter 8 telegraphs the limitations of the paper progression. Transposed to c minor, 3–36 is concerned with issues of both generic figured bass and exact figured bass, as well as with relationships between lower-level keys. The early introduction of Chopin's progression in Chapter 3 might be viewed as a primer for the exhaustive analysis of Chopin's actual composition in Chapter 8 (pp. 252–260).

Bower also taught modal transposition of Church modes in first-semester harmony and even in music fundamentals. This series has retained the early introduction of modal key signatures for the same reason Bower placed it early in his sequence of topics: to underscore the necessity of learning major and minor key signatures immediately; for without this skill, students fail, eventually.

Imagine majoring in literature without knowing the alphabet of the language you are attempting to read. The point is that an easy, simplistic beginning to the study of music *theory* fails to instill in the student the sense of urgency that comes from understanding the importance of learning the musical alphabet, the key signatures.

Bower barraged his students with a lot of difficult material and then added more to that; he was intense and demanding. Bower characterized his own approach as "force feeding." And ultimately, his students became gluttons. Some survived and many did not. But the students who did survive left Bower thinking like a music theorist.

In the early 1970s, a movie called *The Paper Chase*, based upon a novel of the same name, was released and subsequently made into a television series. The story is about the relationship between a young law student and his brilliant, demanding, and virtually impossible to please professor. Students were always on edge with this professor; he was tough and very unforgiving.

The learning experience with Bower was not unlike that depicted in the story. To be sure, Bower was far more gregarious, accessible, and generous with his time than the fictional character in the novel, but the dynamic between teacher and student was similar. It was an extremely exciting period of discovery. In more than thirty-five years, I never left a conversation with Wally without either laughing or learning something; and more often than not, both conditions prevailed.

David B. Nivans, 2016

INDEX

A

5—8 variant, 78–79
6 / 9, 300
abrupt modulation, xi, 221–222, 225, 228, 243, 251–252
accent displacement, 242
acoustical dissonance, 108
add2, 300
add6, 300
add9, 300
added 6th, xii, 289, 294, 299–300
added 9th, xii, 299–300
added-note chord, 285, 288
addition, chords of, 288
Aeolian, 1, 51
Albrechtsberger, Johann Georg, 245
altered chord, 89, 123, 129–130, 290, 295
altered common-tone fully diminished seventh, 131–133, 136
altered dominant eleventh, 295–296
altered dominant thirteenth, 297–298
altered eleventh, xii, 287, 295, 297
altered fifth, xii, 92, 136, 288, 291, 293
altered major eleventh, 297
altered major thirteenth, 297
altered minor eleventh, 296
altered ninth, xii, 287, 291, 293, 297
altered THD, 121–122
altered thirteenth, xii, 287, 295, 298
altered TMD, 110–111, 113–114, 118, 129, 135
antecedent period, 84–85, 117–118
antecedent phrase, vii, 66, 68, 82
apparent chord, vi, xii, 15–17, 19–33 (Chapter 2), 41, 55–56, 96, 101, 104, 106–108, 111–113, 125–126, 132, 149, 175–176, 180, 194, 197, 217, 232, 243–246, 252–254, 256–258, 270, 272, 278–279, 289
apparent chord (non-dominant), vi, 24–31
apparent chordal skip, 177
apparent cross relation, 37, 95, 99–100
applied chord, 32–64 (Chapter 3), 71, 89, 93, 99, 124, 183, 227, 243, 244, 283
applied dominant, vi, viii, 35–39, 42–48, 50, 52, 54–55, 60, 64, 74, 76, 78–79, 93, 99–100, 102, 130, 135–136, 140, 155, 159, 161–162, 167, 170, 172, 179, 182, 185–187, 189, 193, 198, 201–203, 208–209, 211, 215, 222, 227–228, 231, 233, 270, 272, 276, 282–283
appoggiatura, 103, 107–108
approach chord, 58, 60, 62–63, 99, 169, 266
ascending 5—6, ix, 151, 162, 173–175, 178, 180, 182–183, 192, 208, 218–219
ascending 5—6 (becoming 5—10), x, 187–191
ascending 5—6 (becoming 5—8), x, xii, 184–186, 283

ascending 5th sequence, x, 162, 191–196, 198–200
augmentation, 76
augmented 2nd, 2, 53, 93, 95, 97, 102–103, 144, 153, 193, 198, 202, 207, 263
augmented 5th, 27, 102, 294
augmented 6th, vii, viii, 47, 90, 93, 110–111, 112, 114, 115–117, 119–136, 143, 239, 244–249, 256, 261, 266
augmented-major ninth, 292
augmented-major seventh, 9, 11, 13–15, 26, 56, 254, 292
authentic cadence, vi, 58, 61–63, 65, 68, 70–72, 84, 118, 146, 174, 221, 226, 232, 251

B

Bach, Johann Sebastian, 210–220
    Invention No. 13 in A Minor, 210–220
background, 150, 152, 152, 155, 156, 158–159, 205, 216, 218, 235–237, 254, 257, 260, 266–267, 268, 290
back-relating dominant (retroactive dominant), 71, 191, 193, 200, 252
bagatelle, 84, 117–118
balanced binary, 73
Baroque, 32
basic contrapuntal progression (BCP), xiii, 55, 68, 70–71, 81, 205, 221
basic harmonic progression (BHP), xiii, 55, 80–81, 98, 119, 205, 221, 267
basic melodic progression (BMP), xiii, 107, 117–118, 119, 122, 124–125, 150, 159, 174–175, 186, 210, 218, 254, 257–258, 267, 270
Beethoven, Ludwig van, 84, 117–118, 140, 156–157, 159
    Bagatelle No. 1 in G Minor, Op. 119, 84, 117–118
    Piano Sonata No. 21 in C Major, Op. 53 (*"Waldstein"*), 140
    Violin Sonata No. 5 in F Major, Op. 24 (*"Spring"*), 156–157, 159
binary, vii, 71–75, 77, 82, 85–87
binary form (sectional), 72–73
borrowed lowered 3, 5–6, 10–11, 16, 22, 25–26, 28, 150, 222
borrowed lowered 6, 5–6, 21, 24–25, 27, 29, 35, 62, 98, 113, 119, 124, 222
Bower, Wallace Henry, Jr., 303–305
Brahms, Johannes, xi, 222, 234–242, 268
    Intermezzo in A Major, Op. 118, No. 2, xi, 222, 234–242, 268

C

cadential chord, 58, 60–63, 65, 123, 230, 261, 274
Chopin, Frédéric François, ix, xi, 56–57, 82, 143, 145–152, 154–156, 252–260
    Prelude in E Major, Op. 28, No. 9, ix, 82, 143, 145–152, 154–156
    Prelude in E Minor, Op. 28, No. 4, xi, 56–57, 252–260
chord scale, xi, 262–263
chord streams, 244, 247
chordal sequence, 35, 41–42
chords of addition, xii, 276, 285–286, 288–289, 290, 294, 299–300
chord-unfolding scale, 262–263

chromatic bass, ix, 108, 119, 122, 178–182, 185, 208, 247
chromatic passing tone, 35, 89, 96, 103, 119, 178–180, 208–209, 243–244, 258
chromatic pivot, 232–234
chromatic voice exchange, xi, 243–245
chromaticism, v, 1, 17–18, 19, 42–43, 47, 50, 54, 57, 64, 89, 137, 140, 143, 170, 185–186, 198, 202, 221, 254, 281, 289
circle of 5ths, 223
Classic era, 245, 251
closed cadence, 63, 65–66
CLT chord, viii, ix, xiii, 29, 39, 41, 55, 64, 68, 70, 74, 76, 82, 96, 103, 107, 115–118, 123–125, 129, 135, 153, 165, 167, 173, 175, 177–180, 182, 198, 202, 208, 211, 215–218, 231, 239, 241, 254, 274
commercial music, xii, 32, 269, 280, 289, 293, 299
common practice period, 56, 65, 116, 126, 220, 264
common-tone modulation (pivot-tone modulation), 221–222
common-tone fully diminished seventh, viii, 103–104, 106–107, 131, 133–134, 136, 250–251
complete progression, 54–55, 188
consequent period, 84–85, 118
consequent phrase, vii, 66, 82, 85
contextual dissonance, 108
continuous binary, 72–73
continuous period, vii, 71
continuous ternary, 87
contracted dominant, 253, 255–256, 257–258
contraction, 43, 89, 93, 109, 253, 255–256, 257–258, 265, 270, 289
contrapuntal bass, ix, 46–50, 52, 55–58, 101–102, 108, 161, 163–167, 171, 173, 182, 196, 232
contrapuntal cadence, vi, 58, 61, 63, 66, 201, 242, 244, 261
contrapuntal imperfect authentic cadence, 61, 63, 70–71
contrapuntal leading-tone chord (CLT chord), viii, ix, xiii, 29, 39, 41, 55, 64, 68, 70, 74–76, 82, 96, 103, 107, 115–118, 123–125, 129, 135, 153, 165, 167, 173, 175, 177–180, 182, 198, 202, 208, 211, 215–218, 231, 239, 241, 254, 274
contrapuntal perfect authentic cadence, 61, 63
contrapuntal progression, vi, xiii, 37, 54–56, 62, 68, 70–71, 87, 98, 125, 158, 214–215, 227, 254, 267
contrapuntal-structural chord (CS chord), ix, 152–153, 217, 267
contrast, 65
contrasting double period, 84–85, 87
contrasting period, vii, 68, 70–71, 80, 83
conversion dominant, 19–20, 55, 57, 101, 113, 149–150, 155, 175, 177–179, 249–250, 252–254
cross relation, vi, 37–39, 41, 95–97, 99–100, 143, 163–164
cross relation tritone, 165

D

deceptive cadence, 251, 256, 261, 264–265
deceptive resolution, 230, 251, 256, 262, 266

degree inflection, vii–viii, 89–136 (Chapter 5), 167, 272, 288
degree-inflected THD, 167, 288
descending 5—6, vii, x, 77–79, 162, 200–204, 206–207, 264–265
descending 5—6 (becoming 5—8), 78–79, 206–207, 264–265
descending 5th sequence, ix, xii, 43–53, 76, 79, 110, 161–173, 191, 211, 214–215, 218, 226, 272–273, 280, 283
diatonic pivot, 228, 232–233
diatonicism, 1, 89, 230, 289
digression, 74
diminished 3rd, vii, 90, 93–95, 97–98, 110–112, 115, 123, 129–131, 133–136, 142, 145, 198, 261
diminished triad/major 7th, 21, 108
disjunct resolutions, viii, 127
displacement of accents, 242
distance of modulation, xi, 221, 223–226
distant key (distant modulation), xi, 223–226, 228, 232–234, 241, 261, 265
divider, 236–238
dividing dominant, 236–239, 270
dominant eleventh, 294–296
dominant ninth, 109–110, 272, 283, 290–293, 295
dominant thirteenth, 294, 297–298
dominant-family chord, 12, 19, 23, 39, 55, 62, 64, 77, 123, 129, 175, 178, 181, 217, 250
Dorian, 51, 262
double counterpoint, 212–213
double period, 84–85, 87, 117–118
double suspension, 272
double-function chord (DF chord), ix, 158–159, 266–267, 270
doubly diminished triad, 111–112, 117, 129–130, 136
doubly fully diminished TMD, 113–114, 124–125, 131, 136, 143, 247
doubly half-diminished seventh, 112–113, 129–130, 136

E

eleventh chord, xii, 269, 276, 278, 281, 286–287, 289, 291, 294–298, 301
elision, 243, 247, 251–254, 257–258, 261
enharmonic adjustment, 224–226
enharmonic reinterpretation, xi, 223, 243, 245, 250
ethnic augmented 6th chord, vii, 115–116, 122–128, 129, 130, 131, 135–136, 246, 248
exact figured bass, vi, 23, 32–33, 56
exceptional augmented 6th (EA6), viii, 122–123, 128, 135
extended major, v, viii, xiv, 5–8, 10–15, 23, 137–139
extended minor, v, viii, xiv, 3, 6, 8, 13, 137
extended passing chord, 74, 76, 99, 102, 119, 174–188, 227–230, 236, 274–275
extended-diatonic major-minor system, v, 1, 6–7, 13–14, 137
extended-diatonicism, 230

F

false triad, 299
Fauré, Gabriel, 272–275, 280, 284
    Après un rêve, 272–275, 280, 284
figured bass (exact), vi, 23, 32–33, 56
figured bass (generic), vi, 9–11, 16, 19–31, 56, 92, 105, 125–126, 132, 149, 288
flat fifth, flatted fifth, 291–293, 296
flat five, 291
foreground, 210, 240, 251, 252, 254, 255, 257, 268, 284, 290
French 6th, 115–116
French augmented 6th (FA6), viii, 115, 121, 128, 135, 252
frozen nonharmonic tones, xii, 149, 269, 274, 275–276, 280, 289
full cadence, 63, 65–66, 118

G

generic figured bass, vi, 9–11, 16, 19–31, 56, 92, 105, 125–126, 132, 149, 288
German 6th, 115–116
German augmented 6th (GA6), viii, 120–128, 131, 133, 135, 239, 241–250, 256, 261, 277
German doubly augmented 6th (GDA6), 120–122, 124–126, 128, 132, 135, 232, 246, 256, 266
governing tone, governing melodic tone, xii, 156, 158, 205, 216–219, 237, 239–240, 254, 257–258,
    260–261, 264, 266–267, 270

H

half cadence, vi, 58–63, 65–69, 72–76, 80–81, 84–85, 115, 117–118, 123, 135, 146, 252, 258, 261
harmonic ambiguity (harmonic ambiguities), 252, 254, 257
harmonic cadence, 58, 182
harmonic embellishing chord (HEMB chord), 132, 217, 237–238, 261, 264, 270–271, 274
harmonic imperfect authentic cadence, 63, 232
harmonic minor, v, xi, 1–2, 263
harmonic minor chord scale, xi, 263
harmonic perfect authentic cadence, 63–64, 65–76, 80–87, 118, 146, 174, 226, 238, 261, 265–266
harmonic progression, xiv, 95, 236
harmonic rhythm, 74, 118, 211, 214, 242
harmonic sequence, 42, 161, 208
Haydn, Joseph, 80–82, 261
    Sonata No. 35 in C Major (Hob. XVI), Movement I, 80–82
head motive, 79
hemiola, 242
higher power, chords of, xii, 269–301 (Chapter 9)

I

idiomatic usages of the minor mode, 170, 175, 263
imperfect authentic cadence, 61–63, 70–71, 84, 232
incipient ternary, 73, 86
incomplete progression, 54–55, 152, 188
interchangeable counterpoint, 212
interchangeable value, 55
interlocking seventh chords, 42–52, 161–163, 272, 280–285
interlocking voice exchange, 147–148, 155, 241
intermediate harmony, 54, 158, 267
intermezzo, xi, 222, 234–241, 268
interruption, technique of, vii, 66–71, 117–118, 236–237, 253–255, 257–258, 270
invention, x, 210–220
inverted pedal embellishing tone, xiii, 77, 107, 126, 132, 150, 200
invertible counterpoint, x, 212–213
Italian 6th, 115–116
Italian augmented 6th (IA6), 115–120, 122, 127–128, 135, 143, 246–247

J

jazz, iv, xii, 269, 280, 289–290, 293, 295
jumped modulation, 222, 252

L

large form, 65, 66, 87, 156, 222, 234–235, 237
large ternary, 87, 222, 234, 237
lead sheet, iv, 32, 289–301
linear inflection, 89–136 (Chapter 5), 221, 269, 279, 283, 285–288, 300
linear melodic progression (LMP), ix, xiii, 152, 156, 158–159, 218, 236–239
linear modulation, 252
Locrian, 51
lowered fifth, 56, 92, 98, 101, 113, 116, 121, 129–130, 135, 167, 252, 291, 296
lower-level keys, vi, xiv, 35–64 (Chapter 3), 65, 71, 73, 85–87, 89, 107, 136, 140, 146, 156, 158, 180, 182, 187–188, 208, 211, 220, 221–222, 243, 245, 247–248, 250, 252–254, 269, 274
lower-level progression, 54, 56, 187
Lydian, 51, 138, 262

M

main-level key, vi, xiv, 36, 37, 39, 41, 42, 51, 54, 56–60, 62–64, 72, 77, 85, 100, 108, 110, 118, 121, 129, 136, 140, 147, 150, 156, 158, 162, 180, 187–189, 195, 214, 216, 220, 221–222, 238, 240, 244, 252, 264–266, 268
major ninth, 290, 292–293, 297

mediant embellishing (MEMB), viii, ix, 126, 136, 141–142
mediant modulation, 221–226, 232
mediant-related keys, 221–222
melodic minor, v, 1–10, 12–17 (Chapter 1), 29, 137, 164–165, 170, 263–264
melodic modulation, 223–226, 241
melodic sequence, 42–43, 82, 237
middleground, ix, x, 152–153, 155–156, 158–159, 205, 214, 218–220, 221, 236, 238–239, 241, 245, 255–256, 258–260, 265–268, 272, 274–275, 289–290
minor ninth, 290–293, 296
minor thirteenth, 294
Mixolydian, 51
modal dominant, vi, 6–7, 12, 35, 45, 50–53, 78–79, 81, 161–165, 170–172, 184–188, 211, 227, 272, 281–282
modal exchange, 1
modal mixture, 1, 89, 104, 123, 139
mode scale, xi, 262, 264
modulating sequence, 222
modulation, vi, x, xi, 36–37, 60–61, 63–64, 65, 109, 136, 181–182, 208, 211, 220, 221–268 (Chapter 8), 269
motive, vii, 65–66, 79, 239–241
motto, 66
Mozart, Wolfgang Amadeus, 66–80, 106, 228–229, 240
    Sonata No. 5 in G Major (K 283), I, 70–71, 80
    Sonata No. 6 in D Major (K. 284), III, 72–79, 228–229, 240
    Sonata No. 16 in C Major (K. 545), II, 66–69, 106
multiple suspension, 56–57, 259

N

Naples, 94
natural minor, 1–4
Neapolitan 6th, vii, 94–102, 134, 145
ninth chord, xii, 25, 54, 58, 109–110, 269, 270–293, 295–298, 300–301
non-CLT, 103
noncontinuous period, 68–71, 72
noncontinuous sectional period, 70, 72
non-dominant apparent chord, vi, 24–31
non-dominant function, 103, 249–250
nonessential interval, 232
nonharmonic tone, xii, 15–17, 56, 111, 196, 210, 232–233, 235, 238, 258–260, 262, 269, 275, 278–280, 289
non-TMD, 103–108, 250–251

O

ominbus principle, xi, 243–245
one-part form, vii, 68–71, 82–84, 146–148

open cadence, 65, 84–86
outer-voice interval-pattern (OVIP), 161–209 (Chapter 7), 244, 280–285

P

parallel double period, 84–85, 117
parallel minor, 1, 5, 10, 26, 50, 111, 113–114, 124, 137–138, 150, 153, 164, 283, 286
parallel period, vii, 68–69, 83, 252, 270
pedal embellishing, viii, 30, 68, 77, 81, 103, 106, 125–126, 132, 200, 254, 270, 276
perfect authentic cadence, 61–64, 65, 68, 72, 82–87, 118, 146, 174, 226
period, vii, 65–87 (Chapter 4), 117–118, 234
period (noncontinuous), 68, 70–71
phrase, 36–37, 58, 60, 62, 65–66, 68, 71, 73, 240, 251
phrase chain, 82
phrase group, 82–84, 146, 234, 261, 265
Phrygian, 12, 51, 138
Phrygian cadence, 116
Phrygian supertonic, vii, 89, 94, 97–102, 120, 135, 138–139, 142–143, 146, 150–151, 153–154, 235, 274
Picardy third, v, xi, 16, 26, 101–102, 137, 145, 193, 237, 241–242, 274
pivot-chord modulation (pivot chord), xi, 64, 74, 131, 133, 136, 182, 221–222, 225, 227–236, 240–243, 247, 251–252, 261, 264, 266
pivot-tone modulation (common-tone modulation), 221–222, 225, 238, 268
polychord, xii, 295, 300–301
polyphonic melody, 211, 214, 216
post-interruption, 237, 254, 257–258
Poulenc, Francis, 275–276, 280
    Ce doux petit visage, 276
pre-dominant chord, 54–55
pre-interruption, 237, 253–254, 258, 270
primary accent, 35, 42, 103, 107, 147, 162–163, 169, 184, 227, 242, 279
primary borrowing, v, 1–18 (Chapter 1), 89, 98, 129–130, 137–139, 230, 232, 236, 239, 269, 286
principal (melodic) voice, 114, 158, 263
Prokofiev, Sergei, xi, 242, 261–267
    Classical Symphony, Op. 25, III, 261–267

R

raised diminished triad, 111–115
raised fifth, 89, 91–92, 116, 122–123, 134–135, 272–273, 275, 291, 293, 296, 298
raised fully diminished seventh, 114–115, 131, 133
raised submediant, 103–106, 108–109, 134, 136, 138
raised supertonic, 103–108, 126, 128, 131, 134, 136
raised-raised submediant, 104

Ravel, Maurice, 276–277, 280, 301
    Valses nobles et sentimentales, 276–277
related key (related modulation), xi, 221–226, 228, 230, 233
remote key (remote, or removed, modulation), xi, 223–227
repeat sign, 72, 82, 234
repeated period, vii, 80–83, 85
repetition, 65, 82, 85–86, 146, 161, 185, 201, 205–208, 234, 236, 242, 252, 265
retransition, 77, 86
retroactive dominant, vii, 71, 74, 76–79, 146, 148, 159, 191, 193–194, 198, 200, 207, 252, 262, 265
Romantic period, 140, 143, 251
root-position variants, ix, x, xii, 173, 182, 184–191, 206–207, 283
rounded binary, vii, 71, 72–77, 85–87

S

Salzer, Felix, 39, 124, 152–153, 158, 210, 237
SATB, 248, 283
Schachter, Carl, 39, 124
Schenker, Heinrich, 124, 152, 210, 245
Schoenberg, Arnold, 245
secondary accent, 242
secondary borrowing, viii, ix, xi, 89, 94, 97–98, 100, 134, 137–159 (Chapter 6), 221–222, 226, 235,
    237, 240–242, 245, 261, 264
secondary contrapuntal progression (SCP), xiii, 54–55, 98, 125, 205, 214–215, 218–220, 221, 274–275
secondary melodic progression (SMP), ix, xiii, 150, 152, 156
secondary voice, 158, 263, 272, 284
secondary harmonic progression (SHP), xiii, 55, 57, 68, 71, 74, 80–81, 95, 98, 102, 107, 116, 118–119,
    122, 124, 146, 148, 150, 152, 156, 159, 168, 182, 189, 205, 211, 214, 221, 230, 236, 257
sectional binary form, 72–73
sectional ternary form, 87
sequence, vii, ix, 35, 41–53, 74–79, 82, 110, 154, 161–220 (Chapter 7), 222, 225–227, 237, 262–265,
    272, 280–285
sequential modulation, xi, 222, 225–227
sharp fifth (sharp five), 291, 293, 296, 298
single period, 65–71, 80–83, 84
skipped modulation, 222, 252
small ternary, 86–87
sonata, 66–82, 106, 140, 156–157, 159, 228, 240
stationary bass, 15, 30, 104, 106, 125–126, 132, 279
stationary seventh, 45, 161–162, 165
Stravinsky, Igor, 301
    Petrushka, 301
subdividing chord, 68–69, 236
subtonic seventh, v, vi, 9–10, 12–15, 36, 64, 143, 164, 172, 180, 209, 227, 241–245
superposed embellishing melody, 254–261

superposition of the inner voice, 254–261
sus2, 300
suspension, 43, 56–57, 71, 93, 117, 158, 210–211, 252–260, 272–276, 278–279
Swiss 6th, 115, 121
symphony, xi, 242, 261, 264–267
syncopation, 242

T

Tchaikovsky, Peter Ilich, 270–271
    Nutcracker Suite, Op. 71a, Overture, 270–271
Telesco, Paula J., 245
temporary tonic, 35–36, 38, 42–43
ternary form (sectional), 86–87
ternary (incipient), 73, 86
thirteenth chord, xii, 269, 276–278, 281, 285–289, 291, 294–295, 297–298
three-chord pattern, x, 208–209, 241, 264–265
three-part form. 86–87, 234–235, 237
tonal ambiguity, 243, 265
tonal harmonic dominant (THD), vi, vii, xiii, xiv, 12–13, 19–20, 22, 29–30, 35–37, 39, 41–43, 50,
    55–57, 82, 89–93, 95–98, 100–101, 109, 116, 118, 121–123, 125, 131, 133–134, 136, 145–146,
    148, 155, 162–167, 169, 173–174, 176–177, 180, 182, 192–199, 202, 208, 217, 226–227, 231, 244,
    247, 249–250, 253–254, 256–257, 260–261, 266, 270, 274, 280, 300
tonal modulation, 223–226, 228–230
tone melodic dominant (TMD), vi, viii, ix, xiii, xiv, 12–13, 19–21, 29–30, 35, 39–41, 105, 109–118,
    123–125, 129, 135–136, 143, 149, 155, 180, 182, 196, 231, 239, 247, 249–250, 253–254, 300
tone-embellishing melodic succession (TEMB succession), 107, 116, 122, 125
tonic seventh, v, 9–10, 176, 189
tonicization, vi, 36–37, 64, 65
transferred resolution, vi, 48–50, 167
triad contextualization, 7–8, 14–15
tritone, ix, 6–7, 12, 36, 39, 42, 44–47, 50–52, 108, 110, 138, 143, 161–165, 168, 171, 188, 196, 198,
    208–209, 225, 227, 272, 281, 301
tritone modulation, xi, 223–226
two-chord pattern, 42–52, 58, 77, 109, 188, 205, 208–209, 280
two-part form, vii, 71–74, 85–87
two-reprise design, 72

U

unequal 5ths, 27, 38–41, 55, 102, 115, 201–204, 232
unprepared suspension, 259

V

variable-determining voice, 263
variant, ix, x, xii, 78–79, 141, 145, 158, 162, 173, 182–189, 206–207, 243, 245, 265, 283
variation, 65, 68
varied repetition, 82, 85, 146, 234
voice exchange (chromatic), xi, 74, 80–82, 108, 146–151, 155, 210, 216–218, 241, 243–245, 260
voice-leading chord, 35, 146, 150, 168–169, 182, 184, 187

W

Wason, Robert, 245
whole-tone dominant, 90–91, 121–122, 135
whole-tone scale, vii, 90–91

X

X-chord, vii, ix, xiii, 54–57, 64, 68, 71, 74, 81, 95, 97–98, 101, 116, 118–119, 122–125, 134–135, 140, 143–148, 150, 153, 155, 158–159, 162, 168, 174–189, 202, 205–206, 214, 216–219, 227–231, 234, 236–237, 248, 253–261, 267, 274
X-double-function chord (X-DF) chord, 158–159